The American
Economy in
Transition

A Sixtieth
Anniversary
Conference

National Bureau of Economic Research

The American Economy in Transition

Edited by **Martin Feldstein**

The University of Chicago Press

Chicago and London

The University of Chicago Press, Chicago 60637
The University of Chicago Press, Ltd., London

Library of Congress Cataloging in Publication Data
Main entry under title:

The American economy in transition.

   (National Bureau of Economic Research monograph)
   Papers of a conference held in January 1980 marking
the 60th anniversary of the National Bureau of Economic
Research.
   Includes indexes.
   1. United States—Economic conditions—1945–
—Addresses, essays, lectures. I. Feldstein, Martin S.
II. National Bureau of Economic Research. III. Series:
National Bureau of Economic Research. National Bureau
of Economic Research monograph.
HC106.5.A5948   330.973′092   80–17450
ISBN 0–226–24081–9

Contents

Preface

This unusual volume marks the sixtieth anniversary of the National Bureau of Economic Research. In contrast to the technical and specialized character of most NBER studies, the current book is designed to provide the general reader with a broad and critical overview of the American economy. The result is a volume of essays that range from monetary policy to productivity development, from population change to international trade.

A special feature of the volume is the combination of a basic background study on each subject with the personal statements of leading by an outstanding scholar who is an expert on his subject. Each is accompanied by two personal reflections on the changing character of the postwar economy. The distinguished individuals who have written these personal statements have been leaders in shaping national thought and frequently have also been important participants in the forming of government policy and the directing of the private economy. Since the unique mission of the NBER throughout its sixty-year history has been to provide objective and quantitative economic research to serve as a basis for public and private policies, the present combination of background papers and personal statements is a very fitting way for the Bureau to celebrate its anniversary.

The authors of the essays in this volume met for a two-day conference in January 1980. Since the background papers were distributed in advance, much of the discussion at the meeting focused on the personal statements. A very brief summary of the discussion, prepared by Jeffrey Sachs, is included in each section of the volume.

The original idea for an NBER review of the postwar experience of the United States economy was developed in discussions with Dr. John

Sawyer, president of the Andrew Mellon Foundation. I am grateful to Dr. Sawyer for his suggestions and to the Mellon Foundation for its support of this project.

All the participants in the project are grateful to Maureen Kay for her efficient help with the conference and with the preconference distribution of material.

Martin Feldstein

The American Economy in Transition: Introduction

Martin Feldstein

The postwar period began in an atmosphere of doubt and fear. Many economists believed that the nation would slip back into the deep recession from which it had escaped only as the war began. In the decade between 1929 and 1939, real gross national product (GNP) had not grown at all, and the official unemployment rate had reached one-fourth of the labor force. During the war, the economy had returned to full or overfull use of its capacity: real GNP rose 75 percent between 1939 and 1944, while the unemployment rate fell to less than 2 percent. Even many optimists worried that demobilization and the transition to a civilian economy would lead to a new period of long-term stagnation caused by inadequate demand.

Real output did decline as the war ended, and the unemployment rate did begin to rise. Real GNP fell by nearly 20 percent between 1944 and 1947. As ten million men and women left the armed forces, total employment (civilian and armed forces combined) declined by nearly 10 percent and the unemployment rate rose to nearly 4 percent. But the fears and doubts of the "secular stagnationists" were unwarranted. After 1947 the economy began a period of remarkable growth and stability. In the next decade, real GNP rose 45 percent, and in the decade that followed another 48 percent. In only one of those twenty years did real GNP fall by as much as 1 percent, and that was in 1954, when military spending had been sharply reduced. This sustained and rapid expansion had occurred with a relatively stable price level; the annual rise in the consumer price index averaged only 2 percent. The first two decades of the postwar period were a time of unsurpassed economic prosperity, stability, and optimism.

Martin Feldstein is president of the National Bureau of Economic Research and is professor of economics at Harvard University.

The contrast between the strength and achievement of the economy during those years and its poor record since then signals a major change in the performance of the economy over the postwar period. At the aggregate level, real GNP growth slowed from an annual rate of 3.9 percent between 1947 and 1967 to only 2.9 percent between 1967 and 1979. The growth of productivity per man-hour in the private business sector dropped from an annual rate of 3.2 percent during 1947–67 to less than 1.5 percent since 1967 and less than 1 percent since 1973. The average unemployment rate rose from 4.7 percent of the labor force to 5.8 percent. The average rate of consumer price index (CPI) inflation jumped from 2 percent to 6.7 percent (since 1967) with an acceleration to an average of nearly 9 percent since 1973 and over 13 percent in 1979. The Standard and Poor's index of common stock prices, an indicator of both after-tax profitability and investors' expectations about the future of the economy, rose sixfold between 1949 and 1969. Even after adjusting for the rise in the general consumer price level, this index of share prices increased by more than 300 percent. In the decade since 1969, however, the index rose only 10 percent and in constant dollars fell nearly 50 percent. The poor performance of the economy in recent years can also be seen at a less aggregate level: a falling share of national income devoted to net investment and to research and development; increasing pressures and risks in the financial sector; low profitability and an aging stock of plant and equipment in many specific industries; and a deteriorating performance of United States exports.

There is a strong temptation to regard the poor performance of the past decade as the beginning of a new long-term adverse trend for the American economy. It is, however, too early to know whether such an extrapolation is really warranted. Some of the poor record of the 1970s has undoubtedly been due to inappropriate macroeconomic policies adopted during the Vietnam War, to the change in the production policy of the OPEC cartel, and to other disturbances whose impacts will eventually fade away. But the deteriorating performance of the economy may also have more fundamental causes that will not automatically recede. Indeed, some of the sources of our performance may now be so deeply rooted in our social and political system that they cannot be eliminated even when the causes of the problem become better understood. It is clear that there is little hope of reversing the poor performance that has lasted for more than a decade unless the underlying causes are identified and changed.

Many of the papers and comments in this volume point to the expanded role of government as a major reason, perhaps the major reason, for the deterioration of our economic performance. The government's mismanagement of monetary and fiscal policy has contributed to the instability of aggregate output and to the rapid rise in inflation. Government regulations are a principal cause of lower productivity growth and of the decline in research and development. The growth of government income-transfer programs has exacerbated the instability of family life and perhaps the decline in the birthrate. The low rate of saving and the slow growth of the capital stock reflect tax rules, macroeconomic policies, and the growth of social insurance programs.

The expanded role of government has undoubtedly been the most important change in the structure of the American economy in the postwar period. The extent to which this major change in structure has been the cause of the major decline in performance cannot be easily assessed. This introductory essay is certainly not the place to evaluate just how much of our recent problem derives from specific government policies or to assess the positive contributions that government policies have made during the postwar period. Nevertheless, there can be no doubt that government policies do deserve substantial blame for the adverse experience of the past decade. I would like, therefore, to devote these few pages to examining the general character of government policies and of government decision-making that causes it to create problems of the type we have experienced.

Economists generally regard all economic choices as the result of explicit comparisons of costs and benefits. When an individual buys an apple rather than a pear, we assume that he has considered the prices of each and the pleasures that he would expect from the apple and the pear. Even for more complex choices with uncertain future benefits, such as an individual's choice among careers or a firm's choice among investment options, the economist automatically assumes that the decision-maker has considered the possible costs and benefits of the option he selects. Individuals and firms may occasionally be surprised by adverse consequences they had not anticipated, but on average the outcomes should correspond to expectations. Applying such a "rational choice" view to government policies would imply that successive governments made deliberate decisions to accept certain adverse consequences in order to achieve other goals: for example, that the current high inflation was accepted in order to avoid more unemployment; that the low rates of saving and investment were accepted in order to have tax policies and transfer programs that could more equally distribute disposable income; or that the low rate of R&D spending and the fall in productivity were accepted as a consequence of imposing regulations that could protect the environment and the safety of workers.

I find this picture of economically rational choice implausible. I find it much more believable that the adverse consequences of government policies have been largely the unintended and unexpected by-products of well-meaning policies that were adopted without looking beyond their immediate purpose or understanding the magnitudes of their adverse long-run consequences. Expansionary monetary and fiscal policies were adopted throughout the past fifteen years in the hope of lowering the unemployment rate but without anticipating the higher inflation rate that would eventually follow. High tax rates on investment income were enacted and the social security retirement benefits were increased without considering the subsequent impact on investment and saving. Regulations were imposed to protect health and safety without evaluating the reduction in productivity that would result or the effect of an uncertain regulatory future on long-term R&D activities.

Similarly, I believe the government never considered that raising the amount and duration of unemployment benefits to the current high levels to avoid hardship among the unemployed would encourage layoffs and discourage reemployment; that Medicare and Medicaid, introduced to help the elderly and the poor, might lead to an explosion in health care costs; that welfare programs, introduced and expanded to help poor families, might weaken family structures; or that federal aid through the tax laws and through special credit programs to encourage homeownership would have such adverse effects on the cities, precipitating the relocation of business and consequent poverty and other problems for those who remained behind. The list of well-meaning policies with unintended adverse consequences could be extended almost without limit.

Moreover, in many cases the adverse consequences have resulted not from the introduction of fundamentally new programs and policies, but from the fact that old programs are retained and expanded in a changed economic environment. Social security and unemployment compensation were introduced in the 1930s; the differences between the economy then and now would imply corresponding differences in the likely impact of these programs. The high rate of unemployment, the lack of investment demand, and the low rate of personal income tax constituted an environment in the 1930s in which the side effects of social security and unemployment compensation would be relatively innocuous. Today's tight labor market, capital scarcity, and high personal tax rates imply that these programs now impede employment and capital formation. Similarly, our personal and business tax laws were designed for an economy with little or no inflation. The interaction of this tax structure with the current high inflation rates causes extremely high effective tax rates on capital income, a discouragement to saving, and a distortion of investment away from plant and equipment toward housing and consumer durables.

Unfortunately, even when the inappropriateness of old policies is recognized, change is difficult to achieve. Existing programs are maintained even though the same programs would not be adopted today. These programs survive and grow with the help of sympathetic bureaucrats and well-organized beneficiary groups. Loyalties develop to the form of public programs rather than to their basic purpose.

There is a fundamental reason why well-intentioned government policies often have adverse consequences. The government in its decision-making is inherently myopic, more myopic than either households or firms. Political accountability means that a policy will be judged on its apparent effects within as little as two years. A congressman or senator may understand the long-run implications of a policy, but the relevance to him of those long-run effects is very limited if voters look only at the short-run impact. The political process lacks the equivalent of capital assets through which private decision-makers are rewarded or penalized for the long-term consequences of previous decisions. And because the political process does not reward or punish elected officials for the long-term consequences of their actions, there is little or no incentive for these officials to learn about such long-term effects. Political myopia reflects the public's general inability to anticipate the long-run consequences of political decisions and even to associate those consequences when they occur with the policies that caused them. It is not surprising therefore that well-meaning policies frequently have unexpected adverse consequences and that policies with short-run costs and long-run benefits are not adopted.

The nature of the political decision-making process is perhaps most apparent in the development of macroeconomic policy. In the early 1960s, expansionary monetary and fiscal policies were pursued in what might be described as a rational choice based on the Phillips curve analysis that was then widely accepted by the economics profession. But later in the decade President Lyndon Johnson rejected the warnings of his economic advisors that taxes had to be raised in order to avoid an accelerating rate of inflation. Johnson chose to accept an increased long-run inflation rate in order to avoid the short-run political cost of a tax increase. His choice, while perhaps politically rational, was economically myopic. During the 1970s, the government and the monetary authorities focused on the short-run goal of reducing unemployment through expansionary policies that served only to exacerbate the inflationary situation. If escaping from the current high rate of inflation requires a sustained period of increased unemployment and economic slack, the shortsightedness of the political process may make this very difficult to achieve.

The myopia of the political process is also reflected in policies that discriminate against saving and investment. It is significant that pro-investment legislation has always been justified as a way of stimulating short-run demand and thereby reducing current unemployment. There has been little effective support for policies to increase saving and investment in order to expand the capital stock and raise future income. In contrast, tax and transfer policies that favor current public and private consumption have been favored. The long-run benefits of increasing the capital stock apparently lie beyond the political horizon.

If the electoral process makes political decisions inherently myopic, we should recognize this as an intrinsic feature of our democracy. It is important, moreover, to consider this bias in political decision-making in determining the extent of the role that government should play in our economic life.

Of course, politicians do not have a monopoly on myopia. But although some of the political shortsightedness is undoubtedly a response to constituent pressures, the myopia of the political process actually encourages voters to be impatient. Voters demand faster results from the political process than they demand from private activities because they recognize that elected officials are accountable only in the short run. Politicians' promises of "quick-fix" solutions to major social and economic problems also induce voters to expect such solutions and to judge incumbents and candidates by a short-run standard.

The policies that are adopted also bias individuals to be more shortsighted and impatient in their private decisions. Tax policies, credit market rules, and social insurance programs encourage current consumption and a decrease in private provisions for the future. In more subtle ways, government programs that substitute the state for the family cause behavior that weakens the development of the future population: fewer births, more unmarried individuals, more childless couples, and more divorced parents. Of course, to some extent, these government policies may only reflect a growing impatience in the public that stems from other sources. It is impossible to identify the relative importance of different factors, but the government clearly bears substantial responsibility for encouraging and stimulating shortsighted behavior.

To the extent that the poor economic performance of the past decade can be traced to the growing role of government and the inherent myopia of the political process, improvement of our performance will be difficult to achieve. Difficult but not impossible. The public's support for environmental protection and for expenditure on research and development shows that programs with long-run benefits can be politically viable. There are at present some signs of growing public and governmental interest in increasing the rate of capital formation. The Keynesian fear of saving that has dominated thinking on this subject for more than thirty years is finally giving way to a concern about the low rates of productivity increase and of investment. The public has also recognized that the key problem for macroeconomic policy is now inflation, not unemployment. If the public begins to see more clearly the links between current policies and future consequences, there will be less reason to fear the unexpected consequences of myopic decisions.

The 1970s have been a decade of frustrated expectations. The size and influence of the government have grown rapidly, but the public's distrust of government has grown even more rapidly. The economics profession has discovered a new humility as the economy's performance has worsened. As the 1980s begin, there is widespread anxiety about the future. Will this decade be a period of severe economic problems with a major recession, accelerating inflation, or both? Or can the poor economic performance of the 1970s be reversed? The current data on the developing state of the economy are not clear. And, while some events may be outside our control, the success of the economy in the current decade and in the remainder of this century will depend also on whether we choose wisely as we reevaluate and restructure our major economic policies.

1 Postwar Changes in the American Financial Markets

1. Benjamin M. Friedman
2. Milton Friedman
3. A. W. Clausen

1. Benjamin M. Friedman

Financial markets are an integral part of the modern economy. The many and varied activities of financial markets both mirror and induce events in the economic system at large. Only rarely, however, do they serve as ends in themselves. Instead, they facilitate earning and spending, saving and investing, accumulating and retiring, transferring and bequeathing—all activities at the core of economic life. In principle people could do all of these things without financial markets. In practice well-functioning financial markets enable people to do them more efficiently, and few economic events take place without financial counterparts. Financial markets in fact constitute an essential vehicle through which the millions of different participants in the nonfinancial economy continually interact with one another.

The needs and resources, as well as the objectives and concerns, that people bring to financial transactions are always changing. Greater preferences for homeownership, reduced concerns for providing for one's own or one's children's future, or the desire to take advantage of a new production technology, will influence what people seek from the financial markets and hence what takes place there. New public-policy initiatives, and the persistent advance in the technology (especially communications technology) on which the financial markets rely in conducting

Benjamin M. Friedman is professor of economics, Harvard University.

I am grateful to Christopher Piros and Michael Burda for research assistance; to James Duesenberry, John Lintner, Sanford Rose, William Silber, Stephen Taylor, and James Tobin for helpful discussions and comments on an earlier draft; and to the National Bureau of Economic Research and the Alfred P. Sloan Foundation for research support.

their own business, may also effect change in the financial market. Moreover, because every transaction has two sides—a buyer and a seller, or a borrower and a lender—changes in what some people bring to the financial markets necessarily imply changes in what others find there. Hence financial markets act to transmit, not just absorb, the chain of events that originates in the nonfinancial economy, and in so doing they also importantly influence these events. Observing the financial markets therefore provides an additional perspective for understanding nonfinancial developments, even if the more basic origin of those developments is itself entirely nonfinancial.

The experience of the American financial markets in the era since World War II, when compared to the corresponding prewar experience, presents both continuities and contrasts. A time-traveler from 1940, or even 1900, would probably feel more nearly at home on first disembarking in the financial markets than in most other major arenas of 1980 American economic activity. He would immediately recognize major classes of financial market participants and their chief activities, including banks taking deposits and making loans, insurance companies spreading risk and investing in securities, corporations borrowing to finance capital spending, and individuals both saving for their retirement and borrowing to buy houses. The chief items issued and exchanged in these markets are still currency and deposits, stocks and bonds, bills and IOU's. Even the principal financial events that are news today— large government financings, episodes of tight money, stock market rallies, or bulges in the corporate underwriting calendar—are happenings that attracted attention forty and in some cases eighty years ago.

Much of this immediate familiarity, however, would pertain to the surface only. Behind the sameness of the players and their working vocabulary, in many respects the American financial markets are performing (or misperforming) their various functions differently today than they did years ago. Some changes have reflected the changing requirements placed on the financial markets by the nonfinancial economy, while others have reflected government actions, and in a few cases the primary impetus to change has been innovation within the financial markets themselves. The pace of change has not been uniform either. Some differences between today's financial markets and those of forty years ago represent a contrast between the prewar years and the postwar period as a whole, but others represent instead the ongoing process of change that has occurred throughout the postwar era.

The object of this essay is to gain an overview of developments in the American financial markets since World War II, with particular attention to changes that have occurred either between the prewar and postwar years or within the past several decades. Inevitably such an effort must be selective. The primary emphasis here is on the interaction between the financial markets and the nonfinancial economy, in the sense of the demands that the nonfinancial economy has placed on the financial markets and the ways in which the financial markets have responded to these demands. In addition, much of this essay focuses on the evolving role of government in the financial markets and on the changes that it has brought about. Questions pertaining to the internal organization of financial markets and financial institutions, and to financial innovations per se, are also important, but they will receive less attention here.

Section 1.1 briefly sets the background for this analysis by reviewing some significant differences in the underlying economic climate between the prewar and postwar periods. Section 1.2 examines in detail the changes that have taken place in the financing of the economy's nonfinancial activity. Here the dominant trend of the postwar period has been the increasing tendency toward an economy financed by private rather than public debt. Section 1.3 explores changes in the ways in which financial markets have met these needs, with particular attention to the role of financial intermediaries and changes in patterns of intermediation. The dominant trend of postwar developments in this regard has been a continuing increase in the economy's reliance on financial intermediation which, together with a series of innovations, has reduced barriers and frictions interfering with efficient capital allocation. Section 1.4 focuses on changes in the role of government in the financial markets. The major expansion of the federal government's financial activities during the postwar years has been in guaranteeing and intermediating the private sector's debt, as well as in regulating private financial transactions. In addition, section 1.4 provides a brief qualitative account of the ways in which both the conduct of monetary policy and its perception by financial market participants have evolved during the postwar period. Finally, section 1.5 summarizes the principal conclusions of this survey and reemphasizes the interconnections among them.

1.1 Changes in the Underlying Economic Climate

Although the focus of this essay is on changes in financial markets, it is helpful to begin by noting briefly a few of the major changes that have taken place in the underlying climate of nonfinancial economic activity.[1] Three such changes are of particular relevance for understanding what has happened in the financial markets.

First, the American economy in the postwar era has enjoyed much greater stability and prosperity than in the earlier decades of this century. Despite widespread early fears that "secular stagnation" would follow the country's demobilization after World War II, real output and incomes in the American economy in the postwar era turned out to be both stronger and steadier than in the corresponding prewar experience. As the first two columns of table 1.1 show, the postwar years—especially the 1960s—have displayed not only greater economic growth on

Table 1.1   Measures of United States Economic Conditions

Years	Growth of Real GNP		Change in Equity Prices		Rise in Consumer Price Index	
	Mean	S.D.	Mean	S.D.	Mean	S.D.
1911–20	1.7	5.2	−1.1	9.6	8.1	7.4
1921–30	3.1	7.9	11.5	17.0	−1.7	4.0
1931–40	2.6	8.8	−2.1	27.3	−1.6	5.0
1941–50	4.9	8.2	6.3	14.8	5.6	4.8
1951–60	3.3	3.2	12.4	12.6	2.1	2.3
1961–70	4.0	2.2	4.6	10.1	2.8	1.8
1971–78	3.4	3.1	2.6	13.6	6.7	2.5

Sources: U.S. Department of Commerce, Standard and Poor's, and U.S. Bureau of Labor Statistics. This table is in part adapted from Baily (1978).
Note: Data are means and standard deviations, in percentage per annum.

average (as measured by real gross national product) but also a smaller variability of that growth. The pattern of the business cycle, indicated in table 1.2 by the peak-to-trough decline in real gross national product for the thirteen cycles that occurred during the past sixty years, also highlights the increased stability of the postwar period. On the whole, the economy's downturns have been both shorter and shallower.[2] Furthermore, not only has the economy during the postwar period experi-

Table 1.2   Timing and Severity of United States Business Cycle Downturns

Peak	Trough	% Decline in Real GNP.
1918: *Q3*	1919: *Q1*	3.6
1920: *Q1*	1921: *Q3*	8.7
1923: *Q2*	1924: *Q3*	0.2
1926: *Q3*	1927: *Q4*	0.1
1929: *Q3*	1933: *Q1*	29.4
1937: *Q2*	1938: *Q2*	4.1
1945: *Q1*	1945: *Q4*	15.9
1948: *Q4*	1949: *Q2*	1.4
1953: *Q2*	1954: *Q2*	3.3
1957: *Q3*	1958: *Q1*	3.2
1960: *Q1*	1960: *Q4*	1.2
1969: *Q3*	1970: *Q4*	1.1
1973: *Q4*	1975: *Q1*	5.7

Source: U.S. Department of Commerce.
Notes: Peak and trough dates from National Bureau of Economic Research reference cycles; real GNP decline in first seven recessions shown based on annual National Income and Product Accounts data (comparison of 1946 over 1944 for 1945 recession); real GNP decline in last six recessions shown based on quarterly National Income and Product Accounts data.

enced less severe recessions on average, but until 1973 the trend appeared to be toward progressively less severity. After the recessions of 1953–54 and 1957–58, a decade-and-a-half elapsed before another downturn amounted to as much as half of their fairly modest magnitudes.

This enhanced stability of the real economy has both affected and been reflected by financial values. As columns 3 and 4 of table 1.1 show, equity prices in the postwar period, especially until the 1970s, have been less variable than in the prewar period. There have also been fewer nonfinancial corporate bankruptcies since World War II. There have been far fewer bank failures, and—until 1974—essentially no failures at all of large banks.

The realization that the postwar American economy had entered an era of stability and prosperity, instead of returning to the years of chaos and depression, gradually altered both business and consumer thinking in important ways. In addition, the emergence of the United States as the world's dominant military superpower, with attendant responsibilities and privileges in the political and economic spheres, only contributed further to the sense of confidence and expanding horizons. The resulting new perceptions of growth opportunities and new attitudes toward risk-bearing in turn played a major role in bringing about the changing patterns of corporate finance and personal saving that are the subject of section 1.2 below, as well as some aspects of the changing patterns of financial intermediation that are the subject of section 1.3.

A second major feature of the postwar American economy that has importantly affected developments in the financial markets has been price inflation. Whether by cause or by accident, the economy's new-found real prosperity and stability did not come without costs, and among these costs the most readily apparent to almost all of the economy's participants has been the acceleration and increasing volatility of inflation during the second half of the postwar period (see cols. 5 and 6 of table 1.1). The postwar period at first brought an improvement in the stability of prices as well as real incomes, as the rapid and volatile inflation of the immediate postwar years gave way to price movements that were on balance both slower and steadier, especially in the early 1960s. The improvement, however, proved only temporary. Beginning in the mid 1960s prices (and wages) rose more rapidly, leading in time to two episodes of double-digit inflation in the 1970s. Moreover, the faster average rate of price increase during the most recent decade has itself been more volatile.

It is not the purpose of this essay to analyze the reasons for the accelerating postwar American inflation. The focus here is rather on the effects of this new development on the financial markets. Because the greatest acceleration of inflation has come only within the past decade, many key substantive questions about the effects of inflation remain unresolved. Even so, it seems clear already that some of the important financial changes discussed in sections 1.2 and 1.3 below have been due at least in part to the increasing awareness on the part of individuals and businesses of inflation per se, as well as to the rising average interest rate levels that inflation has brought. In addition, several changes in the role of government discussed in section 1.4 have also come about largely as a result of either or both inflation and high nominal interest rates.

Finally, a third feature of the postwar American economic climate that is useful to bear in mind in analyzing this era's financial market changes is the shifting character of the international equilibrium (or disequilibrium). From the beginning of World War I onward, the Western world's international economic balance was highly precarious, and international mechanisms were important in propagating economic disturbances as well as in heightening their severity.[3] In the early years after World War II it looked as if the world economy was at last—or, in the opinion of some who recalled conditions before World War I, again— relatively free from this source of instability. After World War II the world had accepted a de facto dollar standard, and it maintained this convenience even after the return to convertibility of key European currencies in 1958. In addition, until the early 1960s the recovering European economies continually sought both more dollars and more American goods, so that the United States enjoyed not only a strong balance of payments but also the confidence that came from knowing that other countries would gladly absorb dollars in payment for their goods if the American payments balance were not in balance.

This situation changed as the postwar period advanced. America's trading partners increasingly became competitors, and tough competitors at that. Balance-of-payments surpluses changed to deficits. Discussions of how the United States could satisfy the familiar "dollar shortage" disappeared, to be replaced by questions of what, if anything, the United States could do to relieve the "dollar overhang." In the 1970s volatility in the foreign exchange markets again became a major concern, this time with a weak rather than a strong dollar as the center of attention. Questions about the future of the dollar's role in international trade and finance became widespread, especially after the abandonment of dollar-gold convertibility in 1971 and the gradual move to a de facto system of "floating but managed" exchange rates during the next several years. The effective cartelization of the world oil supply in 1973 brought a new wave of payments imbalances and highly skewed accumulations of international reserves, this time far greater in magnitude than any recent experience. On balance, the trend toward ever greater stability in the international economic environment in the first half of the postwar period reversed itself in the second half, although even in the 1970s the situation was far from what it was in the interwar years, and the continuing presence of institutions such as the International Monetary Fund provide a measure of safety that was not there before. This advance and then retreat in the stability of the international economic system, and simultaneously in the strength of the American position in it, have also helped to mold a number of the major changes that have taken place in the American financial markets during this period.   ·

In sum, real economic stability and prosperity, accelerating price inflation, and a more stable but somewhat deteriorating international equilibrium have lain behind much of the development of the American financial markets in the postwar era. Just within the past half decade, however, public confidence in the continuation of the first of these three factors has weakened noticeably. In part this reduced confidence has reflected the growing awareness of inflation and international events, together with a mounting sentiment that these processes must not continue unabated. To whatever extent conditions fostering inflation and a weak dollar had been a source of rapid economic growth, the public has inferred that actions taken to curb them will probably trim the economy's average real performance too. The unanticipated magnitude of the 1973–75 recession, coming as it did after two decades of damping of the economy's business cycle, also exerted a major impact on people's thinking. So too did the series of oil price increases imposed by the cartel. To whatever extent the reliance on inexpensive and plentifully available energy supplies had been a source of rapid growth, the public has feared that both price and quantity actions taken by the foreign oil producers would limit and disrupt future growth. Even simple extrapolations of economic growth on the basis of purely domestic developments such as labor force and productivity also suggested slower growth ahead, since by the 1970s the postwar baby boom had matured, the birthrate had fallen sharply, and the trend rise in productivity had suffered at least one downward shift.[4]

Moreover, economic events have probably not been the sole cause of the decline in confidence in America's economic prospects that set in during the 1970s. Loss of the Vietnam War, apparent erosion of American influence in world affairs, failure to meet domestic social objectives set in the 1960s, increased emphasis on pollution and other intangible costs typically associated with the economic process, and the political trauma of Watergate all contributed to the feeling, widely reported in surveys of business and consumer opinion, that the future looked less bright than the postwar past.

The chief reason why it is useful to emphasize here this most recent apparent shift in attitudes toward the nation's economic climate and prospects is that it provides a clear warning against projecting, as a forecast, any simple continuation of the postwar financial developments described in the remainder of this essay. Within only a decade—a relatively brief interval in the context of the overview attempted here—the American public has sharply changed its perception of the stable growth and prosperity that have been perhaps the central features of their economy's postwar experience. Events may yet prove them right or wrong, but financial behavior responds powerfully to attitudes and perceptions as well as realities. Especially for changes in financial markets, analyzing the past is not equivalent to predicting the future.

1.2   Changes in the Financing of Economic Activity

Individuals, businesses and governments sometimes engage in financial transactions directly with one another, although more often one or more intermediaries stand between them. Nevertheless, because the needs of nonfinancial entities to borrow and lend, to issue liabilities and hold assets, to render and receive payments, constitute the essential raison d'etre of financial markets, in assessing changes in financial markets over a long period of time it is useful to begin by abstracting from the financial intermediation process and directly examining changes in the liability issuing and asset holding behavior of the economy's nonfinancial participants.

1.2.1   The Postwar Rise of the Private Debt Economy

The single development in the American financial markets since World War II that has been most striking from this perspective has been the rise of the private debt economy. Individuals and especially businesses have almost continually increased their degree of reliance on debt in relation to their basic nonfinancial activity. Corporations have relied more on both negotiated loans and market debt issues, in comparison to equity either issued externally or retained internally, to finance their ownership of productive assets and working capital. Individuals have relied more on mortgage credit to finance their houses, and on consumer credit to finance their ownership of durables and even their current consumption. As a result, the indebtedness of the American economy's private sector has risen substantially.

It is essential to ask at the outset whether this pervasive increase in private indebtedness that has taken place during the postwar period has also represented a change in the nonfinancial economy's total propensity to issue debt liabilities (and hold debt assets). The answer is a straightforward negative. The total amount of debt issued by nonfinancial borrowers in the American economy has in fact remained remarkably stable in relation to economic activity throughout the postwar period.[5] Hence the great rise in private debt has mirrored a substantial decline, relative to economic activity, in public debt. Although state and local governments have increased their debt somewhat, an enormous decline (again, relative to economic activity)—in the federal government's outstanding debt has predominated. Hence the postwar rise of the private debt economy has come largel yas the counterpart of a falling off of federal indebtedness.

Figure 1.1 and table 1.3 indicate the general dimensions of the postwar movement to private debt.[6] Figure 1.1 plots, for the years 1918–78, the total outstanding credit market debt issued by the economy's non-financial borrowers, scaled as a percentage of nonfinancial economic activity as measured by gross national product. The figure also plots the respective components of this total debt ratio according to major categories of nonfinancial borrowers in the economy: the federal government, state and local governments, businesses, and households. Table 1.3 presents for closer inspection the underlying data for the postwar years, further distinguishing between corporate and noncorporate businesses and also including, as a memorandum item, debt issued in American markets by foreign borrowers.[7]

The key aspect of the American nonfinancial economy's use of financial markets that stands out sharply in figure 1.1 is the relative stability of its total debt outstanding despite the wide variation of the several components that together comprise the total. Apart from a one-time adjustment associated with the fall of prices at the end of World War I, the nonfinancial economy's reliance on debt, scaled in relation to economic activity, has shown essentially no trend over the past sixty years. At 143 percent as of year-end 1978, the debt ratio was virtually unchanged from 142 percent in 1921. Nonfinancial borrowers' outstanding

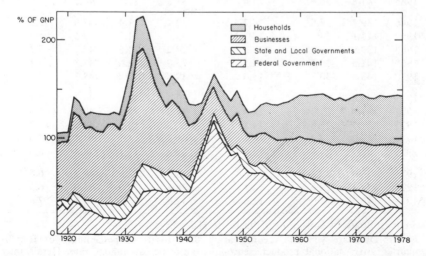

Fig. 1.1   Outstanding debt of United States nonfinancial borrowers.

debt rose significantly in relation to gross national product only during the depression years 1930–33, when gross national product itself not only was well below trend but also was falling too rapidly for the pay-

Table 1.3   Outstanding Debt of United States Nonfinancial Borrowers

Year	Total	Federal Government	State & Local Government	Business Corps.	Other Businesses	Households	Memorandum: Foreign
1946	155.8	103.5	7.0	22.4	7.0	16.0	3.6
1947	145.7	90.6	6.9	23.3	7.0	18.0	5.0
1948	138.4	81.0	7.2	23.7	7.0	19.6	5.2
1949	149.5	84.9	8.4	25.2	7.6	23.5	5.4
1950	133.3	70.8	8.2	23.3	7.4	23.7	4.6
1951	126.9	63.8	8.1	23.5	7.4	24.1	4.3
1952	128.1	61.6	8.7	24.2	7.5	26.1	4.2
1953	134.7	63.0	9.7	25.1	7.5	29.3	4.5
1954	137.0	61.5	11.0	25.5	7.7	31.3	4.4
1955	134.1	56.1	11.3	25.4	7.8	33.4	4.0
1956	133.8	52.0	11.6	26.6	7.9	35.6	4.0
1957	136.2	50.1	12.3	28.1	8.2	37.5	4.2
1958	137.4	49.6	12.9	28.5	8.3	38.2	4.5
1959	141.3	48.3	13.5	29.0	8.7	40.7	4.3
1960	144.0	46.8	14.3	30.5	9.1	43.3	4.6
1961	142.4	45.0	14.3	30.4	9.2	43.5	4.7
1962	143.7	43.8	14.5	30.9	9.6	45.0	4.9
1963	144.0	41.7	14.6	31.0	10.2	46.5	5.1
1964	145.9	40.4	14.8	31.4	10.9	48.5	5.5
1965	141.8	36.8	14.4	31.3	11.1	48.2	5.3
1966	139.7	34.5	14.2	32.1	11.4	47.6	5.1
1967	141.1	34.1	14.3	33.6	11.7	47.5	5.3
1968	139.9	32.7	14.2	34.2	11.6	47.1	5.1
1969	141.5	30.3	14.5	35.8	12.0	47.8	5.1
1970	143.6	30.2	15.0	37.8	12.4	48.3	5.2
1971	143.8	29.8	15.3	37.5	12.8	48.3	5.1
1972	141.9	27.9	14.9	37.4	13.1	48.5	5.0
1973	141.7	25.8	14.3	38.5	13.5	49.6	5.0
1974	144.0	24.8	14.4	41.3	13.7	49.8	5.6
1975	142.7	27.9	14.0	39.4	13.1	48.3	6.0
1976	143.6	29.4	13.6	38.7	12.8	49.2	6.5
1977	144.3	29.0	13.1	38.4	12.8	51.0	6.5
1978	143.3	28.0	12.6	37.8	12.7	52.1	7.4

Source: Board of Governors of the Federal Reserve System.

Notes: Data are year-end credit market debt totals as percentages of fourth-quarter gross national product, seasonally adjusted, at annual rate. Detail may not add to totals because of rounding.

down of debt to keep pace.[8] Otherwise the economy's total nonfinancial debt ratio has remained roughly steady throughout this period. Indeed, as table 1.3 documents in greater detail, the debt ratio has been especially steady during the most recent quarter-century, exhibiting only a slight upward trend and a small amount of cyclicality due to fluctuations of gross national product around its growth trend.[9] From this overall perspective, therefore, the years since World War II have largely represented a continuation of the prewar era.

It is interesting to speculate about the underlying economic behavior that has held the economy's total outstanding nonfinancial debt so steady in relation to its nonfinancial activity. Several different kinds of behavior, not mutually exclusive, may have contributed to this phenomenon. First, the risk of default typically prevents either individuals or businesses from borrowing much in excess of their ownership of (explicit or implicit) collateral, and physical assets constitute the only such collateral that most nonfinancial borrowers can provide. To the extent that private wealth holders in the economy seek to maintain their net worth in relation to their incomes by accumulating more physical assets as they own fewer government-issued financial assets, their ability to issue their own debt will rise as the predominance of government-issued debt declines. Alternatively, some private borrowers may be able to issue as much debt as they want in relation to their incomes, but may also recognize that their liability for future tax payments to support the government's debt service obligations makes the government's debt in some ways equivalent to their own. As their indirect obligations to help service government-issued debt decline, therefore, they become willing to incur an increasing amount of direct obligations for their own debt. Finally, since financial intermediaries must issue their own liabilities approximately in proportion to whatever assets they hold, the amount of debt liabilities that the nonfinancial economy, in total, issues and the amount of financial assets that the nonfinancial economy, in total, holds must be about equal. If private wealth holders in the economy have steady demands for financial assets in relation to their incomes, then the decline of government-issued debt will clear the way for the market as a whole to absorb more private debt, so that this apparent stability on the borrowing side of the financial markets in reality simply mirrors a more fundamental stability on the lending side. Regardless of the relative importance of these (and possibly other) kinds of economic behavior in explaining the stability of the economy's nonfinancial debt ratio, however, that stability has now remained one of the major regularities of the economy's performance over a long period of time.[10]

In sharp contrast to the steadiness of the American nonfinancial economy's overall reliance on debt, the debt issuing behavior on the part of specific categories of nonfinancial borrowers has shown widely divergent patterns. Here the ongoing postwar trend toward ever less federal government debt and ever more private debt in relation to gross national product marks a sharp break from the immediately preceding years. During the 1920s the government was gradually repaying the debt burden it had assumed during World War I,[11] and in these years the private sector was increasing its relative indebtedness. During the 1930s, however, the ratio of the government's debt to gross national product increased by a factor of two-and-a-half (from 18 percent in 1930 to 45 percent in 1940), and during World War II it increased by yet another two-and-a-half (to 119 percent in 1945). The financial system absorbed this rapid relative growth of government indebtedness at first by a temporary increase in the total nonfinancial debt ratio, and then by a sharp reduction in outstanding private debt in relation to economic activity. Since World War II, however, the federal government has again been "repaying" its debt—not by actual repayment from budget surplus, but by the growth (in recent years, mostly the inflation) of economic activity—so that in 1978 the ratio of its debt to gross national product was again down to 28 percent, almost identical to the value in 1918. From the perspective of its total absorption of resources from the financial markets, therefore, the government's posture during the bulk of the post-World War II period has mostly resembled that of the 1920s and has stood in contrast to that of the 1930s and the war itself.

The postwar rise of the private debt economy, following as it did the decline in reliance on private debt during the 1930s and the war years, has mirrored the change in the federal government's behavior. Both businesses and individuals have participated in this postwar resurgence of private debt. The outstanding debt of businesses, which declined in relation to gross national product from 123 percent in 1932 to 29 percent in 1946, has risen in the postwar years to 50 percent in 1978 (in comparison with 84 percent in 1921). The debt ratio for households, which first rose from 15 percent in 1921 to 34 percent in 1932 and then declined to 11 percent in 1944, has risen to 52 percent in 1978. On a short-run basis the data, especially for businesses, exhibit modest cyclical variation in a direction which partly offsets the cyclicality of the government's indebtedness. Nevertheless, over the postwar period as a whole, the trend toward increasing reliance on debt by the private sector has been clear.

In sum, the sustained large-scale turn toward private debt has been one of the principal ways in which the American financial markets in the postwar period have changed, at least in comparison to their more immediate prewar experience. An important question, which this essay leaves unresolved, is whether this resurgence of private debt has primarily constituted merely a return to "normality" after the aberration of the depression and the war or, instead, a shift to a greater "normal" indebtedness than that which prevailed half a century ago. Both factors have no doubt contributed at least to some extent. That the years 1930–45 constituted an aberration, and that a large part of the postwar trend has represented a reversal of that aberration, is certainly plausible enough. Moreover, as the discussion below brings out, after the war the relative indebtedness of some categories of nonfinancial borrowers rose steadily for one or two decades but then reached a plateau for some time, perhaps indicating a completion of the reversal process and re-attainment of the relevant prewar (and pre-depression) norms. Never-theless, the plateauing of businesses' relative indebtedness in the past few years may have been a reflection of cyclical factors rather than longer run forces, and, after a hiatus of over a decade, households have begun to increase their relative indebtedness once again. Even apart from the evidence of experience itself, there are a priori reasons for believing that the progressive development of intermediation in the American financial markets, discussed in section 1.3 below, may have created an environment that is indeed consistent with a higher "normal" private debt ratio than that which characterized the prewar economy.

1.2.2 Specific Nonfinancial Borrowers' Debt-Issuing Behavior

Before going on to examine changes in patterns of intermediation and in asset-holding behavior, it is useful to consider the way in which private debt has come to play this greater role in the financing of economic activity by focusing briefly on the postwar borrowing experience of the principal specific groups whose needs the American financial markets serve.

Businesses

Table 1.4 provides an indication of the changing absolute and relative magnitudes of American nonfinancial corporate businesses' financial needs by presenting data, in dollars and as a ratio to gross national product, showing the average volume of corporations' uses of funds during successive five-year segments of the postwar period to date (and the three-year average for 1976–78). On the whole, the experience of unincorporated businesses has been roughly similar to that of corpora-tions in this regard. Corporate businesses' total uses of funds have grown not only absolutely but also in comparison to the overall scale of the nation's economic activity, although this increase has entirely come in the 1960s and 1970s. Corporations' uses of funds for all purposes first declined from an average 9.9 percent of gross national product during 1946–50 to 9.2 percent during 1956–60 and then rose by more than one-fourth, reaching 11.9 percent during 1971–75. As the memorandum item in the table shows, the nonfinancial activity of the corporate sector, as measured by its gross domestic product, has risen almost continuously

Table 1.4   Uses of Funds by United States Nonfinancial Corporate
                   Businesses

Years	Total Uses	Capital Expenditures		Net Acquisition of Financial Assets		Memorandum: GDP of Nonfinancial Corporate Business
		Total	Plant and Equipment	Total	Liquid Assets	
Billions of Dollars						
1946–50	25.0	18.7	15.5	6.4	1.0	128.4
1951–55	34.2	27.1	23.3	7.1	1.9	192.2
1956–60	42.3	35.1	31.8	7.2	−0.4	250.6
1961–65	62.1	47.7	40.2	14.4	2.3	335.2
1966–70	98.5	78.1	66.6	20.4	1.3	496.8
1971–75	152.6	108.8	97.3	43.8	11.5	741.7
1976–78	224.8	168.3	144.8	56.5	8.7	1113.7
Percent of GNP						
1946–50	9.9	7.5	6.2	2.4	0.3	51.4
1951–55	9.4	7.5	6.4	1.9	0.5	53.1
1956–60	9.2	7.6	6.9	1.5	−0.1	54.3
1961–65	10.3	7.9	6.6	2.4	0.4	55.7
1966–70	11.4	9.1	7.7	2.3	0.1	57.3
1971–75	11.9	8.4	7.5	3.4	0.9	57.2
1976–78	11.7	8.8	7.6	2.9	0.5	58.6

Source: Board of Governors of the Federal Reserve System.
Notes: Data are averages of annual flows, in dollars and as percentages of annual gross national product. Detail may not add to totals because of rounding.

throughout the postwar period, so that at least a part of this greater relative use of funds in recent years may have reflected greater relative nonfinancial activity. Within the overall total, use of funds for purposes of physical investment—including plant, equipment, real estate, inventories, and other real investments—has consistently dominated use of funds for purposes of acquiring financial assets, and has also accounted for most of the increase in total use in relation to gross national product. Nonfinancial corporations have also consistently used some funds to acquire (mostly nonliquid) financial assets, thereby acting in part as financial intermediaries.

Against this background of corporate businesses' needs for funds in their ongoing ordinary nonfinancial activity, table 1.5 presents five-year average data, in dollars and as percentages of total sources of funds, showing how corporations have financed these needs.[12] After World War II the balance of corporate financing first shifted toward internally generated funds including both depreciation allowances and undistributed profits. Beginning in the early 1960s, however, it shifted back toward external funds, including both debt and equity issues. Internal funds provided an average 67 percent of corporations' total funds requirements during 1951–55 and 69 percent during 1956–60, but then fell to only 55 percent during 1971–75. Also over these years depreciation allowances increased in importance, and retained earnings (in other words, internal additions of common equity) decreased in importance, among the sources of internal funds themselves. To the extent that depreciation allowances represent genuine consumption of the capital stock rather than merely a way of redefining profits so as to render them exempt from corporate income taxes, therefore, the decline in the contribution of internally generated funds to the growth of the corporate sector has been even more pronounced than these data suggest.[13] During 1974–77 the effects of the severe business recession and recovery temporarily reversed the trend toward external finance, so much so that corporations' outstanding indebtedness fell from 41 percent of gross national product to 38 percent. Since then, however, corporations have apparently resumed the financing patterns that had predominated for a decade-and-a-half before the unusually deep recession.

A further feature of corporate financial behavior that emerges clearly from table 1.5 is the increase in importance of debt and the correspond-

Table 1.5   **Sources of Funds to United States Nonfinancial Corporate Businesses**

		Gross Internal Funds			Net Increase in Liabilities		
Years	Total Sources	Total	CCA	Undis-tributed Profit	Total	Equity Issues	Credit Market Debt
		Billions of Dollars					
1946–50	30.3	18.6	6.7	11.4	11.8	1.1	5.5
1951–55	35.3	23.5	13.2	9.5	11.8	1.9	6.6
1956–60	47.0	32.6	21.6	10.0	14.4	2.0	10.0
1961–65	69.1	46.0	31.3	13.1	23.1	0.7	14.0
1966–70	111.2	64.5	46.7	16.1	44.7	2.5	30.7
1971–75	182.7	99.7	70.9	25.8	83.0	8.8	50.4
1976–78	267.6	156.3	102.5	49.0	111.2	5.3	73.2
		Percentage of Total Sources of Funds					
1946–50	100.0	61.2	22.2	37.4	38.8	3.7	18.0
1951–55	100.0	66.5	37.2	26.8	33.5	5.4	18.5
1956–60	100.0	69.4	46.0	21.1	30.6	4.3	21.1
1961–65	100.0	66.6	45.3	19.0	33.4	0.9	20.2
1966–70	100.0	59.0	42.8	14.8	41.0	2.3	28.1
1971–75	100.0	54.6	38.8	14.1	45.4	4.8	27.6
1976–78	100.0	58.4	38.3	18.3	41.6	2.0	27.3

Source: Board of Governors of the Federal Reserve System.

Notes: Data are averages of annual flows, in dollars and as percentages of total sources. Detail may not add to totals because of rounding.

ing decline in importance of equity (until the early 1970s) among corporations' external sources of funds. New issues of equity (net of retirements) accounted for an average of nearly 15 percent of corporations' external funds sources during the 1950s but then less than 5 percent during the 1960s, and in three years out of ten during the 1960s equity retirements actually exceeded new issues. Moreover, the data shown in table 1.5 importantly understate both the magnitude and the persistence of the shift to debt finance. What little equity issuance took place during the 1960s typically represented initial public offerings of speculative new ventures aimed at a segment of the investing public that was willing to bear substantial risk. Established corporations largely avoided the equity market. In addition, the bulge of equity offerings during the early 1970s primarily represented only one sector of American industry (public utility companies), and it consisted in large part of preferred shares which are in many respects simply bonds that receive special tax treatment for corporate investors.[14]

Businesses' increasing reliance on debt financing has probably reflected several influences on corporate financial decision-making. To begin, most American businesses emerged from World War II carrying debt that was, in relation to their volume of production and profits, very small in comparison with their prewar experience. As figure 1.1 shows, nonfinancial business indebtedness in relation to gross national product peaked in 1932 and then fell slowly during the remainder of the 1930s. The most rapid decline, however, came during the war years, as the overall business debt ratio fell from 63 percent in 1940 to 27 percent in 1945 (40 percent to 17 percent for corporations). It is at least possible, therefore, that the entire subsequent increase to 55 percent at the 1974 peak (37 percent for corporations) simply represented a slow restoration—which may not yet be complete—of a perceived normal indebtedness that has remained unchanged since before the war. Indeed, by comparison with the standard of the 1920s, the postwar rise in corporate indebtedness has been modest thus far.

Other, more specific explanations are also available, however. First, any private borrower's willingness to incur debt liabilities presumably reflects confidence in the ability to meet these obligations under a wide range of plausible circumstances, including both those particular to the borrower and those general to the economy. As business decision makers became aware of the American economy's distinctly greater stability and prosperity in the postwar era, they probably associated a smaller risk with any given level of indebtedness in relation to either balance sheet or income reference points. Second, the secular acceleration of inflation and rise of nominal interest rates has provided a further incentive for taxable borrowers to increase their indebtedness. As figure 1.2 shows, on average nominal interest rates have about kept pace with inflation,

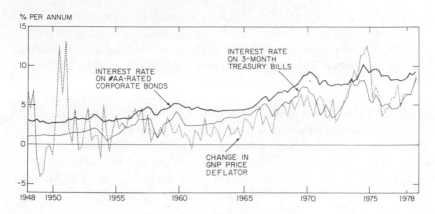

Fig. 1.2   Interest rates and price inflation.

so that "real" interest rates have remained roughly unchanged during the postwar period. Given the deductibility of interest payments against income for tax purposes, however, after-tax "real" interest rates faced by corporate borrowers have been negative almost throughout this period, and have become progressively more negative since the early 1960s —exactly the period of greatest increase in the debt share of total sources of funds.[15] Finally, at least throughout the 1960s, corporate financial decision makers appear to have operated almost continually under the opinion that equities were somehow "undervalued." Especially during the 1960s the belief that equities were undervalued on a widespread basis led not only to the paucity of new equity issues by major corporations but also to such developments as a wave of conglomerate mergers largely financed by debt. In fact, as figure 1.3 shows, equity prices on average had risen sharply during the 1950s and 1960s, both nominally and on a price-adjusted basis. Since then there has been little trend movement nominally and a large decline in real terms, so that any re-

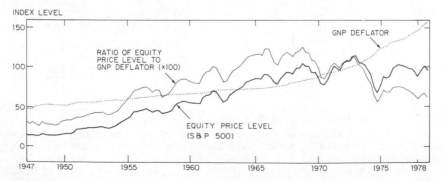

Fig. 1.3   Equity prices and the GNP price deflator.

luctance to issue new equities in the late 1960s because of undervaluation appears (with the benefit of hindsight) to have been misplaced.

Whatever its cause, the shift by corporations from internal funds generation to external financing and from equity to debt within that external financing total, together with similar trends among nonincorporated businesses, has been a major feature of the postwar American financial markets. Table 1.6 presents data showing the total accumulation and also the maturity composition of corporate businesses' outstanding debt. These data show clearly that the large shift to debt financing beginning in the mid 1960s also brought a slow increase in the short-term share of the debt, thereby breaking away from the virtually fixed maturity composition that had prevailed since the end of World War II.[16]

Individuals

The substantial postwar increase in households' relative indebtedness, shown in figure 1.1 and table 1.3, has probably reflected behavioral influences analogous to those identified above as likely causes of the rise

Table 1.6	Outstanding Debt of United States Nonfinancial Corporate Businesses		
Years	Total Credit Market Debt	Long-Term	Short-Term
	Billions of Dollars		
1946–50	60.9	48.6	12.4
1951–55	91.5	72.7	18.7
1956–60	133.9	106.8	27.1
1961–65	191.3	151.9	39.5
1966–70	309.3	238.3	71.0
1971–75	523.4	396.7	126.8
1976–78	760.3	568.8	191.5
	Percentage of Total Debt		
1946–50	100.0	79.7	20.3
1951–55	100.0	79.5	20.5
1956–60	100.0	79.8	20.2
1961–65	100.0	79.4	20.6
1966–70	100.0	77.0	23.0
1971–75	100.0	75.8	24.2
1976–78	100.0	74.8	25.2

Source: Board of Governors of the Federal Reserve System.

Notes: Data are averages of year-end credit market debt outstanding, in dollars and as percentages of the annual total. Detail may not add to totals because of rounding. Long-term debt, with a maturity of over one year, is measured approximately as bonds, multifamily and commercial mortgages, and 40 percent of bank loans. Short-term debt is all other credit market borrowings, including mostly finance company loans, commercial paper, and the remainder of bank loans.

in businesses' reliance on debt. Initially just the return to borrowing standards that had prevailed before the war, then a changing perception of tolerable debt levels as confidence in the economy's stability and prosperity became widespread, and finally the growing after-tax incentive for those in higher tax brackets to borrow as price inflation and nominal interest rates rose together,[17] all contributed to individuals' greater willingness to borrow.

Unlike businesses, however, individuals during the postwar period have increased their outstanding debt well beyond the relationship to gross national product that prevailed during the prewar years. Households' outstanding debt gradually rose from 15 percent of gross national product in 1921 to 24 percent in 1929, then temporarily rose somewhat further in the early 1930s (when gross national product was well below trend), but then stabilized again at an unvarying 25 percent throughout 1936–40. When individuals emerged from World War II with a debt ratio of only 13 percent in 1945 (the low had been 11 percent a year earlier), they presumably felt ample room to borrow heavily. Individuals pushed their indebtedness relative to gross national product past the 25 percent prewar norm as early as 1952, however, and continued to increase it virtually without interruption until 1964 when it reached 48 percent—a level at which it remained almost constant through 1975. Hence it appeared that individuals had reached a new postwar capacity level of tolerable debt. Just during the late 1970s, however, individuals once again began to increase their relative indebtedness. All of these changes in households' indebtedness in relation to gross national product have also represented changes in relation to personal disposable income, which has claimed a steady average of 69 percent of the gross national product, with no trend at all, throughout the postwar period.

Tables 1.7, 1.8, and 1.9 present data for households comparable to that shown in tables 1.4, 1.5 and 1.6 for nonfinancial corporate businesses. First, table 1.7 indicates households' changing financial needs by showing their total uses of funds for all purposes, divided between current consumption of nondurable goods and services and all "investment" type uses—including new residential construction, outlays for durable goods, and financial investment. Whether the evolution of individual behavior documented in table 1.7 constitutes a case for change or continuity within the postwar period is largely a matter of emphasis. Nondurable consumption has remained a steady five-eighths of gross national product, without any trend, since the early 1950s. Households' total nonconsumption uses of funds remained roughly steady at one-fifth of the gross national product until 1970, but has risen sharply since then. Within this total, both durables purchases and residential construction have held a steady relation to overall economic activity throughout, but the net acquisition of financial assets has approximately

Table 1.7 Uses of Funds by United States Households

Years	Total Uses	Nondurable Consumption	Investment Uses of Funds				Memorandum: Personal Disposable Income
			Total	Durable Expenditure	Residential Construction	Net Acquisition of Financial Assets	
			Billions of Dollars				
1946–50	209.7	162.0	47.7	23.0	10.4	14.3	181.4
1951–55	294.1	223.0	71.2	32.4	17.1	21.8	248.2
1956–60	383.8	294.0	89.8	40.0	20.1	29.8	320.2
1961–65	496.2	376.7	119.5	51.8	20.9	46.9	411.7
1966–70	698.4	529.1	169.3	77.5	23.4	68.4	591.9
1971–75	1093.0	805.4	287.5	117.3	40.8	129.4	903.4
1976–78	1670.3	1197.9	472.5	178.8	75.3	218.4	1316.0
			Percentage of GNP				
1946–50	84.2	65.2	19.1	9.1	4.1	5.8	72.9
1951–55	81.2	61.6	19.6	8.9	4.7	6.0	68.6
1956–60	83.2	63.7	19.5	8.7	4.4	6.5	69.5
1961–65	82.5	62.8	19.8	8.6	3.5	7.7	68.5
1966–70	80.5	61.0	19.6	8.9	2.7	7.9	68.2
1971–75	84.3	62.0	22.2	9.1	3.2	10.0	69.6
1976–78	87.4	62.8	24.7	9.4	4.0	11.4	68.9

Source: Board of Governors of the Federal Reserve System.

Notes: Data are averages of annual flows, in dollars and as percentages of annual gross national product. Detail may not add to totals because of rounding.

doubled over the postwar years, rising from an average of 6 percent of gross national product during the late 1940s and 1950s to 10–12 percent in the 1970s. While it is important not to lose sight of the distribution of assets and liabilities—the people who borrow are often not the same ones who accumulate assets—on an aggregated basis the notion that individuals have increased their borrowing (relative to economic activity) either to finance investment in houses and durables or to finance current consumption turns out to be false. Instead, they have borrowed more and simultaneously held more financial assets.

A comparison of households' total uses of funds versus personal disposable income, shown as a memorandum item in table 1.7, indicates that individuals have had to be net borrowers throughout the postwar period. After showing little trend for a quarter-century, the shortfall of disposable income from total uses of funds has increased sharply in the 1970s. The data in table 1.8 show how households have financed their growing needs for funds.[18] Here again the data suggest a long period of stability, followed by some change in household behavior either at the beginning of the 1970s or perhaps the 1960s. Until then the balance of saving and borrowing as sources of funds remained largely unchanged.

Table 1.8   **Sources of Funds to United States Households**

	Gross Personal Saving				Net Increase in Liabilities		
Years	Total Sources	Total	Net Personal Saving	Capital Consumption Allowances	Total	Home Mortgages	Installment and Consumer Credit
	Billions of Dollars						
1946–50	45.4	36.9	21.1	15.7	8.5	4.8	3.6
1951–55	68.2	54.7	27.2	27.5	13.6	8.3	3.9
1956–60	85.9	69.3	29.2	40.1	16.6	10.8	4.0
1961–65	114.6	88.4	39.6	48.8	26.2	15.4	7.6
1966–70	166.6	138.0	71.2	66.8	28.5	15.2	8.0
1971–75	277.3	217.5	110.9	106.6	59.8	37.7	16.0
1976–78	442.1	303.8	141.2	162.6	138.3	86.1	38.9
	Percentage of Total Sources						
1946–50	100.0	81.3	45.6	34.7	18.7	10.6	7.9
1951–55	100.0	80.1	39.8	40.3	19.9	12.1	5.8
1956–60	100.0	80.6	34.0	46.6	19.4	12.6	4.6
1961–65	100.0	77.2	34.6	42.6	22.8	13.5	6.7
1966–70	100.0	82.9	42.8	40.1	17.1	9.1	4.8
1971–75	100.0	78.4	40.0	38.4	21.6	13.6	5.8
1976–78	100.0	68.7	31.9	36.8	31.3	19.5	8.8

Source: Board of Governors of the Federal Reserve System.

Notes: Data are averages of annual flows, in dollars and as percentages of total sources. Detail may not add to totals because of rounding.

More recently individuals have relied more heavily on borrowing, including both mortgages and consumer credit (primarily installment credit[19]). Table 1.9 indicates the accumulation and also the relatively stable composition of this expanding individual debt by type of borrowing. Subject to some variation primarily associated with the pace of homebuilding activity and the movement of house prices, home mortgages have accounted for a fairly steady five-eighths of total household indebtedness throughout the postwar period. Consumer credit has gradually shrunk in relation to the total, while the relatively small amount of borrowing in all other forms has gradually grown.

State and Local Governments

State and local government units gradually increased their outstanding debt from 7 percent of the gross national product at the end of World War II to just over double that in 1971 before allowing it to decline somewhat in the 1970s. Once again, a major portion of this increase in indebtedness constituted a return to prewar norms after the aberration of the wartime years. During the 1920s the state and local government debt ratio had slowly risen from 10 percent to 13 percent, and after some fluctuation in the early 1930s it stood at 13 percent in 1941 also.

Table 1.9   **Outstanding Debt of United States Households**

Years	Total Credit Market Debt	Home Mortgages	Installment and Consumer Credit	Other
		Billions of Dollars		
1946–50	52.7	31.2	17.9	3.6
1951–55	107.2	64.1	36.0	7.1
1956–60	183.3	114.8	56.0	12.5
1961–65	286.6	181.1	84.0	21.5
1966–70	423.0	259.0	126.6	37.4
1971–75	657.0	400.3	195.2	61.5
1976–78	1010.5	637.6	292.7	80.2
		Percentage of Total Debt		
1946–50	100.0	59.2	33.9	6.9
1951–55	100.0	59.8	33.6	6.6
1956–60	100.0	62.6	30.5	6.8
1961–65	100.0	63.2	29.3	7.5
1966–70	100.0	61.2	29.9	8.8
1971–75	100.0	60.9	29.7	9.4
1976–78	100.0	63.1	29.0	7.9

Source: Board of Governors of the Federal Reserve System.

Notes: Data are averages of year-end credit market debt outstanding, in dollars and as percentages of the annual total. Detail may not add to totals because of rounding.

At least until 1960, therefore, the postwar increase was merely a restoration of the previous relative debt level. For the next decade outstanding state and local government debt grew little further in relation to the economy's nonfinancial activity, and in the 1970s it again declined to well within its prewar range.

As table 1.10 shows, the leveling of the state and local government debt ratio in the 1960s and its decline in the 1970s stand in some contrast to the relative size of state and local governments' nonfinancial activity, which continued to grow vigorously through both the 1950s and the 1960s, and leveled off but did not decline in the 1970s. State and local government spending has been the single most rapidly growing component of the nation's total spending since World War II. The great surge in the provision of local public services during this period, much of which was associated with the needs created by the postwar baby boom, more than doubled state and local governments' purchases of goods and services as a share of the gross national product. Only in the 1970s has this growth in spending leveled off, as the demographics have shifted markedly and an increasing number of communities have all but completed their basic social capital installations including schools, hospitals, roads, and sewers.

Table 1.10   **Budget Summary for United States State and Local Governments**

Years	Expenditures Total	Expenditures Purchases of Goods and Services	Net Acquisition of Financial Assets	Total Receipts	Net Increase in Liabilities
		Billions of Dollars			
1946–50	17.2	15.1	1.2	17.4	2.1
1951–55	28.0	25.7	1.6	27.4	4.4
1956–60	43.3	40.4	1.4	42.4	5.3
1961–65	63.8	60.0	3.4	64.1	6.5
1966–70	107.1	100.7	4.3	108.1	9.7
1971–75	185.3	172.6	10.1	194.1	16.0
1976–78	275.2	255.5	20.6	299.2	20.6
		Percentage of GNP			
1946–50	6.8	6.0	0.5	6.9	0.8
1951–55	7.7	7.1	0.5	7.6	1.2
1956–60	9.4	8.7	0.3	9.2	1.1
1961–65	10.6	10.0	0.6	10.6	1.1
1966–70	12.3	11.6	0.5	12.4	1.1
1971–75	14.2	13.3	0.8	15.0	1.3
1976–78	14.4	13.4	1.1	15.7	1.1

Source: Board of Governors of the Federal Reserve System.

Notes: Data are averages of annual flows, in dollars and as percentages of annual gross national product. Detail may not add to totals because of rounding.

The budget data in table 1.10 also show that state and local governments on average have typically kept their total receipts, consisting primarily of tax revenues and federal grants, rising in pace with their increasing total expenditures—including primarily purchases of goods and services, plus small amounts of transfer payments and the excess of interest paid over interest received.[20] Indeed, in the 1970s they have consistently run surpluses.[21] Hence state and local governments' borrowing, which has consisted almost entirely of long-term debt, has served in large part to finance these governments' own investment in financial instruments, especially Treasury securities. In 1978, however, the federal government eliminated the right of state and local governments to earn a positive "spread" by issuing tax exempt (and therefore lower yield) securities in order to hold (without paying taxes) higher yielding Treasury securities. Hence the relationship between state and local governments' debt issues and their budget surpluses or deficits may well become closer in the future than it has been in the recent past.

Foreign Borrowers

Foreign borrowers have played a relatively small, though growing, role in the American financial markets throughout the postwar period.[22] During the late 1950s and early 1960s, discussions of the American balance of payments deficit, which people were just then coming to perceive as a problem, often focused on the strength of the American financial markets and on their ability to extend credit to finance the growth of world trade and development. Even so, as the memorandum column of table 1.3 indicates, outstanding debt issued by foreigners in the American markets first equaled 5 percent of this country's gross national product only in 1963, and it peaked at an only slightly higher ratio after the imposition of capital controls the next year. Moreover, throughout this period and into the 1970s, about half of the foreign borrowing here took the form of loans from the federal government rather than funds advanced by private investors. Foreign debt in American markets did not again reach the 1964 level (in relation to gross national product) until 1974, after the removal of the capital controls. The subsequent growth remained modest through 1978, although the increasing amount of developing country debt owed to American banks has recently raised widespread questions about these banks' exposure to risks associated with foreign lending.

It is interesting to speculate about whether foreign borrowing would have been a more important activity in American markets but for the restrictive government actions taken in the 1960s to prevent capital outflows in the interest of maintaining a stronger dollar. From 1964 until 1974 the Interest Equalization Tax effectively prohibited the sale in the United States of debt securities issued by foreign borrowers other than

Canadian provinces and international institutions such as the World Bank, and from 1965 until 1974 the Federal Reserve's so-called Voluntary Foreign Credit Restraint program limited lending abroad by American banks.[23] These two restrictions—along with the Commerce Department's Office of Foreign Direct Investment program, which from 1965 to 1974 required American companies to finance abroad whatever funds they were investing abroad, and the advent of effective interest ceilings on domestic deposits (discussed in section 1.4 below)—probably provided the chief impetus to the rapid development of the Eurodollar and Eurobond markets. Without these capital controls foreign borrowers almost certainly would have done more financing in American markets, and might have done much more. Since the removal of capital controls the volume of both American banks' lending abroad and foreign issues in the American bond market has picked up sharply, but the Euro markets, now that they are well established, remain the major immediate source of dollar credits to most foreign borrowers.[24] In retrospect it is clear that the capital flow restrictions imposed in the 1960s had the effect of enhancing the competitive position of, for example, the London financial markets over those in New York.

Federal Government

The federal government's reliance on the American financial markets during the postwar period has largely constituted a return to the experience of the 1920s after the aberration of the Depression and the war years. After World War II the government's outstanding debt fell steadily in relation to gross national product until the mid-1970s—from 119 percent in 1945 to 56 percent in 1955, 37 percent in 1965, and a low of 25 percent in 1974. Although the federal government's budget has rarely been in surplus, only during the years 1949, 1953 and 1975–76 did the impact of business recessions on tax revenues and transfer payments enlarge the deficit to such an extent that the government did not "pay down" the public debt in relation to (temporarily shrunken) nonfinancial activity. Nevertheless, the other postwar recessions—in 1957–58, 1960–61, and 1969–70—did produce some slowing, though not a reversal, of the overall postwar decline in the government's debt ratio. The combined effect of the relatively mild 1969–70 recession and the especially severe 1973–75 recession has been on balance to halt much of the decline of the public debt ratio in the 1970s, although the government budget projections for 1979–81 that are available as of the time of writing suggest that this decline may now be in progress once again.

Table 1.11 presents budget summary data relating the federal government's financial needs to its nonfinancial activity. Apart from a one-time jump at the beginning of the 1950s and subsequent fluctuations associated with recessions, federal expenditures have grown slowly but stead-

Table 1.11   Budget Summary for United States Federal Government

		Expenditures				
Years	Total	Purchases of Goods and Services	Transfer Payments	Net Acquisition of Financial Assets	Total Receipts	Net Increase in Liabilities
			Billions of Dollars			
1946–50	36.5	17.2	15.1	−0.8	42.9	−6.3
1951–55	68.8	48.1	16.1	1.6	67.6	3.3
1956–60	85.0	51.5	27.7	0.8	85.0	2.2
1961–65	113.7	63.6	42.7	3.4	111.6	6.5
1966–70	176.1	92.2	72.4	3.7	171.2	10.1
1971–75	277.3	106.9	152.2	6.4	251.9	32.6
1976–78	422.2	142.2	249.8	20.6	379.6	69.4
			Percentage of GNP			
1946–50	14.7	7.0	6.1	−0.7	17.3	−3.0
1951–55	19.0	13.3	4.4	0.5	18.7	1.0
1956–60	18.4	11.2	6.0	0.2	18.4	0.5
1961–65	19.0	10.6	7.1	0.6	18.6	1.1
1966–70	20.3	10.7	8.3	0.4	19.7	1.2
1971–75	21.3	8.3	11.6	0.5	19.4	2.4
1976–78	22.1	7.5	13.1	1.1	19.8	3.7

Source: Board of Governors of the Federal Reserve System.
Notes: Data are averages of annual flows, in dollars and as percentages of annual gross national product. Detail may not add to totals because of rounding.

ily in relation to gross national product throughout the postwar period. Within the overall total, however, the mix between transfer payments and direct purchases of goods and services has radically changed. Except for a brief bulge during the Vietnam War years, the share of gross national product claimed by federal goods and services purchases has fallen ever since the early 1950s. By contrast, during this same period federal transfers—including grants to state and local governments, social security benefits, and all other income support payments—have risen even more rapidly in relation to gross national product. As a result, total expenditures (which also include the excess of interest paid over interest received) have grown modestly in relative size, and their composition is now nearly two-thirds transfers and only one-third direct purchases instead of the reverse twenty years ago.[25]

The federal government typically enlarges its portfolio of directly held financial assets only slowly, so that its borrowing primarily reflects the differences between its total expenditures and its total receipts from tax revenues and social security contributions. After a large surplus during the late 1940s and a small deficit during the Korean War years, the federal government's budget was in balance on average during the late 1950s. Since then the budget deficit has averaged 0.5 percent of the gross national product during the 1960s, nearly 2 percent during the early 1970s and more than 2 percent during 1976–78. Even after allowance for the enlargement of the deficit due to the severe 1973–75 recession, the federal budget deficit has shown a slow but steady tendency to grow in relation to the economy's nonfinancial activity.[26] The result has been the continual slowing—and in 1975–76 the temporary reversal—of the decline in the federal debt ratio that has dominated the postwar period thus far.

The maturity composition of the debt issued by the federal government has also changed substantially during the postwar period, as table 1.12 shows. Federal debt management policy has not only stood in contrast to the pattern of wartime financing but has also undergone several sharp breaks within the postwar years. Especially since the Federal Reserve System's abandonment of bond price stabilization at the beginning of the 1950s, postwar debt management has mostly emphasized short-term rather than long-term financing, driving the mean maturity of the outstanding federal debt down from 113 months in 1946 to a low of only 33 months in 1976. In two distinct periods, however, debt management has gone the other way. During the early 1960s the government lengthened its outstanding debt, from a mean maturity of 50 months in September 1960, to 65 months in January 1965.[27] In addition, beginning in 1976 and continuing through the time of writing, the government has been lengthening its debt once again. The increase in mean maturity from 33 months in January 1976, to 43 months as of September 1979, represents about as rapid a rate of increase as the rate of decrease that predominated on average during the previous thirty years.

1.3 Changes in the Working of the Financial Markets

How have the American financial markets in the postwar period met the changing needs that the economy has placed on them? In any well

Table 1.12   **Maturity of Privately Held United States Treasury Securities**

Year	Mean Maturity	Year	Mean Maturity
1945	116	1975	29
1950	100	1976	33
1955	71	1977	35
1960	58	1978	40
1965	63	1979	43
1970	41		

Source: U.S. Department of the Treasury.
Note: Data are mean values for December (September for 1979).

developed financial system it is useful to distinguish the liability-issuing and asset-holding activity which takes place directly between nonfinancial participants in the economy, whose respective principal business interests lie elsewhere, from that which takes place through an intermediary whose principal business is financial transactions themselves. In general, changes in how financial markets work to meet the requirements of the nonfinancial economy may represent some combination of changes in the economy's overall degree of intermediation and changes in how the intermediaries go about their business. In fact both aspects together have accounted for changes in the American financial system during the postwar era.

1.3.1   The Advance of Financial Intermediation

Throughout their history, but more so during the twentieth century and especially in the years since World War II, the American financial markets have undergone a shift away from direct transactions between nonfinancial borrowers and lenders toward the intervention of financial intermediaries.[28] The development of the commercial banking system and of the life insurance industry in earlier years, and more recently the great expansion of nonbank deposit institutions and both private and public sector pension funds, have been important features of the development of the American financial system.

In the postwar period the continuation and even acceleration of the trend toward intermediated financial markets has hardly been independent of the simultaneous rise in the economy's reliance on privately issued debt. Instead, the two developments have been natural counterparts.[29] In comparison with default-free government obligations, risky private securities impose both information and transactions costs that encourage the economy's development of financial intermediaries. Holders (or potential holders) of private securities must first discover the specific risks that individual claims against private issuers entail, and then monitor these risks on an ongoing basis. These information costs are especially large in the case of negotiated loans like home mortgages, consumer credit, and bank loans to businesses. Not only economies of scale but also the advantages of specialization favor delegating this information gathering and processing function to third parties. An equally important function performed by financial intermediaries holding private securities is the pooling of specific risks. In transforming the direct claims that they hold into the indirect claims that they issue, intermediaries economize on transactions costs so as to facilitate diversification by enabling investors to own interests (indirectly) in a large number of imperfectly divisible assets. In addition, by pooling many individuals' and businesses' needs for liquidity, deposit intermediaries often change the risk characteristics of the aggregate of assets to be held by issuing claims (often explicit or implicit demand claims) that have a shorter maturity than the claims that they in turn hold. Similarly, pension and insurance intermediaries change the aggregate risk structure that insured parties face by pooling actuarial risks.

Individuals are the principal *non*financial holders of assets that represent direct claims on other nonfinancial participants in the economy. Individuals' continued willingness to hold such assets therefore constitutes a retardant to the advance of financial intermediation, while their reluctance to perform this function creates the basic need for intermediation. Figure 1.4 shows how American households have shifted the composition of their financial asset portfolios during the postwar period.[30] Households' aggregate holding of deposit-type liabilities of financial intermediaries have grown continually from the early 1950s to the late 1970s, not only absolutely but in relation to overall nonfinancial economic activity (and personal income). Households' claims on insurance and pension reserves have also grown on balance during the postwar years, although here the growth has been less steady because of the effect of equity price changes on the valuation of these reserves (see again fig. 1.3). By contrast, households' direct holdings of nonintermediated debt have declined in relative terms almost continually since World War II, and their direct holdings of equity claims on business corporations have varied mostly with equity price fluctuations, exhibit-

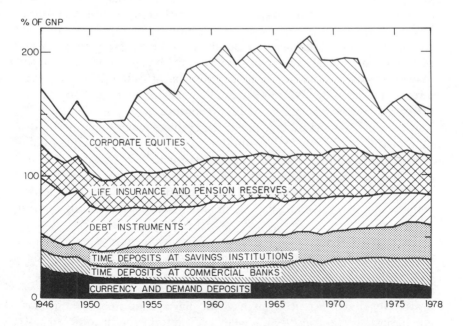

Fig. 1.4   Financial asset holdings of United States households.

ing little overall relative trend.[31] Since the total size of households' financial asset portfolios in relation to gross national product has also shown no overall trend—first declining during the immediate postwar years, then rising sharply in the 1950s, remaining steady through the 1960s, and declining in the 1970s—these patterns of growth and decline in comparison to gross national product also correspond, for the postwar period as a whole, to growth or decline in shares of households' total portfolio.

Households' increasing preference for claims on intermediaries has appeared even more pronounced from the perspective of their accumulation of financial assets. Table 1.13 shows households' net acquisition of various categories of financial assets, both in dollars and as a share of the total. The two features of households' investment behavior that stand out most sharply here are the dominance of deposits throughout the postwar period and the change that took place at the end of the 1950s in households' net investment in corporate equities. Households purchased more equity shares in corporations than they sold in every year during 1946–57, so that the tripling in value of their direct equity holdings over this period represented the combined result of capital gains and positive net purchases. By contrast, households have sold more direct equity shares than they have purchased in every year since 1958, so that capital gains have accounted for more than all of the subsequent increase in total value of their direct equity holdings. Moreover, allowing for the shift from direct ownership of equities to indirect ownership via mutual funds does not alter the fundamental picture of individuals' investment behavior. Households in the aggregate were net purchasers of mutual fund shares during the rise of that industry in the 1960s, but not in sufficient quantity to offset the liquidation of their direct equity holdings. More recently, they have been net sellers of both direct equity holdings and mutual fund shares in every year since 1972. The conclusion remains that equity price movements have accounted for more than all of any increase in the value of individuals' equity holdings. Because equity prices have fluctuated widely but shown little net gain in nominal terms since the mid-1960s (see again fig. 1.3), individuals' aggregate equity portfolio has therefore shown no trend movement in nominal value and has declined in relative value during the last decade and more.

The shift of individuals' investment flows away from equities during the second half of the postwar period probably reflects several considerations in addition to the economies of scale and risk pooling noted above as general advantages of intermediation. Changing birthrates, age distributions, and income levels have all played some role. The increasing government provision of health, education, and income security benefits has also altered the objectives associated with saving for many

Table 1.13   Net Acquisitions of Financial Assets by United States Households

	Total Assets	Currency and Deposits	Equities			Credit Market Debt	Life Insurance and Pension Reserves	Other
			Total	Investment Company Shares	Direct Holdings			
			Billions of Dollars					
1946–50	14.3	3.4	1.0	0.2	0.7	1.2	5.7	3.1
1951–55	21.8	9.7	1.2	0.5	0.7	3.3	7.6	−0.2
1956–60	29.8	13.0	1.0	1.4	− 0.4	6.5	10.6	−1.3
1961–65	46.9	27.8	−1.3	2.1	− 3.4	5.2	14.3	0.8
1966–70	68.4	33.5	−3.3	4.1	− 7.3	15.2	20.6	2.4
1971–75	129.4	79.3	−4.6	−0.2	− 4.4	23.2	34.0	−2.4
1976–78	218.4	126.5	−5.2	−1.0	− 4.2	39.1	65.3	−7.3
			Percentage of Total Net Acquisitions					
1946–50	100.0	23.9	6.4	1.6	4.8	8.1	39.9	21.7
1951–55	100.0	44.5	5.7	2.3	3.4	15.3	35.1	−0.7
1956–60	100.0	43.7	3.5	4.7	− 1.2	21.8	35.5	−4.5
1961–65	100.0	59.4	−2.7	4.6	− 7.3	11.0	30.6	1.8
1966–70	100.0	48.9	−4.8	6.0	−10.7	22.2	30.1	3.5
1971–75	100.0	61.3	−3.6	−0.2	− 3.4	17.9	26.2	−1.9
1976–78	100.0	57.9	−2.4	−0.4	− 1.9	17.9	29.9	−3.4

Source: Board of Governors of the Federal Reserve System.

Notes: Data are averages of annual flows, in dollars and as percentages of annual total net acquisitions. Detail may not add to totals because of rounding.

people. The growing importance of workers' claims on future pension benefits, including job-specific pensions in both the private and public sectors and also social security, has in particular changed many people's need to accumulate assets directly to finance their retirement.[32] Finally, perceptions of the relative returns and risks—including especially inflation risk—associated with different assets have also changed markedly during the postwar period. After the unpegging of bond prices in 1951, fixed-income securities became subject to market risk in addition to inflation risk, and in the 1970s the inflation risk has increased dramatically. As for equities, during most of the 1950s and 1960s, renewed confidence in economic stability and prosperity lessened fears of any collapse of values comparable to that of 1929–33, and in addition many people regarded them as a "hedge" against price inflation.[33] Following the rapid acceleration of inflation and the poor performance of both equity prices and the American economy in the 1970s, however, prevailing opinion has become progressively more skeptical both of the economy's long-run growth prospects and of the usefulness of equities as an inflation hedge.[34] As the correlations presented in table 1.14 show, even during the 1950s and 1960s nominal returns on equities never compensated fully for variations in price inflation.[35] Even so, the table also shows that there has been a noticeable shift in the structure of asset returns and risks in the 1970s.

Although individuals are the dominant nonfinancial holders of direct claims on other nonfinancial participants in the economy, businesses also advance a substantial amount of direct credit, both to individuals in the form of installment and other consumer credit, and to each other

Table 1.14   Asset Returns and Price Inflation

	After-Inflation Total Returns			
	1-Month Bills	20-Year Bonds	Equities	Inflation
1953–78				
Mean	0.41	−0.52	7.09	3.69
Standard deviation	1.41	6.89	20.13	3.12
Correlation with inflation	−0.88	−0.40	−0.61	1.00
1953–72 Subperiod				
Mean	1.02	0.18	10.48	2.36
Standard deviation	0.69	6.59	18.19	1.73
Correlation with inflation	−0.44	−0.30	−0.56	1.00
1972–78 Subperiod				
Mean	−1.62	−2.83	−4.19	8.10
Standard deviation	1.29	8.00	23.87	2.53
Correlation with inflation	−0.97	−0.72	−0.77	1.00

Note: Data in percentages per annum.

in the form of trade credit and commercial paper. Even with the ready availability of business credit cards and charge accounts, however, commercial banks and finance companies have increasingly dominated the consumer credit field. The share of outstanding consumer credit owed to nonfinancial businesses (including corporations and others) has fallen from just over one-third in the early 1950s to just under one-sixth in the 1970s. In addition, business lending via purchases of nonfinancial commercial paper has remained relatively small, so that trade credit—typically equal to 15–18 percent of the gross national product, and mostly borrowed and lent within the corporate sector—remains the primary vehicle for businesses' holdings of direct claims on nonfinancial obligors.

Foreign investors have held a small but growing share of direct claims on nonfinancial participants in the American economy throughout the postwar period.[36] The growth of foreign holdings has been especially rapid during the 1970s, as the persistent American balance of payments deficit has transferred assets abroad, especially to member countries of the international oil cartel. The rapid recent growth has proceeded from a small base, however, so that foreign holdings still represented less than 5 percent of all direct claims against American nonfinancial obligors as of year-end 1978. Nevertheless, the concentration of foreign (especially foreign official) investments in specific instruments has made foreign holdings of particular importance in some American markets. The year-end 1978 share of federal government securities held abroad, for example, was nearly one-sixth.

Figure 1.5 indicates the extent to which the increasing preference for claims on intermediaries by individuals (and, to a lesser extent, other nonfinancial investors) has shifted to intermediaries the task of meeting the needs that nonfinancial participants in the economy have brought to the American financial markets. As of 1978 individuals in the aggregate remained the largest single class of holders of direct claims on nonfinancial borrowers and share issuers—but only by virtue of their continuing domination of the ownership of corporate equities. Because the direct claims that individuals hold consist overwhelmingly of equities (see again fig. 1.4), the household share of ownership of the total of direct claims outstanding has varied with fluctuations in equity prices. Overall, however, the household share has declined, as has the share held by all other nonfinancial investors. As the share of direct claims on nonfinancial entities held by all nonfinancial investors has declined, the share held by financial intermediaries has correspondingly risen. Intermediaries' holdings first accounted for the majority of all direct claims outstanding in the American financial markets in 1969, and they have remained the majority ever since.

Table 1.15 presents flow data indicating the even stronger postwar dominance of intermediaries in meeting the funds required each year by

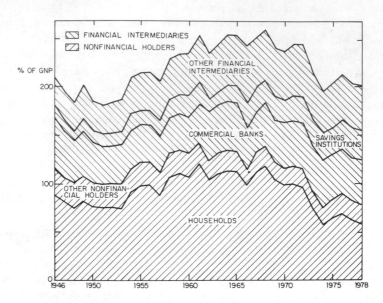

Fig. 1.5   Holdings of claims against United States nonfinancial sectors (including equities).

nonfinancial participants in the economy. Here the main difference from
the pattern indicated in figure 1.5 is that these data exclude equity capital gains, which constituted most of the increase in households' equity
holdings until the late 1960s and more than all of the increase since
then. Apart from accumulating capital gains on equities, individuals and
other private domestic nonfinancial investors have played only a small
and shrinking role in meeting directly the needs that nonfinancial entities
have brought to the financial markets.[37] In large part because of the
growing fraction of those needs that have come in the form of debt
issued by private borrowers, nonfinancial investors have instead accumulated claims on intermediaries and have left to them the task of directly allocating the economy's financial resources.

1.3.2   The Role of Specific Intermediaries

The advance of intermediation in the postwar period has hardly been
uniform. The specialization of American financial intermediaries has
inevitably led to some playing more important roles than others, and
some experiencing more rapid growth than others, as the needs and
objectives of both borrowers and lenders have changed and as government interventions have (intentionally or otherwise) favored first one
kind of institution and then another.

Table 1.15   United States Credit Market Funds Advanced to Nonfinancial Sectors

Years	Total	Private Domestic Nonfinancial Investors	Federal Government	Foreign	Financial Intermediaries			
					Total	Commercial Banks	Savings Institutions	Other
Billions of Dollars								
1946–50	14.2	2.3	1.3	0.1	10.5	1.3	2.7	6.5
1951–55	31.4	5.8	1.7	0.7	23.1	6.6	5.8	10.8
1956–60	40.4	6.8	2.0	1.3	30.4	7.7	8.8	14.0
1961–65	63.1	1.5	5.1	1.0	55.7	20.7	15.0	20.0
1966–70	94.4	9.7	8.6	2.2	73.8	29.4	14.3	30.1
1971–75	189.0	18.3	14.0	10.4	146.3	60.3	40.2	45.7
1976–78	338.1	26.7	23.5	30.8	257.1	92.0	76.4	88.7
Percentage of Total Funds Advanced								
1946–50	100.0	16.2	9.2	0.6	74.0	9.1	19.2	45.6
1951–55	100.0	18.5	5.4	2.3	73.7	20.9	18.4	34.4
1956–60	100.0	16.9	4.7	3.2	75.2	19.0	21.7	34.4
1961–65	100.0	2.3	8.0	1.4	88.2	32.8	23.7	31.7
1966–70	100.0	10.3	9.1	2.4	78.2	31.2	15.1	31.9
1971–75	100.0	9.7	7.4	5.5	77.4	31.9	21.3	24.2
1976–78	100.0	7.9	7.0	9.1	76.0	27.2	22.6	26.2

Source: Board of Governors of the Federal Reserve System.

Notes: Data are averages of annual flows, in dollars and as percentages of annual total funds advanced. Detail may not add to totals because of rounding.

Commercial Banks

The commercial banking system has long stood at the center of economists' interest in financial markets. Even today, despite nearly two decades of increasing emphasis on nonbank intermediaries in financial economics research,[38] discussions ranging from textbook descriptions of the economy to professional evaluations of monetary policy often proceed as if commercial banks were the only intermediaries in the financial markets. This emphasis on the commercial banking system is understandable in part, in view of the special role that banks play in the monetary policy process by virtue of their relationship to the Federal Reserve System. In addition, in the past commercial banks were more dominant in financial market activity than they are today. Before World War II, banks' assets and liabilities dwarfed those of other intermediaries, and before passage of the Glass-Steagall Act in 1933 commercial banks also dominated the American securities business.[39] Until as recently as the early 1970s, commercial banks enjoyed a monopoly on the right to issue checkable deposits.

Since World War II the American commercial banking system has approximately held its own in relation to the scale of nonfinancial economic activity, but it has not participated in the economy's overall postwar expansion of intermediation. The approximate stability of the banking system's relative size is apparent in figure 1.5, and also in the data on commercial banks' assets and liabilities presented in table 1.16. The total size of the banking system in relation to gross national product has shown essentially no trend during the postwar period. Put the other way around, as figure 1.6 shows, there has been little postwar trend in the "income velocity" of the broad *M2* money stock, which consists of most commercial bank deposit liabilities (plus the public's currency holdings), or in the corresponding income velocity of bank credit, which consists of most commercial bank earning assets.[40] This relative stability (actually a slow decline) in the postwar period stands in marked contrast to the prewar years when, over nearly a century, the size of the banking system continually grew in relation to gross national product.[41]

Within the stability of the overall totals, however, the postwar years have also seen substantial shifts in composition on both sides of the banking system's balance sheet. Among bank assets, the most significant development of the postwar period has been the recovery of bank loan portfolios and hence the general resumption of banks' traditional role as "inside" intermediaries. In 1929 loans constituted 73 percent of bank credit. During the depression and then the war years, however, the fall-off in private debt issuing meant that, for all practical purposes, there was little or no loan business to be had. By contrast, the federal government was then issuing debt in record volume, and banks participated in

Table 1.16   Assets and Liabilities of United States Commercial Banks

Years	Financial Assets					Financial Liabilities			
	Total	Treasury Debt	Government Agency Debt	State and Local Debt	Loans	Total	Demand Deposits	Non-CD Time Deposits	CD
Percentage of GNP									
1946–50	54.8	26.7	0.6	2.3	16.0	51.1	35.4	14.0	0.0
1951–55	47.1	17.5	0.8	3.0	18.6	43.8	29.6	12.0	0.0
1956–60	45.1	13.2	0.5	3.4	22.2	41.6	25.8	13.3	0.0
1961–65	47.0	10.6	0.7	4.8	26.1	43.5	22.6	16.6	1.5
1966–70	49.1	6.9	1.1	6.3	30.1	46.0	19.4	19.7	2.2
1971–75	52.7	5.0	2.0	7.1	34.0	49.7	17.1	22.3	4.6
1976–78	50.5	5.1	2.0	5.8	33.6	47.5	14.0	23.3	4.0
Percentage of Total Financial Assets									
1946–50	100.0	48.3	1.1	4.3	29.5	93.2	64.6	25.4	0.0
1951–55	100.0	37.1	1.6	6.5	39.6	93.0	62.8	25.6	0.0
1956–60	100.0	29.1	1.1	7.5	49.4	92.3	57.1	29.7	0.1
1961–65	100.0	22.2	1.6	10.3	55.8	92.7	47.8	35.5	3.3
1966–70	100.0	14.0	2.3	12.8	61.4	93.6	39.4	40.1	4.4
1971–75	100.0	9.4	3.9	13.3	64.6	94.3	32.1	42.3	9.0
1976–78	100.0	10.0	3.9	11.5	66.8	94.1	27.7	46.0	8.1

Source: Board of Governors of the Federal Reserve System.

Notes: Data are averages of year-end amounts, as percentages of annual gross national product and as percentages of annual total assets. Detail may not add to totals because of rounding.

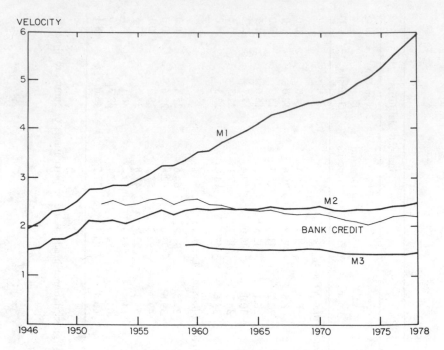

VELOCITY

Fig. 1.6   Income velocities of monetary and credit aggregates.

financing it. By 1935 banks' securities investments exceeded their loan portfolios, and in 1945 investments constituted 79 percent of bank credit. Commercial banks simply were no longer very commercial. The years since 1946 have largely consisted of a reversal of the 1930–45. pattern, with bank loans exceeding securities investments in 1957 for the first time in more than two decades and reaching 73 percent of total bank credit as of year-end 1978.

In rebuilding their loan portfolios and deemphasizing their investments, banks have also both altered the mix of their lending business and changed the character of their securities holdings. Although banks remain a principal source of business credit, and commercial and industrial loans are still the largest single category of bank lending, they no longer dominate bank loan portfolios as they once did. Instead, mortgage credit and other consumer loans now comprise nearly one-third of the total. Especially during the second half of the postwar period, the widespread use of bank-issued credit cards has been a major factor in banks' development of their consumer lending business. Moreover, among business loans per se, the larger banks have increasingly become a major factor in the intermediate-term credit market through the use of explicitly longer maturity loans (in some cases up to ten years) and revolving credits of an implicitly ongoing nature. Total bank investments have grown slowly since World War II, but because of tax incentives banks have so concentrated their investments on state and local government issues that, for a few years in the early 1970s, they held more of these securities than of federal government debt.[42]

Among bank liabilities, the two most significant changes that have occurred during the postwar period have been the continual decline of demand balances and increase of time and savings deposits, relative to either total bank liabilities or gross national product, and the "liability management revolution" that has greatly increased the larger banks' reliance on "bought funds." As figure 1.6 shows, the income velocity of the narrow $M1$ money stock, consisting of currency plus demand deposits, has about tripled over the postwar years as a result of a combination of influences including economies of scale in the public's holding of cash balances, the secular rise in nominal interest rates, and the increasingly widespread use of credit cards and charge accounts.[43] This persistent trend in $M1$ velocity stands in sharp contrast to either the absence of any trend during 1910–30 or the steeply declining trend during 1930–45. Hence only the strong growth of time and savings deposits, including the new negotiable certificates of deposit that first came into existence in 1961, has accounted for the much slower postwar increase in the income velocity of $M2$. Large banks' growing use of such liabilities as certificates of deposit, federal funds, Eurodollar borrowings, commercial paper issues, repurchase agreements and so on—instruments that in some cases represent the development of new financial markets since World War II—has not only changed banks' balance sheets but also facilitated a major change in the feasible aggressiveness of bank lending practices. The enormous postwar expansion of bank loan portfolios, which banks have achieved in part through the competitive use of such devices as loan commitments and medium-term credits, would probably have been impossible if banks had simply continued to follow the classic practice of treating their deposits (and other liabilities) as determined by outside forces.

Finally, it is useful to point out explicitly that because of changes in commercial bank organization, especially during the 1960s, the representation of banks as having merely held their own during the postwar increase in the American economy's degree of financial intermediation relative to economic activity risks understating by a wide margin the growing overall presence of commercial banks in the financial system. After falling by more than one-half between 1920 and 1935, the number of American commercial banks has remained roughly steady at about 14,000. The number of bank branches, however, has risen from some 4,000 to over 32,000 during the postwar years, with most of this growth occurring since 1960. Moreover, especially since the 1970 Amendments to the Bank Holding Company Act, banks have increasingly gone into activities other than their traditional loan and deposit business.[44] Although their direct participation in financial intermediation has not kept pace with the rising postwar trend, commercial banks have increasingly enhanced their importance as more nearly full-service financial institutions.

Nonbank Deposit Institutions

As is clear from figure 1.5, one group of intermediaries that has accounted for much of the postwar increase in American financial intermediation has been the nonbank deposit institutions including savings and loan associations, mutual savings banks, and credit unions. The public's strong demand for consumer-type time and savings deposits has kept these institutions growing rapidly, not just absolutely but in relation to economic activity, during most of the postwar period. In fact, as figure 1.6 shows, their growth has even been great enough to offset the relative decline of the commercial banking system, so that the income velocity of the $M3$ money stock, consisting of $M2$ plus nonbank deposits, has shown a modest downward trend since the beginning of the data series in 1959. Moreover, when extrapolated backward this trend appears to have been a continuation of the downward trend associated with $M2$ during the prewar era when nonbank deposit institutions were not of major importance.

Table 1.17 presents data for the individual deposit (or share) volume and combined asset holdings of the three major groups of nonbank deposit institutions, first in relation to gross national product and then as a share of the total assets of the three groups of institutions together. The vast postwar expansion of the savings and loan industry stands out clearly here. Between the early postwar years and the 1970s outstanding savings and loan shares more than quadrupled as a percentage of gross national product. By 1978 the amount of these shares equaled more than twice the amount of mutual savings bank deposits and credit union shares combined, and also equaled about five-sixths of the amount of consumer-type time and savings deposits held at commercial banks. In comparison with mutual savings banks, the primary factor underlying the more rapid growth of savings and loan associations has probably been mere geography; mutual savings banks are overwhelmingly concentrated in a few states, especially New York and Massachusetts, which have experienced slower than average economic growth during the postwar period. In comparison with commercial banks, the primary factor has probably been the effect of government regulation, in that savings and loan associations did not face deposit interest rate ceilings until 1965 and have enjoyed a one-fourth percent differential over commercial banks since then. The growth of credit unions has been even faster than that of savings and loan associations, but credit unions constitute

Table 1.17   **Assets and Liabilities of United States Nonbank Deposit Institutions**

	Combined Financial Assets			Liabilities by Sector		
Years	Total	Mortgages	Consumer Credit	Savings and Loan Shares	Mutual Savings Banks Deposits	Credit Union Shares
Percentage of GNP						
1946–50	13.4	6.3	0.3	4.7	7.2	0.2
1951–55	15.3	9.7	0.5	6.9	6.6	0.5
1956–60	21.0	15.0	1.0	11.1	7.1	0.8
1961–65	26.9	20.5	1.3	16.0	7.3	1.2
1966–70	27.0	20.9	1.6	16.2	7.2	1.4
1971–75	30.2	22.3	2.1	18.8	7.2	1.8
1976–78	33.1	23.6	2.6	21.7	6.7	2.3
Percentage of Total Combined Financial Assets						
1946–50	100.0	47.4	2.2	32.3	53.5	1.8
1951–55	100.0	63.4	3.3	41.2	43.0	3.0
1956–60	100.0	71.4	4.4	50.0	33.9	4.0
1961–65	100.0	76.4	5.0	54.7	27.1	4.4
1966–70	100.0	77.3	6.0	54.5	26.6	5.2
1971–75	100.0	73.9	7.0	56.0	23.5	6.2
1976–78	100.0	71.4	8.0	58.4	20.2	7.0

Source: Board of Governors of the Federal Reserve System.
Notes: Data are averages of year-end amounts, as percentages of annual gross national product and as percentages of annual total assets. Detail may not add to totals because of rounding.

another example of rapid growth from a small base, and they remain by far the smallest of the three groups of institutions. Mutual savings banks are alone among the three groups in having failed to do more than grow in pace with economic activity. Although mutual savings banks were twice as large as savings and loan associations at the end of World War II, savings and loans were equal in size in 1954 and more than three times as large by 1978.

Because all of these nonbank deposit institutions operate under legal and regulatory constraints governing the disposition of their asset portfolios, their aggregate contribution to meeting the financial needs of nonfinancial participants in the economy has followed a fairly predictable pattern. Savings and loan associations and mutual savings banks typically invest some 80 percent and 70 percent, respectively, of their assets in mortgages, so that these two groups together have become the nation's leading provider of mortgage lending. As of year-end 1978, savings and loans and mutual savings banks together held 45 percent of all outstanding mortgages (in comparison to 18 percent for commercial banks, the next largest class of holders). These institutions are especially predominant in the market for single-family home mortgages, accounting for 55 percent of year-end 1978 loans outstanding. Credit unions, by contrast, have traditionally invested most of their assets in consumer installment loans, and by 1978 they accounted for 14 percent of the outstanding consumer credit.

As the discussion in section 1.4 below emphasizes, the history of American nonbank deposit institutions in the postwar period has been in large part a story of evolving financial regulation, including restrictions on these intermediaries' liability issuing as well as their asset holding. In this context, what may well turn out to be two of the most important changes affecting nonbank financial institutions within the postwar era are only just in progress at the time of writing. The first is the sudden acceleration of the erosion of the deposit interest rate ceilings these institutions have faced since the mid 1960s, following the introduction in mid-1978 of "money market certificates" bearing yields set in relation to those on Treasury bills. Just by late 1979—that is, after less than eighteen months—these new deposit certificates accounted for more than one-fourth of all deposits at savings and loan institutions and almost one-fourth those at mutual savings banks. The second change is the expansion of authority to issue interest-bearing checkable deposits, which nonbank deposit institutions and commercial banks in the New England states received in several steps during 1972–76, and the extension of which to the rest of the country is to be decided by Congress in 1980. Both checking account authority and the freedom from deposit interest rate ceilings are likely to increase greatly the demand for claims on nonbank deposit intermediaries, although the impact of the latter on these institutions' cash flows (and even solvency in some cases) makes it a mixed blessing in the short run.

Nondeposit Intermediaries

Finally, as is also apparent from figure 1.5, a significant part of the postwar increase in the American economy's degree of financial intermediation has stemmed from neither commercial banks nor nonbank deposit institutions but, instead, from intermediaries that issue only nondeposit claims. There are many forms of such intermediaries operating in the American markets, but the most familiar and important among them include life and casualty insurance companies, private and public sector pension funds, independent consumer finance companies and the "captive" finance companies of nonfinancial businesses, equity and money market mutual funds, real estate investment trusts, and security brokers and dealers.

Table 1.18 presents data, analogous to that shown above for the non-bank deposit institutions, for three specific categories of nondeposit intermediaries:[45] life insurance companies, private pension funds, and state and local government pension funds. The reason for focusing in particular on these three groups is not only that they are the largest of the nondeposit intermediaries but also that their respective postwar experiences reflect some interesting contrasts. Because the low interest rates implicitly paid on the savings component of ordinary life insurance has increasingly favored the use of group and other term insurance policies, life insurance companies' total assets held and liabilities outstanding grew little relative to gross national product during the first half of the postwar period, and since then they have been declining in relative terms. Moreover, the relative decline in these companies' life insurance business has been even more pronounced, in that their growth in recent years has consisted disproportionately of pension monies which they

Table 1.18   **Assets of United States Life Insurance Companies and Pension Funds**

	Combined Financial Assets				Financial Assets by Sector		
Years	Total	Equities	Corporate Bonds	Mort-gages	Life Insurance Companies	Private Pension	State and Local Government Pension
Percentage of GNP							
1946–50	24.6	0.8	8.2	4.3	21.2	1.9	1.4
1951–55	26.3	1.6	10.8	6.5	20.8	3.3	2.2
1956–60	31.8	3.4	13.2	8.3	22.3	6.2	3.3
1961–65	36.0	6.1	14.3	9.1	22.3	9.2	4.5
1966–70	36.8	8.3	14.0	9.0	20.6	10.8	5.4
1971–75	35.1	10.2	12.9	6.7	18.4	10.4	6.4
1976–78	33.3	8.7	12.9	5.5	17.3	9.2	6.8
Percentage of Total Combined Financial Assets							
1946–50	100.0	3.3	33.4	17.4	86.4	7.7	5.9
1951–55	100.0	6.0	41.1	24.9	79.1	12.6	8.3
1956–60	100.0	10.6	41.4	26.1	70.0	19.4	10.5
1961–65	100.0	17.0	39.7	25.3	62.0	25.6	12.4
1966–70	100.0	22.6	38.1	24.3	55.9	29.3	14.8
1971–75	100.0	29.0	36.7	19.6	52.4	29.5	18.1
1976–78	100.0	26.2	38.7	16.5	51.9	27.7	20.4

Source: Board of Governors of the Federal Reserve System.

Notes: Data are averages of year-end amounts, as percentages of annual gross national product and as percentages of annual total assets. Detail may not add to totals because of rounding.

manage for other businesses. As of year-end 1978 pension reserves constituted nearly one-third of life insurance companies' total liabilities, up from less than one-tenth in the early postwar years.

By contrast, both private and public sector pensions have experienced extraordinarily rapid growth throughout these years. Tax incentives at both the individual and corporate levels, business personnel policies aimed at reducing worker turnover, features of the collective bargaining process, and other corporate financial objectives have all combined to favor the mushrooming of private pension liabilities since World War II. During most of this period, however, businesses had (and many used) broad latitude to incur pension liabilities without funding them. The 1974 Retirement Income Security Act has subsequently specified minimum standards for the vesting of workers' rights to accumulated pension benefits and for employers' funding of vested pension liabilities.[46] Even so, businesses still have flexibility in choosing the actuarial assumptions underlying the calculation of future benefits, the minimum required amortization of unfunded vested benefits is very slow, and nonvested benefits require no funding at all. Consequently, many businesses continue to carry substantial amounts of unfunded liabilities, so that private pension funds' total assets as shown in table 1.18 substantially understate their liabilities.[47] This understatement has been especially great during the 1970s when many private pension funds' asset portfolios, of which in the aggregate about two-thirds is invested in equities, have suffered an erosion in market value.

State and local government pensions, including both teachers' and other employees' funds, have experienced similar postwar growth. Public sector workers have the same tax incentive to use the pension mechanism to spread income beyond retirement as do private sector workers. Although public sector employers do not have the same tax incentives as do private businesses, in many cases the political process has probably favored the use of pension compensation over current compensation, especially when there is no pressure to raise tax or other revenues immediately to fund the accumulating pension liabilities. In fact public sector pension funds have been and remain substantially underfunded, so that the asset data shown in table 1.18 greatly understate their liabilities also.[48] The continued growth of public sector pensions' assets during the 1970s, in contrast to private pensions, reflects merely the smaller share of assets invested in equities (about one-third in the aggregate) rather than any difference in funding practices.

The asset mix of these insurance and pension intermediaries—and hence their role in financing economic activity—has also undergone important changes since World War II. Regulatory changes in the 1960s allowed many life insurance companies to increase the equity portion of their portfolios, and since the mid-1960s life insurers have largely withdrawn from direct home mortgage lending. State and local government pension funds and especially private pension funds have even more dramatically increased the equity share of their investments. Consequently, these nondeposit intermediaries have increasingly become a major source of both debt and equity funds for corporate businesses. As a result of these portfolio changes, together with the rapid growth of pensions and the (relative) stagnation of the commercial banking system, insurance companies and pension funds combined have come to dominate banks as holders of claims on the American corporate business sector—despite banks' postwar emphasis on loans over investments in government securities. In the early postwar years these intermediaries held only slightly more claims on the corporate sector than did commercial banks, but by the 1970s they held more than twice as much.

It is also important to distinguish the claims on business held by banks, which are overwhelmingly in the form of short- to medium-term loans, from the corresponding claims held by insurance companies and pension funds, which consist mostly of long-term debt and equity securities. These nondeposit intermediaries have traditionally held some three-fourths of all outstanding corporate bonds, and in recent years they have also come to hold nearly one-sixth of all corporate equity. The flow data in tables 1.19 and 1.20 give a further idea of these investors' importance in providing long-term debt and equity capital to American business corporations. In addition to accounting for much or all of the corporate sector's net long-term bond financing throughout the postwar period, since 1960 they have also accounted for more than all of its equity financing, absorbing also the equity holdings liquidated by the household sector. In sum, businesses' equity and bond financing has become increasingly dominated by these investors. Given their high rates of portfolio turnover, especially in comparison with individuals, equity and bond trading has become even more so.

1.3.3   Financial Innovation and the Advance of Market Efficiency

With individuals doing less of the direct lending in the American financial markets and specialized intermediaries doing more, it is not surprising that many aspects of the working of these markets have changed during the postwar years, and that most of these changes have tended to reduce or eliminate barriers to the transfer of financial resources and thereby to render the financial system more efficient than before. One example of this evolution has been individuals' increasing ability to diversify their holdings via mutual funds, pensions, and mortgage pools. Another has been their increased ability to escape interest rate ceilings via negotiable certificates of deposit or money market certificates, and minimum size requirements via money market mutual funds. Still another has been their ability to invest abroad (or for busi-

Table 1.19   Net Issues and Purchases of United States Corporate Bonds

| | | | Net Purchases | | | |
| | Net Issues | | | | | State and |
Years	Total	Domestic Nonfinancial Businesses	Total	Life Insurance Companies	Private Pension Funds	Local Government Pension Funds
			Billions of Dollars			
1945–50	2.9	2.5	4.0	2.7	0.4	0.1
1951–55	4.1	3.5	3.9	2.4	1.0	0.4
1956–60	5.9	4.4	4.7	2.2	1.6	0.9
1961–65	6.4	5.0	6.0	2.6	1.4	2.0
1966–70	15.9	13.9	7.5	2.6	1.3	3.6
1971–75	23.1	17.4	12.9	6.3	1.3	5.3
1976–78	35.0	21.3	27.8	17.6	3.7	6.5
			Percentage of Total Net Issues			
1945–50	100.0	87.8	139.9	93.8	15.1	3.1
1951–55	100.0	86.6	95.6	60.7	24.6	10.3
1956–60	100.0	75.1	79.4	37.6	26.8	15.1
1961–65	100.0	70.8	94.5	40.6	22.0	31.8
1966–70	100.0	87.7	47.5	16.5	8.5	22.5
1971–75	100.0	75.2	55.7	27.1	5.4	23.1
1976–78	100.0	60.9	79.5	50.4	10.5	18.6

Source: Board of Governors of the Federal Reserve System.
Notes: Data are averages of annual flows, in billions of dollars and as percentages of total net issues. Detail may not add to totals because of rounding.

nesses to borrow abroad) as legal barriers have fallen. Especially in conjunction with innovations exploiting new physical technologies, postwar changes in financial intermediation have reduced many of the barriers and frictions that interfere with the capital allocation process.

At least four kinds of friction-reducing changes bear explicit attention. First, wholly apart from the effective reduction of transactions costs associated with increased intermediation, marginal transactions costs in both the direct and the indirect senses have fallen irregularly throughout the postwar period. The fee typically charged for negotiated underwritings of high grade corporate bonds, for example, declined from $10 or more per $1,000 bond in the early postwar years to $8.75 per bond in the late 1950s and has remained unchanged at that level ever since, although underwriting fees for competitively bid bond issues have fallen more substantially in recent years. Bid-asked spreads have fallen from $2.50 or $5.00 to $1.25 or even $0.625 per bond for actively traded government bonds, and the feasible size of transaction at the quoted prices has increased substantially for both government and corporate bonds. Bid-asked spreads for equity issues traded on the New

Table 1.20   **Net Issues and Purchases of United States Corporate Equities**

| Years | Net Issues | | Net Purchases | | | |
	Total	Domestic Nonfinancial Businesses	Sub-total	Life Insurance Companies	Private Pension Funds	State and Local Government Pension Funds
	Billions of Dollars					
1946–50	1.2	1.1	0.4	0.2	0.2	0.0
1951–55	2.2	1.9	0.6	0.1	0.5	0.0
1956–60	2.4	2.0	1.6	0.1	1.4	0.1
1961–65	1.1	0.7	3.1	0.5	2.4	0.2
1966–70	3.4	2.5	7.1	1.3	4.6	1.3
1971–75	10.7	8.8	11.9	3.0	5.9	3.0
1976–78	7.5	5.3	10.2	1.4	5.7	3.2
	Percentage of Total Net Issues					
1946–50	100.0	92.8	31.8	16.6	14.8	0.3
1951–55	100.0	86.6	31.6	5.9	24.9	0.9
1956–60	100.0	82.8	66.5	5.5	58.6	2.5
1961–65	100.0	60.5	310.9	44.4	221.5	21.9
1966–70	100.0	73.3	206.8	36.8	132.7	37.2
1971–75	100.0	82.7	111.6	27.9	55.3	28.5
1976–78	100.0	70.4	136.2	18.0	75.9	42.2

Source: Board of Governors of the Federal Reserve System.
Notes: Data are averages of annual flows, in billions of dollars and as percentages of total net issues. Detail may not add to totals because of rounding.

York Stock Exchange have also declined to a typical $0.25 or $0.125 per share for most issues, instead of the $0.375 per share that was more prevalent some years ago. Effective equity brokerage fees have typically fallen as well, especially for larger trades, although under the fixed minimum commission system the reductions usually took the form of indirect rebates and services provided. Since the Securities and Exchange Commission prohibited fixed minimum commission rates in 1975, average fees on large trades have fallen from $0.15 per share to only $0.08 per share (0.4 percent of principal value). Overall, as a result of natural competitive forces in the financial markets, striking advances in electronic communications and data processing technology, and specific regulatory actions, these and other direct transactions costs have fallen sufficiently that the markets for what are traditionally regarded as "nonliquid" instruments now in fact provide substantial liquidity.[49] In addition, indirect transactions costs at the margin have fallen during the postwar period as nonfinancial businesses have increasingly invested in sophisticated financial staffs, either "in house" or on a retainer basis, and individuals have gained substantially more financial knowledge also.

A second change which has been related to the decline in transactions costs, and which has also served to make markets both more liquid and more efficient in the sense of reducing barriers to financial allocations and reallocations, has been the increasing trend toward negotiability of financial assets. As table 1.21 shows, nonfinancial corporations and finance companies have on balance increased the negotiability of—and hence the potential market for—both their short-term and their long-term debt by substituting commercial paper issues for bank loans and publicly offered bonds for directly placed bonds. In addition, a large part of the postwar trend toward negotiability of financial assets has occurred through the development of new financial instruments. Commercial banks first introduced the negotiable certificate of deposit in 1961, and by the mid-1970s these certificates accounted for some one-tenth of banks' total liabilities. Bank lending has also become more of a straightforward market transaction and less closely tied to bank-customer relations, as in many cases commitment fees have augmented or replaced deposit balances as criteria for extending credit, and the greater flexibility provided by banks' liability management practices has better enabled them to accommodate fluctuating business credit demands (especially through the use of floating-rate loans). The introduction of exchange-traded options and financial futures markets has facilitated hedging and speculating investment postures that previously were either impossible to achieve or possible only via expensive combinations of long and short positions. The development in the 1960s of a secondary mortgage market and the advent of mortgage-backed "pass-through" securities have also rendered home mortgages in effect negotiable and

Table 1.21   **Negotiability of United States Corporate Debt**

Years	Net Corporate Bond Issues		Net Change in Bank Loans and Commercial Paper	
	% Privately Placed	% Publicly Offered	% Bank Loans	% Commercial Paper
1946–50	46.7	53.3	95.7	4.3
1951–55	49.4	50.6	92.8	7.2
1956–60	41.3	58.7	92.1	7.9
1961–65	55.6	44.4	88.4	11.6
1966–70	33.0	67.0	81.1	18.9
1971–75	27.3	72.7	81.6	18.4
1976–78	42.1	57.9	78.8	21.2

Sources: Securities and Exchange Commission and Board of Governors of the Federal Reserve System.
Note: Data are percentages of the respective totals.

have correspondingly increased the range of investors prepared to consider them.

The gradual and piecemeal removal of international barriers to financial transactions, including the American actions already noted above as well as corresponding actions by other countries, has been a third important factor in the postwar development of the American—indeed, the world—financial system. One part of this process has simply been the development of viable financial markets abroad. Most European countries did not even have currency convertibility for current transactions until 1958 (Japan not until 1964). Convertibility for financial transactions has come in individual pieces since then, and it is still incomplete although there is now so much convertibility that massive short-run movements of short-term capital have become a major problem in the international monetary system. Since the removal of the American capital controls, both American and foreign borrowers may again choose whether to raise funds in the American markets or abroad, American banks may choose between domestic and foreign loans, and other American investors may choose whether to buy securities issued at home or abroad. Other countries have also gradually eliminated analogous capital controls—most recently the United Kingdom in 1979. All of these developments have improved the markets' ability to allocate financial resources in comparison with the earlier situation in which banks' participation in the Eurodollar market was the primary vehicle for international capital flows, or even more the situation of the still earlier postwar years before the reopening of foreign financial markets and the use of modern communications technology to connect them with the American markets. In addition, as the example of around-the-clock trading in Eurodollars and Asian dollars suggests, the removal of international financial barriers has also even further enhanced the overall negotiability of many financial assets. The move to floating exchange rates in the 1970s, a subject that lies beyond the scope of this essay, has also been an important part of this entire set of developments.[50]

Financial innovation per se—whether due to technological, regulatory, or entrepreneurial forces—has constituted a fourth major source of postwar change enhancing the efficiency of the American financial system. Given its low capital intensity and highly mobile (and well-educated) labor force, the financial industry is typically able to adopt innovations both more cheaply and more rapidly than can, for example, manufacturing or other production lines of business.[51] Many of the innovations that have been so important in changing the structure and working characteristics of the American financial markets have already appeared in the discussion above. Other examples include such now standard instruments as leveraged leases, variable-rate annuities, corporate bonds subject to call protection, and floating-rate debt issues, as well as instruments that are only just now coming into use like graduated-payment and variable-rate mortgages. Additional markets like those for federal funds and commodity futures are not new in the postwar period, but they now play a far greater role in the financial system than ever before. Adoption of modern electronic technology has already facilitated such innovations as remote terminal banking, and such far-reaching structural changes as the development of a semiautomated national market system for equity trading or an electronic funds transfer system for commercial banking are now visible on the horizon though not yet in place. In every case, these innovations have acted to reinforce the continual trend toward erosion of barriers and frictions that has marked the evolution of the American financial markets since World War II.

Despite this cataloging of the reduction of costs and barriers that have followed from the rise of intermediation together with innovation, however, it would be misleading to suggest that the American financial system has yet (or will soon) realize economists' idealized conception of a perfectly efficient mechanism for allocating financial resources. Many imperfections remain. Perhaps the most striking example of the American financial markets' continuing shortcomings in this respect is the failure, despite the experience documented in table 1.14, to provide an investment vehicle that would (presumably, for a price) guarantee the purchasing power of its holder's capital value.[52] In addition, the home mortgage instrument remains a relatively inflexible instrument despite recent innovations,[53] tax lock-ins remain important despite the changes in inheritance taxes in 1976 and in capital gains taxes in 1978, pension rights remain entirely illiquid, and most individuals face severe liquidity constraints preventing their borrowing against future income in the form of either wages or pension benefits. More generally, the gap between the interest rates that most individuals earn on assets and pay on borrowings is very wide. In sum, the postwar trend has indeed been toward more efficient markets, but at least as of 1979 there is much room left for further development.

1.4   Changes in the Role of Government

In addition to its reliance on the financial markets as a borrower financing its current deficit, the federal government has played a number of other roles in the development of the American financial markets since World War II. Regulatory actions and tax policies have resulted in significant impacts on how the financial markets have been able to do their job. The government's activities as a financial intermediary have affected the allocation (and perhaps the total) of saving in the economy. The monetary policy carried out by the Federal Reserve System has fundamentally shaped the postwar course not only of the financial markets but of the economy as a whole. In sum, despite the decline of the government's role as a direct borrower, the broader changes at work during the postwar era have probably been in the direction of a growing overall influence of government on the American financial markets.

1.4.1 Deposit Insurance and Government Regulation

The proliferation of the federal government's regulatory activities since World War II has touched almost every part of the American economy, and has brought important and far-reaching changes.[54] The financial markets have been no exception in this regard. Some of the most significant innovations in financial market regulation came during the 1930s, as part of the society's immediate reaction to the excesses of the 1920s and their effects during the depression. Others have come since the war. On both counts, however, the postwar experience has been significantly different from what went before.

The single most important development along these lines during this century has been the almost universal adoption of deposit insurance following the inception of both the Federal Deposit Insurance Corporation (FDIC) and the Federal Savings and Loan Insurance Corporation in 1934. Before 1934 the individual depositor had always to regard his deposit holdings as assets subject to default risk, and the wave of bank failures during the early 1930s dramatically demonstrated the potential impact of default not only on individuals' perceptions, and hence their asset-holding behavior, but also on nonfinancial macroeconomic outcomes. After 1934, depositors' losses due to bank failure shrank quickly to miniscule proportion. Bank failures and forced mergers, of which there were hundreds each year during the 1920s and more than 1,000 in each year during 1930–33 (over 4,000 in 1933 alone), suddenly shrank to the double-digit range in 1934 and into single digits per year by the end of World War II. Moreover, from 1934 until the mid-1970s what few bank failures did occur were entirely concentrated among banks with less than $100 million in deposits, and nearly three-fourths of all failures were among banks with less than $1 million in deposits.[55] Even then, more often than not—and especially when a large bank has failed, as in 1974—the FDIC arranged either for a merger or for the assumption of the failed bank's valid assets (and a corresponding share of its liabilities) by another bank, rather than simply pursuing liquidation, so that depositors suffer no loss of liquidity at all. Even in cases of liquidation, the FDIC has typically settled depositors' claims almost immediately. In sum, the advent of deposit insurance has fundamentally changed the nature of the American financial markets.

Federal regulation of banking has not been limited to that incidental to the insurance of deposits. The Federal Reserve System, the FDIC, and the Comptroller of the Currency have shared with the individual state banking commissions the responsibility for regulation and supervision of commercial banks. Important aspects of these activities include inspecting bank operations (and in particular the composition of bank portfolios), ruling on bank merger applications, and regulating the entrance of banks and bank-holding companies into activities beyond traditional banking businesses. Because the fixed-percentage pricing system for deposit insurance implicitly acts as a subsidy to risk-taking, it is possible that the role of bank inspection has been especially important in limiting the risk level of banking, although the available evidence is ambiguous on this question.[56] Bank inspections have in any case become more relevant for limiting risks as banks have moved heavily into international transactions such as exchange market trading and foreign lending. In addition, control over banks' applications to engage in nonbanking activities has become more important as banks and their holding companies have increasingly widened their scope to encompass leasing, credit cards, real estate, insurance and other related activities.

Growth of federal regulation in the postwar era has also extended beyond banks and other deposit intermediaries. The securities legislation of the 1930s, including especially the National Banking (Glass-Steagall) and Securities Acts of 1933 and the Securities and Exchange Act of 1934, not only created a separate securities industry distinct from the commercial banking system but also set down an elaborate set of rules governing securities issuing and trading and established the Securities and Exchange Commission to enforce them. This legislation of course antedated World War II, but many of its effects have appeared only after the war. Disclosure requirements increased, and have continued to increase throughout the postwar years. Public utility companies from 1941 and railroads from 1944 were compelled to seek competitive bids on their new securities—a practice which over time brought major changes in the structure of the investment banking industry.[57] Margin requirements for securities trading, set by the Federal Reserve under authority of the 1933 act, have remained at or above 50 percent since World War II—an especially sharp contrast to the experience of the 1920s. Under the Investment Advisor Act of 1940, the regulation of the postwar securities industry has extended also to asset management as well as the trading and issuing functions. As of the time of writing, the Securities and Exchange Commission is actively considering plans to restructure securities trading so as to develop the nationwide market system mandated by Congress in 1975, and it is possible that the implementation of such a system could eventually even result in a dealer market replacing the auction market that has characterized most American stock exchanges for nearly two centuries.

Federal regulation of the financial markets has also affected non-deposit intermediaries other than securities brokers and dealers. The most recent development along these lines, which bears potentially important implications not just for the financial markets but also for the overall amount and composition of saving in the American economy, is the regulation of private pension funds under the Employee Retirement Income Security Act of 1974. In addition to the minimum pension funding standards already discussed in section 1.3, this legislation further specifies associated fiduciary responsibilities for the management of pension funds' assets. Even within the first few years it has had a noticeable impact on both the amount of pension funding and the composition of pension investments. Given the already increasing role of private pensions in postwar financial intermediation, as discussed above, these changes are of great potential significance for the future.

1.4.2   New Distortions in the Allocative Mechanism

It would be surprising if the increase since World War II in the presence of government, both in the financial markets and more broadly in the economy as a whole, had not brought with it at least some distortions in the economy's allocative mechanism. In fact, as the postwar period has advanced, government actions have directly or indirectly introduced numerous distortions in the financial system's allocation of capital. Several of these distortions, such as the restrictions on international capital flows, have already figured in the discussion of sections 1.2 and 1.3. Nevertheless, it is important to note specifically two aspects of the distortion of capital allocations that have been particularly important since World War II and have differentiated this period from the prewar experience.

The National Banking Act of 1933 introduced deposit interest rate ceilings, in part as a response to banks' alleged overly aggressive bidding for interbank demand deposits during the 1920s. The ceilings have also applied to other demand deposits as well as time and savings deposits, however, so that they have also served as an anticompetitive device to subsidize bank profits and bank borrowers at the expense of bank depositors. Given the postwar changes in the pattern of deposit holding reviewed in section 1.3, the main focus of these ceilings, imposed under the Federal Reserve's Regulation Q and analogous regulations governing nonbank intermediaries, came to be consumer-type time and savings deposits. Moreover, given the growing role of nonbank intermediaries both in issuing such deposits and in mortgage lending, the subsidy has mostly either passed to homeowners or bolstered the lending institutions' (usually inaccessible) reserves.[58]

Apart from the long-run average subsidy transferred from depositors to mortgage borrowers, however, the chief effect of deposit interest rate ceilings has been the introduction of severe volatility into both intermediation and homebuilding through the interaction of these ceilings with the cyclical pattern of short-term interest rate movements. A wholly new postwar phenomenon, experienced for the first time when interest rates on readily available open market investment instruments rose above the prevailing savings deposit ceilings in 1966, was the widespread withdrawal of deposits from both banks and nonbank deposit intermediaries. This "disintermediation" then led to reduced mortgage lending, which after some lag led in turn to a decline in residential construction activity. As figure 1.7 shows, this pattern subsequently recurred in 1969–70 and

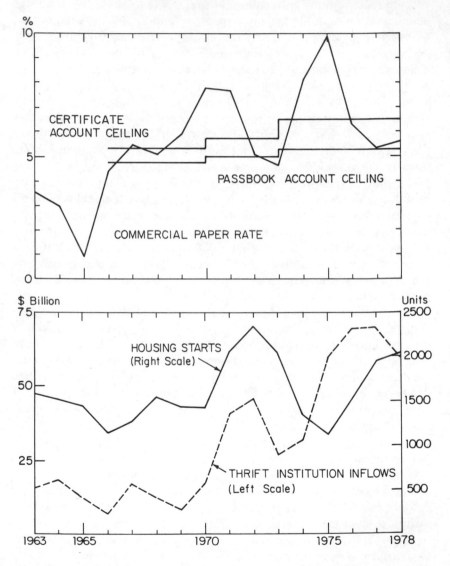

Fig. 1.7   Disintermediation and residential construction.

in 1973–74, with increasing severity except that in these more recent episodes government sponsored intermediaries have increasingly supplemented the funds lost to the mortgage market. Nevertheless, the net result has been the introduction of sufficient volatility into the residential construction industry to make the consequent decline in housing activity a major element in postwar economic downturns.

The second major postwar distortion in the financial markets' capital-allocation mechanism has come from taxes, and in particular from the interaction of taxes with the more rapid price inflation of the later postwar years. The federal government was constitutionally prohibited from imposing income taxes until after passage of the Sixteenth Amendment in 1913, and tax rates remained low by today's standards until World War II. After the great increase instituted to finance the war, tax rates have fallen only slowly during the postwar period. In addition, the effect of inflation over time has been to lower the real income level associated with the higher marginal tax rates.[59]

More importantly, however, because the income tax applies to nominal asset returns—including gains in prices that merely keep pace with inflation as well as whatever premium nominal interest rates include to compensate lenders for the erosion in the real value of their principal —the faster average rates of inflation in recent years have increasingly magnified the associated tax distortions. Given the tax deductibility of nominal interest payments, the after-inflation interest rate on long-term borrowing by medium risk business corporations was negative during ten of the thirteen years 1966–78. Analogously, for an individual investor in the median tax bracket among all American taxpayers, the after-inflation after-tax return on Treasury bills was negative during nine of these thirteen years. Moreover, the presence of deposit interest ceilings has further compounded the effect of taxes and inflation. Not since 1967 have ordinary savings accounts at nonbank deposit institutions returned a positive after-inflation after-tax yield to the investor in the median tax bracket.

As noted in sections 1.2 and 1.3, a variety of tax-related effects have influenced individuals' and businesses' asset-holding and liability-issuing behavior as well as the structure of financial intermediation. Individuals' and banks' preferences for tax-exempt state and local government securities, the postwar emphasis on debt in corporate finance, and the increasing channeling of saving through pensions and other tax-exempt or tax-sheltered vehicles are all attributable, at least in part, to the interaction of taxes and inflation. Within the later postwar years, these effects have also led individuals to restructure their portfolios in yet further ways, shifting from deposit to nondeposit forms of financial assets and, even more, from financial assets to houses and other real investments.[60]

These and other similar distortions, such as those resulting from deposit interest ceilings, have presumably had important effects not just on financial market developments but on economic activity more generally.

1.4.3 The Growth of Government Intermediation and Credit Guarantees

Another important change that has come about within the postwar period, in part as a direct reaction to the distortions noted above, has been the great increase in the federal government's activities as an intermediary for, and also a guarantor of, private credit. The "off-budget" sponsored credit agencies such as the Federal Home Loan Bank System and the Federal Intermediate Credit Bank were in operation before World War II, but the scale of their lending operations was small. As of 1946 all of these agencies combined held only about $2 billion of assets, the majority of which consisted of agricultural loans, and they owed only $2 billion of liabilities. The focus of these agencies' activity turned more toward support for homebuilding after the Federal National Mortgage Association began its lending operations in 1955, but as late as 1960, when their combined assets had reached $11 billion, their total agricultural credit outstanding still exceeded their total housing credit. Only in the 1960s and 1970s, when the interaction of deposit interest rate ceilings with rising nominal interest rates led to the introduction of large-scale support for housing, did government financial intermediation begin to increase rapidly.

Table 1.22 presents data, comparable to that given above for other groups of intermediaries, for the assets of the federally sponsored credit agencies and also the even more recent mortgage "pools" like the Government National Mortgage Association and the Federal Home Loan Corporation. Government sponsored intermediation has grown rapidly, not just absolutely but in relation to gross national product, and by 1978 these intermediaries held more than one-fifth of all outstanding home mortgages and nearly two-fifths of all outstanding farm debt. Moreover, the total housing credit advanced by these intermediaries, which has grown especially rapidly since the onset of periodic disintermediation in the mid-1960s, includes not only direct purchases of mortgages but also Federal Home Loan Bank advances to savings and loan associations, so that the effective amount is even greater. Given its pattern over time, in the absence of this support even the cyclicality of homebuilding shown in figure 1.7 would presumably have been more severe. Federally sponsored intermediaries accounted for 45 percent, 48 percent and 52 percent of the total net extensions of single-family home mortgage credit in the high disintermediation years 1969, 1970, and 1974, respectively.[61]

Federally sponsored intermediaries conduct their business much like private intermediaries, acquiring financial assets on either a loan or

Table 1.22   **Assets of United States Sponsored Credit Agencies and
Mortgage Pools**

Years	Total	Agencies	Mortgage Pools	Housing Credit	Loans to Agriculture
		Combined Financial Assets			
		Percentage of GNP			
1946–50	1.0	1.0	0.0	0.2	0.7
1951–55	1.1	1.1	0.0	0.3	0.6
1956–60	1.8	1.8	0.0	0.7	0.8
1961–65	2.5	2.4	0.1	1.1	1.1
1966–70	3.7	3.4	0.3	2.0	1.4
1971–75	6.3	4.9	1.4	4.3	1.8
1976–78	8.8	5.4	3.5	6.5	2.2
		Percentage of Total Combined Financial Assets			
1946–50	100.0	99.7	0.3	18.7	65.9
1951–55	100.0	98.3	1.6	25.0	58.8
1956–60	100.0	97.8	2.1	38.1	46.6
1961–65	100.0	96.6	3.4	44.5	43.8
1966–70	100.0	91.8	8.2	52.5	39.0
1971–75	100.0	77.3	22.7	68.2	28.6
1976–78	100.0	61.0	39.1	73.1	24.8

Source: Board of Governors of the Federal Reserve System.
Notes: Data are averages of year-end amounts, as percentages of annual gross national product and as percentages of annual total assets. Detail may not add to totals because of rounding.

purchase basis, and in turn issuing their own liabilities. There are at least two important differences, however. One is that government intermediaries do not operate subject to the profit motive alone. While they pursue a profit objective, they do so within the limitations imposed by their charter to support areas of economic activity designated by Congress as public policy priorities.[62] The other key difference is that the liabilities of the mortgage pools and some of the sponsored credit agencies are directly guaranteed by the federal government and accordingly pay interest geared to that on federal government securities. Hence government intermediation also provides some degree of subsidy in the form of access to less expensive (because less risky, by virtue of the guarantee) credit.[63]

The federal government's role as a credit guarantor is not limited to the financial intermediation that it sponsors. Deposit insurance, for example, constitutes the most prevalent form of government sponsored guarantee provided for a fee. Other familiar government sponsored agencies providing guarantees for a fee include the Veterans Administration, the Federal Housing Authority, the Overseas Investors Protection Corporation, the Security Investors Protection Corporation, and most recently the Pension Benefit Guarantee Corporation. The federal government has also sponsored large-scale guarantee programs for diverse borrowers ranging from college students and small businesses to the Lockheed and Chrysler Corporations and New York City. In all, the government's 1978 outstanding credit and credit guarantees—including direct loans, formally guaranteed loans, and other loans by federally sponsored lenders—totaled $440 billion in comparison to $626 billion of direct federal debt obligations outstanding. In addition, the amounts of deposits insured by the FDIC and the Federal Savings and Loan Insurance Corporation were $761 billion and $401 billion, respectively, in 1978.

The postwar growth in the American economy's reliance on federal government intermediation, deposit insurance, and other credit guarantees has probably been to a great extent a counterpart of the government's waning role as a direct borrower. Given the substantial decline (relative to nonfinancial activity) that has occurred in the federal government's outstanding debt, and the corresponding increase in the outstanding debt of private nonfinancial borrowers, the financial markets have increasingly attempted to make private obligations more acceptable to the economy's ultimate wealth holders by converting them into government obligations via government insurance and credit guarantees. Along with the increase in private financial intermediation, the growth of government credit guarantees broadly defined—including some that are merely implicit—have enabled the American financial system to absorb the large postwar shift in the public versus private mix of direct primary debt.

1.4.4 The Evolution of Monetary Policy

Finally, one of the most important, and importantly changing, aspects of the federal government's role in the American financial markets during the postwar era has been the monetary policy carried out by the Federal Reserve System. The changes since World War II in the method of conducting monetary policy, in the effect of monetary policy on the American economy, and in the perceptions of monetary policy held by financial market participants have all been profound.

Although monetary policy developments have been fundamental to the interaction between the American financial markets and nonfinancial economy, a detailed quantitative analysis of the macroeconomic effects of postwar monetary policy lies beyond the scope of this essay.[64] Nevertheless, an essay on postwar changes in the financial markets would be incomplete without some attention—albeit at the qualitative level—to how monetary policy has evolved over these years.

The Federal Reserve System, created by Congress in 1914 as America's first central bank since the 1830s, has responsibility for maintaining the currency and also for the implementation of monetary policy, which along with fiscal policy has constituted one of the two principal engines of government macroeconomic influence during much of this century. As an historical matter, it is interesting to note that the macroeconomic objectives universally associated with monetary policy in the postwar era—and especially the objective of maintaining price stability—received no mention by Congress in the original 1913 Federal Reserve Act. Instead, prompted by the recurrent series of financial crises and panics, most recently in 1901, 1907, and 1913, Congress charged the new Federal Reserve System with the more direct task of preserving stability in the financial markets. More specifically, with the contractionary economic effect of the recent financial panics in mind, Congress instructed the Federal Reserve "to furnish an elastic currency"—exactly the opposite of the anti-inflation objective widely associated with monetary policy and viewed by many people as the chief desideratum of monetary policy today.

The use of monetary policy to achieve broader macroeconomic objectives evolved slowly and cautiously during the prewar years, as economists and Federal Reserve officials gradually came to understand the working of open market operations, now the most important tool of monetary policy but not even contemplated as such in the Federal Reserve Act. The establishment in 1923 of what subsequently developed into today's Federal Open Market Committee led temporarily to an increasing emphasis on open market operations and macroeconomic objectives, but the confusions of the Depression and the associated international monetary problems served to arrest the development of the monetary policy mechanism. During World War II the Federal Reserve facilitated the financing of the huge increase in public debt noted above by supporting the prices of Treasury securities. After the war the reluctance to impose losses on investors who had financed the war effort led to a continuation of the bond price supports, thereby precluding active use of monetary policy for a further half-decade.

The first major postwar change in the posture of American monetary policy came in 1951, when the Treasury-Federal Reserve Accord relieved the central bank of its wartime obligation to peg long-term interest rates. Monetary policy then assumed the macroeconomic role that it has played ever since. Even so, interest rates, especially short-term rates, remained relatively low during much of this period (see fig. 1.2), and the Federal Reserve on balance followed the half-restrictive, half-accommodative policy subsequently known as "leaning against the wind." More specifically, the Federal Reserve primarily keyed its open market operations in the very short run to the net-free reserve position (that is, excess reserves less borrowed reserves) of the commercial banking system. The theory of open market operations underlying this operating strategy—which was based on the relation between sources and uses of bank reserves, and on the assumption of banks' interest-inelastic demands for excess reserves and reluctance to borrow at the discount window—implied that net-free reserves measured banks' willingness to extend loans and create deposits, and hence measured the effect of monetary policy in stimulating or retarding nonfinancial economic activity. In addition, net-free reserves appeared to constitute the perfect "money market" variable—a close proxy for market interest rates (given the level of the Federal Reserve's own discount rate), yet not itself an interest rate and hence not a contradiction of the accord.

For several reasons financial market participants during the 1950s and even the early 1960s did not attach to monetary policy the great importance that they have associated with it in more recent years. The "go-slow" consensus economic philosophy of the Eisenhower years—which Congress never actively opposed, even under the Democratic majorities of the second half of the decade—was broadly consistent with the "sound money" ethos traditionally associated with central banking as well as the more specific "leaning against the wind" policy, which served to dampen cyclical fluctuations of market interest rates as well as to keep them low on average. In addition, although most economists had favored the accord freeing monetary policy, much of the popular thinking of the 1950s emphasized the newfound importance of fiscal policy.

Several changes occurred thereafter, however, that not only heightened market participants' awareness of monetary policy but also changed how monetary policy worked. The emergence of a "guns plus butter" policy, as the Great Society program and the Vietnam War effort peaked simultaneously, had the support of Congress but appeared to be running afoul of the Federal Reserve as interest rates climbed steadily beginning in 1965. Restrictive monetary policy was a major factor, and visibly so, in the macroeconomic policy environment from 1966 on, in part because of the increased sensitivity of the financial markets to interest rate levels as they interacted with the deposit rate ceilings (see fig. 1.7). After 1969 the acceleration of price inflation raised new questions about the relative priority of full employment and price stability in macroeconomic policy making, and the business recessions of 1969–70 and especially 1973–75 placed monetary policy in the middle between the unprecedented double-digit price inflation and the highest unemployment rate of the postwar era. Monetary policy had gradually moved from off stage to on, and then to the center.

Another source of the increasing attention focused on monetary policy during the second half of the postwar period has been a change of attitudes toward fiscal policy. When it emerged during the 1960s that an occasionally flexible fiscal policy was not as sufficient as many people had hoped as a "cure" for business fluctuations, the perception of the potential of monetary policy expanded to fill the apparent need. As is usual in such situations, once opinion began to change it probably went too far in the opposite direction. In the context of an already somewhat polarized economic policy environment, monetary policy therefore became simultaneously the hope of those who opposed whatever they believed to be the current stance of fiscal policy, as well as the target of those who supported that stance but were dissatisfied with the apparent results. Moreover, the question of the fiscal-monetary balance, and therefore the coordination of fiscal and monetary policies, also emerged as issues of some import. Matters of timing came to be perceived as relevant too, as evidence accumulated on the lags associated with the effects of policy actions. Most economists continued to believe that the "outside" lags with which monetary policy influences business activity were longer than the corresponding fiscal policy lags, but the Federal Reserve's compact decision structure shortened the "inside" lag of monetary policy in comparison with the cumbersome Congressional committee process involved in taking fiscal actions.

At the same time, questions arose about the operating methods used to conduct monetary policy per se. Most of the attention centered on the short-run policy of setting the banking system's free reserve position, and then after 1961 on the corresponding short-run policy of setting a short-term interest rate. The essence of the debate was whether this operating method in fact constituted only a short-run guide for open market operations aimed at broader objectives or, instead, had developed into a system of false beacons for policy over the longer run. The main point was that it was not appropriate simply to regard monetary policy as steady or changing because market interest rates (or free reserves) were fixed or moving. What mattered was instead the relationship between observed interest rates and something else—something that was at best difficult to determine. Events played a part here, too, as the acceleration and increasing volatility of price inflation rendered the inference of a "real" market rate of interest ever more difficult. To the extent that allowing for price expectations was basic to interpreting observed (nominal) interest rates as "indicators" of the likely effect of monetary policy on nonfinancial economic activity, calculating such corrections was becoming ever more difficult.

At the beginning of the 1970s, therefore, the Federal Reserve shifted the strategy of its monetary policy yet again—this time to an emphasis on quantitative measures of commercial banking activity in general and on the narrowly defined *M1* money stock in particular. In the late 1960s the Federal Reserve had experimented with a "proviso" approach, according to which short-run open market operations pursued a stated interest rate objective provided that doing so did not cause some aggregate measure to deviate from a predetermined range. In 1970 the Federal Reserve finally adopted an operating strategy based explicitly on monetary targets. The directives governing the conduct of open market operations continued to specify a narrowly constrained short-term interest rate (the federal funds rate), but with the clear understanding that this practice was in large part meant to achieve the targeted rate of monetary growth. Although these directives typically specified target ranges for the growth of several monetary aggregates, as well as commercial bank credit, in practice the focus of policy through the time of writing seems to have been primarily on the narrow money stock.[65]

The Federal Reserve's monetary-targets strategy has subsequently evolved into a fairly well-defined two-stage procedure. First, at the "strategy" level, about once per quarter the Federal Reserve translates its ultimate policy aims (in terms of the economy's growth, employment, price stability, and so on) into a set of desired growth rates for the monetary aggregates over the next year. Because it will choose a new set of desired one-year growth rates three months later, however, only the first quarter of this one-year extrapolation is of direct operational relevance. Second, at the "tactics" level, within the quarter the Federal Reserve determines how best to manipulate the instruments over which it can exert close control (such as nonborrowed bank reserves, or a short-term interest rate) so as to cause the designated monetary aggregates to move in the specified way. In practice the federal funds rate typically served in this instrument role until 1979, when the Federal Reserve initiated a new experiment using the growth of bank reserves as its short-run operating guide. Although the Federal Open Market Committee, which has responsibility for these decisions, meets formally only once a month, it also occasionally uses telephone conferences to make within-month adjustments in the instrument setting aimed at achieving the desired monetary growth, subject only to the need to avoid undue instability in the money market. Apart from occasional variations, the Federal Reserve has essentially continued to pursue its monetary-targets operating strategy along these lines through the time of writing.

In part as a result of the new strategy of open market operations implemented during the 1970s, the short-run volatility of market interest rates sharply increased (see fig. 1.2). These wider interest rate fluctuations in turn have been the source of many of the developments discussed earlier in this essay. Together with the ever higher average level of interest rates during the second half of the postwar period, they have heightened the awareness of monetary policy among nearly all participants in the financial markets. In addition, along with dissatisfaction with macroeconomic outcomes in the 1970s, they have spurred Congress to institute regular "oversight" procedures requiring the Federal Reserve periodically to report its current monetary growth targets through the relevant Congressional committees. The practical ability of Congress to supervise the Federal Reserve's monetary policy in any effective sense, however, appears to be dubious at best.[66]

Finally, a feature of American monetary policy that has also changed several times since World War II has been the degree of influence associated with international considerations. Before the war international financial matters were often at the heart of Federal Reserve policy making. By contrast, during the "dollar shortage" of the early postwar years American monetary policy was largely free to pursue domestic objectives without much regard for international considerations, and the relatively conservative posture of monetary policy (and fiscal policy) during much of the 1950s posed no threat to the country's already strong currency anyway.[67] After the balance of payments had become a major problem in the early 1960s, however, the Federal Reserve began at times to take monetary policy decisions with an eye to their international ramifications. Since then the international constraint on monetary policy making has strengthened and then waned several times. Somewhat surprisingly, although the American role in the international monetary system became a major focus of attention in the early 1970s, with the exchange rate realignment and suspension of dollar-gold convertibility in 1971 and the move to floating exchange rates after 1973, American monetary policy primarily emphasized domestic objectives during these years. By contrast, in the late 1970s (and through the time of writing), despite inconvertibility and floating rates international considerations appear to have exerted more influence over monetary policy than at any time since the early 1960s.[68]

1.5   Summary and Concluding Comments

This essay has documented three major developments that have dominated the American financial markets since World War II.

First, the nonfinancial economy has increasingly relied on private debt financing. At the war's end there was much government debt but little private debt outstanding. Since then both nonfinancial businesses and individuals have greatly increased their indebtedness, while the federal government has sharply reduced its indebtedness, in comparison to the economy's nonfinancial activity. The sustained rise in private indebtedness has represented in part a return to prewar practices after the aberration of the depression and war years and in part the establishment of new norms for indebtedness in relation to incomes. Perceptions of enhanced economic prosperity and stability, greater tax incentives to debt finance under conditions of accelerating price inflation and rising nominal interest rates, increased holdings of physical assets, and the relative decline in government-issued debt per se have probably played some part in accounting for the large relative increase in the nonfinancial economy's private debt.

Second, the economy has increasingly relied on financial intermediaries to hold the claims issued by nonfinancial borrowers. Individuals as well as other nonfinancial investors have allocated a growing share of their portfolios to claims on financial intermediaries, rather than direct claims on nonfinancial borrowers. Even in the holding of corporate equities, the one area traditionally dominated by individual ownership, intermediaries have begun to play a more substantial role. Nonbank deposit intermediaries, including especially savings and loan associations, and private and public sector pension funds have figured prominently in the continuing overall postwar rise in financial intermediation. This increasing degree of financial intermediation has facilitated the increased debt financing of private nonfinancial borrowers and, together with a series of financial innovations, has also helped to break down barriers and frictions interfering with efficient allocation of the economy's financial resources.

Third, in contrast to its declining role as a direct borrower, the federal government has in other ways become more of an influence in the financial markets. The government has increasingly served as an insurer and guarantor of, and an intermediary for, private claims. Federal deposit insurance, instituted shortly before the war, importantly changed the character of private intermediation, and other forms of government credit guarantees have proliferated subsequently. Federally sponsored credit agencies, and more recently mortgage pools, have supplemented private intermediation. Government regulation of the financial markets has also increased in both scope and effect, and market participants have come to attach ever more importance to monetary policy actions as well.

Finally, it is important to reemphasize that these three postwar developments—the rise of the private debt economy, the increasing degree of financial intermediation, and the growing role of the federal government —are not independent phenomena. These three ongoing processes constitute different but closely related facets of the same overall pattern of American financial evolution. Because of the differing risk and liquidity characteristics of public versus private securities, the postwar shift from public to private debt has increased the economy's need for financial intermediation, and the growth and development of that intermediation have in turn facilitated the successful issuance and absorption of ever greater amounts of private debt relative to nonfinancial activity. Similarly, in place of direct government-issued debt, the federal government has indirectly transformed private debt into its own on an increasing scale through a combination of guarantees and federally sponsored intermediation. On balance, over thirty-five years the most important postwar changes in the American financial markets have largely been parts of the same consistent story.

Notes

1. See Gordon's essay in this volume (chap. 2) for a comprehensive treatment.
2. Moreover, the use of annual data for the first seven downturns shown in table 1.2 importantly understates the peak-to-trough decline of real gross national product in comparison to that shown using quarterly data for the six postwar downturns.
3. Kindleberger (1978) provides a lively review of the international propagation of economic disturbances.
4. Perry (1977), Jorgenson (1978), and Perloff and Wachter (1979) documented this shift and offered alternative explanations.
5. Debt issued by nonfinancial borrowers is similar to the concept of "primary securities" introduced by Gurley and Shaw (1960).
6. The data shown here include only those liabilities classified as "credit market debt" in the Federal Reserve Board's flow-of-funds accounts. The debt of the federal government therefore excludes currency and bank reserves but includes the Federal Reserve System's holding of United States government securities ($147.8 billion and $118.6 billion, respectively, as of year-end 1978). For state and local governments, households, and unincorporated nonfinancial businesses, credit market debt in each case constituted 95 percent or more of all liabilities outstanding as of year-end 1978; for nonfinancial business corporations, year-end 1978 total liabilities consisted of 71 percent credit market liabilities, 24 percent trade debt (almost all owed to each other), and 5 percent other liabilities.
7. It is not appropriate to include foreign debt in an analysis of these data from the perspective of the United States economy's liability-issuing behavior. By contrast, if there were some assurance that debt issued by foreign borrowers in United States markets remained in the portfolios of United States investors, then it would be appropriate to include that debt in an analysis from the perspective of the United States economy's asset-holding behavior. (The caveat, of course, would apply as well to debt issued in the United States markets by United States borrowers.)
8. The peak debt/GNP ratio during 1918–78 occurred in 1933, the trough year of the Depression. In addition, much of the household and business debt nominally outstanding during the Depression was of questionable actual value.
9. During 1953–78 the United States debt/GNP ratio has been more stable than the money/GNP ratio. This statement is true regardless of whether one uses annual or quarterly data, either unadjusted or detrended, with money measured as either $M1$ or $M2$; see B. Friedman (1979).
10. See B. Friedman (1979) for a discussion of each of these three behavioral hypotheses and a look at some pertinent postwar evidence.

11. The United States government's debt increased from only $1.2 billion in 1916, the year before the United States entered the war, to $25.6 billion in 1919, the year after the war ended.

12. Apart from a discrepancy due to inadequacies of statistical reporting, the total sources of funds shown in table 1.5 is equal to the total uses of funds shown in table 1.4.

13. Apart from a discrepancy due to inadequacies of statistical reporting, the total sources of funds shown in table 1.5 is equal to the total uses of funds shown in table 1.4.

13. According to U.S. Department of Commerce estimates, reported depreciation allowances *under*stated corporations' true capital consumption by some $2–4 billion annually during 1946–61, then *over*stated it by about the same amount during 1962–73, and since 1974 has *under*stated it again by an increasing amount ($13 billion in 1978). See Feldstein and Summers (1979) for an analysis of the relation between allowable depreciation and true capital consumption under conditions of price inflation.

14. During 1971–76, the years of the equity bulge, public utility companies accounted for 46 percent of total *gross* offerings, and preferred shares accounted for 29 percent of total *gross* offerings. (These data, from the Securities and Exchange Commission, are not available on the net basis used in table 1.5.)

15. For an analysis of this issue see Feldstein (1976) and Feldstein et al. (1978). The more basic point that the corporate tax structure favors debt over equity financing has long been familiar; see, for example, Modigliani and Miller (1963).

16. The rise in short-term indebtedness (which reached 25.7 percent of credit market debt as of year-end 1978) still seems small in comparison with the attention it has received. Moreover, even the small increase that has occurred may be only an illusion if, as seems likely, an increasing share of bank lending is actually intermediate term. The much discussed notion of declining corporate liquidity is captured much better by the relationships among both liabilities and assets. (See data in table 1.4 on funds used to acquire financial assets.) The year-end ratio of the corporate sector's liquid assets to its short-term liabilities has fallen from .86 in 1946 to .68 in 1950, .48 in 1960, .26 in 1970 and a low point of .25 in 1973; after recovering to .34 in 1976, as a consequence of the severe 1973–75 recession, the ratio has fallen again to .27 in 1978.

17. Hendershott and Hu (1979) have documented the growing after-tax incentive for individuals' mortgage borrowing to finance home ownership in recent years, even for those in marginal tax brackets as low as 30 percent. A similar conclusion holds for consumer credit, although here low tax bracket individuals account for more of the borrowing.

18. Apart from a discrepancy due to inadequacies of statistical reporting, the total sources of funds shown in table 1.8 is equal to the total "investment" uses of funds shown in table 1.7.

19. Although installment credit constituted only about one-half of total consumer credit outstanding in the early postwar years, it has so dominated consumer borrowing that, as of year-end 1978, households owed $276 billion of installment credit and only $64 billion of other consumer credit.

20. Since the early 1960s the most rapidly growing expense item of state and local governments has been contributions to their employees' pension funds; see Munnell and Connolly (1976) for a review of this experience. The growth of these pension funds, the subject of section 1.3, has itself been an important development.

21. To avoid confusion it is worth noting explicitly that the *general* funds of state and local governments were in surplus in the 1970s. Since their *pension* funds also run a large current surplus, the state-local government sector has been heavily in surplus on a consolidated basis throughout the postwar period.

22. Because of the enormous size of the United States markets, however, especially in comparison with specific foreign markets, what represents only a small part of lending here may often play a sizable role in meeting the needs of particular foreign borrowers.

23. See Solomon (1977) for a description of the capital controls program and a discussion placing it in the context of the United States economy's postwar foreign economic policy.

24. Remaining barriers to foreign securities issues in the United States market include the withholding tax on interest and dividends paid to foreigners and disclosure requirements of the Securities and Exchange Commission.

25. Because of the cyclicality of transfer payments and the overall weakness of the United States economy in the 1970s, the data shown in table 1.11 slightly overstate the trend increase in both transfers and total federal expenditures in relation to gross national product. See Break's essay in this volume (chap. 9) for a comprehensive review of postwar trends in federal spending.

26. In 1978, the fourth year of the economic expansion, the (calendar year) federal deficit was $28 billion, or 1.3 percent of gross national product.

27. During this same period the Federal Reserve System was trying, via its "Operation Twist," to shorten the mean maturity of the federal debt held by public investors. As table 1.12 shows, the debt management policy predominated. A number of researchers subsequently attempted to analyze the effects of Operation Twist as if it were not offset by debt management policy; see, for example, Modigliani and Sutch (1966; 1967). In light of the prevailing debt management policy, it is not surprising that such efforts were unsuccessful.

28. See Goldsmith (1958; 1969) and Gurley and Shaw (1960) for an analysis of the prewar experience.

29. The interesting question of cause and effect between these two developments lies beyond the scope of this essay.

30. The data plotted in figure 1.4 and used also in table 1.13 refer only to financial assets and hence exclude nonfinancial assets like houses and consumer durables. As of year-end 1978 households' nonfinancial assets, valued at replacement cost, totaled $2.8 trillion (of which $1.5 trillion was residential real estate) in comparison to $4.8 trillion of financial assets. The available current-value data on nonfinancial asset holdings are understandably weak.

31. Moreover, these data overstate households' direct equity holdings in that they do not separate holdings via mutual funds, which grew from an average 2 percent of total equity holdings in 1946–50 to 7 percent in 1971–75.

32. Feldstein (1974), for example, derived a large estimate of social security "wealth" (defined as the present discounted value of expected future benefits) and found evidence of a significant impact of social security on private saving behavior. Although this work and the literature that has followed it have emphasized effects on total saving behavior, there is no reason to expect the composition of asset holding to remain invariant.

33. Some of the best-known examples of this thinking were Greenough (1951) and Advisory Committee (1969).

34. Lintner (1975), Modigliani and Cohn (1979), and Feldstein (1979), among others, have provided analyses of the failure of equity returns to keep pace with inflation.

35. Table 1.14 is adapted from Bodie (1979) and is based on updated annual data compiled by Ibbotson and Sinquefield (1977); see also Bodie (1976). See Cagan (1974) for a more detailed examination of data over a longer time period and for cross-country comparisons.

36. See Hartman (1978) for a review of the participation of foreign investors in the United States financial markets. A distinction documented by Hartman is that, within the category of long-term portfolio (as opposed to direct) investments, foreign investors have mostly bought United States equities while United States investors have mostly bought foreign debt securities.

37. Funds generated internally and retained by corporate businesses also represent a form of investment by the holders of equity shares in those corporations. Given the large household ownership of equities, including retained earnings in the data shown in table 1.12 would greatly increase the share of funds "advanced" by nonfinancial investors, but it would still leave intermediaries as the direct source of well over half of the total.

38. Much of this literature has followed the lead of Gurley and Shaw (1960).

39. Following Glass-Steagall, commercial banks no longer engage in investment banking or broker-dealer activities for publicly offered corporate securities, although they do so for public sector securities, and in recent years they have been increasingly involved in arranging direct placements of corporate securities. In addition, the trust departments of commercial banks continue to be the largest single factor in private asset management.

40. See Fellner and Larkins (1976) for a discussion of the stability of $M2$ velocity, and B. Friedman (1980) for a corresponding discussion for bank credit.

41. The work of M. Friedman (1959) and M. Friedman and Schwartz (1963) explained the downward prewar trend in $M2$ velocity by emphasizing the role of money as a luxury good.

42. Banks' holdings of Treasury securities were essentially flat from 1946 until the swelling of the federal deficit occurred in 1975, so that banks' portfolios of municipals have exceeded their portfolios of Treasuries ever since 1969. Except for 1974–76, all of the growth in banks' holdings of federal government debt has consisted of federal agency securities.

43. See Goldfeld (1973; 1976) for a review of the postwar evidence on money demand behavior.

44. See Rhoades (1976) for a summary of changes in banking structure following the 1970 amendments.

45. In table 1.18, however, the respective size of the three groups is indicated by their total assets because of the lack of historical data on pension funds' liabilities.

46. See Weiss (1976) for a review of the ERISA legislation and its impact.

47. Tepper and Affleck (1974) and Oldfield (1976), among others, have investigated the nature of this underfunding. Although corporations are now required to report (as a footnote to the balance sheet) the difference between pension assets and liabilities for vested benefits, there is no easy way to discover the liability for nonvested benefits.

48. See again Munnell and Connolly (1976).

49. Silber (1977), for example, has analyzed liquidity provided by markets as an alternative to liquidity provided by intermediaries.

50. See Branson's essay in this volume (chap. 3) for a comprehensive treatment.

51. Silber (1975) has developed a theory of financial innovation. For discussions of the impact of specific recent financial innovations, see, for example, Lieberman (1977), Porter et al. (1979), and Lombra and Kaufman (1978).

52. Tobin (1963), for example, called on the government to issue such an instrument long before the major acceleration of inflation. More recently, researchers have sought to discover why the private markets have not provided it; see, for example, Fischer (1975; 1979).

53. See, for example, Modigliani and Lessard (1975).

54. See Caves' essay in this volume (chap. 7) for a comprehensive treatment.

55. Data on bank failures are available from M. Friedman and Schwartz (1963) and successive issues of the FDIC *Annual Report*.

56. For analyses of this issue see, for example, Maisel (1980).

57. The federal government's most ambitious postwar effort to restructure the investment banking industry failed, however, when the government lost the antitrust suit it brought against seventeen leading investment banking firms (*United States* v. *Morgan et al.*) in 1951.

58. An anomaly of these ceilings is that mutual institutions which are in principle owned by their depositors—including savings and loan associations, mutual savings banks, and credit unions—are prohibited from fully distributing earnings to their owners. Earnings above the ceiling rate merely accumulate unless the institution converts to a stock organization (as is legal for savings and loans), in which case they become a windfall to the new owners.

59. Congress has repeatedly adjusted the brackets, but on balance these adjustments have had sufficient redistributive elements to reduce the real income level to which the higher marginal rates apply.

60. Kane (1980), for example, has documented the substantial shifts in individuals' asset holding since the early 1960s.

61. It is possible, however, that the mortgage market receives less as a net addition to available funds than all of the credit provided by the sponsored credit agencies and mortgage pools if they in turn sell their securities to investors who would otherwise have held deposits in thrift institutions. See, for example, the analysis of this question in Jaffee and Rosen (1979).

62. It is important not to draw this distinction too firmly, however. For example, savings and loan associations are constrained to hold at least 82 percent of their asset portfolios in residential mortgages (or other qualified assets). Also, as the discussion above notes, in the presence of deposit interest ceilings limiting the pay-out of earnings to holders of deposit shares, it is not clear what role the profit motive plays in savings and loans' portfolio decisions.

63. See Penner and Silber (1973) for an analysis of the subsidy implicit in federal credit programs.

64. See Gordon's essay in this volume (chap. 2). For more detailed accounts of postwar monetary policy, see M. Friedman and Schwartz (1963), Brunner and Meltzer (1964), Guttentag (1966), Bach (1971), Brimmer (1972), and Poole (1975). Parts of what follows draw on B. Friedman (1977; 1978).

65. Although some observers have alleged that the Federal Reserve's commitment to the monetary growth targets has been largely rhetorical, a steady accumulation of evidence shows that the observed movement of the money stock in relation to its targeted growth path has become a major determinant—on some evidence, the dominant one—of short-run monetary policy operations. De Rosa and Stern (1977), Feige and McGhee (1979), and Lombra and Moran (1979) have all found evidence to this effect.

66. Pierce (1978) and Roberts (1978) have both assessed this effort and drawn essentially negative conclusions.

67. Concerns about the dollar's external position first arose in conjunction with the government's $12 billion deficit in 1958—a peacetime record at the time, and

equal to nearly 3 percent of the gross national product (a relative size not again reached until the 1973–75 recession).

68. See again Solomon (1977) for a detailed account of the role of international factors in United States monetary policy making.

---

2. Milton Friedman

The Changing Character of Financial Markets

World War II may be a meaningful watershed for many aspects of American economic development—though I have my doubts. But two other dates are far more significant for analyzing changes in financial institutions and their role in the economy: first 1933, the end of the Great Contraction and the beginning of a major structural reform of financial institutions; second, the mid-1960s, the beginning of widespread recognition that the immediate problem was not deflationary collapse but rather inflation.

The institutional changes that followed the Great Contraction were designed to reduce the susceptibility of the financial system to collapse; and largely succeeded in doing so. But those very changes made the system ill adapted to cope with inflation. When that danger emerged, further changes in the financial structure occurred that are still far from complete. They too may well be completed after the major need for them has passed.

Post-1933 Changes

My task with respect to the post-1933 changes is eased by a broadbrush evaluation that I made of some of these changes a quarter of a century ago—in chronological time; it seems much longer in psychological time, to borrow Maurice Allais's perceptive distinction.

With respect to changes in the United States banking structure, I wrote:

> Three major changes have occurred in this system since the great depression: first, the establishment in 1934 of the Federal Deposit Insurance Corporation; second, a growth in the importance of government obligations among bank assets; third, a loosening of the links between gold and domestic monetary conditions. These changes have transformed the banking system to an extent that is not generally recognized. . . .
>
> The combined effect of . . . [these changes] is to eliminate as a

Milton Friedman is Senior Research Fellow of the Hoover Institution and Paul Snowden Russell Distinguished Service Professor of Economics at the University of Chicago.

practical possibility anything approaching a collapse of the American banking structure. Insurance rules out an internal drain or banking panic; the importance of government obligations reduces the sensitivity of the stock of money to internal private credit changes; the dethroning of gold reduces its sensitivity to changes in external conditions. It is hard to see how under these circumstances any sharp *decline* in the stock of money could occur except through deliberate action by the monetary authorities to bring one about. This is very different from the situation prior to 1933, when it would have required deliberate action by the monetary authorities to prevent a decline in the stock of money. I hasten to add that none of these changes rules out sharp increases in the stock of money. . . .

After commenting on changes in the fiscal structure and in the psychological climate of opinion, I concluded:

Our present monetary and fiscal institutions are so constructed that anything more than a minor economic recession is extremely unlikely, even if, or especially if, no explicit action is taken by Congress or the Administration. But unless the recession is *exceedingly* minor, explicit action will be taken. The widespread general fear of depression would lead Congress to force such action on any administration whatever its political complexion. . . . Such additional action will be unnecessary. Even more, it will be positively harmful. . . . Measures taken to stem a supposed depression will serve to stimulate the succeeding recovery and to convert it into another round of inflation.

This inflation will not get out of hand; the same built-in stabilizers that would prevent a depression from getting out of hand will also prevent a runaway inflation. Sooner or later another recession will come along. . . . When it does, the same process is likely to be repeated.

The prospect is therefore a period of recurrent bouts of inflation produced by overreaction to the temporary recessions that punctuate the period. How long will this period last? How serious will the inflation be? . . . These questions seem to me to admit of no easy answer. Much depends on accidents of timing and politics, both internal and external.

Economists have known—at least intermittently—for over a century and a half two propositions: first, that by printing enough money you can produce any desired degree of activity; second, that the ultimate result is destruction of the currency. The American public has learned the first proposition. It once knew, but has now forgotten, the second. Only experience is likely to teach it once again.[1]

Experience has been teaching it—and that is the major source of the developments discussed in the next section.

The second change in the banking structure—the increased ratio of government obligations to the total assets of commercial banks—proved temporary in form, though long lasting in substance. As Benjamin Friedman notes in his background paper, the ratio of government obligations to total commercial bank assets has returned to its earlier level, thanks to the reduction, primarily via inflation, in the explicit government debt as a fraction of income. However, the main thrust of the first two changes—assumption by government of responsibility for the security in nominal terms of nominal private assets—has continued. Guarantees have been expanded from deposits in commercial banks and thrift institutions to Federal Housing Administration and veterans' housing loans, Federal National Mortgage Association, Government National Mortgage Association, Federal Land Bank, and Federal Home Loan obligations in the housing area; loans to small businesses and students; securities of New York City; loans to Lockheed and Chrysler. And no doubt this is a highly partial list.

Benjamin Friedman gives an estimate in his background paper of the total amount of some of the outstanding liabilities currently issued or guaranteed by the Federal government. They total nearly three times as much as all direct Treasury obligations. The grand total must by now equal well over half of the total financial assets of the public, and an even larger fraction if the present value of the public's claims to future benefits from social security and from government pensions is included as an asset of the public and a liability of the government.

A corollary is that the decline in the ratio of the funded government debt to national income is highly misleading. Total direct, contingent, and unfunded government debt has almost surely been rising in recent years rather than falling as a fraction of national income. How else explain the decline in the yield differential between corporate Aaa bonds and long-term Treasury bonds?

All of this has to do with *nominal* liabilities and assets. The real value of the physical assets corresponding to nominal liabilities remains subject to all the dynamic forces in a dynamic economy. The guarantee of nominal assets has been accompanied by fluctuations in their real value through variable inflation. Uncertainty has been rechanneled, papered over by a facade of misleading dollar figures.

Federal insurance of bank deposits was accompanied by the adoption of Regulation Q, which prohibited the payment of interest on demand deposits and authorized ceilings on rates of interest that could be paid by depository institutions on other categories of deposits. Regulation Q proved to be a concealed time bomb that had its greatest effect during our second period after interest rates started to respond to inflation. The interest rate limits were largely innocuous for a long time after they were imposed. They were above market rates and so neither performed any positive function nor did much harm.

Similarly, the third change, the reduced role of gold, was finally consummated during our second period, in 1971, though it had considerable impact earlier.

Two developments after 1933 deserve mention to put the changes in the banking structure in perspective.

First, the changes in banking structure were accompanied by a shift in power: from the regional Federal Reserve Banks to the Board in Washington and from the Federal Reserve System to the Treasury Department. The Fed became a largely passive adjunct to the Treasury, playing no active part until the Treasury-Federal Reserve accord in 1951, and, paradoxically, gaining importance through the 1960s as it became a more potent engine of inflation.

The shift of power from monetary to fiscal authorities coincided with a matching shift in economic thinking. The initial shift in power owed nothing to the Keynesian revolution. However, it was strongly reinforced by the changing climate of academic opinion. Research in the Federal Reserve System itself on monetary matters proper largely came to a halt. It was replaced with research on Keynesian lines, which culminated years later in Federal Reserve collaboration in developing a large-scale econometric model in which monetary forces played at most a bit part, entering only via a narrow range of interest rates.

Second, the commercial banking system itself lost power and place to other institutions. The reforms of the 1930s which limited the functions that banks could perform laid the basis for growth in other financial intermediaries and were later strongly reinforced by the impact of Regulation Q. The stress of competition subsequently forced innovation that slowed the decline of commercial banks and altered their operations in the ways that Benjamin Friedman discusses.

A final comment is relevant to the ending of the initial phase and the beginning of the second. The inflationary roller coaster that I predicted in my 1954 talk did not arrive on schedule in the United States (though it did in the United Kingdom). It started in the 1950s but was then aborted by the successive recessions of 1957–58 and 1960, so that, by 1960, inflation was close to zero. Only then did the roller coaster really take off.

That interruption reflected, I conjecture, the accident of a nonpolitical president, Dwight Eisenhower, who was willing to sacrifice his party's, and his vice-president's, presidential prospects in order to cut short the inflationary process. He succeeded, bequeathing to his successor, John F. Kennedy, a noninflationary environment. The process of "recurrent bouts of inflation produced by overreactions to . . . temporary recessions" that had seemed to me imminent in 1954 was then resumed.

That is why it was not until the mid-1960s that inflationary expectations began to become part of the standard outlook of consumers, businessmen, and participants in the financial markets. It has always seemed remarkable to me how late this development occurred and how slowly it proceeded. Even now, after more than two decades, many phenomena in the financial world—particularly, persistent negative real rates of interest—are hard to rationalize except on the assumption that many participants anticipate a fairly prompt return to a noninflationary environment.

Post-1960s

No single year marks the beginning of the inflationary period as sharply as 1933 marks the end of the contraction. Robert Gordon, in his perceptive background paper, picks 1967 and that is probably as good a single date as any. It comes after the beginning of the actual inflationary roller coaster—that is clearly 1960. It comes before widespread recognition that a "new era" was under way. However, it is a good date to mark the beginning of the successive changes in the financial structure that the new era was to bring. That unattractive word "disintermediation" entered the financial vocabulary in 1966, revealing clearly how perverse in a time of inflation were the effects on the financial structure of reforms designed to reduce the evils of deflation.

The rapid rise in the velocity of $M1$ as depositors found ways to economize on non-interest-bearing demand deposits showed that regulation Q was beginning to bite. Similarly, many of the financial changes over the next decade that are referred to by Benjamin Friedman reflected the attempt to evade or avoid Q with respect to both demand and time deposits: negotiable certificates of deposits, negotiable orders of withdrawal (NOW) accounts, automatically transferable savings accounts, special certificates of deposit available to depositors at mutual savings banks and savings and loan associations, money market mutual funds, and so on. Benjamin Friedman emphasizes the extent to which these and other financial innovations contributed to market efficiency. My own reaction is quite different: what a waste of capital and human ingenuity simply to get around restrictions and regulations that should never have been imposed, that were never justified by the ostensible purpose of reducing the vulnerability of the financial system to deflationary pressure and were adopted only because the circumstances enabled commercial banks and other financial institutions to persuade Congress to grant them special privileges they had long sought. In the 1960s and thereafter, the banks were hoisted on their own petard.

Did we really need still another demonstration of how ingenious economic actors are in getting around government restrictions that interfere with their pursuit of self-interest? Was it really a net gain in market efficiency to replace or supplement commercial banks in their function of mediating transactions by savings and loan institutions, mutual savings banks, credit unions, money market funds, Sears-Roebuck, and the telephone company? Or to create a situation in which persons with small sums to invest are struck with rates of return half as large as those available to persons with large sums?

The explosive growth of the Eurodollar market is another example of the same phenomenon. The Eurodollar market was initially established largely as a way to hold dollars not subject to freezing by United States authorities. But its growth was greatly stimulated by regulation Q which could be avoided by borrowing and lending abroad. The attempt to preserve fixed exchange rates through the interest-equalization tax, restrictions on foreign investment by United States enterprises, and on foreign lending by United States banks were even more important. Had the United States cut completely the link with gold earlier and set the dollar free to float, the Eurodollar market would never have attained its present scale. New York, not London would have been the center of world finance and the United States would probably never have drifted into so unsatisfactory an international financial position. Here again, the banking community must bear much of the blame for developments that proved so adverse to its interests. With the notable exception of Walter Wriston, leading bankers were all strong proponents of fixed exchange rates and lobbied for their retention—which meant they also lobbied, though not explicitly, for exchange control.

Benjamin Friedman quite properly emphasizes the growth of private debt and the decline in the ratio of corporate equity to debt. The mystery to me is why debt did not grow still more rapidly under the double spur of tax advantages and the inflation-induced availability of long-term funds at a negative real rate. Individuals and enterprises that borrowed at long term in nominal form have been the major private beneficiaries from inflation. Why were so many so slow to take advantage of the opportunity? The obvious answer is the inertia of the status quo, the long time that it takes for the community at large to adjust its expectations and its behavior to basic changes in its environment—alike a major source of the appeal of inflation to fiscal and monetary authorities, of the damage that inflation does, and of the difficulty of ending inflation. Expectations may be rational, yet take a long time to adjust; markets may be efficient in the technical sense, yet prove highly imperfect estimators of future values; it may not be possible to fool all the people all the time, but it appears to be possible to do so for a surprisingly long time.

An unanticipated consequence of the greatly expanded role of government on both income and capital account has been a return of the cyclical behavior of interest rates to its pre-World War I pattern. Before the

First World War, long-term interest rates typically peaked well after the peak of the business cycle—around mid-recession—and reached their trough well after the cyclical trough—around mid-expansion. This occurred because of the importance of railroad bonds issued to finance extensions of track. Once an extension was started, it was generally expedient to complete it even if business conditions softened. A downturn in the cycle brought a postponement of new track extensions but meant a higher rather than lower demand for bond finance to complete the extensions under way, since there was a decline in current revenues accompanying the constant, or for a time even growing, requirement for capital. As the extensions were completed the demand for finance ebbed, reinforcing the decline in demand elsewhere, and producing by mid-recession a decline in interest rates. Similarly, during an expansion, there was a delay before new track extensions were approved and moved from paper plans to actual construction, so that the demand for finance did not pick up sharply until about mid-expansion.

Since the end of the Second World War the government has increasingly been playing the role that the railroads played earlier as a dominant and lagging element in the market for long-term bond finance. After a cyclical downturn, government demand increases as earlier commitments mature, spending rises on unemployment insurance and similar countercyclical programs, and current tax revenues decline. Interest rates decline only after demand from other sources has fallen enough to offset the higher government demand. A similar sequence in the reverse direction occurs during expansions.

A major institutional change that is still mostly in bud is the widespread indexation of financial contracts for inflation. The shortening of debt periods, floating interest rates, and variable-rate mortgages are all signs of the demand for indexing. An even more dramatic sign is the retreat from financial assets to physical assets—to land, houses, antiques, jewelry, gold, and silver—and the explosive rise in the prices of such assets.

There have been two major obstacles to the issuance of inflation-adjusted securities by private enterprises: first, their ability to borrow at negative real rates of interest through traditional channels; and second, the absence of indexing in the tax structure so that payments to lenders to allow for inflation would not be treated as taxable interest or capital gains. The major obstacle to the issuing of inflation-adjusted liabilities by financial intermediaries is the absence of corresponding assets to serve as their counterpart in the balance sheet.

If the inflationary roller coaster continues, these obstacles will disappear. Nominal interest rates will rise sufficiently to give a positive real yield; the pressure to index the tax system is strong and will become irresistible. The government may even be led to issue inflation-adjusted obligations, which could serve as the counterpart to inflation-adjusted liabilities of financial intermediaries.

Conclusion

I am not nearly so confident now about the longer range future as I was a quarter of a century ago. At that time, the initial stage of a long trend had been passed, so the direction was clear, but the trend was still in its early stages, so it could be expected to continue for a long time. Today that trend is old. It is generating countercurrents of opinion and action. A turn is in the offing. But who knows just when it will occur? As every forecaster is aware, as the Dow theory enshrines, picking turning points is the really hard part of the job.

The turn may come soon. A number of fortuitous circumstances, including mistakes in monetary policy, have, I believe, increased the possibility that 1979 or 1980 will prove the year when inflation peaked in the United States, not in the sense that the inflation will thereafter sink steadily and precipitously to zero, but in the sense that the inflationary roller coaster will change from an upward to a downward trend. In that case, while the trough of inflation in 1981 or 1982 will probably be higher than the preceding trough in 1976, the next peak in the mid-1980s will be lower than the 1979 or 1980 peak. Even if that optimistic outlook is realized, the institutional changes—particularly the indexation of taxes and government borrowing—set in motion by the gradual incorporation of inflationary expectations will continue, though they may not reach full fruition. The continued changes will slow the adjustment to a less inflationary environment—just as the earlier institutional changes slowed the adjustment to accelerating inflation. The role of commercial banks will continue to decline—though the decline may be slowed by a reduction in regulation, particularly the elimination of Q; forms of financial intermediation will continue to proliferate, and new financial instruments will continue to be produced—all, on the initial assumption, to respond to a vanishing problem.

While I now regard this scenario as more likely than I did even six months ago, it still seems to me decidedly less likely than a continued, and indeed even accelerating, upward trend of the roller coaster, with the swings becoming shorter and wider. Inertia is strong. Objections to inflation are weaker than they seem. All of us object to rises in the prices of the things we buy; few of us object to rises in the prices of the things we sell. All of us are eager to end inflation—provided it is done at someone else's expense.

Experience abroad, particularly in Japan and Great Britain, suggests that inflation must reach a rate of something like 25 percent a year before its destructive social effects become so visible, so widespread, as to make it politically profitable to end the inflation.

If that proves the case here, as I fear it will, inflation will come down to perhaps something like 7–9 percent in 1981, and then rise to perhaps 15–20 percent by the mid-1980s. On this scenario, the upward swing of the roller coaster still has another decade or so to run before it becomes politically profitable to end it. That is not a pleasant prospect. However, I do not share the views of those who believe that the outcome will be a runaway hyperinflation (always of course excepting the outbreak of major war, in which case, a wholly different range of possibilities would emerge). The conditions for a hyperinflation are not present now and are almost certainly not going to be present for the foreseeable future.

If the roller coaster does continue on its upward path for another decade or so, the nascent changes in the financial institutions and arrangements could go very far. By then, we shall be living in a financial world where indexation is well-nigh universal for all but very short-term contracts, where financial intermediation of all kinds is a sharply declining industry. The financial markets will be highly efficient, but we shall buy that market efficiency at the cost of physical inefficiency, widespread social unrest, and political instability.

If we cannot long before then summon the political will to end the inflation that only government produces and that only government can end, we shall, in the famous words of Adam Smith, have "to endeavour to accommodate . . . to the real mediocrity of [our] circumstances."

Note

1. "Why the American Economy is Depression-Proof," a lecture delivered in Stockholm in April, 1954. Reprinted in Milton Friedman, *Dollars and Deficits* (Englewood Cliffs, N.J.: Prentice-Hall, 1968), pp. 72–90, quotations from pp. 74, 75, 78, 89, and 90.

3. A. W. Clausen

The Changing Character of Financial Markets in the Postwar Period: A Personal Perspective

Since the postwar period closely coincides with my own thirty years as a commercial banker, my discussion of postwar changes in financial markets will bear the stamp of that personal perspective.

I'll begin by reviewing developments from 1945 to 1960, a time when: mutual funds, savings and loans, and insurance companies invaded the backyard of a sedentary and overly cautious commercial bank-

A. W. Clausen is president of Bank of America.

ing sector; the growth of consumer credit opened vast new markets to financial institutions; and the worldwide dollar shortage came to an end following the declaration in 1958 that major European currencies would henceforth be convertible, paving the way for the rapid growth of trade and multinational activity in the decades to come.

Next I will focus on the 1960s, a period characterized by a flurry of activity and innovation among banks and other financial institutions, including: the emergence of a number of new money market instruments; the advent of liability management in banking; the integration of financial markets on an international scale; formation of one-bank holding companies as vehicles for financial services diversification; and disturbing trends involving our balance of payments and advancing inflation.

The 1970s, my third frame of reference, represents yet another distinct set of developments: the breakdown of the Bretton Woods and Smithsonian agreements and the dramatically increased pressure on the value of the dollar relative to other currencies and gold; the massive recycling of petrodollars following a series of dramatic OPEC price hikes; loan syndications—often for projects in developing countries— of a scope far exceeding previous experience; highly volatile financial markets in the United States and abroad; and a blurring of distinctions between different types of United States financial institutions and between services offered by the financial and nonfinancial sectors.

When I first entered the financial world in 1949, widespread predictions of a depression following World War II were giving way to optimism as the peacetime economy entered an unprecedented period of sustained economic growth. Output per man-hour nearly doubled during the first half of the postwar period, providing the impetus for a 138 percent increase in the gross national product from 1945 to 1960. These gains were facilitated by corresponding increases in American credit markets. During the 1945–60 period, total debt grew 115 percent, to $875 billion.

Not all financial institutions shared equally in the market's largess, of course. Commercial banks, dominated for the most part by conservative managements that were more interested in the size of balance sheet totals than in earnings per share, failed to take full advantage of the opportunities that arose following the war. Insurance companies, mutual funds, savings and loans, and other institutions rushed in to fill the vacuum. By 1960, the banking sector's share of total debt had slipped almost three percentage points.

Savings and loan associations proved especially adept at cultivating the mortgage field. Encouraged by pent-up demand immediately following World War II and subsequently bolstered by government programs such as the Federal National Mortgage Association, mortgage debt grew at a substantial pace throughout the postwar period. From 1945 to 1960, outstanding mortgages increased almost sixfold.

The expansion of Bank of America's mortgage portfolio paralleled this trend. However, most bankers were less eager to participate in the market during the first half of the postwar period, preferring more liquid assets. It wasn't until 1957 that the loan portfolios of commercial banks finally surpassed their holdings of government securities.

Savings and loan associations, adopting a more aggressive stance, doubled their share of the mortgage market during the postwar years. By 1960, they held 29 percent of mortgage debt outstanding. This compared with 20 percent for life insurance companies, 14 percent for commercial banks, 13 percent for mutual savings banks, and 24 percent for all other holders. Commercial banks were more successful in capitalizing on growing demands for consumer installment loans, a relatively young market. Excluding the portion served by retailers, these loans expanded almost twentyfold from 1945 to 1960. The commercial bank share of this $37 billion market had reached 45 percent by 1960.

Banks also began testing the credit card field in the early 1950s. Although early attempts proved unprofitable, Bank of America established a firm foothold in the market with the introduction of BankAmericard in 1958.

However, in attracting time deposits, the savings and loan industry clearly outperformed rival financial institutions during the 1950s. Until the liberalization of Federal Reserve Regulation Q in 1960, commercial banks had been steadily losing ground in this area. From 1945 to 1960, their individual savings deposits increased only 124 percent, to $67 billion, while individual savings at savings and loans rose almost 750 percent, to $62 billion. Then Regulation Q was modified, allowing banks to pay more competitive rates on savings and time deposits. In the years that followed, commercial banks reversed the trend of previous years. For example, they attracted 42 percent of the savings flow from 1960 to 1968, whereas the share going to savings and loans dropped to 26 percent. Life insurance companies, which garnered 31 percent of the savings flow in the 1950s, slipped to a 17 percent share during the 1960–68 period.

The 1960s ushered in a host of other changes that provided banks with new sources of funds, primarily "purchased money" available in large volume at money market rates. As these funds made up an increasingly sizable proportion of bank liabilities by the mid-1960s, the term "liability management" quickly gained currency in financial circles. Carried to its extreme, this concept suggested that banks no longer needed to provide for liquidity in their asset mix. They could simply "buy" the liabilities they needed to meet liquidity or loan demands.

With the introduction of new money market instruments, such as the large denomination negotiable certificate of deposit, the growth of federal funds trading, and the burgeoning of the Eurodollar pool, commercial banks untied themselves from the apron strings of their primary deposit sources—checking and savings accounts. Now they could turn to purchased funds to satisfy the market's growing appetite for credit as the economy boomed and inflation began mounting in the mid-1960s. In the 1950s, the total assets of weekly reporting banks increased by $51 billion, or 53 percent. The corresponding gain in the sixties was $189 billion, a 128 percent jump. By 1970, commercial banking had regained the market share that had been lost during the 1950s.

The dramatic expansion of credit markets in the 1960s coincided with a merging of previously segmented markets and increasing innovation within financial markets. For example, seekers of mortgage funds began venturing beyond the confines of local and regional markets to tap the capital markets. At the same time, household savings also became more mobile, moving from deposit institutions to bond markets and other sectors returning higher yields.

In search of more funds at lower interest rates, corporations also turned increasingly to the money markets, bypassing financial intermediaries. From 1966 to 1969, when the average prime rate increased from 5.2 to 8 percent, the commercial paper market almost tripled—from $13 billion to $32 billion. Bankers and corporate managements both soon learned that "money for hire" has only one allegiance: It goes to the highest bidder offering the least risk. It was quickly dubbed "hot money," and more than once overly dependent banks were burned by it.

Another innovation with far-reaching consequences was the formation of one-bank holding companies that began in 1967 and soon became a vogue. In fact, so popular was this new concept that in the space of but a year, one-bank holding companies grew from almost nothing to encompass one quarter of the total banking assets in the United States. The congeneric was banking's answer to insurance lenders, captive finance companies, and giant corporations that had been trespassing on the traditional turf of banks. It provided an avenue for bank expansion into new fields without running afoul of the Justice Department. However, legislation passed in 1970 curbed bankers' exuberance by restricting operations of one-bank holding companies to specific activities closely related to finance.

Although our subject is American financial markets, many of the forces at work in the United States must be analyzed in a global context. Indeed, the interdependency of international finance had become apparent to American business and financial leaders in the early 1950s. To provide a forum for discussion of major economic, monetary, and fiscal issues affecting the international banking community, the American Bankers Association hosted the first International Monetary Conference in 1954. Initially, the conference brought together chief executive officers of the 50 largest United States banks and 12 to 15 bankers of equal rank from abroad as well as central bank and government officials. The number of foreign bankers in attendance increased each year, and in

1970, the by-laws were changed to make the International Monetary Conference (IMC) a truly international body. The membership has been broadened considerably in the last decade. It currently comprises 116 banks from 23 countries.

The rapid internationalization of finance was powered by two major developments of the 1960s: (1) the dramatic surge of foreign activity by United States-based multinationals; and (2) attempts by the American government to staunch the flow of dollars leaving the country. Because the dollar was overvalued in the 1960s, United States firms found that foreign markets offered extremely attractive investment opportunities. During the latter half of the decade, United States direct foreign investment increased rapidly, mounting to $76 billion in 1970. This compared with direct foreign investment in the United States of but $13 billion.

Devaluations of the dollar in the early 1970s altered the pattern of international investment. Since 1970, the rate of increase in foreign investment in the United States has been outpacing United States investment abroad. At the end of 1978, it totaled nearly $41 billion, a 207 percent increase over the 1970 figure. During the same period, United States direct investment abroad grew by 123 percent, to $168 billion. Naturally, major American banks followed their customers overseas, setting up foreign subsidiaries to service multinational accounts. Soon these banks were deriving a sizable portion of their earnings from abroad.

Except for a branch in London, Bank of America's operations were confined almost exclusively to the United States until 1947. Even as late as 1963, we had only 22 branches abroad. The ensuing years, however, witnessed a phenomenal growth in our international activities. By the end of 1970, our overseas network encompassed 100 branches, 8 representative offices, and 61 subsidiaries and affiliates in 77 countries and territories. Our international assets more than doubled between 1965 and 1970, when they totaled $8 billion. Income from our international activities also climbed steeply, rising to 55 percent of BankAmerica Corporation's profits by 1975. Since then, however, our foreign source income has declined relative to domestic income.

Our shift toward a more international orientation reflected a profound reordering of the global financial structure. In place of compartmentalized national markets, the world was entering an era of highly integrated financial systems that overcame the old limitations imposed by distance and political divisions. This metamorphosis placed the evolving transnational markets on a collision course with some national governments, illustrating once again that changes in the financial environment owe as much to laws, regulations, and similar restraints as to the basic forces of economics.

In the mid-sixties, the United States government began introducing monetary controls aimed at arresting some disturbing trends in the national economy. The inflationary spiral that began its ascent in 1965 was showing little sign of responding to treatment. This, plus the increasing flow of capital abroad and deterioration of the nation's formerly very positive balance of trade, compounded United States balance of payments problems. The nation's official reserve transactions moved from a modest surplus in 1966 to a $3.6 billion deficit in 1967. The following year the situation worsened further as a result of Britain's devaluation of the pound late in 1967, which triggered a run on the dollar. The flight to gold caused the Federal Reserve to tighten voluntary foreign credit restraints and invoke other controls, notably the interest equalization tax.

Instead of keeping dollars at home, these moves by the government acted as a catalyst for the extraordinary development of the Eurodollar market. During a nine-year period of increasing controls that ended in 1974, Eurodollars grew twelvefold, to a gross size of $370 billion. Since then, the market has continued to increase at an average annual rate of 20 to 25 percent.

Ironically, it was this unregulated pool of funds—and the free market mechanism surrounding it—that enabled the international monetary system to rise to the challenge posed by the quintupling of oil prices in 1974. No official mechanism then in place could have resolved the imbalances caused by such an action. The Eurocurrency markets offered the private banking system the flexibility needed to engineer the greatest transfer of financial assets in history with an efficiency that dazzled even supporters of the Euromarkets.

Another, less publicized benefit of these markets is their effect on developing countries. Since they emerged, the Third World has had much greater access to adequate funding for viable projects. The question for the 1980s is what changes will occur in the financial markets in order to accommodate the ever-increasing need in the non-oil-producing Third World to finance the debt burdens caused by higher oil prices and inflation. In 1969, I signed a $245 million syndicated loan for a venture in Papua New Guinea that attracted considerable attention as the then largest privately financed project in history. Today, projects costing billions of dollars are almost commonplace. Much of the funding for these massive projects in the seventies came from the Eurocurrency markets.

A discussion of financial markets in the 1970s would be incomplete without reference to four other developments: (1) concern about overextension of banks following the growth spurt of the sixties; (2) the increasing volatility of markets; (3) the breakdown of the Smithsonian and Bretton Woods accords; and (4) a blurring of distinctions within the financial services industry.

The go-go growth of commercial banks made possible by liability management was a mixed blessing. While effectively meeting rising demands for credit, the rapid expansion of loans and investments in the early 1970s could not continue for long without proportionate additions to equity capital. Balance sheets of commercial banks soon began showing signs of strain. During the first three years of the decade, the assets of major banks expanded at a rate of 15 percent, well above the 9 percent growth of the 1960s. As a result, at the end of 1973, equity capital equaled only 6.5 percent of total bank assets, a considerable decline from 9 percent at the end of 1960. The closure of the United States National Bank of San Diego in 1973, followed by the demise of Franklin National and the international reverberations of the Bankhaus Herstatt failure, further escalated concerns over the soundness of the banking system in this country and abroad.

Against this backdrop, Bank of America adopted a policy of self-restraint in the summer of 1974. In two years, our total assets had risen by more than $15 billion, a gain of 45 percent. And our loan assets had grown by more than 55 percent! Expansion at such a headlong rate clearly could not continue. As a result, we chose to emphasize quality of assets and sustainable growth of earnings over growth for growth's sake. This strategy served us well during the 1974–75 recession and in succeeding years. Other institutions also recognized the need for controlled growth and have adopted similar courses of action.

The return to a more conservative management philosophy led to a gradual erosion in the credit market share of commercial banks during the remainder of the decade, paving the way for more active participation by other intermediaries—especially savings and loans and foreign investors.

Another distinguishing feature of the 1970s is the volatility that infected national and international financial markets during this period. Devaluations of the dollar, the breakdown of the Bretton Woods and Smithsonian agreements, continued high rates of inflation—these and other developments served to undermine confidence in the dollar and encourage speculation.

On the national level, the prime rate offers a useful reference point. From 1934 to 1970, the prime changed thirty-four times, about once a year on the average. Compare this with the three-year period beginning in 1973, when the prime rate changed no less than sixty-six times, or the fifteen changes that occurred in 1979.

Finally, the seventies represented a move away from compartmentalized financial services in the United States and toward a more efficient, nationwide financial market. In the process, we have seen a blurring of the distinctions that traditionally separated competitors within the marketplace. For example, Merrill Lynch, the nation's largest brokerage firm, has developed a Cash Management Account that bears a striking resemblance to a checking account paying a money market rate of interest.

Thanks to pass-through certificates, the mortgage instrument is now relatively marketable. In addition, savings and loan associations are offering construction loans and variable-rate mortgages, as well as housing-related consumer loans. And they can draw funds, when necessary, from the Federal Home Loan Banks. In short, they are becoming more and more like commercial banks.

The desire of savers to receive realistic interest rates has prompted a rush to money market mutual funds and six-month money market certificates. In 1979, for example, the volume of MMCs outstanding more than tripled, exceeding $100 billion by year-end.

And nonfinancial enterprises have been staking out larger claims in financial markets. Sears, Roebuck and Co., for example, earned almost as much from its financial services in 1978 as BankAmerica Corporation. This year Sears intends to go yet another step. To meet some of its capital requirements, it will offer Sears credit card customers an opportunity to buy intermediate term notes through a wholly owned subsidiary.

These and other rumblings in the marketplace portend a shift toward an integrated network that is increasingly efficient at mobilizing and transferring financial resources. Indeed, we already have a nationwide financial services industry on the wholesale level, and I'm convinced it's only a matter of time until the United States has interstate retail banking as well. Electronic funds transfer capabilities and an increasingly mobile population will eventually bring irresistible pressure to bear on the prohibition against interstate banking.

Whatever the future holds, we can be sure there will be no lack of challenges to test the ingenuity, mettle, and resilience of financial markets and the intermediaries that serve them. Chief among these challenges is inflation, which is saddling our economy with a mounting burden of debt and threatening to widen the gap between real gross national product and total credit outstanding. To accommodate demands for future credit and other financial services, financial institutions can be expected to create additional instruments and techniques that will whittle away the remaining impediments to a free flow of funds. Increasing competition, in turn, will produce narrower spreads and greater profit pressures.

In my opinion, this type of environment will favor the consolidation of financial intermediaries, resulting in larger, more diversified institutions that command the resources and leadership qualities required to survive and prosper in an uncertain marketplace. But legislative and regulatory changes will be required to accomplish this. Considering the rough and largely uncharted terrain we've traversed during the past thirty years, I have no doubt that tomorrow's financial systems will be more than adequate to deal with the inevitable future shocks of decades to come. Indeed, the message of the entire postwar period is abundantly clear: Markets will be served. And being terribly prejudiced, I have a personal preference for an active role for the commercial banking industry.

Summary of Discussion

The discussion turned to a number of issues, including the puzzle of low equity and bond yields in an inflationary environment, the changing role of the commercial banks, the growing importance of international constraints in money management, and the role of bank regulation. On the first, Paul Samuelson declared that the greatest puzzle in the area of finance in the past thirty years has been the failure of common stocks to provide an effective inflation hedge. In life-cycle terms, the lower real total yield on equity has substantially raised the real cost of retirement. Samuelson noted a further puzzle in the consistently negative real return to debt in recent years and wondered about the connection between the debt and equity yields. He indicated that Professor Modigliani of M.I.T. claims that both negative yields reflect money illusion of investors, who discount stock prices at the nominal interest rate. Even if the market is vastly inefficient at processing nominal versus real yields, an individual investor may have no way to arbitrage the market error.

Martin Feldstein offered another explanation for low equity and bond yields. The interaction of inflation with the tax rules on depreciation allowances, nominal capital gains, and inventories has lowered the post-tax real rate of return to capital, and therefore the return to equity holders. Low bond yields reflect traditional differentials with equity yields. Walter Wriston declared that the poor performance of stock prices since 1964 reflects an increasingly hostile business environment, with growing regulations and tax burdens. Arthur Okun added that the growing uncertainties about economic performance have led rational investors to bid down equity prices. Okun also joined Feldstein in the view that investors correctly view the combination of taxes and inflation as an effective levy on capital.

Wriston addressed the great changes in the role of commercial banks during the past thirty years. Commercial banks hold a declining share of United States financial assets. In 1946, commercial banks held 57 percent of financial assets in the United States. At the end of 1980, they will likely hold about 37 percent. And Wriston predicted that the downward trend will continue. For example, Sears is beginning to sell commercial paper directly to credit card holders. And while there are 700 million credit cards in America, the commercial banks have less than 15 percent of the cards. General Electric credit will earn more than the Wells Fargo banks, and Sears financial division will earn more in 1980 than Sears retailing. Indeed the entire system of intermediation is moving dramatically away from banks. Wriston declared that the electronic management of funds now allows corporations to maintain nearly zero cash balances and pointed out that the net demand deposits of the clearinghouse banks in New York have not increased in nominal terms in the past five years. Finally, Wriston noted that ten years ago, eight of the world's ten largest banks were resident in the United States. At the end of 1979, there were only three here.

James O'Leary and Arthur Burns suggested that growing world capital mobility and flexible exchange rates have made United States monetary policy increasingly hostage to international events. In coming years, O'Leary predicted, the Federal Reserve Board will not aggressively ease credit in a recession because of fears of large capital outflows and exchange rate depreciation. Milton Friedman, however, was skeptical of this view. He held that monetary policy is freer from international constraints now than under fixed rates. In Friedman's view, the Federal Reserve Board has recently justified its policies on the basis of international events for political convenience rather than as a matter of substance. Friedman said that our main international vulnerability, the dependence on imported oil, is a self-inflicted burden. Our regulations restricting domestic production have made us the "unpaid agents" of OPEC.

On the matter of bank regulation, Burns and Clausen pointed to the difficulties in effecting needed deregulation and reform. Clausen attributed much of the problem to the divergences of interest among small and large banks in the Federal Reserve System in a system in which all banks have an equal vote on changes in regulations. This has shown up in the divergence of views concerning the elimination of Regulation Q, which many small-town banks have ardently fought.

References

Advisory Committee on Endowment Management. 1969. *Managing educational endowments*. New York: Ford Foundation.

Bach, G. L. 1971. *Making monetary and fiscal policy*. Washington, D.C.: The Brookings Institution.

Bailey, Martin Neil. 1978. Stabilization policy and private economic behavior. *Brookings Papers on Economic Activity*, no. 1, pp. 11–50.

Bodie, Zvi. 1976. Common stocks as a hedge against inflation. *Journal of Finance* 31 (May): 459–70.

————. 1979. Purchasing-power annuities: Financial innovation for stable real retirement income in an inflationary environment. Mimeographed. New York: National Bureau of Economic Research.

Brimmer, Andrew F. 1972. The political economy of money: Evolution and impact of monetarism in the Federal Reserve System. *American Economic Review, Papers and Proceedings* 62 (May): 344–52.

Brunner, Karl, and Meltzer, Allan H. 1964. *The Federal Reserve's attachment to the free market concept*. United States House of Representatives, Committee on Banking and Currency, Subcommittee on Domestic Finance, 88th Congress, 2nd Session.

Cagan, Phillip. 1974. *Common stock values and inflation—the historical record of many countries*. New York: National Bureau of Economic Research.

De Rosa, Paul, and Stern, Gary H. 1977. Monetary control and the federal funds rate. *Journal of Monetary Economics* 3 (April): 217–30.

Feige, Edgar L., and McGhee, Robert. 1979. Has the Federal Reserve shifted from a policy of interest rate targets to a policy of monetary aggregate targets? *Journal of Money, Credit and Banking* 11 (November): 381–404.

Feldstein, Martin S. 1974. Social security, induced retirement and aggregate capital formation. *Journal of Political Economy* 82 (September-October): 905–26.

————. 1976. Inflation, income taxes, and the rate of interest: A theoretical analysis. *American Economic Review* 66 (December): 809–20.

————. 1979. Inflation, tax rules, and the stock market. Mimeographed. New York: National Bureau of Economic Research.

Feldstein, Martin S.; Green, Jerry; and Sheshinski, Eytan. 1978. Inflation and taxes in a growing economy with debt and equity finance. *Journal of Political Economy* 86 (April): S53–70.

Feldstein, Martin S., and Summers, Lawrence H. 1979. Inflation and the taxation of capital income in the corporate sector. *National Tax Journal* 32 (December): 445–70.

Fellner, William, and Larkins, Dan. 1976. Interpretation of a regularity in the behavior of M2. *Brookings Papers on Economic Activity*, no. 3, pp. 741–61.

Fischer, Stanley. 1975. The demand for index bonds. *Journal of Political Economy* 83 (June): 509–34.

————. 1979. Corporate supply of index bonds. Mimeographed. New York: National Bureau of Economic Research.

Friedman, Benjamin M. 1977. The inefficiency of short-run monetary targets for monetary policy. *Brookings Papers on Economic Activity*, no. 3, pp. 293–335.

————. 1978. Public disclosure and domestic monetary policy. In *Federal Reserve policies and public disclosure*, ed. Richard D. Erb. Washington, D.C.: American Enterprise Institute.

————. 1979. The relative stability of money and credit "velocities." Mimeographed. Cambridge: Harvard University.

————. 1980. Money and credit targets under the proposed redefinitions of the monetary aggregates. In *Measuring the Monetary Aggregates*. Washington, D.C.: U.S. Congress, House of Representatives, Committee on Banking, Finance and Urban Affairs.

Friedman, Milton. 1959. The demand for money: Some theoretical and empirical results. *Journal of Political Economy* 67 (August): 327–51.

Friedman, Milton, and Schwartz, Anna Jacobson. 1963. *A monetary history of the United States 1867–1960*. Princeton: Princeton University Press.

Goldfeld, Stephen M. 1973. The demand for money revisited. *Brookings Papers on Economic Activity*, no. 3, pp. 577–638.

————. 1976. The case of the missing money. *Brookings Papers on Economic Activity*, no. 3, pp. 683–730.

Goldsmith, Raymond W. 1958. *Financial intermediaries in the American economy since 1900*. Princeton: Princeton University Press.

————. 1969. *Financial structure and development*. New Haven: Yale University Press.

Greenough, William C. 1951. *A new approach to retirement income*. New York: Teachers Insurance & Annuity Association of America.

Gurley, John G., and Shaw, Edward S. 1960. *Money in a theory of finance*. Washington, D.C.: The Brookings Institution.

Guttentag, Jack M. 1966. The strategy of open market operations. *Quarterly Journal of Economics* 80 (February): 1–30.

Hartman, David G. 1978. Long-term international capital flows and the U.S. economy. Mimeographed. Cambridge: Harvard University.

Hendershott, Patric H., and Hu, Sheng Cheng. 1979. Inflation and the benefits from owner-occupied housing. Mimeographed. New York: National Bureau of Economic Research.

Ibbotson, Roger G., and Sinquefield, Rex A. 1977. *Stocks, bonds, bills and inflation*. New York: Financial Analysts Research Foundation.

Jaffee, Dwight M., and Rosen, Kenneth T. 1979. Mortgage credit availability and residential construction. *Brookings Papers on Economic Activity*, no. 3, pp. 333–76.

Jorgenson, Dale W. 1978. The role of energy in the U.S. economy. *National Tax Journal* 31 (September): 209–20.

Kane, Edward J. 1980. Consequences of contemporary ceilings on mortgage and deposit interest rates for households in different economic circumstances. In *The government and capital formation*, ed. George M. von Furstenburg. Cambridge: Ballinger.

Kindleberger, Charles P. 1978. *Manias, panics, and crashes*. New York: Basic Books.

Lieberman, Charles. 1977. The transactions demand for money and technological change. *Review of Economics and Statistics* 59 (August): 307–17.

Lintner, John. 1975. Inflation and security returns. *Journal of Finance* 30 (May): 259–80.

Lombra, Raymond E., and Kaufman, Herbert M. 1978. Commercial banks and the federal funds market. *Economic Inquiry* 16 (October): 549–62.

Lombra, Raymond E., and Moran, Michael. 1979. Policy advice and policymaking at the Federal Reserve. Mimeographed. University Park: Pennsylvania State University.

Maisel, Sherman J., ed. 1980. *Risk and capital adequacy in commercial banks*. Chicago: University of Chicago Press.

Modigliani, Franco, and Cohn, Richard A. 1979. Inflation, rational valuation and the market. *Financial Analysts Journal*, March-April, pp. 3–23.

Modigliani, Franco, and Lessard, Donald R., eds. 1975. *New mortgage designs for stable housing in an inflationary environment*. Boston: Federal Reserve Bank of Boston.

Modigliani, Franco, and Miller, Merton H. 1963. Corporate income taxes and the cost of capital: A correction. *American Economic Review* 53 (June): 433–43.

Modigliani, Franco, and Sutch, Richard. 1966. Innovations in interest rate policy. *American Economic Review, Papers and Proceedings* 56 (May): 178–97.

————. 1967. Debt management and the term structure of interest rates. *Journal of Political Economy* 75 (August): 569–89.

Munnell, Alicia H., and Connolly, Ann M. 1976. Funding government pensions: State-local, civil service and military. In *Funding pensions: Issues and implications for financial markets*. Boston: Federal Reserve Bank of Boston.

Oldfield, George S. 1977. Financial aspects of the private pension system. *Journal of Money, Credit and Banking* 9 (February): 48–54.

Penner, Rudolph G., and Silber, William L. 1973. The interaction between federal credit programs and the impact on the allocation of credit. *American Economic Review* 63 (December): 838–52.

Perloff, Jeffrey M., and Wachter, Michael L. 1979. A production function-nonaccelerating inflation approach to potential output: Is measured potential output too high? In Three aspects of policy and policymaking: Knowledge, data and institutions, ed. Karl Brunner and Allan H. Meltzer. Amsterdam: North-Holland Publishing Co.

Perry, George L. 1977. Potential output and productivity. *Brookings Papers on Economic Activity*, no. 1, pp. 11–47.

Pierce, James L. 1978. The myth of Congressional supervision of monetary policy. *Journal of Monetary Economics* 4 (April): 363–70.

Poole, William. 1975. The making of monetary policy: Description and analysis. *New England Economic Review*, March-April, pp. 21–30.

Porter, Richard D.; Simpson, Thomas D.; and Mauskopf, Eileen. 1979. Financial innovation and the monetary aggregates. *Brookings Papers on Economic Activity*, no. 1, pp. 213–37.

Rhoades, Stephen A. 1976. Changes in the structure of bank holding companies since 1970. *Bank Administration* 52: 64–69.

Roberts, Steven M. 1978. Congressional oversight of monetary policy. *Journal of Monetary Economics* 4 (August): 543–56.

Silber, William L. 1975. A theory of financial innovation. In *Financial innovation*, ed. William L. Silber. Lexington: D. C. Heath.

———. 1977. The optimum quantity of money and the interrelationships between financial markets and intermediaries. *Banca Nazionale del Lavoro Quarterly Review*, March, pp. 87–95.

Solomon, Robert. 1977. *The international monetary system 1945–1976: An insider's view.* New York: Harper & Row.

Tepper, Irwin, and Affleck, A. R. P. 1974. Pension plan liabilities and corporate financial strategies. *Journal of Finance* 23: 1549–64.

Tobin, James. 1963. An essay on the principles of debt management. In *Fiscal and debt management policies*, Commission on Money and Credit. Englewood Cliffs: Prentice-Hall.

Weiss, Randall D. 1976. Private pensions: The impact of ERISA on the growth of retirement funds. In *Funding pensions: Issues and implications for financial markets.* Boston: Federal Reserve Bank of Boston.

2 Postwar Macroeconomics: The Evolution of Events and Ideas

1. Robert J. Gordon
2. Arthur M. Okun
3. Herbert Stein

---

1. Robert J. Gordon

Experience, some people say, is like a light on a caboose, illuminating only where we aren't going. But we scrutinize the past for its elements of prologue, and consolation. [George F. Will, 1979]

2.1 Introduction

The main issues in current discussions of macroeconomic theory and policy are very different from those of the late 1940s. Most shifts in economic opinion can be traced to the impact of changing events on ideas. For example, in some cases the evolution of the economic aggregates helped to decide a debate between schools of thought. In other cases events occurred that could not be understood within the context of existing paradigms and required the invention of new explanations.

The most useful framework for an analysis of postwar changes in *macro*economics is the familiar *micro*economic dichotomy between demand and supply. Most questions in macroeconomics can be usefully divided between issues concerning (a) the determinants and control of aggregate demand and (b) those concerning aggregate supply, that is,

Robert J. Gordon is professor of economics at Northwestern University.

This research has been supported by the National Science Foundation and is part of the NBER's research program in economic fluctuations. I am grateful to Jon Frye for research assistance, and to Martin N. Baily, Alan Blinder, Robert Eisner, Arthur M. Okun, Edmund S. Phelps, Joan Robinson, and Robert M. Solow for their helpful suggestions. Readers should note that the extensive references to "M2" in the text refer to the old definitions, not the new, more comprehensive definitions introduced in January 1980.

the factors that influence the division of changes in aggregate demand between prices and real output. In the early postwar years macroeconomics was almost exclusively concerned with the explanation of aggregate demand within a Keynesian framework that emphasized the need for an activist fiscal policy to offset the instability of private spending. By the end of the 1970s concern with demand management had been pushed aside by two central supply issues—that of explaining and controlling inflation and that of determining the causes and cures of the secular slowdown in the growth of aggregate labor productivity that had occurred in the past decade.[1]

Until 1973 the central area of macroeconomic controversy was the determination and control of aggregate demand. Two main issues were the subject of debate: the relative potency of monetary and fiscal policy and the case for the activist use of discretionary policy as contrasted with a nonactivist policy stance relying on rules. Opinions on the first question shifted almost continuously, from the heavy emphasis on fiscal policy and low regard for monetary policy common in the late 1940s, to an intermediate view that incorporated both monetary and fiscal policy in discussions of the late 1950s and early 1960s, to a common tendency after 1968 to doubt the potency of fiscal policy and assign a strong causal role for monetary changes as initiating fluctuations in aggregate demand growth.

The debate between activists and nonactivists revolved around three further issues: differing beliefs in the inherent stability of private spending, differing beliefs in the potency of price flexibility as an automatic self-correcting force to offset the impact of instability in spending, and differing degrees of trust or distrust in the feasibility of stabilizing government policy actions. The fiscal-monetary and activist-nonactivist debates revolved around logically separate sets of issues. It would have been possible, for instance, to believe that monetary policy was potent and fiscal policy impotent to control aggregate demand, and yet still be in favor of activist monetary policy intervention. Nevertheless, American economists tended to coalesce around either a fiscal-activist or monetary-nonactivist position, with the adjective "Keynesian" often applied to the first group and "monetarist" to the second. Because they tended to believe in the potency both of money's impact on spending and of price flexibility as an automatic stabilizing mechanism, monetarists tended to put more emphasis than Keynesians on variations in monetary growth as the most important cause of variations in the inflation rate, as summarized in Milton Friedman's famous dictum that "inflation is always and everywhere a monetary phenomenon" (1963).

During most of the period before 1973 the intellectual tide shifted in a monetarist direction, both toward a belief in the potency of money and in the defects of policy activism. But since 1973 the advent of supply shocks as a major destabilizing force has caused the monetarist tide to ebb. Supply shocks not only erode the case for the monetarist "rule" that money should grow at a constant rate, but they also open up a new role for fiscal policy in the form of cost-oriented changes in taxes and subsidies to counteract the effect of supply shocks on the overall price level. One element of the monetarist credo—distrust of government actions—remained strongly intact as the decade of the 1970s drew to a close, since the major impact of tax changes had thus far been to raise costs and prices and aggravate economic instability.

A review of the interaction between macroeconomic events and ideas over the 1947–79 era can be organized either by topic or by chronological period. This paper begins by comparing the behavior of important aggregate variables across four subperiods of the postwar era in order to identify the major changes that call for an explanation and that have been the source of changing ideas and doctrines. Subsequently the four subperiods (1947–57, 1957–67, 1967–73, and 1973–79) are examined in more detail. For each interval we identify the economic ideas about which there was a consensus at the beginning of the period, then examine major economic events and trace the impact of unexpected changes on the evolution of theory, policy, and private behavior. We regularly take advantage of historical hindsight by forming judgments on policy mistakes and the desirability of alternative policy actions.

2.2 Essential Features of the Postwar Era

The most important features of the postwar era are well known. In contrast to the century before World War II, the postwar economy has been characterized by much less instability in real output and unemployment together with a tendency toward chronic and persistent inflation. The growth of aggregate demand has been both faster and more stable during the postwar years, with no instance after 1949 in which annual nominal GNP growth actually declined. On the supply side, the responsiveness of prices to fluctuations in nominal GNP growth has gradually diminished (Cagan 1975), and price movements have more and more exhibited sluggish and inertia-dominated behavior that inhibits policymakers from ending inflation through restrictive demand-management policies. Although the willingness of Americans to accept continuing inflation might seem astonishing to a visitor from earlier eras, the dominance of decentralized nonsynchronized wage-setting institutions has given households and firms every incentive to protect themselves against inflation rather than take unilateral action to stop inflation.

2.2.1 The Demand Side

Major features of the postwar era can be traced with the aid of table 2.1, which compares growth rates and ratios of important economic aggregates across seven subperiods spanning the interval between 1923

Table 2.1   Summary of Interwar and Postwar Developments in the American Economy

	1923–29 (1)	1929–41 (2)	1941–47 (3)	1923–47 (4)	1947–57 (5)	1957–67 (6)	1967–73 (7)	1973–79b (8)	1947–79b (9)
I. Annual Growth Rates during Interval									
A. The Demand Side									
1. Nominal GNP	3.3	1.6	10.9	4.3	6.7	6.0	8.6	10.1	7.5
a. money (M2)	4.1	2.5	15.2	5.9	2.8	5.8	8.6	8.7	5.9
b. velocity of M2	−0.8	−0.9	−4.3	−1.6	3.9	0.2	0.0	1.4	1.6
2. Real GNPa	3.1	1.9	2.8	2.4	3.8	4.0	3.4	2.3	3.5
a. nondurable consumption	3.4	1.0	3.9	2.3	2.9	3.7	2.1	3.0	3.3
b. durable consumption and residential investment	1.0	0.5	5.3	1.8	4.3	3.9	7.6	1.7	4.3
c. nonresidential fixed investment	4.4	−1.7	8.3	2.3	3.0	4.6	4.0	1.7	3.5
d. federal expenditures	4.9a	19.5	−6.7	9.3	9.5	3.4	−4.3	0.4	3.2
e. state and local expenditures	4.9a	0.8	0.9	1.9	6.0	5.8	3.6	1.9	4.8
3. Real government transfers to persons	9.1	9.8	17.8	11.6	3.5	7.4	10.0	5.1	6.2
B. The Supply Side									
1. "Natural" real GNP	2.5	2.8	2.7	2.7	3.1	3.5	3.7	3.0	3.3
2. Real GNP	3.1	1.9	2.8	2.4	3.8	4.0	3.4	2.3	3.5
3. Real GNP in private business sector	3.5	1.8	2.9	2.5	3.5	4.5	3.7	2.5	3.6
a. hours	1.1	−0.3	1.1	0.4	0.3	1.3	1.6	1.7	1.1
b. output per hour	2.4	2.1	1.8	2.1	3.2	3.2	2.1	0.8	2.5
4. GNP deflator	0.2	−0.3	8.1	1.9	2.9	2.0	5.2	7.8	4.0

Table 2.1—*continued*

	1923–29 (1)	1929–41 (2)	1941–47 (3)	1923–47 (4)	1947–57 (5)	1957–67 (6)	1967–73 (7)	1973–79[b] (8)	1947–79[b] (9)
II. *Average Values during Interval*									
A. Utilization Variables (Percentage)									
1. Real GNP "gap"									
a. mean	1.2	22.4	−7.6	9.6	0.8	0.8	−0.9	3.1	1.0
b. standard deviation	2.3	10.7	13.5	16.0	4.1	3.0	2.4	2.7	3.3
2. Unemployment rate									
a. mean	3.5	17.4	2.9	10.3	4.3	5.3	4.7	6.8	5.1
b. standard deviation	1.1	6.3	2.9	8.1	1.0	1.0	1.0	1.4	1.4
B. Other Ratios									
1. Nonresidential fixed investment/GNP	11.2	6.6	5.5	7.5	9.7	9.7	10.2	10.2	9.9
2. Government expenditures/GNP	8.8	17.2	34.3	19.4	22.6	26.4	29.7	31.3	26.8
a. goods and services	8.1	14.7	31.4	17.2	18.5	20.8	21.8	20.9	20.3
b. transfer payments	0.7	2.5	2.9	2.2	4.1	5.6	7.9	10.4	6.5

[a]Breakdown of federal and state-local expenditures unavailable in 1920s.
[b]1979 figures refer to the second quarter.

and 1979. The averages for all series before 1947 are shown in column 4, and since 1947 in column 9. The table first examines variables relevant for the determination of aggregate demand growth and then examines the growth of nominal GNP from the supply side. Finally, several ratios are shown, including the mean and standard deviation of the GNP gap and the unemployment rate, as well as the share of investment and government spending in GNP.

It is easiest to think of "aggregate demand" as final sales measured in current dollars, or "nominal final sales." This concept is equal to nominal GNP minus inventory change. Because inventory changes are unimportant over the long intervals examined in table 2.1, line I.A.1 shows the growth rates of nominal GNP itself. It is evident that nominal GNP since 1947 has grown at almost double the rate of the earlier 1923–47 period, and that the difference is even more pronounced if World War II is ignored. Another important feature is the similarity of the growth rates of nominal GNP in the first two postwar subperiods, followed by a substantial acceleration during each of the last two subperiods. Thus, rapid and accelerating growth in aggregate demand stands as one of the most important features of the postwar era.

When we search for an explanation of the four percentage point acceleration in nominal GNP growth between the second and fourth postwar subperiods, we find in the next line that most can be accounted for by an acceleration in the growth of the money supply (the *M2* definition). But the behavior of the money supply is of no help at all in explaining the overall difference between the pre-1947 and post-1947 growth rates of nominal GNP, since monetary growth was exactly the same in the latter period as in the former. Thus an understanding of the reasons for the more rapid postwar growth of aggregate demand cannot simply point to the behavior of money but rather must be based on a more complete explanation in which monetary and nonmonetary factors interact.

The gradual shift in the emphasis on money in explanations of aggregate demand behavior in the last fifteen years reflects a transition in the relationship between nominal GNP and money that occurred at the same time. The postwar era began with monetary explanations in low repute, not a surprising development in light of the loose relation between nominal GNP and monetary growth, particularly in the immediate prewar years 1937–40.[2] During the first decade of the postwar period money played a relatively small role in explaining movements in nominal GNP, and the popularity of the Keynesian multiplier paradigm reflected this fact, with money a mere sideshow forced in most models to exert its full influence on spending through a narrow interest rate channel. But the simultaneous acceleration in nominal GNP and monetary growth beginning in the 1960s gained many new advocates of the notion that money is the prime mover in the determination of aggregate demand.

The traditional multiplier models are built by a "bottom up" procedure that begins with components of spending. Economic instability originates with "autonomous" components of demand, while a major portion of consumption is "induced" and plays the passive role of an obedient child. The motivation for an activist fiscal stabilization policy is rooted in the belief that consumption fluctuations amplify rather than dampen the inherently unstable behavior of autonomous spending. Section I.A.2 of table 2.1 illustrates the erratic growth rate of nonresidential fixed investment in the pre-1947 period that provided the impetus for the dominance of Keynesian thinking, particularly the decade-long cessation in the growth of investment in the 1930s following the ebullient experience of the 1920s.

While nonresidential fixed investment has exhibited substantial fluctuations on a year-to-year basis throughout the postwar years, the *average* growth rates during the first three postwar subperiods exhibit a remarkable stability. In fact consumer investment (line I.A.2.b) has been less stable than business investment (line I.A.2.c), although the growth of both slumped after 1973. Before 1973 federal government expenditure was the primary source of instability across subperiods in the postwar era. In contrast to the 1930s when expanding government expenditures helped to fill the void left by the collapse of investment, postwar fluctuations in government spending have been an autonomous source of instability, largely in connection with the Korean and Vietnam war episodes.

The growing size of government has been associated in recent years with many evils. Thus it is surprising that when federal spending on goods and services is combined with that of state and local government, we find at the bottom of table 2.1 (section II.B) that their *share* in GNP exhibited no increase at all between the 1957–67 decade and the most recent 1973–79 subperiod, after the enormous growth in the share that occurred between the 1920s and the Korean War. The same section at the bottom of the table shows the remarkable stability of the average share of business investment, in contrast to the instability of the share during the interwar years.

If the share of government spending on goods and services has not increased in the 1970s, why has so much public attention been focused on the increasing role of government? The answer lies on the bottom line of the table (II.B.2.6) in the continuous and steady increase in the ratio of transfer payments to GNP, which has swollen from a mere 0.7 percent in the 1920s to more than 10 percent during 1973–79. Combining goods and services with transfer payments, we find that the total share of government spending has increased from 8.8 percent during the 1920s to over 30 percent in the 1970s.

While the increased importance of government has debatable allocative consequences, there can be no doubt that the greater size of government has helped to stabilize the level of economic activity. When real income begins to fall, corporate and individual income tax revenues drop even faster, while transfer payments are either maintained in the case of social security or rise in the case of unemployment benefits and welfare payments. Thus, leaving aside its own contribution to instability during the Korean and Vietnam wars, government has introduced an inertia into the quarter-to-quarter changes in spending that may have made a greater contribution to stability than the commitment to discretionary activism embodied in the Employment Act of 1946.[3]

2.2.2   The Supply Side

Two of the most important measures of the nation's economic performance are real GNP and the unemployment rate. Throughout the postwar era both have been explicit targets of policymakers, and the actual level of each variable has been compared in public policy discussions to target values for each. In the early postwar years this target of policy was called "full employment," although policymakers did not set specific numerical goals for the unemployment rate or real output. Then in the Kennedy-Johnson era an official "interim full-employment unemployment rate" of 4.0 percent was adopted, and Okun (1962) devised a simple method to calculate the "potential" real GNP that was compatible with this numerical unemployment target. No specific behavior of inflation was predicted to accompany the state of full employment; as we shall see, economists in the late 1940s differed regarding the compatibility of full employment and price stability, while the post-1958 Phillips curve framework explicitly warned that a modest but chronic inflation might accompany the achievement of full employment.

Milton Friedman's landmark presidential address (1968), together with two insightful papers by Phelps (1967; 1968) warned that there was an equilibrium unemployment rate that was independent of the inflation rate and outside the control of aggregate demand policy. Friedman's label for this equilibrium condition, the "natural" unemployment rate, was gradually adopted in policy discussions to mean the unemployment rate below which inflation would continuously accelerate.[4] Statistical studies found that the "natural" unemployment rate was higher than the previous 4.0 percent target and had risen considerably after 1963. Although in government documents the corresponding level of real GNP is still called "potential GNP," the overly optimistic record of past official potential GNP estimates, together with considerations of symmetry, suggest that the output which the economy is capable of producing at the natural rate of unemployment be called "natural real GNP," as on line I.B.1 of table 2.1.[5]

Since 1923 the growth of natural real GNP has fluctuated in a narrow range, rising from its minimum annual rate of 2.5 percent achieved in the 1920s to its maximum of 3.7 percent during 1967–73. Actual real GNP grew somewhat more slowly than natural real GNP during the 1923–47 period and slightly faster thereafter, mainly reflecting the evaluation that 1947 did not represent a year of full utilization of capacity.[6] As is shown next in the table, the modest slowdown in the growth of actual real GNP in the 1970s masks a greater deceleration in the growth rate of labor productivity (output per hour), due to the fact that hours have grown rapidly since 1967 while productivity growth has slackened off. The causes of this slowdown in secular productivity growth have eluded economists and stand as one of the major unexplained macroeconomic puzzles.[7]

The inevitable consequence of the acceleration of nominal GNP growth during successive postwar subperiods, combined with the slowdown in real GNP growth, has been an acceleration of inflation that has exceeded in magnitude the acceleration in nominal GNP growth. The entire postwar period has been characterized by a steady rise in prices that has no precedent in the history of the previous two centuries and is made even more remarkable by the observation that the consumer price level was no higher in 1940 than in 1778 (David and Solar 1977, p. 16). While the acceleration of inflation in the 1960s appears to be largely the result of faster monetary growth, the further upsurge in the 1970s cannot be explained solely by the behavior of the money supply.

Inflation, however, cannot be treated merely as a "residual" that by definition equals the difference between nominal GNP and real GNP growth; the acceleration of nominal GNP growth and deceleration of real GNP growth in the 1970s were not two completely independent and exogenous processes. Real output behavior can be influenced by the inflation rate through at least two routes. First, for any given growth rate of nominal GNP, more rapid inflation cuts real GNP growth and tends to induce a recession, reducing the ratio of actual to natural real GNP. Second, inflation has effects on the growth rate of natural real GNP itself, especially when most tax legislation is stated in nominal terms. Inflation tends to raise the real effective corporate tax rate, thus curbing the incentive to purchase business plants and equipment. Through this and other channels, inflation may be partly responsible for the decline in the growth of productivity and in real natural GNP during the latter part of the 1970s, although recent studies indicate that the slowdown in investment explains only part of the productivity story.

The final section (II) of table 2.1 displays means and standard deviations of two measures of the utilization of resources, the "gap" between actual and natural output, and the unemployment rate. These measures contrast the enormous waste of resources during the 1929–41 decade with the much more intensive and stable utilization experience of the postwar years. The closeness of the subperiod mean values of the gap before 1973 to a zero value and the reduction of its standard deviation after 1977 is evident. The subperiod unemployment rate figures have tended to drift upward during the postwar years, reflecting the gradual shifting of the estimated natural unemployment rate used in the definition of natural real GNP, i.e., the unemployment rate considered compatible with the maintenance of stable inflation. An apparent anomaly (to be explored below) is the marked acceleration of inflation after 1973 despite a relatively slack utilization experience; this suggests either that the true level of natural real GNP may be even lower than assumed in the table, or that there is more to the avoidance of inflation than achieving a zero real GNP "gap."[8] For instance a supply shock can simultaneously boost the inflation rate and cause a contraction in real output relative to natural output.[9]

The higher and more stable level of the utilization of resources in the postwar years has been accompanied not just by faster inflation on average, but also by less variability of prices than in earlier decades. Although prices could be counted upon to fall in prewar recessions, there has been no actual decline in the GNP deflator (measured as a four-quarter change) since 1949. Just as the greater role of government has introduced an inertial tendency into aggregate demand behavior, so the greater confidence by firms and workers that severe setbacks will be avoided has led to an inertial tendency in United States wage and price behavior.

Several important shifts in events and ideas stand out in this initial review of postwar trends. First, the increased correspondence between the growth rates of nominal GNP and money, in contrast to their much looser connection before 1947, helps to explain the emergence of monetarism and the diminished emphasis on the simple multiplier framework for the analysis of demand fluctuations. Second, the growth in the size of government after 1947 was mainly reflected in transfer payments rather than goods and services. Increases in transfers, and in the taxes that finance them, both have contributed to economic stability and to taxpayer resistance that has recently increased support for conservative politicians. Third, after 1967 the growth of labor productivity decelerated markedly, with the growth in natural real GNP buoyed only by rapid growth in hours. Together with the relatively high and stable level of utilization of resources achieved during most of the postwar period, the emergence of rapid inflation naturally shifted concern among economists and laymen from finding cures for unemployment to coping with inflation and its consequences. The role of supply shocks in contributing to the high and unstable inflation rate of the 1970s, together with the slowdown in secular productivity growth, created a tilt in the concern and attention of economic thinking toward aggregate supply problems from the dominance of aggregate demand issues that characterized macroeconomics in the postwar years until the mid-1960s.

2.3   The First Postwar Decade, 1947–57

2.3.1   The Conceptual Framework

The central paradigm of macroeconomics as it emerged from the Second World War was the Keynesian multiplier theory and its endorsement of an activist fiscal policy to overcome the inherent instability of private investment. Monetary theory lurked in the shadows, ignored by most economists except in academic exercises based on the simplified Hicksian IS-LM apparatus that allowed an instructor to demonstrate how a low interest elasticity of investment or a high interest elasticity of the demand for money could render monetary policy impotent to cope with a depression.[10]

The major event that had discredited monetary policy was the juxtaposition between early 1938 and late 1940 of a weak economic recovery, explosive monetary growth, complete price rigidity, and a short-term interest rate that had dropped close to zero. Despite a monetary growth rate that was rapid and constant between early 1938 and late 1941, the economy's recovery floundered until defense spending began in earnest in late 1940, after which real GNP suddenly jumped by almost 20 percent in a single year, a chronology that ingrained a deep-seated belief in the potency of fiscal policy and the "pushing on a string" analogy for monetary policy. The acceptance of Keynesian doctrine led in turn to a retrospective deemphasis on the role of monetary factors in the Great Contraction of 1929–33, a view that now appears largely accurate for 1929–31 but seriously misleading for 1931–33.[11]

By current standards monetary policy received little attention in the contemporary literature of the late 1940s. Money was not ignored totally, and many economists took note of the fact that the quantity of nominal money had tripled between 1940 and 1945. The enormous wartime increase in the quantity of money might not avert a postwar depression, however, because the experience of the late 1930s had demonstrated that "idle currency and idle bank deposits do not bid up prices. Someone has to spend to do this. The amount of cash and other liquid assets possessed by the public constitutes only one of the factors that influence the rate of the public's spending" (Seltzer 1945, p. 832). Nevertheless, despite the loose connection between money and income, "there is great risk that the deflationary effects of a radical rise in interest rates might be so severe as to throw the whole economy into a crushing business depression" (p. 844).

This curious inconsistency, with a monetary expansion viewed as impotent and a monetary contraction viewed as too dangerously potent to risk, helped to maintain support for the Federal Reserve's policy of pegging the government bond rate in the late 1940s. Memories looked back not only to the period of monetary impotence in the late 1930s, but also the period after World War I when the economy plunged into a sharp recession in 1920 despite the doubling of the nominal money supply during the war. So great was the influence of the 1919–21 experience (and earlier postwar deflations) that the panel of business economists surveyed by Joseph Livingston (Carlson 1977, p. 33) expected a postwar deflation for six successive semiannual forecasts despite the rapid price increases that occurred through the end of 1948:

Survey Date	Livingston Panel Expectation of 12-Month CPI Change	Actual Change over Following 12 Months
June 1947	−6.64	8.09
December 1947	−0.03	5.82
June 1948	−1.52	0.02
December 1948	−2.48	−3.00
June 1949	−5.58	−1.43
December 1949	−2.25	3.68

In retrospect the exaggerated fears of a postwar depression, with predictions of eight million postwar unemployed common during 1945, reflected a failure to notice a crucial difference between the World War I and World War II experience. While the *nominal* money supply doubled between 1915 and 1920, price controls were sufficiently weak to allow the GNP deflator also to double, leaving the *real* money supply in 1920 slightly below its 1915 value. Controls on prices during World War II were tight enough to limit the 1940–45 increase in the GNP deflator to 30 percent, thus allowing the *real* quantity of money almost to double. As a result the postwar inflation was both inevitable and necessary to achieve a reduction in real balances. Similar statements can be made about the real public debt, which more than tripled between 1940 and 1945. In the context of the swing in opinion from the Keynesian to monetarist paradigm in the late 1960s, we might note that greater attention to the distinction between real and nominal magnitudes would have been helpful in the 1940s as well.

Issues involving aggregate supply received much less attention than those involving the determination and control of aggregate demand. Implicit or explicit in most discussions of aggregate supply was a knife-edge model describing an economy that suffered from either a "deflationary gap" or an "inflationary gap" but was rarely at the delicate point of balance between them. The "gap" terminology was itself ambiguous because a "deflationary gap" was accompanied not by deflation of prices but rather by unemployment and fixed prices. Once again the experience of the late 1930s had been influential, particularly the period between mid-1938 and mid-1940 when an unemployment rate exceeding 15 percent was accompanied by virtually complete price stability.[12] The willingness to assume fixed prices in underemployment cut off the private economy's automatic stabilizing rudder and led to the automatic conclusion that government intervention was necessary to avoid high unemployment.

Inflationary gaps occurred mainly as the result of wars and could be illustrated on the Keynesian multiplier diagram as the consequence of fiscal expansion.[13] The possibility that unemployment and inflation might coexist in a normal situation was only rarely considered; the Phillips curve was still a decade in the future. The unfortunate coincidence of high unemployment and rising prices in the 1933–37 recovery had not been adequately explained or integrated into the basic Keynesian analytical framework.[14] On the other hand, the notion that full employment would bring a transition to an inflationary condition led to considerable concern about the definition of full employment itself. An incorrect estimate of the knife-edge might lead to a "vicious spiral of wages and prices."[15]

Perhaps on no topic does hindsight make the state of economic thinking in the late 1940s seem as archaic as in the area of productivity and economic growth. Productivity growth was not viewed primarily as the wellspring of economic progress, but rather as a source of unemployment. Excessive productivity growth was cited as explaining the paradox that in 1940 and 1941 the United States economy produced substantially more than in 1929 but had a much higher level of unemployment.[16] It was little noticed that the same increase in productivity that had occurred in the 1930s made possible an increase in real private GNP per hour in 1946 of 43 percent over 1929, the last previous peacetime year with an unemployment rate below 4 percent. From our uncomfortable vantage point in the early 1980s with a trend rate of productivity growth of barely one percent, the ability of the economy to generate a two percentage point rate of increase in productivity between 1929 and 1941 must remain something of a mystery in light of the low rate of fixed investment that occurred during the 1930s. Contemporary critics who blame our poor productivity performance on government regulation and on the negative impact of inflation on the incentive to invest stemming from our nonindexed tax system must wonder how productivity managed to grow during the 1930s at double the rate of 1973–78 in spite of an investment/GNP ratio only two-thirds as large.

The lack of attention to productivity and long-term economic growth reflected the obsession with the possibility of underutilized resources and the doubt that the economy could remain along a full-employment path.[17] The enormous achievements of the United States economy during the war must also have impressed economists and others with the high *level* of productive efficiency in the United States economy, particularly in contrast to war-ravaged Europe and Japan. Thus supply constraints and productivity slid well down on the list of economic concerns and became relegated to specialized courses in defense economics.

2.3.2   Major Surprises of the First Postwar Decade

Demand Fluctuations

Major events in the first postwar decade were roughly consistent with the Keynesian multiplier theory of aggregate demand fluctuations. As illustrated in figure 2.1a, where four-quarter rates of change of nominal GNP and money ($M2$) are compared for the 1947–58 interval, monetary growth was much less volatile than that of nominal GNP, so that shifts in nominal GNP were almost entirely accounted for in an arithmetic sense by shifts in velocity. In the context of the theoretical IS-LM paradigm, economic instability stemmed from movements of the IS curve back and forth along a relatively fixed LM curve.

The Korean War was overwhelmingly the most important source of economic instability during the 1947–57 decade. The unexpected North Korean invasion on 24 June 1950 added an explosion of defense spending on top of an already healthy recovery from the 1949 recession. While the Korean War was a *political* surprise, its economic consequences were similar to those of World War II and provided no impor-

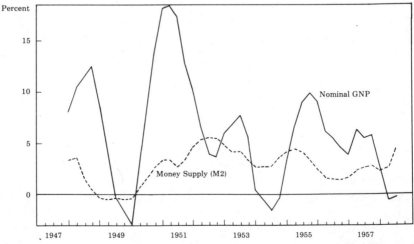

Fig. 2.1a

tant reason to question prevailing economic doctrine. Surely the greatest *economic* surprise of the first postwar decade was the failure of anything resembling a postwar depression to occur, with mild postwar recessions in 1949 and 1954 roughly duplicating in magnitude the minor setbacks of 1924 and 1927. In retrospect the high postwar level of real balances and real government debt was probably the major factor that prevented the long-awaited postwar depression from occurring. Monetarists might note that the downturn in the four-quarter $M2$ growth rate in 1948:2 occurred two quarters prior to the downturn in nominal GNP growth, indicating a possible causative role for money, while the absence of any absolute decline in money during 1949 helped to arrest the economy's decline. There was no similar pattern in monetary growth that helps to explain the timing of the 1954 recession. A monetarist might point to the relatively stable growth performance of $M2$ between 1951 and 1955 as helping to explain why the 1953–55 decline in defense spending had such a short-lived impact on the economy and why the 1955 recovery was so robust.

The Keynesian components-of-expenditure analysis of the timing of economic fluctuations can be set forth with the aid of table 2.2, which illustrates shifts in components of real GNP between key quarters during the first postwar decade. Section B of the table splits real GNP into real final sales and inventory accumulation and points out that the 1949 recession was so mild that there was no decline at all in real final sales. The recession was entirely attributable to a small temporary adjustment in the level of inventories.

An important feature of the 1948–49 episode was the role of government spending in prolonging the length of the expansion through the end of 1948 by offsetting the 1947–48 decline in net exports. The mildness of the 1949 setback itself can be attributed not only to the fortuitous countercyclical swing in total government spending, but also to the timing of the first major postwar restyling of all "big-three" auto models in 1949. The appeal of the new models boosted real final sales of automobiles in 1949:2 fully 38 percent above the 1948 average. This episode stands in contrast to the procyclical swings in auto buying that marked subsequent recessions.

Since the 1949 recession resulted entirely from inventory behavior, a recovery in early 1950 was inevitable as soon as the temporary liquidation of inventories ceased. In fact the 1950 expansion was rapid even before the outbreak of war in June, with consumer investment in autos and houses at the forefront. Once the war began, consumers who had vivid memories of wartime shortages rushed to purchase all types of consumer goods, and the share of consumer durable purchases in real GNP reached a level (9.2 percent) that was not to be exceeded until the first quarter of 1973.

Table 2.2   Real GNP (1972 Prices) and Its Components, Selected Quarters during the First Postwar Decade

	Export Boom 1947:3 (1)	Cyclical Peak 1948:4 (2)	Cyclical Trough 1949:4 (3)	Buying Spree 1950:2 (4)	Cyclical Peak 1953:2 (5)	Cyclical Trough 1954:3 (6)	Auto Boom 1955:3 (7)	Cyclical Peak 1957:3 (8)
A. Natural Real GNP	507.3	524.8	539.2	550.9	601.4	621.0	646.3	691.6
B. Real GNP	468.0	495.9	489.2	542.4	626.2	605.6	660.3	685.6
1. Real final sales	470.9	490.6	496.9	534.4	621.1	609.7	652.5	681.9
2. Inventory change	−2.9	5.3	−7.7	8.0	5.1	−4.1	7.8	3.7
C. Consumption of Non-durables and Services	277.3	282.6	284.7	298.9	322.6	324.6	343.5	367.0
D. Fixed Investment	117.5	117.0	114.6	140.5	128.4	130.9	157.0	154.3
1. Consumer durables	30.3	33.5	38.3	49.9	42.7	42.5	53.9	49.0
2. Residential	21.5	24.2	27.1	35.2	28.4	29.3	35.2	29.3
3. Nonresidential	48.0	51.8	43.5	53.0	55.8	54.8	63.1	67.1
4. Net exports	17.7	7.5	5.7	2.4	1.5	4.3	4.8	8.9
E. Government Purchases	76.0	90.9	97.5	94.9	170.1	154.3	151.9	160.6
1. Federal	36.3	47.9	48.1	44.1	115.9	95.4	87.8	89.9
2. State and local	39.7	43.0	49.4	50.8	54.2	58.9	64.1	70.6

Sources: Natural Real GNP prior to 1955 from Gordon (1978, app. B) and after 1955 from Perloff and Wachter (1979). All other series from National Income and Product Accounts, table 1.2.

From late 1950 on, investment by consumers and businessmen fell back, and the expansion was carried along during its remaining years by a 279 percent increase in federal spending on goods and services which peaked—along with the cycle itself—in 1953:2. In real terms the subsequent recession was more severe than the 1949 episode. Residential construction, net exports, and state and local government all helped to stabilize the economy, and the drop in consumer and business fixed investment was very moderate. The role of monetary policy in converting residential buildings and state-local government into automatic stabilizers is particularly important; dropping nonmortgage interest rates caused funds to be channeled into mortgages and state-local borrowing. Housing starts rose by 40 percent between December 1953 and December 1954, and state-local real spending jumped by 9 percent in a single year.

1955 was a vintage year for the American economy. The automatic stabilizers and stable monetary growth policy had prevented the decline in defense spending from causing a serious setback. With both the Korean War and the danger of postwar depression in the past, households and business firms could contemplate a new era of business prosperity and set out with determination to acquire the higher stock of durable goods that was consistent with this new level of "peacetime permanent income." By mid-1955 real investment had jumped to a level 22 percent higher than had been achieved in the peak 1953 quarter, offsetting almost dollar-for-dollar the 1953–55 drop in federal spending. Further evidence of a fundamental change in expectations is provided by the stock market. The real value of the Standard and Poor's index rose by 102 percent between 1953 and 1959, compared with increases of less than 40 percent in the preceding and following six-year periods.

The 1955 investment explosion was led by consumer purchases of automobiles. Paul Samuelson once announced to an M.I.T. graduate class that he would "flunk anyone who could explain why auto sales in 1955 were so high." A complete quantitative explanation is never likely to be produced, because several of the sources of the 1955 auto boom cannot be quantified rigorously. In addition to the basic accelerator mechanism that makes auto sales depend on the growth of real income, and the effect on expectations of the mildness of the recession, the boom was amplified by a substantial easing in installment credit terms that introduced thirty-six-month installment contracts for the first time, and also by the timing coincidence that all of the "big three" makes introduced radically new models simultaneously in the 1955 model year for the first time since 1949.[18]

Between 1955 and 1957 the expansion changed in character. The countercyclical behavior of residential housing exerted a drag on the expansion, as did the slump in consumer durable sales from the unsustainable 1955 level. The common practice of referring to the 1955–57 expansion as "an investment boom" is completely misleading. It should actually be labeled "an export boom," reflecting the 27 percent surge in real exports between 1955:3 and the post-Suez peak in 1957:1. In contrast, real state-local spending rose by 7.6 percent over the same six-quarter interval, while real business investment grew only 4.4 percent.

Supply Phenomena

Before World War II, price movements mirrored the behavior of nominal GNP, instantaneously absorbing a substantial fraction of nominal spending changes. For instance, falling prices absorbed 51 percent of the 1929–33 drop in nominal GNP. In figure 2.1b we find that the four-quarter rate of change of the GNP deflator shows a similar tendency to mirror nominal GNP changes during the 1947–52 period, with a timing pattern that is virtually simultaneous. Perhaps the most important supply phenomenon of the first postwar decade was the change in the behavior of prices after 1952; the inflation rate no longer responded rapidly to nominal GNP change but rather seemed to be dominated by inertia. Prices hardly responded at all to the spending surge in 1953 and 1955, and to the drop in spending in 1954. Whereas a price decline had insulated real spending in the 1949 recession, the opposite occurred in 1954 when almost the full brunt of the nominal GNP decline was translated into real GNP.

After 1954 the inflation rate displayed the pattern that has become so familiar in the 1960s and 1970s. Price increases responded only sluggishly to the behavior of nominal spending, so that the peak 1957 inflation rate in figure 2.1b occurred six quarters after the peak growth in nominal spending. And over the entire decade between 1954 and 1964

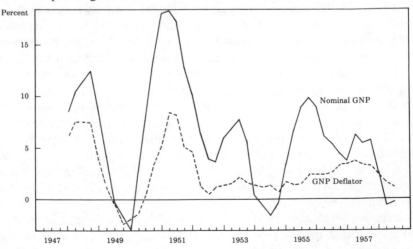

Fig. 2.1b

the variance of inflation was astonishingly low when viewed from the perspective of earlier history. The reasons for this shift in behavior have never been adequately explained. One approach would point to the stability of expectations of the price level: between December 1954 and December 1965 the twelve-month rate of expected price increase by the Livingston panel never went outside the range of zero to 1.25 percentage points. But this observation is not an explanation, since the main reason for the stability of expected inflation must have been the stability of actual inflation.

The assignment of responsibility for the changing behavior of wages and prices remains an unfinished research task. Cagan's careful analysis (1975) of the cyclical behavior of wholesale prices in the 1920s and the postwar years confirms "a gradual decline in price response to recessions over the postwar period." His interpretation is that "an intensification of general anticipations of inflation over the postwar period has lessened the response of manufacturing prices to short-run variations in demand" (p. 55). Sachs (1980) restates Cagan's interpretation by asserting that the new postwar intention to pursue countercyclical stabilization policy shifted expectations toward the belief that recessions would be temporary and that business firms would feel less need to reduce prices to sell their goods. Sachs also emphasizes the growing importance of long-term wage bargaining. By these interpretations the change in the character of the inflation process evident in the 1952–54 period may be traced ultimately both to the Wagner Act of 1935 and the Employment Act of 1946.

The relation between inflation and nominal GNP growth displayed in figure 2.1b has another interpretation. This alternative viewpoint would state that nothing special happened to the inflation process in 1952–54; rather the earlier development of price inertia is disguised by the special events that dominated price behavior in the early postwar era. The immediate postwar disequilibrium between nominal money and the controlled price level led to a temporary surge of inflation after the termination of controls in 1946. And the outbreak of the Korean War in mid-1950 led to a speculative surge in raw materials prices that coincided with a wave of anticipatory buying, creating a short-lived coincidence between nominal GNP growth and price change. The stability exhibited by the inflation rate after 1952 reflected the termination of these special factors and the influence of Korean War price controls rather than any sudden change in underlying behavior. While this account is plausible, and reminds us that any discussion of price movements during 1946–52 must take account of special factors, it nevertheless cannot explain why price behavior was so different in the recessions of 1949 and 1954, and this difference remains the basis for the claim that price behavior underwent a basic change after 1952.[19]

Nominal GNP changes are divided by definition between changes in prices and in real GNP. Thus in figure 2.1b the distance between the upper and lower line represents increases in real GNP. A more revealing display of real GNP behavior is provided by figure 2.1c. The real GNP "gap" is the percentage difference between "natural" and actual real GNP and ranges between a maximum value of 9.2 percent in 1949:4 to a minimum value of −4.3 percent in 1953:1. When the gap is in negative territory the economy is utilizing its resources more intensively than is compatible with the avoidance of accelerating inflation, while a positive gap tends to occur during recessions. Figure 2.1c also displays the relationship of the actual unemployment rate to the "natural" rate of unemployment. Since a zero output gap is defined by the same criterion as the natural rate of unemployment, we find that the actual unemployment rate rises above the natural rate of unemployment in roughly the same quarters as the output gap rises above zero. The close relation between the output gap and the difference between the actual and natural unemployment rates has long been christened "Okun's Law," and ironically the "law" seems to work better after the publication date of Okun's original article (1962) than before.

A comparison of figures 2.1b and 2.1c suggests three outstanding puzzles about aggregate supply behavior in the first postwar decade. First, why was the output gap so high in 1947–48 when unemployment was so low? Second, why was there no acceleration of inflation in 1952–53 in light of the low levels of unemployment and the negative output gap? Third, why was unemployment so much more stable than the output gap in 1955–57?

The first puzzle about the low level of output in 1947–48 can be restated in another way: the unemployment rate was roughly the same in

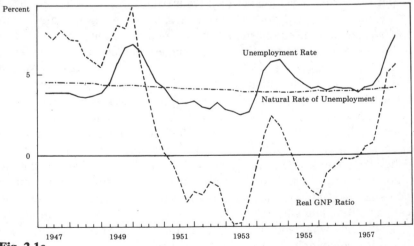

Fig. 2.1c

1948:2 and 1951:1, but real GNP was 15.7 percent higher in the later quarter. The compound *annual* growth rate between the two quarters was 5.4 percent, much faster than anyone's estimate of the long-term growth rate of the economy's "natural" or "potential" real GNP. Because of the absence of any reason why long-term economic growth should have been so much faster between 1948 and 1951 than either before or after, the natural output series used to compute the GNP gap is based on a linear interpolation between 1929 and 1950, accounting for the peculiarity in figure 2.1c that the output gap was large in 1947–48 despite the low level of actual unemployment.[20] Given the fact that the 1948–51 increase in manufacturing real output was 20 percent and in the government sector was 30 percent, I conjecture that a great deal of private and government capital constructed during World War II was temporarily underutilized in 1947–48, due to the low level of defense spending, and that labor was temporarily absorbed in low-productivity service occupations.

The second supply puzzle centers on the low level of inflation in 1952–53 when the unemployment rate was only 3 percent, in contrast to the acceleration of inflation in 1955–57 when unemployment was 4 percent. The only available explanation is that wage and price controls during the Korean War must have been quite effective. While Schultze (1959) proposed an explanation of the acceleration of inflation between 1955 and 1957 based on structural imbalances in the economy, subsequent econometric work finds little in the 1955–57 experience that cannot be explained within a Phillips curve framework.[21] The third puzzle, the failure of unemployment to increase between late 1955 and mid-1957 when the output gap was rising, can be explained by a consistent tendency of business firms to become overstaffed in the last stages of every postwar business expansion.[22]

2.3.3   A Retrospective View of Stabilization Policy

Herbert Stein (1969) has labeled the postdepression commitment to fiscal *stabilization* policy as the "fiscal revolution in America." Yet in the broadest sense fiscal policy has been the most important *destabilizing* influence in the postwar economy. In the first postwar decade the enormous magnitude of the rise and subsequent fall in defense expenditures was the dominant feature of aggregate demand fluctuations, and the expansion of spending for the Vietnam War in 1965–68 destabilized the economy again. By a narrower criterion that takes defense spending as exogenous and outside the purview of discretionary stabilization policy, however, fiscal policy deserves relatively high marks in the 1947–57 decade. Several actions were taken that helped to reduce the variance of income growth, and there were no actions that worked in the opposite direction.

The most important stabilizing action was the rapid move to raise tax rates immediately after the outbreak of war in mid-1950. The natural-employment federal surplus (NES) reached 6 percent of GNP during the last half of 1950, and this helped to dampen the surge of anticipatory buying and accounted for part of the reduction of consumer durable spending that occurred in 1951. After 1950 the NES was allowed to slide from $+6$ percent of GNP to -3 percent by early 1953, a fiscal stimulus that might have been extremely inflationary were it not for the influence of price controls.[23]

Two other stabilizing actions were taken, but in each case the cyclical timing was fortuitous rather than deliberate. Only six months before the 1948 business-cycle peak, Congress passed a large tax reduction over President Truman's veto, but there is no evidence that the proponents of the tax cut foresaw the downturn. Then in 1954 there was a cut in income and excise taxes, but this represented the expiration of wartime-related taxes rather than an activist initiative designed for stabilization purposes. If there was a "fiscal revolution" in the first postwar decade, it was in the willingness to allow the government budget to move into deficit during recessions, thus allowing the automatic stabilizers to work, in contrast to the destructive tax increases engineered by Herbert Hoover in 1932 under the budget-balancing rulebook of pre-Keynesian fiscal policy.

Most discussions of monetary policy in the first postwar decade center on the contrast between the Federal Reserve's pre-Accord-pegging policy and its post-Accord shift to a countercyclical stabilization policy. We have already noted the relative stability of the growth rate of $M2$ in figure 2.1a during the post-Accord 1951–55 period, in contrast to the destabilizing drop in monetary growth during late 1948 and early 1949 as the Fed "accommodated" the economy's decline. The timing of monetary growth between 1953 and 1957 cannot be faulted, with a stabilizing boost in monetary growth in 1954 and decline in 1955–56. Perhaps the main flaw in monetary policy was the acceleration in monetary growth in late 1951 and 1952, which may have partially accounted for the intensity of the last stage of the business cycle expansion in early 1953.

Another view of monetary policy is presented in figure 2.1d, which compares the detrended level of the real money supply ($M2$) with the ratio of actual to natural real GNP (the latter is equal to unity minus the GNP "gap"). To achieve economic stabilization the detrended real money supply should drop when the economy is expanding and should rise during recessions, and so we would hope to find a negative relation between the two series in figure 2.1d. Despite the pegging of interest rates in the pre-Accord period, we see that the negative relation was quite strong throughout the first postwar decade, with real money being allowed to drop substantially during the 1947–48, 1950–51, and 1955–

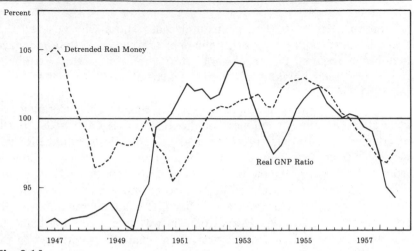

Fig. 2.1d

57 expansions. The expansion in real money in 1949 and 1954 also operated in a stabilizing direction. Once again, the major flaw in the timing of monetary policy was the 1951–53 expansion in real balances.

In retrospect the record of stabilization policy in the first postwar decade, while not perfect, stands out as the best of the four postwar subperiods. The prompt increase in tax rates in 1950 to finance Korean War expenditures contrasts with the failure to take decisive action to reduce the government deficit in 1966. With the exception of the overall destabilizing role of government military expenditures, the basic effect of fiscal and monetary actions was to stabilize the economy. Hindsight allows some quibbling with the behavior of the monetary authorities, but these actions did not have long-run adverse consequences for economic performance as did the mistakes of subsequent postwar subperiods.

2.4 The Second Postwar Decade, 1957–67

2.4.1 The Conceptual Framework

There was no quantum change in the consensus paradigm of aggregate demand behavior in the first two postwar decades. Rather there was a gradual but continuous shift in opinion toward an increased role for money and monetary policy, marked by mileposts including the Patman Committee Inquiry, the report and study papers prepared for the Commission on Money and Credit, the negative reaction of many economists to the downgrading of money in the Radcliffe Report, and the influence of the monetary research of Milton Friedman, his students, and others.[24] As in the case of any body of opinion about the operations of the "real world," the growing belief in the importance of money can be traced to several episodes in the first postwar decade. Those who believed that the large outstanding stock of public debt prevented effective monetary action and required the pegging of interest rates either lost credibility or changed their opinions when the higher interest rates that followed the 1951 Treasury-Federal Reserve Accord failed to have any disastrous consequences for debt management of the economy's performance in general.[25] The relative mildness of the 1954 recession was due partly to countercyclical monetary policy and helped to lessen the belief that monetary policy was only effective in countering inflation and suffered from an asymmetric impotence in dealing with slack demand. The continued acceleration of inflation despite rising interest rates in 1956–57 tempered the belief that monetary policy had unique curative powers to combat inflation. By 1962 Harry Johnson was able to observe that "the wheel has come full circle, and prevailing opinion has returned to the characteristic 1920s view that monetary policy is probably more effective in checking deflation than in checking inflation."

In contrast to the steady process of change in the consensus analysis of aggregate demand, the supply-side framework was completely dominated by the influence of the Phillips (1958) article on the historical United Kingdom relation of wage change and unemployment, together with the Samuelson-Solow (1960) popularization of the "Phillips curve" relation between inflation and unemployment for the American audience. In retrospect the instant success of the Phillips curve framework reflects the inability of the previous "knife-edge" inflationary gap analysis to explain, without resort to ad hoc stories about "cost-push," why inflation accelerated in 1956–57 without excessive overall demand pressure or why it continued at a significant rate during the 1957–58 recession. For the first time since the 1946 Employment Act, economists came generally to recognize that two of the goals of the act, full employment and price stability, might not be compatible. Only if by happy coincidence the negatively sloping Phillips curve crossed the zero-inflation point at an unemployment rate generally regarded as "full" would no policy problem arise. If, however, full employment and price stability were not compatible, policymakers would be forced to choose among a set of second-best points along the Phillips curve. The history of economic policy between 1957 and 1967 can be summarized in the choice during 1957–60 by Republican policymakers of a point relatively far to the southeast along the curve, and the rejection of that point by Democratic policymakers after 1961 in favor of a stimulative "new economics" designed to reach a point further to the northwest.

Another area of change in aggregate supply analysis was the increased attention to growth in output and productivity, and the interrelations between growth, investment, and economic policy. Although little attention was paid to the rapid rates of economic growth being achieved in most European countries, there was great concern—especially after the launching of Sputnik in late 1957—over the rapid growth rate achieved by the Soviet economy and the possibility that the Soviet Union might overtake the United States as an economic power. This new attention to growth as a policy problem brought the theoretical models of Tobin (1955) and Solow (1956) and the empirical work of Solow (1957) and Denison (1962) quickly into the mainstream of the economics curriculum, and the interest in growth went so far that in 1964 James Tobin could write, "in recent years economic growth has come to occupy an exalted position in the hierarchy of goals of government policy" (1964, p. 1).

2.4.2   Major Surprises of the Second Postwar Decade

Demand Fluctuations

In contrast to the first postwar decade when nominal GNP fluctuations were extremely large in relation to fluctuations in monetary growth, and were explained in an arithmetic sense by contemporaneous movements in velocity, in the second postwar decade money ($M2$) and nominal GNP exhibited a much tighter relation, as is illustrated in figure 2.2a. Beginning in the 1960s the velocity of $M2$ (that is, nominal GNP divided by $M2$) displayed a remarkable constancy that lasted until 1977.[26] Another important feature of figure 2.2a is the tendency of money to exhibit a significant lead in advance of turning points in nominal GNP. During the 1958 recovery, 1959 decline, 1961 recovery, 1966 setback, and 1967 expansion, $M2$ displayed a consistent lead of about two quarters, suggesting that money was no longer a sideshow in explaining fluctuations in economic activity but rather was a central driving force.

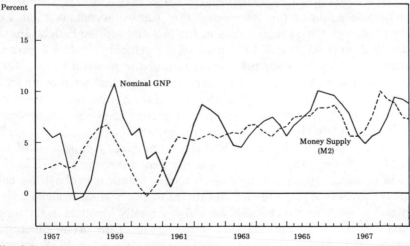

Fig. 2.2a

The change in the relation between money and nominal GNP after 1957, which is surely the most surprising aggregate demand event of the second decade by any *ex ante* criterion, has been little discussed in the literature. Although at first glance the main difference between figures 2.1a and 2.2a might appear to be the decline in *trend* velocity growth after 1957, in fact the *deviations from trend* of nominal GNP and money are much more closely associated in the latter period than the former.

The timing lead of monetary change before nominal GNP change illustrated in figure 2.2a is presumably the source of the finding of the "St. Louis equation," first estimated for this period by Anderson and Jordan (1968), that monetary change is an independent cause of nominal GNP change. The alternative explanation for the close relation between money and spending is that the Federal Reserve "accommodated" autonomous changes in spending as it attempted to maintain a stable interest rate. This second explanation emphasizes the "reverse feedback mechanism" from spending to money that has played a major role in debates regarding the causes of the Great Contraction of 1929–33 (Temin 1976). The timing relationships seem to support a money-to-GNP chain of causation during most of the 1957–67 decade, and a search for independent actions by the Federal Reserve leads to the conclusion that the Fed deliberately tightened money and raised interest rates in 1957, 1959–60, and 1966. But the interpretation of the 1961–66 expansion is more ambiguous.

The standard interpretation of Federal Reserve actions in the early 1960s concentrates on interest rates rather than monetary aggregates as indicators of the tightness or looseness of monetary policy. Thus the most popular explanation of the simultaneous acceleration in money and nominal GNP growth in 1961 is that the Fed passively accommodated an expansion caused by nonmonetary factors. Yet a closer examination casts some doubt on this interpretation of passive accommodation. Far from holding interest rates constant, the Fed allowed the Federal Funds rate to drop from its late 1959 peak of 4.5 percent to below 2 percent in mid-1961 by boosting the growth rate of the monetary base. Then short-term rates were allowed to increase in steps that were compatible with a steady but gradually accelerating growth rate of money until early 1966, when a sudden sharp jump in interest rates was accompanied by an immediate slowdown in monetary growth.

We turn now to table 2.3, which shows the main components of expenditure during the second decade in the same format as table 2.2. The 1958 recession appears to have been almost identical to the 1954 episode in its overall magnitude, as measured by the peak-to-trough decline in real GNP. The two episodes were also virtually identical in the magnitude of the decline in real final sales. The most important difference was in the composition of the decline in expenditures; in 1958 govern-

Table 2.3   Real GNP (1972 Prices) and Its Components, Selected Quarters during the Second Postwar Decade

	Cyclical Peak 1957:3 (1)	Cyclical Trough 1958:1 (2)	Cyclical Peak 1960:1 (3)	Cyclical Trough 1960:4 (4)	Normal Output Reached 1964:2 (5)	Growth-Cycle Peak 1966:1 (6)	Housing Slump 1967:1 (7)
A. Natural Real GNP	691.6	698.6	748.8	766.7	872.0	928.8	968.6
B. Real GNP	685.6	663.4	740.7	731.9	872.0	969.6	994.4
1. Real final sales	681.9	670.2	727.2	735.8	864.0	956.1	979.8
2. Inventory change	3.7	−6.8	13.5	−3.9	8.0	13.5	14.6
C. Consumption of Nondurables and Services	367.0	365.8	397.0	402.5	460.7	501.3	517.6
D. Fixed Investment	154.3	140.2	160.9	157.8	199.9	233.9	218.0
1. Consumer durables	49.0	46.1	52.2	51.5	65.6	80.4	77.5
2. Residential	29.3	28.7	38.2	33.4	44.1	42.7	32.7
3. Nonresidential	67.1	61.2	66.7	65.2	79.9	104.7	103.7
4. Net exports	8.9	4.2	3.8	7.7	10.3	6.1	4.1
E. Government Purchases	160.6	164.2	169.2	175.4	203.5	220.7	244.3
1. Federal	89.9	90.2	89.3	91.7	101.7	106.5	122.6
2. State and local	70.6	74.0	79.9	83.7	101.8	114.2	121.7

ment expenditures rose, whereas in 1954 they had fallen precipitously. The 1958 decline in real *private* final sales was much greater than in 1954.

The 1958–59 recovery in the economy was extremely rapid but was cut short by the steel strike that began in the third quarter of 1959. While the strike doubtless interfered with the momentum of the recovery, it appears in retrospect that the deflationary impact of monetary and fiscal policy during this period was so intense that the expansion would have aborted even without a steel strike.

The most important feature of the 1957–62 period was the sluggish behavior of investment. Consumer durable expenditures did not reach the 1955 peak level again until 1962:1. Nonresidential business fixed investment slumped below its 1957:3 peak until late 1961. In the 1958–60 expansion only residential investment showed any buoyancy.

The 1958–60 expansion presents fascinating problems for proponents of alternative theories of income and investment determination. Present critics who decry the impact of government deficits on investment would find little solace in the laggard 1960 investment performance in light of the high ratio of the NES to GNP reached in 1960. The episode seems to point to a high real interest rate as a major hindrance to investment.[27]

The literature devoted to the 1961–66 business expansion would fill several libraries. The remarkable inertia displayed by the inflation process in the early 1960s allowed virtually all of the faster nominal GNP growth to be transmitted directly to real GNP. And rapid GNP growth over a sustained period of five years (through mid-1966) created an enormous investment boom, as is illustrated in table 2.3. Total real fixed investment rose by 48 percent between the 1960:4 cyclical trough and the 1966:1 peak in the growth cycle (achieved when the ratio of actual to natural real GNP reaches its peak). Both components of real nonresidential investment shared this experience. In their usual fashion both residential investment and net exports peaked relatively early in the expansion.

The second postwar decade ended with a period of monetary restriction. A much discussed and publicized increase in interest rates initiated by the Fed in late 1965 carried the Moody's Aaa rate up from 4.60 percent in November, 1965 (roughly equaling the early 1960 peak) to a temporary peak of 5.49 percent in September, 1966. *M2* growth slowed modestly, although not nearly by so much as 1959–60, and nominal GNP growth followed with only a one-quarter lag.

In the language that was soon to be adopted, the 1966 housing slump represented a classic example of "crowding out" caused by an expansion in government spending during a period of a constant or declining real money supply. The behavior of real money may be determined in turn either by nominal money or the price level, and in 1966 both operated to cause a marked slowdown in real *M2* growth in the four quarters ending in 1967:1. The sum of real government and fixed investment spending grew only 1.7 percent over this same four-quarter period, with most of the increase in real government spending canceled out by a drop in fixed investment, mainly housing expenditures.[28]

Supply Phenomena

Several crucial issues in current macroeconomic debates are dependent on the data displayed in figure 2.2b. Most important, the econometric message that United States inflation fluctuations are dominated by inertia, and depend little on current policy or nominal GNP movements, stands out clearly in the diagram. The 1957–64 period also represents the classic example within the Phillips curve context that high unemployment has only a modest impact on inflation. Despite the fact that unemployment was above the "natural" rate continuously between late 1957 and late 1964, nevertheless the inflation rate decelerated only from 3.3 percent in the four quarters ending in the cyclical peak quarter of 1957:3 to a minimum of 1.3 percent in 1964:1.[29] This small extent of deceleration plays an important role in the objections of those who opposed (in 1969, 1974, and 1979) a rapid deceleration in nominal demand growth to combat inflation. If inertia truly dominates the behavior of inflation, then a slowdown in nominal demand growth that is faster than the maximum possible slowdown in the inflation rate will lead to a slump in real GNP and a period of high unemployment and underutilized resources.

The rapidity of the 1961–66 expansion in real GNP can be viewed from the perspective of figure 2.2c, which compares the behavior of unemployment with that of the real GNP "gap." From a level of +5.1

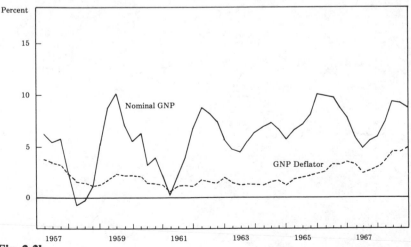

Fig. 2.2b

percent in 1961:1, the gap declined to —4.4 percent in 1966:1, implying that real GNP grew by 9.5 percent relative to its "natural" or trend
level over that five-year interval. At first glance there is nothing in the
juxtaposition of figures 2.2b and 2.2c to contradict the reigning Phillips
curve paradigm of the 1960s, because the acceleration of inflation from
about one percent to roughly 3 percent between 1961 and 1967 would
appear to be compatible with a northwest movement up the stable Phillips curve associated with a decline in unemployment over the same
period from 7 percent to 3.8 percent.

The collapse of the stable Phillips curve after 1967 is sometimes
allowed to obscure the preponderance of data points during 1967 that
supported the policy stance of the administration. Ignoring the lone
voices of Milton Friedman and Edmund Phelps to whom few listened
in 1966, a "natural" unemployment rate is a creation of hindsight wisdom that should not blind us to the environment faced by policymakers.[30] While recognizing that the overall unemployment rate had
been allowed in 1966 and 1967 to slip below the longstanding "full
employment goal" of 4.0 percent, there was little in the behavior of
prices in 1967 to invalidate the notion that the full employment target
was attainable on a permanent basis.

Many features of aggregate economic data in the mid-1960s that then
appeared to represent the dawn of a new era now appear to be the
results of a transient overexpansion of the economy. The high levels of
productivity, the profit share, and stock prices reached in 1965–66 were
particularly ephemeral, both because the overall level of capacity utilization that had made them possible was unsustainable, and also because
both productivity and profits enjoy temporary bulges when output growth
is rapid as a result of lags in hiring and in wage adjustment.

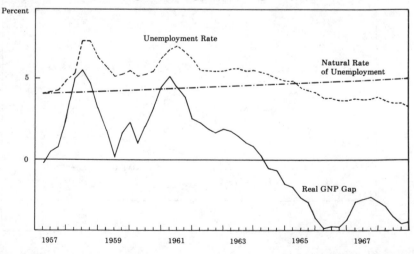

Fig. 2.2c

2.4.3   A Retrospective View of Stabilization Policy

A judgment on the merit of fiscal policy in the second postwar decade naturally begins with the evolution of the NES. Between 1956 and 1963 the NES fluctuated between zero and two percent of GNP, with most quarters recording the higher rather than the lower value. The only major fluctuation over this interval was a brief drop into negative territory during 1958, reflecting the remarkable temporary stimulative expansion of government expenditures.[31] The sharp increase in the NES from −0.5 percent to +2.5 percent of GNP between late 1958 and early 1960 later led to the accusation by Walter Heller (1966) and others that tight fiscal policy had caused the business expansion to abort prematurely through the "drag" of overly high progressive tax rates.

One man's "fiscal drag" is another man's policy to stimulate investment by maintaining the federal budget in surplus. The budget-balancing emphasis of the Eisenhower administration was at least partly based on the desire to encourage business investment and long-term economic growth.[32] There is no necessity for a high natural employment surplus to exert a "drag" on the economy if it is combined with an appropriate monetary policy designed to maintain the economy at its "natural" level of resource utilization. This possibility of tight fiscal and easy monetary policy could have been put into practice in the last two years of the Eisenhower administration but was not, because of the drastic tightening of money that occurred in 1959–60. Thus Heller's critique must be reinterpreted as stating that a high natural employment surplus can be a drag on the economy *if* monetary policy fails to provide the necessary economic stimulus.

The history of fiscal policy during the rest of the second postwar decade consists of the much heralded strategy of the "new economics" of cutting the natural employment surplus by a series of tax reductions, including a major cut in the personal income tax in early 1964, reductions in both excise and personal income taxes in 1965, and new tax incentives for investment introduced in 1962. Between mid-1963 and late 1965 the NES fell from +1.5 to −1.0 percent of GNP in response to the series of tax cuts, and then dropped to −2.2 percent in 1967 as a result of the failure of the administration and Congress to raise taxes promptly to pay for Vietnam expenditures.

There are two available interpretations of the relative roles of monetary and fiscal policy in achieving the vigorous economic expansion of 1961–66, depending on one's view of monetary behavior in 1961–66 as active or passive. The juxtaposition of nominal GNP and monetary growth rates in figure 2.2a could be interpreted as suggesting that the expansion was basically a monetary phenomenon, with the impact of fiscal stimulus evident only in the temporary surge of velocity growth that occurred in late 1965 and 1966. Yet the proponents of fiscal activism would claim that the growth of the money supply was a passive variable that depended on the vigor of the economic expansion. Thus expansionary fiscal policy had its main impact not solely through its *direct* stimulative effect on spending but also *indirectly* by allowing the administration to gain control of the money supply and foster a more vigorous monetary expansion after 1962.

While it is doubtless true that fiscal policy forced the Federal Reserve to accelerate monetary growth, nevertheless the distinction between the direct and indirect multiplier effects of fiscal policy was not sufficiently appreciated in the mid 1960s. Policymakers took literally Arthur Okun's (1968) finding that the multiplier for the 1964 tax cut had been a very large 2.8, not realizing that this figure encompassed not only the direct impact of the tax cut but the indirect effect accomplished by accommodative passive response of the money supply. This misunderstanding had unfortunate consequences in 1968, when the Fed failed to play the accommodative role in supporting tighter fiscal policy upon which the Okun multiplier estimate depended.[33]

The comparison in figure 2.2d between the real money supply and the output ratio provides a simple measure of the stabilizing or destabilizing role of monetary policy. But in the second postwar decade monetary policy deserves failing marks, particularly for the extent of the decline in real balances in 1959–60 even after the economy slumped into recession, for the sluggish growth of real balances in 1960–63 despite the low level of the output ratio, and most notably for the irresponsible expansion of real balances between 1965 and 1968 after real GNP had exceeded its "natural" level.

Throughout the first two decades most discussions of macroeconomic issues assumed tacitly that the United States was a closed economy.

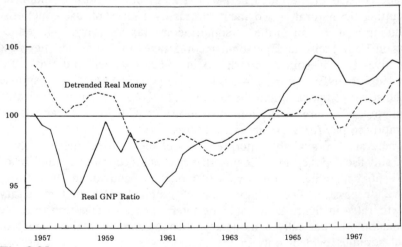

Fig. 2.2d

There were two main sets of influence exerted by the external world on the United States economy. First was the destabilizing effect of two temporary export booms in 1947 and 1956–57 that helped determine the timing and also added to the intensity of the 1949 and 1958 recessions. Second was the shift in 1958 from a long period of dollar shortage to one of dollar surplus, with a continuous loss of official United States reserves over most of the decade after 1958. Because the United States current account was in surplus in every year between 1954 and 1969 with the single exception of 1959, there was general agreement that the balance-of-payments "problem" arose from capital outflows, and that the only solution to the problem was the maintenance of high short-term interest rates. To prevent the balance-of-payments policy objective from interfering with the goal of achieving long-term economic growth, the Kennedy administration fostered the Operation Twist policy of using debt management simultaneously to boost short-term rates while lowering long-term rates.

Subsequent research suggested that Operation Twist had not achieved its objective, and the raw numbers support this conclusion, as for instance the fact that three-month Treasury bill rates were the same in 1956 and 1962 while the Moody's corporate Aaa rate in the latter year was almost a full percentage point higher (not lower as intended). And, in an important reinterpretation of the United States international situation, Despres, Kindleberger, and Salant (1966) concluded that there had been no problem at all. Rather, the United States for many years had been operating as a giant financial intermediary, simultaneously borrowing from foreign governments in a form that created an official balance-of-payments deficit while lending back to foreign nations by buying up long-term foreign assets. The United States came out ahead in this set of transactions when it could earn a higher rate of return on its foreign assets than it paid out in interest on its reserves.

2.5   The Third Postwar Subperiod, 1967–73

2.5.1   The Conceptual Framework

At its zenith in early 1966, an activist view of fiscal policy appeared to have achieved an unassailable victory over its critics. Few in the profession disagreed with Walter Heller's proclamation that "we now take for granted that the government must step in to provide the essential stability at high levels of employment and growth that the market mechanism, left alone, cannot deliver" (1966, p. 9). Since the use of changes in government expenditures for stabilization purposes interfered with allocative considerations, frequent changes in income tax rates became the central policy tool. While the consensus policy paradigm did not neglect monetary policy or deny that monetary tightness could interfere with the pace of economic expansion, monetary policy was basically kept in the background and relegated to a role of maintaining a low and stable level of long-term interest rates to foster the goal of stimulating long-term economic growth. The Democratic advisers in the Kennedy-Johnson administrations had argued that a substantial reduction in the unemployment rate could be achieved at the cost of only a moderate acceleration of inflation, and with an inflation rate of only 3.0 percent in the four quarters ending in 1967:4 their gamble appeared to have paid off.

This policy framework collapsed with amazing speed after 1967 as the result of the interaction of events and economic writings. My graduate school classmates and I were acutely aware of the timing of this turn in the intellectual tide, as we began our first teaching jobs in the fall of 1967 and almost immediately found our graduate school education incapable of explaining the evolution of the economy. The most important ingredient in this intellectual revolution was the influence of the Friedman-Phelps "natural rate hypothesis" (NRH), which denied the ability of policymakers arbitrarily to select any inflation-unemployment combination along a stable tradeoff curve.[34] Instead, below a critical "natural" rate of unemployment the inflation rate would continuously accelerate, adding new urgency to Brainard's contemporaneous warning (1967) that policymakers could not know precisely the multiplier impact of their actions and had to take care to avoid overshooting the target level of real GNP.

Soon after the Friedman-Phelps demonstration that the full employment target of the policy activists might be unsustainable, Andersen and Jordan (1968) struck another blow with empirical equations that implied that fiscal policy had no impact at all on nominal spending over as short a period as a year. Although activist advocates eventually regrouped and presented convincing evidence of fatal statistical flaws in the St. Louis procedure (e.g., Goldfeld and Blinder 1972), their disarray lasted long enough partially to discredit fiscal activism. To add to the overall indictment of fiscal policy provided by the St. Louis equation, Robert Eisner (1969) made an important attack on the efficacy of the temporary tax changes favored by mid-1960s policy activists. Using the framework of Friedman's permanent income hypothesis of consumption, Eisner argued that a temporary income tax cut or surcharge would fail to alter permanent income and thus would have a low spending multiplier. Further, the lag in the effect of fiscal policy might be long and/or unpredictable, with the length of the lag depending on the public's subjective assessment of the likelihood that the tax change soon would be reversed.

These academic criticisms of the activist case might not have been so persuasive if they had not been accompanied by supporting events. Inflation accelerated between 1967 and 1969 far beyond the expectations of activist proponents. Further, inflation failed to slow down in the recession of 1970 and early 1971, as would have been expected along a fixed Phillips curve. The dramatic drop in the personal saving rate in late 1968 and the failure of spending growth to slow appreciably in response to the temporary tax surcharge was consistent both with the St. Louis claim that monetary multipliers had previously been underestimated and fiscal multipliers overestimated, as well as with the Eisner critique.

The continued economic expansion of 1968, even in the last half of the year after the tax surcharge had been introduced, also helped to lead to the de-emphasis of the interest rate as a monetary instrument and to the increased emphasis on monetary aggregates. Once again, it was an economic event that helped popularize an economic idea, in this case Irving Fisher's (1930) distinction between nominal and real interest rates, revived by Mundell (1963) and Friedman (1968). Conventional econometric models, even the newly devised MIT-FRB model with its carefully constructed monetary sector, had neglected the fact that while the demand for money should depend on the *nominal* interest rate, the demand for investment goods should depend on the *real* interest rate. The models thus were unable to explain why investment did not slump in 1968 in response to an increase in the Moody's Aaa rate from the 5.1 percent level recorded in early 1967 to the 6.0–6.5 percent range recorded during 1968.[35]

2.5.2   Major Surprises of the 1967–73 Period

Demand Fluctuations

The relation between money and nominal GNP growth during the 1967–73 interval shared the main features of the 1957–67 decade. A sharp deceleration in the monetary growth rate beginning in early 1969 was followed with about a two-quarter lag by a marked (but less sharp) deceleration in nominal GNP growth. The 1969–70 episode in figure 2.3a seems to repeat the basic pattern of 1959–60, with the minor deceleration of 1966–67 significantly less severe in intensity. The recoveries in monetary growth in 1967–68 and in 1971–72 were also followed with a short lag by recoveries in nominal GNP growth. The major irregularity concerns the period between 1971 and 1973, when two years lapsed between the peak growth of *M2* in mid-1971 and the peak growth in nominal GNP in early 1973. The overall trend growth in *M2* and nominal GNP was about the same over the period, reflecting the constancy in the velocity of *M2* exhibited by the data for the entire period between 1960 and 1977.

Table 2.4 exhibits the main components of real GNP in the same format as for the first two postwar decades. After early 1967 the economy resumed a rapid expansion, with growth in real final sales of about 7.5 percent in the six quarters ending 1968:3. During this interval the growth in federal spending decelerated, and the expansion was fueled by a rapid increase in consumer investment (durables plus housing), an increase that can be explained mainly as a result of the vigorous growth in monetary aggregates over the same period.

The most important issue concerning the behavior of aggregate demand during the 1967–73 period concerns the temporary income tax surcharge that was introduced in July 1968, and since has come to represent the Waterloo of activist fiscal stabilization management. While the charge that the surcharge failed to dampen consumer spending has been debated in a series of econometric articles, the following crude facts of the episode given for the first and last halves of 1968 are suggestive (all dollar amounts are in current prices).

| | First Half | | Last Half | |
	Dollars in Billions	*Percentage of Personal Income*	*Dollars in Billions*	*Percentage of Personal Income*
Consumer durable expenditures	77.3	11.6	82.7	11.8
Consumer nondurable expenditures	445.8	66.6	466.1	66.4
Consumer interest and net transfers to foreigners	13.8	2.1	14.5	2.1
Personal saving	42.4	6.3	33.8	4.8
Personal tax and nontax payments	89.7	13.4	104.4	14.9
Personal income	669.0	100.0	701.5	100.0

The most important finding in this table is that a drop in the share of personal saving in personal income exactly offsets the increase in the share of tax payments. There was no change at all in consumer spending out of personal income, although the share of consumer spending in personal *disposable* income increased from 90.3 to 91.9 percent. A more complete verdict on the episode requires a model to predict what would have been expected to happen to consumer spending, given the behavior of income, wealth, and other variables. The latest conclusion by Blinder (1978) is that "over a one-year planning horizon, temporary taxes are

Table 2.4   Real GNP (1972 Prices) and Its Components, Selected Quarters during the 1967–73 Interval

	Housing Slump 1967:1 (1)	Growth-Cycle Peak 1968:3 (2)	Cyclical Peak 1969:3 (3)	Cyclical Trough 1970:4 (4)	End of Slow Growth 1971:4 (5)	Growth-Cycle Peak 1973:1 (6)	Cyclical Peak 1973:4 (7)
A. Natural Real GNP	968.6	1,021.0	1,052.0	1,098.0	1,130.0	1,188.0	1,219.0
B. Real GNP	994.4	1,061.8	1,083.4	1,071.4	1,120.5	1,229.8	1,242.6
1. Real final sales	979.8	1,052.6	1,070.0	1,068.1	1,116.8	1,218.1	1,217.2
2. Inventory change	14.6	9.2	13.4	3.3	3.7	11.7	25.4
C. Consumption of Nondurables and Services	517.6	550.3	565.2	583.5	598.6	642.8	647.7
D. Fixed Investment	218.0	241.4	249.1	234.2	273.4	320.1	317.4
1. Consumer durables	77.5	90.5	91.6	84.5	103.7	124.9	118.1
2. Residential	32.7	42.8	42.9	43.4	56.4	64.4	54.0
3. Nonresidential	103.7	107.9	115.2	106.0	109.6	128.5	132.4
4. Net exports	4.1	0.2	−0.6	0.3	3.7	2.3	12.9
E. Government Purchases	244.3	260.9	255.7	250.3	251.0	255.2	252.0
1. Federal	122.6	129.5	120.6	108.0	103.2	100.7	94.3
2. State and local	121.7	131.4	135.1	142.4	147.7	154.5	157.7

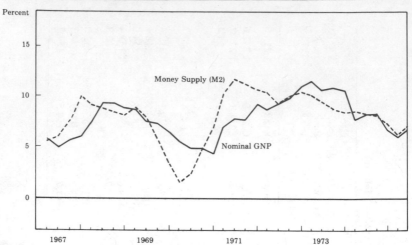

Fig. 2.3a

estimated to have only about 20–60 percent of the impact of permanent taxes of the same magnitude, and rebates are estimated to have only about 10–50 percent of the impact." Both the facts in the table and Blinder's evaluation would appear to support Eisner's initial point that the effects on consumption of temporary tax changes are likely to be weak, uncertain, or both.

After the peak of the growth cycle was reached in 1968:3, the economy moved sideways for the next year. Defense spending had peaked in the summer of 1968, and the modest drop in federal spending over that year was roughly canceled out by a further increase in investment. A surprising feature of the evolution of spending during 1969 and 1970 was the more moderate extent of the decline in housing expenditure than occurred in 1966–67 despite the drastic extent of "disintermediation" that drained money from commercial bank time deposits and from savings institutions. Government spending expanded rapidly in 1966–67 and slumped continuously between mid-1968 and mid-1971, thus "crowding out" housing in the earlier period and "crowding in" housing in the later period.

The mildness of the 1970 recession is evident in table 2.4, with a peak-to-trough decline in real final sales of only $1.9 billion, all of which can be accounted for by the General Motors strike of 1970.[36] In fact the behavior of the economy in 1970 is better described as a "hiatus" than as a recession, and is more than accounted for by the drop in federal defense spending. In the league table of postwar recessions measured by the change in real final sales between the NBER peak-and-trough quarters, 1970 on a strike-adjusted basis was more severe than 1949 or 1960, but less severe than 1954, 1958, or 1975. The automatic stabilizers worked with a vengeance: real personal income in the trough quarter was up 2.2 percent over the peak quarter; real personal disposable income was up even more due to the partial expiration of the tax surcharge.

The subsequent expansion was relatively sluggish in real terms throughout 1971 but then exploded at a frenetic pace through the growth-cycle peak in 1973:1. By far the most remarkable aspect of the expansion was the behavior of real consumer investment, including both consumer durable expenditures and residential investment, which leaped at an enormous annual rate of *16.8 percent* between the trough and growth-cycle peak (adjusted for the 1970 auto strike). Juxtaposing this record with the behavior of monetary growth in figure 2.3a, it is hard to avoid the conclusion that the boom of 1972–73 was primarily due to the influence of the acceleration of monetary growth in 1971, although some credit is due to consumer optimism engendered by the price control program of 1971–72.

By all standards (except the long-run implications of excess demand) 1973:1 was a vintage quarter for the American economy. The ratio of actual to natural output reached almost as high a level as the previous peaks achieved in 1966:1 and 1968:3. Consumer and business investment reached the highest all-time level of the postwar era when expressed as a ratio to natural real GNP. The record achieved in 1973:1 exceeds that of other peak quarters which have been highlighted in this paper.[37] The following figures show the ratio of real consumer and business investment (excluding net exports and inventory accumulation) to real "natural" GNP in percentages for selected quarters.

1973:1	26.8
1950:2	25.1
1978:4	25.0
1966:1	24.5
1968:3	23.6
1955:3	23.5
1960:1	21.0
1948:3	20.9

Several other interesting features of the spending components are evident in table 2.4. After two decades of roughly 6 percent growth in real terms, state and local real spending increased at only 4 percent during 1967–73, and 2.3 percent between early 1973 and late 1978, leading one to ask why the Proposition 13 revolt against excessive spending did not occur earlier. Net exports were much lower during 1968–70 than at any previous time during the postwar period, reflecting the overvaluation of the dollar that culminated in the dollar crisis and Smithsonian Agreement of 1971. The fact that net exports were higher in the peak quarter 1973:1 than in the trough quarter 1970:4 suggests that the intervening devaluations of the dollar had begun to stimulate the United States trade balance.

After early 1973 the economy faltered. A boom in net exports did not succeed in offsetting the continued decline in federal spending and a reduction in consumer investment, so that real final sales were lower in 1973:4 than in 1973:1. The NBER cyclical peak is set in late rather than early 1973 only because of a massive accumulation of inventories that temporarily maintained real GNP, threw the economy's inventory-sales ratio out of equilibrium, and partially explains the severity of the recession during the winter of 1975.

Supply Phenomena

The collapse of the policy paradigm that relied on a fixed Phillips curve occurred in three stages during the period between 1968 and 1971. First, the economy's 1968 recovery from the 1967 slowdown carried inflation up to the 4.5 percent region, in contrast to the inflation rates of 3.2–3.5 percent that had been experienced in 1966 at roughly the same rates of unemployment and resource utilization. This outcome led to general recognition that lags in the inflation process might have been ignored, that the position of the Phillips curve might be sensitive to expectations of inflation, and that there was a long-run Phillips curve with a steeper slope than the short-run schedule. Nevertheless, as long as the steeper long-run curve had a negative rather than vertical slope, there was still a policy tradeoff to be exploited by the policymakers.

The second stage of the collapse occurred during the recession of 1969–70. In contrast to the drop in inflation recorded in each preceding postwar recession and in the growth slowdown in 1967, there was no noticeable decline in inflation during 1970. The change in the GNP deflator over the four quarters ending in 1970:4 (the trough quarter) was 5.0 percent, little different than the 5.2 percent rate recorded during the four quarters of 1969.

Finally, the last stage in the collapse occurred during the first two quarters of the 1971 economic recovery. Despite a sluggish rate of real GNP growth that failed to bring unemployment down from its 6.0 percent peak rate, inflation still refused to abate, and in fact accelerated to a 5.9 percent annual rate. Wage growth accelerated as well, leaving little hope that policymakers could rely merely on high unemployment to achieve any significant deceleration in the inflation process. The early 1971 experience was soon reflected in the verdict of econometric studies that there was no longer any basis for belief that the long-run Phillips curve was negatively sloped rather than vertical.[38] And a more important immediate consequence was that the behavior of wages and prices in the first half of 1971 caused the Nixon administration to give up on

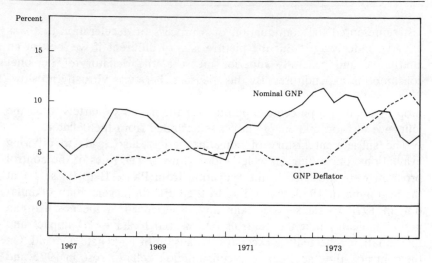

Fig. 2.3b

its policy of "gradualism" and to reverse its previous disavowal of controls by instituting a wage and price freeze on 15 August 1971.

The initial three-month freeze in wages and prices was followed by
several further "phases" of controls with varying rules. A crude verdict
that the program had a temporary impact is provided in figure 2.3b,
which shows that the inflation failed to slow down to any significant
degree in response to the 1969–70 deceleration of nominal GNP growth,
but then dropped substantially in 1972 despite the rapid acceleration of
nominal GNP growth. Another crude verdict can be provided by an
inspection of the annual percentage rates of change over selected intervals of three different measures of consumer prices:

	CPI	Personal Consumption Deflator	Personal Consumption Deflator Net of Food and Energy
1969:3–1970:2	5.9	4.6	4.6
1970:3–1971:2	4.3	4.4	4.5
1971:3–1972:4	3.3	3.4	3.0
1973:1–1974:1	8.7	8.2	5.0
1974:2–1975:1	10.5	9.9	9.8

Some early evaluations of the control program focused on the behavior
of the CPI. Since the CPI had already decelerated very substantially in
the year ending in 1971:2, it was claimed that the controls had no special effect and the relatively low inflation rate of late 1971 and 1972

just represented the continuation of a process of deceleration that was already under way.[39] But the picture is very different if we look at an alternative and generally superior measure, the deflator for personal consumption expenditures. By this measure there was virtually no slowdown in inflation prior to the onset of the controls, and then a sudden drop by about 1.5 percentage points over the next six quarters when the influence of food and energy prices is excluded from the deflator.

The subsequent history of consumer prices also leads to differing evaluations, depending on which index is used. The rules of the control program were loosened in the transition from Phase II to Phase III at the beginning of 1973. According to the CPI, the acceleration of inflation in 1973 to rates faster than any experienced in the post-Korean period indicates that the controls had ceased to have any impact and that inflation reflected the excessive expansion of aggregate demand. On the contrary, the "net" personal consumption deflator rose in 1973 and early 1974 at a rate little different from the 1969–70 experience and suggests that any stimulative impact of demand was canceled out by a lingering effect of the controls.

Subsequent econometric evaluations tend to conclude that the price controls did succeed temporarily in holding down the price level by two to three percentage points during 1972 relative to what would have been expected to occur in the absence of controls *with the same level of resource utilization.* In 1973 the controls had little impact either way, and then after the formal abandonment of controls in 1974:2, the entire earlier effect of controls was dissipated by a rebound in the price level. There was virtually no impact of the controls on wage inflation (except perhaps in the construction industry), so that the controls exerted their effect on inflation only by squeezing profit margins rather than by causing a deceleration of the entire inflationary process.

Between late 1972 and the spring of 1974 there was a rapid acceleration in the overall inflation rate, more than half of which appears to have been caused by an acceleration of food and energy prices, and the remainder by some combination of nominal demand growth and the loosening of controls. Farm prices almost doubled between early 1972 and the summer of 1973 as the result of the simultaneous occurrence of several adverse factors, including the delayed impact of the 1971 dollar devaluation, crop failures in many parts of the world combined with massive sales of United States wheat to the Soviet Union, and a peculiar disappearance of Peruvian anchovies from their normal feeding grounds. The reference to this episode as a "supply shock" here and in other papers does not deny that the worldwide economic boom of 1972–73 may have had some impact on the relative price of food, but rather represents the judgment that most of the unprecedented jump in this relative price stemmed from the upward shift of a supply curve rather than the movement of a demand curve outward along a fixed supply curve. The formation of the OPEC cartel and its impact on oil prices in 1973–74 also seems to have been mainly an autonomous supply shift.

The appearance of supply shifts as a source of changes in the inflation rate, first in the form of price controls and then in the form of an explosion of food and oil prices followed by a postcontrols rebound, was by far the most important economic event of the 1970s. No longer could stable aggregate demand growth insure a stable path of real GNP or unemployment, nor could unstable behavior of real GNP or unemployment be blamed solely on the policymakers controlling aggregate demand. Policy discussions now had to be framed in terms of the optimal degree of "accommodation" of supply shifts by policymakers, who had to be viewed as much less autonomous and powerful in light of the new constraints they faced.

While most of the story of policy responsiveness to supply shocks belongs in the history of the post-1973 subperiod, the issue first becomes relevant during the 1971–73 control interval. Because the temporary success of the controls allowed the inflation rate to slow while demand growth was accelerating, a large gap was opened between the growth rates of nominal GNP and inflation. Real GNP surged ahead, the GNP gap fell close to its postwar minimum, and unemployment declined as well, as shown in figure 2.3c. Far from accommodating the controls program by decelerating the growth of nominal GNP, monetary policymakers allowed the growth of money and nominal GNP to accelerate. In this sense the output boom was caused both by the effects of controls in shifting the division of a given rate of nominal GNP growth toward faster real GNP growth and less price change, and as well by the Federal Reserve in allowing nominal GNP growth to accelerate.

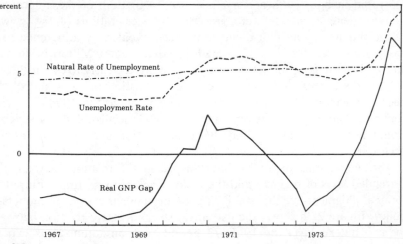

Fig. 2.3c

The 1967–73 period witnessed a substantial increase in the estimated "natural rate of unemployment," the unemployment rate believed to be compatible with steady inflation. The natural rate concept in this paper, based on the work of Perloff and Wachter (1979), shifts upward after 1963 as a result of the demographic changes that raised the overall unemployment rate relative to the rate for "prime-aged" adult males. For instance the unemployment rate of males aged twenty-five and over was an identical 3.0 percent in 1955 and 1974, but the aggregate unemployment rate increased between the two years from 4.2 to 5.6 percent.[40] To the extent that it is valid to infer that the tightness of the prime-aged male labor market has a disproportionate impact on wage and price behavior, this demographic shift helps to explain why the 6.0 percent unemployment rate experienced during 1970 and 1971 had so little downward impact on the inflation process.

It was during the 1967–73 period that concern first surfaced about the behavior of United States productivity growth. Indeed the 1967–73 average growth in output per hour in the private business sector was at an annual rate of 2.1 percent, down from 3.2 percent in the 1957–67 decade. It now appears, however, that this slowdown mainly reflects cyclical phenomena. The rapid growth of productivity between 1957 and 1967 can be partly accounted for by the higher level of resource utilization in the latter year, and productivity in 1973 appears to have been held down by a tendency that seems to surface in the last stage of every business cycle for firms to allow themselves to become overstaffed.[41]

2.5.3 A Retrospective View of Stabilization Policy

Almost nothing can be said on behalf of stabilization policy in the 1967–73 period. Nominal GNP growth was allowed to become much too rapid in both 1968 and again in 1972–73. Both of these accelerations of demand growth were preceded by accelerations of the growth of the money supply that could have been avoided by adherence to a monetary growth "rule" of the type long advocated by Milton Friedman, and both periods of monetary acceleration were clearly irresponsible in light of the overly high level of resource utilization in 1968 and of the need for a monetary deceleration to accommodate the 1971–72 price controls. The 1969 monetary slowdown was needed, but its severity would not have been required if the prior 1968 acceleration had not occurred.

Throughout this paper we have inspected the relation between the detrended level of real *M2* and the ratio of actual to "natural" output to form a judgment on the stabilizing or destabilizing role of monetary policy. Figure 2.3d shows the extremely strong positive relation between the two indexes over the 1967–73 period, with an autonomous expan-

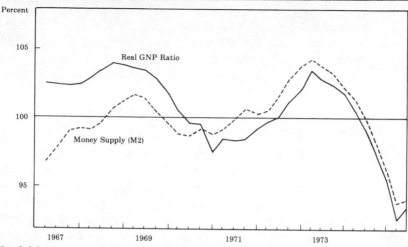

Fig. 2.3d

sion of real balances in 1968 when the output ratio was already too high, a rapid drop in real balances that brought the output ratio below unity, and then another expansion that continued after the output ratio had risen above unity.

The overheated expansion of 1972–73 is perhaps the leading postwar example of Nordhaus's (1975) "political business cycle" in action. The temporary success of the controls in holding down the price level in 1971–72 would have generated rapid growth in real GNP even if nominal GNP had been maintained along a constant-growth-rate path. But the Fed's expansionary monetary policy allowed nominal GNP growth to accelerate, perhaps in the belief that the controls program had allowed an abandonment of caution and the generation of a full-fledged preelection boom. The political business cycle model predicts that policy shifts to restriction immediately after an election, and indeed within three months the controls program had been partially dismantled and monetary growth began to decelerate.

Fiscal policy receives demerits during 1967–73 as well. Real federal government expenditures on goods and services were allowed to drop continuously between mid-1968 and mid-1973, but the speed of decline was most rapid between mid-1969 and mid-1970, thus aggravating the recession, and the decline ceased between mid-1971 and mid-1972, thus intensifying the expansion in total demand. Tax policy appears superficially to have contributed to stability, since the effective personal income tax rate dropped in 1970 and increased in 1972, but there is no visible stabilizing impact of these changes because they were completely offset by opposite movements in the saving ratio. Just as the temporary tax surcharge had not affected consumption appreciably in 1968, so its termination in 1970 had no effect, and taxpayers were smart enough to "pay for" the higher tax collections due to overwithholding in 1972 by cutting their saving rather than their consumption.[42]

2.6   The Fourth Postwar Subperiod, 1973–79

2.6.1   The Conceptual Framework

The year 1973 represents the high-water mark of monetarism. Almost every change in the intellectual consensus in the late 1960s had favored the monetarist position on the issues of both monetary potency and antiactivism, from the accumulating body of evidence that the major source of changes in nominal demand had been prior movements in the money supply, to the demise of the short-run Phillips curve that eliminated the scope for any long-run effect of activist policy on the unemployment rate, to the debacle of the 1968 tax surcharge episode.[43] It is fitting that 1973 ended with the publication of Goldfeld's much cited empirical study that showed the demand for money to be a stable and predictable function of income and interest rates, thus appearing to eliminate instability in money demand as a qualification to the case for a constant-growth-rate rule.

The major effect on economic ideas of the 1973–74 supply shocks was to undermine the case for a constant-growth monetary rule. The theoretical analysis of policy responses to supply shocks, developed by R. J. Gordon (1975a) and Phelps (1978), starts with an appeal to arithmetic—a common feature of all adverse supply shocks is that the division of any given level of nominal GNP is shifted toward a higher price level and a lower level of real GNP.[44] An expansive or "accommodating" demand policy can moderate the impact on real GNP only at the cost of raising the price level and aggravating inflation. Restrictive or "extinguishing" demand policy can moderate the price increase only at the cost of further aggravating the shortfall of real GNP. The choice between an accommodative, extinguishing, or neutral demand policy depends primarily on the nature of wage-setting institutions, on the openness of the economy, and on the relative welfare costs of inflation and unemployment.

The initial impact of an adverse supply shock—e.g., an OPEC price hike—is to raise the share of total spending on the product in question (energy), if its demand is price inelastic. The automatic consequence is that a fixed level of nominal GNP will be devoted more to spending on energy and less to spending on nonenergy goods and services. The reduced amount of nonenergy spending in nominal terms could be reflected in lower real nonenergy output, lower nonenergy prices, or both.

Imagine first that the domestic wage rate is fixed, and nonenergy prices are "marked up" over that wage rate by a constant fraction. Then all of the impact of the supply shock will fall on nonenergy real output. Because the wage rate is unresponsive to aggregate demand, stabilization policy can boost nominal income and thus real nonenergy output without raising nonenergy prices. Policy cannot prevent the overall price level (of energy and nonenergy products together) from rising, but it can prevent the wasteful loss of nonenergy output. The crucial feature allowing this beneficent impact of stabilization policy is the willingness of workers to accept a loss in real wages, that is, in the ratio of their fixed nominal wage to the higher overall price level.

At the opposite extreme, assume that domestic wages are fully and instantly indexed to the overall price level, and the change in the real wage depends only on the pressure of real nonenergy demand in the economy. Then the decline in the real wage required to balance the adverse impact of the supply shock on labor productivity is inhibited by the indexing formula and can be achieved only if stabilization policy allows real nonenergy demand to decline. Complete cost-of-living escalation of the wage rate (or *de facto* real wage rigidity in wage bargaining) thus makes a potentially serious recession and climb in the unemployment rate inevitable in the wake of a supply shock, a feature that several authors have pointed to as explaining the failure of European economies to recover after 1975 as rapidly as in the United States. In such an economy with real-wage rigidity, the economy's short-run aggregate supply schedule is steep, and stimulative aggregate demand policy will cause extra inflation with little benefit in the form of extra real output.

One of the most important phenomena in the United States economy is the inertia displayed by year-to-year changes in the nominal wage rate, resulting from the institution of long-term overlapping wage contracts with decentralized bargaining. While only part of the economy is unionized, the three-year contracts set in the unionized sector tend to set a pattern for important parts of the nonunionized sector. Because the aggregate nominal wage index depends mainly on its own past values, and responds only partially to consumer price inflation and real demand pressure, the aggregate real wage tends to be quite flexible. This creates a case for partial accommodation of supply shocks within the United States institutional framework; the degree of additional inflation caused by such accommodation is modest compared to the real output gained. A serious qualification to accommodation comes mainly from the fact that the United States is not a closed economy, and a greater degree of monetary expansion in the United States than abroad tends to cause a depreciation of the dollar and add extra inflationary pressure to the initial impact of the supply shock. Depending on policy responses in other countries, the United States nevertheless may obtain a real welfare gain by accommodation.

During the 1973–79 decade the analysis of supply shocks consumed relatively little space in academic journals compared to the implications for economic policy of the "rational expectations hypothesis" that firms and households base their decisions on all available information including the past behavior of policymakers. When combined by Sargent and Wallace (1975) with the "Lucas supply hypothesis" (Lucas 1973) that explains output changes by current and prior unexpected changes in prices, the idea of rational expectations led to a theorem that nominal demand policy is impotent to affect real output by any kind of systematic policy that responds regularly to past values of economic variables. Although it caused much ferment in academic circles and many heated conference exchanges, the Sargent-Wallace theorem had little impact on policymakers, because its underlying supply hypothesis depended on instantaneous price flexibility and thus seemed more applicable to price-taking yeoman farmers than to the price-setting institutions of the postwar United States. Since 1954 United States price changes have been dominated by inertia, and it is hard to explain the volatile movements of real GNP by "surprise" changes in the slow-moving aggregate price series.[45]

Another aspect of post-1973 economic performance that influenced prevailing opinion was the inability of earlier studies of the demand for money to explain the evolution of monetary aggregates. These unexplained movements in velocity that Goldfeld soon labeled "The Case of the Missing Money" eroded part of the intellectual underpinning of the case for a contant-growth-rate monetarist rule. As Poole (1970) had shown, instability in the demand for money provides a justification for using interest rates as well as a monetary aggregate as instruments of monetary policy.

2.6.2   Major Surprises of the 1973–79 Period

Demand Fluctuations

The relation between the four-quarter changes in nominal GNP and money displayed in figure 2.4a are not nearly as close as during 1960–73. Not only did the trend velocity of *M2* begin again to grow after a long period of constancy, but the timing of growth peaks in nominal GNP was quite different from that of peaks in money. Between early 1976 and early 1979 *M2* growth was fastest in just the period when nominal GNP growth was slowest, i.e., between late 1976 and mid-1977. On the basis of the widespread prediction in early 1976 that the velocity of *M2* would continue to be stable, monetary policy performed quite

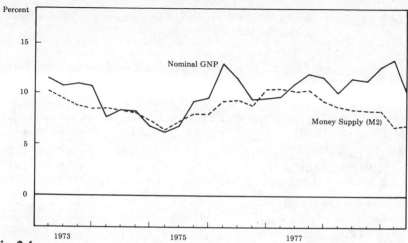

Fig. 2.4a

admirably in keeping the four-quarter change of *M2* growth between early 1976 and early 1979 within the relatively narrow range of 8.5 percent to 10.5 percent. Nevertheless this record of monetary stability did not prevent nominal GNP growth from accelerating to a four-quarter change ending in 1979:1 of 13.3 percent, faster than any similar change recorded during the previous twenty-seven years.

A comparison with similar figures for the earlier postwar subperiods suggests that both nominal GNP and monetary growth were more stable during 1973–79 than before. There were no sharp decelerations in monetary growth as had occurred in 1959–60 or 1969–70. In fact the modest 1975 slowdown in the growth rate of *M2* was less marked than the 1948 and 1966 episodes. The fact that nominal GNP growth slowed down so much more than monetary growth, and rebounded more at the end of the recession, resembles the pro-cyclical fluctuations in velocity that occurred in the 1950s and probably results from the extent of the inventory correction that was required in 1974–75. In any case, nothing in the *nominal* figures plotted in figure 2.4a would indicate to an uninformed reader that the 1974–75 recession was the most serious of the postwar era. The real story of that recession is of instability of prices in one direction and real GNP in the opposite direction.

The components of real GNP in key quarters during the 1973–79 interval are displayed in table 2.5. The severity of the 1973–75 recession is evident both in the behavior of real GNP and real final sales. The final sales decline between the cyclical peak and trough amounted to 3 percent of GNP, as compared to less than 2 percent in both 1954 and 1958. On top of that the shift from inventory accumulation in the peak quarter to nonaccumulation in the trough quarter amounted to 3.5 percent of real GNP, again higher than in any previous recession. The

Table 2.5   Real GNP (1972 Prices) and Its Components, Selected Quarters during the 1973–79 Interval

	Cyclical Peak 1973:4 (1)	Cyclical Trough 1975:1 (2)	Growth-Cycle Peak 1978:4 (3)	Latest Quarter 1979:3 (4)
A. Natural Real GNP	1,219.0	1,262.0	1,428.0	1,461.9
B. Real GNP	1,242.6	1,161.1	1,426.6	1,430.8
1. Real final sales	1,217.2	1,181.6	1,414.6	1,420.8
2. Inventory change	25.4	−20.5	12.0	10.0
C. Consumption of Nondurables and Services	647.7	648.6	768.2	777.8
D. Fixed Investment	317.4	275.9	370.5	370.6
1. Consumer durables	118.1	106.0	152.1	147.0
2. Residential	54.0	35.4	60.0	56.0
3. Nonresidential	132.4	114.4	145.5	148.2
4. Net exports	12.9	20.1	12.9	19.4
E. Government Purchases	252.0	257.1	276.0	272.6
1. Federal	94.3	94.8	99.3	97.6
2. State and local	157.7	162.2	176.6	175.0

decline in real final sales was uniformly severe in each component of consumer and business investment. Because the peak-to-trough growth in state and local government spending was unusually slow by past historical standards, and because federal spending did not increase, the only stabilizing component of expenditure was net exports.

The 1975–78 recovery can be contrasted to the recovery between the 1970 cyclical trough and the 1973 growth-cycle peak. In both cases the recoveries proceeded without any push from federal government spending and were led by consumer and business investment. The main differences between the two expansions were in their intensity and duration; while nominal GNP growth was as rapid during most of the 1975–78 expansion as during 1972–73, there was no controls program to hold down inflation, so that more of the recent expansion took the form of price increases and less the form of real GNP growth. The evolution of the economy after 1978:4 was very similar to that after 1973:1. In both cases there was a sideways movement of real GNP that occurred as a supply-induced acceleration of inflation "used up" the available growth in nominal GNP. The 1979 situation was healthier than that in 1973, however, because there was no spurt of excessive inventory accumulation such as occurred in 1973:4. Nevertheless, the economy collapsed in March 1980, eighteen months after the growth-cycle peak, repeating almost exactly the lag between the 1973:1 growth-cycle peak and the collapse in October 1974.

Supply Phenomena

The role of supply shocks in determining the behavior of inflation and real output growth in the 1973–75 recession stands out quite clearly in figure 2.4b. The four-quarter inflation rate steadily accelerated between early 1973 and early 1975 and then decelerated even faster. A rough estimate is that the peak four-quarter inflation rate of almost 12 percent can be broken down as follows: an underlying 5 percent inflation rate, plus the delayed impact of excessive demand growth in 1973 amounting to about 2 percent, plus an effect of energy and food prices of about 3 percent, plus the effect of the postcontrols rebound of another 2 percent. The precise allocation of these estimates depends on the particular quarter in question, since the direct impact of higher energy and food prices reached its peak at the end of 1973 and the beginning of 1974, while the postcontrols rebound had its greatest effect in the last half of 1974.

Some commentators argue that the rapid deceleration of inflation after the recession trough proves that restrictive demand management can be a very effective anti-inflationary policy within a short period of time. But this interpretation of the inflation slowdown of 1975–76 flies in the face of everything else we know about the postwar period, including the extremely gradual slowdown in inflation during the 1958 and 1960 recessions, the absence of any significant slowdown in 1970–71 prior to the controls, and the transient nature of several components of the 1974 inflation. If OPEC raises the level of the relative price of oil, the

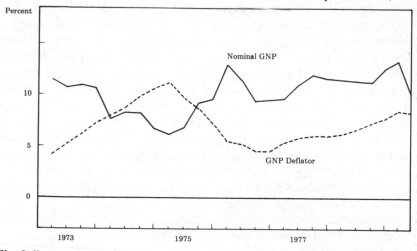

Fig. 2.4b

rate of change of that relative price will temporarily increase and then later decrease. Similarly, the postcontrols rebound was temporary by nature. Thus most of the moderation of inflation in 1975–76 had little to do with restrictive demand policy, although it does seem clear that there was a remaining component that can be attributed to the recession itself.[46]

In 1978–79 inflation accelerated once again almost to the level reached in late 1974 and early 1975. Although the precise details of timing were different, the basic nature of the 1978–79 episode was similar. There was no price controls program to produce a rebound, but there were increases in relative prices of food and energy once again, as well as some effect of the increasing utilization of resources during 1968. But most popular discussions exaggerated both the intensity of the 1979 inflation and the role of excessive demand growth causing it. In 1979:3 the National Income Accounts personal consumption deflator (PCD) increased at an annual rate of 10 percent, of which fully 3.3 percentage points were due to the direct effect of the higher relative prices of food and energy. The net, or energy-and-food-consumption deflator, increased at a rate of 6.7 percent, only about one percentage point faster than its 1976–77 pace, far less of an acceleration than the misleading eight percentage point speedup in inflation as registered by the CPI. Most commentaries on the unprecedented discrepancy between the PCD and CPI emphasized the flaws of the latter rather than the former. As of the third quarter of 1979 there had not yet been any decline in real GNP on a four-quarter change basis as had occurred throughout 1974 and the first half of 1975, reflecting the fact that nominal GNP growth had been faster during 1979 and inflation slower than at the same stage of the 1974–75 cycle. The decline in real GNP finally occurred in 1980:2.

The behavior of unemployment and the GNP gap are displayed in figures 2.4c and d. The duration of the recovery between early 1975 and late 1978 is similar to that between early 1961 and late 1964. Each period finished with the economy arriving at its natural rate of unemployment and output, with the magnitude of reduction in unemployment and the GNP gap greater in the 1975–78 recovery because of the deeper trough of the preceding recession. Then after late 1978 the economy took a totally different turn that after late 1964. Whereas the slow and steady expansion in the earlier episode had been followed by a rapid drop in the GNP gap as Vietnam War spending began, in 1979 the supply inflation used up most of the available nominal GNP growth and caused the GNP gap to increase.

The laments of economic policymakers at their inability to stop supply inflation in 1979 echoed those of 1974. But now in 1979 there was a new supply-side problem. The pace of productivity expansion had progressively slowed during the 1975–78 economic recovery in comparison

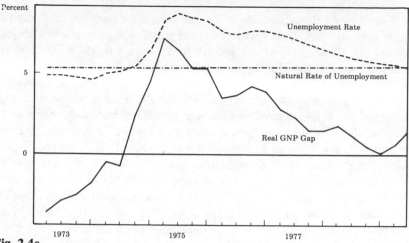

Fig. 2.4c

with the experience in previous recoveries. By late 1979 it appeared that the secular growth rate in productivity might be less than one percent, and a search for the causes of the secular slowdown stimulated a number of studies that were as interesting as they were inconclusive.[47] Because some foreign nations had not suffered as great a slowdown in productivity or as great an acceleration in inflation, the unfortunate supply events of 1978–79 had the healthy effect of forcing chauvinistic United States economists to pay more attention to the condition of the outside world. There was no agreement, however, as to whether the poor United States productivity and inflation performances were related, or whether there was some deeper social problem in American society.[48]

2.6.3   A Retrospective View of Stabilization Policy

Different standards must be applied in judging policymakers who are forced to react to supply shocks and those who live in a relatively peaceful world in which demand instability is the only problem. Since a supply shock in the form of higher prices of food or energy must worsen either inflation or unemployment, and usually both, policymakers cannot hope to escape criticism. Recent evaluations of this policy problem have pointed to the relative rigidity of the United States nominal aggregate wage rate as the central factor allowing an accommodative monetary policy in response to shocks like those faced by the United States in 1973–74 and 1979. And Gramlich's (1979) calculations show that a reasonable weighting of the relative welfare costs of unemployment and inflation makes an accommodative reaction yield a much higher level of social welfare than does an "extinguishing" reaction that attempts to beat the inflation out of the system.

Even among those who do not agree with the details of these studies there appears to be little disagreement that policymakers made a serious mistake in allowing monetary growth to decelerate in 1974–75. The remaining question is whether an acceleration should have been allowed to occur, and if so how much. This debate is unlikely ever to be settled, because it depends not only on one's ability to trust econometric evaluations of the consequences of alternative policies, but one's guess as to whether there would have been a wage acceleration in response to more accommodative policies as occurred in Sweden, Italy, and the United Kingdom.[49] Those who thought that the greater public awareness of inflation would substantially increase the low degree of "pass through" of commodity prices into wages must be amazed by the incredible inertia displayed by data on aggregate wage change in 1979 and 1980. Despite a doubling of the rate of consumer price inflation since 1977 (by the GNP measure), there has been barely one percentage point of acceleration of wage change.

To add to the humility forced upon United States policymakers by their vulnerability to supply shocks and the slow rate of secular productivity growth compared to other nations, the 1978–79 period demonstrated that United States policy can no longer be made on the basis of domestic considerations alone. The Federal Reserve no longer has the latitude to make its decision on the degree of supply-shock accommodation in isolation, because the pursuit of tighter monetary policies in Germany and elsewhere may make it impossible for the Fed to accommodate without causing a substantial erosion in the value of the dollar. Not only does a dollar depreciation directly reduce the real income of United States citizens, but it also tends to have unfortunate political side effects, especially when it induces OPEC oil ministers to increase the posted oil price once again. Nevertheless the stimulus of accommodation to United States real income may still be a wise choice to maximize United States welfare, especially if OPEC sets oil prices in relation to the price of a market basket of its imports from all industrialized nations.

While there was no discretionary increase in government spending on goods and services during the 1974–75 recession, as had occurred in 1958, nevertheless fiscal policy deserves credit for the size and timing of the temporary tax rebate and permanent tax reduction introduced in 1975:2. The criticisms leveled at the 1968 tax surcharge apply as well to the 1975 rebate, although recent studies by Blinder (1978) conclude that there was a nonnegligible stabilizing effect. One may also argue that the tax rebate was larger than would otherwise have occurred because policymakers had absorbed the message of the criticism of the earlier episode. Finally, it might be argued that a tax rebate may have a greater effect than a surcharge even if both are equally recognized as temporary,

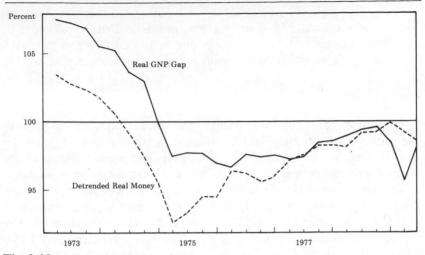

Fig. 2.4d

because some consumers in a recession may face a liquidity constraint.

The increased attention in macroeconomics to the supply side also applies to fiscal policy. Analysts have pointed to the "wedge" that taxes drive between market prices charged by firms and the take-home pay received by workers. To the extent that after-tax wage increases are relatively slow to adjust to the pressure of restrictive demand policy, there may be room for cost-reducing fiscal changes as an anti-inflation device. For instance, if the social security payroll tax tends to be shifted forward to prices to a greater extent than the personal income tax, then a substitution of income-tax for payroll-tax financing of social security would help to decelerate the inflation rate. The Carter administration's economic advisers understood this point well but nevertheless allowed major increases in the payroll tax to take place. This and other cost-increasing measures, sometimes called "self-inflicted wounds," added to the upward pressure on food and energy prices on aggregate inflation. These government-induced supply shocks, including increases in the minimum wage and in the tightness of regulations, as well as in farm price supports, have added to the dilemma faced by the Federal Reserve and increased the chance that the administration will find both inflation and unemployment at record levels (for an election year) in 1980.

Not only did the government inflict wounds on itself and the economy in the late 1970s, but it failed to use fiscal policy creatively to reduce American dependence on imported oil. In Europe and Japan high indirect taxes on energy had long been in effect. These high taxes encouraged energy conservation. In addition, OPEC price increases created a smaller percentage increase in final energy prices—and hence less economic disruption—in Europe and Japan than in the low-tax United

States. As early as 1974 American economists had urged adoption of policies to put heavy taxes on energy and to use the revenue to reduce nonenergy prices (either by subsidies or sales tax rebates).[50]

2.7   Conclusion

In contrast to the interwar period when fiscal policy was faced with the problem of offsetting both a collapse in private spending and the destabilizing impact of monetary restriction and bank failures, in the postwar period external events were the most important single destabilizing force, most obviously in the direct impact of Korean and Vietnam defense expenditures on real GNP and in the effect of the formation of the OPEC oil cartel in the 1970s on inflation and unemployment. The record of stabilization policy is mixed. The three most successful episodes of fiscal stabilization were the prompt increase in taxes to finance the Korean War in 1950, the countercyclical expansion of government expenditures in 1958, and the tax rebate and permanent tax reduction of 1975. Although the 1958 and 1975 episodes had stabilizing effects, nevertheless they were both too little and too late. The most destabilizing fiscal episode was the failure to raise taxes to finance the Vietnam War promptly in 1965–66, leading to deficits and pressure on the Federal Reserve to expand the money supply excessively in 1967 and 1968.

A major theme of this study has been the changing relation between changes in nominal GNP and money. Over the middle part of the postwar era, roughly between 1958 and 1973, accelerations and decelerations in monetary growth regularly preceded movements in nominal GNP growth of roughly the same magnitude. Monetary policy has not only been potent but also inept, bearing responsibility for the unnecessary recession of 1960, the excessive expansion of nominal GNP growth in 1967–68, the recession of 1969–70, and the second episode of excessive growth in 1972–73.

The character of business fluctuations differed both before 1958 and after 1973. In the first postwar decade monetary policy provided a stable framework for an economy that suffered from business cycles as a result of unstable government defense expenditures and to a lesser extent because of autonomous fluctuations in exports. Only during the pre-Accord period did monetary policy aggravate a business cycle, as when it allowed monetary growth to decelerate substantially in 1948. After 1973, demand fluctuations lost their central role as an explanation of business cycles and took second place to supply shocks. Monetary authorities made a mistake in slowing monetary growth in response to the first supply shock episode in 1973–74 but do not bear a major responsibility for the timing of that recession. In 1979 obsolete operating rules for monetary policy (abandoned in October 1979) caused overly slow monetary growth rates in the winter and overly rapid rates in the summer; a relatively stable performance when measured by four-quarter changes was not viewed as stable by speculators, so that the Fed found its freedom of choice regarding the desirable degree of accommodation of the 1979 supply shock was impeded by its sensitivity to external events and opinion.

Economic ideas rarely lead economic events but usually follow them. Although the relation between money and income was quite close after 1958, the monetarist case for policy rules and against discretionary activism did not make much progress as an intellectual framework until the simultaneous coincidence in 1968 of an inflation that accelerated beyond the predictions of existing models, a tax surcharge that failed in its announced mission of slowing the economy, and a presidential address by the most articulate and influential monetarist thinker. After a brief hegemony events once again caused a shift in opinion, and the monetarist tide ebbed under the pressure of supply shocks that added a new reason to question the optimality of fixed monetary growth rules and as new "money demand puzzles" were discovered. Not only were variations in the monetary growth rate incapable of explaining the variations in the inflation rate during the 1970s, but monetarists were forced to cede the frontier of creative policy thinking to nonmonetarist schemes for using taxes and subsidies to counter the impact of the OPEC cartel.

Despite the multitudes of economists who make their living by forecasting the future, and despite the brilliance of a small minority among them, virtually all the "surprises" recorded in this paper have eluded prediction. The predicted postwar deflation and depression failed to occur; the flexibly responding price level that dropped in recessions gave way to the stable Phillips curve tradeoff which in turn gave way to the natural rate hypothesis; the "new economics" of fiscal activism brought not permanent high employment but rather transient job gains at the cost of permanent inflation; an OPEC oil cartel that was initially dismissed as about to collapse and irrelevant for macroeconomics actually ushered in an entirely new way of thinking about economic fluctuations in which aggregate-demand policymakers are hapless passive agents and must cede center stage to supply-side policymakers with their redistributive tax and subsidy schemes; the arrival of flexible exchange rates brought not a new autonomy for the United States but rather a new dependence on the opinions of foreign bankers and speculators.

Nevertheless as the 1980s began it was hard to avoid the conclusion that pessimism had been carried too far. Many United States commentators were so immersed in lamenting American problems that they neglected to notice a different environment in some other nations. Life went on in France and Italy with gasoline at three dollars per gallon, suggesting great potential in the United States for a massive tax on imported oil to be rebated in the form of subsidies or tax reductions on nonenergy goods and services. Productivity growth continued, albeit at a slower rate than before 1973, everywhere but in the United States and the United Kingdom, suggesting that the solution to the United States productivity puzzle might begin by dismantling United States policies that raised costs, discouraged saving, and protected lame-duck industries and companies. Ironically the United States institution of staggered and decentralized wage bargaining which in 1970–71 had impeded the government's fight against demand-induced inflation actually proved to be a blessing in dealing with supply-induced inflation, since sluggish nominal wage adjustment made the United States real wage more flexible than that in most other industrialized countries. As the United States entered the 1980s, a long agenda of positive and forceful economic actions lay gathering dust, awaiting the new broom of a positive and forceful politician.

Notes

1. The dichotomy between aggregate demand and supply factors, while useful for expository purposes, should not blind us to the numerous interactions between demand and supply factors. For instance, how strong are the forces that tend to bring about an equality between aggregate demand and supply? What is the optimal demand management policy in response to a supply shock? R. J. Gordon (1975b) has emphasized the two-way interaction between wage-setting institutions and monetary policy, while Lucas (1976) has stated the general principle that private behavior (on both the demand and supply sides) should depend on policy actions and more generally on the evolution of all economic variables.

2. The loose connection between money and nominal GNP throughout the 1929–41 period is particularly evident in quarterly data, as demonstrated by R. J. Gordon and Wilcox (1980).

3. The increased role of government has reduced the multiplier effect of autonomous changes in spending and thus stabilized the economy. Hickman and Coen (1976, p. 194) estimate a multiplier for changes in real autonomous spending (for five years after the change) of 5.09 under the conditions of 1926–40 and only 2.10 under the conditions of 1951–65. R. J. Gordon (1978, p. 494) has calculated that the automatic fiscal stabilizers absorbed only 5.5 percent of the decline in GNP in 1932, but 36.9 percent in 1975.

4. Many competing labels have been suggested for the state of unemployment that is compatible with steady inflation. Next to Friedman's "natural rate" label, the next most frequently used is probably the NAIRU (Non-accelerating-inflation-rate-of-unemployment) coined by Modigliani and Papademos (1975) and Michael Wachter (1976).

5. Starting with the 1977 *Economic Report of the President* the official Council of Economic Advisers' estimate of potential real GNP has been revised downward by a large amount. For instance, the estimate of potential real GNP in the 1979 report for 1976 is about $90 billion (or 6 percent) lower than the estimate for the

same year in the 1976 report. See *Economic Report of the President* (Washington, D.C.: Government Printing Office, January 1979), chart 7, p. 75. This revision consists partly of a more pessimistic estimate of the long-term growth of labor productivity and partly a less ambitious 5.1 percent unemployment rate criterion in contrast to the old 4.0 percent criterion. The figures shown in table 2.1 for natural real GNP were created by Perloff and Wachter (1979) for 1955–79 and by R. J. Gordon (1978) for earlier years.

6. This judgment is related to the absence of any other explanation of the remarkable growth of real GNP between 1948 and 1951.

7. The most accessible discussion of the puzzle is Denison (1979).

8. Modigliani's (1977) presidential address emphasizes the inability of monetary aggregates to explain the instability of the inflation rate in the 1970s.

9. The consequences of supply shocks are studied in Gordon (1975a) and Phelps (1978).

10. While it does not use the IS-LM apparatus, the discussion of monetary policy in the second edition of Samuelson's textbook (1951, pp. 372–75) is titled "The Inadequacies of Monetary Control of the Business Cycle" and states that "superhuman efforts" are necessary to reduce long-term interest rates and that "investment is likely to be inelastic with respect to the interest rate." Included in the discussion (without qualification) is the famous phrase, "You can lead a horse to water but you can't make him drink" (p. 373).

11. An attempt to provide a statistical estimate of the role of money in the Great Contraction, quarter by quarter, is provided by R. J. Gordon and Wilcox (1980).

12. This stability of prices is particularly evident in the monthly CPI figures for the period between the summers of 1938 and 1940.

13. See Samuelson (1951, pp. 287–88).

14. To Samuelson's credit, he noted this problem (albeit briefly), and wrote: "Even more ominous is the possibility that prices may begin to shoot up long before full employment is reached. As a result full employment may never be reached" (1951, p. 303).

15. Beveridge (1945, p. 200). For a hopeful view that administered contracts and wage bargaining would make prices relatively inflexible and prevent an inflationary spiral at full employment, see Dunlop (1947), a paper that can be cited as a precursor of recent attempts by Phelps and Winter (1970) and Okun (1975) to explain why some wages and prices are administered rather than set in continuously clearing auction markets.

16. See especially Graham (1947).

17. There is no discussion at all in Samuelson (1951) of productivity, economic growth, or economic development, except for treatments of Malthus, depopulation, and secular stagnation.

18. The 1955 model change did not just involve a face-lift. Chevrolet and Plymouth introduced V-8 engines for the first time. The hedonic price literature identifies a very substantial increase in automobile quality relative to price in 1955.

19. A full exploration of this topic is outside of the scope of this paper. For a more complete discussion see Sachs (1980) and Gordon (1980).

20. This interpolation procedure is more intricate than is described in the text and is described in R. J. Gordon (1978, app. C).

21. A unique feature of inflation in 1956–57 is that the acceleration in wages occurred before that in consumer prices. This timing pattern can be explained by wage-price models in which the effective minimum wage is a determinant of wage change, since the largest postwar increase in minimum wage occurred in 1956:1.

22. See R. J. Gordon (1979).

23. The postwar history of the full-employment surplus is given in R. J. Gordon (1978, p. 491).

24. A concise guided tour of contemporary opinion would include Tobin's (1953) review of the Patman Inquiry documents, Gurley's (1960) review article on the Radcliffe Report, Brunner's (1961) review article on the Report of the Commission on Money and Credit, and Harry Johnson's (1962) review article on monetary theory and policy. Prior to the publication of the Friedman-Schwartz monetary history (1963), probably the most influential pieces by Friedman were his original policy statement (1948), the book with his student that helped to revive a new version of the quantity theory (1956), the article on money demand that minimized the role of the interest rate (1959), and the work with Meiselman that set the quantity theory in competition with the Keynesian multiplier approach (1963).

25. A concise contemporary critique of those who opposed flexible monetary policy is contained in Friedman (1951).

26. The velocity of $M2$ was 2.38 in 1960, and 2.43 in 1977. Afterwards velocity rose to 2.51 in 1978 and 2.59 in 1979:3. An adjusted measure of $M2$ that incorporates financial innovations in the late 1970s retains the earlier characteristic of constant velocity—see R. J. Gordon (1979a).

27. Nevertheless, Clark (1979) has recently concluded that the simple accelerator theory outperforms other theories of investment behavior that emphasize the importance of changing interest rates and tax incentives.

28. A diagrammatic illustration of "crowding out" in 1966 is provided in R. J. Gordon (1978, pp. 127–29).

29. The extremes in the four-quarter change in the GNP deflator over the 1957–67 period were a peak of 3.9 percent in 1957:1, trough of 1.3 percent in 1958:3, peak of 2.4 percent in 1959:2, trough of 0.6 percent in 1961:1, peak of 2.1 percent in 1962:4, and trough of 1.3 percent in 1964:1, peak of 3.7 percent in 1966:4, and trough of 2.5 percent in 1967:2. The 1961–62–64 fluctuation provides part of the foundation for the current econometric conclusion that part of the influence of demand on prices represents the effect of the rate-of-change of output, not just the size of the output gap, as shown in R. J. Gordon (1979a). The same paper examines implications of econometric estimates from the 1954–77 period for economic policy in 1979–80.

30. Edmund Phelps reports that his first (1967) paper was written in the first half of 1966.

31. We note that real federal expenditures on goods and services rose by 6.1 percent between the 1957:3 peak cyclical quarter and 1958:4, and then declined by 6.4 percent between 1958:4 and 1960:1. Perhaps more surprising and remarkable is the record of state-local real spending on goods and services, with a 12.6 percent expansion in the first period and only a 0.5 percent rise in the second period, a record that presumably reflects the influence of monetary policy on state-local spending rather than any conscious attempt to pursue an activist counter-cyclical policy. The combined effect of government spending was thus strongly stabilizing, and I believe that the negative correlation of real GNP and real government spending during this episode accounts for much of the finding in reduced-form "St. Louis regressions" of GNP on money and government expenditures that fiscal policy is impotent. In my 1971 article I drew attention to the stabilizing role of government spending in 1958 and the negative correlation of private investment and government spending in 1953–55 as events that explain the low multipliers on fiscal variables in St. Louis-type reduced-form equations. A more general analysis

of the consequences of endogenous monetary and fiscal policy for such equations is presented by Goldfeld and Blinder (1972).

32. See Bach (1971, p. 100), and R. A. Gordon (1974, pp. 133–36).

33. I have previously (1970, pp. 501–5) presented in more detail the argument that the lack of careful specification of the role of monetary policy in contemporary econometric models was directly to blame for the excessive rate of monetary expansion in 1968.

34. Phelps (1967) and Friedman's December 1967 Presidential Address to the American Economics Association made essentially the same point. Although Friedman's presentation had a greater impact and was responsible for the coinage of the "natural rate" terminology, Phelps' 1968 paper attracted considerable attention at the August, 1967, conference of the American Bankers Association.

35. Credit for the distinction between the investment dependence on the real interest rate and money-demand dependence on the nominal interest rate belongs with Mundell (1963).

36. If the auto output figures for 1970:4 and 1971:1 are simply averaged together to eliminate the effects of the strike, we conclude that real GNP would have been $9.9 billion higher and real final sales $5.8 billion higher in 1970:4, thus making aggregate real final sales in that quarter about $4 billion higher than in the peak 1969 quarter.

37. Thus perhaps Paul Samuelson's old challenge to his students to explain automobile sales in 1955 should be replaced by a challenge to a newer generation of econometricians to explain the configuration of investment in 1973:1.

38. In R. J. Gordon (1972, p. 402) I showed that the data points accumulated during 1969 and 1970 had made the econometric wage equation unable to reject the hypothesis that past price change fed through completely to wages, i.e., that the long-run Phillips curve was vertical.

39. Feige and Pearce's (1973) early evaluation that the controls had little effect on prices was based on the behavior of the CPI. R. J. Gordon (1972) and Blinder and Newton (1978) based their evaluations on the behavior of the GNP deflator, especially for the nonfarm sector.

40. These figures come from R. J. Gordon (1978, p. 251), where adjustments in the figures are explained and citations given.

41. In R. J. Gordon (1979b) the slowdown in productivity growth in the 1966:1 1972:4 period relative to the preceding 1947–65 era is only 0.4 percentage points once cyclical corrections are made, and this difference is not statistically significant.

42. Policy actions during this period are examined in detail in Blinder (1979).

43. The major problem for monetarists was the lack of inflation response to slower monetary growth in 1969–70, thus indicating that the economy's automatic powers of "self-correction" were weak.

44. Gramlich (1979) provides a clear exposition of what he calls the Gordon-Phelps model and sets it in the context of a welfare-maximizing policymaker. Blinder (1980) extends the analysis to deal with alternative OPEC pricing regimes.

45. It is evident from figures 2.1b, 2.2b, 2.3b and 2.4b that changes in real output have *preceded* price changes, leaving little room for unexpected price movements to *explain* output changes.

46. The wage and price equations presented in R. J. Gordon (1979a) indicate that roughly half of the impact of a recession on the inflation process is proportional to the rate of change of unemployment, and the other half to the level of unemployment relative to natural unemployment. Thus inflation tends to decelerate when unemployment is rising, while in the first stages of the recovery, when

unemployment is falling but still well above the natural rate, inflation tends to be relatively constant, as in 1961–63 and 1976–77.

47. See Denison (1979) for the widest ranging discussion of the problem. Other papers either appear in or are cited in the second 1979 issue of the *Brookings Papers on Economic Activity*.

48. Symptomatic of the new concern was the press attention given to Vogel (1979).

49. For such econometric evaluations, see Eckstein (1978). Other studies are discussed in Blinder (1979).

50. A discussion of fiscal devices to offset supply shocks is contained in R. J. Gordon (1975a, pp. 194–96). An early advocate of a tax on imported oil to extract part of OPEC's monopoly profit was Houthakker (1976).

---

2. Arthur M. Okun

Postwar Macroeconomic Performance

I would emphasize the following salient features of the postwar macroeconomic record:

1. Throughout the postwar era, real economic activity has displayed much more stability than it did in earlier United States history.

2. For the first twenty or twenty-five years of the postwar era—but not since then—that greater stability was accompanied by more rapid progress with especially strong growth of both output and productivity.

3. While the superior real performance from the mid-forties to the mid-sixties was not achieved at the expense of a serious departure from price stability, the record since then shows a dramatic and unprecedented chronic inflation accompanying the deterioration of real performance.

4. In subtle but important ways, both the good news and the bad news of the postwar era reflect the categorical imperative of policymaking established at the beginning of that era—namely the avoidance of an encore of the Great Depression.

The Stability of Real Activity

Throughout the postwar era including the seventies, economic activity has been far more stable than it was in previous United States history. The standard deviation of real GNP around its growth trend in 1946–76 was about one-fourth as large as it had been in 1900–45, and only half

Arthur M. Okun, who died while this book was in press, was a senior fellow of the Brookings Institution.

The views expressed are the author's and are not necessarily those of the officers, trustees, or other staff members of the Brookings Institution.

as large as in the "golden age" of 1900–16, 1920–29, omitting wartime and depression years in the prewar era (Baily 1978). The contrast in the cyclical chronology is equally striking: the average duration of business-cycle expansions between 1854 and 1937 was twenty-six months, and that of recessions twenty-one months. From 1945 to 1975, expansions averaged forty-eight months in length and recessions, eleven months. Thus, the economy spent only 19 percent, rather than 45 percent, of the elapsed time in recession. The longest and deepest postwar recession (1973–75) was shorter than the median prewar recession and less severe than four of the nine recessions of the 1900–38 period.

This quantum jump in stability—this taming of the business cycle—must, in my judgment, be credited to public policy. It was made in Washington. I suspect that the largest single stabilizing development stemmed from a change that was not designed to enhance macroeconomic stability, namely the increased size of the public sector as a share of GNP. That compositional shift created a large component of the total economy that was not sensitive to cyclical fluctuations and that resisted multiplier-accelerator interactions. On the income side, the counterpart to the growth in the public sector was the increase in marginal tax rates, which cut the size of investment multipliers. The growth of transfer payments also created important automatic stabilizers: unemployment insurance benefits alone have bolstered private purchasing power *during recession periods* by more than the total of discretionary stimulative fiscal actions of the postwar era. The absence of the financial panic element that was a hallmark of prewar recessions reflects, in part, the development of federal deposit insurance and other types of federal financial regulation as well as the willingness and ability of the Federal Reserve to contain the ripple effects of major failures and defaults.

Private decision makers gradually realized that the government had the tools of demand management to prevent catastrophes of depression magnitude. And that recognition helped to alleviate, and ultimately to end, the fears of an encore of the thirties, which were intense at the beginning of the postwar era. The perceived reduction of catastrophe risks, in turn, contributed to less volatile shifts by decision makers in response to those fluctuations that did emerge, as Baily suggests.

Fiscal and monetary policy were geared up appropriately to avoid catastrophes, but their record in dealing with the relatively minor accidents that in fact occurred is mixed. Gordon ably traces that experience in his background paper. I shall merely underline a few of the lessons. Some of the better stabilization performances came early in the postwar era. An appropriately large federal surplus was maintained during 1947 and 1948. In terms of macroeconomic stabilization, the Korean War was by far the best managed military emergency in United States history

—presenting a sharp contrast with the subsequent Vietnam experience. But, during recession periods, fiscal policy was uniformly slow on the trigger. Indeed, it is fair to conclude that no significant discretionary stimulative fiscal action was adopted while the economy was still in recession. A borderline case was the tax cut enacted in March 1975, which was the month of the business-cycle trough. Most of the strongly stimulative fiscal actions were taken in the first year of recovery. On occasions, these worked effectively to promote the restoration of prosperity; on others, they may have overdone the job—providing a stimulus that was too much too late. Antirecessionary expenditure programs like public works seem to have operated with a lag of half a cycle. (It may be easier to stretch the lag to a full cycle than to cut it appreciably!)

The outstanding applications of restrictive budgetary policy occurred in the fiscal years 1957, 1960, and 1974. And all of these were cases of too much too late. At the end of the fiscal years 1957 and 1960, celebrations on the achievement of federal budgetary surpluses were followed immediately by mourning over the onset of recession. The lessons inferred from those experiences contributed to the general acceptance of federal deficits as a normal and appropriate state of affairs in the sixties and the seventies.

Monetary policy as well was too slow on the trigger in reacting to recessions. The growth rate of money remained below average right through the trough of most recessions, even in those cases when (as Gordon emphasizes) it accelerated relative to the peak of the previous expansion. Often, like fiscal policy, monetary policy turned markedly expansionary during the first year of recovery. A generally accommodating stance was maintained for too long during several expansions, followed by shifts to restraint that were too much too late.

The record provides some illuminating examples of bad and good applications of the fiscal-monetary mix. In the face of the massive fiscal stimulus of butter and Vietnam guns, the Federal Reserve in 1966–67 demonstrated that it could do the whole macro job. Tightening enough to generate a virtual cessation of money growth, it achieved a nonrecessionary slowdown that cooled inflation. But the macro success was accompanied by serious micro distortions: a collapse in homebuilding, an acute mortgage famine, a general contraction of availability in credit markets, and major capital losses on bonds and equities. Then in late 1967 and 1968, monetary policy was clearly too stimulative because the Federal Reserve refused to risk an encore of these distortions. A good mix performance is illustrated by the 1964–65 tax cuts, when fiscal policy played an active role and monetary policy carried an accommodative role. That strategy was superior to the alternatives of relying on a unilateral fiscal stimulus or on a unilateral monetary stimulus. In the latter case, in order to provide an equivalent stimulus, interest rates would have had to be reduced substantially, thereby risking an overstimulus to homebuilding and exacerbation of the balance-of-payments problem.

I read the undistinguished record of cyclical stabilization as suggesting ample opportunities for improvement. We have to try harder—not cease the effort.

Deteriorating Growth Performance

Until recently, the greater stability of the postwar era was accompanied by more rapid progress. The average annual growth rate of real GNP was 3.8 percent from 1948 to 1973, far surpassing the average rate of 2.8 percent for 1909–29 and 2.3 percent for 1929–48. Moreover, when allowances were made for the size of the "net gap" under these trend lines connecting prosperity years, the superiority of postwar performance is even clearer: the net gap averaged zero for 1948–73; it averaged 5 percent of GNP in 1909–29 and 12 percent of GNP in 1929–48. Finally, output per hour worked rose at an average rate of 3 percent per year through most of the postwar era, a substantial improvement over the 2 percent par for the course in the earlier periods.

For 1973–78, however, the annual growth rate of real GNP averaged only 2.5 percent. And that growth was accomplished only as the result of an especially rapid increase in the labor force and employment, while the trend growth of output per hour worked apparently slowed to a mere one percent a year. The productivity slowdown has generated a vast amount of interesting economic research, which is often inconclusive. One important consensus finding is that slower growth of capital per unit of labor accounts for *part but only part* of the slowdown. That slower growth of the capital-labor ratio in turn has two components. If the ratio of investment to GNP in recent years had matched its historical average, the capital-labor ratio would have displayed unusually slow growth in view of the especially rapid growth of the labor force. In fact, in the latter part of the 1973–75 recession and for some considerable time in the subsequent recovery, the ratio of business fixed investment to GNP ran considerably below its historical average.

Chronic Inflation

The other outstanding dimension of deteriorating economic performance in recent years is the rapid and accelerating pattern of inflation since the mid-sixties. The chronic inflation that has survived slack and recession is an unprecedented experience for Americans. Fourteen years ago, when the United States economy (and, incidentally, the reputation of economists) looked brightest, Gardner Ackley (1966, p. 176) warned: "It is easy to prescribe expansionary policies in a period of slack. Managing high-level prosperity is a vastly more difficult business and requires vastly superior knowledge." The price record demonstrates that we have not had the skill to manage high-level prosperity.

Actually, in terms of the ability of the federal government to forecast and control the course of *nominal* GNP, demand management has been especially successful in the past decade. The official annual "Troika" forecasts of nominal GNP were distinctly more accurate in the seventies than they had been in the sixties—with an average absolute error of 0.75 percent compared to 1.3 percent. (This brings up to date a fact previously noted by William Fellner. I assure you that the improvement should not be attributed to a lower quality of the people doing the Troika forecasting in the sixties!)

In fact, control over nominal GNP is all that monetary and general fiscal policy can be expected to achieve. They cannot control the "split" of the growth of nominal GNP between its real and its inflation components. But errors in forecasting the split have been serious and costly. In 1970, 1971, 1973, 1974, and 1979, inflation was *under*predicted by a percentage point or more while the growth of real GNP was *over*predicted by a point or more. The year 1974 is the most egregious case: the nominal GNP forecast was nearly perfect, with offsetting errors of about two and a half percentage points each for the GNP deflator and real GNP.

The big errors in assessing the split stemmed initially from continued econometric reliance on the short-run Phillips curve. It was hard to cast aside a tool that had traced the United States record so well from 1954 through the late sixties. And it was easy to ignore the Friedman and Phelps attack on the stability of the short-run Phillips curve, and their prophetic warning (issued at a time when the Phillips curve was still performing admirably) that the curve would come unstuck in a prolonged period of excess demand. Unfortunately, most of the profession (including me) took too long to recognize that. Since 1970, the Phillips curve has been an unidentified flying object and has eluded all econometric efforts to nail it down.

A second major contributor to the split errors was the widespread misassessment of the inflationary significance of supply shocks, such as those in food during 1973 and in fuel during 1974 and 1979. Paradoxically, the theory that correctly predicted the shifting Phillips curve implied incorrectly that the rising prices of these items would be offset by reductions in other prices—with no significant effect on the price level at given utilization rates. Indeed, it is now clear that the shocks generate not merely a "one-shot" rise in the price level but a further inflationary chain reaction through the influence of consumer prices on wages. Here again, the policymakers and much of the profession ignored timely warnings and constructive policy prescriptions, offered, in this case, by Gordon, Perry, and me.

The third major source of split errors was the inadequate recognition of the inertial patterns of wages (and prices) in the sectors governed by implicit and explicit contracts. The experience of 1974–75 reinforced previous evidence that the first-year effect of cutting nominal GNP by $1 is a reduction between 10¢ and 20¢ in the inflation bill and a reduction in output between 80¢ and 90¢. The stark verdict emerges that, unless that split can be improved, an attack on inflation pursued solely by monetary-fiscal restraint would cost roughly $200 billion of production per point of reduction in the inflation rate.

Policymaking has suffered even more from an incorrect qualitative assessment of the broader implications of inflation than from the quantitative errors in forecasting inflation. The costs of perceived inflation are not extra trips to the bank, as most models would have it, but rather a crawl away from money. The entire system of transactions in the United States economy has been built on the dollar as a unit of account and a yardstick. Because the price level at the start of World War II was just about where it had been at the end of the Civil War, people took money seriously. The nominal unit became the foundation of our financial system, our accounting system, our corporate and personal planning and scorekeeping, our tax system, and our explicit and implicit contracts.

The crawl away from money proceeds along many lines: pressures for cost-of-living escalators; the erosion of model-year pricing and orders with guaranteed prices at delivery; the scrapping of pricing formulas that rest objectively on historical costs; the agonizing, slow shift to last in–first out (LIFO) accounting; and the transformation of capital budgeting to incorporate explicit though highly uncertain inflation forecasts.

In asset markets, portfolios shift away from long-term, fixed-interest nominal assets toward the time-honored refuges from inflation—readily resalable tangible assets such as real estate, precious metals, and art objects. But the inflation hedges are far less liquid and involve much higher transactions costs than do nominal assets. And even the most sophisticated investor cannot construct a portfolio whose real value will be neutral with respect to the inflation rate. Moreover, because various categories of prices and wages respond with differential sensitivity to the general price level, inflation is inevitably nonneutral in its micro effects: it must change relative prices and relative wages and must reshuffle real incomes in an arbitrary and haphazard way.

The obsolescence of the capital invested in the dollar as a yardstick and the enforced lottery in the income distribution make inflation extremely unpopular. Yet the government seems incapable of solving the problem; and rationally grounded fears grow that the era of chronic inflation will end ultimately only through either a prolonged deep recession or a prolonged application of stultifying price and wage controls. In this environment of uncertain and pessimistic expectations, is it really a mystery why common stocks are depressed, why capital spending is not ebullient and why it is focused on short-term projects, or why the public's confidence in our basic institutional structure and its future has plummeted?

There are ample grounds for the suspicion (previously voiced by Denison and Fellner) that various aspects of our chronic inflation may account for some of the puzzle of the productivity slowdown. In coping with the uncertain value of the dollar, buyers and sellers face genuine increases in their real transactions costs. Managerial effort is diverted from the promotion of productivity to the development of nonmonetary yardsticks. The search for inflation hedges may distort the composition of investment. Uncertainty shrinks the time horizon and creates an aversion to long-lived projects, which may embody particularly large elements of technical change. Research and development budgets may get squeezed as well in an era of mounting inflation for the same reason that desserts vanish from table d'hôte dinners. These are all conjectures, but they deserve serious investigation in the continuing effort to resolve the productivity puzzle.

A Concluding Perspective

The postwar era began with widespread anxiety about a relapse into another Great Depression. The categorical imperative of policy was to avoid such a relapse; and the success must be measured, not in dollars of real GNP, but in the very survival of United States capitalism. The formulators of the Employment Act of 1946 focused on avoiding catastrophe, but they achieved much more than that: the taming of the business cycle.

Did the crusading zeal to prevent depression bring on the subsequent disease of chronic inflation? Not in the gross ways sometimes alleged. The economy was not generally overheated: Gordon shows a net average gap of real GNP in each of the three postwar decades, relative to his estimates of the "natural" unemployment rate. Nor were investment and saving shortchanged in favor of public or private consumption: the ratio of business fixed investment to GNP compares favorably with the prewar era, and the ratio of gross private saving to GNP in years of prosperity has faithfully obeyed Denison's Law. (I note with envy that that is the one law of an economist that survived the seventies.)

But, in subtle ways, I believe that depression mentality fostered inflation vulnerability. There was an imbalance in policy: it is inconceivable that a four-year recession would have been tolerated in the way that a four-year boom was tolerated in the late sixties. And when an economy is made depression-proof and deflation-proof, private expectations and conventions become asymmetrical, introducing an inflationary bias into the system. Moreover, there was an asymmetry in the development and deployment of the macroeconomics: our analysis of the determinants of employment and output was and remains far superior to our understanding of fluctuations in the price level and their consequences. There was an imbalance, and it must be corrected through greater emphasis on the price level in the economic policymaking (and the economic analysis) of the eighties.

Bibliographical Note

The stability of postwar economic activity and the growing perception of that stability are documented in Martin Neil Baily, "Stabilization Policy and Private Economic Behavior," *BPEA, 1:1978*, pp. 13–33. The role of monetary policy during business cycles is discussed in George L. Perry, "Stabilization Policy and Inflation." In *Setting National Priorities: The Next Ten Years*, edited by Henry Owen and Charles L. Schultze (Washington, D.C.: Brookings Institution, 1976), pp. 289–93. The quotation on managing prosperity is from Gardner Ackley, "The Contribution of Economists to Policy Formation," *Journal of Finance* 21 (May 1966): 176.

Fellner's analysis of the accuracy of "Troika" forecasts of nominal GNP can be found in William Fellner, *Towards a Reconstruction of Macroeconomics: Problems of Theory and Policy* (Washington, D.C.: American Enterprise Institute, 1976), pp. 118–24.

Discussions of the contribution to overall inflation from supply shocks appear in Robert J. Gordon, "Alternative Responses of Policy to External Supply Shocks," *BPEA, 1:1975*, pp. 183–204; statement of George L. Perry, in *The 1974 Economic Report of the President*, Hearings before the Joint Economic Committee, 93d Cong. 2d sess. (Washington, D.C.: Government Printing Office, 1974), pt. 2, pp. 542–45; and Statement of Arthur Okun, in *Multinational Corporations and United States Foreign Policy*, Hearings before the Subcommittee on Multinational Corporations of the Senate Committee on Foreign Relations, 44th Cong. 1st sess. (Washington, D.C.: Government Printing Office, 1975), pt. 11, pp. 64–65. Chronic inflation is cited as possibly accounting for the recent slowdown in productivity in Edward F. Denison, *Accounting for Slower Economic Growth: The United States in the 1970s* (Washington, D.C.: Brookings Institution, 1979), pp. 135–36; and William Fellner, "The Declining Growth of American Productivity: An Introductory Note." In *Contemporary Economic Problems: 1979*, directed by William Fellner (Washington, D.C.: American Enterprise Institute, 1979), pp. 4–6.

3. Herbert Stein

Changes in Macroeconomic Conditions

One of the changes that has come over macroeconomics in the postwar period is indicated by the fact that this session is the last on the program. Surely that would not have happened ten or fifteen years ago. Then macroeconomics was the centerpiece of economics. It was the thing we understood and knew how to manage. Now we know that we don't do it very well, either as science or as policy. Moreover, and this is more important for economists, the suspicion is growing that there may not be any macroeconomics. Macroeconomics may only be a lot of microeconomics, the statistically aggregated consequences of microeconomic decisions.

Despite these uncertainties, I will talk about what we have been talking about as macroeconomics for the past thirty or forty years. I would like to relate some of the experiences of one who has been preaching macroeconomic policy during the whole postwar period under review here and from that standpoint explain some of the changes that have occurred in common thinking about the subject. I shall start with the early statements about macroeconomic policy by the Committee for Economic Development, which is a convenient approach for several reasons. The timing is appropriate because these statements came out mostly in the years from 1944 to 1948. The statements were more explicit in their economic and political reasoning than most of that time. They were representative of a certain school of thought, which used to be called "modern conservative" or some such combination of words, and the evolution of this brand of thinking is itself a matter of some contemporary interest. Also, of course, I have more personal contact with this body of thought than with any other of that period.

We were, in the first place, obsessed with the unemployment problem and with high employment as a target of economic policy. This was, of course, the common condition, and the Committee for Economic Development (CED) was less obsessed than others. In fact, after the earliest statements the CED always insisted on using the term "high employment" rather than "full employment," because full employment seemed too ambitious an objective, entailing too much danger of inflation and of government intervention in the free market. Nevertheless, CED did accept the primacy of the employment objective. For example, when it wrote about reform of the tax structure it called its proposal a tax pro-

Herbert Stein is professor of economics at the University of Virginia.

gram for high employment, and it discussed international economic policy with primary emphasis on its effects on domestic employment.

Moreover, the CED, like almost everyone else at the time, believed that the condition of high employment could be defined by a single statistic, the unemployment rate as then measured, and that the rate corresponding to high employment would, for all practical purposes, remain constant. They also thought that they knew what the number was, within a narrow range. When the committee was working on its key statement on budget policy, which called for running a small surplus at high employment, it debated whether it should define high employment as 4 percent or 5 percent unemployment. Almost twenty years had passed since the last period of extended peacetime high employment, and we had no reliable employment-unemployment statistics for the earlier periods. All we had were some horseback estimates by Sumner Slichter that the sum of seasonal and frictional unemployment would be 4 percent of the labor force. This was not, however, compelling evidence, and the committee could just as well have said 5 percent as 4 percent. The way the committee picked on 4 percent illustrates how such things are done by practical people. The committee wanted to recommend that there should be a surplus at whatever level of employment it defined as high employment. The reason it felt obliged to recommend a surplus was that it wanted to recommend use of the cash-consolidated budget, rather than the administrative budget which excluded the trust accounts and which was in more common use. But if it recommended only balancing the cash-consolidated budget it would be accused of wanting a deficit in what many people still considered the true budget, and the committee was unwilling to face that. But, given its desire to show a moderate surplus, doing that at 5 percent unemployment would require higher tax rates than doing it at 4 percent unemployment, and the committee, which included some big taxpayers, was unwilling to recommend higher taxes. So they settled for 4 percent unemployment as the definition of high employment.

This was one of the early identifications of 4 percent unemployment as the high employment target and was, I think, highly influential. By the mid-1950s, and possibly earlier, this number had become firmly established in public thinking, for no other reason, as far as I can see, than that it was conventional and to challenge it was to risk being called hardhearted. This fixation on the 4 percent unemployment rate, from which we became liberated only slowly, and are not yet fully freed, has been a major obstacle to clear thinking about macroeconomic policy during the years when I was in the government as well as at other times.

Of course, we later learned that, whatever confused idea we may have had about the meaning of high employment at the beginning, we had no good reason ever for thinking it was 4 percent. Also, if it ever had been

4 percent, it undoubtedly changed, and increased, substantially after 1955. Moreover, the changes resulted not only from exogenous forces but also from policy measures, like unemployment compensation. Moreover, the amount of misery connected with unemployment, and the feeling of guilt and responsibility on the part of the community as a whole, all changed. We also came to see that the measurement of unemployment, as disclosed by our survey techniques, had little economic significance and that the distinction between being unemployed and being out of the labor force was slight.

For all of these reasons the use of unemployment as a target of macroeconomic policy became much more controversial, uncertain, and ad hoc than it had seemed to us in 1947. In fact, subsequent developments raise the question whether we did not make a fundamental mistake then in taking unemployment or any other real magnitude as a target of macroeconomic policy. We would probably have done better to fix our attention on stabilizing some nominal variable, like nominal GNP or the price level or the rate of change of either. If we had done that the market would have given us whatever rate of employment could be permanently achieved and we would have escaped the inflationary consequences of trying to achieve an employment rate that was not permanently sustainable.

Contrary to the impressions given by some recent writing, the people of the early postwar period knew that the economy grows, that its growth is a good thing and that its growth can be influenced by public policy. That is, they were not ignorant of the supply side of the economy, even though they were understandably preoccupied, after the 1930 experience, with getting the supply utilized.

The attitudes of the CED differed from presently fashionable notions about the supply side in important respects. CED regarded the demand-side and supply-side problems as existing in two separate boxes. The demand-side problem was one of short-run stabilization. The CED did not believe that any significant contribution to the short-run problem could come from the supply-side measures because their effects would be too small and too slow.

Businessmen have a strong propensity to argue for supply-side solutions to demand-side problems because they like to argue that if you will cut taxes on us we will produce more and that will cure both unemployment and inflation. The supply-side argument is a way of arguing that what is good for us is good for you. I always remember a discussion of this at a CED meeting in 1947 or 1948 when some of the businessmen were arguing for productivity-increasing measures as the solution for inflation. Jacob Viner made what still seems to me the cogent point that the Federal Reserve could do more to create inflation by a stroke of a pen in one day than all their productivity-increasing effort could do to check inflation in a decade.

In the business community outside the CED and in the Republican party at that time there were people who took what is now the standard supply-side view. That is, during the debates over tax reduction they argued that tax cuts would increase production, cure inflation, prevent a recession, and raise the revenue. They were Lafferites before there was a Laffer curve and possibly before there was a Laffer. Insofar as there was any basis for this, other than wishfulness, it was a romantic memory of the days of Andrew Mellon, just as today's Lafferism is based on a romantic memory of the days of John Kennedy. However, CED did not go along with this.

Even if we leave aside the more extravagant claims of supply-side economics there are important issues about national policy towards growth which have persisted throughout the postwar period. These issues became especially prominent in the late 1950s and early 1960s and have come to the fore again in the last few years.

Some of you may remember this earlier period when there was a competition among presidential hopefuls to see who could promise the highest growth rate. As I remember, the competition was won by Nelson Rockefeller, who offered 5 percent a year, which did not, however, get him the presidency. Around this time CED produced a statement on economic growth which deserves a footnote in the history of economic thought because Edward Denison did the background research. Drafting this statement was a long struggle between the businessmen who wanted to make vague but expansive promises of the addition to growth that would result from certain policy changes, especially in the field of taxation, and the economists who were more reserved and skeptical. This stimulated Denison to try to measure the determinants of economic growth and led to the Denison studies that are now familiar to all of you.

The first publication of Denison's results was in a paper that he and I wrote in 1960 for President Eisenhower's Commission on National Goals. The main point was that the difference between a growth rate of 3 percent and a rate of 4 percent was not one percent as commonly thought at the time but 33.3 percent. This meant that in some sense we would have to increase the total of resources devoted to producing growth—the investment, the research, the education, and so on—by one-third, which seemed a tall order and raised the question whether it would be worthwhile. In fact, we concluded in 1960 that making the American economy grow faster was not one of our top-priority objectives.

This question looks a little different today than it did twenty years ago. Then we thought we had a built-in growth rate of 3 percent a year.

Today we don't know what we have. One can, I think, make a stronger case for trying to promote growth now than in 1960. Also, there are a number of measures that would be desirable on other grounds and that would also promote growth—such as tax changes to reduce the discrimination against investment and anti-inflationary policy. However, beyond that it is not easy to find growth-promoting measures that are clearly worth their cost—especially in view of the mystery about the causes of the slowdown in productivity growth.

Of course, the big problem which we did not adequately assess in the immediate postwar years was the inflation problem. It would be wrong to think that we were unaware of the problem. In fact, much of what we said was dictated by fear of it. A primary reason for our resistance to functional finance and discretionary fiscal policy was that, in the political process, it would lead to endless inflation. But in our naïveté we meant by endless inflation an endless rise of the price level, not an endless increase in the rate of increase of the price level.

Neither were we ignorant of the possibility of having inflation and excessive unemployment at the same time. The people in CED in the early days were much impressed with the experience of 1936–37 in this respect, and one of the first items on CED's research agenda was a study of what we then called the inflationary dilemma. Our efforts in this field never came to any fruition, however, because we never discovered anything very convincing, or perhaps because we were too reluctant to say what had to be said.

But in any case, we thought we were talking about inflation rates of 2 or 3 percent as a possible cost of high employment. I remember an occasion, I believe in 1950, when Sumner Slichter wrote a newspaper article saying that we should accept an inflation rate of 3 percent in order to have high employment. To the CED this was shocking, and also embarrassing because Slichter was chairman of our Research Advisory Board.

The critical question is how we got from such a situation in which 2 or 3 percent inflation was necessary for high employment, if we were ever in such a situation, to one in which a much higher and possibly accelerating rate is necessary. I have not heard anything in yesterday's or today's discussion of the structure of the American economy to explain that. I remain of the opinion that the main reason we have such a high rate of inflation, and find it so difficult to reduce, is that we now have a history of a high rate of inflation and that the announcement of government intentions to curb the inflation has little credibility. Therefore, I think that the early CED emphasis on fiscal and monetary restraint against inflation was correct and our mistake was in not realizing how critical it was. We did not recognize how difficult it would be to reverse course once we had gotten on the inflationary path, and therefore how essential it was not to set foot on that path. This is, to me, a reminder of how essential it is to get off that path before we move much further along it.

I must confess that the businessmen who were the members of the CED had a hankering to deliver sermons about the necessity for business and labor to behave responsibly, which translated to mean that labor should not demand such big wage increases. The staff did manage to keep such sermons muted, at least while I was there, but I nevertheless regret them.

CED was in those early days a strong believer in the effectiveness of monetary policy. We felt confirmed in that view by the behavior of the economy immediately after the war ended. The prevailing expectation of economists who belittle the importance of money was that there would be a severe postwar depression. CED held the contrary opinion that the large stock of money and other liquid assets accumulated during the war would sustain demand when wartime controls were relaxed. This turned out to be correct.

Although CED continued to emphasize the role of monetary policy it never proposed any rule of monetary policy that would complement the rule of budget policy on which it set so much store. My explanation for this may be too cynical, but I think not. The difference was that the businessmen of CED felt themselves to be outside the budget-making process and unrepresented in it. On the other hand, many of them were bankers. Many were directors of Federal Reserve Banks. All were friends of directors. That is, they wanted rules to govern a budgetary process from which they felt excluded but not to govern a monetary process of which they felt themselves a part. Still, I think that the logic of the general CED outlook, with its skepticism of the political process and mistrust of forecasting, pointed to having a monetary rule as well as a budgetary rule.

I had an opportunity to observe at first hand the possibility of running fiscal and monetary policy by rules when I came into the government in January 1969. Paul McCracken, who was the chairman of the Council of Economic Advisers, believed in a rule of budget policy much like the CED rule and he admitted, in an early press conference, to being Fried-manesque. I agreed with him on both scores. This kind of thinking was congenial to Mr. Nixon. In fact, he was an early believer in rational expectations. That is, he didn't believe that the government could fool the private sector for long.

Nevertheless, as you all know, we didn't follow any consistent rule. Of course, we weren't responsible for monetary policy, but we had ideas about it, and we couldn't even keep these ideas in line with any rule. There were several reasons for this. For one thing, the behavior of the statistics was disconcerting. During the first six or seven months of 1969 we wrote the president a number of memos saying that it would soon be necessary to get the Federal Reserve to raise the rate of growth of the money supply from 2 percent to 4 percent a year. But when the revised money supply figures came out in August we learned that they had been growing at more than 4 percent during the first half, which gave us the feeling of shooting at an erratically moving target.

There were, however, more important difficulties.

First, while you can show advantages to staying on a steady fiscal monetary path once you are on it, if you are not on it or have never been on it the movement to the path is not prescribed by the rule, and it rarely seems a good time to make that movement.

Second, even though one can demonstrate that adherence to some rule may give the best results on the average over a long period of time the policymaker is responsible for only a short period of time and the temptation to try to beat the system and do better than the rule during that period is irresistible.

Third, in our case, after the president was led by George Shultz to enunciate a rule of budget policy something like the old CED rule, which unfortunately caused Mr. Nixon to announce that he was now a Keynesian, that rule found no support in the country. The business and financial leaders, who should have welcomed the rule, hooted and hollered that it was just an excuse to run a deficit and returned to muttering about balancing the budget.

Fourth, this left the administration all alone, deserted by the fiscal conservatives and attacked by the Democrats and most economists in 1972 for not expanding the economy fast enough. The pressure to bend a rule which nobody but us cared about was too strong.

I do not say these things to excuse our failure to make a more determined effort to establish durable rules of fiscal and monetary policy but rather to try partially to explain it. Our experience with rules of macroeconomic policy raises one of the two main questions I would like to close with. I think that the history of the past twenty years shows the need for rules and limits of policy to be even greater than it seemed in the early postwar days. That is because the cure of inflation is now very much tied up with the credibility of policy. It will be necessary now not only to follow an anti-inflationary policy but also to convince the country and the world that we will follow such a policy continuously. The question is how can we show that. How can we establish new rules of policy and show that we will stick by them? Is there any middle ground between completely ad hoc discretionary policy and constitutional amendments that, even if they could be achieved, would be much cruder than we would like? Is it possible to achieve a degree of public understanding, political self-restraint, and responsible national leadership which will support a consistent credible policy? I don't know the answer to that.

My second and final question, which I can't answer either, is whether it is possible to preserve the free economic system by moderation and gradualism. The basic philosophy of CED in its early days was that it would sustain the free system by correcting its defects and abandoning its shibboleths. Thus, we would abandon traditional rules of budget balancing in order to help stabilize the system. We would support a progressive income tax in order to make the system more acceptable to the public. We would seek responsible—i.e., nonmarket—behavior of labor and business in order to forestall government controls.

Arthur Smithies once said that we in the CED were Fabians. He meant, I believe, that we, like the Fabians, were going to socialism slowly. The Fabians wanted to get there and the CED did not want to get there. But the end would be the same, and CED would have helped to reach it. CED's budget rule would not have prevented fine tuning but would have paved the way for it. CED's concession to progression in the tax system would have legitimized demands for more. CED's talk about responsible private behavior would have provided the rationale for controls and quasi controls.

I don't know whether another strategy would have been more effective. Would a more extreme and doctrinaire stance have slowed down the trend of policy to which many around this table have objected in the last two days or would it simply have left the arena of decision making exclusively to those who preferred that trend? On another day I would like to hear some wise discussion of that question.

Summary of Discussion

Alan Blinder noted that the links between inflation and relative price changes occur in two directions. Inflation probably changes relative prices, for as Okun has indicated, some prices can adjust more rapidly than others. But on the other hand, relative price changes, such as the oil price increase, also tend to exacerbate inflation. There is a facile tendency, Blinder indicated, to blame inflation for the costs of the relative price change. Blinder also held that indexation in the tax rules and the financial system could substantially reduce the costs of inflation and make it easier to fight inflation through contractionary policy.

References

Andersen, Leonall C., and Jordan, Jerry L. 1968. Monetary and fiscal action: A test of their relative importance in economic stabilization. *Federal Reserve Bank of St. Louis Review* 50:11–24.

Bach, G. L. 1971. *Making monetary and fiscal policy.* Washington, D.C.: The Brookings Institution.

Beveridge, William H. 1945. *Full employment in a free society.* New York: Norton.

Blinder, Alan S. 1978. Temporary taxes and consumer spending. NBER Working Paper no. 283. New York: National Bureau of Economic Research.

———. 1979. *Economic policy and the great stagflation.* New York: Academic Press.

———. 1980. Supply-shock inflation: Money, expectations, and accommodation. In *Development in an inflationary world,* ed. M. J. Flanders and A. Razin. New York: Academic Press.

Blinder, Alan S., and Newton, William J. 1978. The 1971–1974 controls program and the price level: An econometric post-mortem. NBER Working Paper no. 279. New York: National Bureau of Economic Research.

Brainard, William. 1967. Uncertainty and the effectiveness of policy. *American Economic Review* 57: 411–25.

Brunner, Karl. 1961. The report of the Commission on Money and Credit. *Journal of Political Economy* 69: 605–20.

Cagan, Phillip. 1975. Changes in the recession behavior of wholesale prices in the 1920s and post-World War II. *Explorations in Economic Research* 2: 54–104.

Carlson, John A. 1977. A study of price forecasts. *Annals of Economic and Social Measurement* 6: 27–56.

Clark, Peter K. 1979. Investment in the 1970s: Theory, performance, and prediction. *Brookings Papers on Economic Activity* 10: 73–113.

David, Paul A., and Solar, Peter. 1977. A Bicentenary contribution to the history of the cost of living in America. *Research in Economic History* 2: 1–80.

Denison, Edward F. 1962. *The sources of economic growth in the United States and the alternatives before us.* Washington, D.C.: Committee on Economic Development.

———. 1979. Explanations of declining productivity growth. *Survey of Current Business* 59: 1–24.

Despres, Emile; Kindleberger, Charles P.; and Salant, Walter S. 1966. The dollar and world liquidity: A minority view. *Economist,* vol. 218 (5 February).

Dunlop, John T. 1947. Wage-price relations at high-level employment. *American Economic Review* 37: 243–53.

Eckstein, Otto. 1978. *The great recession*. Amsterdam: North-Holland.

Eisner, Robert. 1969. Fiscal and monetary policy reconsidered. *American Economic Review* 59: 897–905.

Feige, Edgar L., and Pearce, Douglas K. 1973. The wage-price control experiment—did it work? *Challenge*, vol. 16.

Fisher, Irving. 1930. *The theory of interest*. New York: Macmillan.

Friedman, Milton. 1948. A monetary and fiscal framework for economic stability. *American Economic Review* 38: 245–64.

———. 1951. Comments on monetary policy. *Review of Economics and Statistics* 33: 186–91.

———. ed. 1956. *Studies in the quantity theory of money*. Chicago: University of Chicago Press.

———. 1959. The demand for money: Some theoretical and empirical results. *Journal of Political Economy* 67: 327–51.

———. 1963. *Inflation: Causes and consequences*. New Delhi: Asia Publishing House.

———. 1968. The role of monetary policy. *American Economic Review* 58: 1–17.

Friedman, Milton, and Meiselman, David. 1963. The relative stability of the investment multiplier and monetary velocity in the United States, 1897–1958. In *Stabilization policies*, ed. Commission on Money and Credit, pp. 165–268. Englewood Cliffs, N.J.: Prentice-Hall.

Friedman, Milton, and Schwartz, Anna. 1963. *A monetary history of the United States, 1867–1960*. Princeton: Princeton University Press.

Goldfeld, Stephen M. 1973. The demand for money revisited. *Brookings Papers on Economic Activity* 4: 577–638.

Goldfeld, Stephen M., and Blinder, Alan S. 1972. Some implications of endogenous stabilization policy. *Brookings Papers on Economic Activity* 3: 585–640.

Gordon, R. A. 1974. *Economic instability and growth: The American record*. New York: Harper and Row.

Gordon, Robert J. 1970. The Brookings model in action: A review article. *Journal of Political Economy* 78: 489–525.

———. 1971. Notes on money, income, and Gramlich. *Journal of Money, Credit, and Banking* 3: 533–45.

———. 1972. Wage-price controls and the shifting Phillips curve. *Brookings Papers on Economic Activity* 3: 385–421.

———. 1975a. Alternative responses of policy to external supply shocks. *Brookings Papers on Economic Activity* 6: 183–206.

———. 1975b. The demand for and supply of inflation. *Journal of Law and Economics* 18: 807–36.

————. 1978. *Macroeconomics*. Boston: Little, Brown.

————. 1979a. Monetary policy and the 1979 supply shock. NBER Working Paper 418, January 1980. Cambridge: National Bureau of Economic Research.

————. 1979b. The "end-of-expansion" phenomenon in U.S. short-run productivity behavior. *Brookings Papers on Economic Activity* 10: 447–61.

————. 1980. Characterizing shifts in the cyclical flexibility of wages and prices since 1900. *American Economic Review* 70. In press.

Gordon, Robert J., and Wilcox, James. 1980. Monetarist interpretations of the Great Depression: An evaluation and critique. In *Contemporary views of the great depression*, ed. K. Brunner. Rochester: University of Rochester.

Graham, Benjamin. 1947. National productivity: Its relationships to unemployment-in-prosperity. *American Economic Review* 37: 384–96.

Gramlich, Edward M. 1979. Macro policy responses to price shocks. *Brookings Papers on Economic Activity* 10: 125–78.

Gurley, John G. 1960. The Radcliffe report and evidence. *American Economic Review* 50: 672–700.

Heller, Walter W. 1966. *New dimensions of political economy*. New York: Norton.

Hickman, Bert G., and Coen, Robert M. 1976. *An annual growth model of the U.S. economy*. New York: American Elsevier.

Houthakker, Hendrick S. 1976. *The world price of oil*. Washington, D.C.: American Enterprise Institute.

Johnson, Harry G. 1962. Monetary theory and policy. *American Economic Review* 52: 335–84.

Lucas, Robert E., Jr. 1973. Some international evidence on output-inflation trade-offs. *American Economic Review* 63: 326–34.

————. 1976. Econometric policy evaluation: A critique. In *The Phillips curve and labor markets*, ed. K. Brunner and A. H. Meltzer, pp. 19–46. Vol. 1 of a supplementary series to the *Journal of Monetary Economics*.

Modigliani, Franco. 1977. The monetarist controversy or, should we forsake stabilization policies? *American Economic Review* 67: 1–25.

Modigliani, Franco, and Papedemos, Lucas. 1975. Targets for monetary policy in the coming year. *Brookings Papers on Economic Activity* 6: 141–63.

Mundell, Robert A. 1963. Inflation and real interest. *Journal of Political Economy* 71 (June): 280–83.

Nordhaus, William D. 1975. The political business cycle. *Review of Economic Studies* 42 (April): 169–90.

Okun, Arthur M. 1962. Potential GNP: Its measurement and significance. In *Proceedings of the Business and Economic Statistics Section*, pp. 98–104. American Statistical Association.

————. 1968. Measuring the impact of the 1964 tax reduction. In *Perspectives on economic growth*, ed. Walter W. Heller. New York: Random House.

————. 1975. Inflation: Its mechanics and welfare costs. *Brookings Papers on Economic Activity* 6: 351–90.

Perloff, Jeffrey M., and Wachter, Michael L. 1979. A production function-nonaccelerating inflation approach to potential output: Is measured potential output too high? In *Three aspects of policy and policymaking: Knowledge, data and institutions*, ed. K. Brunner and A. H. Meltzer, pp. 113–64. Vol. 10 of a supplementary series to the *Journal of Monetary Economics*.

Phelps, Edmund S. 1967. Phillips curves, expectations of inflation and optimal unemployment policy over time. *Economica* 34: 254–81.

————. 1968. Money-wage dynamics and labor-market equilibrium. *Journal of Political Economy* 76: 678–711.

————. 1978. Commodity-supply shock and full-employment monetary policy. *Journal of Money, Credit, and Banking* 10: 206–21.

Phelps, Edmund S., and Winter, Sidney G., Jr. 1970. Optimal price policy under atomistic competition. In *Microeconomic foundations of employment and inflation theory*, ed. Edmund S. Phelps et al. New York: Norton.

Phillips, A. W. 1958. The relation between unemployment and the rate of change of money wage rates in the United Kingdom, 1861–1957. *Economica*, n.s., 25 (November): 283–99.

Poole, William. 1970. Optimal choice of monetary policy instruments in a simple stochastic macro model. *Quarterly Journal of Economics* 84: 197–216.

Sachs, Jeffrey. 1980. The changing cyclical behavior of wages and prices, 1890–1976. *American Economic Review* 70: 78–90.

Samuelson, Paul A. 1951. *Economics*. 2d ed. New York: McGraw-Hill.

Samuelson, Paul A., and Solow, Robert M. 1960. Analytical aspects of anti-inflation policy. *American Economic Review* 50: 177–94.

Sargent, Thomas J., and Wallace, Neil. 1975. Rational expectations, the optimal monetary instrument, and the optimal money supply rule. *Journal of Political Economy* 83: 241–57.

Schultze, Charles L. 1959. *Recent inflation in the United States*. In *Study of employment, growth, and price levels*, Joint Economic Committee, Study Paper no. 1. Washington, D.C.: Government Printing Office.

Seltzer, Lawrence H. 1945. Is a rise in interest rates desirable or inevitable? *American Economic Review* 35: 831–50.

Solow, Robert M. 1956. A contribution to the theory of economic growth. *Quarterly Journal of Economics* 70: 65–94.

————. 1957. Technical change and the aggregate production function. *Review of Economics and Statistics* 39: 312–20.

Stein, Herbert. 1969. *The fiscal revolution in America.* Chicago: University of Chicago Press.

Temin, Peter. 1976. *Did monetary forces cause the Great Depression?* New York: Norton.

Tobin, James. 1953. Monetary policy and the management of the public debt: The Patman inquiry. *Review of Economics and Statistics* 35: 118–27.

————. 1955. A dynamic aggregate model. *Journal of Political Economy* 63: 103–15.

————. 1964. Economic growth as an objective of government policy. *American Economic Review* 54: 1–20.

Vogel, Ezra. 1979. *Japan as number one: Lessons for America.* Cambridge: Harvard University Press.

Wachter, Michael L. 1976. The changing cyclical responsiveness of wage inflation. *Brookings Papers on Economic Activity* 7: 115–59.

Will, George F. 1979. The illusion of progress. *Newsweek* 94:59.

3

Trends in United States International Trade and Investment since World War II

1. William H. Branson
2. Herbert Giersch
3. Peter G. Peterson

1. William H. Branson

3.1 Introduction and Summary

At the end of World War II the United States was by far the dominant industrial economy in the world. With industrial capacity largely destroyed in Europe and Japan, the United States produced more than 60 percent of the world's output of manufactures in the late 1940s. As a result, the United States was a net exporter of manufactured goods of all kinds; historically the United States was a net importer of consumer goods, but in 1947 there was a net export surplus of $1 billion in that category. Thus in the immediate postwar years, the pattern of United States trade was distorted by a relative strength in manufacturing that was transitory. The recovery of the European and Japanese economies in the 1950s and 1960s, and the growth of manufacturing capacity in the developing countries in the 1960s and 1970s inevitably reduced the United States share of world output and of world exports. The evolution of United States trade patterns since World War II has been strongly

William H. Branson is professor of economics and international affairs at Princeton University.

I would like to thank Jacques Artus of the IMF, Christopher Bach and Howard Munad of the United States Department of Commerce, and Arthur Neef of the United States Department of Labor for providing data and advising on its interpretation, and the National Science Foundation for research support. Robert Baldwin and Robert Stern provided useful comments, and thanks also go to Howard Kaufold and Iqbal Zaidi for invaluable research assistance, and to Joyce Mix for typing and organizing.

influenced by these initial postwar conditions. By the 1970s, trade patterns reflecting underlying comparative advantage had been restored, and the United States was once again an importer of consumer goods.

The United States international investment position just after World War II was miniscule. In 1950, its private long-term assets abroad totaled $17.5 billion; foreign investment in the United States was $8 billion. Thus while the United States was very open to trade at that point, there was little international ownership of assets. The United States long-term foreign asset and liability positions have both grown steadily at about 10 percent per year since 1950. This has resulted in an internationalization of investment over the same period in which the United States lost its dominant position in trade.

This paper presents and analyzes the data on the trends in United States international trade and investment since World War II. From this data we can perceive a shrinking United States fraction of manufacturing output and exports, a return to and strengthening of lines of comparative advantage, and balanced and rapid growth in long-term investment. We can also see increasing volatility of trade and long-term investment in the 1970s, along with a real depreciation of 25 percent in the weighted United States exchange rate.

Section 3.2 sets the framework for this analysis by studying trends in the United States position in the world economy since 1950. The United States trend real growth rate has been the lowest in the industrial world, while the European and Japanese economies recovered. Its share of manufacturing output shrank from 1950 to the 1970s, while its share of manufactured exports stabilized at about 13 percent since 1970. United States costs have risen at a rate that is about average for the industrial countries, and the dollar devaluation of the 1970s has resulted in a significant real depreciation.

Section 3.3 studies the trends in United States trade and comparative advantage since World War II against the background of data going back to 1925. The postwar export bulge was eliminated by the mid-1950s, and a stable pattern of trade emerged. It shows export surpluses in capital goods, chemicals, and agriculture and deficits in consumer goods and nonagricultural industrial inputs. Trade in automotive products switched from surplus to deficit in 1968, and of course energy imports soared in the 1970s. At the four-digit end-use code level one can also discern patterns of trade that are consistent with the internationalization of investment and production.

Trends in long-term investment position are summarized in section 3.4. It shows a picture of remarkably steady and balanced growth, with international assets and liabilities both growing at 10 percent or so a year. The data on direct investment are disaggregated by country and industry. United States investment abroad has been increasingly directed toward Europe, whose share of total United States direct investment rose from 15 percent in 1950 to over 40 percent in 1977. To a large extent, direct investment has gone to the industrial economies, rather than to the developing countries. Foreign investment in the United States has been mainly European throughout, with a share of 66 percent in the 1950s and the 1970s.

Developments in the balance of payments, reserves, and exchange rates are discussed in section 3.5, which shows a trend from surplus to deficit in the United States basic balance (current account plus long-term capital), and a marked increase in the volatility of the basic balance (as measured by time series variance) from the 1960s to the 1970s. This increase in volatility has raised significantly the size of variation in reserves that would be needed to fix exchange rates. The result has been *more* movement in reserves with "floating" rates in the 1970s than with "fixed" rates in the 1960s.

It is difficult to summarize briefly the impression created by this intensive review of the data, but perhaps it is worth a try. At the end of World War II the United States dominated an industrial world that was tied together economically mainly by trade. This was clearly a temporary position, at least in hindsight. Gradually, over thirty-five years, the other industrial countries have caught up with the United States, restoring a kind of economic balance to the world picture. At the same time, international investment has thickened the connections of the United States to the world economy. My impression is that the United States has moved from a position of dominance to being one of several roughly equal centers, with increasingly tight economic interconnections among them.

3.2 Broad Trends in the United States Position in the World Economy

At the end of World War II, the United States was the dominant industrial producer in the world. With industrial capacity destroyed in Europe—except for Scandinavia—and in Japan and crippled in the United Kingdom, the United States produced approximately 60 percent of the world output of manufactures in 1950, and its GNP was 61 percent of the total of the present (1979) OECD countries. This was obviously a transitory situation. During the 1950s the European economies recovered and rebuilt capacity, competing with the United States in world markets. Japan entered the competition in a major way in the 1960s, and in the 1970s several developing countries became significant in terms of aggregate world output and trade in manufactures.

Thus during the thirty-five years since World War II, Europe, Japan and then the less developed countries (LDCs) have grown faster than the United States in terms of real GDP and industrial output, both aggregate and per capita. This has resulted in a shrinking United States share of world output and exports and a closing of productivity differentials.

As its competitors' capacity grew faster than that of the United States, real depreciation of the dollar was required to keep trade and current account balances in line. This depreciation was delayed by monetary arrangements under the Bretton Woods agreements, which resisted change in the dollar exchange rate. Thus instead of a gradual real *depre*ciation, a small real *ap*preciation appeared in the late 1960s, contributing to a growing trade imbalance. Once the Bretton Woods system broke down, a significant real depreciation of the dollar occurred during the 1970s, helping to restore balance in trade among the industrial countries.

By 1980, the United States will have moved from a position of dominance to a position of equality or symmetry among groups of industrial countries. Its share of OECD real GNP is now (1979) 39 percent, and its share of world industrial production is about 35 percent, compared with 40 percent as late as 1963. Its share of world exports of manufactures has fallen from 29 percent in 1953 to 17 percent in 1963 and 13 percent in 1976. The weighted real exchange rate of the United States (in index terms, 1975 = 100) has depreciated from around 83 in 1961 to 106 in 1978. The United States economy is now part of a world of nearly symmetric interdependence.

Data are presented below that describe and summarize the change in the United States position in the world economy since World War II, examining first comparative trends in production, then competitiveness and trade, and finally exchange rates. These data set the framework for subsequent analysis of trends in United States international transactions.

3.2.1   Measures of Trends in Output

Real GDP

United States real GDP has grown more slowly along trend than that of the other major industrial countries since World War II. Table 3.1 shows index numbers for real GDP for seven major countries: the United States, Canada, Japan, France, West Germany, Italy, and the United Kingdom. The data are indexed to 1967 = 100. Among these countries, only the United Kingdom had a slower growth rate to 1967 (27 percent per year versus 3.5 percent for the United States). This is also true of the period since 1967, during which the United States growth rate has been 2.3 percent per year.

Real GDP per Capita and per Worker

More interesting than aggregate real GDP data are real GDP per capita and per worker. These summarize both income per capita and productivity trends in terms of domestic prices and over the entire economy.

Table 3.2 shows index numbers for GDP per capita in the same set

Table 3.1 **Index of Real Gross Domestic Product, Own Country Price Weights, 1967 = 100**

Year	United States	Canada	Japan	France	Germany	Italy	United Kingdom
1950	53.0	43.6	21.3	44.0	33.6	39.4	62.0
1955	65.1	56.3	33.0	53.8	52.7	52.6	72.2
1960	73.2	68.5	49.7	68.6	76.7	68.8	81.5
1965	91.8	90.3	80.2	90.8	97.7	88.3	95.4
1966	97.4	96.7	88.9	95.5	100.2	93.4	97.5
1967	100.0	100.0	100.0	100.0	100.0	100.0	100.0
1968	104.4	105.6	114.1	104.3	106.3	106.3	103.6
1969	107.1	111.1	128.0	111.5	114.6	112.3	105.3
1970	106.8	114.0	142.8	117.9	121.5	118.0	107.7
1971	109.8	121.9	150.2	124.3	125.4	119.8	110.4
1972	116.2	129.0	164.3	131.7	130.0	123.6	112.7
1973	122.5	138.8	180.6	138.7	136.3	132.1	121.8
1974	120.9	143.7	180.0	143.2	137.1	137.8	119.8
1975	119.5	145.5	182.5	143.7	134.4	133.0	117.8
1976	126.4	153.9	194.1	150.3	141.1	140.5	121.9
1977	133.0	158.3	204.2	154.9	144.9	143.4	123.6
1978	138.4	163.8	216.0	159.6	149.4	146.9	127.9

Source: Department of Labor.

Table 3.2 **Index of Gross Domestic Product per Capita, 1967 = 100**

Year	United States	Canada	Japan	France	Germany	Italy	United Kingdom
1950	69.5	64.9	25.7	52.1	42.4	44.4	67.4
1955	78.3	73.2	37.1	61.3	63.5	56.9	77.6
1960	80.5	76.0	53.3	74.4	82.1	72.2	85.0
1965	93.9	93.7	81.8	92.3	98.8	89.5	96.4
1966	98.4	98.4	89.9	96.3	100.4	94.0	98.0
1967	100.0	100.0	100.0	100.0	100.0	100.0	100.0
1968	103.3	104.0	112.7	103.5	105.9	105.7	103.1
1969	105.0	107.8	125.0	109.8	113.1	111.0	104.4
1970	103.6	109.1	138.1	115.1	118.7	115.8	106.5
1971	105.4	115.3	142.1	120.2	121.3	116.8	108.8
1972	110.6	120.7	153.2	126.2	124.9	110.6	110.7
1973	115.7	128.3	166.1	131.9	130.4	126.7	119.4
1974	113.3	131.0	163.4	135.3	130.9	130.9	117.4
1975	111.2	130.6	163.6	135.1	128.8	125.5	115.4
1976	116.7	136.4	172.1	140.8	135.9	131.8	119.6
1977	121.9	138.8	179.3	144.6	140.0	133.8	121.3
1978	126.2	142.3	187.9	148.4	144.5	136.5	125.6

Source: Department of Labor.

Table 3.3   Average Annual Growth Rate of Real GDP per Capita
                   (in Percentages)

Country	1950–55	1955–60	1960–65	1965–70	1970–75	1975–78
United States	2.38	0.55	3.08	1.97	1.42	4.22
Canada	2.41	1.27	3.67	3.04	3.60	2.86
Japan	7.34	7.25	8.57	10.47	3.39	4.62
France	3.25	3.87	4.31	4.42	3.20	3.13
Germany	8.08	5.14	3.70	3.67	1.63	3.83
Italy	4.96	4.76	4.30	5.15	1.61	2.80
United Kingdom	2.82	1.82	2.52	1.99	1.61	2.82

of industrial countries, and table 3.3 gives the five-year average growth rates. In terms of per capita GDP, the United States growth rate is slightly lower than that of the United Kingdom, and much lower than those of the other major countries. The growth rate summary in table 3.3 shows a general deceleration of growth in the industrial world, throughout the period 1950–78, with the United States growth rate consistently slower than the others.

Tables 3.4 and 3.5 show index numbers and the growth rate summary for real GDP per employed worker, coming closer to a home currency

Table 3.4   Index of Real GDP per Employed Person, Own Country Price
                   Weights, 1967 = 100

Year	United States	Canada	Japan	France	Germany (2)	Italy	United Kingdom
1950	68.2	65.8	29.4	45.9	44.3	41.6	68.1
1955	77.7	78.0	40.5	56.0	60.9	53.3	75.8
1960	83.4	85.4	55.2	71.0	76.4	65.1	84.0
1965	96.8	98.4	83.6	91.9	94.4	87.6	94.4
1966	99.7	99.4	90.8	95.9	100.9	94.5	96.2
1967	100.0	100.0	100.0	100.0	100.0	100.0	100.0
1968	102.2	103.8	112.0	103.4	106.2	106.6	104.2
1969	102.4	105.9	124.4	109.0	112.9	113.8	105.9
1970	101.6	107.6	137.2	114.3	118.2	119.3	109.0
1971	104.3	112.4	143.4	119.7	121.7	121.4	113.8
1972	107.4	115.5	156.4	125.8	126.5	127.6	115.5
1973	109.9	118.1	167.7	130.8	132.4	135.3	122.2
1974	106.7	117.2	167.8	134.0	135.6	138.4	120.1
1975	107.0	117.5	170.6	136.9	137.4	132.9	118.9
1976	109.7	121.7	179.8	142.4	145.8	139.5	122.8
1977	111.7	123.0	186.7	145.8	150.1	141.6	124.2
1978	112.0	123.2	195.1	150.0	154.8	144.4	128.1

Source: Department of Labor.

Table 3.5   **Average Annual Growth Rate of Real GDP per Employed Worker (in Percentages)**

Country	1950–55	1955–60	1960–65	1965–70	1970–75	1975–78
United States	2.61	1.42	2.98	0.97	1.04	1.52
Canada	3.40	1.81	2.83	1.79	1.76	1.58
Japan	6.41	6.19	8.30	9.91	4.36	4.47
France	3.98	4.75	5.16	4.36	3.61	3.05
Germany	6.36	4.53	4.23	4.50	3.01	3.97
Italy	4.96	4.00	5.94	6.18	2.16	2.77
United Kingdom	2.14	2.05	2.33	2.88	1.74	2.48

productivity measure. The United States growth rate in these terms is relatively slower than in terms of GDP per capita. Over the entire period 1950–78, the United States growth rate was 1.7 percent per year; the next slowest was the United Kingdom with 2.2 percent.

Manufacturing Output per Hour

More precise estimates of trends in productivity are given in tables 3.6 and 3.7, for output per hour in manufacturing. Since manufactures are an important component of tradable goods, this brings us closer to fundamental movements in relative competitiveness, as well. In table 3.6 we can see that the United States and United Kingdom trends in manufacturing productivity have been about the same over the entire period; the United States growth rate for 1950–78 is 2.4 percent per year, while that for the United Kingdom is 2.5 percent. Both are well below the trends in the other countries. Table 3.7 shows the general deceleration in productivity growth; the United States is consistently low.

Tables 3.1 through 3.7 document the fact that the United States growth in output and productivity in manufacturing since 1950 has been slower than that of the other major industrial countries. This is the case even before adjustment for the major movements in exchange rates and the terms of trade in the 1970s. This phenomenon has permitted the other industrial countries to converge toward the United States level of productivity as of the late 1970s. The data imply a decline in the United States share of world output as the others catch up in productivity terms.

Shares of World Manufacturing Output

Calculation of shares of world manufacturing output is difficult because we have no firm data on the world aggregate. Thus any share calculation gives the share of a given country in total output of a group of industrial countries known to produce perhaps 90 percent of the world total. Share calculations have become even more difficult in the 1970s with the growth of manufacturing in the newly industrializing

Table 3.6   Index of Output per Hour in Manufacturing, 1950–78,
                   1967 = 100

Year	United States	Canada	Japan	France	Germany	Italy	United Kingdom
1950	65.0	51.6	21.5	43.9	37.3	35.0	62.5
1951	67.1	53.7	26.8	46.2	38.5	39.0	62.6
1952	68.3	55.2	28.2	47.7	42.1	40.6	60.0
1953	69.5	57.1	32.1	50.2	45.1	42.6	62.9
1954	70.6	59.6	34.3	51.6	47.0	44.9	64.9
1955	74.1	63.4	36.0	54.2	50.0	48.8	66.9
1956	73.5	66.1	38.4	57.7	51.3	51.5	67.0
1957	75.1	66.5	41.9	58.6	55.8	52.5	68.6
1958	74.7	68.8	39.2	60.9	58.6	53.4	69.8
1959	78.0	72.5	45.6	65.3	63.3	57.5	72.7
1960	78.9	75.1	52.6	68.7	67.8	61.2	77.0
1961	80.8	79.2	59.3	71.9	71.4	66.1	77.7
1962	84.5	83.3	61.9	75.2	75.8	73.2	79.6
1963	90.5	86.5	67.1	79.7	79.3	75.2	83.9
1964	95.2	90.3	75.9	83.7	85.2	79.6	89.8
1965	98.3	93.7	79.1	88.5	90.7	88.5	92.5
1966	99.7	96.9	87.1	94.7	93.9	94.4	95.8
1967	100.0	100.0	100.0	100.0	100.0	100.0	100.0
1968	103.6	106.8	112.6	111.4	106.9	107.9	107.3
1969	104.8	113.1	130.0	115.4	113.4	116.1	108.6
1970	104.5	114.7	146.5	121.2	116.1	121.7	108.8
1971	110.1	122.9	151.0	127.6	121.4	125.2	113.2
1972	115.7	128.5	162.3	135.1	128.7	135.3	121.5
1973	118.8	134.3	181.2	142.5	136.6	151.7	127.6
1974	112.6	136.6	181.7	146.6	145.0	159.7	127.7
1975	118.2	133.3	174.6	150.7	151.3	152.9	124.2
1976	123.4	139.4	188.7	163.6	160.3	165.9	127.9
1977	127.5	146.1	199.2	171.7	160.3	165.9	126.5
1978	128.9	152.2	215.7	180.2	175.3	172.7	128.6

Source: Department of Labor.

countries (NICs) among the LDCs. Therefore I show here two sets of share data. The first is across an aggregate of ten major industrial countries since 1950; the second is across an OECD estimate of world output since 1963.

Shares of total manufacturing output across ten major OECD countries since 1950 are shown in table 3.8. Share data can be computed from underlying data supplied by the U.S. Department of Labor by one of two ways. The first is to use real output data by country, converted to a common valuation using a fixed nominal exchange rate. This is the method used for table 3.8, using 1967 exchange rates. The implicit PPP

Table 3.7   **Average Annual Growth Rate of Output per Hour in Manufacturing**

Country	1950–55	1955–60	1960–65	1965–70	1970–75	1975–78
United States	2.62	1.26	4.40	1.22	2.46	2.89
Canada	4.12	3.39	4.43	4.04	3.01	4.42
Japan	10.31	7.58	8.16	12.33	3.51	7.05
France	4.21	4.74	5.06	6.29	4.36	5.96
Germany	5.86	6.09	5.82	4.94	5.30	4.91
Italy	6.65	4.53	7.38	6.37	4.56	4.06
United Kingdom	1.36	2.81	3.67	3.25	2.65	1.16

assumption in this calculation is that nominal exchange rate movements, at least along trend, have followed relative price movements. The second way to perform the calculation would be to use nominal output data and convert them at current exchange rates. If the PPP assumption 1950–78, the United States growth rate was 1.7 percent per year; the were correct, the two calculations would be the same. But if the assumption is incorrect, the nominal cum current rate calculation will distort the share data.

In table 3.8 we see that the United States share of major industrial countries' total manufacturing output has indeed been shrinking—from 62 percent in 1950 to 44 percent in 1977. The countries gaining shares within the table 3.8 subset were certain European countries in the 1950s and 1960s, and Japan in the period since 1955.

The share data of table 3.8 omit manufacturing output in the developing countries, including the Southern European OECD. However, a

Table 3.8   **Shares of Total Manufacturing Output in Ten Industrial Countries, 1950–77**

Countries	Percentage Share of Total						
	1950	1955	1960	1965	1970	1975	1977
United States	61.9	58.1	50.5	50.1	43.6	42.5	44.0
Canada	3.5	3.4	3.3	3.5	3.4	3.7	3.6
Japan	2.1	3.5	6.3	8.0	13.1	13.2	13.4
Denmark	0.7	0.5	0.6	0.6	0.7	0.7	0.7
France	7.6	7.1	8.1	8.1	8.9	9.8	9.6
Germany	10.1	14.1	17.2	16.7	17.2	16.5	16.0
Italy	2.2	2.5	3.1	3.1	3.7	4.3	4.3
Netherlands	1.8	1.9	2.2	2.1	2.3	2.3	2.2
Sweden	2.0	1.7	1.9	1.9	1.9	2.0	1.6
United Kingdom	8.2	7.2	6.9	5.9	5.3	4.9	4.5

Source: Department of Labor.

major development of the 1970s has been growth of output in the NICs. This has brought them into competition with the industrialized countries in markets for manufacturing, raising fears of a "new protectionism." Table 3.9 provides estimates of the distribution of world output of manufactures since 1963, including the LDCs.

In the first row of table 3.9 the United States share of world output falls from 40 percent in 1963 to 37 percent in 1970 and 35 percent in 1975–76. The rise in 1977 is probably due to the United States recovery that was not matched by European growth. The 1980–81 slowdown

Table 3.9   **Geographical Distribution of World Industrial Production Percentages and Index Numbers**

	1963	1970	1973	1974	1975	1976	1977
Major Industrial Countries							
United States	40.25	36.90	36.59	36.30	34.97	35.42	36.90
Japan	5.48	9.28	9.74	9.28	8.88	9.06	9.14
Germany	9.69	9.84	9.19	8.95	8.98	8.97	8.85
France	6.30	6.30	6.25	6.35	6.25	6.25	6.15
United Kingdom	6.46	5.26	4.78	4.61	4.67	4.29	4.16
Italy	3.44	3.49	3.29	3.43	3.28	3.41	3.33
Canada	3.01	3.01	3.08	3.16	3.17	3.08	3.08
Newly Industrializing Countries							
Spain	0.88	1.18	1.37	1.48	1.47	1.43	1.56
Portugal	0.23	0.27	0.30	0.31	0.31	0.30	0.32
Greece	0.19	0.25	0.30	0.30	0.33	0.33	0.33
Yugoslavia	1.14	1.25	1.31	1.43	1.60	1.53	1.62
Brazil	1.57	1.73	2.10	2.25	2.47	2.49	—
Mexico	1.04	1.27	1.30	1.38	1.54	1.44	1.45
Hong Kong	0.08	0.15	0.18	0.17	0.17	0.21	—
Korea	0.11	0.22	0.32	0.41	0.51	0.63	0.69
Taiwan	0.11	0.23	0.34	0.33	0.37	0.42	0.46
Singapore	0.05	0.06	0.08	0.08	0.09	0.09	0.10
Total "Gang of 4"	0.35	0.66	0.92	0.99	1.14	1.35	—
Total NICs	5.40	6.61	7.60	8.14	8.86	8.87	(9.28)
Other developed countries[a]	10.99	9.72	9.83	9.73	10.58	9.90	9.29
Other developing countries	8.98	9.59	9.65	10.05	10.36	10.75	9.30
India	1.21	1.11	1.03	1.04	1.15	1.17	1.19
Argentina	0.94	1.07	1.09	1.14	1.18	1.06	1.06
World	100.0	100.0	100.0	100.0	100.0	100.0	100.0
World (1970 = 100)	66.0	100.0	121.0	122.0	115.0	125.0	129.0

Sources: *The Growth of World Industry*, and *Monthly Bulletin of Statistics*, United Nations; IMF Statistics; Secretariat estimates.

Notes: The Eastern bloc is excluded from all World calculations. Figures for 1970 represent value added; those for other years are based on industrial production indexes.

[a]All other OECD countries plus South Africa and Israel.

will restore the United States share relationship. Most of the other developed countries in the top tier of table 3.9 have also had shrinking shares in the 1970s. In this decade the gainers have been the NICs, shown in the middle tier in the table. On aggregate, their share has risen from 5.4 percent in 1963 to 6.6 percent in 1970 and about 9 percent in 1975–77. Thus in terms of share of world output in manufacturing, those of the ten NICs have nearly doubled from 1963–77.

An interesting subset of the NICs is the Gang of Four: Hong Kong, Korea, Taiwan, Singapore. Their share of world manufactures output has risen from 0.4 in 1963 to 0.7 in 1970 and 1.4 in 1976, a tripling in fifteen years. Thus the major gainers during the 1970s have been the industrializing LDCs collectively, with the United States share shrinking from 37 percent to 35 percent of the estimated world total.

3.2.2   Trends in Competitiveness

With manufacturing capacity and output growing relatively rapidly in Europe, Japan, and the LDCs, a significant improvement in United States competitiveness would have been required to hold the United States share of world markets. During the period 1950–70, in general, United States costs relative to those of its competitors, adjusted for exchange rate changes, did not decline. The result was a shrinking United States share of world trade in manufactures. After 1970, the depreciation of the United States dollar led to an improvement in United States competitiveness of about 40 percent (1970–78), and the United States share of world manufactures exports stabilized at about 13 percent.

Index numbers for unit labor costs in manufacturing, adjusted for exchange rate changes, are shown in table 3.10 for seven major industrial countries. Their growth rates are summarized in table 3.11. During the period 1950–70 the increase in unit labor cost in the United States was in the middle of the league. Over that twenty-year period the average annual growth rate of unit labor cost in the United States was 2.6 percent, the same as Italy, faster than Canada, Japan, and France, and slower than Germany and the United Kingdom. In table 3.10 it is clear that the growth rate of unit labor cost in Germany is exaggerated by the choice of 1970 as the terminal year; the 1950–69 growth rate is 2.8 percent, almost the same as that of the United States. Thus during the Bretton Woods period, while the rest of the world expanded capacity relative to the United States, unit labor cost in the United States rose at about the same rate as did that of its competitors.

This flat relative trend is confirmed in the IMF-weighted competitiveness indexes. Table 3.12 shows the ratio of the United States unit labor cost to a trade-weighted average of fourteen competitors' unit labor costs, adjusted for exchange rate changes. This is an index of cyclically adjusted relative "normal" unit labor cost, computed by the IMF. Fol-

Table 3.10   Indexes of Unit Labor Costs in Manufacturing, United States Dollar Basis, 1950–78, 1967 = 100

Year	United States	Canada	Japan	France	Germany	Italy	United Kingdom
1950	69.4	75.2	83.2	69.1	61.1	70.6	54.7
1951	73.9	84.9	85.0	84.2	68.3	69.4	59.3
1952	77.3	97.6	93.3	94.3	66.7	71.9	67.7
1953	80.2	98.6	86.0	92.3	65.3	73.6	68.3
1954	82.5	100.8	88.1	94.8	64.7	72.7	69.9
1955	81.6	96.4	87.9	97.2	64.8	72.3	72.3
1956	87.5	97.7	85.9	98.4	68.3	73.9	78.6
1957	90.8	106.3	82.7	86.9	70.2	75.2	81.4
1958	95.4	106.8	90.1	81.5	72.7	77.8	85.7
1959	94.8	106.5	86.1	79.3	73.2	75.2	84.9
1960	97.7	106.9	82.5	81.5	76.5	76.5	85.5
1961	98.3	99.7	84.7	85.8	84.7	78.3	91.1
1962	97.7	92.4	92.8	90.3	90.7	83.4	93.7
1963	94.2	91.4	95.6	94.2	92.8	96.1	92.8
1964	93.4	90.9	94.8	96.4	93.3	101.0	92.7
1965	92.6	92.0	102.5	98.2	94.4	97.1	98.6
1966	95.4	96.0	102.5	97.7	100.4	95.1	103.0
1967	100.0	100.0	100.0	100.0	100.0	100.0	100.0
1968	103.3	100.6	103.8	101.2	99.1	99.0	86.9
1969	108.7	102.1	107.2	96.7	103.5	104.3	92.6
1970	116.5	111.7	113.2	96.7	125.7	119.2	104.8
1971	117.6	116.1	130.7	102.9	142.8	135.6	117.4
1972	118.1	122.0	159.7	118.4	164.3	152.2	125.7
1973	123.2	127.0	195.2	146.3	211.7	172.5	130.2
1974	143.1	147.7	237.3	157.7	236.2	182.6	154.7
1975	152.4	166.6	284.8	206.2	268.5	245.1	196.2
1976	158.2	187.4	285.3	195.1	265.4	212.5	182.9
1977	166.6	183.7	326.5	207.5	299.4	234.9	196.9
1978	179.4	175.8	412.0	243.9	358.3	270.4	249.0

Source: Department of Labor.

Table 3.11   Average Annual Growth Rate of Unit Labor Cost in United States Dollars (in Percentages)

Country	1950–55	1955–60	1960–65	1965–70	1970–75	1975–78
United States	3.2	3.6	−1.1	4.6	5.3	5.4
Canada	5.0	2.1	−3.0	3.9	8.0	1.8
Japan	1.1	−1.3	4.3	2.0	18.5	12.3
France	6.8	−3.5	3.7	−0.3	15.1	5.6
Germany	1.2	3.3	4.2	5.7	15.2	9.6
Italy	0.5	1.1	4.8	4.1	14.4	3.3
United Kingdom	5.6	3.4	2.9	1.2	12.5	7.9

Table 3.12   **Index of United States Weighted Relative Unit Labor Cost, 1975 = 100**

Year	Relative Cost Index	Year	Relative Cost Index
1961	152.6	1970	144.8
1962	151.8	1971	137.0
1963	151.0	1972	123.9
1964	151.2	1973	110.1
1965	148.1	1974	105.8
1966	147.5	1975	100.0
1967	148.1	1976	105.1
1968	151.4	1977	104.2
1969	151.2	1978	96.5

Source: International Monetary Fund.

lowing the table, the United States showed a small improvement in the mid-1960s, which was eliminated by 1969, when the index stood at 151.2 compared with 152.6 in 1961. Then the depreciation of the dollar beginning with the German float of 1969 brought relative unit labor cost down to 100 by 1975 and 96.5 by 1978.

3.2.3   Shares of World Trade in Manufactures

With competitors' capacity growing and no significant improvement in unit labor cost, over the period since 1950 the United States has lost 55 percent of its share of the world market for manufactures. In 1953, 29 percent of global manufactured exports were from the United States: by 1976 its share had shrunk to 13 percent. This reduction is striking enough to warrant detailed attention here.[1] To set the framework for the detailed look at United States trade in section 3.3, I will describe in some detail trends in world manufacturing trade, with particular emphasis on the relative market shares of major competitors during the 1953 to 1976 period. The description is divided into two parts. The first is an examination of changes in trade shares of total manufactures over three periods: 1953–59, 1959–71, and 1971–76. The second focuses on trends in three basic manufacturing categories: chemicals, machinery and transport equipment, and other manufactures.

Total Manufactures

Movements in the distribution of world exports of total manufactures for the period 1953–59 are shown in table 3.13. There we see that the United States share fell from 29.2 percent in 1953 to 13.2 percent in 1976. The share has been relatively constant at 13.2–13.4 percent throughout the 1970s.

Table 3.13   Distribution of Exports of Manufactures (SITC 5–8)

Country	1953	1956	1959	1962	1965	1968	1971	1974	1976
Total ($ millions)	37,738	51,721	61,400	79,330	109,730	150,070	226,670	483,070	585,260
					Percentage of Total				
Developed[1]	88.0	83.5	82.1	81.6	82.0	83.1	83.9	83.7	83.1
LDCs[2]	7.0	6.6	5.3	5.3	5.8	5.8	5.5	7.8	8.0
CPEs[3]	5.0	9.9	12.6	13.1	12.1	11.0	10.4	8.4	8.9
Developed									
Western Europe	49.0	50.1	53.7	54.4	54.7	53.0	54.7	54.9	54.0
EEC	—	—	31.9	33.5	34.4	34.4	35.8	*44.9	44.0
EFTA	—	—	20.3	19.2	18.4	17.2	17.2	* 8.2	8.0
Germany	9.7	12.2	15.6	14.8	15.4	14.8	15.4	16.3	15.5
United States	29.4	23.0	18.7	17.6	15.8	15.8	13.4	13.2	13.2
Canada	5.0	4.3	3.9	3.5	3.7	4.9	4.6	3.4	3.5
Japan	2.8	4.2	4.9	5.5	7.1	8.1	10.0	10.9	10.9
Other	1.9	2.0	1.2	0.6	0.8	1.4	1.3	1.4	1.5
LDC									
Africa[4]	1.6	1.4	1.3	1.2	1.3	1.3	0.9	0.9	0.6
Latin America	1.6	1.6	1.2	1.1	1.2	1.6	1.4	1.9	1.6
Middle East	0.3	0.4	0.4	0.3	0.4	0.2	0.2	0.5	0.4
Asia[5]	3.5	3.2	2.4	2.6	2.8	2.7	2.9	4.5	5.4
NIC3[6]	0.9	0.9	0.8	0.9	1.2	1.5	1.8	2.4	3.0

*Reflects admission of the United Kingdom, Ireland, and Denmark to the EEC and their departure from the EFTA.
[1]Developed market economies: United States, Canada, Japan, Western Europe, Australia, New Zealand, and South Africa.
[2]All countries excluding developed countries and CPEs.
[3]Eastern Europe, USSR, People's Republic of China, Mongolia, North Korea, North Vietnam.
[4]Excludes South Africa and Rhodesia.
[5]Excludes developed countries and CPEs.
[6]Republic of Korea, Hong Kong, Singapore (data for Taiwan were not available for the entire period).

1953–59. Two-thirds of the decrease in United States market share since 1950 occurred between 1953 and 1959. The U.S. share decreased by 8.7 percent (36 percent of the 1953 share) during this period. Canada and the LDCs together lost 2.8 percent (23 percent of their 1953 share). Most of the gain went to the centrally planned economies (CPEs), Germany and Japan.

Most of the CPEs' increase was due to the rapid postwar expansion of their own market, i.e., most of the increase was in trade among the CPEs. Although Germany's growth can be attributed to rapid growth of the West European economies, it should be noted that the rest of Western Europe's market share *declined* during the period, while Germany's increased by almost 6 percent (60 percent of the 1953 share). Clearly Germany was increasing its position in the European market and capturing a larger share of non-European markets. Japan's share increased by 2.1 percent (75 percent of the 1953 share), beginning a trend which continued until 1974. Three of the LDC regions lost market shares while the Middle East's remained unchanged.

Table 3.14 displays the growth rates of real exports for 1953–76. The deflator used is the export price index for all manufactures. Therefore, the deflated values include changes in the relative price of a region's manufactures as well as volume growth. During the 1953–59 period United States export growth was nil, and the LDCs and Canada also had very slow growth.

1959–71. During the 1960s the U.S. lost market shares at a slower pace. Germany and the CPEs stopped penetrating markets as the lead passed to Japan and the other members of the Common Market. Japan doubled its share from 5 percent to 10 percent of the world market. The non-German EEC countries gained 4 percent of the market. Canada's growth was due entirely to the rapid increase in machinery and transport equipment during 1965–71. Examination of bilateral flows reveals that this was due mainly to the effects of the 1965 Auto Agreement between Canada and the United States.

An interesting pattern developed among the LDCs during this period. Overall they gained only 0.2 percent of the world market. The Middle East and Africa lost; Latin America gained slightly; non-NIC Asia lost; but the NICs more than doubled their market share.

1971–76. During the final five years the United States share remained constant at 13.2 percent. The shares of Japan and Germany changed only slightly. The most dramatic movement was the increase in Asian and NIC shares. All of the growth in the LDCs' share was captured by Asian countries (2.5 percent increase in market share), and half of that is concentrated in the three NICs. The growth of Asian exports appears to have been at the expense of the CPEs, Canada, and Africa. Had the

Table 3.14 Average Annual Growth Rates (in Percentages) of Manufactured Exports, Constant (1970) World Prices

Country	1953–56	1956–59	1959–62	1962–65	1965–68	1968–71	1971–74	1974–76	1953–59	1959–71	1971–76	1953–76
World	10.6	5.5	7.6	10.2	9.8	9.8	11.4	3.6	8.0	9.3	8.2	8.7
Developed[1]	8.7	4.9	7.4	10.4	10.3	10.2	11.2	2.1	6.8	9.6	7.5	8.4
LDCs[2]	8.1	−1.6	7.5	13.6	9.4	7.9	25.6	3.3	3.1	9.6	16.2	9.2
CPEs[3]	39.3	14.1	9.1	7.2	6.5	7.8	3.8	4.1	26.1	7.6	3.9	11.3
Developed												
Western Europe	11.5	7.9	8.1	10.4	8.6	11.0	11.5	1.8	9.7	9.5	7.5	9.1
EEC	—	—	9.4	11.1	9.8	15.0	—	1.7	—	11.3	—	—
EFTA	—	—	5.7	8.5	3.4	9.8	—	1.4	—	6.8	—	—
Germany	19.5	14.3	5.8	11.7	8.4	11.2	13.5	0.6	16.9	9.2	8.2	10.9
United States	1.9	−1.5	5.3	6.3	9.7	4.1	10.4	2.5	0.2	6.3	7.2	4.9
Canada	5.2	2.3	3.5	12.2	20.8	7.7	0.8	3.4	3.7	6.5	1.8	4.7
Japan	27.4	11.2	11.6	19.8	14.9	17.6	14.5	2.4	19.0	15.9	9.5	15.3
Other	11.4	−11.6	−11.6	17.7	*33.8	7.4	12.5	4.8	−0.8	10.6	9.4	7.3
LDC												
Africa[4]	6.9	3.8	4.0	14.2	7.1	−0.5	9.8	−11.2	5.3	6.1	0.9	4.7
Latin America	9.4	−4.3	4.2	13.7	20.7	6.1	23.2	−3.9	2.3	11.0	11.5	8.8
Middle East	12.1	7.4	1.8	16.1	*12.0	10.8	50.9	−2.1	9.7	3.6	26.9	9.9
Asia[5]	7.7	−3.9	10.7	12.7	8.6	11.8	29.2	8.8	1.7	10.9	20.6	10.4
NIC3[6]	13.0	1.7	11.5	18.5	24.5	16.9	22.3	10.4	7.2	17.8	17.4	14.9

*Reflects admission of the United Kingdom, Ireland, and Denmark to the EEC and their departure from the EFTA.
[1] Developed market economies: United States, Canada, Japan, Western Europe, Australia, New Zealand, and South Africa.
[2] All countries excluding developed countries and CPEs.
[3] Eastern Europe, USSR, People's Republic of China, Mongolia, North Korea, North Vietnam.
[4] Excludes South Africa and Rhodesia.
[5] Excludes developed countries and CPEs.
[6] Republic of Korea, Hong Kong, Singapore (data for Taiwan were not available for the entire period).

data for Taiwan been available, the concentration of market share in the NIC category would be even higher.

Chemicals

The pattern of change in trade shares of chemicals (about 10 percent of the total) has been quite different from that for all manufactures. This is shown in table 3.15. Over the 1953–76 period the LDCs, CPEs, and Japan have captured little, if any, increased share of the world market. The major shift has been a combined loss by the United States and Canada of 12 percent and a 9 percent gain by Western Europe. Almost 5 percent of the market has been captured by Germany. The last two years of data reflect a slight reversal of the trend; the United States and Canada gain and West Europe and Japan lose.

Machinery and Transport Equipment

Exports in machinery and transportation equipment have grown from 50 percent of total United States manufactures exports in 1953 to 64 percent by 1976. Table 3.16 illustrates that since 1956 the developed countries have maintained their aggregate market share, about 87 percent.

Although United States exports have grown rapidly they have not kept pace with world growth in this category. During the 1950s the United States lost almost 16 percent of the world market. Half of this went to the CPEs and most of the remainder to Western Europe, especially Germany. The United States share diminished more slowly in the 1960s. Between 1959 and 1971 the United States lost 5.9 percent, the CPEs lost 4 percent, and Western Europe 2 percent. Of this 12 percent, Japan gained 7 percent (thereby *tripling* its market share in twelve years), Canada gained over 4 percent (mainly due to the Auto Agreement with the United States), and the LDCs gained 1 percent.

Japan continued to increase its share in the 1970s and was joined by the Asian countries, which tripled their share in five years. The burden of these gains was not concentrated on the United States. During the 1971–76 period the United States lost only 1 percent of the market while more serious losses were sustained by Western Europe, Canada, and the CPEs.

Other Manufactures

Trade patterns in other manufactures are shown in table 3.17. Here the United States lost two-thirds of its 1953 share by 1976. Most of the loss came in the 1950s: since 1962 the loss has been moderate and of decreasing importance to the overall United States position in manufactures. During the 1950s the big gains were made by Japan, the CPEs,

Table 3.15   Distribution of Exports of Chemicals (SITC 5)

	1953	1956	1959	1962	1965	1968	1971	1974	1976
% of World Manufacturing	9.3	10.1	10.9	10.7	11.1	11.3	10.7	13.3	11.7
Total ($ millions)	3,518	5,198	6,668	8,460	12,220	16,970	24,210	64,110	68,440
Country				Percentage of Total					
Developed[1]	87.8	87.8	87.3	86.2	86.9	88.5	88.8	88.2	88.2
LDCs[2]	7.8	4.7	3.9	4.1	4.2	3.7	3.9	5.8	5.3
CPEs[3]	4.4	7.5	8.8	9.7	8.9	7.8	7.3	6.0	6.5
OPEC	—	—	—	—	—	—	0.3	0.9	0.9
Developed									
Western Europe	55.7	54.8	56.8	57.7	59.2	60.3	62.5	64.7	64.0
EEC	—	—	35.4	36.9	38.8	41.2	42.7	*55.2	54.6
EFTA	13.6	15.0	20.7	20.0	18.9	17.6	18.3	* 7.9	8.0
Germany			16.6	17.1	17.0	18.4	18.7	18.9	18.3
United States	23.8	24.5	22.8	22.2	19.6	19.4	15.9	13.8	14.6
Canada	4.9	5.1	3.7	2.4	2.4	2.4	2.4	1.7	2.1
Japan	1.8	2.0	2.5	3.1	4.5	4.8	6.2	6.3	4.0
Other	1.6	1.4	1.5	0.8	1.2	1.6	1.8	1.7	3.5
LDC									
Africa[4]	2.0	1.4	1.3	1.3	1.0	0.6	0.7	0.6	0.5
Latin America	2.6	1.7	1.1	1.3	1.3	1.7	1.8	2.3	2.2
Middle East	0.3	0.2	0.3	0.2	0.5	0.2	0.2	1.0	0.9
Asia[5]	2.9	1.4	1.3	1.3	1.4	1.1	1.2	1.8	1.7
NIC3[6]	2.6	1.2	0.5	0.5	0.4	0.7	0.8	1.0	0.8

*Reflects admission of the United Kingdom, Ireland, and Denmark to the EEC and their departure from the EFTA.
[1] Developed market economies: United States, Canada, Japan, Western Europe, Australia, New Zealand, and South Africa.
[2] All countries excluding developed countries and CPEs.
[3] Eastern Europe, USSR, People's Republic of China, Mongolia, North Korea, North Vietnam.
[4] Excludes South Africa and Rhodesia.
[5] Excludes developed countries and CPEs.
[6] Republic of Korea, Hong Kong, Singapore (data for Taiwan were not available for the entire period).

Table 3.16   Distribution of Exports of Machinery and Transport Equipment (SITC 7)

	1953	1956	1959	1962	1965	1968	1971	1974	1976
% of World Manufacturing	36.7	38.4	39.7	41.8	41.6	43.6	45.9	42.6	47.6
Total ($ millions)	13,855	19,859	24,360	33,140	45,690	65,640	104,050	205,670	278,350
Country				Percentage of Total					
Developed[1]	92.5	86.7	84.9	86.4	85.9	86.8	87.8	87.2	87.9
LDCs[2]	1.2	1.1	0.6	0.8	0.9	1.0	1.4	3.2	3.4
CPEs[3]	6.3	12.3	14.8	12.8	13.2	12.1	10.8	9.6	9.1
OPEC	—	—	—	—	—	—	—	0.1	0.2
Developed									
Western Europe	47.9	48.8	54.7	56.3	55.2	50.9	52.6	51.5	51.0
EEC	—	—	30.8	33.7	34.4	33.3	34.9	*43.1	42.8
EFTA	12.1	15.0	22.9	21.4	19.5	16.8	16.6	*7.1	6.9
Germany			17.6	18.5	20.3	17.3	17.8	18.5	17.4
United States	40.3	33.4	24.6	24.3	21.9	22.0	18.7	18.6	17.8
Canada	2.5	1.6	1.7	1.8	2.6	5.9	5.8	4.3	4.3
Japan	1.4	2.4	3.3	3.8	5.8	7.5	10.2	12.3	13.4
Other	0.4	0.5	0.6	0.3	0.4	0.5	0.5	0.5	0.4
LDC									
Africa[4]	—	—	—	0.1	0.1	0.1	0.1	0.1	—
Latin America	—	—	0.1	0.1	0.1	0.2	0.4	0.7	0.7
Middle East	0.1	—	0.1	—	0.1	0.1	0.1	0.2	0.2
Asia[5]	.9	.8	0.4	0.6	0.6	0.5	0.8	2.2	2.5
NIC3[6]	0.1	0.1	0.1	0.2	0.3	0.4	0.6	1.3	1.5

*Reflects admission of the United Kingdom, Ireland, and Denmark to the EEC and their departure from the EFTA.

[1]Developed market economies: United States, Canada, Japan, Western Europe, Australia, New Zealand, and South Africa.

[2]All countries excluding developed countries and CPEs.

[3]Eastern Europe, USSR, People's Republic of China, Mongolia, North Korea, North Vietnam.

[4]Excludes South Africa and Rhodesia.

[5]Excludes developed countries and CPEs.

[6]Republic of Korea, Hong Kong, Singapore (data for Taiwan were not available for the entire period).

Table 3.17   Distribution of Exports of Other Manufactures (SITC 6 and 8)

	1953	1956	1959	1962	1965	1968	1971	1974	1976
% of World Manufacturing	53.9	51.4	49.3	47.6	47.2	45.0	43.4	44.2	40.7
Total ($ millions)	20,357	26,610	30,290	37,730	51,820	67,460	98,410	213,290	238,470
Country				Percentage of Total					
Developed[1]	85.0	80.3	78.9	76.3	77.5	78.3	79.0	79.0	77.1
LDCs[2]	10.8	11.0	9.4	9.5	10.6	11.0	10.2	12.9	14.2
CPEs[3]	4.2	8.7	11.7	14.2	11.9	10.8	10.8	8.1	8.6
OPEC	—	—	—	—	—	—	—	0.4	0.3
Developed									
Western Europe	48.6	50.2	52.3	51.9	53.2	53.1	55.1	55.3	54.6
EEC	—	—	32.1	32.5	33.2	33.8	35.1	*43.4	42.5
EFTA	—	9.7	18.2	17.1	17.2	17.4	17.6	* 9.4	9.3
Germany	7.4	15.0	10.9	11.0	10.7	11.6	12.1	13.5	12.4
United States	22.9	15.0	12.5	10.6	9.5	8.7	7.3	7.8	7.5
Canada	6.6	6.1	5.7	5.2	4.9	4.5	3.9	3.1	3.0
Japan	3.9	6.0	6.8	7.6	8.9	9.6	10.7	10.8	9.9
Other	3.0	3.0	1.5	1.0	1.0	2.4	2.0	2.0	2.1
LDC									
Africa[4]	2.5	2.4	2.4	2.3	2.5	2.5	1.9	1.8	1.2
Latin America	2.5	2.7	2.0	1.9	2.0	2.8	2.3	2.9	2.4
Middle East	0.5	0.6	0.7	0.6	0.7	0.3	0.3	0.6	0.6
Asia[5]	5.3	5.3	4.3	4.8	5.2	5.3	5.5	7.6	9.9
NIC3[6]	1.1	1.5	1.5	1.7	2.1	2.8	3.3	3.8	5.4

*Reflects admission of the United Kingdom, Ireland, and Denmark to the EEC and their departure from the EFTA.
[1] Developed market economies: United States, Canada, Japan, Western Europe, Australia, New Zealand, and South Africa.
[2] All countries excluding developed countries and CPEs.
[3] Eastern Europe, USSR, People's Republic of China, Mongolia, North Korea, North Vietnam.
[4] Excludes South Africa and Rhodesia.
[5] Excludes developed countries and CPEs.
[6] Republic of Korea, Hong Kong, Singapore (data for Taiwan were not available for the entire period).

and Germany. During the 1960s leadership passed to other West European countries along with Japan.

From 1968 to 1976 a major shift occurred in this category. The United States market position stabilized, Japan's growth was nil, and the Asian LDCs made all of the market gains. Since 1968 the Asian LDCs have captured 4.6 percent of the market; of this three NIC countries have taken more than half, 2.6 percent. This is the category of manufactures most important to Asian and NIC penetration of manufactured exports.

Summary

Since 1953 the United States has experienced a major reduction of its share of world trade in manufactures. During the 1950s the gains were made by Western Europe, especially Germany, the CPEs, and Japan. During the 1960s Japan's share increased very rapidly while growth of Western Europe slowed and the CPEs actually lost market shares. In the 1970s the growth centers were the Asian LDCs, especially the newly industrializing countries. Japan's share continued to increase but at a much slower rate than in the earlier periods.

The movements of market shares have been different amongst the three categories of manufactures: chemicals, machinery and transport equipment, and other. Japan's performance has been led by the second category while the third has been most important to the LDCs.

3.2.4   Trends in Effective Exchange Rates

The combination of growing capacity in the rest of the world relative to the United States and roughly comparable cost developments led to a significant drop in the United States share of world exports in manufacturing from 1950 to 1970, as shown in section 3.2.3 above. This in turn built up pressure for a devaluation of the United States dollar. Since, under the Bretton Woods system, a dollar devaluation was effectively ruled out, the United States trade balance deteriorated after reaching a peak surplus in the early 1960s. As pressure accumulated, eventually the system broke down in 1970–71. Section 3.5 will examine monetary developments in detail, while here we will focus on movements in the *real effective exchange rate* as an adjustment mechanism that was frozen during the period 1950–70, but has worked reasonably well since.

Measures of Exchange Rates

When we consider exchange rate adjustment, we must keep in mind two distinctions. First, we can consider bilateral or effective rates. Bilateral exchange rates are the relative prices of individual currencies; an effective rate is the average price of a group of currencies. For example, we can consider the bilateral rates of the United States dollar in relation to the Swiss franc or the Canadian dollar, or in terms of an effective rate that averages the United States dollar price of these bilateral rates. With some bilateral rates rising and some falling, an effective rate will generally show less movement than most bilateral rates. We see this in figure 3.1.

The second distinction differentiates between nominal and real exchange rates. These can be either bilateral or effective. The nominal rate is simply the home currency price of foreign exchange. The real rate is the nominal rate adjusted for movements of the relevant price levels. Thus if the United States dollar price of the deutschemark (DM) rose by 10 percent over a given period, this would be a nominal devaluation of the United States dollar. But if United States prices rose by 10 percent relative to German prices over the same period, there would be no change in the real dollar-DM rate. Analysis of short-term monetary developments usually focuses on *nominal bilateral* rates; analysis of long-run adjustment in a country's overall trade normally focuses on the *real effective* rate.

Adjustment in the Real Effective Rate

Table 3.18 shows index numbers for the United States nominal effective exchange rate in column 1, relative wholesale price indexes (WPIs) in column 2, and real effective exchange rates in column 3 for the period 1961–78. The period breaks clearly into two subperiods: 1961–70 where the three series are fairly constant, and 1970–78 where the effective rates fall substantially.

During the 1960s the United States WPI fell slightly relative to the weighted average of the other industrial countries, from 102.6 in 1961 to 98.4 in 1970. This reflects the middle-of-the-road performance of unit labor cost shown above in table 3.11. The effective nominal exchange rate also fell slightly during this period—an *up* valuation or appreciation of the United States dollar as other exchange rates moved. The combination of a small relative price improvement and an equally small effective appreciation in nominal terms resulted in almost no movement in the real effective rate. From 82.9 in 1961, it rose to 85.9 in 1965 then returned to 83.0 in 1969. Thus over the 1960s there was essentially no adjustment in the real effective rate as the United States lost trade shares.

Beginning in 1971 nominal bilateral rates began to move substantially, and the United States real effective rate began to adjust. Figure 3.1 shows the movements of four United States bilateral rates and the United States nominal effective rate. The bilateral rates shown are the United States dollar price of the Swiss franc, Japanese yen, Canadian dollar, and pound sterling. These are important rates that span the experience of the 1970s. The effective nominal United States rate is the weighted

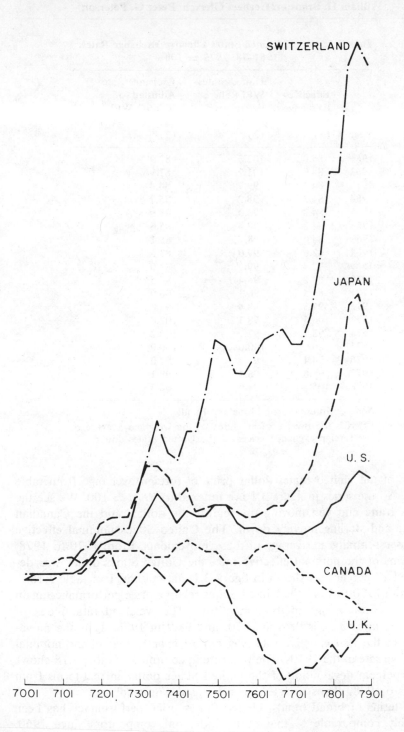

Fig. 3.1   Bilateral and effective nominal exchange rate.

Table 3.18   United States Effective Exchange Rates,
1961–78, 1975 = 100

Year	Effective Exchange Rate[a] (1)	United States WPI Relative to Competitors (2)	Exchange Rate Adjusted for Relative WPI $(3) = (1) \div (2) \times 100$ (3)
1961	85.0	102.6	82.9
1962	84.3	101.7	82.9
1963	84.2	99.7	84.4
1964	84.2	98.2	85.7
1965	84.2	98.0	85.9
1966	84.2	98.4	85.6
1967	84.0	98.7	85.1
1968	82.6	99.0	83.5
1969	82.4	99.3	83.0
1970	83.2	98.4	84.5
1971	85.5	98.3	86.9
1972	92.3	98.4	93.8
1973	100.3	98.3	102.0
1974	98.1	97.9	100.2
1975	100.0	100.0	100.0
1976	94.4	97.3	97.0
1977	95.6	96.4	99.2
1978	105.3	98.9	106.4

Source: International Monetary Fund.
[a]This is the inverse of an index of the weighted average of the foreign exchange prices of the United States dollar.

index of the United States dollar price of foreign exchange from table 3.18. All the series in figure 3.1 are indexed to 1970 = 100. We see the Swiss franc and yen moving up against the dollar, and the Canadian dollar and sterling moving down. The United States nominal effective rate is essentially an average of these movements. From 1970 to 1978, in terms of the nominal effective rate, the United States dollar was devalued 27 percent, as shown in figure 3.1 and column 1 of table 3.18.

From 1970 to 1978 the United States relative price performance again matched the average of its competitors. The weighted ratio index of WPIs in table 3.18 is 98.4 in 1970, and 98.9 in 1978. Thus the movement in the real effective rate was almost exactly that of the nominal effective rate in the 1970s. The real rate in column 3 of table 3.18 shows a 26 percent devaluation of the United States dollar in real terms from 1971 to 1978, almost exactly the same as the nominal rate.

In terms of broad trends, United States price performance has been roughly comparable to that of its industrial competitors since 1960. During the decade 1960–70, the nominal effective United States rate was essentially constant (with a small upward creep due to an occasional devaluation in one of the other countries), and so was the real effective rate. With capacity growing abroad, the United States lost trade shares. In the 1970s, movement in the nominal effective United States rate brought about a real effective devaluation of over 20 percent, and the shrinkage of export shares halted. It appears that the real effective rate has worked as an instrument for adjustment, and that its movements have come through movements in the nominal rate with roughly parallel price performance.

3.3   Trends in the Composition of United States Trade

At the end of World War II the pattern of United States trade was distorted by the fact that industrial capacity had been significantly reduced in the other major advanced countries. Trade in consumer goods provides a good example of this distortion. In every year from 1925 to 1938 the United States was a net importer of consumer goods (see table 3.19). But in 1946 the United States emerged from the war as a net exporter, and in 1947 the surplus on consumer goods was $1 billion. As industrial capacity was rebuilt in Europe and Japan, the surplus shrank steadily, and in 1959 the United States again became a net importer, with a deficit in consumer goods that has grown steadily since then. This example is typical of the pattern we see in the long-run data on the composition of trade. During the years since 1950 the composition of United States trade has moved back toward its longer run base of comparative advantage. By the mid-1960s we see growing surpluses in trade in capital goods, chemicals, and agriculture, and deficits in consumer goods and nonagricultural industrial supplies and materials. Trade in automotive products switched from surplus to deficit in 1968.

This section examines the long-term trends in commodity composition of United States trade, using end-use data developed by the Commerce Department. Section 3.3.1 analyzes the aggregate data by major end-use categories. These show the broad trends just described. Section 3.3.2 studies the disaggregated data, down to the four-digit level. At that level one can see the effects of product cycles, international rationalization of the location of industry, and international location of stages in processing within an industry, for example.

Section 3.3.3 moves to consider the implicit factor composition of trade, and finds that the United States, on balance, is a net exporter of the services of human capital and an importer of labor services. Thus the broad picture that emerges in this section is an increasing international division of labor along the lines of comparative advantage, with the United States showing strength in goods that are intensive in human capital.

Table 3.19   **United States Trade Balances by End-Use Commodity, 1925–78**
($ Millions)

| | Industrial Supplies and Materials | | | | |
Year	Agricultural Goods	Fuels and Lubricants	Chemicals	Other	Capital Goods
1925	355	473	−37	−345	399
1926	52	634	−22	−418	422
1927	154	484	−14	−352	454
1928	186	494	−20	−309	516
1929	−78	517	−6	−370	618
1930	15	433	3	−271	518
1931	−45	243	5	−221	312
1932	54	188	16	−136	123
1933	67	211	17	−200	127
1934	23	244	26	−111	207
1935	−158	260	31	−237	251
1936	−333	275	26	−310	325
1937	−459	395	22	−184	486
1938	19	403	34	−33	512
1939	−267	403	64	−63	570
1940	−399	323	136	217	945
1946	1,082	587	262	−100	1,628
1947	1,604	1,013	553	890	3,144
1948	645	713	476	−600	2,523
1949	864	379	464	−460	2,456
1950	−810	174	354	−1,632	2,033
1951	−499	787	479	−1,494	2,356
1952	−706	605	376	−1,705	2,585
1953	−1,258	274	334	−2,227	2,705
1954	−936	136	533	−1,500	2,699
1955	−625	102	620	−1,571	2,817
1956	272	220	746	−1,689	3,470
1957	495	297	857	−926	4,087
1958	−202	−544	829	−1,412	4,292
1959	−260	−699	914	−2,515	4,026
1960	857	−739	1,128	−1,227	4,949
1961	980	−933	1,133	−1,098	5,217
1962	741	−1,080	1,187	−2,021	5,685
1963	1,068	−956	1,313	−2,010	5,781
1964	1,699	−1,069	1,627	−1,793	6,424
1965	1,516	−1,264	1,504	−2,989	6,581
1966	1,570	−1,270	1,627	−3,634	6,756
1967	1,139	−1,127	1,729	−3,359	7,531
1968	230	−1,457	2,075	−4,574	8,292
1969	190	−1,584	2,044	−3,945	9,013

Table 3.19—*continued*

	Industrial Supplies and Materials				
Year	Agricultural Goods	Fuels and Lubricants	Chemicals	Other	Capital Goods
1970	533	−1,390	2,231	−3,394	10,457
1971	888	−2,068	2,045	−5,913	10,871
1972	1,560	−3,180	2,114	−7,183	10,955
1973	7,967	−6,373	3,156	−6,299	13,760
1974	10,527	−21,913	4,946	−7,527	20,663
1975	11,414	−21,880	5,163	−5,010	26,126
1976	10,471	−29,913	5,509	−7,470	25,198
1977	8,804	−40,218	5,572	−10,950	25,358
1978	13,258	−38,415	6,596	−15,055	26,771

Year	Consumer Goods	Automotive Products	Other	Military Goods	N.F.C.
1925	−107	323	−475	5	92
1926	−144	326	−558	6	81
1927	−152	395	−381	5	87
1928	−138	506	−279	6	76
1929	−173	544	−275	8	55
1930	−92	282	−153	7	40
1931	−63	151	−78	5	25
1932	−40	78	−29	5	18
1933	−45	92	−50	6	0
1934	−28	192	−97	12	11
1935	−37	232	−126	10	11
1936	−33	245	−202	14	26
1937	−38	353	−291	22	−39
1938	16	275	−146	37	18
1939	21	259	−176	54	−5
1940	68	258	−320	169	−1
1946	592	551	−153	97	221
1947	958	1,147	−183	174	231
1948	599	904	−204	249	142
1949	519	759	−115	306	175
1950	310	723	−381	441	112
1951	445	1,180	−689	1,260	144
1952	352	968	−508	2,244	175
1953	329	945	−198	3,773	116
1954	310	1,019	−122	2,522	81
1955	143	1,191	−293	1,568	41
1956	113	1,250	−223	2,035	0
1957	126	1,010	−175	1,823	−147
1958	119	568	−60	1,111	−207
1959	−261	343	−214	936	−319

Table 3.19—*continued*

Year	Consumer Goods	Automotive Products	Other	Military Goods	N.F.C.
1960	−505	633	−99	804	−274
1961	−448	805	−5	792	−167
1962	−821	780	−14	914	−112
1963	−831	882	63	954	−80
1964	−943	962	90	881	22
1965	−1,506	990	107	1,170	−109
1966	−1,877	444	146	1,155	−107
1967	−2,102	150	145	952	−325
1968	−3,041	−842	113	963	−349
1969	−3,883	−1,400	56	1,502	−244
1970	−4,670	−2,242	135	1,230	230
1971	−5,530	−3,521	173	1,335	58
1972	−7,600	−4,207	111	1,038	206
1973	−8,175	−4,542	73	1,385	556
1974	−8,096	−3,798	139	2,015	916
1975	−6,735	−1,596	297	2,782	860
1976	−9,248	−4,911	312	2,413	697
1977	−12,979	−6,554	165	3,041	1,175
1978	−17,894	−9,853	343	4,341	1,392

Year	Total	Year	Total
1925	1,025	1950	2,788
1926	763	1951	5,959
1927	1,058	1952	6,078
1928	1,436	1953	6,519
1929	1,300	1954	6,788
1930	1,154	1955	6,335
1931	606	1956	8,886
1932	467	1957	10,373
1933	451	1958	7,326
1934	749	1959	5,117
1935	557	1960	9,199
1936	357	1961	9,982
1937	661	1962	9,167
1938	1,463	1963	10,424
1939	1,280	1964	12,958
1940	1,930	1965	11,020
1946	5,833	1966	10,490
1947	11,411	1967	10,619
1948	7,081	1968	8,310
1949	6,931	1969	1,749

Table 3.19—*continued*

Year	Total	Year	Total
1970	3,120	1975	11,422
1971	−1,659	1976	−6,939
1972	−6,185	1977	−26,585
1973	1,508	1978	−28,516
1974	−2,125		

Source: OBE 1970, table 5 (exports) and table 6 (imports); BEA 1977, table 2.2.

3.3.1   Long-term Trends in United States Trade by Aggregate End-Use Categories

A useful perspective on developments in United States trade can be obtained by reviewing its longer run trends by end-use commodity categories. The OBE data on trade are broken into six summary categories: foods, feeds, and beverages (0); industrial supplies and materials (1); capital goods (2); automotive products (3); consumer goods (4); and military goods (5) (OBE 1970; BEA 1977). This section considers these aggregate end-use categories. Selected three- and four-digit categories are examined in table 3.22 to observe more detailed movements in trade.

Initial Assumptions and Hypotheses

Two basic questions arise in analyzing and presenting the OBE data: How should the data be disaggregated—in terms of both categories to be used and degree of detail? And how should exports and imports be related to each other?

To a large extent, the answer to the first question involves the way the OBE organizes the data. This disaggregation makes sense if the course of trade in subcategories is more similar *within* major categories than *across* major categories. Thus a decision was made to disaggregate, within the end-use framework, as far as possible to see whether similar trade patterns obtain *within*, and dissimilar patterns *across*, categories.

The second question called for focus on trade balances by commodity groups. This focus, of course, does not suggest that all categories "should" show surpluses, or that categories showing large and growing deficits display "weakness" that necessarily should be corrected by policy action. The net balance of payments should be in equilibrium on whatever basis is thought appropriate, while within it some items show deficits, and others surpluses. Furthermore, the basic notion of comparative advantage implies that the United States should be a net importer of some goods and a net exporter of others.

But even at the finest level of statistical disaggregation that is available, it appears that most goods are subject to two-way trade. Thereby, the notion of comparative advantage becomes the proposition that the United States should be a *net* exporter of goods in which it has a comparative advantage—whether it derives from resource endowment, technological advantage, or education embodied in human capital—and a *net* importer of goods in which it is at a disadvantage.[2] Thus it is natural to focus on net exports by commodity group in an analysis that attempts to reveal something about movements in United States comparative advantage and trade.[3]

Trends in Aggregate End-Use Categories

Table 3.19 shows net exports for ten major export end-use categories for the years 1925–78, excluding the war years 1941–45. In the table, total nonagricultural industrial supplies and materials are disaggregated into three parts: fuels and lubricants; chemicals; and a residual component. This disaggregation is necessary for two reasons. Fuels and lubricants include as major subcategories crude petroleum and semifinished petroleum products and natural gas. Throughout the period trade in these categories was heavily influenced both by natural resource advantages and by government policies. The oil price increases of the 1970s show up here. Chemicals are shown separately because they are the only three-digit category among nonagricultural industrial supplies and materials to show a surplus consistently since World War II.

Agricultural goods. Exports and imports of agricultural goods are shown in figure 3.2. From 1925 to 1972, the United States trade balance in agricultural goods typically fluctuated in a range from a surplus of $1.5 billion to a deficit of $1.2 billion. Deficits dominated in the 1950s, and there were small surpluses throughout the 1960s. A major change in United States agricultural trade came in the years 1972–74. Exports rose from $9.5 billion in 1972 to $22.2 billion in 1974, and the surplus went from $1.6 to $10.5 billion. Of the increase, approximately $5 billion was in wheat and feed grains, and the other $4 billion was scattered across other commodities. The 1972–74 increase is associated with the boom in agricultural prices in those years. However, exports stayed in the $22–24 billion range in 1974–77, and rose to $30 billion in 1978, with the surplus rising to $13.3 billion in 1978. Thus food prices do not account for the persistence of the change. During the mid-1970s United States agricultural trade moved from a position typically near balance to a surplus of $10–14 billion.

Fuel and lubricants. Trade in fuel and lubricants is shown in figure 3.3. It consistently showed a small surplus from 1925 through 1957. This was replaced in 1958 by a deficit, which grew fairly steadily to 1970. The deficit began to increase progressively in 1971, with major jumps to $22 billion in 1974 and $40 billion in 1977–78. On the basis of the first two quarters of 1979, the fuels and lubricants deficit for the year is about $50 billion. The increase in the deficit in recent years is, of course, due to the oil price increases. In the period 1946–70, however, trade in fuel and lubricants followed a pattern frequently seen in United States trade in industrial supplies and materials and in consumer goods. There was a significant postwar bulge in the export surplus, which then

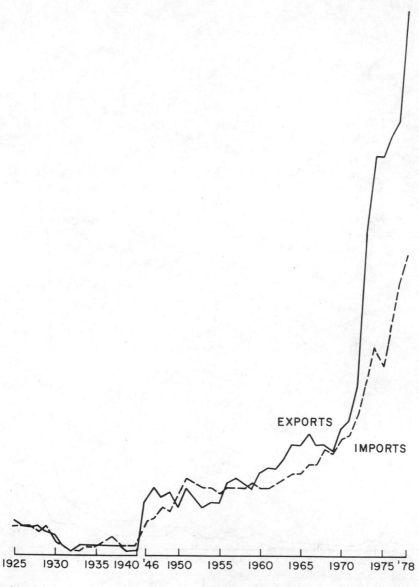

Fig. 3.2   United States exports and imports of agricultural goods, 1925–78.

diminished to balance in the mid-1950s, and a growing deficit in the 1960s. This is a sign of comparative advantage being reestablished in the postwar economy.

Chemicals. A different pattern appears in chemicals (including fertilizers but excluding medicinal preparations), shown in figure 3.4. From

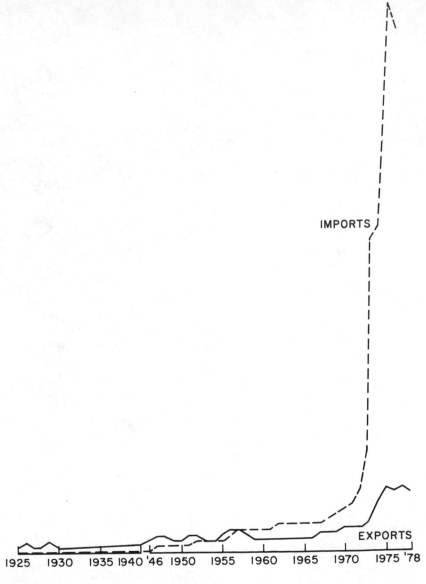

Fig. 3.3   United States exports and imports of fuels and lubricants, 1925–78.

1925 to 1937 trade in these products was roughly balanced. Then in 1938–40 a small but growing surplus appeared. After the war, exports started off substantially above imports, which were roughly at their pre-war level, then grew substantially faster than imports throughout the period 1946–68. From 1968 to 1972, the surplus stabilized at about $2

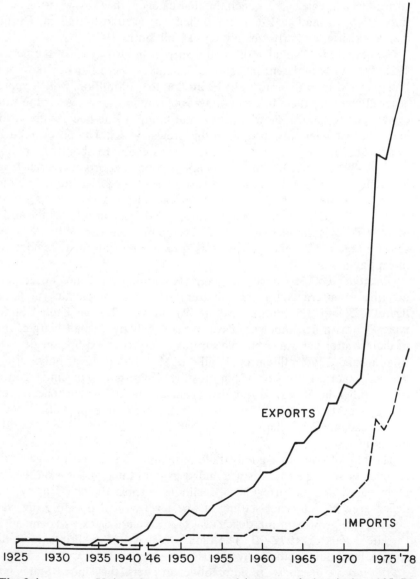

Fig. 3.4   United States exports and imports of chemicals, 1925–78.

billion. Then, with the increase in the price of oil, the principal input into chemicals, the surplus rose to the level of $5–5.5 billion in 1974– 77, and $6.6 billion in 1978.

Other nonagricultural industrial supplies and materials. The category of other industrial supplies and materials is a heterogeneous group of products, as can be seen in table 3.19. Most of them have shown deficits throughout the period 1925–70. Some of the more interesting subcategories will be discussed in the section on disaggregated trade patterns. On aggregate, the deficit in this category has grown irregularly since 1946. In the late 1960s, the deficit was around $4 billion. During the 1970s, it grew fairly steadily to $15 billion in 1978.

Capital goods. Capital goods had a surplus in every year of the period 1925–70. As is apparent in figure 3.5, imports were flat before World War II, varying in the range of $10 million to $40 million, while exports generally were in the $400 million to $600 million range. After the war, capital goods exports showed the typical bump in the late 1940s, yielding a much higher surplus than in the prewar years. The postwar bulge disappeared in 1950, and the surplus grew steadily to about $11 billion in 1971–72. From 1972 to 1975, capital goods exports increased from $17 billion to $36 billion, and the surplus rose by $15 billion. The distribution of the $19 billion increase in capital goods exports is shown in table 3.20. Exports to Western Europe and Canada rose significantly. More striking is the increase to the developing countries and OPEC. As shown in table 3.20, the increase was spread across all the subcategories of capital goods.

Consumer goods. Consumer goods (excluding food and beverages) describe a pattern completely different from that of capital goods, as figures 3.5 and 3.6 confirm. Before World War II, the United States typically was a net importer of consumer goods by a small margin. Immediately after the war, a sizable surplus emerged as exports quadrupled from around $250 million to $1 billion. After this postwar bulge disappeared, exports grew slowly but steadily. Imports of consumer goods, on the other hand, have expanded at an increasingly rapid pace, overtaking exports in 1959. The deficit has increased exponentially ever since, reaching $5 billion in 1970–71, $10 billion in 1976, and $18 billion in 1978.

The plot of consumer goods trade in figure 3.6 suggests two generalizations. First, once the postwar bulge in consumer goods exports had disappeared and the irregularly declining surplus dwindled away, the deficit grew steadily, not settling at one level as it had before the war. Second, the growth in the deficit was not a result of excess demand in the late 1960s or 1972–73. The data reveal it in the shrinkage of the surplus beginning in the early 1950s.

Automotive products. In automotive products, the United States had a surplus every year until 1968, but since then has had an increasing deficit. There was a small but steady surplus before World War II, following a pattern quite similar to that of capital goods (see fig. 3.7). After the war the familiar export bulge appeared but was eliminated by the early 1950s. Exports grew erratically from 1953 to 1962, and at a

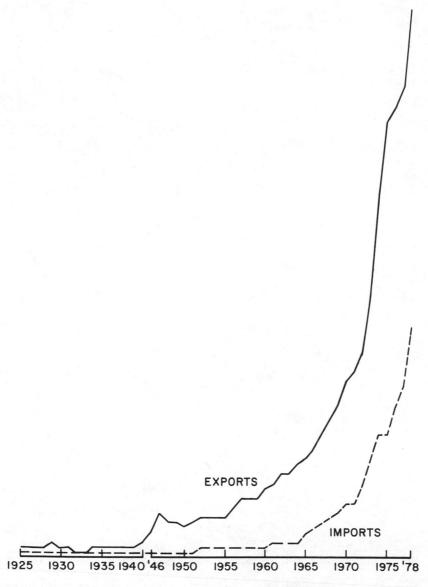

Fig. 3.5   United States exports and imports of capital goods, 1925–78.

smoothly increasing rate after that. Imports did not appear at a significant level until about 1955. They then grew at an increasing rate—with a relapse in 1959–61—and overtook exports in 1968, generating a deficit that has been growing ever since. The deficit on automotive products

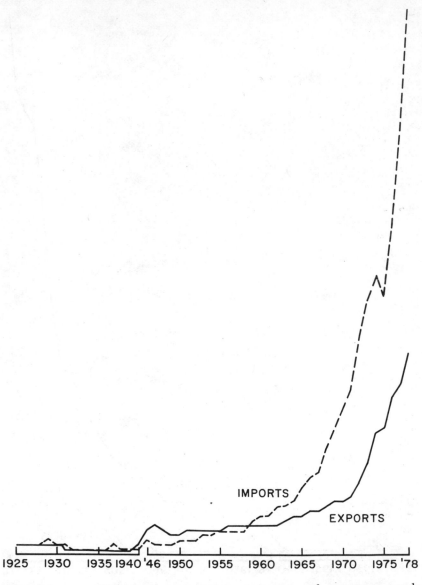

Fig. 3.6   United States exports and imports of consumer goods, 1925–78.

jumped from the $5 billion level in 1976 to nearly $10 billion in 1978. Over that period imports increased by $8.2 billion, while exports grew by $3.2 billion. The geographic division of the change is shown in table 3.21. The increase in trade with Canada reflects continued rationaliza-

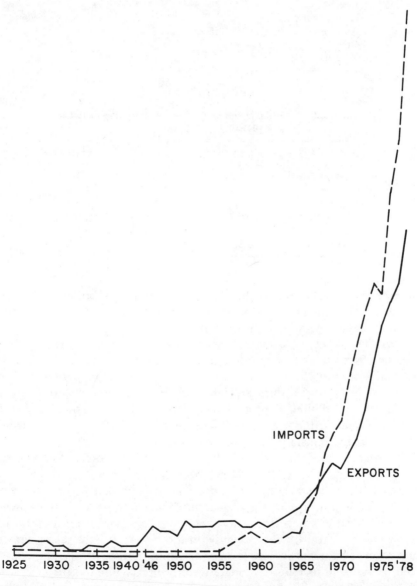

Fig. 3.7   United States exports and imports of automotive products, 1925–78.

Table 3.20   Change in Capital Goods Exports, 1972–75 ($ Billions)

Area	Increase in Exports
Western Europe	$ 4.9
Eastern Europe	0.7
Canada	2.7
Japan	0.5
Latin America	3.6
Australia, New Zealand, South Africa	1.1
Other Asia and Africa	5.5
Total	$19.0

Table 3.21   Change in Trade in Automotive Products, 1976–78 ($ Billions)

Area	Exports	Imports	Balance
Western Europe	0.3	2.0	−1.7
Canada	1.7	2.5	−0.8
Japan	0	3.4	−3.4
Latin America	0.7	0.2	+0.5
Other	0.5	0.1	+0.4
Total	3.2	8.2	−5.0

tion of the industry across the Canada-United States border following the Auto Agreement of 1965. The major shift has come in the deficit vis-à-vis Japan, with Western Europe next.

Military goods. Trade in military goods is shown in figure 3.8. Imports of aircraft and parts have grown erratically to about $150–200 million a year in 1975–78. Exports have had two major periods of expansion. In 1950–53, during the Korean War, exports rose from $0.4 billion to $3.8 billion. Exports then shrank to a level of about $0.8–1.3 billion a year in the period 1958–73. Since 1974, exports have again grown rapidly, reaching $4.3 billion in 1978.

Summary. The data of table 3.19 give a strong impression that United States trade since World War II has been characterized by growing surpluses in chemicals and capital goods and growing deficits in consumer goods and industrial materials. Once the immediate postwar adjustment to 1950 or so was finished, a clear pattern of comparative advantage in these goods emerged. More recently, in the 1970s we have seen a growing deficit on automotive products and surplus in agriculture. These also can be assumed to reflect comparative advantage. Finally, the oil price increases of the 1970s have produced a $40 billion deficit in fuels, and military sales show a $4 billion surplus.

3.3.2   Disaggregated Patterns of Trade in Manufactured Goods

Patterns of United States trade in manufactured goods, disaggregated into thirty-four end-use commodity groups, are outlined in table 3.22.[4] The table attempts to summarize the movements of exports and imports

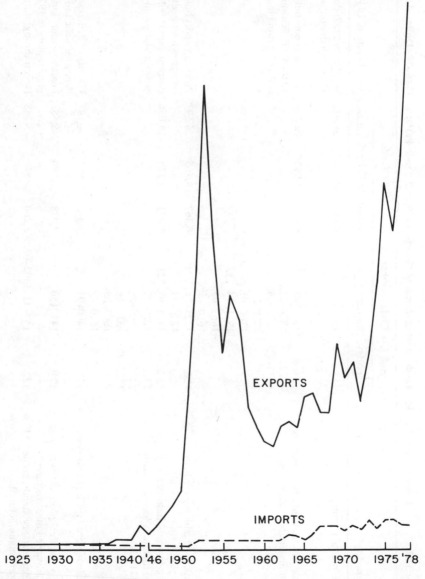

Fig. 3.8   United States exports and imports in military goods, 1925–78.

Table 3.22   United States Foreign Trade in Manufactured Goods, 1978, and Trade Patterns, 1946–78 (Dollar Amounts in Millions)

Commodity[a]	End-Use Code Number		1978 Trade			Trade Pattern, 1946–78
	Exports	Imports	Exports	Imports	Surplus	
Fuels and lubricants	11	10	4,499	42,915	−38,415	Surplus to 1957; deficit growing since 1958 with discontinuous jumps after 1973.
Nonagricultural industrial supplies and materials, except fuels	12 less 1273, 1275–77[b]	11, 1203, 121, 1220–22, 1225–26, 1230–31, 1300–01, 1311, 14, 15, 1603–05, 1610	26,433	34,892	−8,459	Postwar export bulge and resurplus 1946–47; deficit since 1950 except 1961 and 1975; rapid import growth since 1975.
Chemicals, excluding medicinal preparations	125	1225–26, 1230–31	10,362	3,765	6,597	Postwar export bulge; surplus throughout; growing rapidly since 1972.
Nonagricultural industrial supplies and materials less chemicals and fuels	12 less 125, 1273, 1275–77[b]	11, 1203, 121, 1220–22, 1300–01, 1311, 14, 15, 1603–05, 1610	16,071	31,126	−15,056	Postwar export bulge; deficit since 1948; growing sharply in 1977–78.
Basic material for iron and steel	120	1400–01	845	993	−147	Usually in deficit since 1946; no tendency for deficit to grow.
Iron and steel products excluding advanced manufactures	121	141, 150	2,028	7,590	−5,563	Postwar export bulge; deficit since 1962; grew rapidly in 1977–78.
Other primary metals, crude and semimanufactured	122	142–43, 1402–03	3,260	8,648	−5,388	Deficit throughout; growing in 1970s.

Table 3.22—continued

Commodity[a]	End-Use Code Number		1978 Trade			Trade Pattern, 1946–78
	Exports	Imports	Exports	Imports	Surplus	
Finished metal shapes and advanced manufactures	123	151, 152	1,534	1,494	40	Postwar export bulge; surplus to 1965, near balance 1966–73, surplus since.
Lumber, wood, pulp, and paper, including newsprint	124	11, 1300–01, 1311	4,804	8,001	−3,197	Deficit throughout. Rapid import growth 1976–78.
Industrial textile fibers, yarn, fabric	126	121, 1203	2,245	1,683	563	Postwar export bulge; surplus to 1962; deficit growing rapidly 1965–76, reversed in 1972–74.
Other nonagricultural industrial materials	127 less 1273, 1275–77[b]	1220–22, 1603–05, 1610	1,354	2,717	−1,363	Deficit throughout, growing since 1971.
Capital goods, less automotive[c]	2	2	45,952	19,181	26,771	Surplus throughout; growing rapidly to $26 billion in 1975; level since.
Electrical machinery	20	200	8,110	5,860	2,251	Surplus generally growing since 1946; exports growing rapidly since 1971.
Construction and contracting machinery less nonfarm tractors	210 less 2104	2011	4,429	2,333	2,095	Surplus growing to $4 billion in 1975; decreasing since.
Nonelectrical industrial machinery	211	2010, 2012	12,890	4,275	8,614	Surplus growing rapidly to 1975; level at $8–9 billion since.
Machine tools and metal working machinery	2112	2010	1,161	969	192	Surplus growing rapidly to 1975; declining since.
Industrial machinery less machine tools and metal working machinery	211 less 2112	2012	11,729	3,306	3,306	Surplus growing rapidly to 1975; level since; jump in exports 1972–75.
Agricultural, scientific, and business machinery less tractors	212 less 2120	2015–16, 2018	9,949	3,982	5,967	Surplus growing since 1959; rapid growth since export take-off in late 1960s.

Table 3.22—*continued*

Commodity[a]	End-Use Code Number		1978 Trade			Trade Pattern, 1946–78
	Exports	Imports	Exports	Imports	Surplus	
Agricultural machinery, except tractors	2121	2015	1,249	507	742	Balance to 1973; rapid growth of exports since 1974.
Business machinery	2122	2016	5,241	2,143	3,098	Little trade to 1960; surplus growing exponentially since.
Scientific and medical instruments and equipment and tools for photo and other service industries	2123, 2124	2018	3,459	1,332	2,126	Post-war export bulge and surplus throughout; growing rapidly since 1968.
Tractors, nonfarm, and farm and garden tractors and parts	2104, 2120	2013, 2014	2,497	929	1,568	Surplus throughout; rapid export growth 1972–75.
Civilian aircraft, engines, and parts	220	21	7,283	982	6,302	Little trade to 1958; rapid export growth since 1965.
Complete aircraft, civilian	2200	2100	3,616	231	3,385	Rapidly growing surplus since 1958.
Civilian aircraft, engines, and parts, except complete aircraft	220 less 2200	2101	3,667	751	2,916	Exports and surplus growing rapidly since 1967.
Automotive vehicles, parts and engines	3	3	14,460	24,314	−9,854	Postwar export bulge and surplus to 1967; deficit growing since 1968.
Passenger cars, new and used	300	300	3,691	13,674	−9,982	Deficit growing since 1957; exponential import growth since 1972.
Trucks, buses, and special-purpose vehicles	301	301	2,768	3,709	−939	Postwar export bulge, surplus to 1967; deficit since 1968 except after export jump in 1973–75.
Automotive parts	31	302	7,998	6,930	1,068	Surplus throughout, fluctuating in $0.5–1.7 billion range since 1955.
Consumer goods, less automotive	4	4	10,272	28,166	−17,894	Postwar export bulge and surplus; deficit since 1959; increasing exponentially.

Table 3.22—continued

Commodity[a]	End-Use Code Number		1978 Trade			Trade Pattern, 1946–78
	Exports	Imports	Exports	Imports	Surplus	
Consumer durables, manufactured	400	41	4,602	14,551	−9,949	Postwar export bulge and surplus to 1954; growing deficit since then.
Electrical household appliances and radios and so forth	4000, 4001	4103, 4104	1,685	4,705	−3,020	Surplus to 1961; rapid import growth and growing deficit since product cycle.
Nonelectric cooking and heating equipment	4002	4101, 4102	572	1,851	−1,278	Postwar export bulge, deficit growing steadily since 1951.
Clocks, watches, jewelry, and antiques	4003	4108, 4109	555	2,841	−2,286	Deficit growing exponentially throughout.
Toys and sporting goods	4004	4100, 4105, 4107	766	3,749	−2,893	Deficit growing exponentially since 1950.
Other consumer durables, manufactured	4005	4106, 410A	1,024	1,404	−379	Postwar export bulge; trade roughly balanced since 1950.
Consumer durables, nonmanufactured[a]	401	421	493	2,231	−1,739	Deficit growing steadily throughout.
Consumer nondurables—textiles, except rugs	410	400	883	5,357	−4,474	Postwar export bulge and surplus to 1954; imports and deficit growing rapidly since 1975.
Consumer nondurables, except textiles	411	400	4,294	5,892	−1,599	Postwar export bulge and surplus to 1968; deficit growing irregularly since 1970.
Footwear, luggage, apparel of leather, fur, rubber, plastic	4110	4010, 4011	196	3,215	−3,019	Postwar export bulge and surplus to 1954; deficit growing steadily since then.
Medicinal and pharmaceutical preparations	4113	4012	1,521	699	821	Surplus throughout, growing rapidly since 1967.
Other consumer nondurables	4111–12, 4114	4013	2,552	1,978	575	Surplus except 1970; rapid export growth since then.

See following page for sources.

of manufactured goods down to the level represented by four-digit end-use codes. Selected commodities serve as illustrations of four general points.

From Raw Inputs to Finished Products: Steel

Within a given industry, such as steel or petroleum, the United States trade balance tends to move from deficit to surplus along the industrial scale from raw materials to semifinished products to finished products. Iron and steel and finished metals provide a good example.

The trade balance in iron and steel is depicted in figure 3.9. In basic materials, there was a surplus in the 1930s, but almost continuous deficits have existed after 1946, widening since 1960. In iron and steel products, except advanced manufactures, a prewar surplus widened after the war, and then narrowed, giving way to balance in the early 1960s, but a deficit opened from 1963 onward. Finally, in unfinished metal shapes and advanced metal manufactures the United States still has a small surplus after a few years of deficit in the period 1966–73.[5]

This description makes clear that the United States has become basically a net importer of steel with basic inputs and semifinished products in deficit and a small surplus in advanced products by 1978. While the United States has steadily lost its comparative advantage in iron and steel in general, the figure also suggests that, the more advanced the stage of production, the longer the United States trade advantage is maintained.[6]

Textiles: Postwar Export Bulge and 1970s Rationalization

In several commodities the United States characteristically had a balanced or deficit trade position before World War II, enjoyed a substantial surplus with a major increase in exports just after the war, and then

---

Sources: OBE 1970, table 5 (exports) and table 6 (imports); BEA 1977, table 2.2, and data tape provided by OBE. OBE's criterion for splitting off end-use categories below the one-digit level is generally the volume of trade in a category. For this reason, export and import categories do not generally match one for one. The development of the trade balances by commodity, described in the table, followed the export end-use breakdown, and matched imports to exports as closely as possible. Thus the first two columns of the table give the export end-use description and code number, and the third column gives the import end-use code numbers covering the same commodity as the second column's export end-use code number.

[a]Commodity descriptions are for export end-use code numbers, as described in OBE 1970.

[b]Groups 1273 and 1275–77 are subgroups of other nonagricultural industrial commodities that are a heterogeneous group and very difficult to match to an import category. In 1968, these groups accounted for $686 million of exports.

[c]Total includes other transportation equipment, not shown separately below.

[d]This nonmanufactured category is included in the table because of its relative importance in foreign trade.

lost it in a growing deficit after 1950. Also, in several commodities in the 1970s we can see the effects of international reallocation of the location of production, with labor-intensive stages of manufacturing moving away from the United States. A good example of these patterns is presented by textiles, both industrial and consumer textiles, as reflected in the trade balances shown in figure 3.10.

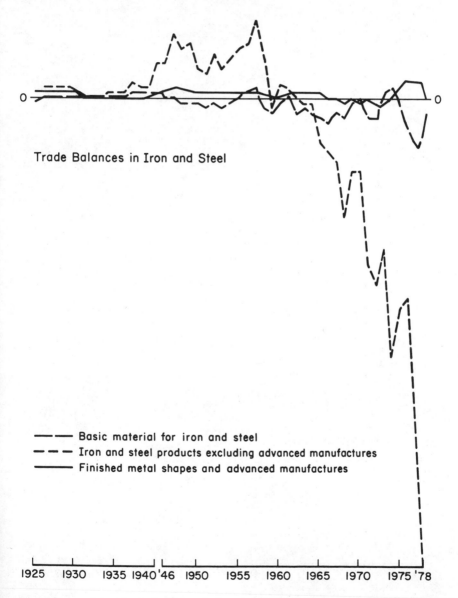

Fig. 3.9   Trade balances in iron and steel, 1925–78.

The postwar export bulge in textiles disappeared by 1949, leaving exports essentially flat at $500 million to $600 million in industrial textiles and $150 million to $200 million in consumer textiles from 1950 on, with little growth in the latter in the 1960s. Imports, however, grew in both cases. Consumer textile imports rose slowly from 1947 through 1954 and increasingly rapidly after 1954, while industrial textile im-

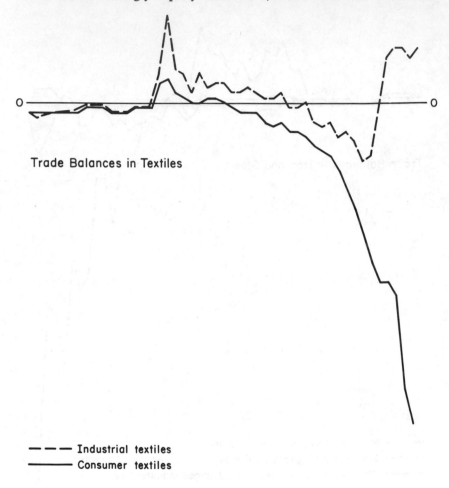

Trade Balances in Textiles

- - - - Industrial textiles
———— Consumer textiles

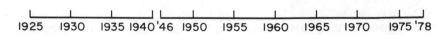

Fig. 3.10   Trade balances in textiles, 1925–78.

ports grew irregularly from 1949 to 1961 and extremely rapidly after that. The United States became a net importer of consumer textiles in 1955 and of industrial textiles in 1963.[7]

Since 1972, imports of consumer textiles have taken another significant jump, and trade in industrial textiles has moved back into surplus. At the consumer end, imports rose from $1.9 billion in 1972 to $5.4 billion in 1978, with the deficit moving from $1.2 billion to $3.6 billion. At the industrial end, however, exports rose from $0.9 billion in 1972 to $2.2 billion in 1978, while the balance moved from a $0.5 billion deficit to a $0.6 billion surplus. The United States is now an exporter of the industrial good and an importer of the consumer good.[8]

The Product Cycle: Household Appliances

Disaggregation to the four-digit level makes it possible to determine the pervasiveness of the product cycle phenomenon. In his seminal paper, Raymond Vernon (1966) suggested that trade in manufactured goods typically follows a cycle in which the United States is first a net exporter as a good is introduced and "shaken down," and then becomes a net importer as production of the good becomes standardized and moves abroad to minimize production costs. Since the product cycle involves patterns of trade in individual commodities, the likelihood that it can be observed increases with disaggregation of the data.

Household appliances are a good illustration of the product cycle (see fig. 3.11). After World War II there was a bulge in exports in 1946–48, and then growth from $109 million in 1949 to $261 million in 1956. Export growth slowed after 1956, and imports accelerated beginning in 1959. By 1962 the product cycle had reached the net import stage.[9]

The product cycle is, of course, a microeconomic phenomenon, observable at the four-digit level at best. That it *can* be observed at that level of aggregation suggests, however, that it is a fairly widespread phenomenon and should be taken into account in trade projections. At any point in time, commodities in which a substantial trade surplus exists may be in the maturing phase of the cycle with shrinking surpluses, while products just entering it may be at trade levels too small to seem significant. Thus the existence of the product cycle may tend to bias trade projections made on a commodity-by-commodity basis in a pessimistic direction (in the sense of small surpluses).

The 1970s Boom in Capital Goods Exports

In the aggregate data of figure 3.5, we saw that capital goods exports made a discontinuous jump from 1972 to 1975. The jump was spread across all the subcategories of capital goods except agricultural, scientific, and business machinery, where steady rapid growth continued. The increase in three subcategories is shown in table 3.23. There we see that the developing countries and OPEC took the biggest fraction of the increase, followed by Western Europe and Canada. The change in capital goods exports may point toward future growth as demand continues to rise in the LDCs and OPEC.

Consistency within Aggregates: Capital and Consumer Goods

Finally, the disaggregated data on trade in capital goods and in consumer goods exhibit strikingly similar patterns within the aggregate categories. Throughout the period 1946–78, in each category of capital goods, the United States typically has had a surplus, which has grown substantially since the early 1950s. The only exception is agricultural machinery. In the consumer categories, the United States typically had a deficit before the war and a surplus just after it. The surplus then shrank to balance in the middle or later 1950s and a growing deficit developed in the 1960s. Thus the patterns of trade are similar within

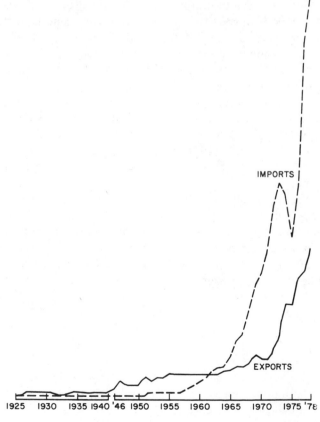

Fig. 3.11   United States exports and imports of household appliances, 1925–78.

Table 3.23   **Change in Exports of Selected Capital Goods, 1972–75**
                  ($ Millions)

Area	Electrical Machinery	Construction Machinery	Nonelectrical Industrial Machinery
Western Europe	668	599	1,626
Eastern Europe	66	80	389
Canada	283	357	922
Japan	100	61	180
Latin America	624	487	1,266
Australia, New Zealand, South Africa	110	194	333
Other Asia and Africa	1,099	1,208	1,472
Total	2,950	2,446	6,188

end-use aggregates and dissimilar across them, confirming the usefulness of the OBE categorization.

Conclusions from the Long-Term Data

From this survey of the long-term data, it appears that the United States has a growing comparative trade advantage in capital goods and chemicals but is at a disadvantage in consumer goods and other industrial supplies and materials. In consumer goods, the United States typically had a deficit from 1925 to 1938, and after a postwar surplus, returned to a deficit position starting in 1959. In some industrial supplies and materials—fuels and lubricants, basic materials for iron and steel, and their products—the United States was a net exporter before World War II and became a net importer thereafter.

Part of the movement from surplus to deficit in consumer goods and nonchemical industrial supplies and materials since the late 1940s has been due to the loss of a temporary advantage after World War II. This seems to be the case in consumer goods and textiles, although the trade deficit continued to increase even after the postwar advantage disappeared in the mid-1950s. In these areas, as well as in steel and petroleum, the loss of the postwar advantage merely reinforced the more fundamental loss in competitive advantage.

3.3.3   Sources of the United States Comparative Advantage in Manufactured Goods

As we have seen in sections 3.3.1 and 3.3.2, the United States has been a net exporter of capital goods and chemicals since World War II, with surpluses increasing rapidly since the late 1960s. In nonfuel, non-agricultural industrial supplies and materials the United States has likewise been a net importer since World War II. After a post-World War II bulge in exports of consumer goods, by 1960 the United States had become a net importer in that category, with deficits growing in the 1970s. In its trade in automotive products, the postwar surplus turned to deficit in the late 1960s. Within each of these categories there are complications and exceptions to the general trend. Notable among these is the pattern caused by international rationalization of the location of production, a phenomenon appearing in the trade data only since 1970. This can be seen in the growing export of auto parts and import of complete autos or in the export of industrial textiles and import of consumer textiles, for example. But the basic pattern of trade in the period beginning in 1970 is clear; the United States exports chemicals and capital goods, and imports consumer goods, automobiles, and nonfuel, nonagricultural industrial supplies and materials.

Presumably this very stable pattern of trade results from underlying relative advantages the United States has in chemicals and capital goods and disadvantages in consumer goods, automobiles, and other industrial supplies and materials. If the trade pattern showed large random fluctuations, we might not search for an underlying pattern of sources of comparative advantage. But with a stable pattern of trade, we look for a stable underlying basis for it.

In the immediate post-World War II period, trade analysts focused on a two-factor, capital and labor, model of comparative advantage, assuming that the United States trade pattern would reflect a heavy endowment of capital. This assumption was refuted by Leontief (1953). Gradually, after fifteen years of confusion and further analysis, a new consensus has appeared, which focuses on the role of human capital as the principal source of United States comparative advantage.

Capital Labor and Human Capital

The classical factor-endowments theory of international trade, generally associated with Heckscher and Ohlin, predicts that a country will export goods whose production is intensive in the use of primary input factors with which it is relatively well endowed, and import goods whose production intensively uses factors in which it is relatively poor. In the usual two-goods, two-factors, two-countries models, this dictum means simply that a country better endowed with capital than with labor should export goods whose production is capital-intensive and import goods that are labor-intensive. Since the United States has a high ratio of capital per employee, this proposition was generally taken to mean that its exports would be more capital-intensive than its imports.

This assumption was refuted by Leontief in 1953, when, using the 1947 input-output coefficients, he showed that United States exports are less capital-intensive in production than are the goods it imports. Leontief's findings were subsequently confirmed by Leontief (1956), using 1951 data, and by Hufbauer (1970) and Baldwin (1971), who used the 1963 input-output coefficients. Hufbauer showed that they also hold for manufactured goods separately.

Leontief suggested that his findings were due to higher labor productivity in the United States than in its trading partners. In support of this conjecture, in his 1956 paper he showed that production of United States exports employed relatively more skilled labor than did production of import-competing goods. At about the same time, Irving Kravis (1956) published a paper showing that leading United States export industries paid, on average, higher wages than leading import-competing industries. Both Leontief's conjecture and Kravis's findings point to the importance of a third factor of production in explaining United States trade patterns. If the high productivity of United States workers were due to a relatively large endowment of capital (physical capital, that is), then United States net exports should, by the factor proportions theory, be capital-intensive. But if there were a third factor involved, namely human capital, then a relatively high endowment of human capital relative to physical capital could explain both Leontief's and Kravis's results within a three-factor H-O model. This was noted by Gary Becker (1964).

A consensus was developing by the mid-1960s that an important explanation of the Leontief paradox was that the usual two-factor version of the Heckscher-Ohlin model was too simple. An analysis of trade in manufactured goods must be couched in terms of at least three inputs: physical capital, human capital, and raw (or uneducated) labor. In this case, the United States, because of its higher levels of education and training, may be relatively better endowed with human capital than with physical capital. In a two-factor model this situation would lead to United States exports of labor-intensive goods; a three-factor model might reveal that the United States exports goods that embody a high amount of human capital per man. The role of human capital in comparative advantage and trade was developed in a fundamental paper by Kenen (1965).

Since 1965, work on the human capital approach to Leontief's paradox has followed two tracks. One assumes that, in a cross-section, wage differentials reflect differences in human capital, following the spirit of Kenen's article. Thus Bharadwaj and Bhagwati (1967) as well as Hufbauer (1970), find a role for wage differentials as representing human capital in explaining trade. The other approach attempts to measure differences in human capital across industries by proportions of employees in various skill classifications. This is the route taken recently by Baldwin (1971), and earlier by Keesing (1966).

The first approach should be preferable if human capital is, in fact, reflected in earned income. If human capital is correctly valued, and this value accrues as earned income, wage differentials should fully capture the effects on productivity of differences in human capital per person.

The presence of, say, a high proportion of scientists in an industry should make that a high-wage industry, with the capitalized value of the excess of that wage rate over the wage of an uneducated person measuring the human capital input. In this event, the wage, or human capital, differential should capture the contribution of the input of human capital to production, or to trade advantage. Only if the scientists contribute something extra, in excess of their wage, to production should a "skill ratio" of scientists to total employees add to the ability of the human capital measure to explain variations in output or trade advantage.

Thus if wage rates accurately reflect differences in human capital, the capitalized value of the average wage above the wage of raw labor can serve as a measure of human capital in explaining net exports. If, in addition, a skill ratio is significant, it reveals that the skilled personnel are, in a sense, contributing more to comparative advantage than their market-determined wage indicates.

By the mid-1970s, the human capital explanation of the basis for United States comparative advantage was broadly accepted in the economics literature, as reflected in the paper by Bertil Ohlin (1977) and the comments thereon. A brief summary of one set of empirical results that supports this view follows.[10]

Empirical Estimates

In a paper that studied the composition of inputs into United States trade in manufactured goods, Branson and Monoyios (1977) found that in its trade, the United States exports the services of human capital and, marginally, physical capital, and imports the services of unskilled labor. For 1963 and 1967, they developed data matching the inputs of physical capital (K), human capital (H), and labor (L) in manufacturing industries to trade in commodities produced by these industries. They then performed cross-section regressions of net exports of commodities on the inputs of the industries. A representative sample of their results is shown in table 3.24.[11] The first column in the table identifies the dependent variables net exports (NX), exports (X), or imports (M). The next three columns show the estimated coefficients of K, H, L, and the constant terms of the regressions in that order. The numbers in parentheses under the coefficients are the t-ratios. Those marked with one asterisk identify coefficients that are significantly different from zero at the 5 percent confidence level, while those with two asterisks are significant at both the 5 percent and 1 percent levels. In the sixth column the multiple correlation coefficient R^2 for the regression is given and in the last column, the identifying number for the equation.

The simple r^2 in the sample data between NX and H is equal to 0.32. In equation 2–1 in table 3.24 both K and H are introduced as independent variables. While the coefficient of H is positive and highly signifi-

Table 3.24   **Estimates of Regression Equations at the Three-Digit SITC Level**

Dependent Variables	Independent Variables					Equation Number
	K	H	L	C	R^2	
NX (1963)	−0.04	0.03		−2.29	0.34**	2–1
	(1.63)	(5.31)**		(0.08)		
NX (1963)	−0.05	0.04	−0.67	18.54	0.45**	2–2
	(2.18)*	(6.87)**	(3.99)**	(0.72)		
X (1963)	0.01	0.03	−0.44	37.56	0.53**	2–3
	(0.61)	(5.39)**	(2.58)*	(1.45)		
M (1963)	0.06	−0.01	0.23	19.02	0.40**	2–4
	(5.58)**	(2.88)**	(2.77)**	(1.48)		
NX (1967)	−0.04	0.04	−0.69	19.05	0.34**	2–5
	(2.33)*	(6.02)**	(3.21)**	(0.53)		

cant, that of K is negative and not even marginally significant; the R^2 for regression stays practically unchanged from 0.32 to 0.34. When L is entered into the regression in equation 2–2 the size and sign of the coefficients of K and H are not affected while their significance is increased slightly so that K becomes marginally significant. The coefficient of L is negative and significant, and R^2 rises from 0.34 to 0.45.

Equation 2–3 of the table shows that industries with high gross exports are human capital intensive in production, other things being equal. Physical capital input is not significant. On the other hand, equation 2–4 indicates that the United States imports goods whose domestic production intensively uses physical capital and labor relative to human capital. The signs of the coefficients are the reverse of 1–2 and all three coefficients are significant although the fit of the regression is not as good as when X is the dependent variable.

The Branson and Monoyios results confirm that the United States exports human capital and imports unskilled labor in its trade in manufactured goods, at least in 1963–67. Since sections 3.3.1 and 3.3.2 showed that the mid-1960s pattern of trade became even clearer in the 1970s, there is no reason to expect that the Branson-Monoyios results do not still hold. This conclusion is supported by the Stern and Maskus (1979) study that considers the 1958–76 time-series data.

Summary

Combining the evidence on trends in United States trade in sections 3.3.1 and 3.3.2 with the results on United States comparative advantage in this section, we obtain the following broad picture of United States trade patterns. The United States exports chemicals and capital goods and imports consumer goods, nonfood, nonfuel industrial supplies and materials, and automobiles. In this exchange the United States exports the services of human capital—i.e., skilled or educated labor—and perhaps physical capital and imports the services of unskilled labor.

Thus human capital and unskilled labor play a clear role in the formation of United States comparative advantage. Good examples are aircraft on the export side, which are extremely human capital intensive but not very intensive in physical capital, and consumer textiles on the import side. Physical capital plays a more neutral role, combining relatively more with human capital in exports and unskilled labor in imports. Good examples may be chemicals on the export side and consumer electronics on the import side.

In the ten years or so after World War II, the United States had a false boom in exports of goods that are relatively labor intensive in production. But after the mid-1950s comparative advantage reasserted itself with the growth of industrial capacity in Europe and Japan. The United States trade pattern moved back to a base in comparative advantage discussed just above. In the 1970s, growth in industrial capacity in the LDCs seems to be generally along lines of their comparative advantage. This is strengthening the pattern of United States trade in a world of increasing specialization and interdependence.

3.4   Trends in Long-Term Investment

During the period since World War II there has been significant growth in United States long-term investment abroad and foreign long-term investment in the United States. Both United States long-term claims on foreigners and liabilities to foreigners have grown at an annual rate of about 9 percent during the period 1950–77. Within this balanced growth of the aggregate long-term investment position there have been significant changes in composition in terms of type and location of United States foreign investment and type and geographical source of foreign investment in the United States. The following section presents the data on the long-term United States investment position compiled for the years 1950–77.

3.4.1   United States Aggregate Investment Position

The aggregate United States long-term foreign investment position is summarized in table 3.25. There we see that United States private plus government long-term claims have grown from $28.3 billion in 1950 to $264.4 billion in 1977, while long-term liabilities have risen from $8 billion to $94 billion. The United States net long-term position was $170.5 billion in 1977. Over the twenty-seven-year period for which we have data, United States total long-term claims have grown at an annual rate of 8.3 percent (table 3.25, cols. 1 and 2) and United States liabili-

Table 3.25   United States Long-Term Assets and Liabilities, 1950–77
                    ($ Billions)

Year	U.S. Private Long-Term Assets (1)	U.S. Government Long-Term Credits (2)	U.S. Long-Term Liabilities (3)	Balance (1)+(2)−(3)
1950	17.5	10.8	8.0	20.3
1955	26.8	12.4	13.4	25.8
1960	44.4	14.1	18.4	40.1
1965	71.0	20.3	26.4	64.9
1970	105.0	29.6	44.7	89.9
1975	174.4	39.8	80.7	133.1
1977	216.6	47.8	93.9	170.5

ties have grown at the annual rate of 9.1 percent. The distribution of
United States claims has shifted from government toward private. In
1950 private claims were 62 percent of the total; by 1977 this ratio had
risen to 82 percent.

3.4.2   Distribution and Growth of United States Long-Term
Assets and Liabilities

United States Assets

Table 3.26 shows the breakdown of the United States long-term private asset position from table 3.25 into direct investment, investment
in foreign bonds and stocks, and other long-term investment. Roughly,
the definitional division between direct investment and stock ownership

Table 3.26   United States Private Long-Term Foreign Assets ($ Billions)

Year	Total	Direct	Foreign Bonds	Foreign Stocks	Other
1950	17.5	11.8	3.2	1.2	1.4
1955	26.7	19.4	3.0	2.4	1.9
1960	44.4	31.9	5.5	4.0	3.1
1965	71.0	49.5	10.2	5.0	6.4
1970	105.0	78.2	13.2	6.4	7.2
1971	114.5	83.0	15.9	7.6	8.1
1972	127.8	90.5	17.1	10.5	9.7
1973	139.8	101.3	17.4	10.0	11.1
1974	151.0	110.1	19.2	9.0	12.7
1975	174.4	124.0	25.3	9.6	15.4
1976	198.3	136.4	34.7	9.5	17.8
1977	216.6	148.8	39.2	10.1	18.5

is 10 percent control; once that level of ownership is reached, all further investment in that firm is direct.

Growth rates of United States foreign assets are summarized in table 3.27. There we see that the United States private long-term asset position has grown in a very balanced way since 1950. The sole exception is slower-than-average growth in ownership of foreign stock at an annual rate of 7.8 percent. In table 3.26 we see that stock-ownership peaked in 1972 at $10.5 billion; the growth rate for 1950–72 was 10 percent.

United States direct investment abroad has grown at a remarkably steady rate. During the 1950s the direct investment position grew at a 10 percent rate; during the 1960s the growth rate was 9 percent; and from 1970 to 1977 it was 9.2 percent. Thus long-term United States investment abroad has proceeded at a very stable rate of 9–10 percent throughout the entire, sometimes turbulent, period.

United States Liabilities

The disaggregation of United States long-term liabilities to foreigners is shown in table 3.28, and the growth rate summary is given in table 3.29. Within an aggregate growth rate of 9.1 percent over the period, foreign investment in United States private and government bonds grew by 15.9 percent, and direct investment grew by 8.5 percent.

Foreign investment in United States bonds started from the low base of $181 million in 1950, and grew with two big jumps, in 1955–60 and 1965–70. From 1965 to 1971 foreign bond ownership rose tenfold to nearly $10 billion. Direct investment has gone through a growth cycle, beginning at 8 percent in 1950–55, falling to 5 percent in 1960–65, and rising to 13.5 percent per year in the 1970s. Foreign investment in United States corporate stock has grown at an annual average rate of 9.7 percent, fluctuating between a high of 16.2 percent in 1950–55 and a low of 4.9 percent in 1965–70.

Table 3.27	Average Annual Growth Rates of United States Private Long-Term Foreign Assets (in Percentages)						
Item	1950–77	1950–55	1955–60	1960–65	1965–70	1970–75	1975–77
Long-Term Private, Total	9.3	5.5	10.2	9.4	7.8	10.2	10.8
Direct Investment	9.4	10.0	9.9	8.8	9.2	9.2	9.1
Foreign Bonds	9.3	−0.7	11.9	12.2	5.2	13.1	21.9
Foreign Corporate Stocks	7.8	14.6	9.8	4.7	4.9	8.0	2.7
Other	9.7	6.3	9.9	14.5	2.4	15.3	9.1

Table 3.28   **United States Long-Term Liabilities to Foreigners ($ Billions)**

Year	Total	Direct	Bonds	Corporate Stock	Other
1950	8.0	3.4	0.2	2.9	1.5
1955	13.4	5.1	0.3	6.6	1.5
1960	18.4	6.9	0.6	9.3	1.6
1965	26.4	8.8	0.9	14.6	2.1
1970	44.8	13.3	6.9	18.7	5.9
1971	50.1	13.9	8.6	21.4	6.1
1972	60.8	14.9	10.9	27.8	7.1
1973	74.3	20.6	12.6	33.5	7.7
1974	67.6	25.1	10.7	24.2	7.6
1975	80.7	27.7	10.0	35.3	7.7
1976	92.6	30.8	12.0	42.9	7.0
1977	93.9	34.1	13.4	39.7	6.7

Source: *Survey of Current Business.*

Table 3.29   **Average Annual Growth Rates of Foreign Long-Term Assets in the United States (in Percentages)**

Item	1950–77	1950–55	1955–60	1960–65	1965–70	1970–75	1975–77
Long-Term Total	9.1	10.3	6.3	7.2	10.6	11.8	7.6
Direct Investment	8.5	8.0	6.2	4.8	8.2	14.7	10.4
Bonds	15.9	7.2	18.4	6.0	41.2	7.5	5.7
Corporate Stock	9.7	16.2	6.9	9.0	4.9	12.7	5.9
Other	5.6	.0	0.8	6.0	20.8	5.2	−6.7

3.4.3 United States Investment Abroad

The data on United States direct investment abroad can be disaggregated by industry and area. The geographic breakdown is Europe, Canada, Japan, Latin America, and other, while the industry breakdown is mining and smelting, petroleum, manufacturing, and other. The disaggregated data on direct investment are given in table 3.30 for the total, and tables 3.31 through 3.35 for the geographic areas. The shares of United States direct investment on each geographical area are given in table 3.36.

Turning first to the industry disaggregation of total direct investment, we see a steady growth of the direct investment position throughout the

Table 3.30   **United States Direct Investment, Total ($ Billions)**

Year	Mining and Smelting	Petroleum	Manu-facturing	Other
1950	1.1	3.4	3.8	3.4
1955	2.2	5.9	6.6	4.7
1960	3.0	10.9	11.2	7.7
1965	3.8	15.3	19.3	10.9
1970	6.2	21.7	32.3	18.0
1971	6.7	24.2	35.6	19.7
1972	7.1	26.3	39.7	21.2
1973	6.0	27.3	44.4	26.0
1974	6.1	30.2	50.9	31.3
1975	6.5	26.2	55.9	35.6
1976	7.1	29.7	61.1	39.4
1977	7.1	30.9	65.6	45.2

Source: *Survey of Current Business.*

Table 3.31   **United States Direct Investment in Europe ($ Billions)**

Year	Mining and Smelting	Petroleum	Manu-facturing	Other
1950	0.0	0.4	0.9	0.3
1955	0.0	0.8	1.7	0.5
1960	0.0	1.7	3.8	1.1
1965	0.0	3.4	7.6	2.9
1970	0.0	5.5	13.7	5.2
1971	0.0	6.2	15.6	5.8
1972	0.0	6.9	17.6	5.9
1973	0.0	8.5	20.8	8.9
1974	0.0	10.0	23.8	10.7
1975	0.0	11.4	26.0	12.1
1976	0.0	13.4	28.7	13.7
1977	0.0	13.9	31.4	15.2

Source: *Survey of Current Business.*

Table 3.32   **United States Direct Investment in Canada ($ Billions)**

Year	Mining and Smelting	Petroleum	Manu-facturing	Other
1950	0.3	0.4	1.9	0.9
1955	0.9	1.4	3.1	1.4
1960	1.3	2.7	4.8	2.4
1965	1.8	3.4	6.9	3.2
1970	3.0	4.8	10.1	4.9
1971	3.2	5.1	10.6	5.1
1972	3.5	5.3	11.6	5.4
1973	2.7	5.3	11.8	5.8
1974	2.8	5.7	13.4	6.4
1975	3.1	6.2	14.7	7.1
1976	3.2	7.2	16.0	7.6
1977	3.2	7.7	16.7	7.8

Source: *Survey of Current Business.*

Table 3.33   **United States Direct Investment in Japan ($ Billions)**

Year	Mining and Smelting	Petroleum	Manu-facturing	Other
1950	0.0	0.0	0.0	0.0
1955	0.0	0.0	0.0	0.1
1960	0.0	0.0	0.0	0.2
1965	0.0	0.0	0.3	0.4
1970	0.0	0.5	0.7	0.2
1971	0.0	0.6	1.0	0.2
1972	0.0	0.9	1.2	0.3
1973	0.0	0.9	1.4	0.4
1974	0.0	1.4	1.5	0.4
1975	0.0	1.3	1.6	0.5
1976	0.0	1.6	1.7	0.5
1977	0.0	1.5	1.9	0.6

Source: *Survey of Current Business.*

Table 3.34   **United States Direct Investment in Latin America ($ Billions)**

Year	Mining and Smelting	Petroleum	Manu- facturing	Other
1950	0.6	1.2	0.8	1.8
1955	1.0	1.6	1.4	2.2
1960	1.2	2.9	1.6	2.7
1965	1.1	3.0	2.7	2.5
1970	2.1	3.9	4.6	4.1
1971	2.1	4.2	5.0	4.5
1972	2.1	4.3	5.6	4.8
1973	1.7	3.0	6.5	5.3
1974	1.4	3.6	7.5	7.1
1975	1.5	3.3	8.6	8.7
1976	1.6	2.9	9.2	9.8
1977	1.6	3.4	10.0	12.8

Source: *Survey of Current Business.*

Table 3.35   **United States Direct Investment in Other Countries ($ Billions)**

Year	Mining and Smelting	Petroleum	Manu- facturing	Other
1950	0.1	1.3	0.2	0.3
1955	0.3	2.2	0.5	0.5
1960	0.5	3.7	0.8	1.3
1965	0.9	5.5	1.8	1.9
1970	1.0	7.0	3.1	3.5
1971	1.3	8.0	3.5	4.0
1972	1.5	8.9	3.7	4.9
1973	1.6	9.6	4.0	5.5
1974	1.8	9.6	4.7	6.6
1975	2.0	3.9	5.1	7.2
1976	2.2	4.6	5.4	7.8
1977	2.2	4.3	5.7	8.7

Source: *Survey of Current Business.*

Table 3.36   **Distribution of United States Direct Investment by Area (in Percentages)**

Year	Europe	Canada	Japan	Latin America	Other
1950	.15	.30	.00	.38	.17
1955	.15	.35	.01	.31	.18
1960	.20	.34	.01	.26	.19
1965	.28	.31	.01	.19	.20
1970	.31	.29	.02	.19	.19
1971	.32	.28	.02	.18	.19
1972	.32	.27	.03	.18	.20
1973	.37	.25	.03	.16	.20
1974	.38	.24	.03	.16	.19
1975	.40	.25	.03	.18	.15
1976	.41	.25	.03	.17	.15
1977	.41	.24	.03	.19	.14

period at 9.4 percent per year. There was a slowdown of growth in assets in mining and smelting and petroleum after 1970, steady growth in manufacturing at about 10 percent per year over the entire period, and an acceleration in other investments after 1970. Manufacturing investment grew from 32 percent of the total in 1950 to 44 percent in 1977.

United States direct investment in Europe grew at a 13 percent annual rate, 1950–77. Mining and smelting investment in Europe was nil, and the three other categories show balanced growth, each increasing at a 13–14 percent annual rate. In table 3.36 we see that Europe's share of total United States direct investment rose from 15 percent in 1950 to 41 percent in 1977.

In Canada, United States investment in petroleum had the highest growth rate, 10.8 percent over the entire period. United States investment in Japan grew at 11.9 percent from a tiny base in 1950. By 1977 the Japanese share of United States direct investment was still a miniscule 2.7 percent. The United States direct investment position in Latin America grew at an annual rate of 6.8 percent from 1950 to 1977. Investment in Latin America was concentrated in manufacturing, with a 9.4 percent growth rate, and with a 7.3 percent growth rate in other. In the share table, we see a cycle in the Latin American position. It fell from 38 percent in 1950 to a low of 16 percent in 1973, and then began to rise to 18.6 percent by 1977.

To summarize, the United States direct investment position grew remarkably steadily during the period 1950–77. There was a movement away from resource-based investment, except in Canada, toward manufacturing and other investment. The major growth area remains Europe, whose share of the total rose from 31 percent in 1970 to 41 percent in 1977. After a long period of relative decline, United States investment in Latin America also shows acceleration since 1973 or so.

3.4.4   Foreign Direct Investment in the United States

The foreign direct investment position in the United States can be disaggregated geographically by investment from Europe, Canada, Japan, and other, and by industry into petroleum, manufacturing, insurance and finance, and other. The disaggregated data by industry are given for total foreign direct investment in the United States in table 3.37, and for each area in tables 3.38 through 3.41. The distribution of shares by geographic source is shown in table 3.42.

Total foreign direct investment in the United States has risen from $3.4 billion in 1950 to $34.1 billion in 1977. This is 23 percent as large as United States direct investment abroad. The growth rate of the direct foreign investment position in the United States doubled in the 1970s compared to the previous two decades: 7.1 percent per year in the 1950s, 6.5 percent in the 1960s, and 13.5 percent in the 1970s. The distribution of the total across industries has moved from insurance and finance towards the other three categories. The petroleum share rose from 12 to 19 percent, manufacturing from 34 to 40 percent, and other from 23 to 34 percent, while the share of insurance and finance fell from 31 to 7 percent.

In the share distribution of table 3.42, we see Europe fairly steady at 65 to 70 percent over the period, Canada falling from 30 to 18 percent, Japan growing from nil as late as 1973 to 5 percent in 1977, and other growing from 4 to 11 percent. As foreign direct investment in the United States accelerated in the 1970s, the Canadian and European shares fell, and the Japanese and other shares rose. Table 3.43 shows the distribution of the increase in foreign investment from 1970 to 1977. There we see that even as the Japanese and other shares rose, the bulk of the increase in investment position came from Europe. The rising shares of Japan and other began from a very small base.

To summarize, foreign direct investment in the United States rose in the 1970s relative to the trend of 6–7 percent growth of the 1950–70 period. The distribution moved away from finance toward manufacturing, petroleum, and other, essentially from finance toward nonfinancial firms. While foreign investment in the United States is only a quarter of United States investment abroad, we may be seeing the beginning of the internationalization of ownership of United States industry.

Table 3.37   **Foreign Direct Investment in the United States ($ Billions)**

Year	Total	Petroleum	Manu-facturing	Insurance and Finance	Other
1950	3.4	0.4	1.1	1.1	0.8
1955	5.1	0.9	1.8	1.5	1.0
1960	6.9	1.2	2.6	1.8	1.3
1965	8.8	1.7	3.5	2.2	1.4
1970	13.3	3.0	6.1	2.3	1.9
1971	13.9	3.1	6.7	2.6	1.5
1972	14.9	3.3	7.3	2.9	1.4
1973	20.6	4.8	8.2	1.9	5.6
1974	25.1	5.6	10.4	1.3	7.8
1975	27.7	6.2	11.4	1.6	8.4
1976	30.8	5.9	12.6	2.1	10.1
1977	34.1	6.6	13.7	2.3	11.5

Source: *Survey of Current Business.*

Table 3.38   **Direct Investment in the United States by Europe ($ Billions)**

Year	Petroleum	Manu-facturing	Insurance and Finance	Other
1950	0.3	0.7	0.9	0.3
1955	0.7	1.0	1.3	0.4
1960	1.0	1.6	1.5	0.6
1965	1.5	2.2	1.7	0.7
1970	2.8	4.1	1.8	0.9
1971	2.9	4.5	2.0	0.9
1972	3.0	4.8	2.3	0.9
1973	4.1	4.8	1.5	3.5
1974	4.7	6.1	1.0	5.0
1975	5.5	6.7	1.2	5.2
1976	5.0	7.4	1.6	6.1
1977	5.5	8.4	1.8	7.0

Source: *Survey of Current Business.*

Table 3.39 **Direct Investment in the United States by Canada ($ Billions)**

Year	Petroleum	Manu-facturing	Insurance and Finance	Other
1950	0.1	0.5	0.2	0.4
1955	0.2	0.7	0.2	0.5
1960	0.2	0.9	0.2	0.6
1965	0.2	1.2	0.4	0.6
1970	0.2	1.8	0.3	0.8
1971	0.2	2.0	0.3	0.8
1972	0.2	2.2	0.4	0.7
1973	0.4	2.3	0.2	1.3
1974	0.5	2.9	0.2	1.5
1975	0.6	3.1	0.2	1.5
1976	0.7	3.4	0.2	1.6
1977	0.7	3.4	0.2	1.7

Source: *Survey of Current Business.*

Table 3.40 **Direct Investment in the United States by Japan ($ Billions)**

Year	Petroleum	Manu-facturing	Insurance and Finance	Other
1950	0.0	0.0	0.0	0.0
1955	0.0	0.0	0.0	0.0
1960	0.0	0.0	0.0	0.0
1965	0.0	0.1	0.0	0.0
1970	0.0	0.1	0.0	0.1
1971	0.0	0.1	0.1	−0.4
1972	0.0	0.1	0.1	−0.3
1973	0.1	0.1	0.0	−0.1
1974	0.0	0.3	0.0	0.0
1975	0.0	0.3	0.0	0.2
1976	0.0	0.3	0.0	0.8
1977	0.0	0.3	0.0	1.3

Source: *Survey of Current Business.*

Table 3.41   Direct Investment in the United States by Other Countries ($ Billions)

Year	Petroleum	Manu-facturing	Insurance and Finance	Other
1950	0.0	0.0	0.0	0.1
1955	0.0	0.0	0.0	0.1
1960	0.0	0.1	0.1	0.1
1965	0.0	0.0	0.1	0.1
1970	0.0	0.1	0.1	0.1
1971	0.0	0.2	0.1	0.1
1972	0.0	0.2	0.2	0.1
1973	0.2	1.0	0.2	0.9
1974	0.3	1.0	0.1	1.4
1975	0.1	1.3	0.2	1.5
1976	0.2	1.5	0.3	1.6
1977	0.3	1.5	0.3	1.6

Source: *Survey of Current Business.*

Table 3.42   Distribution of Foreign Investment in the United States by Area (in Percentages)

Year	Europe	Canada	Japan	Other
1950	.66	.30	.00	.04
1955	.66	.30	.00	.03
1960	.68	.28	.00	.04
1965	.69	.27	.01	.02
1970	.71	.23	.02	.03
1971	.74	.24	−.02	.03
1972	.75	.23	−.01	.03
1973	.68	.20	.01	.11
1974	.67	.20	.01	.12
1975	.67	.19	.02	.11
1976	.65	.19	.04	.11
1977	.67	.18	.05	.11

Table 3.43   Increase in the Foreign Direct Investment Position in the United
                    States, 1970–77 ($ Billions)

	Change in Liabilities to
Canada	2.9
Europe	13.1
Japan	1.5
Other	3.3
Total	20.8

3.5   The Change in Balance of Payments and Exchange Rate Arrangements, 1960–78

Sections 3.3 and 3.4 reviewed trends in trade and investment since World War II against the background of section 3.2. They showed that the dominant United States economic position of the 1950s eroded subsequently, perhaps in a return to more normal historic patterns. This section briefly reviews the major changes in monetary arrangements, as they reflect or affect the changing structure of the United States economy. It does not present a full-scale review of international monetary developments.[12] Rather, it focuses on two major structural changes since 1960. One is an increase in the underlying volatility of the United States "basic balance," defined as the current account plus net long-term capital flows, from the 1960s to the 1970s. The other is the shift from fixed exchange rates in the 1960s to managed floating rates since 1973. To an extent, these two changes have a cause-and-effect relationship. The increase in variability of the basic balance is an economic fact that makes the equilibrium exchange rate more variable over time. This is one of the reasons for the emergence of the system of managed floating, to permit use of the exchange rate to absorb some of this variability.

3.5.1   Intervention and Exchange-Rate Flexibility

During the period 1971–73, between President Nixon's speech of 15 August 1971, which ended gold convertibility of the dollar, and March 1973 when "generalized floating" of the major currencies began, there was a major shift in United States exchange rate policy. This was one of the two major structural changes affecting reserve and exchange rate relationships during the period. Most commentators agree that after March 1973 the world had completed a shift to more or less managed floating among major currencies, but there is disagreement on whether this period began in 1971 or 1973. During that interim period we experienced a type of "mini" Bretton Woods system in which the German and Japanese authorities attempted to hold their exchange rates fixed at the values decided in the Smithsonian Agreement of December 1971.

Before 1971, central banks generally intervened by buying or selling reserves in the foreign exchange markets to hold exchange rates within bands of specified width around parity values. After 1973, exchange rates were allowed to vary toward market equilibrium rates but with official intervention following guidelines or rules that generally have not been made public. To clarify the discussion of intervention versus flexibility, and the subsequent analysis of the effects of a change in the volatility of underlying determinants of the equilibrium exchange rate, we turn to the analytical framework of figure 3.12.

An Analytical Framework

Figure 3.12 shows the interaction between the basic balance (B), short-term capital movements (S), the exchange rate $(e$, in dollars per unit of foreign exchange, the weighted nominal rate), and net changes in reserves (R). The balance of payments identity in these terms can be written as

$$B - S = \Delta R.$$

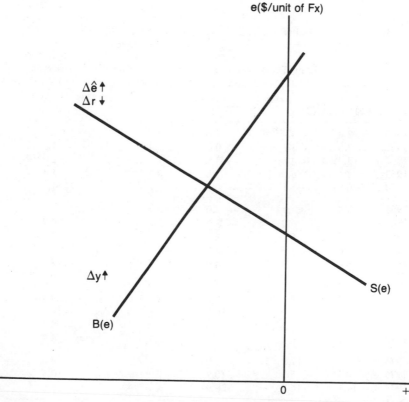

Fig. 3.12   Basic balance and short-term capital.

Here, and in figure 3.12, B is the *surplus* on basic balance, S is the *deficit* on short-term capital, and R is the *increase* in reserves. The basic balance is the current account surplus less net long-term capital outflow, and short-term capital is defined over private transactions. Data for these aggregates are given in table 3.44. The B and S curves in figure 3.12 are drawn in the negative quadrant because the basic balance has generally been in deficit since 1960.

The basic balance function $B(e)$ in figure 3.12 has a steep positive slope reflecting the effect of an increase in e (devaluation of the dollar) on the current value of the trade balance. An increase in income Y would shift B up, yielding a larger current account deficit at any given value of the exchange rate. The $B(e)$ function takes as given other determinants of the basic balance, including lagged values of the real exchange rate. The short-term capital function $S(e)$ has a flat negative slope reflecting the sensitivity of short-term capital inflows as the exchange rate changes *relative* to the expected rate e. An increase in expected rate shifts $S(e)$ up, as the surplus on short-term capital is reduced; an increase in domestic interest rates shifts it down.[13]

Table 3.44   United States Balance of Payments ($ Billions)

Year	Current Account (1)	Long-Term Capital Surplus (+) (2)	Basic Balance (1)+(2) (3)	Short-Term Capital Net Outflow (+) (4)	Change in Reserves (3)−(4) Net Income (+) (5)
1960	2.8	− 4.4	− 1.6	1.8	− 3.4
1961	3.8	− 3.7	0.1	1.4	− 1.3
1962	3.4	− 4.6	− 1.2	1.5	− 2.7
1963	4.4	− 6.0	− 1.6	0.3	− 1.9
1964	6.8	− 7.1	− 0.3	1.2	− 1.5
1965	5.4	− 7.4	− 2.0	−0.7	− 1.3
1966	3.0	− 6.0	− 3.0	−3.2	0.2
1967	2.6	− 6.7	− 4.1	−0.7	− 3.4
1968	0.6	− 2.9	− 2.3	−3.9	1.6
1969	0.4	− 4.4	− 4.0	−6.7	2.7
1970	2.3	− 6.3	− 4.0	5.9	− 9.9
1971	− 1.4	− 9.1	−10.5	19.2	−29.7
1972	− 5.7	− 5.1	−10.8	−0.6	−10.2
1973	7.1	− 7.9	− 0.8	4.5	− 5.3
1974	2.1	− 6.1	− 4.0	4.7	− 8.7
1975	18.3	−17.3	1.0	5.4	− 4.4
1976	4.6	−15.3	−10.7	−0.2	−10.5
1977	−14.1	−14.8	−28.9	6.1	−35.0

Source: Survey of Current Business.

Operation with Fixed Exchange Rates

If foreign central banks are committed to intervention at a given weighted nominal United States exchange rate (from the United States point of view) $\bar{e}$ then the difference between the B and S functions of figure 3.12 at $\bar{e}$ gives the effect on net United States reserves. For example, in figure 3.13, if the dollar rate is fixed at $\bar{e}$, below the market equilibrium value, the basic balance deficit is larger than the short-term capital surplus, and the resulting intervention to hold the exchange rate at $\bar{e}$ reduces net United States reserves by the difference $B - S = R$, which is negative. A tightening of United States monetary policy, shifting $S(e)$ down, would reduce the reserve loss, as would a United States recession that shifts $B(e)$ down.

If the parity rate $\bar{e}$ were above the market equilibrium rate, then intervention would result in gain in United States reserves, $R > 0$. An easing of United States monetary policy or expansion of demand would reduce the size of the reserve change in this case.

The average level of the United States reserve position over time will depend on whether the weighted parity rate $\bar{e}$ tends to be below or above

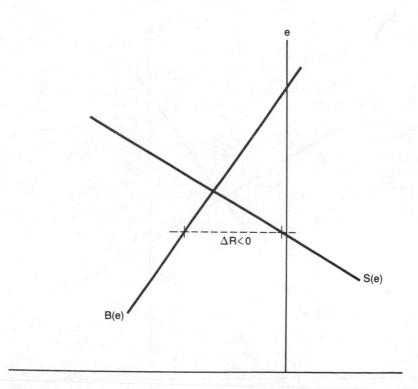

Fig. 3.13   Intervention with a fixed rate.

the market equilibrium rate in figure 3.13. In section 3.2, we saw that during the 1960s the United States share in world export markets decreased while the United States experienced roughly average price performance internationally. In figure 3.13 this development would be interpreted as a drift toward the left of the $B(e)$ function, with an increasing basic balance deficit at any given exchange rate. As a result, the market equilibrium nominal exchange rate drifted up along the $S(e)$ function, and the equilibrium real exchange rate moved along with it. It was this pressure of cumulative reserve loss and a growing gap between the equilibrium rate and the parity rate that led to the breakdown of the fixed rate system in 1971.

Operation with Flexible Exchange Rates

A system of cleanly floating exchange rates is defined as one with no intervention, that is $\Delta R = 0$. In this case the nominal exchange rate will find its market equilibrium value e^* where $B(e) = S(e)$, as shown in figure 3.14. There have been only a few short periods of completely clean floating since 1971. One clean float came in March 1973 when

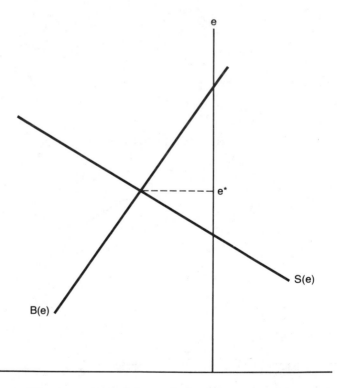

Fig. 3.14   Floating rate, no intervention.

intervention had become unsustainable and rates were so far from market equilibrium that they had to be floated to see where the equilibrium was. Other periods of minimal intervention have come when the $B(e)$ and $S(e)$ functions remained stable for a period of time and as a consequence exchange rates remained stable without intervention. One such period came during 1975, when the weighted nominal United States exchange rate rose 1.25 percent (fig. 3.1, 1975:1–1976:1), and United States reserves fell by only $4.4 billion (table 3.44).

Partial Intervention or "Leaning against the Wind"

Generally in the period since 1971, exchange rates have been neither fixed nor cleanly floating. Instead we have had a period of generally managed floating, in which central banks have intervened to slow the movement of the rate, effectively resulting in partial adjustment of the actual rate when the equilibrium rate moves. This intervention policy, called "leaning against the wind" in foreign exchange markets, is illustrated in figure 3.15.[14] There the initial market rate is e^*_0. A leftward shift of $B(e)$ from B_0 to B_1 would raise the market equilibrium rate to

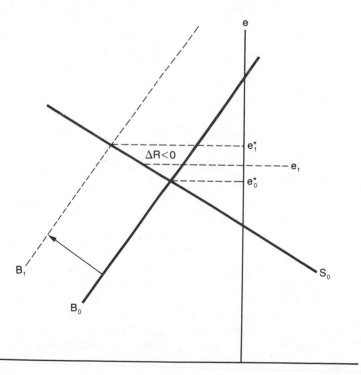

Fig. 3.15   "Leaning against the wind."

e^*_1. If the rate of change of e from e^*_0 to e^*_1, is viewed as too large by foreign central banks or the Fed, intervention could hold the rate at some intermediate value e_1. The resulting reserve loss to the United States would be ΔR, in figure 3.15.

An example of this policy appears in the data for 1977–78 in figure 3.1 and table 3.44. The United States basic balance deficit increased from $11 billion in 1977 to $29 billion in 1978 (table 3.44). This was accompanied by an increase in the weighted nominal exchange rate of 12.6 percent from 1977:4 to 1978:4 *and* an increase in reserve loss from $11 billion in 1977 to $35 billion in 1978 as central banks slowed the movement in the exchange rate.

It should be clear from the example of 1977–78 that observed reserve movements can be larger under managed floating than under fixed rates, if the stability of the $B(e)$ function changes across periods. When $B(e)$ is relatively stable, fixed rates may be maintained with little intervention as long as the parity rate is close to the market equilibrium rate on average over time. But if $B(e)$ becomes unstable, larger interventions are required. If these become too large for central banks to countenance, they move to managed floating. This permits the exchange rate to absorb some of the shock of $B(e)$ disturbances. For example, in figure 3.15 the ΔR that would be to hold the rate at e^* as B shifts from B_0 to B_1 is much larger than the intervention under managed floating.

Thus a significant increase in the volatility of the current account or the basic balance could move the system from fixed rates to managed floating. Here the structural change in policy regime in the 1970s could be traced to a change in the underlying structure of the economy. We now turn to evidence of such an increase in basic balance volatility.

3.5.2   Volatility of Underlying Exchange Rate Determinants

The annual data for United States balance of payments aggregates since 1970 are shown in table 3.44. There the data are arranged to correspond to the framework of figures 3.12 through 3.15. The basic balance surplus of column 3 is $B(e)$; the short-term capital outflow of column 4 is $S(e)$, and the change in reserves of column 5 is ΔR. The basic balance shows deficits every year except 1961 and 1976; the reserve column shows losses every year except 1966, 1968, 1969. The current account column generally shows surpluses. The exceptions are the cyclical recovery years of 1971–72 and 1977–78. It is interesting to note that cyclical fluctuations rather than movements in the price of oil have dominated movement in the current account in the 1970s.

The increase in volatility in the basic balance from the 1960s to the 1970s is evident in table 3.44. From 1960 to 1969 the range of variability of the basic balance was $4.2 billion, from a surplus of $0.1 billion in 1961 to a deficit of $4.1 billion in 1967. But from 1970 to 1978 the range widened to $30 billion, from a $1 billion surplus in 1975 to a deficit of $28.9 billion in 1977. The time-series standard deviation of the basic balance increased from $1.4 billion in 1960–69 to $9.4 billion in 1970–77.[15] Thus there was a significant increase in the volatility of the basic balance from the 1960s to the 1970s. This resulted both from the increase in variation of the price of oil and the international business cycle, and from a jump in the net outflow of long-term capital in the last half of the 1970s.

By comparison with the basic balance, the increase in variability of the balance on short-term capital from the 1960s to the 1970s is small. The range of variation in the short-term capital balance of table 3.44 in the 1960s is $8.5 billion; in the 1970s it rose to $19.2 billion, including the massive outflow in 1971 when the fixed rate system gave way. If we exclude 1971 as a unique event, the range of variation from 1970 to 1978 is $6.2 billion, *less* than in the 1960s. The standard deviation of the short-term capital time series for the 1960s is $2.8 billion. For the 1970s it is $6.1 billion including 1971 and $2.9 billion excluding it. Thus there has not been a significant increase in the volatility of short-term capital in the 1970s.

The reserve column of table 3.44 shows significantly greater net interventions in the 1970s than in the 1960s. During the 1960s, annual changes in the net United States reserve position varied from the $3.4 billion increase in the tight-money year of 1967 to a $2.7 billion decrease in 1969. Since the regime of managed floating began in 1973, foreign central banks have absorbed dollars every year, slowing the rate of devaluation of the dollar. As a consequence, the net United States reserve position has decreased each year, with the biggest change since 1973 coming with the $35 billion accumulation of official dollar holdings abroad in 1977.

The increase in intervention, in quantitative terms, from the 1960s to the 1970s is not evidence of increased fixity of exchange rates. Rather, the variability of the underlying determinants of the exchange rate, especially the basic balance, has increased significantly. As a result, the intervention that would be needed to hold rates fixed has increased substantially. Thus we see larger interventions in the "floating rate" system of the 1970s than in the "fixed rate" system of the 1960s, even as movements in exchange rates now absorb some of the pressure of variation in the basic balance.

The data of table 3.44 support the view that the variability in exchange rates since 1973 is largely the result of underlying variability in the basic balance. As the basic balance is perceived to change, the exchange markets forecast the consequences for exchange rates, and the pressure appears as an immediate movement of the rate. Thus in interpreting balance of payments and exchange rate fluctuations in the 1970s, we should go back to underlying economic determinants of movements in the basic balance.

Notes

1. The data and an initial draft of this section were contributed by Dennis Warner of Michigan State University and NBER, using OECD trade data.

2. Strictly speaking, in a list of commodities ordered from those with maximum net exports to those with maximum net imports, the United States has a comparative advantage in producing the goods higher on the list relative to those lower on the list.

3. Disaggregation of the end-use data in an analysis focusing on net exports runs into the problem that, beyond the two-digit level, export and import categories do not match. This arises because a major criterion the OBE used for creating subcategories was the contribution of an item to the value total in its major category, and this criterion was applied separately on the export and import sides. In disaggregating beyond the two-digit level, therefore, the analysis here basically follows the export end-use categories, assigning import categories to the relevant export groups. For a discussion of the rationale and structure of the end-use groupings, see OBE (1970 pp. vii–xviii).

4. The analysis here focuses on trade in manufactured goods, for several reasons. First, and perhaps most important, trade in agricultural goods is greatly affected by nonmarket activities, mainly government subsidy and import programs in all the developed countries, and the P.L. 480 agricultural aid program in the United States. This general intervention is much more extensive in agricultural trade than in trade in manufactured goods, and could easily obscure underlying trends in comparative advantages. In addition, the cross-section data used to assess the basis for United States comparative advantage in the mid-1960s relate only to trade in nonagricultural goods, although they include trade in goods from the mining industry.

5. A similar pattern can be seen in the petroleum industry. The United States has had a deficit in crude petroleum trade since 1946, a deficit in semifinished petroleum products since 1949, and a surplus in finished petroleum products that has been shrinking from a $520 million peak in 1951 to a deficit of $114 million in 1976.

6. This could, of course, be due either to a basic United States comparative advantage in more advanced manufacturing or to an effective tariff structure that favors it.

7. Trade in footwear, luggage, and apparel of leather, fur, rubber, or plastic has followed a pattern quite similar to that of consumer textiles.

8. A similar pattern is observable in trade in automotive goods, with a surplus in parts and a deficit in finished product.

9. The same product cycle can also be observed in man-made fibers and in synthetic rubber. By 1963 the United States was a net importer of fibers, and by 1966 trade in synthetic rubber was roughly balanced. For examples of the product cycle at a disaggregated level, see Seev Hirsch (1965) and Louis T. Wells, Jr. (1969).

10. After this paper was completed, I received a copy of Stern and Maskus (1979). Their work, on cross-section and time-series data for 1958–76, is in close agreement with the results reported here.

11. This is table 2 in Branson and Monoyios (1977). In verifying their results they also provide scaled regressions to adjust for heteroskedasticity and probit regressions, at the two-digit and three-digit SITC levels.

12. See Branson (1979c) for a year-by-year description of international monetary developments since 1965 and their effect on the theory of international finance.

13. The implicit model of figure 3.12 is the standard asset-market model of exchange rate determination. The curves of figure 3.12 represent end-of-period positions, given beginning-of-period asset stocks. See Branson (1979a) for the asset-market model and Buiter (1979) for an analysis in a period model.

14. This policy was first analyzed in Branson (1976). There is ample empirical evidence that intervention policy has followed this approach in general. See, for example, Branson-Halttunen-Masson (1977) for Germany and Amano (1979) for Japan. This policy rule is explicitly built into the Flex 1 econometric model of Japan, which is discussed by Amano.

15. The F-statistic for the increase is 32.8 compared to 3.1 at the 5 percent level and 5.1 at the 1 percent level.

---

2. Herbert Giersch

The United States in the World Economy— A European Perspective

The first half of the sixty-year period to which the NBER can look back saw the decline of the "Pax Britannica." During the same time the United States economy rose to a position that enabled it to become, after World War II, the center of a worldwide system of relatively free international transactions, sometimes called the "Pax Americana," the OECD area, or, simply, "the West." This system is now being gradually transformed into a tripartite system, with Japan in Asia and the European Community as the other two centers. As a symbol of America's leadership role in rebuilding the Western world's economy, one may simply look at the fact that the United Nations and the institutions created under the Bretton Woods agreement established their headquarters on the east coast of the United States. Would the same location necessarily be selected today?

The United States economy qualified for undisputed leadership in rebuilding the world economy for a number of valid reasons, including the fact that it ranked highest among all Western countries in the follow-

Herbert Giersch is president of the Institute of World Economics of the University of Kiel.

ing areas: share in world GDP or in world manufacturing output (60 percent); share of world exports (20 percent); the state of technology and the level of productivity in a large number of industries; independence of raw material imports, including energy; and military strength and lack of military vulnerability.

United States leadership was readily accepted in the West. At least from the perspective of former enemy countries it was combined with apparent generosity. The U.S.:

1. Gave aid to war-ravaged and starving Europe, including West Germany where a Morgenthau plan had been expected rather than Marshall Aid
2. Pursued a constructive policy towards postwar Japan, later supported by United States demand for procurement during the Korean War
3. Made positive contributions to worldwide tariff reductions in successive GATT rounds and to trade liberalization within Europe (EPU and OEEC)
4. Extended sympathy towards European economic integration (EEC) despite its discriminatory implications for the United States
5. Pursued a policy of keeping imports relatively free, including imports from countries in a catching-up process, at exchange rates favorable to those in need of overcoming a dollar shortage, thus creating or permitting conditions for export-led growth, e.g. in Japan and Germany
6. Was a source of foreign direct investment which enabled the other countries to benefit from a unilateral transfer of technical knowledge

It is difficult for an outside observer to judge how much of the generosity was a reflection of basic liberal or libertarian attitudes and how much of it has to be imputed to United States national interest during Cold War conditions with the East.

In many respects the United States economy became a model that offered itself for imitation. This refers not only to technology, but also to sociopolitical characteristics such as free markets for goods and ideas, monopoly control, competitive behavior and other features congenial to an open society and representative democracy. However, United States trade policy often remained protectionist enough to prevent domestic adjustment processes where they would have been unpopular. With regard to agricultural products the United States favored free trade for its export products and opposed it for products on the import list (Kindleberger 1976/77), and the export of capital was not unrestrained after 1945.

United States leadership or hegemony (as Shonfield [1976] calls it for the period 1950–65) was likely to be a temporary phenomenon of rather short duration, mainly for reasons I believe to be inherent in the nature of a decentralized world market system. United States superiority was eroded in the following ways:

1. Relatively free trade in goods, assets, and knowledge enabled other countries with a large, potentially productive stock of human capital to catch up with the United States; this happened in Europe and, under the stimulus of Japanese economic growth, in Asia and nowadays particularly in those NICs that have abandoned import substitution policies to take advantage of dynamic linking (concentration on products with a high income elasticity of world demand).
2. More and more producers in catching-up countries succeeded in switching from technological imitation to genuine innovations, thus overtaking their United States competitors in such fields as cars (Germany), motorcycles, steel, rail transportation, shipbuilding, and consumer electronics (Japan).
3. Economic growth in the West reduced the United States share in world output and exports.
4. Multilateral market penetration raised the openness of the United States economy (imports in relation to GNP).
5. And, debatable domestic policies increased America's vulnerability to external supply shocks (energy).

It is true that the United States economy's comparative advantage in the international division of labor is in land-intensive agricultural products and, in manufacturing, in goods requiring a large input of human capital in combination with much physical capital; but the United States economy is no longer alone in advanced manufacturing and has, therefore, fewer opportunities for earning monopoly gains in world markets. With relatively great freedom in international trade, investment, and transfer of technology there is also no longer any tight complementarity between United States research and United States labor: knowledge produced in the United States can well be combined with efficient management and labor elsewhere. Thus, organized labor in the United States will have to learn to adapt to the emergence of an open economy. (Perhaps in a more distant future government will have to recognize that it operates in competition with governments elsewhere, given the increasing importance of international investment and the increasing international mobility of people embodying special skills and other forms of highly productive human capital with positive externalities.)

The most important symbol of America's loss in superiority is the decline of the dollar in international currency competition. Of course, under United States leadership the Bretton Woods system had all the properties of a currency cartel: stable or sluggishly adjusted prices (exchange rates) expressed in, or tied to, a hegemonial currency, the supply of which had barometric or leadership functions for the supply policies of the other members of the "club"; this worked relatively well as long as the dollar was freely convertible into gold at a fixed price or deserved full confidence because of the relative stability of its purchasing power in terms of American goods and services. As a reward for monetary leadership the United States could, comparable to a bank, earn seigniorage gains in the form of a deficit in its basic foreign balance. While some American economists thought that the expanding world economy needed more international liquidity—in addition to gold production for monetary use—than the United States could supply without destroying confidence, thus propagating the creation of SDRs, some countries actually felt compelled to accumulate more dollar claims than they wanted to add to their reserves, given the exchange rate and their desired monetary policies. The dollar glut began to emerge in the early 1960s. As the exchange rate adjustments which the situation required were too limited in geographic scope (Germany and the Netherlands in March 1961) and absolutely inadequate in size, a transatlantic disequilibrium developed in money and finance as well as in trade and production. This led to the collapse of the exchange rate cartel in the early 1970s and to the emergence of what has been called a "nonsystem" or a "system of managed floating" and what I consider to be a lively competition among currencies, with some currency areas expanding (yen, deutschemark, Swiss franc) at the expense of the dollar area.

Among the factors which may have contributed to the decline of the dollar, I would like to suggest the following for consideration:

1. Those restrictions on United States banks (regulation Q, no interest payment on minimum reserve requirements, etc.) which induced the expansion of banking operations outside the United States.
2. The choice by United States policymakers after 1961 to shoot for a point on the Phillips curve that implied less unemployment and more inflation than the economy had experienced during 1957–60 (see Gordon, chap. 2 of this text, pp. 00) and an increasing rate of actual price inflation, despite guidepost policies to repress it and despite a tendency to export it to some other countries on the de facto dollar standard.
3. The tendency of the United States foreign balance (basic balance) to show a worsening deficit between 1962 and 1972, rarely matched by imports of short-term capital, notwithstanding the Kindleberger-Salant Hypothesis, and leading to an increasing loss of reserves, as shown in Branson's table 3.43. This occurred despite government interventions to slow down the outflow of short-term capital (Operation Twist) and of long-term capital (Interest Equalization Tax and the Federal Reserve's Voluntary Foreign Credit Restraint Program), including direct investment (see Friedman, chap. 1 of this text, p.

91) ; and despite government efforts to sell, and to obtain prepayment for, military equipment, and to prevent gold conversion of official foreign claims by exchange rate guarantees (Roosa Bonds), by moral suasion, and even by a threat to withdraw United States troops from strategically important sites in Germany.

The reference system, or normative system, against which this development of the United States foreign balance should be judged would include the following criteria:

1. As a rich country, the United States ought to run a surplus on current account to enable or to support an outflow of long-term capital to countries where the potential marginal product of capital is higher because of an apparent capital shortage.
2. As an advanced country the United States has a role to play as a supplier of services, including the supply of financial intermediations.
3. As a supplier of world money, the United States must be ranked number one in maintaining price level stability, or must be almost as successful in this respect as its close competitors; under currency convertibility it must fully anticipate, in its policy decision-making process, the loss in seigniorage gain (interpreted by some as a vicious circle) that is bound to occur when an inflation tax is imposed on dollar holders, domestic or foreign, and when that tax can be avoided by holding other currencies.

As a supplier of services, the country can afford some overvaluation of the exchange rate on the basis of production costs for standardized internationally traded goods (Heckscher-Ohlin goods). The country must be prepared to let the production of standardized goods, which are neither capital intensive nor skill intensive, outmigrate to less developed countries closer to the periphery of the system. LDCs can then be good capital importers and can earn the foreign exchange needed for servicing the increasing foreign debt. The rich capital-exporting country will then also find an expanding market for its capital goods in LDCs, hopefully for capital goods which incorporate a technology appropriate for countries suffering from a capital shortage and an abundance of unskilled labor. In this light, the overvaluation of the dollar during the sixties can hardly be criticized.

As a supplier of world money the United States should have, as mentioned above, refrained from an easy-money policy for employment purposes. This constraint requires a public understanding that the level of employment in the country as a whole in any one sector, industry, region, or firm essentially depends upon the relation between real wages and productivity (the latter, of course, adjusted for changes in the terms of trade). The monetary authority is then free to care for the international competitiveness of its own product—money—as a store of value.

In a small open economy with an independent currency, there is less temptation to solve the employment problem by means of unanticipated inflation. This is perhaps the basis of strength of the Swiss franc. The strength of the deutschemark rests on the traumatic experience of two war and postwar inflations (one open, one repressed) and on a consensus supported by a tripartite understanding between labor, business, and government that imputes to organized labor at least some indirect responsibility for price level stability and high employment. In the United States the labor market seems to be too polypolistic for such arrangements. On the other hand it seems also to be too heterogeneous to permit full employment at relative wages and wage differentials that are compatible with prevailing views about fairness and justice (minimum wages). But, contrary to Europe, the United States seems to have some downward flexibility of real wages, or a type of money illusion that offers itself for exploitation by policymakers. Moreover, the United States is large and still so similar to the model of a closed economy that proponents of Keynesian employment strategies were rarely aware of the additional upward flexibility of prices which flexible exchange rates have introduced into the system via the prices of internationally traded goods. Complaints about this disadvantage of flexible rates are an implicit admittance of the great help which United States full employment policies in the 1960s had received from the fact that the United States could (temporarily) export inflation (lengthen the price and wage lag) at the expense of its leadership role (or hegemonial power) in international monetary matters.

In the 1960s the dollar became grossly overvalued, not in relation to Third World currencies, but in relation to Europe and Japan. In the absence of accepted normative criteria we may also say that the 1960s gave Europe and Japan a competitive advantage vis-à-vis the United States, perhaps as a fair return for the stability they were induced to export (the inflation they had to import).

What happened can be summarized in four points.

1. Europe benefited from an accelerated inflow of investment, technology, and entrepreneurship (called the "American Challenge" in a widely read book by Sevran-Schreiber [1967]), only partly reflected in the balance on current account. This development destroyed United States monopoly positions in many fields and led to a deterioration of the United States terms of trade and hence to a decline in United States incomes relative to European incomes.

2. Countries such as Germany were induced to build up their international sector (exports and import substitutes) in response to what appeared as an ever increasing export market (a "black hole in the world economy"); this was done at the expense of the domestic

sector and presumably accelerated economic growth (as we measure it).

3. The induced expansion of the international sector in Germany led to an export-biased growth in Europe's center, partly at the expense of economic growth in the south of Europe which suffered from an insufficient inflow of capital and an excessive drain of workers.

4. Economic growth in the United States became import-biased and, I venture to assert, slower than it could have been.

The 1970s saw a process of correcting the transatlantic imbalance. To describe and explain this process, let me emphasize six points:

1. The decline of the effective dollar exchange rate (exchange rate adjusted for relative WPI in Branson's table 3.33) after 1969, notably between 1971 and 1973

2. The even more drastic devaluation of the dollar in relation to European currencies, particularly the Swiss franc (Branson, fig. 3.1) and the deutschemark (not shown in Branson), which gained more than 100 percent in nominal terms and 80 percent on an inflation-corrected basis (WPI 1979 over 1969)

3. An accompanying change in the relation between hourly wage costs in manufacturing in the United States, on the one hand, and in West Germany and other European countries on the other hand (Giersch 1979, p. 641)

4. A rise in the United States share of total manufacturing output of the West and a corresponding decline of the German share (Branson, table 3.8)

5. A decline in employment in German manufacturing (about one million jobs during the seventies), combined with a slowdown of industrial growth and a reacceleration of the growth rate of industrial output per hour (Branson, table 3.7) when much of the adjustment took place (1970–75)

6. A reversal of the transatlantic flow of direct investment, with United States firms being less attracted to Germany (and the European continent) and German (and European) firms being more attracted by investment opportunities in United States manufacturing (see also Branson, p. 244)

The structural implications of this adjustment problem for West Germany had been clearly recognized at an early stage (e.g., Fels; Schatz; and Wolter 1971). A similar transpacific adjustment problem likely existed at the same time. These structural phenomena, to my knowledge, were practically ignored in the international economic policy discussions which took place at various levels after the 1975 world recession.

Today, the assessment of the United States role in the world economy cannot be sufficiently comprehensive without mentioning oil. In this context the following points readily come to mind. The United States has been a leader towards an oil-intensive civilization. The rest of the world has little sympathy for a policy which keeps the relative price of oil in the United States lower than it is elsewhere (a policy described as perverse by Milton Friedman in a recent issue of *Newsweek*) and leaves the role of leadership toward a less oil-intensive civilization to other countries. Permissiveness vis-à-vis short-run domestic populist pressures may have medium-run disadvantages for the United States economy's international terms of trade when world demand for producers' and consumers' durables with incorporated energy-saving technology will be booming.

The NICs will be a challenge for the United States as well as for other old industrialized countries. Structural adjustment to imports from the NICs and from those to become NICs in the next decade, is likely to be essential for all advanced countries. Economists should know, and explain to others, that this is a positive sum game as exemplified by the postwar reconstruction of the Western world economy.

If, as Keynes observed, defunct economists have more policy influence than vested interests, the United States and West Germany should not be too unhappy that their economic and political elites have switched from the doctrines of Alexander Hamilton and Friedrich List to the ideas of a philosopher-economist of Scottish origin. However, it is worth watching current attempts of Cambridge (England) economists to apply the infant industry argument for protection to senile industries, and to countries where such industries are plentiful. Such proponents of a new protectionism are likely to find increasing resonance in advanced countries under adjustment pressure. The danger that this will produce negative external effects on the growth of international transactions and the increase of real incomes deserves to be a matter of concern.

3. Peter G. Peterson

The World Economy and Us: Some Comments

Dr. Giersch, my limitless capacity for indiscretion forces me to say to you that as sophisticated as your analysis has been of what happened, you may have raised to a level of conscious and even benevolent policy

Peter G. Peterson is chairman of the board and president of Lehman Brothers, Kuhn, Loeb.

what at least in the 1960s was more a matter of ignorance and inadvertence on the part of the United States.

What I am referring to is this: Certainly during much of the 1960s a good deal of our foreign policy and foreign economic policy—in the face of obvious evidence of seriously distorted exchange rates and a profound change in America's competitive position—was remarkably benign, indeed innocent. I think it is fair to say that much of our foreign policy establishment in the 1960s would have operated on one of two premises: (1) we did not have a significant foreign economic problem even in economic terms, and (2) even if we did, it was not truly significant in relation to our other strategic, foreign policy interests. Therefore, while I would agree with your analysis of what happened, I am not entirely sure that I would agree with your analysis of why it happened, and whether in the 1960s it really was as conscious a policy as you would suggest.

My comments about international economics will be quite brief. Milton, I have to tell a story on you and me to illustrate why this is appropriate. You have probably forgotten a lunch meeting that you and I had at the time George Shultz called me in the very late 1970s and said, "We want you to come down to the White House to take on a job as Assistant for International Economic Affairs." I asked Milton if I should take this job. No one has ever accused Milton of excessive ambiguity and he may have forgotten that he gave me a very unambiguous, "No." I said, "Why not, Milton?" And he said, "Well, if you have floating exchange rates, the job is unnecessary, and if you don't, it is impossible, and I think at your age in life you should not take a job that is either unnecessary or impossible." Incidentally, he may have been right that it was a nonjob.

In any event, when I went down there I found profoundly different perceptions as to whether we even had an international economic problem. On the one hand, there were those in the Commerce Department who felt that our problem had so metastasized that the United States was about to become a service economy and therefore the solution was quotas on virtually everything. On the other hand, many in the State Department were tending to ask, as I indicated earlier, "What problem are you talking about?". I decided to put together hurriedly a series of charts that showed what had happened to the position of the United States in the global economy in the last twenty or thirty years and to define what the problem was. And perhaps all I achieved was to add to the growth rate of the audiovisual industry. I don't know. In any event, preparing for this meeting I decided to update some of this material. I will save you the horrors of another audiovisual show, and I have only a marginal contribution to what William Branson has already done very ably.

I would like to emphasize two or three aspects of what has happened since 1970. I think that since the various so-called Nixon economic shocks of 15 August 1971, which is a threshold date in many, many ways, it has become conventional in this country in talking about our trade picture to sound and act as though we alone have had an oil deficit problem. So, I thought it might be interesting to look at Japan, which obviously imports relatively much larger amounts of oil, and look at the configuration of its trade picture since 1970. What this tends to show is that Japan in addition to having a much more serious oil deficit problem than the United States has, of course, had a much enlarged trade deficit in food that has gone from about $4 billion to $12 billion from 1970 to 1978. Our trade picture, of course, would be much more negative had our foodstuff balance not gone from virtually half a billion dollars surplus in 1970 to a $12.5 billion surplus in 1978. In addition to that, of course, the raw materials deficit in Japan's foreign trade picture has gone much more negative from $5 or $6 billion in 1970 down to a $15 billion deficit in 1978.

Also, very interesting to note when you consider the relative size of the economies, is that Japan's fuel deficit since 1970 has gone from roughly $4 billion to over $31 billion; the United States deficit, in a much larger economy has gone from $2 to $38 billion. So, relatively speaking, I think we sometimes forget the much larger oil import burden they have carried in relation to their GNP. The obvious question is: What have they done to achieve their impressive trade surplus? Obviously, I need to say a few things about manufactured exports. From 1970 to 1978, our trade balance has gone from about $1 billion in surplus to a $4 billion deficit in manufactured goods. Japan's surplus on manufactured goods has gone from a $13 billion surplus to $76.5 billion, or a $63 billion larger surplus in manufactured goods than they had in 1970, in spite of the exchange rate changes. And Germany's manufactured goods trade surplus has gone from $12 to $55 billion at a time when our surplus has gone down. To be sure, our situation has improved somewhat in recent months but the comparative data are not yet available.

Next, technology. I won't say much more than Edwin Mansfield said in his paper about our relative role of technological innovation, but clearly something is going on in that area. The Department of Commerce has had a set of numbers on what I call technology intensive products. These definitions are not perfect, but they are at least consistent and I think the trends are so significant as to suggest that something is going on here. These technology intensive manufacturers have always been the principal source of United States export strength as you might expect, but what's happened since 1971 in regard to those products is to me quite interesting. I got a fair amount of initial comfort out of the fact that in the aggregate our surpluses on those technology-intensive products had gone from about $4 to $19 billion during this period. However, when I examined the composition of that surplus, I discovered that the vast increase in those surpluses has been to OPEC countries and other LDC countries. However, if you look at our trade in those technology intensive products with West Germany and Japan, here is what you see. In the case of Japan in particular, this deficit has gone from $2 billion in 1970 to $13.5 billion on the higher technology products since 1970.

And there are just a couple of additional points I would make about this technology situation in terms of patent trends. I agree with Professor Mansfield that patents are hardly a universal measure, but they must indicate something; at the very least that some people decided some idea was worth at least going to the Patent Office and getting a patent for if nothing else. In the last ten or eleven years our patents in absolute terms have gone down about 10 percent or so. Also, if you look at the four areas of high technology that have traditionally been an important source of exports for this country and, of course, internal strength— machinery, electronics, communication, and scientific instruments—in those fields generally our patents have gone either flat or down in the last ten years. But Japan's have gone up 400–500 percent, and West Germany's have risen substantially too. Now clearly theirs are from a much lower base, but I believe there is something important going on here in this technology innovation front.

There is another thing that has not been publicized, but I hear about it more and more from businessmen. Increasingly I hear that foreign manufacturers, particularly in Japan and in Germany, have an added degree of quality and reliability in their products that gives users, particularly less sophisticated users, a sense of added confidence in the use of those products. For example, a recent study on Japanese versus United States color television sets strongly suggests that the Japanese have achieved the twin objectives of added reliability and lower production costs.

If you go back to 1970, and I am focusing on manufactured goods because I think not as much study has been done in that area as should have been, it may interest you to know that the United States and West Germany were roughly identical in respect to absolute levels of exports of manufactured goods in that year. However, today, we are now at $94 billion, and the Germans are now at $125 billion, or roughly a third higher than we are in absolute terms at the present time. The Japanese are now where we are. Back in 1960 they were only at $4 billion; we were exporting four times as much in goods as they were. I am simply trying to make the point that in the manufacturing exports arena something very significant has happened.

I don't know what we can do about exports, and I am sure in this group there may be a debate as to whether we should do anything.

Exports have always been a "mego" subject in America. One of the few intellectual contributions of the Nixon Administration, some might say the only one, was the concept of mego (mego stands for "my eyes glaze over"). Exports are clearly not a mego subject in other countries. George Shultz had Helmut Schmidt in California this summer and it fascinated me to listen to the informed way in which the chancellor talked about his country's exports. He did not consider it irrelevant or embarrassing or trivial to know the major export orders that his country was trying to get. He seemed briefed on all the major deals to the United States. It is not a subject that America's leaders have displayed much interest in.

To take another example, I was asking Paul Samuelson whether selling savings bonds was as unrespectable in classical economic circles as ever, and he assured me he thought it was. We spend an enormous amount of time in the Treasury and other places selling savings bonds. I wonder what would happen if we spent as much time in the export areas. While in some of our more sophisticated companies at the chief executive officer level the export potential is perceived, I think there are still quite a few companies that are shocked when they see how much of the exports of a lot of their competitors are to the Third World.

Let me briefly touch on the problem and potential of the Third World and its implications. You perhaps know that our exports are growing much faster to LDCs than to the rest of the world. But many people are surprised to know that in some of our more sophisticated industries, such as chemicals and machinery, LDCs are now accounting for 40 percent to 50 percent of the total exports to the United States. An OECD study showed that all the growth of manufactured goods in the last four or five years was to LDCs. This raises the whole engine of growth concept and whether LDCs could be a source of less inflationary growth for the developed countries.

A key problem, however, is the one of the ballooning debt and deficits of the Third World and their implications to the global economy. I have spent about ten weekends in the past two years, not too happily, in some state of schizophrenia, paranoia, or other assorted psychic disorders, on the Willy Brandt Commission. Two-thirds of the membership, very able members, may I say, are from the Third World from such exotic places as Tanzania and Upper Volta. But in the course of our work we asked the IMF to look at the oil-related LDC deficits and do a projection to 1985. You may or may not have much confidence in these estimates, but they point out that whereas the internal debt of these countries now aggregates about $250 to $300 billion even before the last two price increases of the last three weeks, it is conservative to estimate that this number will be up to at least $350 billion by 1985. Thus, there are IMF estimates now, that have not been published, of $600 to $700 billion in aggregate debt of oil-importing LDCs. This raises to me significant questions about whether the private banking system can or should really fund this level of proposed debt, and if they don't can their economies adjust to these relative prices? One of the ideas I tried to promote on this Brandt Commission is that among the brilliant public relations achievements of the last ten years has been that of the OPEC countries portraying themselves as brothers and friends of the South in the North-South confrontation. And, I wonder why the OPEC countries could not be induced to broaden their portfolio and do some direct lending to the non-oil-developing countries—or at the very least share some loan guarantees, and of course contribute much more in direct aid. This problem of aggravated debt is one I don't think we can ignore.

Third, I don't think we can have any discussion of international economics without discussing the very fragile supply of oil from OPEC over the next several years. Conventional estimates of how much oil we would be getting from OPEC in the 1980s were, on the low side, 35 million barrels and, on the high side, 45 million barrels. But I think it is clear that we may be in the range of the high twenties for a whole series of reasons. I think OPEC has discovered it can produce less and get more. Also, the young princes want to have something to do later in their lives.

There are very important political and psychological elements that have not been discussed but which I think are very real. It is now clear that some of the leaders of certain OPEC countries may feel their lives, both politically and psychologically, may be at stake if progress isn't made on this Palestinian issue, and that may have a tendency to "focus their minds" with regard to the use of the oil weapon. Thus, I don't see how we can talk very seriously about the future of the global economy without facing the very clear possibility that oil supplies may be both inadequate and very unstable. I hope that the current situation in Afghanistan helps to clarify in our minds the fact that reasonable security of oil supplies is clearly a political and military security issue, and not simply an economic question of price.

Finally, I can't resist the temptation to say something that George Shultz and Arthur Okun have alluded to when they talk about the political landscape of the United States. We have an incredible tendency in meetings like this to preach to the choir and talk to each other about the need for investment, productivity, savings, and the like. I think the truth of the matter is that it is easy for me and perhaps Walter Wriston and others to blame the television media and the news media for some of our problems. They share in it, but I think the business community has to take a great deal of responsibility for the attitudes that exist in the public about business and investment. I think the Business Roundtable has done a fine job in Congress, much better than they used to, but I think we are just doing a D-minus job with the public. When I say this to some of my business friends they tell me they have given X number of speeches in the last six months on free enterprise to several public high schools in the area. What we seem to forget is that networks are *news* media, and news media are not interested in dull platitudinous speeches on the free enterprise system. They are interested in *news*. And businessmen have a remarkable capacity when central issues come up to become silent.

I was reminded of this on the Chrysler matter recently. Forty-two out of forty-three or forty-four of the Business Roundtable in their private sessions talked to each other about what a horrendous precedent the British Leyland action set. At least a statement was put out, but not signed by any individual. It was a kind of public statement, but Senator Proxmire's Committee tells me they had great difficulty getting individuals to testify on the issue. Walt Wriston's testimony was vastly more relevant, courageous, and eloquent as usual than mine, but I finally also decided that something had to be said about this. And I think some changes were made at least at the margin in the way the Chrysler plan is going to be implemented, such as instituting review boards and financial viability tests. All I am trying to suggest is that I think it is too easy for businessmen to suggest that there is a problem "out there" about perceptions of the business system. Until some of us in the business world forget some of our collegial relationships with each other (in the case of the Chrysler matter, two of our esteemed competitors told me candidly that they were afraid to say anything because some of their clients would not like it). We will always have a reason when a public, controversial issue comes up to say nothing. I really think that we have to look at the so-called media problem as resulting from our lack of courage and willingness to say anything that is newsworthy as another source of the problem.

Summary of Discussion

A variety of topics in international economics were probed. Walter Wriston strongly challenged the notion that growing LDC debt represents a serious threat to the world economy. The fears of widespread defaults by LDCs after the 1973 oil price increase were widely held. Calmer voices arguing that world financial markets would function well could not be heard in the din. But the fact is that the financial markets operated as Wriston expected, and no serious problems of default have arisen. The record of debt is better for the LDCs than for many United

States industries. Indeed, the dollar and gold reserves of the non-oil-exporting LDCs are $30 billion greater than before the OPEC price increase. And it is as true today, in Wriston's view, that the "burgeoning" LDC debt in coming years is a nonissue. Debt rescheduling by LDCs is not a matter for hand wringing; it is what the United States Treasury does every time it sells a treasury bill. The only real economic issue in Wriston's view is whether the exports of LDCs and their cushion of gold and dollar reserves will continue to give them access to financial markets. And that is a very different issue from a "$600 billion problem." Peter Peterson disagreed to this extent: he said this needed to be looked at on a country by country basis. He believed there might well be countries, perhaps a considerable number, which would have significant problems getting financing.

David Packard offered an optimistic appraisal of the increasing ability of firms to export to the Japanese market. In the past year, alone, the Hewlett-Packard Company has doubled its exports to Japan, to a level that is almost comparable to its exports to Germany. What remains for American businesses is that they become more aggressive in pursuing openings in the Japanese market.

Richard Caves stressed that many apparent problems of United States competitiveness and the decline in the United States share of world output and trade, merely reflect developments in the rest of the world. It is the rapid growth abroad, not necessarily our poor performance, that underlies the drop. Peter Peterson disagreed. He believed that our performance in share of manufactured exports, while improving recently, had reflected both the serious relative decline in relative growth in manufacturing productivity and less effective export programs by United States companies.

References

Amano, A. 1979. Flexible exchange rates and macroeconomic management: A study of the Japanese experience in 1973–78. Mimeographed. Kobe University.

Baldwin, R. E. 1971. Determinants of the commodity structure of U.S. trade. *American Economic Review* 61 (March): 126–46.

Becker, Gary S. 1964. *Human capital.* New York: Columbia University Press.

Bharadwaj, R., and Bhagwati, J. 1967. Human capital and the pattern of foreign trade: The Indian case. *Indian Economic Review*, n.s., 2 (October): 117–42.

Branson, William H. 1976. "Leaning against the wind" as exchange rate policy. Mimeographed. Geneva: Graduate Institute of International Studies.

———. 1979a. Exchange rate dynamics and monetary policy. In *Inflation and employment in open economies*, ed. Assar Lindbeck. Amsterdam: North-Holland.

———. 1979b. Monetary and fiscal policy with adjustable exchange rates. Mimeographed. Study prepared for the U.S. Congress, Joint Economic Committee.

Branson, William H.; Halttunen, H.; and Masson, P. 1977. Exchange rates in the shortrun: The dollar-deutschemark rate. *European Economic Review* 10 (December): 305–24.

Branson, William H., and Monoyios, N. 1977. Factor inputs in U.S. trade. *Journal of International Economics* 7 (May): 111–32.

Buiter, Willem H. 1979. *Temporary equilibrium and long-run equilibrium*. Outstanding Dissertations in Economics series. New York: Garland.

Fels, G.; Schatz, K. W.; and Wolter, F. 1971. Der Zusammenhang zwischen Produktionsstruktur und Entwicklungsniveau, Versuch einer Strukturprognose für die westdeutsche Wirtschaft. *Weltwirtschaftliches Archiv* 106, no. 1: 240–78.

Giersch, H. 1979. Aspects of growth, structural change, and employment: A Schumpeterian perspective. *Weltwirtschaftliches Archiv* 115, no. 4: 629–52.

Hirsch, Seev. 1965. The United States electronics industry in international trade. *National Institute Economic Review*, no. 34 (November): 92–97.

Hufbauer, Gary C. 1970. The impact of national characteristics and technology on the commodity composition of trade in manufactured goods. In *The technology factor in world trade*, ed. R. Vernon, pp. 145–232. New York: Columbia University Press.

Keesing, Donald B. 1966. Labor skills and comparative advantage. *American Economic Review* 56 (May): 249–58.

Kenen, Peter B. 1965. Nature, capital, and trade. *Journal of Political Economy* 73 (October): 437–60.

Kindleberger, C. P. 1976/77. U.S. foreign economic policy 1776–1976. *Foreign Affairs* 55, no. 2:395–417.

Kravis, Irving B. 1956. Wages and foreign trade. *Review of Economics and Statistics* 38 (February): 14–30.

Leontief, W. 1953. Domestic production and foreign trade: The American capital position re-examined. In *Readings in international economics*, ed. R. E. Caves and H. G. Johnson. London: George Allen and Unwin.

————. 1956. Factor proportions and the structure of American trade: Further theoretical and empirical analysis. *Review of Economics and Statistics* 38 (November): 386–407.

Ohlin, B.; Hasselborn, P. O.; and Wijkman, P. M., eds. 1977. *The international allocation of economic activity.* New York: Macmillan.

Servan-Schreiber, J. J. 1967. *Le défi americain.* Paris: Denöel. Published in English as *The American Challenge.* New York: Atheneum, 1979.

Shonfield, A. 1976. Introduction: Past trends and new factors. In *International economic relations of the Western world 1959–71,* ed. A Shonfield. Vol. 1. *Politics and trade.* London: Oxford University Press.

Stern, Robert M., and Maskus, K. 1979. Determinants of the structure of U.S. foreign trade, 1958–76. Mimeographed. University of Michigan.

U.S. Department of Commerce, Bureau of Economic Analysis (BEA). 1977. *U.S. merchandise trade—exports and imports—classified by BEA end-use categories, 1965–1976.* Washington, D.C.: Government Printing Office.

U.S. Department of Commerce, Office of Business Economics (OBE). 1970. *U.S. exports and imports classified by OBE end-use commodity categories, 1923–1968.* A supplement to the *Survey of Current Business.* Washington, D.C.: Government Printing Office.

Vernon, Raymond. 1966. International investment and international trade in the product cycle. *Quarterly Journal of Economics* 80 (May): 190–207.

Wells, Louis T., Jr. 1958. Test of a product cycle model of international trade: U.S. exports of consumer durables. *Quarterly Journal of Economics* 83 (February): 152–62.

4 American Population since 1940

1. Richard A. Easterlin
2. Victor R. Fuchs
3. Simon Kuznets

---

1. Richard A. Easterlin

Before World War II it was confidently assumed that American population growth was grinding to a halt (Hansen 1939; Whelpton 1947). This assumption was subsequently belied by the huge upsurge in population growth following World War II, described by one scholar of the postwar period as "perhaps the most unexpected and remarkable feature of the time" (Hickman 1960, pp. 161–62). This population boom, which peaked in the late fifties, has been followed by an equally surprising population "bust." Although few scholars in the late 1950s expected the undiminished continuation of the high growth rates prevailing at that time, no one foresaw the rapidity and depth of the subsequent decline. This boom and bust pattern of population growth is one of the most dramatic and unanticipated developments of the post-World War II period with far-flung social and economic ramifications.

Although the growth rate itself is the most startling feature of the postwar population record, it is not the only surprise. The recent upsurge in illegal immigration has received increasing attention. So too have new developments in internal migration—the movement to nonmetropolitan areas and the Sunbelt. Even mortality, the most slighted subject in population studies, has produced its share of surprises—the 1954–68 plateau in death rates now appears to have been pierced in a substantial and startling way.

Richard A. Easterlin is professor of economics at the University of Pennsylvania.

I am grateful for helpful comments to Eileen M. Crimmins, Ronald D. Lee, Peter Lindert, and Morton Owen Schapiro, and for comments and assistance to Lisa M. Ehrlich, Mahmoud S. Issa, Aline S. Rowens, and Steven Spear. Research support for this paper was partly provided by NICHD Grant HD–05427.

This chapter outlines these developments in postwar American population growth and touches on some of their cause-effect relations to changes in the economy and society more generally. Primary attention will center on the swing in the population growth rate and the associated change in marriage and childbearing, but there will be some discussion of mortality and migration as well.

4.1 Population Growth and Fertility

Swings in the rate of population growth are not new in American experience. For as far back as the record reliably goes—and probably before—there have been marked surges and relapses in the rate of population growth.[1] Before 1940 these movements (often designated Kuznets cycles in honor of Nobel prizewinning economist Simon Kuznets who pioneered their study) were around fifteen to twenty-five years in duration and due largely to corresponding movements in immigration (fig. 4.1).[2] What is notable about the post-1940 swing is its duration, about forty years instead of twenty, and the fact that it is attributable to a fertility movement—a baby boom and bust—rather than to immigration.

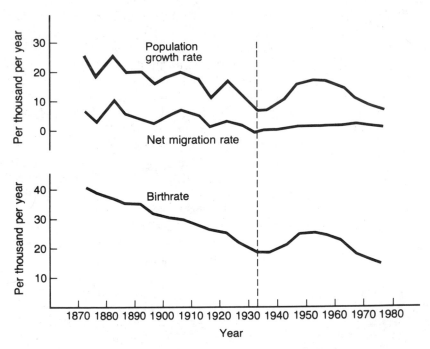

Fig. 4.1   Swings in population growth, migration, and fertility. Data from table 4.A.1.

Such an immense swing in American fertility is unprecedented, as figure 4.1 makes clear, and any attempt to explain the recent swing in population growth must focus on this fertility movement.

4.1.1   Causes of the Fertility Swing

What are the causes of the baby boom and bust? No one knows for sure, but there are numerous speculations, including one for which I am responsible. Since I am partial to my own theory, I will stress it here. But first I should like briefly to discuss some of the other arguments that have been advanced.

Birth Control Technology

A number of hypotheses focus on the baby bust since 1960, and leave the baby boom unaccounted for. This is true of what might be called for short, "the pill hypothesis."

In June 1960 the long-sought-after oral birth control pill was authorized for use, and since then use of the pill has grown rapidly. The late 1960s saw the introduction of the intrauterine device (IUD) and a widespread liberalization in abortion laws. To many writers these developments in access to or availability of new means of fertility control—especially the innovation and spread of the oral pill—are the key to the baby bust (Westoff and Ryder 1977, p. 340).

As plausible as this seems, there are a number of reasons to question this assumption. Well before the introduction of the pill most young American families were using contraception. Population surveys on contraceptive practice in the 1950s show this to be the case (see Whelpton, Campbell, and Patterson 1966, chap. 5). The pill was largely a substitution of a new method for old ones. For some households—especially Catholic households—the pill may have been a more effective means of preventing conception. But experience shows that if the motivation to limit fertility is strong, so-called inefficient methods can be used effectively. A valuable new study by Jean Claire Ridley (in process) reveals that the primary contraceptive methods used by couples in the 1930s to achieve the unprecedented low fertility of that period were the so-called "inefficient" ones of condom, withdrawal, and douche.

The "pill hypothesis" leaves unexplained the pre-1960 baby boom. This was hardly a period of retrogression in the ability of Americans to control their fertility. On the contrary, World War II assured that many more young Americans than ever before were systematically educated in techniques of fertility limitation (chiefly the condom) as part of their indoctrination in the Armed Forces. Yet the postwar fertility rate soared despite more universal knowledge on how to prevent conception.

The pill and other changes in contraceptive availability since 1960 may have had some "add-on" effect in reducing fertility. But, for the reasons just noted, it seems likely that the rapid spread of these new techniques, rather than being a principal cause of the fertility decline, was itself a response to other, more fundamental, factors making for lower fertility.

Women's Sex Role Attitudes and Status

Another popular explanation—again of the baby bust, but not of the baby boom—is what might be called the New Woman hypothesis. This view asserts that a drastic shift has occurred in young women's views on their proper roles in life in an antinatal, prowork direction. The emerging modern woman is seen as well educated, career oriented, and financially independent—freed from the wheel of marriage and childbearing. Evidence of this, it is said, is the sharp increase since 1960 in work outside the home among young women, especially wives, the counterpart of their plunging fertility. As additional support for the changed status of women, it is claimed that "educational differences between the sexes have greatly diminished" (Westoff 1978).

So far as education is concerned, rather than women having improved their status compared to men, the truth is just the opposite. In the 1940s and 1950s young women enjoyed a slight educational advantage over young men. Since then the differential has shifted in the opposite direction, and currently young men enjoy a slight educational advantage over young women.[3]

As for attitudes toward sex roles, there is no doubt that in recent years there has been a questioning as never before of traditional views. And there are real signs of change. Certainly schools are doing more to treat students equally regardless of sex; and businesses, colleges, and other institutions are trying to expand opportunities for women. Also, surveys show that increased proportions among both sexes are in favor of equal labor market rights for women and of making important household decisions jointly (Mason 1973; Thornton and Freedman 1979). However, on the issue of whether there has been a fundamental shift in views among the population generally as to the principal roles that husband and wife should play in the family, the answer suggested by the evidence is negative. Today, as they reach adulthood most men and women envisage the traditional arrangement in which the man in the family is a full-time worker throughout his life, while the woman drops out of the labor force to have two or more children whom she raises at home, at least until they reach school age. The woman is expected to work outside the home before childbearing and also, in most cases, to return to the labor force after the children reach school age. But the job the woman expects to hold is usually a traditional "female job," just as the man expects to hold a traditional "male job." Here are the results of some recent surveys of young adults, the group for whom significant change, if it has occurred, is most likely to be noticeable (survey dates and age groups vary somewhat because of differences among the surveys):

1. There has been little backing away from the ideal of motherhood for young women. In 1977, three out of every four *single* women aged 18 to 21 expected to have at least two children; among married women in this age group, the proportion was four in five (U.S. Bureau of the Census 1978, p. 27). As demographer Judith Blake (1974) has pointed out from studying similar survey responses on ideal family size, despite the large decline in the birthrate, Americans today, including young Americans "are highly tolerant of large families and noticeably intolerant of the one child family or childlessness" (p. 36).

2. A national sample of high school seniors from the class of 1977 was asked how it felt about different work situations for husbands and wives with preschool children (Herzog, Bachman, and Johnston 1978). Out of four possible ratings (not acceptable, somewhat acceptable, acceptable, desirable), seven out of ten considered a situation in which both partners work full time as not acceptable, and over half of the remainder gave this situation the second lowest rating (somewhat acceptable). In contrast, the traditional arrangement—husband works full time, wife doesn't work—received the two highest ratings from four students in five (desirable, acceptable) with the division between the two ratings about equal. Male respondents tended to be more traditional than female in their evaluations, but the difference by sex was very small.

3. In 1979 a national cross-section of teenagers aged 13 to 18 was asked, "As of right now what kind of work do you think you will do for a career?"[4] The job aspirations of teenagers are likely to be unrealistic, of course, with an emphasis on glamorous occupations; hence one cannot take the responses as indicative of the lines of work that will actually be pursued. What is interesting, however, is the difference between boys and girls in their responses. Here are the top ten career choices of each:

Rank	Boys	Girls
1	Skilled Worker (e.g., Mechanic)	Secretary
2	Doctor, Dentist	Doctor, Dentist
3	Lawyer	Musician, Artist
4	Musician, Artist	Nurse
5	Professional Athlete	Teacher
6	Electronics career	Stewardess
7	Military career	Accountant, Auditor
8	Businessman	Lawyer
9	Aviation industry career	Social worker
10	Architect	Psychologist

There are some indications of new aspirations among young women as evidenced by the appearance in the girls' top ten of the occupations of doctor, lawyer, and accountant. A comparison of the two lists, however, shows a substantial difference in the occupational orientation of the two sexes—only three occupations appear on both lists, and the girls' list is dominated by what have been traditional female occupations (secretary, teacher, nurse, stewardess, social worker).

4. Somewhat more realistic are the responses of women 21 to 24 years old, who were asked the following question in 1975: "Now I would like to talk to you about your future job plans. What kind of work would you like to be doing when you are 35 years old?"[5] Note that the question relates to an age when for most women all of their children would already be in school, and this predisposes the respondent to reply in terms of work outside the home. Despite this, only slightly more than half (56 percent) actually specified some job plans, 31 percent answered "married, keeping house, raising a family," and 13 percent said "don't know." Among those who did have plans to be working outside the home, the most frequently named jobs that they would "like to be doing" were in traditional female occupations. The ten leading ones were:

1. Teacher	6. Hospital attendant
2. Secretary	7. Typist
3. Nurse	8. Bookkeeper
4. Social welfare worker	9. Artist, Art teacher
5. Practical nurse	10. Sewer or Stitcher

Together these ten occupations accounted for more than half of those women with job plans. Again, the impression conveyed is that most young women continue to think along traditional lines.

There are doubtless some young women who conform to the New Woman model cited above. But the evidence clearly indicates that for the bulk of the female population the shift from childbearing to work outside the home cannot be attributed to any drastic shift in underlying attitudes on women's "proper" roles in life.

Women's Employment Opportunities as the Cause of the Fertility Decline

Seemingly related to the New Woman hypothesis, but, in fact, quite different is an explanation advanced by William P. Butz and Michael P. Ward. They argue that "young women's fertility has been strongly influenced by increasing demand for female labor" (1977, p. 18). "The prolonged economic expansion of the 1960s, with rising wages and job opportunities, induced increasing numbers of women to work outside their homes, and correspondingly, to forgo, or at least delay, having children. . . . After the 1970 recession, real wages resumed their steep rise and women went to work in record numbers instead of having children" (Butz and Ward 1978, pp. 9–10). According to this view, it is not a change in women's attitudes that accounts for their altered work and fertility behavior, but a change for the better in their job opportunities that has pulled them out of the home and into the labor market, and thereby reduced childbearing.

This theory is at variance with a number of facts of the female labor market in the post-World War II period. Both historically and at present, the overall demand for female labor has been primarily dependent on the growth of a limited number of occupations in the professional, clerical, sales, and service fields. Compared with the growth of jobs generally, women's occupations did not expand more rapidly in the years after 1960 when young women's labor force participation rose more rapidly than before (Easterlin 1978). Hence the demand for female labor was not unusually favorable after 1960, and women were not disproportionately pulled into the labor market by demand conditions. Corroboration is provided by the descriptions of opportunities in women's occupations in the Labor Department's *Occupational Outlook Handbook*. The handbooks of the 1950s use terms such as "serious shortage" (elementary school teachers, 1951), "excellent prospects" (secretaries, 1951), and "many thousands of job opportunities" (sales clerks, 1959). In contrast, those of the 1970s describe women's opportunities in much more guarded terms. Also, if demand for young women in the labor force were unusually favorable since 1960 one would expect to find their wages rising compared with men's and their relative unemployment rates falling. In fact, by both of these measures, the relative position of women appears to have deteriorated since 1960.[6] Finally, if the demand for female labor were unusually favorable during this period, one would expect the growth in labor force participation to be similar for all age groups of women because of the high degree to which older and younger women are substitutes for each other. In fact, the rise in young women's participation has been accompanied by a slowing or cessation in that of older women. Figure 4.2 shows the percentage of women in the labor force from 1890 to 1975. The contrasting pattern for younger and older women occurred in the two decades before 1960 as well, except that then it was the older women whose labor force rates rose rapidly and the younger women's hardly at all. Subsequently I shall suggest the reasons for this inverse pattern, which has appeared only since 1940. For the present purpose, it is sufficient to note that the proposed explanation of the fertility swing in terms of major new female employment opportunities leaves this important development wholly unaccounted for.

The Relative Income Hypothesis

What, then, is the reason for the postwar fertility swing? In my view, the interpretation that is most plausible, and consistent with a wide range of evidence, is what has been termed the "relative income" hypothesis.

Positive attitudes toward marriage, childbearing, and other aspects of family formation and growth reflect confidence in the future by young adults. Decisions regarding family formation depend crucially on how the "typical" young couple assesses its prospects for achieving the economic life-style to which the partners aspire; this will be called here the couple's "relative income." The more favorable this assessment, the freer will a couple feel to marry and raise a family, and the less will be the pressure on the young woman during the family forming years to couple work outside the home with childbearing and childrearing.

There are two elements entering into the judgment about the couple's prospects for achieving its desired life-style. One is the potential earning

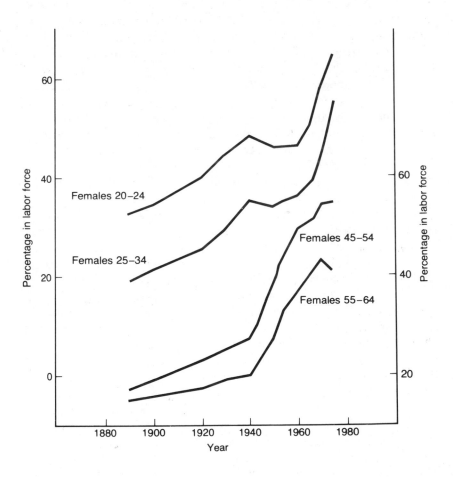

Fig. 4.2   The trend in women's work outside the home. Data from table 4.A.2.

power of the partners; the other is their material aspirations. It is the ratio between the two that determines judgments on the ease or difficulty of forming a household, and this ratio can vary because of changes in the numerator, denominator, or both. Thus an optimistic outlook may arise from exceptionally high earnings prospects for the couple, unusually low material aspirations, or a combination of the two. Let us look at numerator and denominator in turn.

Factors in the earnings outlook. How does a young couple judge its earnings prospects? Clearly many considerations are involved that will vary markedly from one couple to the next, such as energy, ambition, education, "connections," and so on. But whatever the list one might think up in advance, it is certain that the actual experience of "working and getting" will dominate in judgments on the earnings outlook. A couple may think its prospects are good or bad, as the case may be, but the ultimate test is the labor market itself. For most young adults there is an interval of several years between starting work and marrying. A recent United States Labor Department study (1970, p. 122) shows that labor market knowledge among young adults is positively associated with years of exposure to the labor market. Thus there is a period of some length in which valuable information is accumulated that provides an important basis for projecting the future. If jobs are easily acquired, wages good, and advancement rapid, the future will look rosy; if times are bad, the opposite will be true.

The formation of material aspirations. While the labor market may be the principal teacher of earning prospects, one's family of origin is the most plausible instructor of life-style. By life-style, I mean how the material standards of young adults are formed—why one generation of young adults, say, views a car as a luxury and the next, as a necessity. My argument is that the expectations of young adults about how they ought to live are largely the unconscious product of the material environment that they experienced during their upbringing. In other words, economic aspirations are unintentionally learned or "internalized" by virtue chiefly of one's exposure in one's parents' home. And this environment is very largely shaped by the economic circumstances of one's parents, the income in one's family of origin. Thus a child raised in an affluent suburban home in a life-style centered on automobile trips to school, shopping, friends, movies, and so forth comes to view the automobile as an integral part of everyday life.

One may cite, of course, a number of other factors affecting aspirations, including religious training, formal education, neighborhood environment, the influence of peers and relatives—the multitude of circumstances that enter into what sociology calls the "socialization experience"; that is, the long years of transition from being a young protected child in the bosom of the family to becoming a functioning independent adult member of contemporary society. But many of these factors— where one lives, what school one attends, who one's peers are—are also determined in important part by one's parents' income. Nor should style fads be confused with trends in material aspirations. The current craze for casual dress, epitomized by the international market for Levi's, is not a rejection of material affluence by the young, as a look at the price tags on Levi's quickly testifies. Today's youth may prefer a more casual style, but not a less costly one—witness the cost of "necessities" like stereos, vans, and rock concerts.

Relative versus absolute income. A couple's assessment of its earnings potential might be thought of as its *absolute* income outlook. But the same absolute amount of income may look quite different to two couples differing substantially in their "economic" socialization experience. To one couple, from an affluent background and with consequently high material standards, a sum of $20 thousand might leave the couple feeling pinched; whereas to another, from an impoverished background and with low material desires, it could look like Easy Street. The same argument would apply to a comparison between two different points in time. To a second generation, $20 thousand might not mean as much as to a first generation—even if the purchasing power of the sum were the same —because the first generation comes from wealthier backgrounds and consequently has formed more ambitious material expectations. A study by Lee Rainwater (1974) based on Gallup Poll surveys that asked the question, "What is the smallest amount of money a family of four needs to get along in this community?" found that the amount, expressed in dollars of the same purchasing power, increased by one-third between 1954 and 1969. Why did respondents at the second date think that so much more was needed to get along? The answer is clear. The survey at the second date reflected respondents' experience with more affluent conditions, and this experience elevated the standards by which respondents judged the minimum amount necessary to get along.

This reasoning can be distilled into a fairly simple *relative* income notion. Relative income, the relation between earnings and aspirations, can be defined in simple ratio terms as:

$$\text{relative income} = \frac{\text{earnings potential of couple}}{\text{material aspirations of couple}}.$$

To simplify matters, I propose to approximate this by:

$$\text{relative income} = \frac{\text{recent income experience of young men}}{\text{past income of young men's parents}}$$

In the latter formulation, the recent income experience of young men in the labor market is taken as shaping the assessment of the couple's earnings prospects; the past income of their parents as establishing their aspirations. In the numerator I focus on the male side of the labor market, because in most families the man's income accounts for the major share of the total over the life cycle. Also as we shall see the economic fortunes of young men and women tend to fluctuate together.

Testing the relative income theory. The argument so far can be summarized quite simply in terms of this relative income concept: as the relative income of young adults rises, they will feel less economic pressure and hence freer to marry and have children; as their relative income falls, they will feel increasing economic stress, and marriage and fertility will decline. Is there evidence to support this view?

The answer is yes. The data available to estimate relative income are hardly ideal, and are poorer before 1957 than after, but what we have shows a pattern consistent with the swing in fertility (fig. 4.3). Relative income is estimated here in the following way. For the period from 1957 the numerator, the young man's earnings outlook, is estimated on the basis of his prior earnings experience; the denominator, the material aspirations of the couple, from the incomes in their families of origin, on the assumption that their parents' living levels played an important

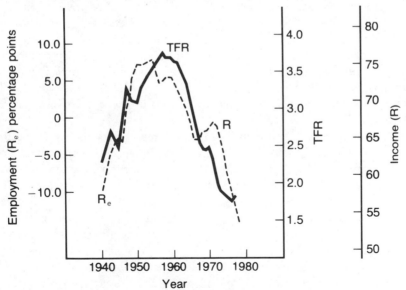

Fig. 4.3   Relative income and fertility. Fertility is represented by TFR and relative income by R and R_e. R_e is an approximation to relative income based on employment data. Data from tables 4.A.3 and 4.A.4.

part in shaping the couple's material standards. For example, the 1957 value of relative income is 73 percent. Consider a typical young man under twenty-five years old at that date who was thinking about marrying and forming a family. If he and his partner aspired to a standard of living that (whether they were aware of it or not) corresponded roughly to the income levels of their families of origin when they were growing up, the young man's prospective income would in itself support 73 percent of that desired level of living. Twenty years later, according to the chart, the man's prospective income, though absolutely greater, would support only 56 percent of the level of living desired by the couple. Thus, young adults in the 1970s find themselves under considerably greater economic stress than those in the late 1950s, in the sense of the male primary breadwinner's ability to support the couple's aspirations. This has led, in turn, to deferred marriage and reduced childbearing within marriage, both of which enter into the fertility decline shown in figure 4.3. There is, of course, nothing sacred about the particular values of 73 and 56 percent—one can think of reasons why the numbers ought to be higher or lower. What is important here is the *change* in the numbers, which indicates that a systematic shift for the worse has occurred in the factors that make up a young man's ability to support a household.

Relative income and relative numbers. Why has the relative income of young men deteriorated so much in the past two decades? Appropriately for this chapter the answer is primarily a demographic one—the relative income of young men has fallen as their relative numbers have grown. In 1955 for every four men between the ages of thirty and sixty-four there were two between the ages of fifteen and twenty-nine; in 1977, there were three—an increase by 50 percent in the ratio of younger to older men.

How does the relative number of young men affect their relative income? The answer is, through altering the balance of supply and demand. Imagine that there is some typical proportion between the jobs of younger and older workers, and as the economy expands these jobs grow at about the same rate, that is, the demand for younger and older workers grows equally. Suppose now that the supply of younger compared with older workers changes noticeably over a period of a decade or so. At a time when the relative supply of younger workers is high, competition among the young will be intense and employers can be choosy. For younger workers to find satisfactory jobs may take considerable time and effort, salaries may be disappointing, and rates of advance up the career ladder frustratingly slow. Conversely, when younger workers are in short supply, it is the employers who find themselves competing, and younger workers are in a position to pick and choose.

Employers will be much more likely to snap up those seeking jobs, and they will more readily offer higher wages to attract the needed workers.

We can read this story of demand and supply in statistical averages that summarize the earnings experience of individuals. Because older men are further up the career ladder than younger men, older men's earnings are typically above average, and younger men's below. However, when the number of younger workers grows relative to older ones, the wages of the young fall even farther below the average while those of older men rise farther above. As shown in figure 4.4, this is what happened between the mid-1950s and 1977.[7]

It should be emphasized that the subject here is the *relative* earnings of the young. In absolute terms, full-time working men in their early twenties in 1977 earned almost one-third more than their counterparts in 1955, even after adjustment for the sharp increase in the cost of living. But it is the relative income situation that is critical in shaping much of young adults' behavior as well as their feelings of well-being.[8]

The altered relative position of young men shown by the earnings data is repeated in statistics on the unemployment rate—the ratio for each age group of unemployed workers to those in the labor force. A higher

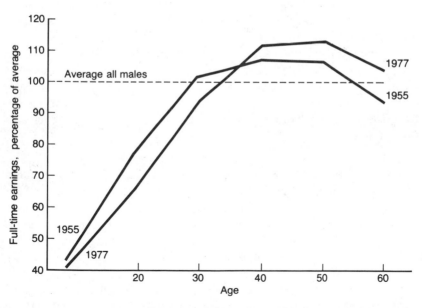

Fig. 4.4   The earnings of younger men compared with older men, 1970s versus 1950s. For each date, earnings at the age shown at the bottom of the figure are expressed as a percentage of the average for all ages (the horizontal broken line). Data from table 4.A.5.

unemployment rate for younger workers than for older ones is normal, because of such factors as the newness of younger workers in the job market or the tentativeness of their job commitments. In the 1970s, however, the relative position of younger workers was noticeably worse than in the 1950s. Thus the weight of numbers sharply aggravates the relative unemployment as well as relative earnings disadvantage of the young. It is as though young and old were at opposite ends of a seesaw, with the ends of the seesaw corresponding to their earnings (or employment) levels. The seesaw is always tilted against the young. But when relatively more young workers are piled on their end, the seesaw tilts even more against them.

These changes in younger men's relative earnings and unemployment rates reflect shifts in the supply of young versus old relative to normal demand. If wages were highly flexible, the effect of changes in relative numbers would be confined to rates of pay alone. But minimum wage laws, unemployment compensation, and similar conditions limit downward pressure on wages, so that the "numbers effect" shows up both in earnings and unemployment rates.

If younger male workers could substitute easily for older, then a relative abundance of younger men would simply result in their shifting into older men's jobs without any adverse effect on their relative earnings and unemployment. But younger men are not good substitutes for older men, primarily because the two groups are at different stages on the career ladder. Older workers have acquired more skills, have greater experience with the internal workings of the firm in which they are employed, and are likely to be viewed by the employer as more reliable and responsible. Union restrictions and employer job specifications differentiating among workers on the basis of age reinforce the lack of substitution.[9]

Women's labor market experience. I have focused so far on younger men. The economic experience of younger women parallels that of the men. For example, in 1955 the earnings of women in their early twenties who were full-time, year-round workers were almost the same as those of women aged 45–54; by 1977, the earnings of the younger group had fallen to 82 percent of those of the older group (table 4.A.5). Similarly for unemployment rates: between the 1950s and 1970s the unemployment rate of females aged 20–24 rose relative to that of females aged 45–54. As Gertrude Bancroft has pointed out, in the 1950s because of their scarcity in the labor market, younger women could pick and choose among jobs, and avoid lower paying types of work.[10] This has not been true in the seventies when the relative supply of younger women was vastly greater.

Relative numbers and fertility. The available empirical approximation to relative income is quite crude. Hence an alternative test of the relative income hypothesis is to compare fertility directly to the relative number of young men, on the assumption that the latter is chiefly responsible for variations in a couple's relative income.

Figure 4.5 measures relative numbers by the ratio of the male population aged 30–64 to that aged 15–29. The increase in this measure to 1955–60 indicates a growing scarcity of younger relative to older men; the subsequent decline in the measure, a growing abundance. Note how the fertility curve moves in a fashion consistent with the hypothesis. Before 1955–60 an increasing scarcity of young men and consequent improvement in their life chances is accompanied by a rise in fertility; after 1955–60 an increasing abundance of young men is paralleled by a decline in fertility. The conclusion pointed to by both figures 4.3 and 4.5 is the same: the evidence supports the relative income hypothesis, both for the baby boom and the baby bust.

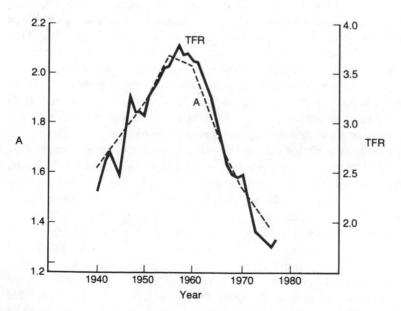

Fig. 4.5   Relative numbers and fertility. Fertility = TFR. A = relative number of males 30–64 to males 15–29. Data from table 4.A.4.

Relative numbers and female labor force participation. Figure 4.2 brought out the differing patterns in the uptrend of labor force participation for younger and older women in the two decades before and after 1960. Between 1940 and 1960 the labor force participation of younger women shows little change while that of older women rises abruptly. (The wartime boost in labor force participation rates is not shown in figure 4.2 so that long term trends will stand out more clearly.) After 1960, it is younger women who show the abrupt increase in labor force participation, while the growth of participation among older women slows noticeably. These contrasting movements can also be explained by the relative income hypothesis.[11]

Consider the situation of a young man and woman who are contemplating marriage. Although both are working full-time, their relative income situation, let us say, is poor, in the sense that both partners find it difficult to make as much as they feel they need to live in the way they'd like. What can they do to improve their economic situation? For each of them, there are possibilities such as seeking extra training to improve job advancement prospects or "moonlighting," that is, taking on a second job. But the most obvious adjustment over the long run is a reallocation of the woman's work time from the home to the labor market. For couples who expect to start having children as soon as they are married, this means putting off marriage so that the woman can work a longer time. For married couples it may mean putting off childbearing. For those who have children, it may mean trying to combine childbearing and childrearing with work outside the home. Or it may mean stopping at fewer children than were desired so that the wife can return to the labor market sooner than planned. In all of these cases, the solution to the economic pressures that the couple feels is increased labor force participation for the woman. This option is not available to the man because the couple is already planning on his continuous labor force participation throughout the family forming years.

The relevance of this reasoning to the post-World War II movement in young women's work outside the home is obvious. In the 1950s young workers were in unusually short supply—this was the "scarcity generation" born in the low birth rate period of the 1930s. For both men and women, job opportunities at good wages were plentiful and unemployment rates relatively low. It proved relatively easy to earn enough to satisfy life-style aspirations. This contrasted sharply to the pre-World War II situation when demand for labor of all types was low, jobs hard to find, and young persons had a hard time "making ends meet," which is another way of saying "living as they would like to." The favorable experience of young adults in the fifties encouraged earlier marriage and childbearing in two ways. First, a number of young adults found it possible to accumulate fairly rapidly a savings "nest egg" or to acquire goods that would eventually be used in establishing a home. Second, the favorable employment and earnings experience of young men and their relatively rapid job advancement increased couples' confidence that the man in each household would be able to support its needs and that the woman could give up her job so that the couple could start a family. Thus in the 1950s the high relative income of couples due to their small numbers led to a sharp departure from pre-World War II trends. Couples could get married earlier and women leave the labor market sooner to start raising a family.

In the 1970s large relative numbers of young adults have produced the opposite effect. Relative to their life-style aspirations young men and women today find the economic going tough. As shown by the crude relative income measure above, a young man's ability to supply a couple's needs has declined on the average, by close to one-third (fig. 4.3). Since women's economic experience is affected similarly by increased relative numbers, the ability of young women to contribute to the couple's desired living levels has correspondingly declined. Hence young persons are under much greater economic pressure. We have seen some response to this on the part of men, such as increased "moonlighting." But the more pervasive response has been on the female side through much more rapidly increased labor force participation.

What about older women? Why, in the light of the similar trends for older and younger women before World War II, has the period since the war been marked by opposing movements for the two age groups? The key to the answer is provided by the fact that older women and younger women do essentially the same types of work. In contrast to the situation among males, older women are not typically on a higher rung of the career ladder than younger women. This means that from an employer's point of view there is a high degree of substitution possible between younger and older women, though young women are somewhat preferred for several reasons, among them, their superior education.

Consider now the post-1940 labor market for women as a whole. The demand for female labor was expanding steadily with the growth of the economy, creating new openings for teachers, secretaries, cashiers, sales clerks, and so on. After World War II because the relative income situation of young adults was so good, the normal growth in labor force participation of younger women was interrupted as couples opted for marriage and a family at higher rates than previously. With young women failing to come foreward at the normal rate, employers turned increasingly to older women to fill the gap. In Gertrude Bancroft's words: "Faced with a restricted number of women in the age groups that they normally favor, employers were forced to turn to other ages for their labor supply" (1958, p. 80).[12] The result was a disproportionate growth in work outside the home for older women, as they benefited from the incremental demand left unfilled by younger women. It is worth quoting more fully Bancroft's description of this period:

> With the strong demand for labor during most of the 1950s, based in part on the defense program, middle-aged and older women free to take jobs outside the home were the only substantial source of additional workers. In all probability, if they had not been available and if traditional attitudes about the suitability of both married and middle-aged women for many jobs had not broken down, the high levels of employment of the 1950s could never have been achieved. [P. 132]

What about the subsequent turnaround in the sixties and seventies—the accelerated growth in work outside the home for younger women and the slowdown in growth for older women? The key to the answer is the reversal in young adults' relative income as their relative numbers increased. As young couples' relative income progressively deteriorated, young women flooded the labor market at above normal rates, taking advantage of the continuing growth in demand for female labor and partly displacing the normal growth in older women's work outside the home.

It is possible also that the movements for older women have reflected a relative income influence of their own (Wachter 1977). Before 1960, the relative income situation of *older men* (which is essentially the inverse of that for younger) was adverse, and the wives of the older men were under greater pressure to work. After 1960 the relative income situation of older men improved as that for younger men deteriorated, thus reducing the pressure for their wives to work.

Relative numbers, psychological stress, and social conditions. Marriage, fertility, and women's work outside the home are not the only conditions sensitive to the economic pressures felt by young adults. Another way to test the relative income hypothesis is to see whether there are other conditions among young adults that indicate swings in stress consistent with the argument. Figure 4.6 shows that there are. Before the late fifties homicide and suicide rates among young men were low or declining. Thereafter, they rose, at first gradually, and then, starting around the mid-sixties, quite sharply. In contrast, the suicide rate for men aged 45–54 declined from 1960 on, and the homicide rate rose only mildly.[13]

Increased stress among young adults in the past two decades is evident in a variety of other social conditions as well.[14] The drinking of alcoholic beverages by young persons has increased noticeably. This has doubtless been one connecting link between stress and the rise in suicide and homicide rates just noted. It has also contributed to increased mortality due to accidents, especially motor vehicle accidents.

Another indication is the rise in illegitimacy rates, which is due in considerable part to the fact that legitimation by marriage of premarital
conceptions has dropped noticeably, partly because of the increased
difficulty young men are experiencing in their ability to support a family. Divorce rates among young adults have also risen at above average
rates, reflecting the strains that economic pressures are placing on marriages. Although other factors have influenced these social conditions,
the pattern of worsening since 1960 that they show in common is consistent with the view that young adults have been experiencing increased
stress as their relative numbers have grown.

Relative numbers and economic stability. Changing demographic conditions have also aggravated the problem of economic stabilization in the

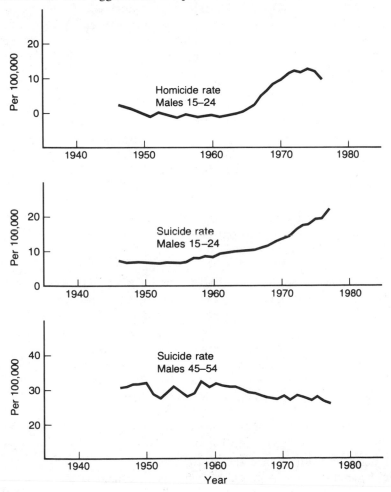

Fig. 4.6   Crime and suicide rates. Data from table 4.A.6.

last two decades.[15] A rise in the relative number of young adults tends to raise the economy-wide unemployment rate for two reasons. As has been mentioned, the unemployment rates of younger workers are typically higher than those of older workers. Because the economy-wide rate is an average of the rates for younger and older, a rise in the share of younger workers in the total labor force will raise the average. Also, as we have seen, an increase in the relative number of young workers raises their own unemployment rate, and this further increases the economy-wide unemployment rate.

An increase in the general unemployment rate due to changed labor supply conditions is not as susceptible to correction by the usual monetary and fiscal policies as is a rise in unemployment due to inadequate demand. Monetary and fiscal policies aim to raise the total level of spending and thereby stimulate output and employment. If the source of increased unemployment is a disproportion between younger and older workers, however, firms will find it difficult to hire new workers in the right proportion of skilled older workers to unskilled younger workers, because there are not enough older skilled workers to go around. Under these conditions, the response of firms to increased demand is therefore more likely to be increased prices rather than expanded output and employment. More rapid price inflation and increased unemployment—so called "stagflation"—are thus likely to occur together. Many other factors of course, have been responsible for the last decade's stagflation, but it is clear that changed demographic conditions have been a contributing factor.

Pre-1940. The discussion so far has been confined to the period since 1940 and for good reason. It is only since 1940 that the effect of relative numbers has played such a dominant role in shaping the conditions of young adults. Before World War II the demand for labor fluctuated widely from one decade to the next. If labor demand was grossly deficient, the benefit of scarce numbers was swamped by general unemployment. As for boom periods, any potentially beneficial effect of scarce numbers was wiped out by free immigration. Before the mid-1920s, if the domestic demand and supply situation produced a tight labor market—plentiful job prospects at good wages—it served as a green light turning on the flow of traffic from abroad. The potential benefit to young American men of a major boom was lost in the influx of European workers.[16]

All this has been changed by federal laws drastically altering the historical relations between labor demand and supply. On the supply side federal legislation since the 1920s has had the effect of sharply restricting immigration in periods when labor demand is high. On the demand side, the Employment Act of 1946 committed the federal government to maintaining a high and growing level of labor demand through monetary and fiscal policies. The feasibility of the government's accomplishing this was helped by the substantial rise in the relative importance of federal government expenditures in the post-World War II economy compared with the prewar economy. Although immigration and fluctuations in labor demand have not wholly ceased, their magnitudes (even including illegal immigration) compared with the past are much smaller. In contrast, the magnitude of swings in the proportion of younger to older adults is strikingly greater than in the past. The result has been a major shift in the comparative roles of these factors in shaping the fortunes of young adult Americans.

Post-1980. If the relative income hypothesis is correct, then, under the new conditions of post-World War II American society, a self-generating cycle in the birthrate may have been born. In simplest terms the reasoning is as follows. The birthrate at any given time is largely determined by the relative number of younger to older adults (fig. 4.5). But as shown in figure 4.7, the relative number of younger to older adults is itself an echo of the birthrate about twenty years earlier. Thus we have a historical situation which can be represented diagramatically as follows:

	1920–40	*1940–60*	*1960–80*	*1980–2000*	*2000–2020*
Persons $\frac{15-29}{30-64}$		Decline ↓	Rise ↓	Decline ↓	etc.
Birthrate		Decline ↗ Rise	↗ Decline	↗ Rise	↗ etc.

This shows that the fertility decline of 1920–40 caused in 1940–60 a decline in the relative number of young adults, and the effects of that, in turn, gave rise to a concurrent baby boom. The baby boom of 1940–60, in turn, caused a rise in the relative number of young adults twenty years later, and a consequent baby bust. The baby bust of 1960–80 will itself cause another turnaround in the proportion of younger adults, a decline from 1980 to 2000, and thus lay the basis for a new baby boom at that time. That baby boom—of 1980–2000—would in turn, cause a rise in 2000–2020 in the proportion of young adults and lead to a new baby bust. And so on into the future.

If one short-circuits the mediating role in the diagram of the proportion of young adults, one sees directly that the birthrate in any given twenty-year period is causing an opposite movement in itself in the next period. Thus we arrive at a self-generating fertility movement lasting forty years, if one counts both boom and bust phases. Along with these fertility movements would be corresponding cycles in a wide variety of socioeconomic phenomena, reflecting variations in the relative income of young adults. And, to return to the rate of population growth, with which this section started, this implies that American population growth in the future, as in the past, would be marked by sizable fluctuations, although the length of the fluctuations would be longer than in the past and the reasons for them different. The size of the American population would, in consequence, continue to grow in roughly stepwise fashion.

This argument is, of course, speculative. But, in contrast to others that are current, it is based on a theory that is consistent with a wide range of evidence over the past forty years.

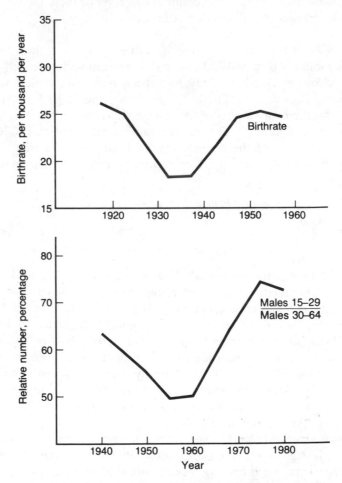

Fig. 4.7   The lagged effect of the birthrate on the relative number of younger men compared with older men. Data from tables 4.A.7 and 4.A.8.

4.2   Mortality

Mortality change in the post-1940 period falls into three clearly demarcated periods.[17] Up to the mid-1950s there was a phase of unprecedented improvement chiefly due to the diffusion of a succession of newly discovered antibiotic "wonder drugs," first introduced in the 1930s. Then there was a period of leveling off, so pronounced that it led analysts at the National Center for Health Statistics in 1964 to caution that "the death rate for the United States has reached the point where further decreases as experienced in the past cannot be anticipated" (HEW 1964, 42). As reasonable as this statement seemed at the time, it was very shortly undercut by events. After 1968 a new decline in mortality set in at rates like those of the two decades before 1954. Even more remarkable is the age pattern of this recent decline. Rates of improvement at the older ages are higher than in the earlier period, and are perhaps the highest ever, while young adult mortality has shown very little change. Infant and child mortality, however, has declined at about the same pace as earlier. By race, whites continue to have lower mortality than blacks, but the differential has declined, and black females now have higher life expectancy than white males. In contrast, for both races the differential by sex has continued to widen in favor of females.

4.2.1   Trends and Differentials

The crude death rate, the number of deaths per year divided by the total mid-year population, is not a good measure of mortality improvement, because it is affected by the age distribution of the population. For example, even if the mortality rate at each age remained the same, the crude death rate would increase if the proportion of elderly persons in the population grew. The "age-adjusted death rate" is free of distortions caused by shifts in the age distribution and is thus a better indicator of the rate of improvement in mortality. The trend in this rate has been sharply downward since the mid-1930s, except for the protracted plateau from 1954 to 1968 (fig. 4.8). The crude death rate has followed a similar course, but the gradient has been lower because of an upward trend in the share of older persons in the population.

Historically, mortality improvements have been highest at younger ages and lowest at older, and this was true of the advances in the 1936–54 period (fig. 4.9). Between 1954 and 1968, improvement came virtually to a halt at all ages except those under 15, and even for these, the advances were less than in the earlier period. Indeed, there was an upward trend in mortality rates of males above age 15 in almost every age group between 1954 and 1968. Since 1968 rates of improvement at all ages other than 15–34 have approached or exceeded those of the 1936–

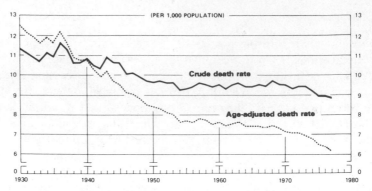

Fig. 4.8   Crude and age-adjusted death rate, 1930–77. Data from HEW (1979).

54 period. Rates of decline for young adults, however, have lagged behind noticeably.

The mortality improvement since 1936 translates into an average advance in life expectancy at birth of almost fifteen years, from 58.5 years in 1936 to 73.2 in 1977. As is well known, however, life expectancy varies considerably by race and sex within the population. The excess of white life expectancy over that of "all other races," as the category is called in the official statistics, has been more than halved since 1936, as shown by the following figures for both sexes combined, in years (HEW 1979; 1977):

	1936	*1977*
White	59.8	73.8
All Other Races	49.0	68.8
White Minus all Others	10.8	5.0

The trend in this differential has been far from steady, and during the period from 1954 to 1968 when national mortality leveled off, there was actually a slight widening. On the other hand, the recent narrowing has been at a faster rate than in the pre-1954 period. Differences in mortality by race are usually attributed chiefly to the more favorable social and economic circumstances enjoyed by whites, and the narrowing observed since the sixties in both black-white income differences and mortality is consistent with this.

In contrast to the differential by race, that by sex widened steadily throughout the period. In 1936 for both races female life expectancy at birth exceeded male by around four years; by 1977 the differential had risen to about eight years. This differential is generally believed partly to reflect differences between the sexes in their consumption and the kind of work they do and partly, biological factors (Fuchs 1974, p. 50; Siegel 1978).

4.2.2 Causes and Effects

Although living levels may partly account for some point-of-time differentials in mortality, their relationship to the general trend in mortality is, at best, uncertain. This is most apparent from the historical perspective of the mid-nineteenth century. From 1850 to 1900 the long term rate of economic growth as measured by real per capita income—the economic magnitude whose improvement is most often presumed responsible for mortality decline—was just about the same as in the twentieth century. Yet in the nineteenth century, mortality rate improvement, if it occurred at all, was quite modest (Easterlin 1977). The rapid decline which set in toward the start of the twentieth century seems principally due—here as in Europe—to the diffusion of public health improvements (Stolnitz 1955), followed in the 1930s by the discovery and spread of antibiotics. By the 1950s, as the incidence of infectious disease was reduced to fairly low levels, the mortality decline virtually

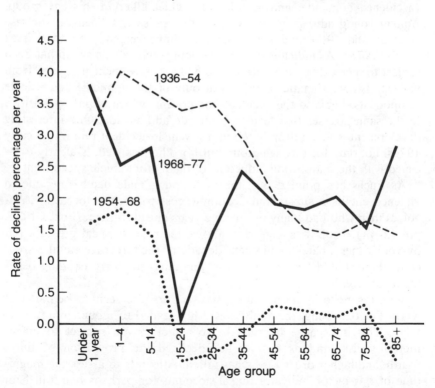

Fig. 4.9   Age pattern of mortality decline in three periods. Data from table 4.A.9.

ceased, despite the persistence of high growth in real GNP per capita. Then, in the last decade mortality reduction at a rapid rate resumed, although there was a noticeable drop in the rate of economic growth.

The causes of this recent unforeseen mortality decline have not as yet been adequately investigated, but it seems clear from data on death by cause that some important new factors are at work. Since 1968 deaths resulting from cardiovascular diseases have dropped at a surprising rate, and this has been the chief reason for the dramatic decline in mortality at older ages (HEW 1979). Noticeable declines in mortality from infectious diseases have also occurred in this period, but this factor is no longer the main source of mortality improvement as it was in the 1936–54 period. The reduction in mortality from cardiovascular diseases may partly reflect new medical care developments both in identifying high risk cases and in the treatment of such diseases. It may also reflect lifestyle changes in the population, involving reduction of cigarette smoking, improved diet, and greater exercise.

The failure of mortality to decline among young adults, especially males, reflects the trend in a quite different cause, deaths from violence (accidents, homicide, and suicide), the chief killer in this age group. Among young adults, mortality from this cause has been on the rise since around 1960, and has offset mild improvements in other areas (Weiss 1976). As indicated in the preceding section, this group has been subject to increasing economic stress, and the movement in deaths from violence is symptomatic of this—not only of the homicide and suicide components, but also the accident component, which is partly sensitive to the same stresses that lead to homicide and suicide. One interesting development is that a drop in the motor vehicle accident rate in the early 1970s, not only for this age group but for others as well, is clearly associated with the nationwide reduction of the motor vehicle speed limit.

As Fuchs has pointed out, the high young male death rate due to violence entails a substantial economic cost to society, because it involves men who had many productive years ahead of them (Fuchs 1974, pp. 42–43). If, as was suggested above, the psychological pressure felt by young men abates in the next decade as their relative numbers decline, there should be a reduction in this rate with corresponding benefits to society.

With regard to infant mortality, new factors also seem to be partly at work. For one thing, the "baby bust" has tended to reduce infant mortality. This is because later births to a mother are subject to higher mortality risk, and as fertility has declined the proportion of third, fourth, and higher order births has fallen. Attempts to assess the magnitude of this factor indicates that it accounts for perhaps one-fourth of the recent decline (Morris, Udry, and Chase 1975; Wright 1975). If fertility turns up substantially again, this source of infant mortality reduction will be removed. Possibly longer intervals between births have also contributed to the decline in infant mortality.

The recent mortality improvements at older ages have already led to a substantial upward revision in the projected population aged 65 and over at the turn of the century. The most recent (1977) projection is that this group will number 31.8 million, over 10 percent more than was projected only a decade ago. Close to half (45 percent) will be aged 75 and over (Siegel 1978, pp. 17, 19). If labor force participation rates of older men continue to decline, including those for men under 65, this will add to recent mortality reductions in raising further the prospective size of the *retirement* population.

Because of the sex differential in mortality, the older population is always disproportionately composed of women. Among those 65 and over in 1976 there were about seven men for every ten women; by 2000, the proportion could be two to three (Siegel 1978).

The share in the total population of those 65 and over in the year 2000 depends, of course, partly on the outlook for fertility. The latest Census Bureau projection, based on a conservative fertility projection, is for a slight increase by 2000—from a 1976 value of 10.7 percent to between 11.3 and 12.9 percent. If there is, in fact, a new baby boom then this proportion might not rise at all.

Mortality changes since 1940 have had only a minor effect on the rate of population growth, and this will continue to be true. This is partly because the crude death rate has not fluctuated over a wide range as has the fertility rate (cf. figs. 4.3 and 4.8). Moreover, mortality is already at a fairly low level, and as we have seen, the effect on the crude death rate of further reductions in mortality at given ages is partly offset by the growth in the proportion of the population at older ages.

Additional declines in mortality rates will have only a limited impact on life expectancy. This is because mortality rates in early and middle life have already been reduced to quite low levels, and most future mortality improvement would necessarily be concentrated at older ages, the principal exception being the effect of eliminating deaths from violence among young adults. For example, it is estimated that elimination of mortality from cancer of all types would raise life expectancy at birth 2.5 years; from heart disease, 5.9 years.[18] Given that the maximum life-span for humans is about 100 years, there is clearly an upper limit to the improvement possible, short of discovery of the Fountain of Youth.[19]

4.3   The New "New Immigration"

For much of its history, the United States prided itself on being the "melting pot" of the world, and not without cause—the net inflow of 24 million persons from 1840 to World War I is unmatched in the history of the world. By 1920, nineteenth century immigrants and their descendants had doubled the size of the American population compared with that which would have resulted from the colonial stock of 1790 alone (Easterlin 1980b). However, from a worldwide point of view the ingredients considered appropriate for the melting pot were rather narrowly defined. The era of American independence started with a population almost wholly of northwest European origin (predominantly British), and this remained true down to the Civil War (fig. 4.10). As the nineteenth century wore on, the origins of immigrants shifted increasingly to southern and eastern Europe as population growth surged upward in those areas with the onset of modern economic development. This growth in southern and eastern European immigration, characterized by contemporaries as the New Immigration, became a subject of growing concern, and, eventually in the 1920s, the target of restrictive legislation with national origins quotas. Earlier, incipient flows from Asia to the Pacific Coast had been substantially terminated by legislation and treaties which sought to stem the "Yellow Peril." From the 1920s to the 1950s the makeup of the American population in terms of racial mix and national origin remained essentially fixed. The 1920s restrictions also had the effect of substantially reducing the total flow of immigrants, especially relative to population (see fig. 4.1).

In the last two decades, however, dramatic changes have occurred in the immigration picture—what might be called the *new* New Immigration has come into being. In the 1960s persons of Latin American and Asian origin accounted for over half of *legal* immigration, and, in the first half of the seventies, for almost three-fourths (fig. 4.10). In 1972–76, the seven leading countries of origin of immigrants were, in descending order: Mexico, the Philippines, Korea, Cuba, India, Taiwan, and the Dominican Republic (U.S. Congress 1978).

To an important extent this change is the result of the Immigration Act of 1965, which shifted the basis of American immigration policy from a national origins criterion of quota allocation to one based on considerations such as labor skills, reuniting families, and humanitarian concerns (e.g., providing asylum for political refugees). The new policy affected not only national origins, but a number of other characteristics of immigrants as well (although some of these changes had been foreshadowed in the McCarran-Walter Act of 1952).[20] As compared with the period of free immigration before World War I, the proportion of females and of married persons rose considerably, reflecting the priority given to reuniting families and the importance of refugee or quasi-refugee movements. Also, the occupational composition of immigration shifted sharply in the direction of higher skill. For example, in the 1960s the proportion of immigrants in professional occupations was close to one-fourth, compared with a mere 1 percent in 1901–10; the proportion

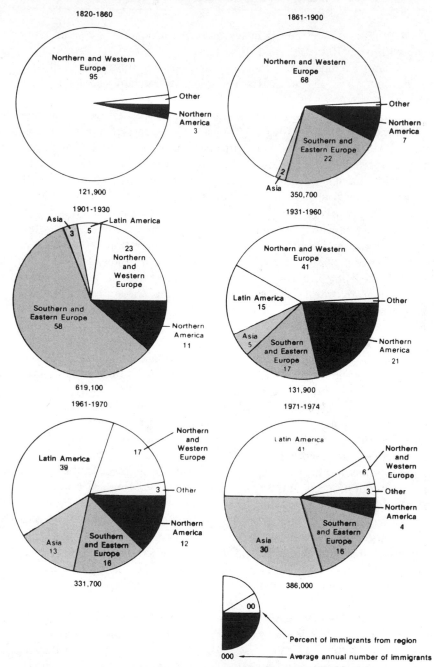

Fig. 4.10   United States immigrants by region of origin, 1820–1974.
Data from Leon F. Bouvier, Henry S. Shryock, and Harry
W. Henderson, "International Migration: Yesterday, To-
day, and Tomorrow," *Population Bulletin* 32, no. 4: 3–42
(Washington, D.C.: Population Reference Bureau, Inc.).

who were laborers and domestic servants was around 20 percent, compared with over 70 percent in 1901–10.

Much more publicized in the popular press has been recent illegal immigration. This, of course, is not a new phenomenon—so-called wetbacks were a prominent concern in the 1950s. Although relevant facts about illegal immigration are hard to come by, a few tentative generalizations can be made.[21] Illegal immigration appears to be increasing, and the principal countries of origin of these immigrants are much the same as for legal immigration—Mexico, for example, is estimated to account for about 60 percent of illegal immigrants. In contrast to legal immigrants, illegal aliens are largely unskilled, many of them being agricultural wage workers. So far as Mexicans are concerned, there is a considerable two-way movement across the United States-Mexico border, indicating that a significant share of the migration is temporary, although on balance the net flow is to the United States. Rather than illegal aliens being a burden to the American taxpayer, as some have claimed, the opposite appears to be true—illegal aliens are more likely to pay taxes than they are to receive the benefits of government-supported facilities and services.

Since 1950 the volume of net *legal* immigration has averaged 300 to 400 thousand per year, with the highest levels occurring mostly in the 1960s. It is possible that net illegal immigration in the last decade-and-a-half may be of comparable magnitude.[22]

Of the nation's estimated growth in population of 15 million between 1970 and 1979, net legal immigration accounted for a little over one-fifth (U.S. Bureau of the Census 1979). Allowance for illegal immigration would raise the growth in total population size and the share contributed by immigration, perhaps to one-third. In contrast, in the 1950s, legal immigration accounted for somewhat over one-tenth of population growth. The increased importance of immigration as a source of population growth is partly due to the inflow of illegal aliens, but chiefly to the drop in domestic fertility. Currently, the percentage of United States population that is foreign born is 5 percent; this compares with 13 percent in 1920. If fertility rates remain at their current low levels, the percentage of foreign born will start to grow.

Illegal immigration and most legal immigration today is stimulated by the opportunities for employment at comparatively attractive wages offered in the United States, as was true of immigration before World War I (Briggs 1975; M. Wachter 1978). Moreover, in the next decade employment opportunities for unskilled labor are likely to grow—hence the prospect is for continued high levels of illegal as well as legal immigration (M. Wachter 1979). However, conditions in the country of origin are also important in determining the size of the flow. As noted previously, the New Immigration before World War I was partly a result of higher rates of population growth in southern and eastern Europe that occurred as the process of modern economic growth spread to those areas. Viewed in perspective, the new New Immigration is a continuation of this historical pattern, as modern economic development accompanied by high population growth extends to Latin America and Asia. That such "push" factors are important is shown by the low levels of immigration from Mexico to the United States before World War II, despite the absence of legal restrictions.[23]

4.4   The New Internal Migration

The geographic distribution of American population has so far gone through two great epochs and today appears to be on the verge of a third. The first, that of agricultural settlement of the country, was largely completed by 1860 although it stretched on until the end of the nineteenth century. Overlapping this in time and eventually superseding it was the cityward movement of population, which started to grow in the first half of the nineteenth century and continued at a rapid rate until the last decade or so (Davis et al. 1972, chap. 5). So powerful was this movement that rural depopulation had become a pervasive phenomenon by the mid-twentieth century.

It seems likely that we are now at the brink of a third great epoch— one of repopulation of a number of previously rural areas. The first clue to this was the emergence of "suburbanization" in the first quarter of this century. More recently the return to rural areas has, in addition, taken the form of population growth in rural areas not bordering on major cities (so-called nonmetropolitan areas) and the shift to the Sunbelt.[24] Fifty years hence it is possible that the history of American population distribution will be seen as a paradoxical succession of settlement, abandonment, and resettlement.

4.4.1   Recent Developments

The shift to the Sunbelt is shown clearly by comparing, as in table 4.1, regional population growth and net migration rates in the fifties, sixties, and seventies (Beale and Fuguitt 1978, chap. 8). In every period the South and West lead in rate of population growth, and the lead widens noticeably over time (col. 1). This is chiefly the result of internal migration. Throughout the period the Northeast and the north central region have low or negative rates of net migration, while the South and West have positive rates—that is, net in-migration—except for the 1950–60 decade in the South (col. 5). By the seventies the South moved into a virtual tie with the West for leadership in rates of population growth and net in-migration.

Table 4.1 Annualized Population Change and Net Migration Rates (per 1,000) by Metropolitan Status and Adjacency Status: Census Regions 1950–60, 1960–70, and 1970–75

| | Annualized Population Change | | | | | Annualized Net Migration Rates | | | | |
| | | | Nonmetro | | | | | Nonmetro | | |
	Total (1)	Metro (2)	Non-Metro (3)	Adjacent (4)	Not Adjacent (5)	Total (6)	Metro (7)	Non-Metro (8)	Adjacent (9)	Not Adjacent (10)
Northeast										
1950–60	12.4	13.2	7.0	7.8	4.9	0.8	1.7	− 4.6	− 3.2	− 8.2
1960–70	9.4	9.5	8.1	9.9	3.2	0.7	0.8	− 0.2	− 2.5	− 6.0
1970–75	1.5	−0.3	13.0	13.7	11.0	−2.7	−4.5	8.5	9.5	5.7
North Central										
1950–60	14.9	20.9	3.6	7.7	−0.2	−0.3	4.5	− 9.3	− 4.8	−13.4
1960–70	9.2	12.2	2.7	5.8	−0.3	−1.4	0.3	− 5.1	− 2.4	− 7.8
1970–75	3.6	2.4	6.3	6.0	6.0	−2.9	−5.1	1.8	1.4	2.3
South										
1950–60	15.2	28.6	−1.4	1.0	−3.5	−2.8	10.0	−18.5	−16.1	−20.7
1960–70	13.3	20.0	3.0	4.8	1.3	1.2	7.0	− 7.8	− 5.9	− 9.6
1970–75	15.4	17.0	12.7	14.7	10.7	7.6	8.5	6.1	8.1	4.1
West										
1950–60	32.6	38.6	14.0	15.0	13.4	16.0	22.5	− 4.2	− 1.9	− 5.6
1960–70	21.6	24.8	9.3	16.2	4.9	9.2	12.4	− 2.9	− 4.6	− 7.7
1970–75	15.7	13.6	23.9	27.9	21.2	7.4	5.5	15.1	19.5	12.1

Source: Fuguitt and Voss, 1979, table 5, p. 8.
Note: Metropolitan status is as of 1974.

Equally noteworthy are developments in the relative growth within each region of metropolitan versus nonmetropolitan areas. In the 1950s metropolitan growth exceeds nonmetropolitan in every region, and the nonmetropolitan areas are net exporters of population to metropolitan (cols. 2, 3, 7, and 8). By the 1970s the situation has almost completely turned around. Nonmetropolitan growth rates are higher than metropolitan in every region except the South (cols. 2 and 3). In the Northeast and the north central region there is net out-migration from metropolitan areas and net in-migration to nonmetropolitan; in the South and West the trends in migration rates are in the same direction as in the North, but because the metropolitan areas of these regions are beneficiaries of the regional population shift to the Sunbelt, they continue to show net in-migration to both metropolitan and nonmetropolitan areas.

In part the resurgence of nonmetropolitan areas reflects the process of suburbanization. This is shown by the population growth and migration trends for nonmetropolitan areas bordering on metropolitan (cols. 4 and 9). In part, however, the resurgence reflects a quite unexpected development, a turnaround in areas not bordering on the metropolitan sector. In every region these "nonadjacent" nonmetropolitan areas show net out-migration in the 1950s and 1960s—though usually at a lower rate in the 1960s—but in the 1970s they show net in-migration (col. 10). Correspondingly, population growth rates which had been low and declining in these areas—in some cases actually negative as rural depopulation occurred—turned sharply upward in the 1970s (col. 5). Indeed, in every region except the South, population growth was higher in these nonmetropolitan areas than in the metropolitan, although growth in the nonmetropolitan areas adjacent to the metropolitan sector was usually highest.

4.4.2   Work, Residence, and Play in the Location of the American Population

What are the reasons for the shift to the Sunbelt and nonmetropolitan areas, and will it continue? There are, of course, special factors at work such as the stimulus to locate in the South because of its relatively low wages (cotton textiles) or natural resource endowments (petrochemicals), and government decisions regarding the location of military, space, and educational activities. But the shift appears to reflect also the emergence of longer term factors connected with the process of economic growth. These will be stressed here, because they bear particularly on the prospective continuation of the new migration pattern. To understand them, it is necessary to see first how the earlier tides in the movement of American population—settlement and urbanization—were connected with economic growth.

Throughout the history of mankind residence decisions have been dominated by place of work, and this is true of the epochs of settlement and urbanization in the United States. The settlement phase of American population distribution is a reflection of the immense agricultural opportunities offered by America's land. That the key factor was one of *economic* opportunities is clearly evidenced by the absence of substantial settlement in the vast but economically submarginal interior lands of Australia and Brazil.

Starting in the nineteenth century a major new set of economic possibilities was added to the pursuit of agricultural opportunity. The British Industrial Revolution ushered in the era of modern economic growth. The key element in this was the widespread implementation of the long-envisaged possibilities of mechanized production that were made possible by new inventions in power (the steam engine) and industrial materials (especially wrought iron and later steel). The impact of these developments on the location of economic opportunities was profound. Prior to the Industrial Revolution, the prevailing manufacturing technology typically involved little more than hand tools and could be carried on in the shop or home. Because of this, manufacturing was fairly widely dispersed over the land. The new industrial technology shifted the balance sharply in favor of urban locations. This was partly because the new technology had sizable economies of scale, and factories, unlike shops, required access to substantial markets as outlets for their products. It was partly because the new technology was geared initially to a narrow set of resource requirements, primarily coal and iron ore, that were much less ubiquitous than the agricultural and forest resources on which preindustrial technology was based. Hence location was favored at or near the sources of the new industrial inputs or at transport points that made these resources cheaply accessible.

The result was the creation of new business and job opportunities in urban centers and a corresponding response to these opportunities in the geographic distribution of the American work force and population. This was reinforced by several factors. First, application of the new steam and iron technology to internal transportation led to invention of the railroad. The rail network that eventually came into being sharply accentuated the economic advantages of those places at key junctions in the network. Second, what are called "agglomeration" economies added to the opportunities in urban centers. For example, industries serving consumers, such as printing and publishing, were attracted to cities by the concentration of workers and consumers that had been induced by the new technology. Finally, the new technology had an impact on location via consumer demand, because it gave rise to an unprecedented growth in per capita income. With income rising, consumer demand grew proportionately more rapidly for high-income-elasticity nonagricultural products than for low-income-elasticity agricultural products. Because production of the former is more concentrated in urban areas, the result was further to expand the job opportunities in urban areas and hence their attractiveness to the population.

As this process continued into the mid-twentieth century, the counterpart of urbanization came to be rural depopulation. For example, of the over 3,100 counties in the United States, in each of the two decades between 1940 and 1960 about half experienced absolute declines in population. Modern economic growth was "de-settling" the areas filled up only a century earlier, and concern over rural decay started to grow.

However, modern economic growth, through its continuing impact on technology, per capita income, and leisure time, was already undoing its own handiwork, by breaking the ties that had previously bound the consumer's residence to his place of work.[25] The new forces can best be understood if one considers the impact of economic growth in this century on the relative advantages of rural and urban areas with regard to: (1) residential preferences of consumers; (2) recreational preferences of consumers; and (3) locational decisions of business firms.

With regard to residential preferences, there is considerable evidence that many urban Americans prefer rural or semirural living, although some like it coupled with proximity to urban centers (Fuguitt and Zuiches 1975, p. 493). The technological breakthrough that opened up the possibility of reconciling the economic advantages of urban location for businesses with the residential preferences of consumers was the automobile, although the horsedrawn trolley and electric streetcar were forerunners of the automobile.[26] Higher consumer income was necessary to realize this possibility because of the cost of purchasing and operating an automobile. Modern economic growth supplied this need and contributed further via shortened working days that left time for lengthy commutation. Nor should one overlook another major technological development, electricity transmission, that supplied the power so vital for modern household operation to dispersed residential communities.

With regard to the recreational preferences of the American consumer, it is clear that modern economic growth has tipped the balance in favor of rural areas. Urban centers have special advantages for certain types of recreation—most notably spectator sports like baseball and football. Cultural activities such as opera and live theater are perhaps other examples, but they depend on an elite not a mass market. The crucial technological development affecting recreation was television, which brought spectator sports and movies into the home, thereby drastically lessening the need for urban residence to enjoy these pursuits. On the other hand, the recreational activities offered by rural areas, such as camping, picnicking, and water sports, inhere in their very setting. Even recreational activities closer to home, such as softball, tennis, and golf, typically favor rural over urban residence. As George Katona (1964, chap. 25) has pointed out, outdoor recreation is the most distinctive feature of American leisure-time activities. This predisposes many households toward rural areas. Modern economic growth today permits the realization of this preference, not only via new technology, but also by giving households the money and time to pursue it.

The manifestation of these residential and recreational preferences is nowhere clearer than in the locational patterns of the retirement population—a group largely freed from the constraint of place of work. Several studies have shown that one of the groups centrally involved in the new pattern of American population distribution is retirees. As we have seen, improved longevity is a concomitant of economic growth (though for the most part not directly caused by it), and the span of retirement years will rise further in the future. The result will be to reinforce the new trends in location already apparent.[27]

So far, the discussion has centered on how economic growth has affected the relative advantage of rural and urban areas with regard to consumer residential and recreational preferences. How has twentieth-century economic growth affected the location of business firms? In the nineteenth century, modern economic growth spurred urban concentration by endowing cities with drastic new advantages over rural locations. The twentieth century has seen a sharp reduction in this. The progress of modern technology has greatly diversified industrial materials—witness the shift from ferrous to nonferrous metals and plastics, and energy inputs from coal to petroleum, natural gas, and other sources. The innovation of an electric power network has contributed to a more even geographic distribution of power costs. The rigid rail transport network has been supplemented and replaced by truck transportation and a far-flung network of highways. New possibilities of information transmission and processing via the telephone and computer have opened up. Such developments, it seems safe to say, have increased the number of firms that are "footloose" vis-à-vis those whose locational decisions are tied to narrow resource input requirements. Moreover, agglomeration economies of urban areas have turned into diseconomies as pollution and congestion have grown. Even the trend in consumer demand has turned against urban-based activities, as expenditures on services, which can usually be produced equally well in small and large communities, have grown relative to those on manufactured products. All of this means that in contrast to the nineteenth century, the location of business firms in this century is less bound by technology to a limited urban network and is more responsive to consumer preferences, not only as manifest in product markets, but also as evidenced in worker preferences for more attractive working locations.

Economic historians sometimes distinguish between a *first* Industrial Revolution based on the steampower/coal/iron-and-steel technology of the nineteenth century, and a *second* Industrial Revolution, associated with the innovation of the internal combustion engine, electrical power, and chemical developments of the twentieth century. The locational mandate of the First Industrial Revolution was urban concentration. The Second Industrial Revolution is now starting to make its effect felt in the form of rural repopulation, though, of course, this will entail new urban centers in formerly rural areas, and will not uniformly embrace all rural places. This new technological era of modern economic growth, coupled with continued growth in consumer income and leisure has broken the link that throughout mankind's history chained consumer residence to the economic dictates of place of work. For the first time, industrial location is being shaped in important part by consumers' locational preferences rather than the other way around. Although little recognized by planners and nonplanners alike, the market has been at work on problems of excessive urban growth and rural decay, and America is now beginning to see the first signs of this in the new directions of population movement.

4.5 Concluding Remarks

Every aspect reviewed here of post-1940 American population change has been characterized by major unforeseen developments. Contrary to expectation, fertility and the rate of population growth surged upward after World War II and then, starting around 1960, turned around and plummeted downward in equally startling fashion. In the last decade, mortality rates, after a period of leveling off, have unexpectedly started to fall sharply, with especially surprising declines occurring at older ages. There has been a dramatic increase in illegal immigration, and, for the first time in American history, the majority of immigrants—legal and illegal—are of non-European origin. Internally, the historic trend toward growing urbanization appears to have been reversed, and a number of rural areas not adjacent to cities have shown renewed population growth, much to everyone's surprise.

These developments in fertility, mortality, and migration have had important effects on the labor markets of younger and older workers and of skilled and unskilled, and have aggravated the problem of economic stabilization in recent years. Also, through their effects on demand, they have altered the composition of output and the allocation of resources, and, via relative wages, the distribution of income. In turn they have themselves been shaped by ongoing social, economic, and technological developments.

There was a time when population growth and distribution seemed reasonably predictable, but post-World War II experience has disproved that view. In recent decades population has emerged as a dynamic force, shaping and being shaped by social and economic conditions.

Appendix

Table 4.A.1   **Average Growth Rate of Population by Component of Change, 1870–1978 (per Thousand per Year)**

Period	Rate of Population	Net Migration Rate	Birth Rate	Death Rate
1870–1955				
1870–75	25.5	6.7	40.8	21.8
1875–80	18.3	3.4	38.8	23.8
1880–85	25.4	10.1	36.9	21.0
1885–90	19.9	5.8	35.3	20.6
1890–95	20.1	4.5	34.3	19.5
1895–1900	16.3	2.8	31.6	18.8
1900–05	18.5	6.0	30.0	17.6
1905–10	19.8	6.9	29.6	16.6
1910–15	17.5	5.3	27.5	14.7
1915–20	10.5	1.1	26.1	16.2
1920–25	16.9	3.6	25.0	11.3
1925–30	12.5	2.0	21.5	10.6
1930–35	7.0	−0.4	18.3	11.0
1935–40	7.2	0.2	18.3	11.3
1940–45	10.6	0.5	21.2	10.9
1945–50	15.6	1.3	24.5	9.9
1950–55	16.9	1.2	25.2	9.6
1950–1978				
1950–55	17.2	1.8	24.8	8.9
1955–60	17.0	1.8	24.6	9.4
1960–65	14.5	1.9	22.2	9.4
1965–70	10.6	2.2	18.1	9.5
1970–75	8.3	1.7	15.8	9.5
1975–78	7.6	1.6	14.9	8.8

Sources: 1870–1955: except as noted below, Kuznets, 1958, p. 37, table 1, col. 4; p. 39, table 3, col. 5; p. 41, table 5, col. 7; and p. 43, table 6, col. 5 (underlying unrounded quinquennial estimates were used). However, for net migration, 1910–40 data were from Simon Kuznets and E. Rubin, *Immigration and the Foreign Born* (New York: NBER, 1954), pp. 95–96, table B–1. For 1940–55, estimates for all series were revised somewhat, the chief differences from the original source being inclusion of armed forces deaths overseas and keeping the scope of the net migration estimate the same as for the pre–1940 period.

1950–78: U.S. Bureau of the Census, 1977, p. 7; U.S. Department of Health, Education and Welfare, *Monthly Vital Statistics Report: Births, Marriage, Divorce and Deaths for June 1978* (12 September 1978). U.S. Bureau of the Census, *Estimate of the Population of the United States to July 1, 1978*, series P–25 no. 729 (Washington, D.C.: Government Printing Office, August 1978).

Note: The sum of the components does not exactly equal total increase, because net migration refers to alien arrivals less departures and thus includes some non-migratory movements. Pure migration estimates are not available prior to 1910.

Table 4.A.2   Labor Force Participation Rates of Females by Specified Age Groups, 1890–1975

Year	20–24 (1)	25–34 (2)	45–54 (3)	55–64 (4)
1890	32.7	18.8	17.4	14.8
1900	34.2	21.7	19.1	16.0
1920	40.0	25.7	22.8	17.7
1930	44.3	29.1	24.6	18.7
1940	48.1	35.3	27.3	20.0
1950	46.1	34.0	38.0	27.0
1955	46.0	34.9	43.8	32.5
1960	46.2	36.0	49.8	37.2
1965	50.0	38.6	50.9	41.1
1970	57.8	45.0	54.4	43.0
1975	64.3	54.6	54.6	41.0

Source: 1950–75: *Employment and Training Report of the President* (Washington, D.C.: GPO); 1890–1940: extrapolation of 1950 value in ibid., by percentage point change shown in Bancroft (1958, p. 207).

Table 4.A.3   **Annual Average Total Money Income of Families with Head 14–24 Years Old as Relative of Prior Income of Families with Head 45–54, 1957–78 ($ of 1964 Purchasing Power)**

Head 14–24 Years Old		Head 45–54 Years Old		Relative Income (2) ÷ (4)	
Period (1)	Income (2)	Period (3)	Income (4)	Year (5)	Percentage (6)
1950–54	3,596	1947–53	4,917	1957	73.1
1951–55	3,687	1948–54	5,028	1958	73.3
1952–56	3,814	1949–55	5,203	1959	73.3
1953–57	3,956	1950–56	5,439	1960	72.7
1954–58	4,033	1951–57	5,641	1961	71.5
1955–59	4,132	1952–58	5,830	1962	70.9
1956–60	4,210	1953–59	6,011	1963	69.7
1957–61	4,222	1954–60	6,204	1964	68.0
1958–62	4,241	1955–61	6,404	1965	66.2
1959–63	4,282	1956–62	6,602	1966	64.8
1960–64	4,414	1957–63	6,795	1967	65.0
1961–65	4,625	1958–64	7,019	1968	65.9
1962–66	4,824	1959–65	7,288	1969	66.2
1963–67	5,032	1960–66	7,564	1970	66.5
1964–68	5,289	1961–67	7,874	1971	67.2
1965–69	5,485	1962–68	8,205	1972	66.5
1966–70	5,520	1963–69	8,566	1973	64.4
1967–71	5,506	1964–70	8,872	1974	62.1
1968–72	5,523	1965–71	9,175	1975	60.2
1969–73	5,532	1966–72	9,507	1976	58.2
1970–74	5,492	1967–73	9,814	1977	56.0
1971–75	5,377	1968–74	10,017	1978	53.7

Sources: Richard A. Easterlin, "Relative Economic Status and the American Fertility Swing," in *Family Economic Behavior: Problems and Prospects*, ed. Eleanor Bernert Sheldon (Philadelphia: Lippincott, 1973), p. 185, table 12, cols. 5 and 6. Recent data were kindly provided by Dr. Campbell Gibson, U.S. Bureau of the Census. The choice of dates used in constructing the relative income measure is explained in ibid., pp. 182–86.

Table 4.A.4   **Total Fertility Rate, 1940–77, Relative Employment Experience of Young Adult Males, 1940–55, and Ratio of Males Aged 30–64 to Males Aged 15–29, 1940–75**

Year	Total Fertility Rate (1)	Relative Employment Experience (2)	Ratio, Males 30–64 / 15–29 (3)
1940	2.30	−10.2	1.586
1941	2.40	− 8.6	
1942	2.63	− 5.8	
1943	2.72	− 4.4	
1944	2.57	− 3.2	
1945	2.49	− 2.9	
1946	2.94	− 3.3	
1947	3.27	0.4	
1948	3.11	3.5	
1949	3.11	6.1	
1950	3.09	7.2	1.840
1951	3.27	7.0	
1952	3.36	7.2	
1953	3.42	7.5	
1954	3.54	7.6	
1955	3.58	6.7	2.014
1956	3.69		
1957	3.77		
1958	3.70		
1959	3.71		
1960	3.65		1.994
1961	3.63		
1962	3.47		
1963	3.33		
1964	3.21		
1965	2.93		1.716
1966	2.74		
1967	2.57		
1968	2.48		
1969	2.45		
1970	2.47		1.509
1971	2.28		
1972	2.03		
1973	1.90		
1974	1.86		
1975	1.80		1.351
1976	1.76		
1977	1.83		

Table 4.A.5   Median Income of Year-Round Full-Time Income Recipients by Sex–Age Group as Percentage of Average, 1955 and 1977

Age Group	1955 (1)	1977 (2)	Age Group	1955 (1)	1977 (2)
All Males	100.0	100.0	*All Females*	100.0	100.0
14–19	43.3	40.1	14–19	83.8	63.9
20–24	77.7	65.0	20–24	101.2	85.1
25–34	101.7	93.8	25–34	104.4	108.3
35–44	106.5	111.9	35–44	104.5	105.3
45–54	106.0	113.0	45–54	102.4	103.7
55–64	93.4	104.0	55–64	93.6	100.4

Sources: 1955: U.S. Bureau of the Census, *Current Population Reports*, series P–60, no. 23 (Washington, D.C.: Government Printing Office, November 1956), table 3, p. 13. 1977: U.S. Bureau of the Census, *Current Population Reports*, series P–60, no. 116 (Washington, D.C.: Government Printing Office, July 1978), table 10, p. 16.

Sources to Table 4.A.4: Total fertility rate: Easterlin 1968, p. 247, col. 4; and Campbell Gibson and Martin O'Connell, U.S. Bureau of the Census. Relative employment experience: Richard A. Easterlin, "Relative Economic Status and the American Fertility Swing," in *Family Economic Behavior*, ed. Eleanor Sheldon (Philadelphia: Lippincott, 1973), p. 195, table 6, cols. 5–6. Age ratio: U.S. Bureau of the Census, *Current Population Reports*, Series P–25 as follows: for 1940–50—no. 98, p. 115; for 1955—no. 265, p. 25; for 1960—no. 286, series C, p. 42; for 1965—no. 519, p. 20; for 1970–75—no. 614, pp. 11–16.

Table 4.A.6   Death Rates from Homicide and Suicide, Males Aged 15–24, and Death Rate from Suicide, Males, Aged 45–54, 1946–77 (per 100,000)

Year	Males 15–24		Males 45–54
	Homicide (1)	Suicide (2)	Suicide (3)
1946	12.2	7.4	30.3
1947	11.9	6.6	30.5
1948	11.3	6.6	31.5
1949	10.1	6.7	31.6
1950	9.6	6.5	32.0
1951	9.0	6.5	28.5
1952	9.9	6.5	27.9
1953	9.6	6.5	29.2
1954	9.3	6.7	31.0
1955	8.5	6.3	29.7
1956	9.4	6.3	28.3
1957	8.9	6.4	28.6
1958	8.8	7.4	32.1
1959	9.0	7.7	31.0
1960	9.1	8.2	31.6
1961	8.8	7.9	31.0
1962	9.0	8.5	30.9
1963	9.0	9.0	30.7
1964	9.9	9.2	29.9
1965	10.7	9.4	29.1
1966	12.0	9.7	28.5
1967	14.3	10.5	27.9
1968	16.4	10.9	27.3
1969	18.0	12.2	27.2
1970	19.0	13.5	27.9
1971	20.6	14.0	26.8
1972	21.5	15.7	28.0
1973	20.7	17.0	26.9
1974	22.1	17.1	26.6
1975	21.2	18.9	27.9
1976	19.1	18.5	26.2
1977	19.4	21.8	25.6

Sources: 1946–60: National Center for Health Statistics, HEW, *Vital Statistics Rates in the United States: 1940–1960*, no. 1677 (Washington, D.C.: Public Health Service, 1968), table 63.

1961–75: National Center for Health Statistics, HEW, *Vital Statistics of the United States*, Annual Yearbook (various issues), vol. 2, *Mortality*, part A.

1976–77: Unpublished data from Mortality Division of National Center for Health Statistics.

Table 4.A.7   Crude Birthrate, 1915–60

Period	Rate (1)	Period	Rate (1)
1915–20	26.1	1940–45	21.2
1920–25	25.0	1945–50	24.5
1925–30	21.5	1950–55	25.2/24.8
1930–35	18.3	1955–60	24.6
1935–40	18.3		

Sources: 1915–55: Kuznets, 1958, p. 37, table 1, col. 4; table 3, col. 5; p. 41, table 5, col. 7; and p. 43, table 6, col. 5 (underlying unrounded quinquennial estimates were used). 1950–60: U.S. Bureau of the Census, *Current Population Reports*, series P–25 (Washington, D.C.: Government Printing Office, September 1977), no. 706, p. 7. The break in the series in 1950–55 is due to the shift in sources.

Table 4.A.8   Male Population Aged 15–29 as Percentage of That Aged 30–64, Actual 1940–75 and Projected 1980

Date	Male Population Aged 15–29 (1) (000)	30–64 (2)	Ratio, 15–29 / 30–64 (percentage) (3)
1940	17,442	27,664	63.0
1950	17,216	31,761	54.4
1955	16,772	33,781	49.6
1960	17,794	35,478	50.2
1965	21,151	36,295	58.3
1970	25,262	38,115	66.3
1975	28,793	38,908	74.0
	Projected		
1980	30,426	42,184	72.1

Sources: 1940–95: U.S. Bureau of the Census, *Current Population Reports*, series P–25 (Washington, D.C.: Government Printing Office) as follows: for 1940–55—no. 98, p. 115; for 1955—no. 265, p. 25; for 1960—no. 286, series C, p. 42; for 1965—no. 519, p. 20; for 1970–75—no. 614, pp. 11–16; for 1980—no. 704, series 2, pp. 40–60.

Table 4.A.9   Percentage Change per Year in Age-
Specific Death Rates, Three Periods,
1936–77

Age	1936–54	1954–68	1968–77
Under 1	−3.0	−1.6	−3.8
1–4	−4.0	−1.8	−2.5
5–14	−3.7	−1.4	−2.8
15–24	−3.4	+0.6	0.0
25–34	−3.5	+0.5	−1.4
35–44	−2.9	+0.2	−2.4
45–54	−2.0	−0.3	−1.9
55–64	−1.5	−0.2	−1.8
65–74	−1.4	−0.1	−2.0
75–84	−1.6	−0.3	−1.5
85+	−1.4	+0.6	−2.8

Source: 1936–54: National Center for Health Statistics, HEW, *Vital Statistics Rates in the United States, 1940–60*, no. 1677 (Washington, D.C.: Public Health Service, 1968). 1968–77: National Center for Health Statistics, Monthly Vital Statistics Department, *Final Mortality Statistics, 1977* (Washington, D.C.: Public Health Service, 1979).

Notes

1. The analysis in this part is developed more fully in Easterlin (1980a).
2. See Kuznets 1958; 1961.
3. Shown below is the trend since 1940 in the median years of school completed by men and women aged 25–29:

	1940	1950	1960	1970	1977
Males	10.1	12.0	12.3	12.6	13.0
Females	10.5	12.1	12.3	12.5	12.8
Excess of Males over Females	−0.4	−0.1	0	0.1	0.2

Data are from U.S. Bureau of the Census (1950; 1960; 1970; 1977, table 1, p. 7).
4. Data supplied by Gallup Poll.
5. Tabulation of unpublished data from the National Longitudinal Survey of Young Women. The original national sample was of females, aged 14–24 in 1968; the same women were then surveyed again in 1975 at ages 21–31.
6. For data on unemployment rates, see the following: 1957–66—BLS (1967, table 51, pp. 84–85). 1967–77—BLS (1977, table 54, pp. 109–10). 1978—BLS (1978, table A–3, p. 21). For information on the earnings gap between men and women, see U.S. Department of Labor, Women's Bureau (1976; 1975, pp. 126–27). Unfortunately, no studies are available covering the full period that standardize adequately for relevant factors such as education.
7. The chart is confined to year-round full-time workers to get as nearly as possible to salary or pay *rates*.
8. The relative income measure in figure 4.3 is not exactly the same as relative earnings in figure 4.4. Nevertheless, the movement of the relative income measure is largely shaped by the change in the relative number of young men.

9. The sizable employment and earnings effects of recent shifts in the relative numbers of younger and older men and the low elasticity of substitution between them, even after controlling for other pertinent factors such as education, have been demonstrated in a number of recent studies. *On earnings*, see Freeman (1979), Lee (1978a), Welch (1979), and Wachter (1977). *On employment*, see Anderson (1978; 1977), and Wachter (1976).

10. According to Bancroft (1958): "The abundance of white-collar jobs which did not require extensive training attracted an increasing proportion of young women and made it possible for them to avoid the lower-paid or less desirable types of work" (p. 82).

11. See also Wachter (1972).

12. See also Bancroft (1958, p. 30).

13. See the homicide arrest data in FBI (1960 through 1976).

14. See Easterlin (1980a, chaps. 5 and 6). See also Preston and McDonald (1979).

15. For further discussion, see Easterlin, M. Wachter, and S. Wachter (1978) and the references they cite therein.

16. For a fuller discussion of experience before World War II, see Easterlin (1968).

17. This section on mortality is partly based on a paper by Eileen M. Crimmins (1980).

18. Siegel 1978, p. 15. See also Preston (1974).

19. Research on aging is the modern, more promising equivalent of this. See the National Academy of Sciences (1979), p. 447.

20. Keely 1975. See also American Association for the Advancement of Science (1966).

21. U.S. Congress 1978, pp. 1–3. See also Bustamante (1977).

22. The Scheuer Committee Report suggests that the current consensus on the population of undocumented aliens in the United States is around 3 to 6 million (U.S. Congress 1978, p. 2). If one takes the mid-value, 4.5 million and assumes most of these persons came in the past fifteen years, then net immigration per year would average 300 thousand.

It is possible that this guess is on the high side. A recent paper by David Heer (1979) estimates the annual net flow of undocumented Mexican immigrants to the United States in 1970–75 at between 82,000 and 232,000 persons.

23. A recent analysis suggests that a shift in Mexican government agricultural policy favoring capital-intensive techniques was also an important stimulus to illegal immigration. See Jenkins (1977).

24. The "Sunbelt" as usually defined includes Virginia, North Carolina, South Carolina, Georgia, Florida, Alabama, Mississippi, Arkansas, Louisiana, Texas, Oklahoma, Missouri, New Mexico, Arizona, and California.

25. Some time ago Simon Kuznets (1964) emphasized the growing role of consumer preferences in affecting the spatial distribution of population. Ann R. Miller (1977) has pointed out the consistency of new patterns of migration by occupation with Kuznets' hypothesis.

26. The impact of the automobile on population distribution is stressed in a number of studies. See, for example, Downs (1979) and Guest (1979).

27. The importance of recreational and retirement factors in the new migration patterns has been brought out in a number of recent studies, among them are: McCarthy and Morrison (1979), Fuguitt and Voss (1979), Williams and Sofranko (1979), Fuguitt and Zuiches (1975), Biggar (1979), and Morrison and Wheeler (1976).

2. Victor R. Fuchs

Continuity and Change in American Life

The celebration of the National Bureau's sixtieth birthday is an opportune time to stop and take stock of where we are as a people, how we got to our present condition, and where we are likely to be going. This paper does not deal with all aspects of American life, but emphasizes demographic variables broadly defined to include not only the size and composition of the population, but also where and how we live and when and how we die. The United States in 1980 is surely a very different country from the one that Wesley Mitchell, Edwin Gay, Malcolm Rorty, N. I. Stone, and the other founders of the NBER knew in 1920. We must, however, guard against exaggerating the magnitude or novelty of recent developments. As we review the changes that have occurred since 1950, it is useful to consider the extent to which they are a continuation of earlier trends. Such comparisons not only serve to highlight the continuity in our demographic history, but also help to identify those recent changes which do represent a sharp break with previous experience.

In this paper I examine selected demographic variables grouped into four categories: (1) population size and composition, (2) fertility, (3) mortality, and (4) the family.[1] Tables C4.1 through C4.4 present the trends in these variables from 1950 to 1980 (actually the closest years to 1980 available) and, data permitting, compare them with rates of change from 1920 to 1950. Trends for the subperiods 1950–65 and 1965–80 are also shown. I offer brief comments on many of the trends and conclude the paper with a discussion of the phenomena that seem to me to have the most significant long-run implications for the economy, namely changes in family life.

Throughout I follow a Rip Van Winkle approach to the data, concentrating on broad secular changes between benchmarks rather than becoming enmeshed in the ups and downs of the intervening years. Let us suppose an economic demographer had fallen asleep in 1950 and had awakened just a few days ago. When he (or she) examines the latest statistics, what does he (or she) find?

Victor R. Fuchs is professor of economics at Stanford University.

Helpful comments from Robert T. Michael and research assistance by Nicholas Dyer are gratefully acknowledged. Financial support was provided in part by grants to the NBER Health Economics Program from the Robert Wood Johnson Foundation and the Henry J. Kaiser Family Foundation.

Table C4.1 Selected Demographic Variables, 1920, 1950, 1965, 1980: Population Size and Composition

	Year				Rate of Change (% per Annum)			
Variable	1920	1950	1965	1980	1920–50	1950–80	1950–65	1965–80
Population (millions)	106	151	194	218[b]	1.18	1.31	1.67	.90
Percentage:								
Under 21	42.5	35.4	40.7	35.4[c]	−.61	.00	.93	−1.16
21–64	52.9	56.5	49.8	53.6[c]	.22	−.20	−.84	.61
65 or over	4.6	8.1	9.5	10.8[c]	1.89	1.07	1.06	1.07
Northeast	28.0	26.1	24.5	22.8[e]	−.23	−.50	−.42	−.60
North central regions	32.1	29.4	27.9	26.8[e]	−.29	−.34	−.35	−.34
South	31.2	31.2	31.0	32.3[e]	.00	.13	−.04	.34
West	8.7	13.3	16.6	18.2[e]	1.41	1.16	1.48	.77
Nonwhite	10.3	10.5	11.9	13.4[e]	.06	.90	.83	.99
Cities over 500,000	15.4	17.5	15.9[h]	15.6[e]	.43	−.46	−.96[i]	−.13[j]
Other urban	36.2	46.7	53.9[h]	59.9[e]	.85	1.00	1.43[i]	.70[j]
Rural	48.4	35.8	30.1[h]	24.5[e]	−1.01	−1.52	−1.73[i]	−1.37[j]
Nonwhite in:								
Northeast cities over 500,000	3.8	11.0	16.5[h]	24.9[f]	3.54	4.08	4.05[i]	4.12[k]
North central cities over 500,000	4.9	13.8	24.3[h]	32.6[f]	3.45	4.30	5.66[i]	2.94[k]
Black in:								
SMSA* central cities		12.3	20.6[g]	22.7[e]		2.27	3.22	.88
SMSAs outside central cities		5.4	4.2[g]	5.6[e]		.13	−1.57	2.62
Outside SMSAs		10.8	9.8[g]	8.9[e]		−.72	−.61	−.88

[a]1979; [b]1978; [c]1977; [d]1976; [e]1975; [f]1970; [g]1966; [h]1960; [i]1950–60; [j]1960–75; [k]1960–70.
*Standard Metropolitan Statistical Area.

Table C4.2 Selected Demographic Variables, 1920, 1950, 1965, 1980: Fertility

Variable	Year				Rate of Change (% per Annum)			
	1920	1950	1965	1980[b]	1920–50	1950–80	1950–65	1965–80
Crude Birthrate (per 1,000)								
Total	27.7	24.1	19.4	15.3[a]	− .46	−1.68	−1.45	−2.46
White	26.9	23.0	18.3	13.8	− .52	−1.96	−1.52	−2.57
Nonwhite	35.0	33.3	27.6	21.1	− .17	−1.75	−1.25	−2.44
Births per 1,000 Women, Aged 15–44								
Total	117.9	106.2	96.6	65.8	− .35	−1.84	− .63	−3.49
White	115.4	102.3	91.4	62.2	− .40	−1.91	− .75	−3.50
Nonwhite	137.5	137.3	133.9	87.6	.00	−1.73	− .17	−3.86
White 1st & 2d birth order	61.4	65.6	51.9	46.9	.22	−1.29	−1.56	− .92
White 3rd & higher birth order	54.0	36.7	39.6	15.3	−1.29	−3.37	.51	−8.65
Nonwhite 1st & 2d birth order	65.0	64.1	62.4	61.2	.05	− .18	− .18	− .18
Nonwhite 3rd & higher birth order	72.5	73.2	71.4	26.4	.03	−3.92	− .17	−9.04
Births per 1,000 Unmarried Women, Aged 15–44								
Total		14.1	23.5	24.7		2.16	3.41	.45
White		6.1	11.6	12.7		2.82	4.28	.82
Nonwhite		71.2	97.6	78.1		.36	2.10	−2.03
Births to Unmarried Women as Percentage of All Births								
Total		3.9	7.7	14.8		5.13	4.53	5.94
White		1.7	4.0	7.7		5.81	5.70	5.95
Nonwhite		16.8	26.4	45.2		3.81	3.01	4.89

[a] 1977.
[b] all 1976, except as noted.

Table C4.3   Selected Demographic Variables, 1920, 1950, 1965, 1980: Mortality

Variable	Year				Rate of Change (% per Annum)			
	1920	1950	1965	1980[b]	1920–50	1950–80	1950–65	1965–80
Crude Death Rate (per 1,000)								
Total	13.0	9.6	9.4	8.8[a]	−1.01	−.32	−.14	−.50
White	12.6	9.5	9.4	9.0	−.94	−.21	−.07	−.40
Nonwhite	17.6	11.2	9.6	8.2	−1.53	−1.20	−1.03	−1.43
Age-Adjusted Death Rate† (per 1,000)								
Total	14.2	8.4	7.4	6.3	−1.75	−1.11	−.85	−1.46
White male	14.2	9.6	9.1	8.0	−1.30	−.70	−.36	−1.17
White female	13.1	6.5	5.3	4.4	−2.34	−1.50	−1.36	−1.69
Nonwhite male	20.4	13.6	12.2	10.7	−1.35	−.92	−.72	−1.19
Nonwhite female	21.0	10.9	8.3	6.4	−2.19	−2.05	−1.82	−2.36
Life Expectancy at Birth								
White male	54.4	66.5	67.6	69.7	.67	.18	.11	.28
White female	55.6	72.2	74.7	77.3	.87	.26	.23	.31
Nonwhite male	45.5	59.1	61.1	64.1	.87	.31	.22	.44
Nonwhite female	45.2	62.9	67.4	72.6	1.10	.55	.46	.68
Life Expectancy at Age 65								
White male	12.2	12.7	12.9	13.7	.14	.28	.08	.55
White female	12.7	15.0	16.3	18.1	.54	.72	.55	.95
Nonwhite male	12.1	12.7	12.6	13.8	.18	.30	−.08	.83
Nonwhite female	12.4	14.5	15.5	17.6	.53	.73	.43	1.16
Infant Mortality (per 1,000 Live Births)								
White	82.1	26.8	21.5	13.3	−3.73	−2.69	−1.47	−4.37
Nonwhite	131.7	44.5	40.3	23.5	−3.62	−2.46	−.66	−4.90

Table C4.3—*continued*

Variable	Year				Rate of Change (% per Annum)			
	1920	1950	1965	1980[b]	1920–50	1950–80	1950–65	1965–80
Death Rate by Cause (per 100,000)								
Crude								
infectious diseases	386.1	60.5	37.6	36.5	−6.18	−1.94	−3.17	−.28
circulatory diseases	365.3	508.8	509.5	453.9	1.11	−.44	.01	−1.05
neoplasms	83.2	139.2	153.2	176.2	1.62	.91	.64	1.27
accidents and violence	85.8	76.8	72.4	68.5	−.37	−.44	−.39	−.50
other	379.6	174.7	167.3	154.9	−2.57	−.46	−.29	−.71
Age-adjusted†								
heart disease		307.6	273.9	216.7		−1.35	−.77	−2.13
lung cancer		12.8	23.0	33.5		3.70	3.91	3.42
other cancer		112.6	104.0	98.8		−.50	−.53	−.47
other		408.5	338.1	278.5		−1.47	−1.26	−1.76

†Age adjustment by direct method using 1940 United States age distribution.
[a]1977.
[b]all 1976 except as noted.

Table C4.4   Selected Demographic Variables, 1920, 1950, 1965, 1980: The Family

Variable	Year				Rate of Change (% per Annum)			
	1920	1950	1965	1980	1920–50	1950–80	1950–65	1965–80
Percentage of Women Ever Married:								
Ages 20–24	54.0	67.7	67.9[y]	52.4[b]	.75	−.91	.02	−1.99
Ages 25–29	76.8	86.7	89.5[y]	82.0[b]	.40	−.20	.21	−.67
Median Age at First Marriage:								
Male	24.6	22.8	22.8	24.2[b]	−.25	.21	.00	.46
Female	21.2	20.3	20.6	21.8[b]	−.14	.25	.10	.44
Divorce Rate per 1,000 Married Women	8.0	10.3	10.6	21.1[c]	.84	2.66	.19	5.74
Persons per Household	4.33	3.47	3.40	2.87[b]	−.74	−.68	−.14	−1.30
Percent Living Alone:								
All adults		3.9	7.3	10.8[b]		3.64	4.18	3.01
Widows 65 and over		24.5	43.2	65.3[b]		3.50	3.78	3.18
Never married, ages 25–34		5.1	16.3	30.5[b]		6.39	7.75	4.82
Labor Force Participation Rate, Married Women, Spouse Present:								
Children 6–17 only		28.3	42.7	55.6[c]		2.50	2.74	2.20
Children under 6		11.9	23.3	39.3[c]		4.42	4.48	4.36

[y]mean of 1960 and 1970.

Population Size and Composition

First, our newly awakened colleague would probably be surprised by the size of the United States population in 1980; it is now 30 percent larger than the "medium" forecast and 15 percent above the highest forecast made by the Bureau of the Census in 1947 (Whelpton 1947). This is not because the rate of growth from 1950 to 1980 was much greater than from 1920 to 1950 (1.3 versus 1.2 percent per annum), but because extrapolation of pre-1950 trends suggested that further deceleration in growth was likely. Such deceleration is readily evident since 1965; it was the 1950–65 population boom (approximately equal to the turn-of-the-century rate of growth) which confounded post-World War II forecasts.

The age distribution of the population in 1980 is not very different from what it was in 1950, although there were some large changes during the intervening years. The *percentage* of the population sixty-five or over has increased somewhat, but this is not a new phenomenon. Moreover, the rate of growth of the *number* of elderly was actually more rapid from 1920 to 1950 than since 1950, and more rapid from 1950 to 1965 than from 1965 to 1980.[2]

The regional shift in population, also much discussed in recent years as if it were something unusual, loses much of its novelty when examined against a background of earlier trends. The relative shift from the Northeast and the north central regions to the West is a familiar story; one new regional development is the relative growth of population in the South since 1965.

One demographic variable which does show marked change in the past three decades is the percentage of the nonwhite population. Between 1920 and 1950 the racial composition of the population was virtually constant, but since 1950, white and nonwhite growth rates have differed by a full percentage point per annum. The interaction between this differential and shifting geographical patterns has produced some of the most marked demographic changes of the post-World War II era.

Until the middle of this century there was a strong long-term shift in population from rural areas to urban areas, including the big cities.[3] After 1950 the relative decline of rural areas continued, but the relative growth of big cities was reversed. Since then, all of the relative growth has been concentrated in smaller cities or in urban areas outside of city limits. The one group that continued to head for the big cities was the nonwhites, with the result that by 1970 one in four residents of large cities in the Northeast was nonwhite, and in the north central region the proportion was one in three. Taking all SMSA central cities in the United States as a group, blacks accounted for 23 percent of the population in 1977, up from 12 percent in 1950.

Given the legacies of slavery, segregation, and discrimination, these demographic trends have had enormous economic and social impact. As one observer wrote in 1964: "Except for the worldwide population explosion itself, the movement of Negroes from the southern part of the United States has without a doubt been the greatest and most significant sociological event of our country's recent history" (Hamilton 1964, p. 294).

In 1977 the median age of blacks was 24.1, compared with 30.3 for whites. Thus, even if age-specific birth and death rates become identical for blacks and whites, there will be a substantial differential in the rate of natural increase for many years to come. Although considerable progress has been made in civil rights, several questions must still be faced. Can the cities cope with such a disproportionate share of the poorest and most disadvantaged members of our society? Will racial discrimination in housing outside the central cities be reduced enough to permit a less segregated residential pattern?[4] How rapidly will racial differences in education and income decrease?

Fertility

Changes in the size and composition of the population depend upon differential trends in fertility, mortality, and migration. With respect to fertility, our modern Van Winkle would note with interest (but probably not shock) that the American birthrate is at a historic low. The decline since 1950 has been far more rapid than in the previous thirty years, but the 1980 rate is not far out of line with extrapolations covering a much longer period. The fertility decline has been much larger for birth orders three and above than for first and second births. The trend away from large families was evident in 1920–50 as well, but has been particularly marked since 1965.[5]

This reduction in the variance in family size is of major demographic importance. Consider for instance, birthrates in 1976 compared with 1936, the previous low point of United States fertility. For white women (and probably for nonwhite women as well), *all* of the decrease was in births of third order or higher. The rate per 1,000 women aged 15–44 for first and second birth orders rose slightly, from 46 to 47, but the rate for the higher orders fell from 28 to 15. One clear consequence of these trends is that many fewer children will have to share parental resources with large numbers of siblings. If, as some observers believe, such sharing contributes to physical, social, and intellectual deficits in some children, the next generation should, in this respect, be much better off.[6]

One extraordinary trend in American life is the rise in the birthrate for unmarried women at a time of generally decreasing fertility. Such births, relatively rare in 1950, now account for 8 percent of white births and almost one in two of nonwhite births. A small part of the increase (about one-eighth) can be attributed to the rising proportion of births to women under twenty years of age (who have always had the highest percentage of babies born out of wedlock), but most of the increase reflects higher percentages at every age.

Mortality

United States death rates were lower in 1980 than in 1950 at all ages and for both sexes and races. The rate of decline was greater for females than for males, and greater for nonwhites than for whites. These differential trends were also evident in 1920–50, but the decrease in nonwhite death rates in recent decades has been particularly striking and has been the major factor in the rise in the proportion of nonwhites in the population. To be sure, nonwhite fertility has been substantially higher than white fertility during the past thirty years, but this differential was equally evident in the years 1920–50. The nonwhite-white differential in rate of natural increase (excess of births over deaths), which was 3.1 per 1,000 in 1920, had risen to 8.1 by 1976. Between those dates the racial difference in birthrates actually declined slightly, from 8.1 to 7.3, but the difference in death rates declined dramatically from +5.0 to —0.8 per 1,000.

Since 1950, and especially since 1965, the rate of increase in life expectancy at age 65 has been unusually rapid for all sex-race groups. This is particularly noteworthy inasmuch as the rate of increase in life expectancy at birth was much smaller after 1950 than before that date. Because death rates at younger ages are now quite low, future declines in mortality will result primarily in additional years being lived at older ages. This is very different from the effect of mortality reductions in the first six decades of this century when *half* of the additional person-years were lived at ages 25–60 and another one-fourth below the age of 25 (Fuchs 1978). Each additional year of life expectancy at age 65 adds more than 5 percent to the cost of retirement benefits. One way that society may choose to deal with this is to raise the age at which benefits can be collected and thus reverse the trend toward earlier retirement.

Infant mortality, usually a useful indicator of social and economic well-being, fell much more slowly 1950–65 than in 1920–50, but has fallen very rapidly since 1965. No one has been able to explain satisfactorily the 1950–65 retardation, nor is there any consensus regarding the reasons for the unprecedented rate of decline since 1965.[7] Another puzzle is the failure of infant mortality to decline more rapidly for nonwhites than for whites prior to 1965. The racial gap might have been expected to narrow over time if the white-nonwhite economic gap did not, because the income elasticity of infant mortality moves toward zero as income rises and because barriers to medical care for nonwhites have been substantially reduced. It is possible that improvements in statistical coverage of nonwhite infant deaths (as the percentage of babies delivered in hospitals rose) offset some narrowing of the race differential. Since 1965, nonwhite infant mortality *has* declined more rapidly than has white.

The differential trends in death rates by cause are striking, particularly the rapid decline in the rate for diseases of the circulatory system (cardiovascular and cerebrovascular) since 1965 compared with a rapid rise from 1920 to 1950. According to the noted medical historian, Henry Sigerist, "Each civilization creates its own diseases." He might have added "and sooner or later tries to deal with them." As the great killers of the first quarter of this century, influenza, pneumonia, tuberculosis, diphtheria, and other infectious diseases, succumbed to economic development and medical progress, their places were taken by heart disease and cancer. Now the peak seems to have been passed for heart disease. It is not clear how credit for the improvement should be allocated between changes in medical care and changes in life-style, but it is clear that age-specific death rates have fallen 20 to 25 percent in the past ten years.

Very recently, even lung cancer mortality has stopped rising for white males 35–54, and would almost surely fall for all groups who gave up cigarette smoking. Although heart disease and cancer account for more than half of all deaths, accidents and violence (suicide and homicide) are emerging as the greatest contributors to health costs (medical care plus indirect costs of morbidity and mortality) in American society. In 1975 the economic cost of accidents and violence was 62 percent larger than the cost of cancer and only 17 percent below the cost of all cardiovascular diseases (Berk, Paringer, and Mushkin 1978). The costs are so high because many of the accident and violence victims are young, with much of their potential production still ahead of them. Reduction of these costs must be sought in the social as much as in the medical arena.

The Family

Many of the greatest changes in recent decades have been in "family life," although even here there is a danger of exaggerating the novelty of contemporary phenomena. For instance, the propensity to marry— as evidenced by the percentage of women ever married at given ages, or by the median age at first marriage—while substantially lower in 1980 than in 1950, is at approximately the same level as in 1920. The divorce rate has soared since 1965, but the novelty is in the rate of change, not direction, which has been upward throughout the century.

Average household size has continued to shrink; the rate of decline since 1950 has been about the same as in the preceding thirty years. In recent decades the major factor has been a decrease in the number of *adults* per household through divorce, and especially through a rise in the proportion of adults who live alone. This proportion has increased for almost every age-sex group and the rise has been particularly important in absolute numbers for widows 65 and over and never-married men and women 25–34 (Michael, Fuchs, and Scott 1980).

The increase in divorce (and in the proportion of births to unmarried women) has resulted in a substantial percentage of children not living with both parents. In 1977 among whites, 15 percent of children did not live with both parents, and among nonwhites, 53 percent did not.[8] Even when children do live with both parents there has been a marked change in family life because of an increase in female labor force participation. This increase has been particularly remarkable for married women with spouse present who have children at home. The child who lives at home with a father who is in the labor force and a mother who is not is now becoming the exception rather than the rule.

These changes in family life seem to me to have significant long-run implications for our economy and our society. To develop my thesis fully would take far more space than is available here; I can only state in simplified form the main lines of the argument:

1. Recent changes in the family, while possibly subject to cyclical variation, have a clear secular trend. Although Easterlin's relative income hypothesis is appealing, I do not expect changes in cohort size alone will induce major reversals in female labor force participation or bring about baby-boom fertility rates.[9] The absolute rise in value of women's time in the market (Mincer 1962; Becker 1965), improvements in contraception (Michael 1977), the growth of a service economy,[10] and the general weakening of most hierarchical relations[11] seem to me to be producing changes in sex roles which are significant and long lasting.

2. Recent changes are an extension of a long-term cumulative reduction in the scope and magnitude of functions performed within the family. The first activities to move outside—production of food, clothing, fuel, and other staples—were taken over by business firms. More recently, many responsibilities such as education, health care, and social insurance have been assumed by the state. Within the next decade we will probably see another major role transfer—care of the young—which is, in many respects, the quintessential family function.

3. The market system, which is the most efficient and most conducive to individual freedom yet devised, does not itself provide a sufficient basis for the organization of society. Its success over the last 200 years is attributable in good part to the existence of strong nonmarket institutions such as the family, which has been the primary agent of socialization and, in conjunction with religion, the primary source of values and beliefs. The decline of the family and the growth of government will

seriously jeopardize the market system and associated political, social, and cultural freedoms.

To conclude, most of the demographic changes of the past thirty years are not sharp departures from earlier trends and pose no insurmountable problems for the economy. The financial burden of a rise in the number of elderly, for instance, could be accommodated by small gradual in- creases in the age at which social security benefits begin. In a few in- stances, however, such as the growth of the nonwhite population in major cities, and the decline of the traditional family, the changes have been so marked as to warrant urgent consideration. In the long run, a healthy economy requires a healthy society. The NBER would be faithful to the aspirations of its founders if, in the coming decade, it gave high priority to the economic analysis of social problems.

Notes

1. Given Easterlin's excellent survey paper, I have felt free to be selective in coverage both with respect to variables and time periods. I regret that limitations of space precluded consideration of the future of immigration, a subject of great potential importance.

2. When a variable is presented as a proportion (e.g., percent ≥ 65) rather than in absolute form, considerable care should be taken in interpreting the rate of change measured in percentage per annum. Since a proportion is bounded by zero and 100 percent, the rate of change can be very large near zero and must be very small near 100 percent. The rate of change of the absolute value of a variable that has been expressed as a proportion can easily be obtained by adding the rate of change of the proportion to the rate of change of the total population. E.g., if *percent* ≥ 65 increased at 1.89 percent per annum 1920–50 and the total popula- tion increased at 1.18 percent per annum, then the *population* ≥ 65 increased at 3.07 percent per annum. The comparable figure for 1950–80 is 2.38 (1.07 + 1.31). The comparable rates for 1950–65 and 1965–80 are 2.73 and 1.97 percent per annum, respectively.

3. "Big cities" are defined in this paper as having populations over 500,000.

4. In Standard Metropolitan Statistical Areas (SMSAs) outside central cities, the percentage of blacks is very low (5.6 percent in 1977), but has started to rise.

5. The increase in the relative importance of first and second order births is partly attributable to a relative increase in the number of females under twenty- five, but even after adjusting for changes in age distribution there has been a large decline in higher order births.

6. See, for instance, De Tray (1978). He concludes that "holding income, the opportunity cost of the mother's time, and the parents' educational level constant, there is a quantitatively and statistically strong negative partial relationship be- tween a couple's fertility and the amount of education their children receive" (p. 36).

7. "Success has many fathers." Some possible reasons are: improvements in neonatology, better contraception, legalized abortion, Medicaid, and mother-child health centers in poor neighborhoods.

8. In 1968 the percentages were 11 and 42.

9. A primitive formulation of the relative income hypothesis led me in 1956 to predict a decline in United States fertility (see Fuchs 1956). This was a very special situation, however, involving a deep depression followed by a postwar boom.

10. The service sector (defined to include trade; finance, insurance and real estate; services; and government) has provided seven out of every eight additional jobs in the United States since 1948. These are the jobs that offer the greatest opportunities for women.

11. E.g., parent-child, employer-employee, teacher-student, priest-layperson.

---

3. Simon Kuznets

Notes on Demographic Change

These notes raise questions about the economic consequences of demographic trends, consequences in terms of what the trends imply for the rate of economic advance and for the distributive aspects of economic growth. These are questions rather than answers, for lack of firm basis for the latter; and even the questions are selective. The two trends chosen for comment are: the long-term decline in birthrates, associated largely with increasing control of intramarital fertility; and the long-term rise in the proportion of population in advanced ages (65 and over), associated largely with the recent impact of health technology in reducing mortality at the higher ages.

The natural concentration in Professor Easterlin's paper on the recent, forty-year swing in fertility, left little room for noting the underlying downtrend. Yet it is conspicuous in Easterlin's table 4.A.1, from the 1870s to World War II; and even within the swing itself, the average birthrate declined, from 22.3 per thousand in the four quinquennia of 1935–55 to 19.5 per thousand in the twenty-three years from 1955 to 1978. The consensus of the present projections suggests further decline. According to the latest, 1978, assessment (medium variant) by the United Nations, the average for 1955–60 to 1975–80 (the latter weighted by half) of 19.8 per thousand will drop to an average of 15.8 for 1975–80 (weighted by half) through 1995–2000.[1] Two comments should be added. First, the marked decline in fertility was observed in, and projected for, many other countries, in some of which it dropped to much lower levels than in the United States (e.g., the United Kingdom, France, Germany, and Sweden). Second, with the age composition moving toward the older, and higher mortality ages, the crude rate of natural increase dropped more relatively than the crude birthrate. Thus, for the United States, the birthrate drops from an average of 37.9 per thousand

Simon Kuznets is professor of economics, emeritus, Harvard University.

for 1870–75/1885–90, to the projected rate of 14.2 in 1995–2000, a decline of 62 percent; the rate of natural increase drops from 16.3 to 4.4 per thousand, by 73 percent.

The other trend to be noted is the sustained rise in the proportion of population 65 years old and older. To go back just to 1930, we find a steady rise in the proportion from census to census, from 5.4 percent in 1930 to 9.9 percent in 1970; and the recent projections move the proportion from 10.5 percent in 1975 to 12.7 in the year 2000.[2] The relative rise is far greater than would be produced as a secondary effect of the fall in the birthrates, and hence of the proportions of the very young. This is shown clearly when we observe the share of the next to the oldest group, 55–64, which rises from over 6.8 percent in 1930 to 9.1 in 1970, and is projected to only a slightly higher share in the year 2000.

In turning now to economic consequences of the long-term decline in fertility, one may note first that, given the limited universe in which we live, and the marked decline in mortality due to scientific advance and economic progress, a reduction of fertility was to be expected. And one could view it as a free and rational response of would-be parents to higher survival rates of children and to the value of greater investment of human capital in a smaller number of offspring. But this does not mean that some of the consequences of the downtrend in fertility and of the associated decline in the rate of natural increase, may not be problematic. The decline in the proportion of new entrants into, and of the younger groups in, the labor force may result in sluggish mobility, in an inadequate response to new employment and growth opportunities afforded by technological innovations. And the reduced growth rate in total product may have a damping effect on entrepreneurial capital formation because of lowered growth horizons.

A more interesting aspect of birthrates, and—for posttraditional societies, of the associated rates of natural increase—is their negative correlation, within a country, with the income level of the parental pair (or more strictly, of the family or household—income on a per capita or per consuming unit basis). That the poor tend to have more children, and with the death rates at lower secular levels, more *surviving* children, has been observed repeatedly; and there is some evidence for it for recent decades in the United States. If so, the contribution of the lower income groups, the poorer classes in the population, to new additions to the population and eventually to the labor force, is appreciably greater than their weight in the parental population. Several consequences follow. First, if we assume that the growth rate (G) for product per worker, from one generation to the next, is the same for the offspring of the lower and the higher income groups, say 3 percent per year or 81 percent over a span of two decades, the growth rate for the total body of workers would be *below* this assumed rate—because of the rise in the proportion of the low income groups. Second, if, retaining the assumed overall rate of 3 percent per year for the initial, parental population, we modify the growth rate to make it higher for the lower income offspring and lower for the higher income offspring, thus reducing the initial income inequality, the shortfall in the growth rate of per worker product for the total labor force would be even greater. Thus, other conditions being equal, the negative association between income levels and rate of natural increase makes either for lower rates of growth of product per worker, or for widening income inequality, or for both.[3]

The data easily at hand refer to racial or ethnic groups, characterized by substantially lower than average income per capita. Thus, the 1970 census shows the proportion of the black population to total of 11.1 percent; but the ratio of the black group aged 0–4 to total population aged 0–4 was 14.2 percent (see the series in the *Historical Statistics* volume cited in note 2). In March 1978 the average family comprised 3.33 persons, of whom 1.10 were related children under 18 years of age. But the average white family averaged 3.28 persons, of whom 1.04 were related children, while the average for a black family was 3.77 persons of whom 1.59 were related children under 18. The black family population accounted for 11.5 percent of total family population, and for 14.7 percent of related children under 18. But the money income per person was $3.2 thousand in black families and $5.7 thousand in white. A similar case of higher propensity to have children is found for families with head of Spanish origin: the average number of persons per family was 3.88, of whom 1.66 were related children, and the per capita income of $3.4 thousand was 40 percent below that for all families.[4]

The economic and social class differences in birth and fertility rates just suggested are an important subject for further study; and so are the economic and social class differences in mortality, which are negatively correlated with the per capita income level of the families or households involved. Such further analysis would make it possible to deal more insightfully with the problems raised by concentration of births and of eventually resulting additions to the working population in the lower income levels. But, in the present connection one might push speculation further and ask whether the combination of declining fertility and mortality, in the typical pattern associated with economic growth and the demographic transition, is not likely to make, in some phases, even greater concentration of new population and new labor force in the lower income families; and thus aggravate the task of integrating the additions, without limiting effect on growth of product per worker or without worsening inequality in the income distribution.

This possibility can again be illustrated by using crude birth and death rates for a racial group, viewed as a proxy for the lower income and social components in the population. Comparing whites and nonwhites (the latter including races other than black, but greatly dominated by the latter), we find that for 1921–30, the crude vital rates (per 1,000) were: for births—23.6 for the white population, and 31.9 for nonwhite; for deaths—11.1 for white and 16.6 for nonwhite; for rates of natural increase—12.5 and 15.3 respectively, a spread of 2.8 points per thousand. The death rates used here are for total population, and the differential mortality for the younger groups could be different; but the general bearing of the illustration may be valid. By 1961–70, the rates were: births at 18.8 and 27.3 per thousand for the white and nonwhite populations; death rates at 9.5 and 9.7 per thousand, for the two groups; and the rates of natural increase were 9.3 and 17.6, respectively, a spread of 8.3 points per 1,000.[5] The spread in the rates of natural increase, the rates most relevant here, widened partly because the birthrates for the nonwhites declined somewhat less than for the white population; but largely because in the diffusion of lower mortality, the drop in the death rates for the nonwhite group was so much larger and mortality rates for the two groups converged to almost equality. With the ratio of nonwhite population to total in 1930 at 10.2 percent, and rising to 13.0 percent by 1970, the proportion of the nonwhite population aged 0–4 to total population of that age class rose from 11.4 percent in 1930 to 15.9 percent in 1970. The eventual effect would obviously be to raise substantially the proportion of nonwhites in the additions to the labor force.

All of the parameters above need revision, and the suggested inferences are illustrative. They are intended to stress that during the long-term decline of the birth and death rates, the higher proportion of off-spring of the lower income groups surviving to join the country's labor force, higher than in the parental population, means pressure making for a more limited growth of product per worker or for widening inequality of income. In some phases of this process, the pressure may be greater, either because the income-origin mix in the addition to working population becomes more biased toward the lower income groups; or because the initial income inequality has widened; or for other reasons (e.g., changes in requirements for labor force participation, raising the levels of education and skill required to levels not easily accessible to children of the poor).

The reduction in fertility obviously had a variety of other consequences, among them the recent and increasing rise in the rate of participation of women in the labor force. And there are also the obvious effects on the age and sex structure of the population viewed as groups of consumers, with the resulting shifts in the structure of total consumer demand—decline in the relative importance of some consumer goods and rise in that of other goods. But let me turn now to the second trend selected for comment, the long-term rise in the proportion of population in the advanced ages.

Three aspects of this rise were noted in Professor Easterlin's paper. First, within the group of 65 and over, the older subgroups rose proportionately more than the younger. Thus, the share of the 65–74 age group in total population rose from 5.58 percent in 1950 to 6.50 percent in 1975, and is then projected to rise to 6.91 percent in the year 2000; the share of the 75 and over group rose from 2.56 percent in 1950 to 3.99 percent in 1975, and is projected to rise to 5.75 percent in 2000. The share of the younger group rises by less than two-tenths; that of the older group more than doubles.[6] Second, the widening difference in favor of women in life expectation at advanced ages means that, within the total group of 65 and over, the share of women and their excess over men has increased. Thus, the ratio of women to men, within the 65 and over group, rose from 1.02 in 1950 to 1.44 in 1975, and is projected to 1.50 in the year 2000. Third, the excess of women over men grew conspicuously more within the older subgroups. Thus, the ratio of women to men in the 65–74 age class rose from 1.02 in 1950 to 1.30 in 1975, and drops somewhat to 1.27 in the projection to year 2000; the ratio of women to men within the 75 and over age class rises from 1.21 in 1950 to 1.71 in 1975, and is projected to 1.85 by the year 2000.

Partly because of the progressive aging within the 65 and over group, but largely because of factors on the demand side, the labor force participation rates for the male group declined sharply since 1950, and are projected to decline further. Those rates (based on census data) were as high as 68 percent in 1890, declined to 41 percent by 1950, and dropped, in just two decades, to 25 percent in 1970 (see *Historical Statistics, 1976*, Series D29–41, p. 132). The International Labor Office (ILO) data indicate a movement of the labor force participation rates for males 65 and over from 45 percent in 1950 to 26 percent in 1970, and then project a further decline to 19 percent in the year 2000.[7] Both sources show very low rates of participation for women aged 65 and over, ranging from 7 to 10 percent in the census data, hovering below 10 percent in the ILO data, and projected to about 9 percent in the year 2000. Given the differences in the level of participation rates between the two sexes, and rising proportions of females, the combination of the two sexes yields (in the ILO data) a decline for the total participation rate from 26 percent in 1950 to 16 percent in 1970, and a projection to 12 percent in the year 2000.

The reduction of mortality at the advanced ages might have meant also reduction of morbidity; and, at a given age, say in the 65–74 age class, better health and greater productive capacity than before. If so, one may ask why the drastic fall in the labor force participation rates for the older males, and why the failure of the very low rates for older females to rise. Was it because of increasing obsolescence of the knowledge and skill of the older groups, induced by changes in the requirements for effective employment on the demand side? Or, less likely, was it due to favorable changes in the asset position of the aged (or in welfare policies) that made a shift to earlier retirement from the labor force feasible and preferable? The substantial rise in the proportions of the aged in the total population, and further projections of it (which may turn out to be understatements because of breakthroughs in health technology), assign to the question of working capacity and propensity of the aged, indeed of their role in society, large and increasing weight.

Another question relates to the two problems implied in a rising proportion of aged. The first is the likely increase in the share of the aged with shortages of income or wealth relative to needs. While it is not feasible to document this possible trend, several groups of factors appear to have made for it. One is connected with the unforeseen character of the relevant mortality trends and of other economic circumstances—which could have rendered earlier rational plans for financing retirement seriously deficient (because of extension of life, but not of work; and of the effects of inflation particularly on the nonworking aged). Another is implied in the convergence of death rates for poorer and richer groups in society, with the result that the proportions of lower income groups within the total group of 65 and over might have increased.[8] The third is suggested by the recently marked trend on the part of the aged to live separately, in single or two-person households, implying a weakening of the family ties between the active generations and their aged parents; and reduction in the possibly ameliorative effects of intra-larger-family sharing. It is hardly surprising that in the greater concern in recent decades over consumption deficiencies among the lower income groups, particular attention had to be paid to the aged among them.

Even assuming adequate provision for consumption needs of the aged, the other possible problem—increased excess of their consumption over the contribution of their labor and capital to total product—remains. Indeed, the real dissaving involved in such excess may only be increased by transfer and other policies properly oriented to sustain consumption by the aged. The concern here is not with the intricacies of the estimate of such excess. If, simply, one assumes the realistic possibility of a discrepancy, positive or negative, between a given human unit's consumption and the contribution of its labor and capital to total product, it is possible to argue that the rising proportion of the aged in total population—with their limited labor force participation and the likely growth of the poorer subgroups among them—means an increasing weight of the real dissaving, at least in absolute magnitude. The question then arises as to the weight of such dissaving relative to national product; or, better, relative to the net positive savings that may be generated in the economy by groups and institutions other than those represented by the aged.

The notes above stressed the consequences of selected demographic trends; and the need, in considering them, to distinguish the differing incidence among the several socioeconomic groups within the country. Demographic trends are long, so that changes are gradual and are likely to be overshadowed by the shorter term economic and political changes and their reflections. Yet one must emphasize that demographic trends, because of their biological bases, imply substantial constraints within which people must act. Thus, only women in childbearing ages can produce children (at least until another method is devised); breakthroughs in health technology are not predictable responses to economic investment, and some mortality differentials (e.g., between women and men) are not yet subject to human control; and various age and sex groups differ widely as producers and as consumers. To be sure, the constraints of the long biological cycle, from birth to death, are partly modified by society's institutions and dominant views. But this makes it all the more important to be able to appraise the economic consequences of these *changing* constraints, in their impact on economic advance, on the distribution of this advance among the several socioeconomic groups, and on the institutional adjustments that may be called for.

Notes

1. See United Nations, *World Population Trends and Prospects by Country, 1950–2000: Summary Report of the 1978 Assessment* (New York: United Nations, 1979), tables 2–A and 2–B, pp. 47–56.

2. These and other data in the paragraph are: for 1930–70, from U.S. Bureau of the Census, *Historical Statistics of the United States, Colonial Times to 1970, Bicentennial Edition, Part 1* (Washington, D.C.: Government Printing Office, 1975), Series A–119–34, pp. 15–18; for 1975–2000, U.S. Bureau of the Census, "Illustrative Projections of World Population to the 21st Century," *Current Population Reports*, Series P–23, no. 79 (Washington, D.C.: Government Printing Office, 1979), table 2, part U, p. 39.

3. See Simon Kuznets, "Income-Related Differences in Natural Increase: Bearing on Growth and Distribution of Income," in *Nations and Households in Economic Growth: Essays in Honor of Moses Abramovitz*, ed. Paul A. David and Melwin W. Reder (New York: Academic Press, 1974), pp. 127–46.

The illustrative data used in this earlier paper are not available over a long time span; and I am using here data on racial and ethnic minorities, with lower average incomes, in comparison with the white majority with its higher average income. The comparisons are rough and cannot be pursued here with adequate attention to the limitations of the data.

4. The data are from U.S. Bureau of the Census, *Current Population Reports*, Series P–60, no. 118 (Washington, D.C.: Government Printing Office, 1979), table 2, pp. 14–19.

5. The data here and in the rest of the paragraph are from *Historical Statistics* (Washington, D.C.: Government Printing Office, 1976), Series A–119–34, pp. 16–18; Series B–5–10, p. 49; and Series B–160–80, p. 59.

6. In addition to the Census Bureau projection referred to in note 2, and covering the span from 1975 to 2000, we used for 1950–75 the United Nations' age and sex distribution of population according to the 1973 assessment (this involves projections to 1970 and 1975, but these are close to the Bureau of Census later date. The source is United Nations, Population Division, "Population by Sex and Age for Regions and Countries, 1950–2000, as Assessed in 1973: Medium Variant," ESA/P/WP.60 (mimeographed), (New York: United Nations, 1976), p. 97.

7. See International Labour Office, *Labour Force Estimates and Projections, 1950–2000*, 2d ed. (Geneva, 1977), vol. 4, tables 2, 5, pp. 9, 76.

8. The share of black population in the total, for all ages, rose from 9.7 percent in 1930 to 11.6 percent in 1977; the share within the 65 and over group rose from 5.6 percent in 1930 to 8.2 percent in 1977 (see *Historical Statistics, 1976*, the series referred to in note 2); and *Statistical Abstract of the United States, 1978*, Washington, D.C.: Government Printing Office, 1978, table 29, p. 29). The sharper rise of the share of the lower income, black, population in the aged group, is striking.

Summary of Discussion

In leading off the discussion, Wilbur Cohen developed some of the implications of the demographic shifts for income support programs. First, as the life expectancy of women continues to grow over that of men, there will be an increasing number of 75–90 year old widows, putting an added strain on the social security system. This will be exacerbated by a general aging of the population and a decline in the labor force share of younger workers. The increasing number of births out of wedlock will tend to increase economic inequality, while the decline in number of large families may reduce poverty and inequality.

A number of participants speculated on the causes and consequences of the decline in extended families and the apparent decline, more generally, in family values. Robert Gordon pointed to welfare provisions as a major influence in the decline of two-adult households in American inner cities. A more favorable effect, Gordon stated, has resulted from the social security system, which has reduced dependence of older individuals on younger family members. Milton Friedman, on the other hand, saw social security as a detrimental influence on social trends. He declared that as children stopped contributing voluntarily to the support of their parents, and began contributing through a system of government fiat, a serious erosion of family values became inevitable.

Samuelson ventured the judgment that, although the 1945–80 data are broadly consistent with the Easterlin model of an every-other-generation cycle in population growth generated by changes in economic security and opportunity of young adults resulting from changes in their *relative* numbers, the power of that evidence to give one confidence in the hypothesis is weak. It is almost as if one had but two or three data points in the relevant scatter of cycles. It would seem safer to regard Easterlin's point as just one of many and not one strong enough to dominate the rest. If economics is to describe the dynamics of demography, the fad and fashion theory of skirt length may be as germane as the doctrine of invariant indifference and preference contours.

References

American Association for the Advancement of Science. 1966. The new immigration. *Annals* (September).

Anderson, Joseph M. 1977. An economic-demographic model of the United States labor market. Ph.D. diss., Harvard University.

————. 1978. Population change and the American labor market: 1950–2000. In *Consequences of changing U.S. population: Baby boom and bust*, vol 2, pp. 781–804, U.S. House of Representatives, hearings before the Select Committee on Population. 95th Congress, 2d session. Washington, D.C.: Government Printing Office.

Bancroft, Gertrude. 1958. *The American labor force: Its growth and changing composition*. New York: John Wiley.

Beale, Calvin L., and Fuguitt, Glen V. 1978. The new pattern of nonmetropolitan population change. In *Social democracy*, ed. Karl E. Taeuber, Larry L. Bumpass, and James A. Sweet, chap. 8. New York: Academic Press.

Becker, Gary S. 1965. A theory of the allocation of time. *Economic Journal* 75, no. 299 (September).

Berk, A.; Paringer, L.; and Mushkin, S. J. 1978. The economic cost of illness fiscal 1975. *Medical Care* 16, no. 9 (September): 786.

Biggar, Jeanne C. 1979. The sunning of America: Migration to the Sunbelt. *Population Bulletin* 34, no. 1: 1–44. Washington, D.C.: Population Reference Bureau, Inc.

Blake, Judith. 1974. Can we believe recent data on birth expectations in the United States? *Demography* 11, no. 1 (February): 25–44.

Briggs, V. M. 1975. Mexican workers in the United States labor market. *International Labor Review* 112, no. 5: 351–68.

Bustamante, Jorge A. 1977. Undocumented immigration for Mexico: Research report. *International Migration Review* 11, no. 2 (spring): 149–77.

Butz, William P., and Ward, Michael P. 1977. *The emergence of countercyclical U.S. fertility*. Santa Monica: The Rand Corporation.

————. 1978. *Countercyclical U.S. fertility and its implications.* Santa Monica: The Rand Corporation.

Crimmins, Eileen M. 1980. The changing pattern of American mortality decline, 1940–1977. Paper presented at the annual meeting of the Population Association of America, Denver, Colorado, 11 April 1980.

Davis, Lance E., et al. 1972. *American economic growth: An economist's history of the United States.* New York: Harper and Row.

De Tray, Dennis. 1978. Child schooling and family size: An economic analysis. R–2301–NICHD. Santa Monica: The Rand Corporation (April).

Downs, Anthony. 1979. The automotive population explosion. *Traffic Quarterly* 33, no. 3 (July): 347–62.

Easterlin, Richard A. 1968. *Population, labor force, and long swings in economic growth: The American experience.* New York: Columbia University Press.

————. 1977. Population issues in American economic history: A survey and critique. In *Recent developments in the study of business and economic history: Essays in honor of Herman E. Kross,* ed. Robert E. Gallman, pp. 131–58. Greenwich, Conn.: Johnson Associates.

————. 1978. What will 1984 be like? Socioeconomic implications of recent twists in age structure. *Demography* 15, no. 4 (November): 431–32.

————. 1980a. *Birth and fortune: The impact of numbers on personal welfare.* New York: Basic Books, 1980.

————. 1980b. Immigration: Economic and social characteristics. In *Harvard encyclopedia of American ethnic groups.* Cambridge: Harvard University Press, forthcoming.

Easterlin, Richard A.; Wachter, Michael L.; and Wachter, Susan M. 1978. Demographic influences on economic stability: The United States experience. *Population and Development Review* 4, no. 1 (March): 1–21.

Federal Bureau of Investigation (FBI). 1960–80. *Uniform crime reports.* Washington, D.C.: Government Printing Office.

Freeman, Richard B. 1979. The effect of demographic factors on age-earnings profiles. *The Journal of Human Resources* 14, no. 3 (summer): 298–318.

Fuchs, Victor R. 1956. Population growth concepts and the economy of tomorrow. *Proceedings of the Annual Dean's Day Program.* New York University, School of Commerce (December). Reprinted in *The Commercial and Financial Chronicle,* 13 December 1956.

————. 1974. *Who shall live?* New York: Basic Books.

————. 1978. A note on the demographic and economic consequences of reductions in mortality (mimeographed).

Fuguitt, Glen V., and Voss, Paul R. 1979. *Growth and change in rural America*. Management and Control of Growth Series. Washington, D.C.: The Urban Land Institute.

Fuguitt, Glen V., and Zuiches, J. J. 1975. Residential preferences and population distribution. *Demography* 12, no. 3 (August): 491–504.

Gallup Poll. Princeton: Institute of Public Opinion.

Guest, Avery M. 1979. Patterns of suburban population growth, 1970–75. *Demography* 16, no. 3 (August): 401–15.

Hamilton, Horace C. 1964. The negro leaves the South. *Demography* 1, no. 1: 273–95.

Hansen, Alvin W. 1939. Economic progress and declining population growth. *American Economic Review* 29, no. 1 (March): 1–15.

Heer, David M. 1979. What is the annual net flow of undocumented Mexican immigrants to the United States? *Demography* 16, no. 3 (August): 417–23.

Herzog, A. Regula; Bachman, Jerald G.; and Johnston, Lloyd D. 1978. High school seniors' preferences for sharing work and family responsibilities between husband and wife. Ann Arbor: Institute for Social Research, University of Michigan.

Hickman, Bert G.. 1960. *Growth and stability in the postwar economy*. Washington, D.C.: The Brookings Institution.

Jenkins, J. Craig. 1977. Push/pull in recent Mexican migration to the U.S. *International Migration Review* 11, no. 2 (spring): 178–89.

Katona, George. 1964. *The mass consumption society*. New York: McGraw-Hill.

Keely, Charles B. 1975. Immigration composition and population policy. In *Population: Dynamics, ethics, and policy*, ed. P. Reining and I. Tinker. Washington, D.C.: American Association for the Advancement of Science.

Kuznets, Simon. 1958. Long swings in the growth of population and in related economic variables. *Proceedings of the American Philosophical Society* 102: 25–52.

———. 1961. *Capital and the American economy: Its formation and financing*. Princeton: Princeton University Press.

———. 1964. Introduction. In *Population redistribution and economic growth, United States 1870–1950*, ed. H. T. Eldridge and D. S. Thomas. Vol. 3. Philadelphia: The American Philosophical Society.

Lee, Ronald. 1979a. Causes and consequences of age structure fluctuations. The Easterlin hypothesis. Paper presented at the International Union for the Scientific Study of Population Conference on Economic and Demographic Change: Issues for the 1980s. Helsinki (August).

———. 1979b. Economic aspects of age structure—Introductory statement. Paper presented at the International Union for the Scientific

Study of Population Conference on Economic and Demographic Change: Issues for the 1980s. Helsinki (August).

Mason, Karen Oppenheim. 1973. Studying change in sex-role definitions via attitude data. *American Statistical Association: Proceedings of the Social Statistics Section*, pp. 138–39.

McCarthy, Kevin F., and Morrison, Peter A. 1979. *The changing demographic and economic structure of nonmetropolitan areas in the United States.* R–2399–EDA. Santa Monica: The Rand Corporation (January).

Michael, Robert T. 1977. Two papers on the recent rise in U.S. divorce rates. NBER Working Paper no. 202. New York: National Bureau for Economic Research (September).

Michael, Robert T.; Fuchs, Victor R.; and Scott, Sharon R. 1980. Changes in the propensity to live alone: 1950–1976. *Demography* 17 (February): 39–56.

Miller, Ann R. 1977. Interstate migrants in the United States: Some social-economic differences by type of move. *Demography* 14, no. 1 (February): 1–17.

Mincer, Jacob. 1962. Labor force participation of married women. In *Aspects of Labor Economics.* Princeton: Princeton University Press.

Morris, Naomi M.; Udry, Richard J.; and Chase, Charles L. 1975. Shifting age parity distribution of births and the decrease in infant mortality. *American Journal of Public Health* 65, part 1 (April): 359–62.

Morrison, Peter A., and Wheeler, Judith P. 1976. Rural Renaissance in America? The revival of population growth in remote areas. *Population Bulletin* 31, no. 3: 1–28. Washington, D.C.: Population Reference Bureau, Inc.

National Academy of Sciences. 1979. *Science and technology: A five-year outlook.* A report for the National Science Foundation (April), pp. 411–76.

Preston, Samuel A. 1974. Social and demographic consequences of various causes of death in the United States. *Social Biology* 21 (summer): 144–62.

Preston, Samuel A., and McDonald, John. 1979. The incidence of divorce within cohorts of American marriage contracted since the Civil War. *Demography* 16, no. 1 (February): 1–25.

Rainwater, L. 1974. *What money buys.* New York: Basic Books.

Ridley, Jeanne Clare. In process. A study of low fertility cohorts in the United States. Kennedy Institute, Center for Population Research, Washington, D.C.

Siegel, Jacob S. 1978. *Current population reports.* Special Studies Series P–23, no. 78. U.S. Congress, House Select Committee on Aging.

Prospective trends in the size and structure of the elderly population impact of mortality trends, and some implications. Washington, D.C.: Government Printing Office.

Stolnitz, George J. 1955. A century of international mortality trends. *Population Studies* 9, no. 1 (July): 24–55.

Thornton, Arland, and Freedman, Deborah. 1979. Changes in the sex role attitudes of women, 1962–1977: Evidence from a panel study. *American Sociological Review*, 44, no. 5 (October): 832–42.

U.S. Bureau of the Census. 1950. 1960. 1970. *Census of population* Volume I. Washington, D.C.: Government Printing Office.

———. 1977. Educational attainment in the United States: March 1977 and 1976. *Current Population Reports*, series P–20, no. 314. (December), pp. 1–12. Washington, D.C.: Government Printing Office.

———. 1978. Fertility of American women: June 1977. *Current Population Reports*, series P–20, no. 325 (September), pp. 1–76. Washington, D.C.: Government Printing Office.

———. 1979. Estimates of the population of the United States and components of change: 1940–1978. *Current Population Reports*, series P–25, no. 802 May. Washington, D.C.: Government Printing Office. 1–14

U.S. Bureau of Labor Statistics (BLS). 1967. *Handbook of labor statistics, 1967.* Bulletin no. 1955. Washington, D.C.: Government Printing Office.

———. 1977. *Handbook of labor statistics, 1977.* Bulletin no. 1966. Washington, D.C.: Government Printing Office.

———. 1978. *Employment and earnings, July 1978.* Vol. 25, no. 7. Washington, D.C.: Government Printing Office.

U.S. Congress. House. Select Committee of Population. 1978. *Legal and illegal immigration to the United States.* Serial C, 95th Congress, 2d session (December). Commonly referred to as the Scheuer Committee Report.

U.S. Department of Health, Education, and Welfare (HEW). 1964. *The change in mortality trend in the United States.* National Center for Health Statistics. Series 3, no. 1. (March). Washington, D.C.: Government Printing Office.

———. 1977. Life tables. In *Vital statistics of the United States*, 1976. Vol. 2, sec. 5: 5–15. Hyattsville, Md.: National Center for Health Statistics.

———. 1979. Final mortality statistics, 1977. *Monthly Vital Statistics Report* 28, no. 1 (supplement) (11 May), pp. 1–35. Hyattsville, Md.: National Center for Health Statistics.

U.S. Department of Labor. 1970. *Career thresholds*, vol. 1. Manpower Research Monograph no. 16. Washington, D.C.: Government Printing Office.

U.S Department of Labor, Women's Bureau. 1975. *Handbook on women workers*. Bulletin no. 297. Washington, D.C.: Government Printing Office.

———. 1979. *The earnings gap between men and women*. Washington, D.C.: Government Printing Office.

Wachter, Michael L. 1972. A labor supply model for secondary workers. *Review of Economics and Statistics* 54, no. 2 (May): 141–51.

———. 1976. The changing cyclical responsiveness of wage inflation. *Brookings Papers on Economic Activity* 1: 115–67.

———. 1977. Intermediate swings in labor-force participation. *Brookings Papers on Economic Activity* 2: 545–76.

———. 1978. Second thoughts about illegal immigrants. *Fortune*, 22 May, pp. 80–82.

———. 1979. The labor market and immigration: The outlook for the 1980's. Paper prepared for the Interagency Task Force on Immigration. Discussion Paper no. 40. Center for the Study of Organizational Innovation (February).

Welch, Finis. 1979. Effects of cohort size on earnings: The baby boom babies' financial bust. *Journal of Political Economy* 87 (October): 65–74.

Westoff, Charles F. 1978. Some speculation on the future of marriage and fertility. *Family Planning Prespectives* 10, no. 2 (March/April): 81.

Westoff, Charles F., and Ryder, Norman B. 1977. *The contraceptive revolution*. Princeton: Princeton University Press.

Weiss, Noel S. 1976. Recent trends in violent deaths among young adults in the United States. *American Journal of Epidemiology* 103, no. 4. 416–22.

Whelpton, Pascal K. 1947. *Forecasts of the population of the United States, 1945–1975*. Washington, D.C.: Government Printing Office.

Whelpton, Pascal K.; Campbell, Arthur A.; and Patterson, John E. 1966. *Fertility and family planning in the United States*. Princeton: Princeton University Press.

Williams, J. D., and Sofranko, A. J. 1979. Motives for the immigration components of population turnaround in non-metropolitan areas. *Demography* 16, no. 2 (May): 239–56.

Wright, Nicholas H. 1975. Family planning and infant mortality rate decline in the United States. *American Journal of Epidemiology* 101, no. 3: 182–87.

Errata

The following corrections should be made to chapter 5

Page 368, last line—for "p. 42" read "p. 546"; add additional data source: BLS 1979a, table 42, p. 134, and table 147, p. 502.

Page 378, table 5.6—add additional source: Joe Russell, "Changing Patterns of Employment of Nonwhite Workers," in L. A. Ferman, J. L. Kornblah, and J. A. Miller, *Negroes and Jobs* (Ann Arbor: University of Michigan Press, 1968).

Page 382, table 5.7, line 13—for "doctorate women" read "doctorate workers"

Page 385, section heading 5.9.1—read "Level and Composition of Unemployment"

Page 387, line 10—add: "All the data except those in figure 5.4f are from *Employment and Training Report of the President 1979*; the education data are from Bureau of Labor Statistics, *Special Labor Force Reports,* various years."

5 The Evolution of the American Labor Market, 1948–80

1. Richard B. Freeman
2. John T. Dunlop
3. R. F. Schubert

1. Richard B. Freeman

Since World War II, the labor market in the United States has experienced significant changes in the composition of the work force, the type of work performed, institutional rules of operation and structure of wages, and employment and unemployment. Some of the changes continue historic trends. Others, however, have diverged from developments of earlier decades to create new labor market conditions and problems. In this paper, I identify seven of the most important changes, document their magnitude, and seek to estimate their impact on the economy. The seven changes are:

1. A Decreasing Rate of Growth of Real Wages and Labor Productivity

For the first time in recent American economic history, the real (constant dollar) pay and average output per worker have failed to increase substantially over an extended period of time. From 1900 to 1966, real earnings increased by 2.1 percent per annum. From 1966 to 1978, real compensation per man-hour increased by just 1.7 percent per annum. Output per worker grew by 2.4 percent from 1900 to 1966, compared to just 1.8 percent from 1966 to 1978. Slackened growth of real earnings and productivity in the 1970s represents one of the major changes in the United States labor market.

Richard B. Freeman is professor of economics at Harvard University.

I have benefited from the comments of Orley Ashenfelter, H. G. Lewis, and J. T. Dunlop.

2. A Changed Age, Sex, and Educational Composition of the Work Force

Continuing historic trends, the percentage of the work force that is female and the percentage with high school and college training have increased, while the labor participation rate of older men has declined. The age structure of the work force was also altered as a result of the post-World War II "baby boom." These demographic changes make the typical worker in the latter part of the twentieth century different from the typical worker in earlier decades and have led to different market problems.

3. A Significant Change in the Composition of Labor Demand and Employment

Continuing long-term historic trends, the fraction of workers employed in white-collar occupations, in government, and in the service industries increased in the period under study, while the fraction working as factory operatives or laborers, and in agriculture, declined. In specific individual sectors, marked changes occurred in the composition of employment, with the number of workers in some industries (e.g., coal) decreasing in early postwar years and then increasing in the later years, while the converse occurred in other industries (e.g., education). In a strikingly new development, the growth of demand for educated workers fell short of the growth of supply, with the result that the quality of jobs obtained by the educated declined. The sizable changes in employment by industry and occupation highlight the flexibility of the work force in response to dynamic changes in demand for labor in a modern economy.

4. A Declining Proportion of Workers in Trade Unions

In 1954, 35 percent of nonagricultural workers in the United States were in trade unions; in 1974, only 26 percent were so organized—a decline in the extent of union organization of comparable magnitude to the decline in the percentage of those organized in the 1920s. The decline in the proportion organized is the result of two divergent trends: a steep fall in the proportion of *private* wage and salary workers who are organized, even in traditional union strongholds, and a sharp rise in the proportion of *public* sector workers who are organized. Thus, unionism has become less prevalent and qualitatively different than in the immediate post-World War II period.

5. Changes in the Rules and Procedures of Operation of Firms and Unions

Three important sets of forces have fundamentally altered the way in which companies hire, fire, promote, and otherwise treat workers: equal opportunity and affirmative action legislation by the federal government;

other federal laws such as those pertaining to occupational health and safety; and the advent of computerized personnel files. These forces have transformed the personnel practices of companies to an extent unprecedented since the onset of the scientific management movement from the 1890s through the 1920s. They have had a particularly significant effect on the way enterprises treat minority and women workers.

6. *An Altered Structure of Wages*

Differentials in wages by race, age, education, and occupation have undergone fundamental changes in the postwar period. The wages of young workers have fallen relative to the wages of older workers. Blacks have gained relative to whites. The composition of the wage package has also altered, with fringes becoming an increasingly large share of labor cost. Sizable medium-term changes in the differentials paid different groups of workers highlight the flexibility of wage structures.

7. *Changes in the Rate and Composition of Unemployment and its Relation to Wage Inflation*

The average rate of unemployment in the United States drifted upward in the period under study. In the 1950s, unemployment averaged 4.5 percent; in the 1970s, 6.2 percent. The fraction of the unemployed who are young workers, particularly young minority workers, has risen noticeably as has the fraction in high-skill groups. The rate of change in money wages coincident with given levels of unemployment rose over the period, destroying the once widely held belief in the existence of a stable Phillips curve linking wage inflation to unemployment.

5.1 Plan of Study

What are the quantitative dimensions of the seven changes sketched out above? To what extent do the changes represent continuance of past labor market developments or fundamentally new patterns of change? What caused the seven major changes?

These are the questions that will be considered here. This paper will first analyze the magnitude of each of the seven changes and the extent to which they represent a continuation of historical trends or fundamentally new economic developments and then try to determine the cause of the changes and their meaning for the operation of the United States economy.

5.2 Change 1: Growth of Real Earnings and Labor Productivity

Perhaps the most disturbing post–World War II trend in the American labor market has been the notable retardation in the growth of real wages and output per man-hour that began in the late 1960s. As table 5.1 shows, long-term increases in real compensation per man-hour on

Table 5.1   Retardation in the Rate of Growth of Productivity and
                   Real Earnings

	Compound Annual Rates of Change (in Percentages)		
	1900–66	1947–66	1966–78
Productivity			
1. Output per man-hour (NBER)	2.40	3.39	—
2. Private business sector output per hour of all persons (BLS)	—	3.30	1.83
Real Earnings			
3. Annual earnings	2.14	2.90	—
4. Compensation per man-hour	—	3.30	1.71
5. Average hourly earnings, private industry	—	2.36	0.84

Sources: Line 1—U.S. Bureau of the Census, Historical Statistics, Part I, Series
D–683, Washington, D.C.: GPO, 1975, p. 162.
Line 2: BLS 1979c, table 79, p. 229, with 1978 from Monthly Labor Review 102
(August 1979): 103, table 31 (1947–66 based on hours worked concept from la-
bor force data with 1978 estimated from 1977–78 from change in output per hour
using established data.)
Line 3: U.S. Bureau of the Census, Historical Statistics, Part I (1975), Series D–
726, p. 164 for 1900–60; Series D–722, p. 164, deflated by E–135, p. 210. I cal-
culated the growth rate from 1900–60, then from 1960–66, and used the final
figure to calculate 1900–66. A similar procedure was used to get 1947–66.
Line 4: BLS 1979c, table 80, pp. 231–32 with update from Monthly Labor Review,
August 1979, table 31, p. 103. Because of slight inconsistencies among the series,
I used the percentage change from 1977–78 in the Monthly Labor Review to update the series.
Line 5: Monthly Labor Review, August 1979, p. 81 for average hourly earnings
and p. 89 for consumer price index deflator in 1978 with earlier figures taken from
BLS 1979c, table 118, p. 399.

the order of 2.1 percent per annum, which had risen in the 1947–66
period, declined to just 1.7 percent from 1966 to 1978. The rate of
growth of real average hourly earnings (a measure which is widely used
but is not totally adequate, since it excludes fringe benefits) fell from
2.4 percent (1947–66) to just 0.8 percent (1966–78). Concomitant
with the decline in real earnings was a sharp fall in the growth of output
per man-hour.

Is the retardation in the growth of real earnings and productivity the
result of sectoral shifts in the economy, such as the reduced flow of
workers out of agriculture or the shift into services? Analysis by the
United States Bureau of Labor Statistics (BLS) suggests that 22 percent
of the reduction in growth from 1947–66 to 1967–78 can be attributed
to sectoral shifts (Mark 1979), a percentage which falls far short of
accounting for the bulk of the retardation. That sectoral changes are not
the prime force at work is documented by the fact that productivity

growth has decreased in most industries: in forty-seven of the sixty-two industries for which the BLS calculates productivity, rates of change in output per employee hour were lower from 1966 to 1976 than from 1947 to 1966. Similarly, while rates of change in earnings differ for various groups of workers (see the discussion of change 6) only in coal was the rate of increase in real earnings higher post-1969 than pre-1969.[1] The seventies' retardation is not the result of the changing industrial mix of the economy.

The retardation in growth rates is also not directly explicable by the sluggish state of the economy in the 1970s. Regression analyses of the log of real earnings or productivity per man-hour on a trend variable, a 1970 trend, and a measure of business cycle, the level of unemployment, yield significant negative 1970 trend coefficients. Comparable regressions using a first difference format and using different trend breaks yield similar results.[2]

Accepting the retardation of growth as real, what factors can be adduced to explain the pattern of change?

Selected factors to account for the 1950s slowdown have been suggested by Edward F. Denison, who used standard growth accounting methods to evaluate the decline in productivity. Table 5.2 presents the results of his analysis for the period 1948–73 and 1973–76. While Denison's period is shorter than that covered in table 5.1 and suffers from reflecting cyclical (the 1974–75 recession) as well as secular patterns and other problems, his estimates offer the best available evaluation of the magnitude of factors at work.

With respect to labor inputs, Denison finds little impact from changes in workers' hours and attributes on the decelerated growth rate: the sizable increase in the educated work force in the period, which tends to raise growth, is balanced off by the decrease in labor input due to fewer hours worked and the changing age-sex composition of employment. Extending these calculations over a longer period of time is unlikely to greatly alter the results (see change 2).

With respect to the other major input, capital, Denison's calculations suggest only a modest role for slower capital formation per person in the retardation. From 1948 to 1973 Denison finds a growth of capital per person employed of .35 points, compared to .24 points from 1973 to 1976, a modest retardation of .11 points compared to the decline in productivity of 2.97 points. Using different data, Mark (1979) obtains an even stronger result as he finds that "the capital-labor ratio grew at about the same rate from 1966 to 1976 as it did from 1947 to 1966" (p. 198), eliminating it as an explanatory factor.

Three other possibilities for explaining the retardation deserve attention. First is the decline in expenditures on research and development (R&D) relative to national output. While the drop in R&D may have

Table 5.2   National Income per Person Employed in Nonresidential
Business: Growth Rate and Sources of Growth 1948–73
and 1973–76

	1948–73	1973–76	Change
Growth Rate	2.43	−0.54	−2.97
Contributions to growth rate in percentage points			
Total factor input:			
Changes in workers' hours and attributes:			
hours	−.24	− .54	− .30
age-sex composition	−.17	− .25	− .08
education	.52	.88	.36
Changes in capital and land per person employed:			
inventories	.10	.02	− .08
nonresidential structures and equipment	.29	.25	− .04
land	−.04	− .03	.01
Output per unit of input[a]			
Improved allocation of resources[b]	.37	− .01	− .38
Changes in the legal and human environment[c]	−.04	− .44	− .40
Economies of scale	.41	.24	− .17
Irregular factors	−.18	.09	.27
Advances in knowledge and miscellaneous determinants[d]	1.41	− .75	−2.16

Source: Edward F. Denison, *Accounting for Slower Economic Growth: The United States in the 1970s,* The Brookings Institution, 1979, table 7–3. (To be published)
[a]Contributions to the growth rate shown in subsequent lines are restricted to effects upon output per unit of input.
[b]Includes only gains resulting from the reallocation of labor out of farming and out of self-employment and unpaid family labor in small nonfarm enterprises.
[c]Includes only the effects on output per unit of input costs incurred to protect the physical environment and the safety and health of workers, and of costs of dishonesty and crime.
[d]Obtained as a residual.

complex effects on the economy, estimates of its contribution to the retardation of growth using standard growth accounting suggest only a modest impact (Denison 1979; Griliches 1973).

Second is what Denison calls "changes in the legal and human environment," due in large measure to governmental regulation (see change 6). While there is general agreement that regulations have reduced measured productivity, estimates of the degree to which this is true are difficult to obtain. Those of Denison indicate that costs incurred to protect the physical environment and health and safety of workers may explain as much as 13 percent of the retardation (−.40/−2.97).

The third, and most controversial factor, is the rise in energy prices. Some analysts place great weight on the increase in energy prices and resultant decline in energy used in their analyses of productivity (Jorgenson and Hudson 1978). The fact that the timing of the drop in productivity and real wages was concentrated after 1973, which is roughly coincident with the rise in oil prices due to OPEC, tends to support this interpretation. On the other hand, other analysts (Perry 1978; Denison 1979; Bruno and Sachs 1979) attribute a smaller impact to the rise in energy prices, largely because energy use has not declined dramatically and does not constitute a large share of national product.

As table 5.2 shows, the bottom line in Denison's calculations for productivity growth in the 1970s, like those for earlier times, leaves the final explanation open to question, for the key factor is changes in the residual "advances in knowledge and miscellaneous determinants," which dropped from positive 1.41 to negative —.75 in the period covered. In sum, while there is general agreement that there was a marked break in trend in productivity and real wage growth in the period covered, the cause and possible long-term persistence of the change remain open to question. Is the retardation a phenomenon unique to the United States in the post-1967 period, or is it a more general process?

Table 5.3 presents evidence on the growth of productivity and real wages in several developed countries and in the United States which suggests that the retardation has characterized most of the developed countries and is thus more likely due to worldwide economic trends than to developments specific to the United States.

Table 5.3   **Compound Annual Increase in Output per Hour and Real Hourly Earnings in Manufacturing, 1960–77**

	Output per Hour in Manufacturing		Real Hourly Earnings of Production Workers in Manufacturing	
	1960–67	1967–77	1960–67	1967–77
United States	3.4	2.4	1.5	0.9
Belgium	5.2	8.2	5.2	5.5
Canada	4.2	3.7	2.0	3.6
Denmark	6.0	6.4	4.1	5.1
France	5.5	5.5	3.4	5.1
Germany, F.R.	5.7	5.4	5.5	4.5
Italy	6.3	4.0	5.1	7.8
Japan	9.6	7.5[a]	4.1	7.4
Netherlands	5.8	7.9	6.4	4.5
Sweden	6.8	4.6	4.0	3.2
United Kingdom	3.8	2.4	2.5	1.8
Austria	—	—	4.7	5.7
Switzerland	—	—	3.7	3.2
Norway	—	—	3.1	4.5

Source: BLS 1979c, table 164, p. 582 and table 168, p. 586.
[a]Based on 1967–76.

What stands out in table 5.3 is the fact that both before and after the period of retardation, the growth rate of the United States was exceedingly dismal: worse than that of every country save the United Kingdom. Moreover, though in earlier decades slower growth in the United States might be attributed largely to higher initial levels of productivity and real earnings, such an explanation has decreasing validity. Despite serious problems of comparison due to exchange rate fluctuations, there is no doubt that the United States no longer has a major advantage in real income over other major developed countries: by the latest BLS comparisons, in fact, the United States had lower compensation per hour worked than did Belgium, Germany, the Netherlands, and Sweden.[3] Finally, it also is important to realize that the more sluggish increases in real wages in the United States compared to other developed countries are partially attributable to the rough constancy of labor's share of compensation in the United States in the period, compared to an upward trend in labor's share in several of the other countries.[4]

Since growth of productivity and real wages is the essence of economic progress, the declining rates of increase in the 1970s represent a potentially major economic problem. Productivity advances are necessary for improving average living standards and make numerous national goals easier to attain. Reduction of poverty, increased real defense spending, allocation of a greater share of desirable jobs to women and minorities, and increased support of older persons is easier, most would agree, in a rapidly growing economy than in a sluggish one. In the late 1950s, the Rockefeller Brothers issued a report comparing the growth of the United States to that of the Soviet Union and called for a major effort to raise the United States growth rate. If the falloff in the 1970s represents a new secular pattern of productivity growth rather than a temporary phenomenon, national attention should perhaps focus once more on policies to strengthen productivity growth.

5.3   Change 2: The Composition of the Work Force

In 1978 there were over 103 million persons aged 16 and over in the United States work force, of whom 100.4 million were in the civilian work force. Forty-one percent of the work force were women; nearly half were less than 35 years of age; and about one-fourth were between 16 and 24; approximately one in three had attended college for at least one year and one in six was a college graduate; over 70 percent were high school graduates; and about 10 percent may have been illegal aliens.[5]

Thirty years earlier, the composition of the labor force was quite different with relatively fewer women, young persons, and highly educated workers. The labor force participation rate of married women with spouse present more than doubled over the period, and the proportion of married women in the labor force with children under six nearly tripled. The participation of men, by contrast, fell, especially those in the 55 to 64 age bracket and nonwhite men. In the span of only three decades, the work force had changed to a remarkable extent (see fig. 5.1).

The most important change was the influx of women into the job market, particularly of married women with children. In the early part of the post-World War II period, most of the increase occurred among older women, many of whom were returning to work as their children reached school age. Nearly 80 percent of the growth in the female work force between 1947 and 1965 resulted from increased numbers of women aged 35 and over, whose labor force participation rate rose sharply. By contrast, in the late 1960s and early 1970s, the major source of growth of the female work force was among younger women, with 77 percent of the increase coming from persons less than 35 years old. From 1965 to 1977, the participation rate of women aged 20 to 24 rose from 50 percent to 67 percent while that of women aged 25 to 34 rose from 39 percent to 60 percent (BLS 1979c, p. 34).

The increased participation of women in the work force was related, presumably partly as cause and partly as effect, to several important social developments. The downward trend in fertility that followed the postwar baby boom was undoubtedly linked to the change in participation, though the influx of women with children into the work force makes it clear that the link is not the predominant factor at work. Similarly, the growth in the number of female-headed homes, which was especially sizable among blacks, is also likely to have been closely tied to increased female participation. By 1978 only 23 percent of homes fit into the traditional stereotype husband-wife homes with men employed and no other household member in the work force.[6]

On the job side, the female work force was associated with a marked increase in part-time jobs, which are largely filled by women. In 1950, 16 percent of persons with work experience over the year were part-time workers; in 1975, 12 percent, and in 1977, 21 percent (BLS 1979c, p. 12).

Because of the changes in fertility noted above, there was a remarkable shift in the age structure of the work force. In the 1950s, the proportion of the work force below 35 years of age was relatively small because of the low birthrate during the Depression. In the mid-1960s, however, the number of younger workers began increasing at unprecedented rates due to the postwar baby boom. The proportion of workers under 35 years of age jumped from 35 percent to 50 percent in the span of only one decade. As the proportion of the young going on to higher education increased in the period, much of the growth in the labor force of younger workers occurred among the college trained. In 1966, there

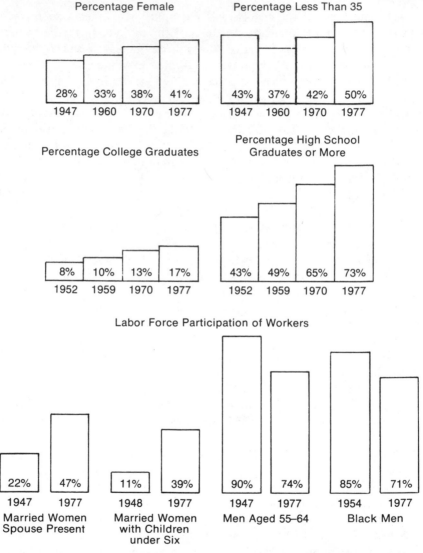

Fig. 5.1   Fractions of work force. Data from BLS 1979c, table 1 (percentage female), table 3 (age data), table 4 (male participation rate), table 12 (education data), table 14 (female participation rate).

were 0.49 male college graduates aged 25 to 34 per graduate thirty-five years of age and over; by 1976 the ratio had jumped to 0.78 (BLS 1977).

The large size of the youth population has had several socioeconomic consequences. It has, as will be seen later, altered the earnings of younger relative to older workers and made youth unemployment a major national concern. Coupled with 1960s' increases in the proportion of young choosing to go on to college, the increased number of youths sparked a large expansion of the education sector and a "golden age" for colleges and universities. Because crime is an activity disproportionately conducted by the young, it also raised rates of criminal activity (Freeman and Medoff 1980).

Despite the extraordinary increase in the number of young persons and growth in their labor participation rate, youth unemployment did not rise dramatically in the period studied. Among white youth aged 16 to 19 the number employed rose from 4.1 million in 1964 to 7.0 million in 1977 as the proportion employed actually increased. Among minority youth, however, the proportion in the labor force and the proportion employed fell while the proportion unemployed rose. The differential employment prospects facing white and black youth became one of the major problems of the decade (BLS 1979c, table 15).

One of the most surprising labor force changes shown in figure 5.1 is the marked drop in the participation of adult males, particularly older men and nonwhite men. In 1954, 86 percent of men 16 and over were in the work force; in 1977, 79 percent. Among nonwhites the decline was even more precipitous, from 85 percent in 1954 to 71 percent in 1977. The downward trend in nonwhite male participation is the major discordant pattern in a period of broad nonwhite economic advance. Both among whites and nonwhites the drop in participation was concentrated among older men, with the participation of all 55 to 64-year-old men falling by 16 percentage points.

The principal qualitative change in the labor force in post-World War II years was the increased educational attainment of workers. In contrast to the situation before World War II, high school graduation became common among the young, and a substantial fraction of young men and women chose to go on to college during the 1960s. Between 1954 and 1969, the proportion of 18 to 19-year-old men going to college rose from 30 percent to 44 percent while the proportion of 18 to 19-year-old women going to college increased from 23 percent to 36 percent. As a result of increased enrollments, in the late 1960s and the early 1970s, the number of graduates grew rapidly. From 1966 to 1974, the number of bachelor's degrees granted doubled, while the number of master's degrees and doctorates increased at nearly the same pace. The boom was accompanied by sizable changes in the fields of study and occupations of new graduates, with some specialties like law or MBA management enjoying extraordinary growth and others such as engineering experiencing different patterns of change.

At the outset of the 1970s, however, enrollment in higher education began leveling off. The proportion of 18- to 19-year-old men in college dropped to just 34 percent by 1974; whereas in 1969 there were 0.5 graduate level enrollees per college graduate aged 22 to 29, and in 1975, there were 0.4 enrollees per bachelor's graduate in the 22 to 29-year-old age bracket. In some PhD specialties, enrollments and degrees granted fell by as much as 40 percent. Stabilization or decline in enrollment rates among the young did not, however, reduce or even greatly affect the rate of increase in the overall educational attainment of the work force. Even with the rates of the 1970s, the average education of the labor force rose noticeably. This was because of a continued sizable difference in years of schooling between retiring and entering workers. The proportion of college workers among the young, but not in the work force as a whole, stabilized.[7]

5.3.1   Causes of Change 2

The economic model of labor supply, in which supply decisions reflect economic incentives, can be used to analyze changes in female participation, male participation, and educational investments. In the simple economic model, changes in labor force participation are caused by changes in market wages and in the value of time spent working at home (the 'shadow wage' for household activities). Increases in market wages will raise labor participation (substitution effect), while increases in the value of working at home, due to higher income of other household members, will reduce participation (income effect).

Improvements in household technology, which take the form either of new machines or techniques or of lower prices for given techniques, can increase or decrease work activity depending on the extent to which they substitute for household time, among other things.

The basic effort to explain participation rate patterns follows a two-stage procedure. First, the effects of the wages of women and of their husbands on participation are estimated by cross-sectional (more recently, longitudinal) data. Then the changes in these explanatory factors over time are multiplied by their estimated effects to assess the impact of the changes on participation. Because the wages of men and of women have risen at roughly the same rate over time, the model requires greater female responsiveness to female wages than to the incomes of their husbands to account for the upward trends in participation. While most studies have found that women react more to their own wages than to their husbands' earnings, the differences have not been sufficiently large to explain the bulk of increased female participation.[8] Addition of other factors, such as number of children, does not greatly enhance the ability to track the trend. Perhaps most discouragingly, the most recent results for the 1970 Census of Population show that the economic factors "which together once explained three-quarters of the variation in wives' participation rates across SMSAs (Standard Metropolitan Statistical Areas) now account for only one-third of it. Many of the variables are no longer significant, and the strength and explanatory power of all except the unemployment variable have declined" (Fields 1976, p. 576). We are far from accounting for the rise in the participation of women in terms of simple economic factors.

One possible missing element from standard models is the nature of household technology. The household sector is surprisingly capital intensive. In 1975 the average household had $6,900 in consumer durables. From 1952 to 1975, the accumulation of durables increased by 5.4 percent per annum.[9] Refrigerators, washing machines, and related equipment became increasingly prevalent in the home. Although cause and effect cannot be readily disentangled, the growth of fast-food services and other restaurants have come to offer a more readily available (and chosen) alternative for one of the main household products. In the absence of estimates of the quantitative effect of these factors (and of the substitution between time and goods in household production), however, we can do no more than speculate about the effect of technology in "freeing" women's time.

Another possible missing element, which must be brought into the story with care, is attitudinal changes, potentially associated with the women's liberation movement of the late sixties and seventies. That there were significant changes in attitudes over the period is apparent from diverse opinion surveys. As late as 1967, 44 percent of first-year college women and 67 percent of first-year college men thought "a woman's place is best at home." In 1974 only 19 percent of entering college women and 40 percent of entering college men agreed with that view (Freeman 1976, p. 168, fig. 29). Clearly, it had become (for whatever reason) more socially acceptable for women to devote themselves to careers as opposed to marriage and family. The extent to which these changes in attitudes were caused by or caused the labor force patterns is difficult to determine.

The basic economic model can also be used to analyze the decline in the labor participation of older men. One important economic factor that can be expected to reduce participation of men sixty-five and over has been the expansion of social security coverage, which places a higher tax on earnings after that age. Another factor likely to lower older male participation is private pension plans, which have also become more widespread in recent years (Skolnik 1976) and which typically provide strong incentives to leave the job, often in the form of mandatory retirement. Indeed, mandatory retirement provisions are sufficiently wide-spread as to constitute a major institutional provision in labor contracts (Lazear 1979). Recent changes in the law regarding vesting of pensions and mandatory retirement (see change 6) may provide an important "test" of how private pensions and mandatory retirement rules in fact affect retirement decisions.

Most empirical studies find sizable response parameters to economic variables in retirement behavior, with older men estimated to be more sensitive to wages or nonwage income than men in general (Cain and Watts 1973). Although detailed analysis of the effect of social security on retirement is just beginning, the evidence seems to support the attribution of a considerable effect to the social security mode of retirement pay (Boskin and Hurd 1978; Boskin 1977; Burkhauser and Turner 1978; Pellechio 1978; Quinn 1977). Recent analysis of the work incentive effects of social security—the strong dependence of benefits on final years' pay, which can increase participation—does, however, raise some doubts about its impact (Blinder, Gordon, and Wise 1979).

The puzzling drop in the labor force participation of black men has been explained in part by another component of social security: disability insurance (SSDI). About half of older black men out of the labor force are recipients of SSDI. Because of their concentration in blue-collar jobs with substantial risk of job-related injuries and lower wage rates, black men turn out to have been more affected by the program than white men (Leonard 1979). Still, a significant proportion of their decline in participation remains unexplained.

Finally, the human-capital analysis of investment in skills provides a reasonably successful explanation of the changes in the qualifications of the work force. In the human-capital model, decisions to obtain a certain level of schooling or skill are made by comparing two income streams: the stream that results from the investment and the stream that would obtain in its absence. If, at a given interest rate r, the present value of the former exceeds the latter plus the direct cost of the investment, the individual is expected to choose the investment. Because about two-thirds of the private cost of education turns out to consist of foregone income, as opposed to direct costs, the analysis directs attention to differences in the wages of more and less qualified persons as the major factor in investments in schooling.

Analyses of the link between enrollment patterns suggest that much of the postwar expansion and the seventies' contraction in the higher education system can be attributed to changes in economic incentives, measured by wages or other indicators of rates of return. The growth of enrollments in the 1960s was spurred by improved earnings opportunities for college graduates while the decline of enrollments in the 1970s appears to be the result of the falling return to college workers (see change 5). Cross-section (Rosen and Willis 1979) and time series (Freeman 1975) analyses find sufficiently high elasticities of response as to account for the bulk of the changes in male enrollments in terms of the economic model. The slowdown in doctorate production also appears explicable in terms of the economic factors at work in that market, although, in this case, nonprice factors, notably the difficulty of obtaining academic employment, may be as important as wages in causing changes (Freeman 1980a). Finally, the selection of particular fields of study has also been found to respond to market factors with, for example, relatively many students choosing education in the 1960s when the school system was expanding and few choosing this concentration in the 1970s when the teacher's job market deteriorated (Hebl 1978). Though by no means without problems, the economic analysis does appear to provide a good handle on the changing educational attainment of the work force.

Overall, if one single conclusion about the labor force is to be drawn from the post-World War II experience, it is that the labor supply undergoes substantial dynamic shifts and evinces high supply responsiveness in several dimensions and thus cannot be viewed as a stable, inflexible component of the labor market. Much of the variation of course, rises from marginally attached groups—young persons, women, older workers—rather than from the prime-age male workers.

5.4 Change 3: Demand and Employment

Figure 5.2 highlights some of the most significant changes in the composition of employment in the post-World War II period. With respect to occupations it shows a massive shift in employment from blue-collar work, including agricultural, to white-collar work, particularly into professional, technical, and clerical jobs. Note, however, that the rate of expansion of the white-collar sector levels off noticeably in the 1970s. Between 1950 and 1960 the proportion in white-collar jobs increased by four percentage points; between 1960 and 1970, the increase is by seven points, whereas from 1970 to 1978 it is just three points. Among professionals the slackened rate of increase in the 1970s is even more striking: after increasing by three points between 1950 and 1960 and by four points between 1960 and 1970, the professional share of employment was virtually unchanged between 1970 and 1978.

The slowdown in the growth of professional and white-collar employment at a time when the number of college graduates was increasing rapidly caused a major "underemployment" problem in the college job market. As table 5.4 shows, there was a substantial downgrading in the types of jobs held by graduates, with fewer holding professional and technical positions and more in blue-collar and lower level white-collar jobs. The modest increase in the proportion of male graduates in managerial positions and the sizable increase in the proportion of women in those jobs is, it should be stressed, dwarfed by the decline in the proportion in technical and professional jobs. The Bureau of Labor Statistics predicts that in the next decade or so the demand for professionals will continue to expand more slowly than supply, creating an even greater underemployment problem.

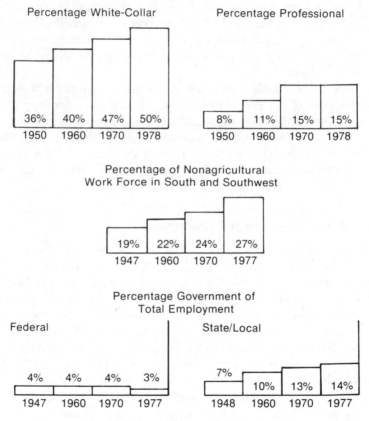

Fig. 5.2   Employment distribution. Data for 1950–70 white-collar and professional from U.S. Bureau of Census 1975, p. 139; for 1978 white-collar and professional, from BLS 1979a, pp. 172, 174; government data from BLS 1979c, table 50 with the total employment from table 1, regional data from table 52, with total nonagricultural employment from table 42. South and Southwest defined as regions IV and VI and Arizona and Nevada from region IX. See table 52, p. 159 for precise definitions of regions.

Table 5.4 **Percentage Distribution of Occupations of Employed College Graduates, 1968–78**

Occupations	Men			Women		
	1968	1978	Δ	1968	1978	Δ
Professional and technical	60.6	52.1	−8.5	81.1	65.0	−16.1
Managers and administrators	22.2	24.5	1.8	4.1	8.7	4.6
Sales workers	6.8	8.9	2.1	1.2	4.6	3.4
Clerical workers	4.4	4.7	0.3	10.6	15.4	4.8
Craft workers	2.2	3.9	1.7	1.2	1.9	0.7
Other blue-collar workers	1.3	2.7	1.4	1.2	1.9	0.7
Service workers	1.1	2.1	1.0	1.5	3.8	2.3
Farm workers	0.9	1.2	0.3	0.3	0.5	0.2

Source: Brown, 1979, p. 58, table 5.

The reduction in the quality of jobs and in the relative earnings of the more highly educated could be expected to cause a drop in the job satisfaction of more highly educated workers, and, according to the University of Michigan Quality of Work Survey, such appears to have been the case. Whereas in 1969 college workers scored higher than high school workers on an overall job satisfaction index by a considerable amount, in 1977 they scored much lower than in 1969 and no higher than high school workers.[10] A major burden has been placed on employers to adjust to the new availability of college graduates for jobs that have traditionally been held by the less educated and to the distorted age structure of the college work force.

Figure 5.2 also displays one of the most important changes in the industrial distribution of the work force: the doubling in the state and local governments' share of employment in the postwar period. By 1977 one in seven workers was employed by state and local governmental bodies compared to one in fourteen three decades earlier. One-third of the growth of employment over the entire 1948–76 period is attributable to expansion of the public sector (including federal employees). At the other end of the spectrum there was a continued shift of the work force out of agriculture, leaving just 3.8 percent of employed workers in that sector in 1976, and a drop in the self-employed, nonagricultural labor force (BLS 1979c, table 42, p. 134, table 34).

The increased importance of the governmental labor force in the economy has raised a whole host of industrial relations problems. Consider, for example, the following type of issue. A locality forbids public workers from striking. This same locality reaches an agreement with the public workers on a certain wage settlement after collective negotiations, but the citizens of the locality refuse to raise taxes to pay for this wage settlement. The public sector workers cannot strike. Should wages be raised to the negotiated levels? If not, should the public sector workers be permitted to strike to pressure voters to meet the agreement? What should be done? A wide variety of answers to these questions have been employed by various states. As yet, there is no general agreement as to the best mode of dealing with public sector industrial relations problems.

Another widely heralded shift in employment, shown in figure 5.2, is the relative decline of employment in the Eastern and Midwestern industrial belt. The fastest growing regions of the country were the South, Southwest, and, to a lesser extent, the West Coast. Many industries moved into the South and Southwest in this period, locating new plants in such states as Texas, Louisiana, Florida, Arizona, and Colorado. Industrialization of those areas and loss of employment in New England and the Midwest became a subject of considerable controversy, due to, in part, the federal government's alleged spending decisions which favored the Sunbelt over the Snowbelt.

The shifts in jobs among occupations, industries, and areas are the tip of an iceberg of changes in employment in the job market. Among disaggregated categories there were large changes in employment, with some groups growing rapidly and others declining and with the growth sectors of one decade often being the declining sectors of the next and vice versa. Schoolteaching, for example, was a booming occupation in the 1960s but not in the 1970s. Employment in aircraft and parts rose by 184 percent from 1950 to 1969 and then fell by 42 percent from 1969 to 1977. Employment in all mining dropped from 901,000 in 1950 to 619,000 in 1969 and then shot up to 837,000 in 1978.[11]

It is important to recognize that the changes in the composition of employment are more extensive than the changes in the structure of wages. The standard deviation of log changes in employment in three-digit Census of Population occupations from 1960 to 1970 was .39 compared to a standard deviation in the log changes of earnings in those occupations of .13. Similarly, the standard deviations in log changes in employment among two-digit manufacturing industries far exceeded those in wages. From 1961 to 1977 (which have roughly similar cyclical conditions) the standard deviation on log changes in production worker employment in twenty two-digit durable and nondurable industries was .25, while the standard deviation in the log changes of average hourly earnings, exclusive of overtime, was .09.[12]

One of the fundamental features of the United States economy appears to be much greater variability in employment by sector than in earnings by sector. Though the wage structure changes over time, it has greater stability than employment.

5.4.1   Causes of Change 3

The principal cause of the structural change in employment among occupations and industries appears to be *dynamic shifts in demand for labor*, which alters employment along relatively elastic supply schedules. While there are other possible explanations for the concordance of large changes in employment with more modest changes in wages, the demand/elastic-supply interpretation of the patterns appears to offer the best explanation of the observed phenomenon (Freeman 1980b). Some of the shifts in demand are attributable to broad economic swings, such as growth of demand for some goods rather than others, while others are attributable to technological changes.

5.5   Employment and Productivity

Considerable concern has often been expressed about the effect of technological change on the level of employment in industry. Does employment increase or decrease in industries undergoing significant technological progress? The impact of differential increases in productivity and industry of employment is twofold. All else being the same, industries with large increases in productivity will experience relative declines in employment since fewer workers are needed for production. But all else will not remain the same. An industry with substantial gains in labor productivity will find that labor costs per unit of output and total costs decline rapidly. The decline in cost causes prices to fall and induces consumers to purchase more of the industry's output. Hence, the decline in labor demand associated with the need for fewer workers per unit of output may be offset by the increased demand for output.

Empirical evidence for the United States in the postwar period indicates that the employment creating effect of the growth of output is roughly offset by the disemployment effect of rapid productivity gains. Specifically, the correlation between changes in output per employee hour and employee hours in the industries for which the BLS calculates productivity indexes is a bare $-.03$ (BLS 1979c, table 81). Thus, rapid productivity is essentially unrelated to growth of employment by sector. Technological change alters the distribution of employment among industries and occupations, but does not have the feared effect of creating significant loss of jobs in sectors with rapid productivity growth.

5.6   Change 4: Unionism

Collective organization of the United States labor force has changed substantially in the postwar period. Since the mid-1950s, the fraction of private sector workers who are unionized has fallen gradually while, by contrast, organization of public sector workers has jumped enormously. These two changes have altered the labor movement in the country and the operation of the labor market.

The two divergent patterns and their net impact on unionization in the country are depicted in figure 5.3, which records the fraction organized in the private and public sectors and in the country overall. In 1956 the BLS data showed 34 percent of private nonagricultural workers to be organized; by 1974 the fraction had dropped to 26 percent. In the public sector, organization grew from 12 percent in 1956 to 19 percent in 1974, reaching 34 percent if members of associations, like the National Education Association, are included as union members. Because the majority of workers are private employees, the overall percentage has also fallen.

Data on the success of unions in National Labor Relations Board (NLRB) representative elections tell a similar story about the diminution of private sector unionism in the United States. In 1950 unions won 74 percent of NLRB elections; in 1976 their victory rate was below 50 percent. The fraction of eligible-to vote workers in elections won by unions fell even more sharply as unions had increasing difficulty in elections in large establishments. Barely one-third of workers in elections were in districts won by unions. As a result, the ratio of workers organized as a consequence of the NLRB elections to the total nonagricultural private work force fell from 1.7 percent in 1950 to a bare 0.3 percent in 1977.[13]

While trade unions have contracted in earlier time periods—notably the 1920s when the percentage of nonagricultural workers organized fell from 20 percent to 12 percent—the drop in the 1950s to the 1970s represents a sharp break with the long-term trend and a pattern in marked contrast to the growth or stability of unionism in other developed countries, including Canada, where many of the same unions and firms operate.

What explains the erosion of private sector organization of the United States labor force? One important factor has been the demographic and employment changes in the composition of the work force. The proportion of workers who have historically tended to be less organized—women, the young, Southwestern workers, white-collar workers—have grown while the proportion in the traditionally organized categories have fallen. Estimates by Freeman and Medoff suggest that about 60 percent of the decline in unionism can be explained by such structural changes (1976, p. 24, table 4).[14] Still, even among blue-collar workers in traditional strongholds of unionism, there was a sizable drop in union coverage. The following figures show the percentage of production workers covered by collective bargaining (BLS 1979c, table 157, p. 42):

	1958	1960	1970	1974–76
Metropolitan areas	—	73	—	61
Northeast	—	77	—	66
Manufacturing	67	—	61	—
Electrical manufacturing	73	—	58	—
Petroleum refining	89	—	74	—

Ratio of Union Workers to Nonagricultural Employment*

	1958	1960	1970	1974–76
Transportation and public utility	81	81	73	69
Contract construction	84	79	73	69

*These figures are merely illustrative, since the concepts and sources of the data are quite different.

A second major factor underlying the erosion of unionism among private wage and salary workers has been increased managerial opposition, abetted in part by changes in the law. In the early years of the Wagner Act, employers were severely limited in what they could say or do to oppose unionism. Since the late 1940s, however, legal enactment (Section 8C) of Taft-Hartley and diverse NLRB and Supreme Court decisions regarding management right to "free speech" in opposition to unionism has significantly altered the nature of the election process. Nowadays, managements contest elections, making extensive efforts to convince workers to vote against union, and often employing specialized labor-management consultants to advise or run their campaigns. In Canada, where the same unions and management often deal with one another but where the method of recognizing unions does not allow for management campaigns against organization, trade union organization of the work force has grown.

Quantitative data from the AFL-CIO and the National Industrial Conference Board (NICB) suggest that active management opposition has significant effects on the success of unions. According to the AFL-CIO study, unions won 97 percent of elections with no opposition compared to 30 percent to 40 percent in which management opposition was extensive. According to the NICB study, unions won 85 percent of elections in which companies made either no effort or a limited effort in the form of a written letter opposing organization; they won 51 percent of those in which the company held antiunion meetings but only 34 percent of those in which companies communicated their opposition in writing or by holding group and individual meetings. Although the validity of these studies suffers from the possibility that management might not fight when the outcome is a foregone conclusion in the union's favor, both union and management officials place great stress on the impact of opposition, and particularly on the use of expert labor/management consulting firms.

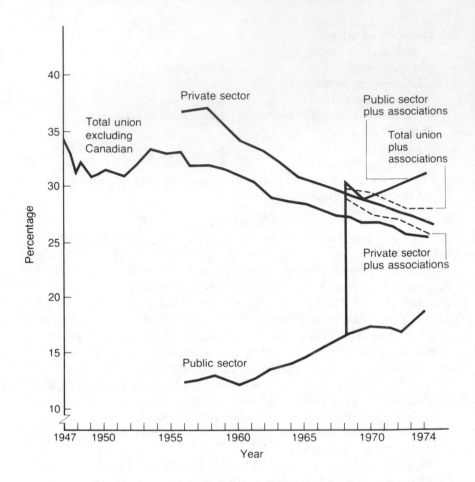

Fig. 5.3   Union organization of the nonagricultural sector, 1947–74: union members per hundred nonagricultural employees. Data for total from BLS 1979c, table 150, p. 507. Public sector estimated by multiplying the percentage of union members in the public sector from table 147, pp. 498–503, by the total proportion by the ratio of nonagricultural employment to government employment from table 42, p. 134. Data for public sector including associations obtained by multiplying public sector figures by the ratio of union plus association membership to union membership from U.S. Bureau of Labor Statistics, *Directory of National Unions and Employee Associates* (Washington, D.C.: Government Printing Office, 1975), table 15, p. 70. Private sector and private sector plus association figures calculated using the same tables and methodology. Total association data from *Directory*, table 6, p. 63.

In addition to legal opposition, however, there has been a marked increase in illegal opposition to unions. The number of cases under section 8(a) (1) of the Taft-Hartley amendment—those involving discrimination in employment to discourage unions—has skyrocketed from 4,472 in 1950 to over 26,000 in fiscal 1977 while the number of 8(a) (3) cases—firing for union activities—has risen from 3,213 in 1950 to over 16,000 in 1976. The penalty for breaking these provisions of the law are sufficiently slight as to be only a moderate deterrent to companies strongly opposed to unions. Statistical analysis finds a significant negative correlation between unfair labor practices or other indications of managerial opposition and union success (Ellwood and Fine 1980; Freeman and Medoff 1976). Finally, in certain cases, even when management has lost an election, it may bargain so as never to sign a collective agreement.

A third potential cause of the diminished success of private sector unionism is the growing similarity in personnel practices between organized and nonorganized companies, especially among the largest enterprises. Many large nonunion firms pay union-level wages and have work conditions comparable to those in organized plants, such as job bidding systems for positions, seniority rules on layoffs, and grievance procedures. This is particularly the case in firms that have some organized plants and some nonorganized plants. In addition, to some extent at least, unions may be suffering from the fact that increased governmental regulation of the labor market and funding of worker benefits (see change 5) have also eroded the payoff to joining a union.

Another factor which may contribute to the changed position of unions has been a drop in favorable attitudes toward the institution. Beginning roughly in mid-1957, when the McClellan Labor-Management Relations Committee began its sensational hearings, stories dealing with labor in the major newspapers, *Time*, and *Newsweek*, became unfavorable. In public opinion surveys by Gallup, responses to the question, "In general, do you approve or disapprove of labor unions?," show a steady deterioration in favorable attitudes as follows:

Period	Average Approval
1950–1957 (Sept.)	75%
1957 (Sept.)–1959	68%
1960s	68%
1970s	60%

This drop in public approval for unions has occurred within broad occupational categories (professional and business, white-collar, blue-collar, and farmers). According to Gallup, it has dropped most rapidly in the past decade among adults under thirty.

Even with changing attitudes, however, a relatively large fraction of nonunion workers would like to be unionized. Kochan found that in the 1977 Quality of Employment Survey 39 percent of blue-collar workers would vote for union representation in their workplace if an election were held, while 28 percent of white-collar workers, excluding the self-employed and managers, would also vote for unions. "Perhaps the most striking finding was that 67 percent of all black and other minority workers would vote to unionize" (Kochan 1979, p. 25). While *all* of these workers could be in plants where even in the absence of management campaigns to discourage organization the majority of workers would vote down unions, it is more likely that at least some are in plants that would be organized if institutional procedures were different.

Will private sector unionism continue to diminish in the future? The answer to this question is unclear. On the one hand, even modest efforts to reform the labor laws in the United States in such a way as to reduce the ability of management to discourage unionism, (e.g. the Labor Law Reform of 1978) have been defeated. On the other hand, unionism has traditionally grown in sudden spurts which were never predicted by experts.

What are the economic effects of a proportionately smaller trade union movement? From the perspective of the monopoly "face" of unionism the decline can be expected to reduce the monopoly misallocation of resources resulting from unionism and, to the extent that union monopoly wage gains depend on the fraction of the labor force organized (Freeman and Medoff 1979), also reduce the union wage advantage. On the other hand, however, reduced unionism can be expected to affect adversely many of the positive effects of strong unionism—lower dispersion of earnings among workers; lower quit rates; and higher productivity due to pressures on management to reduce costs in organized firms. As the United Mine Workers organization and industrial relations in coal have deteriorated, productivity in union mines has fallen sharply. The broader social effects of a diminished trade union movement remain to be seen.

5.6.1 Public Sector Unionism

While private sector unionism has declined, public sector unionism has grown rapidly. The largest union in the AFL-CIO is that of the State, County and Municipal Workers. Teachers have become one of the most highly organized occupations in the country. In most cities, policemen and firemen negotiate for wages and work conditions. About half of the federal work force is organized. This organization of public sector workers brings the United States closer to other developed countries, where unionism of government employees has long been important, and alters the face of the American labor movement. Public sector unions rely on political rather than economic muscle to obtain desired benefits. Public sector unions are usually not allowed to strike. Negotiated settlement must be approved, in many cases, by bodies that decide taxes. As noted earlier, these distinct characteristics create new industrial relations issues.

What explains the success of unionism in the public sector compared to the diminution of organization in the private sector? A good case can be made that the direct cause of union success in the public sector has been explicit changes in the law regarding public sector labor relations. First, states with laws that are more favorable to public sector collective bargaining have the highest proportion unionized. Second, and more importantly, over time public sector organization has grown rapidly in states following passage of the more favorable laws and has not grown rapidly in states which maintain laws that discourage public sector unionism. In one study, it was found that organization of police increased sizably following passage of a law that required localities to meet and confer with unions (Lauer 1979). Third, at the federal level, President Kennedy's Executive Order 10988 and ensuing policies toward unionism clearly precipitated the successful organization of federal employees. While the political and attitudinal changes that underlie the new laws may be properly viewed as the fundamental causes of the increased public sector unionism, new laws appear to be a necessary condition for organizational success.

Concomitant with an increase in unionization in the public sector has been a growth of strikes among public employees, including white-collar workers such as teachers. In 1956 BLS data show that outside of education there were just 27 work stoppages in the public sector; in 1976 the number of stoppages was 378. For the education sector, National Center for Education Statistics (NCES) data reveal only two teacher work stoppages (involving just 210 people) in 1959 compared to 218 stoppages (involving 182,300 teachers) in 1975 (NCES 1978, table 4.9, p. 182). Despite the illegality of public sector strikes in most states, teachers and other public sector workers (except for police and firemen) have come to view the strikes as a legitimate mode of seeking contract changes.

Most studies of the effects of public sector unionism on the pay of public employees have found moderate differences between the wages of public sector workers in cities that are organized and cities that are not (see Lewin 1977), a surprising result in view of the widespread concern over the power of public sector unions and the belief that absence of competition for government functions would create inelastic demands for union services and thus allow them great power in bargaining (Wellington and Winter 1972). One reason for the modest estimated effect of public sector unions appears to be the extensive "spillover" of wages across cities as a result of the extensive reliance of local governments on comparability comparisons in wage setting (Ehrenburg and Goldstein 1975). A nonunion city near a union city in the same state is likely to pay wages similar to those in the union city. One study has found that while police in union and nonunion cities in the same state receive roughly similar pay, police in highly unionized states obtain a considerable advantage over those in less organized states, suggesting that public sector unionism has indeed had sizable economic consequences that escape detection from city comparisons (Lauer 1979). Other studies have found that public sector unions have larger effects on fringe benefits than on direct pay (Gustman and Segal 1977; Ichniowski 1978; Edwards and Edwards 1979).

5.7   Change 5: Governmental Regulations

One of the major changes in the labor market in post-World War II years has been an increased role of governmental regulations in determining market behavior and outcomes. In the area of collective bargaining, legislative enactment and NLRB and court decisions have brought internal union affairs and the bargaining process under greater regulation than ever conceived by the proponents of the Wagner Act. In the area of personnel policy, the antibias and affirmative action rules of the federal government have revolutionized employee selection, promotion, and remuneration policies. In the area of workplace conditions, occupational health and safety acts and environmental policies have brought governmental rules and regulations into the workplaces of thousands of enterprises. Compensation has also been affected, both by equal pay legislation and regulation of pension plans. Finally, through its taxation and social welfare programs, the government has altered the rewards from working and the floor beneath which those who cannot work may fall.

5.7.1   Regulation of Collective Bargaining

In the period under study, two major pieces of labor legislation were enacted by the United States Congress. The Taft-Hartley Act attempted to redress what was viewed by many as an imbalance in the labor law favoring unions. The main purpose of the Landrum-Griffin Act was to regulate the internal affairs of trade unions to guarantee democratic procedures and reduce the possibilities of corruption. The laws, interpreted by the National Labor Relations Board, the Representative of Labor (expressly responsible for the Landrum-Griffin Act), and the courts have established the method of determining union representation, modes of bargaining and conflicts, and internal union practices.

Representation

As noted in change 4, court rulings and the Taft-Hartley "free speech provision" have greatly expanded the extent to which employers can campaign against unions in NLRB elections, making the electoral process more an adversary procedure than had previously been the case. In addition, the Taft-Hartley Act outlawed closed-shop clauses, which made union membership a prerequisite for a job, and permitted states to outlaw the union shop, which required membership after employment. Evidence suggests that these changes have contributed to the gradual diminution of private sector unionism (Freeman and Medoff 1976; Ellwood and Fine 1980).

Bargaining Topics and Procedures

The government has also come to play a role in determining the subjects of collective bargaining, prescribing *mandatory topics* about which parties must bargain (as opposed to permissive topics, which they can choose not to discuss), and outlawing other topics. When the Supreme Court ruled in 1949 that pensions were a mandatory topic, there was a sharp increase in the proportion of the wage bill going to pensions in unionized industries. In the 1964 Fibreboard Case (which made contracting out a mandatory bargaining topic under certain conditions) the Supreme Court noted the extent to which the original intent of the Wagner Act (to get parties into a room to negotiate, but not to affect the substance of the negotiations) had been changed. "There was a time when one might have taken the view that . . . the courts have *no* power to determine the subjects about which parties must bargain. . . . Too much law has been built upon a contrary assumption."[15]

A second, more complex legal obligation on the two parties is "bargaining in good faith." In several important decisions, the NLRB and the courts have outlawed certain forms of bargaining—such as Boulwarism (the General Electric strategy of making its first offer the full and final offer and engaging in a tough propaganda program to sell the offer to workers)—and have sought to interpret the state of mind called "good faith." As there are no obligations to reach an agreement, however, it is unclear what effect the duty to bargain has on negotiations.[16]

5.7.2   Weapons of Conflict

The Taft-Hartley Act outlawed certain forms of conflict, making it an unfair labor practice for unions, as well as managements, to coerce employees, for instance by mass picketing, to engage in secondary boycotts, and to strike for jurisdictional purposes. The Landrum-Griffin Act added "hot cargo" clauses (in which management agrees to refuse to deal with other enterprises having labor disputes) to the list of illegal weapons of conflict.

5.7.3   Internal Union Practices

Far-reaching federal controls on the governance of unions were established by the Landrum-Griffin Act, passed following the sensational McClellan Committee hearings on criminal elements in trade unions: the electoral procedures in unions were brought under the law; a "bill of rights" was enacted to guarantee normal democratic freedoms to members; trusteeships over locals were restricted; and union leaders were ordered to report certain financial transactions.

To some extent the extensive and detailed regulation of collective bargaining and internal union democracy may be a necessary concomitant of the use of government-regulated elections to establish unions. Once the government has set up a procedure for organizing, next it can reasonably be expected to concern itself with the process and outcome.

5.7.4   Antibias Regulation of Personnel Policies

No institutional change has transformed the labor market more than the outlawing of discriminatory employment practices by Title VII of the Civil Rights Act of 1964 and the requirement that federal contractors engage in affirmative action under Executive Order 11246. "The world of the personnel manager was changed drastically as the EEO and the courts have enforced and implemented Title VII of the Civil Rights Act" (Miner and Miner 1978, p. 4). Many traditional modes of recruiting, testing, and selecting workers were ended by the Equal Employment Opportunity (EEO) laws, replaced by affirmative action searches and "fast tracks" to promote women and minorities. As table 5.5 indicates, a whole set of new personnel practices was initiated as a result of the EEO pressures of the government. As stated in the Bureau of National Affairs (1976):

> Equal Employment Opportunity (EEO) Programs complete with Affirmative Action Plans (AAP) are viewed as "a fact of life" by nearly all employers, and the personnel function has changed in a variety of ways as a result of the government's efforts to enforce the employment provisions of the act. [P. 1]

The muscle behind the EEO effort has been the court decisions, which first tended to weigh heavily the interests of protected groups as opposed to other workers. Through the early 1970s most court decisions tended to favor active equal employment and affirmative action programs. In the mid and late 1970s, however, the tone of court decisions changed. Instead of Griggs Power, which came down heavily against employment tests with disparate effects, there was *Washington* v. *Davis*, which sup-

Table 5.5   **New Personnel Practices Resulting from EEO**

Company Programs and Regulations	Percentage of Companies
1. Have *Formal* EEO Programs	86
Including Affirmative Action Plan	
(of those subject to OFCCP regulations)	96
2. Have Had Investigation or Other Action under Title VII	63
3. Have Made Changes in Selection Procedures for	
EEOC Reasons:	60
in testing procedures	39
in revised job qualifications	31
in application forms	20
in recruiting techniques	19
4. Have Instituted Special Recruiting Programs:	
for all minority workers	69
for minorities in professional/managerial positions	58
5. Have Instituted Programs to Insure EEO Policies	
are Implemented	
communications on EEO policy	95
follow-up personnel or EEO office	85
training sessions on EEO	67
periodic publications of EEO results	48
EEO achievements included in performance appraisals	33
6. Have Instituted Special Training Programs	
for entry-level jobs	16
for upgrading	24
for management positions	16

Source: Bureau of National Affairs Personnel Policies Forum, *Equal Employment Opportunity: Programs and Results*, PPF Survey No. 112, March 1976 (*lines 1–2*: table 9, p. 15; *line 3*: table 3, p. 4; *line 4*: table 1, p. 9; *line 5*: table 6, p. 9; *line 6*: table 5, p. 8).

ported tests for the District of Columbia police force. Instead of finding discrimination on the basis of statistical disparities, additional information on specific cases of discrimination was also required in several cases. In the Weber Case the entire notion of voluntary affirmative action that involved inverse discrimination came under attack. The decision of the court in favor of Kaiser Steel and the Steelworkers may have drawn the bounds, however, on the changed direction of court decisions.

There is a wide variety of evidence indicating that governmental equal employment efforts have substantially improved the economic position of black workers. As table 5.6 indicates, there was a marked acceleration in black economic progress post-1964, when the federal antibias effort began (Title VII of the Civil Rights Act outlawing discrimination took effect on 1 July 1965). As might be expected given

Table 5.6   Ratios of Nonwhite to White: Economic Position and Annual Changes in Ratios 1949–64 and 1964–76

	Year			Annual Change	
Males	1949/50	1964	1976	Before 1964	After 1964
Median wages and salaries:					
all workers:	.50	.59	.73	0.6	1.2
full-time, year-round workers:	.64[a]	.65	.77	0.1	1.0
Median income: Professionals	.57	.69	.84	1.1	2.1
Relative number of:					
professionals	.39	.45	.65	0.4	1.8
managers	.22	.22	.41	0.0	1.7
Females					
Median wages and salaries	.40	.58	.97	1.8	3.5
All workers:					
Full-time, year-round workers:	.57[a]	.69	.99	1.3	2.3
Relative number of:					
professionals	.47	.60	.83	0.9	2.1
clericals	.15	.33	.69	1.3	3.3

Source: Incomes from U.S. Bureau of Census, Current Population Reports, Consumer Income Series P–60. Employment from Census of Population, 1950 and U.S. Department of Labor, Handbook of Labor Statistics, 1977.
[a]1955.

pressures of affirmative action programs to place and promote minorities into higher level jobs that were previously closed to them, many of the gains were concentrated among the better educated and skilled. For the first time in American history, blacks began to obtain managerial and professional jobs in major corporations. The most rapid gains were made, it is important to recognize, by young blacks and by black women, both of whom attained rough economic parity with whites in many markets. Finally, most studies of the employment of blacks have found greater increases in employment in companies influenced by federal antibias and affirmative action pressures than in companies that are less influenced by such pressures (Burman 1973; Ashenfelter and Heckman 1976; Heckman and Wolpin 1976; see Goldstein and Smith 1976 for an exception).

While most would agree that at least some of the post-1964 black economic progress results from the effect of antibias laws on company employment practices, some have cited other factors as being important as well. Welch and Smith (1975) stress improvements in the quality of education obtained by blacks, while Butler and Heckman (1977) suggest that reduced work force participation of black relative to white workers may also have contributed to the observed changes.[17]

Though apparently less affected, the position of women appears to have also improved, in some respects, by the federal laws. Some women were moved into traditionally male occupations and others benefited from special promotion policies designed to alleviate underrepresentation in high level jobs.

5.7.5 Computerization

In addition to EEO pressures, the personnel practices of major corporations were also greatly affected by new computer techniques developed in the postwar period. For the first time, companies computerized available personnel files (some put together as a result of court cases regarding discrimination) which permits more detailed and rigorous tracking and analysis of internal labor markets. The new technology has begun and will continue to transform personnel policy into a more integral part of corporate policy-making.

5.7.6 Other Market Regulations

The federal government enacted several other major pieces of legislation regulating the labor market in the period under study. Among the most important were:

(a) The Coal Mine Health and Safety Act (1969), which established dust and ventilation standards in mines and compensation for victims of black lung disease. In the years following the Act, fatality rates fell among bituminous coalworkers, apparently, at least partially as a result of the regulations (Connerton 1978).

(b) The Occupational Safety and Health Act of 1970 (OSHA), which requires that places of employment be free from "recognized hazards that are causing or are likely to cause death or serious physical harm to employees" and mandates the Department of Labor to promulgate and enforce occupational health and safety standards. Despite the significant powers given to OSHA and efforts of the agency to monitor work places, it is generally agreed that OSHA failed to live up to its potential for reducing job injury and disease. There is an increasing realization of the complexities involved with health and safety problems, which will not yield to simplistic strategies based on simple approaches (see Ashford 1976; Smith 1976; Viscusi 1980).

(c) The Employee Retirement Income Security Act (ERISA), which mandates that all retirement plans be vested after ten years. It established financial standards for pensions and provided federal insurance for pension plans. As is often the case with governmental regulations, in addition to its planned effects on pension plans, ERISA appears to have had unanticipated effects causing a number of plans of small companies to be closed down.

(d) Extension of Minimum Wage coverage. While the level of the minimum wage has not changed relative to average wages, the fraction of the work force covered has increased greatly, which can be expected to increase its effect. In 1947, 56 percent of workers were covered by the minimum wage; by 1968 the fraction covered had risen to 79 percent.

(e) Age Discrimination in Employment Act, which outlaws discrimination against workers between the ages of forty and seventy, and the Rehabilitation Act of 1973, which outlaws discrimination against handicapped workers.

5.7.7 Spending and Taxation

In addition to direct regulations, the government has influenced the operation of the labor market through its social insurance and welfare manpower training and taxation policies. In the post-World War II period, many new programs were initiated and expenditures on existing programs increased while tax rates rose significantly.

In 1960 the United States federal expenditure on manpower programs was approximately $250 million; in 1975 expenditures were over $5 billion a year, more than a twentyfold increase. The legislative cornerstone of this expansion is the Comprehensive Employment and Training Act of 1973 (CETA), with its subsequent amendments, which is designed to provide training, employment, and related services for economically disadvantaged, unemployed, and underemployed persons. The major titles of CETA authorize: a nationwide program of employment and training services, including training, employment, counseling, testing, and placement administered for the most part by state and local governments; transitional public service employment and other manpower services in areas with high rates of unemployment; nationally sponsored training and job placement programs for such special groups as youth, criminal offenders, persons of limited English-speaking ability, seasonal farmworkers, and others with particular market disadvantages; the Job Corps program of intensive education, training, and counseling for disadvantaged youth; and temporary emergency public service jobs to reduce the impact of high unemployment. For persons on welfare, the Work Incentive (WIN) program is designed to provide comparable aid in obtaining skills and finding jobs. In 1976 there were about 2.5 million persons in CETA programs and over two million registered for WIN. While the results of studies of manpower training programs are not uniformly positive, it appears that trainees may have benefited from their experience, though the return to the investment may not be extremely high (Ashenfelter 1978).

Other programs gave direct financial aid to persons unable to work or temporarily out of work. Public social welfare expenditures, broadly defined—the most important of which is Aid to Dependent Children, which provides money largely for families lacking a male head of household—increased drastically in the 1960s and 1970s, from 10 percent of

GNP in 1960 to 19 percent in 1975. Other major programs include social security disability insurance, and workmen's compensation, which assist persons injured at work. Another set of programs seeks to provide funds for particular types of purchases. In 1976, $5.6 billion were given in food stamps to help low income families with food coupons. These stamps can be used only for purchases of food. Medicare similarly provides funds for the medical expenses of older persons. Yet another, unemployment insurance, provides money for persons who have lost their jobs.[18]

The effects of these various programs are twofold. On the one hand, they clearly raise the economic well-being of persons suffering economic distress. One estimate of the net effect of the welfare programs suggests that upwards of sixteen million persons have been raised above the official poverty level.[19] On the other hand, the programs also reduce the incentive to work and thus reduce labor force participation.

On the taxation side, the gap between before and after tax earnings has grown steadily in the post-World War II period, as a result of increases in income, social security, and other taxes. In 1949 taxes took up 23 percent of net national product; in 1975 taxes amounted to 33 percent of net national product (NNP). In 1949 the individual federal income taxes were 7.6 percent of NNP, while social insurance taxes accounted for 2.3 percent. By 1979 the income tax share was 11.5 percent and the social security share 7.2 percent. While there does not exist a set of widely accepted estimates of the effect of taxes on the quantity, quality, and effort devoted to work, many believe that the increased gap between what employers pay and what workers receive in earnings has significantly affected the market.[20]

5.8 · Change 6: Structure and Composition of Wages

Once thought of as relatively inflexible, the structure of wages in the United States, by which I mean the differentials paid workers categorized in various ways, underwent significant change in the post-World War II period. Educated workers, young workers, and many highly skilled workers had slower increases in wages than less educated, older, or less skilled workers in the 1970s after more rapid increases in the 1950s and 1960s. Black workers, as noted, had greater increases in earnings than white workers. While differentials may not have changed as rapidly as might be desired for optimal allocation of workers or elimination of discriminatory differences, there is no gainsaying the flexibility of relative wages in responding to the changes in the supply-demand balance. Table 5.7 summarizes evidence on some of the principal changes in the wage structure in post-World War II years.

Table 5.7   Changes in the Structure of Earnings in the United States

	Ratios of Earnings	
	1968	1975–79
Education[a]		
College/high school men		
all	1.53	1.38[b]
25–34	1.38	1.16[b]
Age		
Men 25–34/men 45–54		
all	.85	.79[c]
college	.72	.61[c]
Industry		
Mining/all private	1.11	1.28[d]
Construction/all private	1.53	1.32[d]
Specific Skills Group		
R&D doctorate women/all full-time workers	2.68	2.47[c]
Professors/all full-time workers	2.50[e]	2.20[f]

Sources: R. Freeman, "Effect of Demographic Factors on Age-Earnings Profile," *Journal of Human Resources*, vol. 14 (Summer 1979), table 2; ———. "The Facts About the Declining Economic Value of College," *Journal of Human Resources*, vol. 15 (Winter 1980), table 1; U.S. Department of Labor, *Employment and Training Report of the President 1977*, Washington, D.C.: GPO, 1978, table C–3, and *Monthly Labor Review*, vol. 102 (August 1979), table 14.

[a]Education data for 1977 has been adjusted for change in imputation procedure in 1975.
[b]1977.
[c]1975.
[d]1979.
[e]1969–70.
[f]1975–76.

5.8.1   Education

One of the most widely heralded changes in the structure of wages has been the decline in the advantage received by college graduate men. As table 5.7 shows, from the 1950s through the 1960s, college men earned a sizable differential over men with just high school training. In the 1970s, however, the differential eroded rapidly—part and parcel of the declining occupational position of graduates depicted in table 5.3. The drop in the advantage to college workers was most pronounced among the young, with starting bachelor's graduates in several cases earning much less in real terms in the mid-1970s than comparable workers earned at the end of the 1960s. For instance, the real pay for beginning B.S. science majors dropped by 21 percent from 1969 to 1975 and that of social science or humanities majors by 23 percent.[21] Since the direct costs of college rose in the period, the rate of return to college graduates fell markedly, which in turn lowered enrollment rates among young persons.

The principal cause of the decline in the relative earnings of young college graduates appears to be the enormous increase in the number of graduates in the 1970s—the result of the high fraction of (baby boom) young persons enrolling for higher education—rather than decreased demand for college relative to high school graduates. Viewed strictly from a human-capital investment interpretation, however, an alternative explanation of the change can be developed: namely that the wages of young graduates have fallen because graduates are making greater investments in on-the-job training as a means of coping with the increased supply. This view suggests that the earnings of the workers who graduated in the 1970s will rise rapidly in the 1980s (Welch and Smith). While the long-term significance of the depressed college market of the 1970s thus will not be clear for some time,[22] the changes of the period show dramatically the impact of supply and demand on relative earnings and investments in skills.

Another important change in the structure of wages has been a marked twist in age-earnings profiles. As table 5.7 shows, in 1968, 25 to 34-year-old men earned 15 percent less than 45 to 54-year-old men. By 1975 the differential had risen to 21 percent. Among college men, the ratio of 25 to 34-year-olds' earnings to those of 45 to 54-year-olds fell from .72 in 1968 to .61 in 1975. The remarkable increase in the income advantage of older over younger male workers in the period appears to be primarily due to the changed age composition of the work force noted earlier, apparently because younger and older male workers are imperfect substitutes in production. It previously eased the inflow of the large numbers of young workers of the period into employment and enabled the market to adjust to the baby-boom cohort without massive increases in youth unemployment. It may also have created, however, a lifetime "cohort earnings gap" for the entrants of the 1970s. Whether the sizable drop in the earnings of the young in the 1970s will persist, however, remains to be seen (Welch and Smith 1978).

5.8.2 Specific Skills Groups

Workers in certain occupational and industrial groups also experienced marked changes in earnings relative to other workers in the postwar period. In the 1960s, construction average hourly earnings zoomed, rising from 1.26 times those in manufacturing in 1947 to 1.56 times those in manufacturing in 1969, only to fall to 1.37 times those in manufacturing by 1979. Scientists, engineers, college faculty, and doctorate personnel enjoyed substantial increases in income in the sixties and sluggish increases in the seventies. Workers in the oil industry had sizable gains in the 1970s, as did those in coal.

Overall, the pattern of the 1970s was toward lower differentials between more and less skilled workers, in contrast to stable or rising differentials in the 1950s and 1960s. As in other changes in the wage structure, the prime reason appears to be shifts in the demand for those workers compared to the supply.

Finally, as noted earlier, one of the major changes in the wage structure occurred along the racial dimension. Black-white differences diminished significantly, apparently as a result of increased demand for labor spurred by governmental EEO efforts.

5.8.3 Significance

The finding that relative wages have changed in the postwar period in response to labor market conditions suggests that the price system has at the least operated in the right direction in rewarding and allocating workers among sectors. According to the postwar experience, large increases in numbers of workers in particular groups, relative to demand, produced sizable drops in wages relative to those of other workers, while large decreases had the opposite effect.

5.8.4 Composition of the Wage Bill

Table 5.8 documents another important change in the pattern of wage payments in the United States: the increased importance of fringe or supplementary benefits. By 1977 over one-third of compensation in major companies consisted of fringes, with pension plans, vacation and holiday pay, and health insurance constituting the bulk of privately agreed-upon fringes and social security, the most important component of legally required payments.

There are several reasons for the growth of fringe benefits: the tax advantages which accrue to most fringes, increased worker desires for certain benefits as incomes rise, union pressures for fringes following rulings that fringes are valid bargaining topics (fringe benefits are a larger share of wage bills in union than in nonunion companies), and changes in social security and other laws.

While there are serious problems in international comparisons of wage bills, particularly with regard to the institutional structure of work forces (distinction between regular and temporary workers, for example), available data suggest that the tendency for a larger share of compensation to take the form of fringes is not unique to the United States, and that the ratio of supplementary payments to earnings in the United States is by no means high on an international scale. For example, the following figures show the comparative ratios of additional compensation to hourly earnings for 1960 and 1978 (BLS 1978).

	1960	*1978*
United States	18.0	34.5
Italy	71.7	93.4
Germany	35.0	60.9
United Kingdom	26.5	29.4
Canada	15.4	24.1
Sweden	16.0	60.7
France	54.5	75.7

The increased role of supplementary or fringe benefits has substantially changed the nature of renumeration for work and complicated the meaning to be attached to "wages." Whether workers behave differently when a sizable proportion of their pay does not appear in the weekly pay check than when it does has not been seriously investigated, however.

5.9   Change 7: Unemployment and Wage Inflation

From the point of view of national policy two basic labor market problems plague national economics: unemployment and hourly wage inflation. In the post-World War II period under study, the level of unemployment drifted upward, the composition of unemployment changed, and there was a significant change in the level of wage inflation and its link to unemployment and aggregate economic activity.

5.9.1   Level of Composition and Unemployment

The level of unemployment in the United States appears to have increased in the 1970s relative to the 1950s and 1960s. From 1950 to 1959 unemployment averaged 4.5 percent per year, with a range from 2.9 percent to 6.8 percent. From 1960 to 1969, the average was slightly higher at 4.8 percent, with a range from 3.5 percent to 6.7 percent. From 1970 to 1977, however, unemployment averaged 6.3 percent, with a range from 4.8 percent to 8.5 percent.[23] Analysis of the unemployment rates of separate groups of workers shows that, while changes in the demographic composition of the work force have contributed to the higher rate, the upward drift in the 1970s is not primarily the result of the changing mix of workers but is, instead, a phenomenon found among virtually all groups of workers, though it is more pronounced among some than among others. While part of the upward drift in unemployment rates may be attributable to changes in unemployment insurance, which leads some workers to remain on unemployment compensation for large periods of time due to the receipt of funds while out of work, most analysts would attribute the higher rates of unemployment to the state of the aggregate economy—in particular, the level of demand for labor (itself affected by changes in oil and other natural resource prices) and to governmental macroeconomic policy. Most other major countries have also experienced an increase in unemployment rates in the 1970s, pointing to world market conditions as an underlying cause of the problem.

The incidence of unemployment in the United States has also changed significantly, with young workers in general and black teenagers in particular having higher rates of unemployment relative to other workers

Table 5.8   **Changes in the Composition of the Wage Bill in Large Companies: Fringe Benefits as a Percentage of Payroll Expenses**

	1951	1977	Change
Total	18.7	36.7	+18.0
1. Legally Required Payments	3.5	8.5	+5.0
a. OAS(DH)I	1.4	5.4	+4.0
b. Unemployment compensation	1.4	1.5	+0.1
c. Workmen's compensation	0.6	1.5	+0.9
d. Railroad retirement tax, etc.	0.1	0.0	−0.1
2. Pension, Insurance, & Other Agreed-upon Payments	5.4	12.7	+7.3
a. Pension plan premiums, etc.	3.6	5.9	+2.3
b. Life insurance premiums, etc.	1.4	5.9	+4.5
c. i. separation or termination pay allowances	*	**	—
ii. salary continuation or long-term disability	**	0.2	—
d. Dental insurance premiums	**	0.2	—
e. Discounts on goods and services	0.2	0.1	−0.1
f. Employee meals	***	0.2	—
g. Miscellaneous	0.2	0.2	—
3. Paid Rest Periods, Etc.	1.9	3.5	+1.6
4. Payments for Time not Worked	6.0	9.8	+3.8
a. Paid vacations	3.2	5.0	+1.8
b. Holidays	2.0	3.2	+1.2
c. Sick leave	0.6	1.2	+0.6
d. Payments for National Guard duty, jury, Death in family, other personal, etc.	0.2	0.4	+0.2
5. Other Items	1.9	2.2	+0.3
a. Profit sharing	0.7	1.1	+0.4
b. Employee thrift plans	***	0.4	—
c. Bonuses	1.0	0.4	−0.6
d. Employee education expenditures	***	0.1	—
e. Special wage payments ordered by courts, payments to union stewards, etc.	0.2	0.2	0.0
Total as ¢/Hour	31.5	226.4	+194.9
Total as $/Year-Employee	644.0	4692.0	+4048.0

Source: U.S. Chamber of Commerce, *Employee Benefits* 1951 and 1977.

*< .05%.

**not included.

***included in 2g miscellaneous in 1951.

than in the past, exacerbating the concentration of and inequality in unemployment. On the other end of the spectrum, white-collar workers and more highly educated workers have also had higher rates of unemployment relative to others than in the past.

The changing patterns of unemployment rates over time is examined in figure 5.4 in terms of the rates of unemployment for selected groups of workers and the rates predicted by regression of those rates on those of other workers. When the deviation between actual and predicted rates rises over time, the rate of the specified group worsens relative to the other group, and converse is true if the deviations decline over time.

The figure shows the following:

1. A moderate increase in the employment rate of 16 to 19-year-old white young persons at given levels of total unemployment in the 1960s but not in the 1970s.
2. A more surprising and less noticed increase in the unemployment of 25 to 34-year-old white men relative to older workers, possibly attributable to demographic forces.
3. A marked increase in the unemployment rate of black teenagers relative to the total unemployment rate. The causes of the extraordinary deterioration in the employment position of these youths

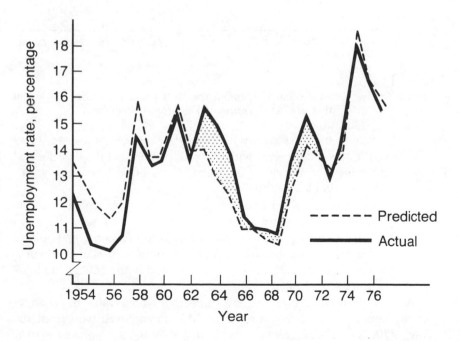

Fig. 5.4a   Actual unemployment for 16–19 year old whites versus that predicted from total unemployment rate.

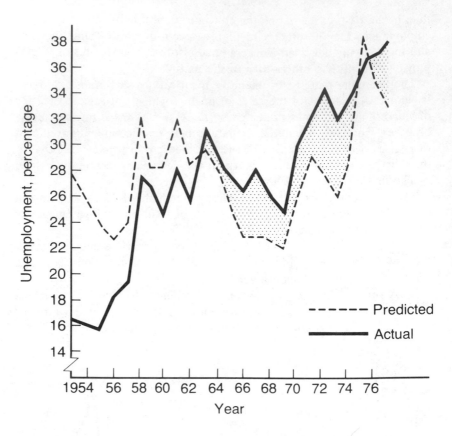

Fig. 5.4b   Actual unemployment for 16–19 year old nonwhites versus that predicted from total unemployment rate.

has yet to be satisfactorily explained. Whatever the causes, however, few would disagree with the proposition that the deteriorated employment of nonwhite youth constitutes one of the major socioeconomic problems of the period.

4. An increase in the unemployment rate of white-collar workers relative to blue-collar workers.

5. An increase in the unemployment rate of professional and college trained workers relative to the less skilled and less educated workers, yet another indicator of the turnaround in the college job market discussed earlier.

As a result of the changed pattern of unemployment rates and changes in the composition of the work force, the unemployed worker of the late 1970s had very different characteristics than the unemployed worker in earlier years. The unemployed worker of the late 1970s was more likely to be young, black, and also highly educated and skilled than in the past.

The changing composition of unemployment suggests the need for different policies to aid the jobless than in the past. Young unemployed workers, particularly minority youth in inner cities, have a greater need for job training and related skill acquisition than the unemployed experienced heads of households of previous periods. Unemployed professional, managerial, and other white-collar or college educated workers also represent a new problem, for which existing policies may be inadequate.

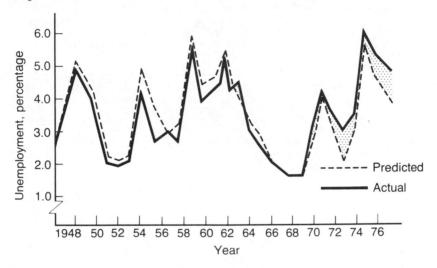

Fig. 5.4c   Actual unemployment for 25–34 year old white men versus that predicted from 35–44 year old white male rate.

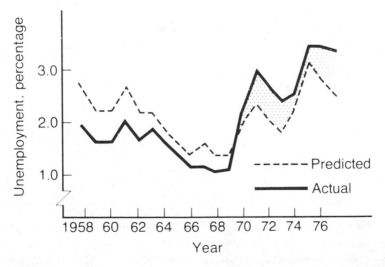

Fig. 5.4d   Actual white-collar unemployment versus that predicted from blue-collar unemployment rate.

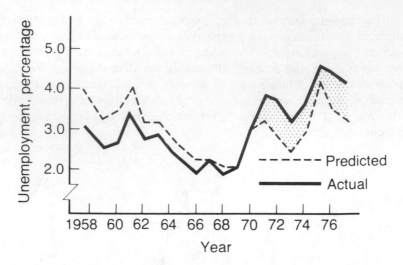

Fig. 5.4e   Actual unemployment of professional, technical, and kindred workers versus that predicted from blue-collar unemployment rate.

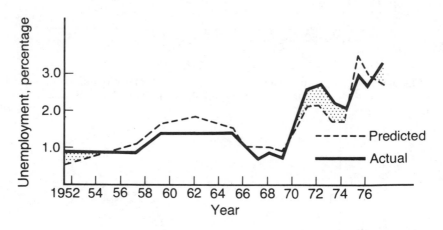

Fig. 5.4f   Actual unemployment of college graduates (four or more years) versus that predicted from high school graduate (four years) rate.

5.9.2   Wage Inflation

Concordant with the upward drift in unemployment over the postwar period has been an increase in the average rate of wage inflation, creating a substantial policy problem. From 1950 to 1959, hourly compensation of all persons in private businesses increased by 5.1 percent per annum; from 1960 to 1969, hourly compensation of all persons in private business increased by 4.9 percent per annum; from 1970 to 1977, the rate of increase was 7.1 percent. As figure 5.5 shows, the increase in wage inflation in the 1970s despite increased unemployment appears to have significantly raised the Phillips curve relation which once guided thinking on the unemployment-inflation problem. Whereas in the 1950s and the 1960s a level of unemployment of 6.0 percent to 7.0 percent was associated with wage inflation of 4.0 percent to 5.0 percent, in the 1970s it was associated with wage increases nearly twice as high. While it is not universally agreed that the experience of the 1970s proves that there is no long-term stable tradeoff between unemployment and hourly wage inflation, there is no doubt that whatever relation exists is quite unstable and an inadequate guide to policy.

More detailed analyses of the cyclical behavior of wages have shown a further change in the responsiveness of wage to unemployment and

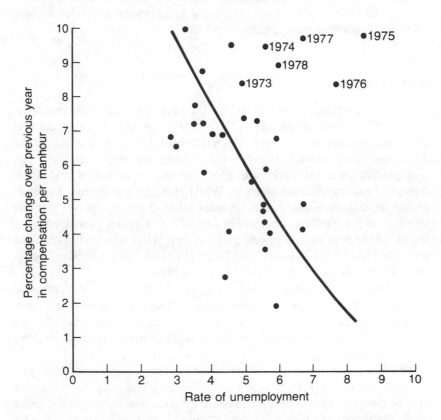

Fig. 5.5   The relation of unemployment to changes in money wages in the United States, 1948–79. Data from U.S. Department of Labor 1978, tables G–2, A–19.

aggregate cyclical conditions in the period under study: a sizable decline in the reduction in the rate of wage inflation associated with a given shortfall in aggregate activity. According to one set of estimates, the effect of unemployment on the rate of change in wages has become significantly lower in the postwar period than in the earlier part of the twentieth century (Sachs 1978). One important reason for the declining cyclical sensitivity of wages is the spread of long-term collective bargaining contracts. At the outset of the postwar period most contracts covered a one-year period. By the 1970s, most major industrial agreements were written for a three-year period. Wages set over a three-year period are likely to be unresponsive to unemployment or other measures of market conditions except in the year the contract is signed. Other factors, such as effective macroeconomic policy, have also been cited as potential causes of the decreased cyclical responsiveness of wages (Sachs 1978). The upward shift and reduced slope of the unemployment-wage change schedule make aggregate economic policy more difficult, which directs attention to a more disaggregated and sectoral approach to both unemployment and wage inflation problems.

5.10   Conclusion

"Each generation believes itself on the verge of a new economic era, an era of fundamental change" (NBER 1929, p. ix). In three decades examined in this study, seven major changes have taken place in the American labor market, significantly altering the wages, employment, and institutions at the workplace. First, the rate of growth of real wages and productivity declined sharply. While some of the decline is attributable to sectoral shifts in employment—the changing age-sex composition of the work force, changes in capital-labor ratios, increased regulation, changes in energy prices, and reduced R&D effect—for the most part, the retardation in growth is a story of changes in the famous "residual," about which, by definition, we know little.

Second, there have been sizable demographic changes in the composition of employment: more women workers, more young workers, more educated workers, and fewer older male workers. In part these changes can be explained by changes in labor market incentives, but at least some remain a puzzle.

Third, the composition of employment has changed substantially, with the number of workers in white-collar and skilled jobs, in the South and Southwest, and in local and state government employment rising while the number in blue-collar and lower skilled jobs has declined. One noticeable pattern has been that employment in skilled areas has fallen short of the growth of the supply of educated labor, with a resultant drop in the quality of jobs held by the educated. Another is for employment changes to vary more across sectors than wage changes.

Fourth, the trade union share of the work force has diminished substantially, with a sharp drop in the proportion unionized in the private sector overpowering a rise in the proportion organized in the public sector. Changes in the age-sex-skill mix of the work force explain perhaps 60 percent of the decline in private sector organization, but increased managerial opposition and effectiveness in contesting NLRB elections is also important in accounting for the diminished number of private sector unionism. Growth of public sector organization appears to be closely linked to changes in public sector labor relations laws.

Fifth, governmental regulation of the labor market and of the internal operation of management and labor has been greatly expanded. Equal employment legislation and affirmative action requirements have changed the personnel function. A wide variety of acts, such as the Occupational Health and Safety Act or the Employee Retirement Insurance Security Act, have changed the "rules" of labor market behavior, in some cases with sizable effects on basic economic factors.

Sixth, the structure of earnings has been significantly altered by shifts in the demand/supply balance. In the period studied, college graduates, particularly the young and those in the educational sector, young male workers, and those in several highly skilled occupations have suffered declines in relative earnings. Black workers have significantly gained compared to white workers. Fringe benefits increased in importance in the wage package.

Seventh, the composition of unemployment and its relation to wage inflation has also undergone major change. Young black workers and highly educated men have come to bear a greater share of unemployment. The rate of inflation consistent with particular levels of unemployment has increased rapidly.

5.10.1   Comparisons with 1929 NBER Conference

The changes delineated in this paper can be fruitfully compared to those examined half a century earlier at the 1929 NBER Conference on Recent Economic Changes, in which Leo Wolman wrote a section on labor. Which of the seven changes are similar to those cited in the earlier volume? To what extent do our changes represent continuation of long-term developments and to what extent do they significantly diverge from historical changes? Answers to these questions should provide perspective on the nature of changes in the post-World War II period.

Four of our changes, while different in some cases in direction, have definite parallels with those in the earlier period.

In 1929, as in 1979, the changing demographic structure of the work force, due to declining birth rates and immigration was of some concern.

In 1929, however, the increased participation of women was not given serious attention.

Similarly, in 1929, as in 1979, patterns of change in the composition of employment—increases in white-collar and skilled jobs, declines in farming—received attention. While the 1970s may be relatively unique in that growth of employment in skilled areas has fallen short of the growth of educated labor there is nothing surprising in the existence of significant shifts in employment among sectors.

Sizable changes in the wage structure were also observed in the 1929 volume. Though the direction and nature of changes differed fundamentally between the periods, changes in relative wages appear to be a hallmark of the United States labor market.

Decline in unionization in the 1920s parallels to some extent the decline in the post-World War II period, though here more fundamental differences also arise. In the 1920s, the total number of union members, as well as the union share of the work force fell, whereas in the post-World War II period, union membership rose, while the proportion of workers covered fell. Moreover, there was nothing in the 1920s comparable to the spurt in public sector organization in the later period. Still, in the period covered by this essay and in the earlier period, declines in unionization were a major development.

Three of our seven changes, by contrast, seem to differ greatly from those stressed in the 1929 volume.

First, the latter period experienced increased governmental regulation of the labor market and of the internal operations of management and labor. Governmental intervention in the market following World War I seems to have been sufficiently modest as to draw virtually no attention from analysts. Peacetime growth of governmental regulation in the recent decades appears to be a relatively unique development.

Second, the concern of the 1970s over the growth of real wages and productivity had no parallel in the earlier period of time. In the 1929 conference, continued rapid advance of the economy was assured by all: "The spread of higher living standards [is] not new, but in its degree and scope it has taken on new importance" (NBER 1929, p. xi). The loss of confidence in growth, due to the sluggish performance in the 1970s, is a strikingly new development.

Third, the 1970s saw a drift upward in both unemployment and rates of wage inflation, constituting the aggregate economic problem of that decade. By contrast, in 1929, there was little concern with overall levels of unemployment (which were viewed as satisfactory) or with inflation, due to an "increasing tendency" toward price stability.

Finally, it is important to remember that all of the labor market changes stressed in the 1929 conference were, of course, completely overshadowed by the change about to occur—the Great Depression, the development of which no analyst managed to foresee. I hope the changes examined in this paper will not be overshadowed by forces escaping current attention that will yield a new economic disaster.

Notes

1. This can be seen by examining the earnings by industry data in BLS (1979c, table 92). In coal the rate of increase in real earnings rose from 1.6 percent (1950–69) to 1.8 percent (1969–77), using the CPI Deflater.

2. Regression of the log of output per man-hour (O) on unemployment (U), trend (T) and trend post-1970 (T70) yielded:

$$O = 3.97 + \underset{(.001)}{.003T} - \underset{(.003)}{.010U} - \underset{(.002)}{.012T70} \qquad R^2 = .995$$

Regression of the log of real compensation per man-hour (C) on the same variables yielded:

$$C = 3.97 + \underset{(.0004)}{.031T} - \underset{(.001)}{.019T70} + \underset{(.002)}{.000U} \qquad R^2 = .998$$

An alternative way of showing the changed trend in productivity growth and real wages is to assume that they follow a random walk with a drift and analyze changes (Δ) in the variables. (Suggested by Orley Ashenfelter.) The results of this calculation are given below:

$$\Delta O = -.005 - \underset{(.001)}{.005T70} + \underset{(.003)}{.008U} - \underset{(.003)}{.007\Delta U} \qquad R^2 = .366$$

$$\Delta C = .02 - \underset{(.001)}{.003T70} + \underset{(.003)}{.002U} - \underset{(.002)}{.004\Delta U} \qquad R^2 = .270$$

3. BLS 1978. If one correlates the rate of growth of real wage for 1967 to 1977 with the level of real wages in 1967 in that document, one does find a negative Spearman rank correlation of −.55, indicating that there is a pattern for slower growth in higher wage countries. However, less than 25 percent of the country variation in real wage growth can be explained by variation in initial levels.

4. Thus the United States lags more in real wage growth than in productivity growth.

5. All figures are from BLS (1979c) except for the illegal alien figure which is a rough estimate from M. Piore (pers. comm.).

6. Estimated by multiplying the percentage of all households composed of husband-wife families by the percentage of those families with husbands in the labor force and wives not. A comparable figure for 1955 was 46 percent. See BLS (1979c, table 27) and U.S. Department of Commerce (1977, table 50).

7. See Freeman (1976a) for these and related data.

8. See, for example, Ashenfelter and Heckman (1974, pp. 73–86). For a review of the time series literature see J. Mincer (1966).

9. Figures for 1975 were estimated by dividing current (1975) dollars of consumer durables of $497 billion as reported in the U.S. Bureau of Census (1977, p. 428, table 695), by 71.1 million households (p. xiii) with 1952 data for trend

from U.S. Bureau of Census (1975, p. 252), and (1960, p. 15). The 1952 value was $2,079 (in 1958 dollars).

10. This is based on an index of job satisfaction rather than a single measure. See Quinn and Staines (1978, table 18.5).

11. BLS 1977 (pp. 4, 313). See BLS (1979a, p. 75) for coal mining, and BLS (1978, p. 64) for aircraft and parts.

12. The data for three digit census occupations are from Freeman (1980b). The other data were calculated from BLS (1979c, table 45 and table 95).

13. Data from 1977: numbers in elections won by unions from NLRB (1977, p. 294); numbers of nonagricultural workers from BLS (1979c, table 42). Data for earlier years in Freeman and Medoff (1976).

14. This estimate is obtained by calculating the unionization rate one would expect in one year given the fractions organized of various demographic groups in another year.

15. U.S. Supreme Court decision in Fibreboard Case.

16. Dunlop and Bok (1970) among others, have argued that the duty to bargain has little impact. For a contrary view see Ross (1965).

17. For a survey of the literature see Freeman (1980c). The Butler and Heckman (1977) survey is unfortunately marred by use of incorrect data, which leads to an underestimate of the effect of post-1964 governmental policy.

18. Social insurance statistics taken from U.S. Bureau of the Census (1977, line 459, p. xvii; line 630, p. xix).

19. Calculated from data in Paglin (1977).

20. Calculated from data in Tax Foundation (1977, tables 15, 21, and 82).

21. See Freeman (1976a) for this and other related evidence on the falling value of college.

22. According to some analysts, the college job market will improve for new graduates in the 1980s when the supply of new degree recipients falls.

23. Calculated from data in BLS (1979c, table A–1).

---

2. John T. Dunlop

The Changing Character of Labor Markets

The introduction by the Committee on Recent Economic Changes to John Maurice Clark's *Strategic Factors in Business Cycles* published by the National Bureau of Economic Research in 1935 contains at least two ideas for this anniversary. First, the committee addressed "the great question that we face as a nation: which factors are and which are not amenable to purposive control by public or private agencies?" (p. xi).

Clark stated that "a factor may be said to have strategic importance if it has real power to control other factors, and . . . it has peculiar strategic importance if, in addition, we have power to control it; if it is not, like the weather, beyond the reach of anything we can do." (pp. 6–7).

The quality of being amenable to purposive control depends on the

John T. Dunlop is Lamont University Professor, Harvard University.

time frame. If one regards strategic factors as subject to control in a five- or ten-year framework, one is dealing with a moderate economic term in which to secure a turnaround, but an aeon in political time, normally beyond the perspective or concern of our political process. In this conflict between economic and political time lies one of our nation's most paralyzing characteristics of the period under review.

The second idea stated in the committee's introduction is reflected in the composition of this conference:

> Effective results can be achieved only by putting to work the results of scientific analysis and continued statistical investigation in the realm of practical affairs. What is perhaps more needed at the present time than anything else is the development of the means of coordinating and utilizing the experience of men of affairs and the results of economic research. [P. x]

This theme deserves separate consideration in the present conference, since today, those engaged in research and those making public policy are neither listening to each other nor communicating much that is relevant to one another.

The idea of strategic factors, amenable to purposive control, suggests that we might examine Prof. Richard B. Freeman's list of changes or factors operative in the period 1948–80—as well as those of other papers—with this concept in mind. The idea of factors that are controllable is also a fruitful framework in which to view the future, provided one is open-minded as to means of control or persuasion. Several of Freeman's list of changes are clearly not to be classed as strategic, although this appraisal in no way minimizes their importance in generating other significant changes. The changed composition of the labor force (change 2)—age, sex, and educational features—as well as change in the composition of labor demand and employment and the wage structure (change 3 and part of change 6) are clearly forces that have to be largely accepted in any decade. It would have been appropriate for Freeman also to develop the shifts in employment regionally and between the suburbs and central city and to place emphasis upon the growing significance of undocumented aliens.

The following discussion treats several of Freeman's other categories of change (changes 4 and 5 and part of change 7) that might be regarded as strategic in the period of a decade in the sense of being amenable to purposive control. (Change 1 concerning real wages and productivity is passed over here since there is a whole session related to that topic.)

Freeman's Change 4: Declining Proportion of Workers in Trade Unions

The number of employees in labor organizations is a strategic factor in that it is subject in a decade's perspective to influence by the policies and activities of public and private managements, by governments as rule-makers, and by labor organizations themselves in their organizing activities and collective bargaining policies. American management has generally been more hostile to the presence of unions in enterprises than have managements in other advanced Western countries. One of the key questions for the decade ahead is whether more managements will find this historic bias unsatisfactory on balance in dealing with challenges to management in the political and international arena in such areas as corporate governance, trade policy, regulatory processes, regional development, and taxation issues. Some larger enterprises may find a moderation of hostility and more accommodating approaches to be desirable. The "neutrality letter" of General Motors, restricting forms of hostility permitted by law, is illustrative of this possibility.

Labor and management do not adequately recognize that union policies in collective bargaining are themselves one of the strategic ways in which union growth is influenced, at times adversely. Union capacity to extract gains in collective bargaining is often greater than its capacity to organize domestic or foreign competition, resulting in the gradual erosion of a highly organized sector. In the 1920s, railroads, coal mining, and construction—among the highest organized sectors—suffered declines in union organization, in part as a result of the consequences of collective bargaining policies, while employment grew in the new unorganized industries such as automobiles, electrical manufacturing, rubber, and glass. In the 1970s, employment again eroded under highly organized union agreements in such industries as meat-packing, steel, construction, master-freight trucking, and maritime, while employment expanded in unorganized service industries, such as professional employment and clerical occupations, and at the same time shifted to the sunbelt that was resistant to union representation. It is a fundamental problem to collective bargaining in the decade ahead to transform bargaining structures in many key organized sectors, such as trucking, steel, construction, rubber, and retail food, in which employment is eroding under agreements (see Weber 1979, p. D–2). Separate provisions or agreements may be required, for instance, to cover local cartage, short hauls, and special products in the trucking industry rather than to include these under the master-freight agreement as at present, and separate provisions likewise may be more appropriate for rubber plants, other than those devoted to tires and tubes, that produce rubber belting or footwear.

Public policy in legislation and administration in numerous ways affects the climate for union growth and the opposition of managements. Union growth is influenced by many external factors, but the policies of labor organizations, managements, and government constitute a strategic factor.

It is somewhat ironical that nowhere does Freeman tell us the absolute numbers of union members, only the declining proportion of nonagricultural workers reported as dues-paying members of unions. But the fact is that unions and employee organizations, such as the National Education Association (NEA) or the baseball players who act like unions, increased their dues-paying membership by 60 percent, or 9 million members, in the period 1948 to date, thus expanding membership from 15 to 24 million. The 1920s were a very different era since there was a marked absolute decline from a peak of 4.8 million members in 1920 to 3.2 million in 1930, and 2.8 million in 1933 (Troy 1965, pp. 1–2). (The percentage of nonagricultural employees members of unions declined from 19 to 11 percent.)

The share of the nonagricultural work force in labor organizations, moreover, is scarcely an all-purpose measure of union strength or influence—at the workplace, in a community, or in the larger society—on compensation, on the role of the strike, on legislative matters, on voting patterns, on the role of retired members who are not counted, or on public opinion or the community. It is hard to believe that labor organization influence in the society today, in the year of the National Accord, is one-fourth less in some gross sense, than it was in 1948, one year after the Taft-Hartley Act was enacted.

Labor organizations and collective bargaining have been major factors contributing to the homogenization of the rules of work places under the direction of larger enterprises in the postwar period, whether organized or not. A major influence of labor organizations has been on the managers and their policies in larger unorganized establishments. In larger companies, particularly those that encompass both organized and unorganized establishments and units, considerable attention is directed by managers to see that wages and salaries, benefits and policies relating to employment, promotions, layoffs, transfers, and a host of personnel rules do not favor one group over others in similar occupations. Union membership figures, or fractions of the labor force paying union dues, cannot reflect this influence. Other factors have been working in the same direction, such as the training of managers, the professionalism of personnel, and public policies, but the dominant influence has been collective bargaining and potential organization.

There is a strange lacuna in Freeman's recital (in change 5) of the major enhancement of government regulations in the labor market of the period 1948–80. He refers to equal employment opportunity legislation, OSHA, pension plan regulation, and the expanded scope of the obligation to bargain under the National Labor Relations Act. He fails to relate this expansion in regulation to the legislative role of organized labor despite its falling rate of growth in dues-paying membership. He might also have included statutes and regulations against age discrimination, the handicapped, social security and disability legislation, and minimum wage and hours laws. The Civil Rights Act of 1964 contains Title VII only because George Meany insisted, on behalf of the labor movement, that it be included. On the eighth floor of the AFL-CIO building hangs an exhibit with 100 pens used by President Johnson in the middle 1960s to sign major legislation advocated by the labor movement. Legislative programs of the Federation, from its inception a hundred years ago, have encountered opposition from management and others, but their success cannot narrowly be related to the percent of the work force paying dues to unions.

The patterns of union growth constitute a large subject for a brief commentary. Econometric models have not been very helpful, in my view, and Freeman is correct that "unionism has traditionally grown in sudden spurts which were never predicted by experts."[1] Over the past hundred years, labor organization in this country has grown appreciably in a relatively few years, no more than one-fourth of the total years—1884–86; 1896–1901; 1916–20; 1933–37; 1940–48; 1951–53. The normal state of affairs has been that the labor movement has had to run hard to stand still. Major breakthroughs to new industries, occupations, and locations seem to take place under the impact of special social and political circumstances that are often long-term in the making.

Freeman's Change 7: Wage Inflation and Economic Policy-Making

In my experience the procedural fundamental of a policy of wage restraint in a period of inflation in this country is the sympathetic involvement of leading representatives of labor organizations and management. The substantive fundamental of a wage restraint program is various standards that allow the gradual restoration of historical relativities in wages, salaries, and benefits, or the attainment of those which are emergent or which correct the distortions created by the stabilization program itself, often in an earlier phase (Dunlop and Fedor 1977, pp. 235–59). (The wage differentials created by different standards for COLA—cost of living adjustments—and non-COLA increases in the 1978–79 program are illustrative.)

There have been two quite different types of wage restraint programs in public policy in this country.[2] The first group is represented by the programs of World War II, the Korean War period, the Construction program of 1971–74, and some aspects of 1971–74 which involved genuine participation of labor and management. These programs have involved overt recognition of multiple standards for various elements of compensation, direct involvement in dispute resolution and considerable attention to individual case situations. These programs have typically been built upon a general statutory authorization that always has been made more detailed by Congress over the course of the program. The second type of wage restraint program includes the guidepost period of 1962–66, much of Phase II of 1971–72, and the 1978–79 program. These programs have involved concentration upon a single guidepost number for all elements of compensation, a labor-cost approach to restraint, little or no labor and management participation (except for the outset of Phase II in 1971), and a rejection of concern with dispute resolution and the process of developing policy through case consideration. The single standard necessitates a cost approach to all compensation which distorts benefits very considerably in work groups of different compositions, as in the costing of pensions for a young or old work force. These programs have been labeled voluntary rather than compulsory, but that distinction has now been greatly confused.

The industrial-relations fraternity has led the first approach, and the guidepost wing of the macroeconomic profession has designed and led the second, and it appears that never the twain shall meet or communicate. The macroeconomics profession is designing and advocating still other devices which it regards as effective to restrain wage inflation, such as TIP, tax-based income policies (see Rees 1978, pp. 453–90), anti-inflationary tax-credit compacts (Eisner) and MAP, market method antiinflation plan (Lerner). This is the point at which the 1935 wisdom of the Committee on Recent Economic Changes needs to be recalled: "What is perhaps more needed at the present time than anything else is the development of the means of coordinating and utilizing the experience of men of affairs and the results of economic research."

The task of serious discussion and consensus building at a policy level in this country is made virtually impossible by virtue of the Advisory Committee Act and its interpretations and administration, which require open meetings with full access by the press and media. As compared to other advanced industrial countries we have seriously handcuffed ourselves to reach consensus on such vital matters as general economic policy, including wage restraint, among major interest groups of the nation. Yet frank and continuing discussion among representatives of labor, management, and government is essential if structural questions are to be seriously addressed that are at the bottom of many features of inflationary tendencies—these include questions of taxation, trade, productivity, the duration of collective agreements, introduction of technical change, reform of bargaining structures. Such discussions are indispensable to generate ideas, develop common approaches, and shape institutional changes. Legislative or executive fiat or expert pronouncement are ineffectual.

As one element of economic policy, wage restraint in voluntary or compulsory forms will not work save for a very brief period, indeed measures to achieve the result will have perverse results, unless a large measure of genuine consensus and participation in any program is developed in the labor and management communities.

Notes

1. See Dunlop (1948, pp. 163–93; 1958, pp. 25–54).
2. Let me state for the record again, that direct wage or price restraint is a limited purpose tool of great complexity with only marginal restraining consequences at best and with serious adverse and disruptive consequences most generally.

---

3. R. F. Schubert

Postwar Changes in the American Labor Market

Since the end of World War II, the American economy and its labor market have clearly undergone important changes. The question to which this paper is directed is whether the labor market at the beginning of the 1980s is different in significant ways from the labor market at the beginning of the postwar period. In my opinion, the answer probably is in the affirmative. However, I would also suggest that it can persuasively be argued that the changes which have taken place should not be seen as radical shifts in direction or watersheds but rather as developments consistent with the general evolution of our labor market, our economy, and our society at large.

It should be noted at the outset that the frame of reference selected for reviewing the changes which have occurred will be the steel industry labor force (specifically Bethlehem Steel's employment history) with the belief that this perspective is probably consistent in many ways with the labor market as a whole. It should also be understood that there are some obvious forces which, although not specifically discussed, have clearly been at play in the overall postwar labor market. Among these are: the general shift in the proportions of private versus public sector employment and the concurrent increase in the percentage of white-collar jobs; the impact of collective bargaining tempered by the realization that labor unions have had declining success over the last ten or fifteen years in terms of the proportion of the American work force that they represent; the influx of young adults into the labor market resulting from the post World War II "baby boom"; a dramatic increase in imported goods; and the numerous effects of escalating inflation on every aspect of our economy.

I leave it to the experts—the economists and sociologists—to debate the specific influences of these forces for change. This paper, aims, in-

R. F. Schubert is president of Bethlehem Steel Corporation.

stead, at helping to define the postwar changes in the labor market by capsulizing some of the changes that have occurred in a representative sector of the labor force—the steel industry. The changes have been extensive. And, while some have been subtle, the majority are more obvious and the impact of each of them poses difficult questions for our future:

In comparing the average Bethlehem steelworker of 1949 with a similar steelworker today, the following differences are apparent:

1. *A significant increase in real wages*
   Over the thirty-year period since 1949, the level and composition of steelworker income, broadly defined, has changed significantly. Employment costs, which include nonwage compensation as well as wage and salary payments, have, after adjustment for inflation, risen almost 300 percent over the period in question. This has been accompanied by a dramatic increase in the "benefits"–to–payroll ratio. In 1949, benefit costs for production workers in the steel industry were equal to 3 percent of payroll costs. Today, that percentage has risen to 26 percent. In the case of Bethlehem's health care program instituted in 1950, for example, the company's contribution at that time was less than 50 percent of the cost of coverage, whereas today Bethlehem picks up 100 percent of the cost of the much more extensive program.

2. *An increase in the level of education*
   While 1949 data is not readily available to specifically document this change, we know that the average steelworker of today is much more apt to be a high school graduate than his or her counterpart of thirty years ago, and today many of our employees have some post high school training. As an example, one of our major plants found that 130 of the last 1,100 hired into entry-level production and maintenance jobs, or 10 percent of those hired, had graduated from a four-year college.

3. *A shorter work life*
   Besides entering the work force later due to extended periods of education, the steelworker of today is choosing to retire earlier than ever before. In 1949, the average Bethlehem pensioner was more than sixty-eight years of age and received a monthly pension of $165 in 1978 dollars. In 1978, our average steelworker was retiring nine years earlier, at age fifty-nine, and received a pension of $655, four times more than that received by his 1949 counterpart.

4. *An increase in the amount of leisure time*
   Besides spending fewer years at his job, the steelworker of today also spends fewer days at his job each year than did the 1949 steelworker; through the postwar years our employees have re-

ceived more and more holidays and more vacation time off. In 1949, the typical steelworker had six holidays a year and received one, two, or three weeks of vacation, depending upon his service (three weeks were granted after twenty-five years with the company). Today, a steelworker receives eleven holidays a year and vacations ranging from one to five weeks, with extra "extended vacation" weeks once every five years amounting to three weeks for shorter-serviced employees and eight or nine weeks for longer-serviced employees.

5. *An increase in the number of female workers*

The influx of women into the labor force and the removal of barriers to their participation in traditionally male-only jobs have had a noticeable impact on the steel industry. For example, in 1949 women constituted approximately one-half of a percent of Bethlehem Steel's production work force. Today, that percentage has risen to about 4.5 percent. Also, historically, most women employed by Bethlehem in the postwar period worked in office and clerical positions but, increasingly, the company has hired women as management trainees and has hired them for, or promoted them to, previously all-male higher-level supervisory and management positions.

6. *A decrease in concern over job security*

The average steelworker of today seems less concerned about layoff than was an employee circa 1949 because of the excellent benefits accruing to an unemployed worker today from private and public sector programs. And, while there is much legitimate speculation about the effects such benefits to the unemployed may have on their interest in actively seeking work, it suffices to say at this juncture that laid-off steelworkers today will, in most cases—through State Unemployment Compensation (UC) and Bethlehem Supplemental Unemployment Benefits (SUB)—receive an income of approximately 65 percent of their gross earnings for temporary periods of unemployment of, in some cases, up to 104 weeks. Compared to 1949, when laid-off employees received only 24 weeks of UC benefits equal to about 33 percent of their wages, the employees of today are afforded considerable security against cyclical economic fluctuations.

In general, it is clear that the changes noted in our work force since 1949 have been substantial, and they have generally proven very positive changes for Bethlehem employees. As a company, we employ a work force that is better educated and more comfortable financially than our work force of thirty years ago. Ironically, these same changes have caused some paradoxes, and these paradoxes signal warnings for the future.

1. While the steelworker of today is better educated than he was thirty years ago, his education has in some instances increased faster than has the demand for jobs requiring higher levels of education, the result being that a number of people have had to settle for positions below the level for which they were prepared.

What effect will this elevated level of education of our production workers have on future job satisfaction? How can we adapt our human-resources training so as to motivate people who may feel overeducated and who may, hence, in the future react negatively to employment in positions which they perceive to be inferior to those for which they were trained and those to which they had aspired?

2. While the worker of today is considerably more comfortable financially than his or her counterpart of thirty years ago, a good portion of this personal financial improvement has been obtained at the expense of profits and retained earnings for capital investment. Higher employment costs are, of course, not totally to blame for the industry's plight, but there is little doubt that they have been a major contributor to the decline in profit margins and funds available for investment. In the last ten years the American steel industry invested in capital expenditures $22 billion—*twice* what it earned. But during the next ten years, the American steel industry will have to spend *six* to *seven* times what it earned in the past ten years—$60 to $70 billion—if it is to remain technologically competitive, reduce its energy costs and improve its productivity. Therefore, all concerned must take a hard look at the proper tradeoffs in employment cost and new investment.

3. While over the last thirty years advancing technology and an expanding economy have created thousands of jobs throughout the country, many of which have been filled by a whole new sector of our population—women—their success in attaining jobs has to a certain extent aggravated the problem of another category of Americans—unemployed youth, many of whom are becoming lost in the ranks of the structurally unemployed.

4. While, again, the steelworker of today has, among other advantages, a much improved wage and benefits package and a better work environment, there seems to be concurrently a lesser degree of job satisfaction and work motivation than thirty years ago.

What does this issue of lower job satisfaction and work motivation portend for the future? What steps do we take to make work more meaningful for our employees and, again, what can be done about improving worker motivation? There would seem to be a direct correlation between these issues and our nation's lagging productivity growth.

These four paradoxes, though probably mirrored in the labor market generally, are matters of particular concern for the steel industry's future. There is one further paradox which I will consider and this too clearly affects not only Bethlehem and the steel industry, but most segments of American industry as well. This is the problem of lagging productivity growth.

Lagging productivity growth is a societal problem that can only be solved if we see it as such and are committed to work together to overcome it. The problem arises at a time when as a country we've made great strides in the work place for our employees. However, with all of the positive benefits, the productivity growth of the 1950s and early 1960s—the Golden Age of Productivity—is slipping away from us. And a drop from a 3.2 percent annual increase in our nation's rate of growth up through 1965, to a much less desirable rate of one percent since 1973, could translate into some unpleasant predictions for our standard of living in the coming decade.

This problem is one of the most serious for my industry, and while there are many ideas being promulgated concerning the factors contributing to the productivity problem, there clearly is no panacea. But as I see it there are a couple of things that we in the business community can do to help. We can work on improving the vocational training, the skills training, of our younger work force and of the minorities and women whom we will hire. We can also develop more innovative human resources techniques to try to reverse the trend we detect toward lower worker motivation.

Both the private and public sectors must join forces to keep each other better informed of what jobs will be available in the future and what training can be planned to meet those needs. We can also work together on a national industrial policy or strategy so desperately needed to generate the capital which industry *must* have to maintain a competitive posture. And with some of that capital we can strive to return to the pre-1973 level of commitment to research and the development of new technology and equipment. And, of course, more capital and improved technology in the end will mean more jobs—real jobs—and, we hope, lasting jobs.

That is really the bottom line. More jobs. More jobs to address a problem that's probably bigger even than our nation's productivity problem, and growing all the time. It is the labor-market problem of the 1980s—the structurally unemployed.

And interestingly enough, many of the suggestions made for addressing the nation's lagging productivity are also possible solutions for this bigger problem. Foremost among these is the need to work together. There must be a commitment on the part of the public and private sectors to communicate needs and potential cooperative solutions. That commitment must be manifested in terms of a stable flow of government funds to the private sector for manpower training and development programs during periods of an expanding economy when the private sector has career opportunities. And the commitment must also include a strategic plan for a quick and efficient transfer of government fund allocations from the private sector to public sector job creation programs during those periods when the economy dampens. We must also work together to improve our capital formation so we can create more jobs and target groups to train for those jobs. Conceivably, we in industry can even use some of our plants and skilled craftsmen during slower times to train youths in the trades that will be expanding in the upswing.

I don't mean to make the solution sound simple, for we all know that it is not. Unemployment is a labor-market problem that has been with us long before the postwar period. But the problem of youth unemployment—of structural unemployment—is even more severe. It may indeed be a time bomb with an ever-shortening fuse. And the only way to begin to defuse it is to pool our ideas, our energy, and our resources with an unequivocal commitment and unflagging resolve.

Summary of Discussion

The themes of wage inflation and demographic shifts in the labor force dominated the discussion. Arthur Okun declared that wage restraint is difficult to achieve because of externalities in the wage-setting process. He urged that we consider using an incentive system, perhaps through the tax code, to provide the right signals to private parties in wage setting. Now, parties simply do not pay attention to the social interest in holding down wages and prices. Okun suggested that the problem partly results from the willingness of the government to underwrite, or bail out, parties agreeing to excessive wage settlements. In the steel negotiations, for example, the industry anticipates government policies for protection from international competition. Schubert retorted that the steel industry's problems have been caused, not solved, by government. He cited price restraints, outmoded depreciation laws, the regulatory burden, and the failure of the government to enforce trade laws against dumping as sources of the industry's problems.

Alan Blinder challenged John Dunlop's view that macroeconomists have spearheaded the past programs of statutory wage-and-price controls. Men of affairs created the programs, Blinder suggested, largely over the opposition of academic macroeconomists. Herbert Stein opposed any system of wage restraints built on an agreement between government and organized labor. He criticized the 1979 "accord" between the Carter administration and the AFL-CIO as undemocratic, for it made the leaders of organized labor, with its twenty-five million members, the unelected representatives of the entire labor force. Robert

Gordon declared that the main effect of the Carter administration's wage guidelines during the past two years has been to drive a wedge between wages of workers in large establishments, whose wages are restrained by the guidelines, and other workers, whose wages are not.

James Schlesinger pointed out the difficulties of achieving wage restraint in an economy with low or negative productivity growth. The presence of rising living standards is an important lubricant to a successful controls program.

Many participants addressed the problem of youth unemployment. Gordon noted that results of the recent NBER Conference on Youth Employment (May 1979) showed that white youth unemployment is not a severe problem. When the number of white out-of-school unemployed youths is measured as a proportion of the white youth labor force *plus* youths in school, the adjusted unemployment rate stands at about 5 percent, near the level of adult unemployment. On black unemployment Gordon felt that zoning laws in suburban areas prevent young workers from living near new suburban factories, thus hindering job creation for central city workers. He contrasted this situation with that of many European cities, where working-class suburban neighborhoods have sprung up near suburban factory sites. Martin Feldstein stressed that much of the black youth unemployment problem has resulted from the decline of rural agriculture and the urbanization of black youths in the past thirty-five years. Richard Freeman reported research results which show that unemployed black youths eventually get absorbed into the adult labor market, though possibly not with the quality of jobs they might have found without the unemployment spell.

Victor Fuchs addressed demographic changes at the other end of the age distribution, noting that slower economic growth and the increasing age of the United States labor force will threaten the financial stability of the social security system over the next twenty years. He proposed that the age of eligibility for retirement benefits be raised two months per year for the next eighteen years, increasing the eligibility age three years by the year 2000.

Wilbur Cohen discussed another major structural shift in the labor market: the tremendous growth of the unemployment insurance system. In the last thirty years, Cohen noted, the coverage of the unemployment insurance system has moved far beyond industry, so that it is nearly universal today. The maximum duration of benefits has grown from 16 to 20 weeks in 1948, to 39 weeks today. In some special congressional income support systems, such as those relating to airlines and railroads, benefits may be provided for five years, or even until retirement! Cohen declared that these special programs may have a major impact on work incentives in the United States labor force.

References

Ashenfelter, A. 1979. Estimating the effects of training programs on earnings. *Review of Economics and Statistics* 60 (February):47–57.

Ashenfelter, Orley, and Heckman, James J. 1974. The estimation of income and substitution efforts in a model of family labor supply. *Econometrica* 42 (January): 73–86.

———. 1976. Measuring the effect of an antidiscrimination program. In *Evaluating the labor market effects of social programs,* ed. Orley Ashenfelter and James Blum. Princeton, N.J.: Industrial Relations Section, Princeton University.

Ashford, N. 1976. *Crisis in the workplace.* Cambridge: MIT Press.

Blinder, Alan S.; Gordon, Roger H.; and Wise, Donald E. 1979. Reconsidering the work disincentive effects of social security. Mimeographed. Princeton, N.J.

Boskin, Michael J. 1977. Social security and retirement decisions. *Economic Inquiry* 15, no. 1 (January): 1–25.

———. 1978. The effect of social security on early retirement. *Journal of Public Economics* 10 (December): 361–77.

Brown, S. C. 1979. Educational attainment of workers: Some trends from 1975 to 1978. *Monthly Labor Review* 102 (February):54–58.

Bruno, Michael, and Sachs, Jeffrey. 1979. Supply vs. demand approaches to the problem of stagflation. National Bureau of Economic Research Working Paper, no. 382. Cambridge, Mass.: NBER.

Bureau of National Affairs. 1976. *Equal employment opportunity programs and results.* Personnel Policies Forum, Survey no. 12. Washington, D.C.: Bureau of National Affairs.

Burkhauser, Richard V., and Turner, John A. 1978. A time-series analysis on social security and its effect on the market work of men at younger ages. *Journal of Political Economy* 86 (August): 701–15.

Burman, George. 1973. The economics of discrimination: The impact of public policy. Ph.D. diss., University of Chicago.

Burstein, P. 1978. Equal opportunity legislation and the income of women and nonwhites. Unpublished paper. New Haven: Yale University.

Butler, R., and Heckman, J. 1977. Government's impact on the labor market status of black Americans: A critical review. In *Equal rights and industrial relations,* ed. L. J. Hausman, O. Ashenfelter, B. Rustin, R. F. Schubert, and D. Slaiman, pp. 235–81. Madison, Wisc.: Industrial Relations Research Association.

Cain, G., and Watts, H. 1973. *Income maintenance and labor supply.* Chicago: Markham.

Clark, John Maurice. 1935. *Strategic factors in business cycles.* New York: National Bureau of Economic Research.

Connerton, M. 1978. Accident control through regulation: The 1969 Call Act. Ph.D. diss., Harvard University.

Denison, E. F. 1979. Explanations of declining productivity. In U.S. Department of Commerce, *Survey of Current Business* 59 (August): 1–24.

Dunlop, John T. 1948. The development of labor organization: A theoretical framework. In *Insights into labor issues,* ed. Richard A. Lester and Joseph Shister, pp. 163–93. New York: Macmillan.

———. 1958. The American industrial relations system in 1975. In *U.S. industrial relations: the next twenty years,* ed. Jack Stieber, pp. 25–54. East Lansing: Michigan State University Press.

Dunlop, J., and Bok, D. 1970. *Labor and the American community.* New York: Simon and Schuster.

Dunlop, John T., and Fedor, Kenneth J., eds. 1977. *The lessons of wage and price controls—the food sector.* Cambridge: Harvard University Press.

Edwards, L., and Edwards, F. N. 1979. The effect of unionism on the money and fringe components of public employees: The case of municipal sanitation workers. Unpublished paper, Columbia University Press.

Ehrenberg, R., and Goldstein, M. 1975. A model of public sector wage determinations. *Journal of Urban Economics* 2 (June): 223–45.

Ellwood, D., and Fine, G. A. 1980. The impact of right-to-work laws on union organizing. National Bureau of Economic Research Working Paper. Cambridge: NBER.

Fields, J. 1976. A comparison of intercity differences in the labor force participation rates of married women in 1970 with 1940, 1950, and 1960. *Journal of Human Resources* 11 (fall): 568–76.

Freeman, R. 1976a. *The overeducated American.* New York: Academic Press.

———. 1976b. The depressed college job market: Issues and implications. Unpublished paper. Cambridge, Mass.

———. 1979. The effect of demographic factors on the age-earnings profile in the U.S. *Journal of Human Resources* 14 (summer): 289–318.

———. 1980a. The facts about the declining economic value of college. *Journal of Human Resources* 15 (winter): 124–42.

———. 1975. Overinvestment in college training. *Journal of Human Resources* 10 (summer): 287–311.

———. 1980b. Employment opportunities in the doctorate manpower market. *ILRR* 33 (January): 185–87.

———. 1980c. An empirical analysis of the fixed coefficient "manpower requirements" model, 1960–1970. *Journal of Human Resources* 15 (summer). In press.

————. 1980d. Black economic progress post-1964: Who has gained and why? In *Low income labor markets*, ed. S. Rosen. Chicago, University of Chicago Press.

Freeman, R., and Medoff, J. 1976. The dwindling of private sector unionism. Unpublished paper.

————. 1978. The percentage organized-wage (POW) effect. National Bureau of Economic Research Working Paper, no. 305. Cambridge: NBER.

————. 1980. The youth labor market problem in the U.S.: An overview. National Bureau of Economic Research Working Paper. Cambridge: NBER.

Garfinkel, I. The quality of education and cohort variation in black-white earnings differential. *AER*, 70 (March): 186–91.

Goldstein, Morris, and Smith, Robert S. 1976. The estimated impact of the anti-discrimination program aimed at federal contractors. *Industrial and Labor Relations Review* 29 (July): 523–43.

Griliches, Z. 1973. Research expenditures and growth accounting. In *Science and technology in economic growth*, ed. B. R. Williams. New York: Hartford Press.

Gustman, A., and Segal, M. 1977. Interstate variations in teacher's pensions. *Industrial Relations* 16, no. 3 (October): 335–44.

Hebl, J. 1979. A look at the 20th century market for public elementary and secondary school teachers. Senior thesis, Harvard College.

Heckman, James J., and Wolpin, Kenneth. 1976. Does the contract compliance program work? An analysis of Chicago data. *Industrial and Labor Relations Review* 29 (July): 544–64.

Ichniowski, C. 1980. Economic effects of the firefighters' unions. *Industrial and Labor Relations Review* 33 (January): 198–211.

Jorgenson, D. W., and Hudson, E. A. 1978. Energy prices and the U.S. economy 1972–1976. *Data Resources U. S. Review* (September), pp. 877–97.

Kirchner, William. N.d. Statement as Director of Organization, AFL-CIO to the Special House Subcommittee on Labor.

Kochan, T. 1979. How American workers view labor unions. In U. S. Department of Labor, *Monthly Labor Review* 102 (April): 23–31.

Lauer, H. 1979. The economic effects of the policemen's unions. Senior thesis, Harvard College.

Lazear, E. 1979 Why is there mandatory retirement? *Journal of Political Economy* 87 (December): 1261–84.

Leonard, J. S. 1979. The social security disability program and labor force participation. National Bureau of Economic Research Working Paper, no. 392. Cambridge: NBER.

Lewin, David. 1977. Public sector labor relations: A review essay. *Labor History* 18, no. 1 (winter): 133–44.

Mark, J. 1979. Productivity trends and prospects. In *Work in America: The decade ahead,* ed. C. Kerr and J. Rosow. Van Nostrand Reinhold.

Mincer, J. 1966. Labor force participation of married women. In *Prosperity and unemployment,* ed. R. Gordon. New York: Wiley.

Miner, M. G., and Miner, J. B. 1978. *Employee selection within the law.* Washington, D.C.: Bureau of National Affairs.

National Bureau of Economic Research (NBER). 1929. Recent economic changes in the U.S. New York: McGraw-Hill.

National Center for Education Statistics (NCES). 1979. *The condition of education 1978.* Washington, D.C.: Government Printing Office.

National Industrial Conference Board (NICB). 1970. White-collar unionization. New York.

National Labor Relations Board (NLRB). 1978. *42nd annual report.* Washington, D.C.: Government Printing Office.

Paglin, M. 1977. Transfer in kind: The impact on poverty, 1959–1975. Hoover Institution Conference on Income Redistribution. Unpublished. Stanford, Calif.

Pellechio, Anthony T. 1978. The effect of social security on retirement. National Bureau of Economic Research Working Paper, no. 260. Cambridge: NBER.

Perry, G. G. 1978. Potential output: Recent issues and present tides. Reprint 336. Washington, D.C.: The Brookings Institution.

Quinn, R. P., and Staines, G. L. 1977. *The 1977 quality of employment survey.* Ann Arbor: Survey Research Center.

Rees, Albert. 1978. New policies to fight inflation: Sources of skepticism. *Brookings Papers on Economic Activity* 2: 453–90.

Rosen, S., and Willis, R. 1979. Education and self selection. *Journal of Positive Economy* 87, no. 5 (October), pt. 2, pp. 27–36.

Ross, P. 1965. *The government as a source of union power: The role of public policy in collective bargaining.* Providence: Brown University Press.

Sachs, J. 1978. The changing cyclical behavior of wages and prices: 1890–1976. National Bureau of Economic Research Working Paper, no. 304. Cambridge: NBER.

Skolnik, Alfred M. 1976. Private pension plans, 1950–74. *Social Security Bulletin* 39 (June): 3–17.

Smith, Robert Stewart. 1976. *The Occupational Safety and Health Act: Its goals and its achievements.* Washington, D.C.: American Enterprise Institute for Public Policy Research.

Tax Foundation. 1977. *Facts and figures on government finances, 1977.* Washington, D.C.: Tax Foundation.

Troy, Leo. 1965. *Trade union membership, 1897–1962.* NBER Occasional Paper 92. New York: National Bureau of Economic Research.

U.S. Department of Commerce, Bureau of the Census. 1947–77. *Current population reports*. Consumer Income Series P–60. Washington, D.C.: Government Printing Office.

———. 1954. *Census of the population 1950*. Washington, D.C.: Government Printing Office.

———. 1961. *Historical statistics of the United States, colonial times to 1957*. Series A–242. Washington, D.C.: Government Printing Office.

———. 1975. *Historical statistics of the United States, colonial times to 1970*. Part 1, series D–182–232, series F–373. Washington, D.C.: Government Printing Office.

———. 1976. *Statistical Abstract of the United States, 1976*. 97th ed. Washington, D.C.: Government Printing Office.

———. 1977. *Statistical abstract of the United States, 1976–77*. 98th ed. Washington, D.C.: Government Printing Office.

———. 1978. *Statistical abstract of the United States, 1977–78*. 98th ed. Washington, D.C.: Government Printing Office.

———. 1978. *Statistical abstract of the United States, 1977–78*. 99th ed. Washington, D.C.: Government Printing Office.

———. 1978. *The Budget of the U.S. Government*. Washington, D.C.: Government Printing Office.

U.S. Department of Labor. 1977. *Employment and training report of the president, 1977*.

———. 1977. *Handbook of labor statistics 1977*.

———. 1978. *Employment and training report of the president, 1978*.

U.S. Department of Labor, Bureau of Labor Statistics (BLS). 1977a. *Employment and earnings, U.S. 1909–1975*. Washington, D.C.: Government Printing Office.

———. 1977b. *Educational attainment of workers*. Washington, D.C.: Government Printing Office.

———. 1978a. *Employment and Earnings*, vol. 25, no. 3 (March).

———. 1978b. *Estimated hourly compensation of production workers in manufacturing: Ten countries, 1960, 1965–1978*. Washington, D.C.: Government Printing Office.

———. 1979a. *Employment and earnings*. Washington, D.C.: Government Printing Office.

———. 1979b. *Monthly Labor Review*, vol. 102, no. 8 (August).

———. 1979c. *Handbook of labor statistics 1978*. Bulletin 2000. Washington, D.C.: Government Printing Office.

Viscusi, W. Kip. 1980. *Employment hazards*. Cambridge: Harvard University Press.

Weber, Arnold R. 1979. Cost to industries of old labor ties. *New York Times*. 19 December.

Welch, F. 1973. Black-white returns to schooling. *American Economic Review* 63, no. 5 (March): 893–907.

————. 1978. Effects of cohort size on earnings: The baby boom babies' financial bust. Cambridge University Conference on Income Distribution, March 1978.

Welch, F., and Smith, J. 1975. Black/white male earnings and employment: 1960–1970. U.S. Department of Labor, R–1666–DOL–June 1975.

————. 1978. The overeducated American: A review article. Rand Paper Series. Santa Monica: Rand Corporation.

Wellington, H. H., and Winter, R. K. 1972. *The unions and the cities*. Washington, D.C.: The Brookings Institution.

6 The Level and Distribution of Economic Well-Being

1. Alan S. Blinder
2. Irving Kristol
3. Wilbur J. Cohen

1. Alan S. Blinder

6.1 Introduction and Preview

The more things change, the more they remain the same.

The ultimate purpose of an economy, it may fairly be said, is to enhance the material well-being of its people. In the philosophical pecking order, such a crass and narrow goal may not appear as lofty as, let us say, inner peace and spiritual uplift. But, as has oft been remarked, it is difficult to feed the soul while the stomach is empty.

Because of the absolutely central position of the task of producing more and better goods, and distributing them equitably (what a loaded word that is!) among the citizenry, the topics of the other chapters in this book may justifiably be considered subservient to this one. Changes in the financial system, in taxation and public expenditure, in the structure of industry, or in international economic relations are all most

Alan S. Blinder is professor of economics at Princeton University.

My gratitude goes to C. R. Lindsey for skillful and diligent research assistance; to my NBER reading committee, Stanley Lebergott and Eugene Smolensky, for much good advice; and to Edgar Browning, Sheldon Danziger, Angus Deaton, Richard Easterlin, Benjamin Friedman, Victor Fuchs, Roger Gordon, Harvey Rosen, and Timothy Smeeding for helpful suggestions. I should also acknowledge the National Science Foundation for support over the years for my research on income distribution. None of these persons or institutions, however, is an accomplice in the conclusions. Finally, the occasion of this volume (and helpful hints from Milton Friedman and Arthur Burns) prompts me to point out that the NBER was started to learn "the facts" about income distribution in the United States. Apparently the task was more difficult than the founding fathers realized; but we are still working on it!

415

naturally appraised by asking how much they contribute to economic well-being. Thus this chapter may, without stretching the imagination too far, be thought of as the "outputs" produced by the other chapters' "inputs." At least this is the preeminence I claim for my topic.

How well has the United States economy performed the two central tasks of raising living standards and enhancing economic equality during the postwar period? The basic story is simple enough to summarize in a few words, though complex enough to require volumes for a complete account. Where the *average level* of economic well-being is concerned, the record is one of steady *improvement*. Not an unblemished record to be sure, and not as spectacular a record as the postwar "economic miracles" of Germany and Japan, but a creditable record nonetheless.

However, when we turn to consider the *distribution* of economic welfare—economic equality, as it is commonly called—the central stylized fact is one of *constancy*. As measured in the official data, income inequality was just about the same in 1977 (the last year for which data were available when this was written) as it was in 1947. Though this seems a straightforward conclusion, it actually conceals a host of controversies and puzzles. For the stability we observe in the income distribution is not the result of a boring, static economy, nor the result of some "natural economic law," as Pareto (1897) thought. Rather it is the result of a confluence of powerful forces, some pulling toward greater equality and some pulling toward greater inequality, which together produced a great underwater swirl while causing barely a ripple on the surface.

For example, the American population experienced substantial demographic changes during this thirty-year period. The causes of these changes were varied, complex, in part obvious and in part obscure, but in any case well beyond the scope of this chapter.[1] What matters for our purposes is that, given the way income distribution data are compiled, these demographic shifts would have produced a substantial trend toward greater inequality had not other factors intervened. It will not be giving away the plot to suggest that government transfer programs played a major role in that intervention.

Even the basic stylized fact that income inequality has remained constant since World War II has not gone unchallenged. It has been argued, for example, that if we measured income more comprehensively than we do, or if we measured it over periods longer than a year, a clearer trend toward equality would emerge. As we shall see, seemingly mundane issues like how to define and measure income are of considerable importance in appraising the economy's postwar performance; and they also raise some surprisingly profound (and perhaps insoluble) issues.

Since this chapter is a long one, it will be useful to provide a reader's guide at the outset. Section 6.2 disposes briefly of some preliminary issues of measurement—the measurement of welfare, the measurement of income, and the measurement of inequality. The next two sections, which constitute the bulk of the paper, address the two central topics of the chapter—postwar trends in the *level* of income (section 6.3) and its *inequality* (section 6.4). Section 6.4, in particular, examines in some depth the controversies alluded to above. Section 6.5 then takes up several peripheral aspects of the distribution of income which seem to be of special interest—poverty, black–white income differentials, and male–female income differentials. Finally, in section 6.6, the myopic concentration on income is remedied by examining postwar developments in nonincome aspects of well-being such as leisure, wealth, and health. Section 6.7 offers some brief concluding remarks.

6.2 Preliminaries

6.2.1 From the Sublime to the Ridiculous

The essay begins with a strategic retreat which moves farther and farther from a concept that is interesting but unmeasurable (welfare) and closer and closer to a concept that is measurable but possibly uninteresting (money income as defined by the U.S. Bureau of the Census). Like most strategic retreats, this one does accomplish something. But it must be admitted that its direction is dictated more by expedience than by principle. The retreat takes place in several stages.

The first step is to admit that man does not live on bread alone. Political freedom, peace, inner tranquillity, a happy family life, and so on may be far more important to many people than the bill of goods and services they consume. Still, it would be the height of folly for an economist to write an essay on these more ephemeral aspects of human welfare. On grounds of comparative advantage, therefore, I will for the most part restrict my attention to what is normally considered *economic* well-being.

The second step is to concede that there is little scientific basis for deciding how much "utility" any specific individual gets at any particular time, and even less for deciding whether Laurel gets more or less than Hardy. Two avenues therefore remain open. We can look at levels and distributions of items which are presumed to yield utility, such as consumption goods and leisure time. Or we can look at peoples' opportunities, as summarized by their endowments and the prices they face, on the assumption that people with more generous opportunities achieve correspondingly higher levels of satisfaction.[2]

While part of our army will stop to fight the battle here, most of it will retreat one step more—to the use of current income to summarize the whole opportunity set. Now we know this is not quite right. Two individuals with identical opportunities will have different incomes if their preferences differ.[3] Ill health may mean that more current income is necessary to achieve any given level of satisfaction, or a large store of accumulated wealth may mean that less is necessary. While several of these qualifications will be dealt with in what follows, the data dictate that the analysis be conducted mainly in terms of income.

6.2.2   The Measurement of Income

Perhaps the worst news is saved for last. The only reasonably consistent time series of income distributions covering a long period comes from the annual *Current Population Survey* (CPS), which uses an income definition that is far from the economist's (or anyone else's) ideal.[4] Economists define an individual's income as the amount he could consume without depleting his wealth—the sum of his expenditures plus any increase in his wealth. What does the CPS offer us? Basically, a distribution of money income in which some sources of income are grossly underreported, capital gains are excluded, cash transfers are included but transfers in kind are excluded, and from which no deduction is made for income and payroll taxes. Measured income thus falls far short of the ideal concept of income. Given the wide cleavage that already exists between well-being and even this ideal concept of income, one might well wonder if our data do not leave us with a grin without a cat. I proceed nonetheless in this essay to analyze the grin. However, some time will be spent in section 6.4 questioning whether a better measure of income might tell a different story about postwar trends in income inequality.

Our interest in the level and distribution of *income* clearly is motivated by a belief that we can use these two numbers as approximate indicators of economic *welfare*. Specifically, we would like to believe that higher or more equally distributed incomes mean that society is "better off." Having decided, for lack of a superior alternative, to use census money income, the next step is to decide on the recipient unit. Whose incomes shall we study?

This question, which may seem foolish and "academic" at first, is in fact very important because of the demographic changes mentioned earlier. For it appears that one of the items that Americans have purchased with their postwar prosperity has been the privilege of living apart from their relatives. Think what happens, for example, when higher living standards and/or more generous public transfer programs enable junior, or grandma and grandpa, to move into an apartment of their own. A new economic unit is formed, with a rather low income, thus bringing down the average level of income and raising its inequality. Both economic indicators will therefore signal a deterioration in welfare, though we may presume that these changes in living arrangements actually make the parties involved better off.[5]

We therefore must exercise extreme caution in interpreting postwar trends in income distribution. The Census Bureau offers separate income distributions for *families* ("a group of two or more persons related by blood, marriage, or adoption and residing together") and for *unrelated individuals*, as well as a *pooled* distribution that combines both types of units. In this essay, we will pay attention to each of these distributions and to the interrelationships among them.

Further perplexities enter when we ask another question: why should we be interested in distributions of *annual* incomes instead of incomes measured over some alternative accounting period? One answer is straightforward and prosaic: that's the way the data come. But a deeper question is not so easily answered. If we could measure income over any accounting period we wished, what accounting period would be best?

It seems clear that periods like a day or a week are far too short to generate meaningful data on income inequality. All of us have weeks of zero income (at least on a cash accounting basis), without being "poor" in any real sense. So longer periods are necessary. But why stop at a year? Clearly a year is far too short an accounting period to place many people meaningfully within the income distribution. For example, since investment in human capital typically leads to rising age-earnings profiles, many people who are quite well off in a lifetime sense may appear quite "poor" during certain years. For these and other reasons many economists, including myself (1974; 1976), have been attracted to the distribution of *lifetime* incomes, though even this choice is not unobjectionable.

As we shall see, there is evidence that income distributions over multiyear accounting periods display less inequality than income distributions for a single year. More important, there is reason to believe that a stronger trend toward equality might emerge if somehow we were able to measure the distribution of lifetime income.

6.2.3   The Measurement of Inequality

There are many ways to measure how "equal" or "unequal" any given distribution of income is;[6] but the availability of data dictates that we concentrate on two. The first is straightforward and requires no elaboration: we can examine trends in the shares of total income accruing to specific income groups, such as the poorest fifth or the richest fifth, for example. The second is something called the *Gini ratio* and requires some explanation.[7]

Income distributions are typically displayed in a convenient graphical device invented by M. O. Lorenz (1905); two such *Lorenz curves* are depicted in figure 6.1. To construct a Lorenz curve, begin with a square whose dimensions represent 100 percent. Along the horizontal axis, mea-

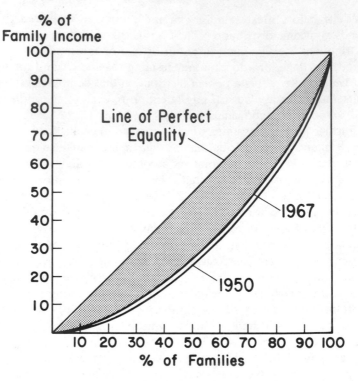

Fig. 6.1   Two Lorenz curves for family income.

sure the cumulative percentage of consumer units, starting from the poorest; along the vertical axis, measure the cumulative share of income received by these units. Data on income shares then appear as points within the square, and the curvilinear line connecting them is the Lorenz curve.

Every Lorenz curve has four basic properties:

1. It must begin at the origin, since zero units have zero income
2. It must end at the upper-right corner of the diagram since 100 percent of the units must receive all the income
3. If incomes were distributed equally, the Lorenz curve would be a diagonal line connecting these two points, since the "poorest" 20 percent of units would receive 20 percent of the income, the "poorest" 40 percent would receive 40 percent, and so on
4. In a real economy, in which significant income differentials exist, the Lorenz curve will "sag" downward from this diagonal line representing perfect equality. The reason is straightforward. If there is any inequality at all, the poorest 20 percent of units, for example, must receive less than 20 percent of the income, and the poorest 40 percent must receive less than 40 percent.

Lorenz curves are useful in depicting inequality because curves that lie *closer* to the diagonal represent distributions with *less* inequality. This is also illustrated in figure 6.1 which shows, for the family income distribution, the most equal and most unequal distributions during the entire postwar period. (The fact that they are so close together illustrates the aforementioned stability of the income distribution.) In fact, the area between the Lorenz curve and the diagonal (shaded in fig. 6.1), expressed as a fraction of the area beneath the diagonal,[8] is often used as a summary measure of inequality. This fraction is called the *Gini ratio*, after its inventor Corrado Gini (1936), and it is clear that higher Gini ratios connote greater inequality.

Since Gini ratios appear so frequently in this essay, a word on their interpretation is in order. The Gini ratio is a purely mechanical measure of inequality, while our interest in inequality is as an indicator of social welfare. Suppose in comparing two income distributions we find that distribution *A* assigns less income *both* to the poorest 20 percent of families *and* to the richest 20 percent than does distribution *B*. (Distribution *A* naturally has to assign more income to the middle 60 percent of families.) Which distribution has more "equality"? Clearly *A* is more equal at the upper tail (the rich are not quite so rich), but *B* is more equal at the lower tail (the poor are not quite so poor). But which distribution is "better"? It is clear that the answer is unclear. It depends on whether society attaches more importance to income differences at the high or low end of the income distribution. But the Gini ratio (or, for that matter, any summary statistic) tolerates no such ambiguity. It will state, for example, that the Gini ratio for distribution *A* is .36 while that for distribution *B* is .37. For this reason, we must take care in pronouncing distributions with lower Gini ratios as "better."

There is, however, one important circumstance in which the Gini ratio *can* be relied upon to rank different income distributions properly. This is the case where the Lorenz curves do not cross (as in fig. 6.1), for then the more unequal distribution will always get the higher Gini ratio. The conclusion then is this. When Lorenz curves cross, the Gini ratio may rank income distributions incorrectly, and thus cannot be taken very seriously. However, when Lorenz curves do not cross, such misrankings cannot occur and the Gini ratio provides useful information. Fortunately for us, most of the inequality comparisons we have to make are between Lorenz curves that do not cross.[9]

6.3   Trends in the Level of Income and Consumption

I turn now to the first of the two major concerns of this chapter: What has happened to the average level of economic well-being in the United States since World War II? As noted earlier, I will at first stealthily translate this question to: What has happened to the average level of *income*?, postponing the consideration of nonincome aspects of well-being to section 6.6.

The basic story is, of course, extremely well known. The postwar United States economy has generally produced growth of per capita incomes, though that growth has been punctuated by periodic recessions.[10] This stylized fact is illustrated in figure 6.2, which charts the behavior of real disposable income per capita from 1947 to 1978. The trend in consumption, naturally enough, has followed the trend in income rather closely. But the aggregate data conceal some dramatic changes in patterns of consumption.

6.3.1   The Growth of Incomes, 1947–77

Many serious shortcomings of census income were mentioned in section 6.2. Fortunately, in studying trends in the *level* of income, we need not restrict ourselves to census income since much better measures are available in the national income accounts (NIA).

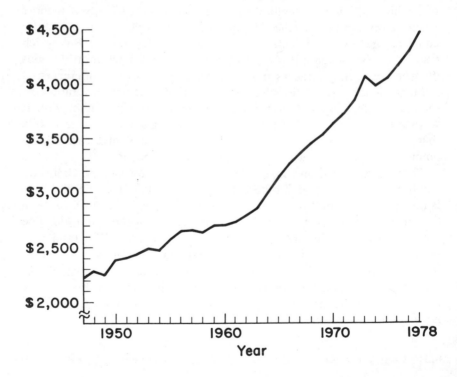

Fig. 6.2   Real disposable income per capita, 1947–78 (in 1972 dollars).

The NIA concept that comes closest to census income is personal income (PI). And it is easy to remedy several problems with census income by supplementing personal income with other NIA data. First, as a crude way of accounting for (a smoothed version of) capital gains, we can add corporate retained earnings to personal income. Second, we can put personal income on a more consistent posttransfer but pretax basis (like census income) by including not only the employee's share of the payroll tax but also the employer's share. Making both these changes in the NIA data leads me to an income concept that I call *augmented personal income.*[11]

A more fundamental problem with census income, however, is the illogic of adding in transfers but failing to deduct the taxes that pay for them. This is easily remedied in the aggregate data by deducting both personal income taxes and payroll taxes (both shares) from augmented personal income to arrive at an income concept that I call *augmented disposable income.*[12]

The decade-by-decade annual growth rates in real census income, real augmented personal income, and real augmented disposable income[13] are presented in table 6.1. Not surprisingly, for the postwar period as a whole the growth rates of census income and augmented personal income are almost identical, while the growth rate of real augmented disposable income is about one-third of a percentage point less. Compounded over thirty years, these figures mean that from 1947 to 1977 real augmented personal income per family increased 95 percent, while real augmented disposable income per family increased 77 percent. The gap is accounted for by an increasing burden of personal taxation (with, presumably, a corresponding increase in public services.)

Table 6.1   **Annualized Growth Rates (in Percentages) in Real Income per Family and per Unrelated Individual, by Three Different Definitions**

Period	Census Income		Augmented PI[a]		Augmented DI[a]	
	per Family	per UI	per Family	per UI	per Family	per UI
1947–77	2.22	2.14	2.25	2.17	1.92	1.84
1947–57	1.83	1.00	2.18	1.35	1.97	1.14
1957–67	3.01	2.71	3.01	2.72	2.68	2.39
1967–77	1.84	2.72	1.56	2.44	1.11	1.98

Sources: Computed by the author from data in U.S. Bureau of the Census, *Current Population Reports*, series P–60, no. 118; *Survey of Current Business*, July 1979; and *The National Income and Product Accounts of the United States, 1929–1974.*

[a]Augmented PI and augmented DI are defined in the text. It was assumed that each of these aggregates was divided between families and UIs in the same proportion as census income.

When we break the thirty-year period down into decades, the close agreement between census income and augmented personal income starts to melt away. More importantly, a striking difference between the postwar economic progress of families and unrelated individuals (UIs) emerges. For both groups, and for any of the income measures, the middle decade (which was dominated by the long boom of the 1960s) exhibited the strongest growth. But the rankings of the other two decades is reversed. Apparently, families fared much better than unrelated individuals between 1947 and 1957, while unrelated individuals fared much better than families during the most recent decade. Why? The reasons are to be found in the demographic shifts summarized in tables 6.2 and 6.3. These tables show that while demographic changes during 1947–57 were mostly minor for families, unrelated individuals became more likely to be female or elderly. By contrast, during the last decade unrelated individuals became much less likely to be female, while more families became female headed. (Both groups became younger on average.)

Where Did It Come From?

Naturally, all the components of personal income participated in the postwar growth, though certainly not equally. Table 6.4 shows that

Table 6.2   **Selected Changes in Family Structure, 1947–77**

Characteristic	1947	1957	1967	1977
Average Number of:				
Persons	3.64	3.65	3.67	3.33
Children	1.19	1.37	1.41	1.10
Earners			1.67	1.66
Percentage Headed by:				
Male	90.0	90.6	89.3	85.6
Female	10.0	9.4	10.7	14.4
Percentage Having:				
Two members	30.6	32.1	33.9	38.5
Three members	25.2	21.5	20.6	22.1
Four members	20.1	20.5	19.0	20.6
Five members	11.4	12.6	12.5	11.0
Six or more members	12.7	13.4	14.0	7.9
Percentage Headed by Person:				
Age 14–24	5.0	5.2	6.3	6.7
Age 25–34	22.8	22.1	19.7	23.5
Age 35–64	60.7	59.8	59.8	55.4
Age 65 and over	11.5	12.9	14.2	14.4
Percentage on Farms	17.5	11.0	5.4	3.8

Sources: *Current Population Reports*, Series P–60, no. 118; Series P–20, nos. 21, 80 and Technical Paper no. 17.

Table 6.3	Selected Demographic Changes among Unrelated Individuals, 1947–77 (in Percentages)			
	1947	1957	1967	1977
Males	45.1	39.1	36.9	43.3
Females	54.9	60.9	63.1	56.7
Earners	65.5	67.2	61.8	63.7
Age 14–24	10.1	9.3	11.6	17.8
Age 25–34	13.0	11.8	9.3	19.7
Age 35–64	46.5	45.8	40.5	30.8
Age 65 and over	30.4	33.0	38.6	31.7
Living on Farms	11.8	6.2	2.6	1.7

Sources: *Current Population Reports*, Series P–60, nos. 5, 30, 59, 118, and Technical Paper no. 17.

wages, interest, and transfers accounted for greater shares of augmented personal income in 1977 than was true in 1947, whereas proprietor's income, rents, and corporate profits accounted for smaller shares.[14]

Where Did It Go?

The concept of augmented personal income as defined here can be divided into three principal uses:

1. Spending: the sum of personal consumption expenditures, interest paid to businesses, and transfers to foreigners, *minus* indirect taxes.
2. Saving: personal saving as in the NIA *plus* retained earnings.

Table 6.4	Sources of Augmented Personal Income, 1947–77					
	Percentage Share					
Year	Wages[1]	Proprietor's Income	Rents	Interest	Corporate Profits[2]	Transfers
Postwar Average	67.6	10.9	2.7	5.7	5.6	7.5
1947	64.5	17.9	2.6	3.6	5.5	5.9
1957	68.7	12.0	3.3	4.6	5.5	5.8
1967	67.7	8.7	2.8	6.5	6.7	7.5
1977	67.7	5.9	1.4	8.3	4.5	12.2

Source: National income accounts.

[1]Compensation of employees.

[2]Corporate profits (with inventory valuation adjustment and capital consumption adjustment) minus corporate tax liabilities. This is equal to the sum of dividends and retained earnings.

3. Taxes: personal taxes as in the NIA *plus* contributions for social insurance *plus* indirect taxes. (This can be viewed as purchases of public consumption.)

Using this three-way split, table 6.5 shows that spending has commanded a dwindling share and taxes have commanded an expanding share during the postwar period. The share of savings exhibits no trend, though saving rates were unusually low in three of the last four years. Closer inspection of these data reveals that the share of consumption stabilized between 62 and 63 percent around 1966 or so, and the share of taxes stabilized near 30 percent around 1968. Thus, since 1968 American consumers have paid about 30 percent of their gross incomes to the tax collector, saved about 7 percent, and spent the remaining 63 percent.

6.3.2   Patterns of Consumption, 1947–77

So income and consumption have grown mightily over the postwar period. How have American consumers spent this largesse? An examination of postwar changes in consumption patterns is interesting for the profile it draws of the American way of life. And it also holds a few surprises. A logical place to start is with changes in budget shares. What fraction of each dollar of consumer spending was spent on various items in 1947 and 1977? Which items commanded an increasing share of the consumer's budget and which a decreasing share?

Table 6.6 contains some answers; but there are too many numbers in this table for it to "speak for itself," and many others hidden in the data that underlie it. Let us see what story these data tell.

Table 6.5   **Uses of Augmented Personal Income, 1947–77**

Year	Percentage Share		
	Spending[1]	Saving[2]	Taxes[3]
Postwar average	65.5	7.6	26.9
1947	72.4	4.7	22.8
1957	66.7	8.0	25.4
1967	62.2	9.7	28.1
1977	62.9	5.7	31.3

Source: U.S. Bureau of Economic Analysis (1976) and *Survey of Current Business*, July 1979.

[1]Personal outlays less indirect taxes.

[2]Personal savings plus retained earnings.

[3]Personal taxes plus contributions for social insurance plus indirect taxes.

Table 6.6   **Selected Budget Shares, 1947 and 1977 (in Percentage Points)**

Item	Share of Total Consumer Spending		Change
	1947	1977	1947–77
Food[1]	34.7	21.8	− 12.9
Purchased meals	6.7	5.2	− 1.5
Alcoholic beverages	5.3	2.4	− 2.9
Housing—Rent	9.9	15.5	+ 5.6
Owner occupied	5.2	10.4	+ 5.2
Tenant occupied	3.5	4.0	+ 0.5
Household Operation	14.6	14.6	0
Household appliances	1.8	1.0	− 0.8
Electricity	0.9	2.1	+ 1.2
Fuel oil and coal	1.8	1.1	− 0.7
Telephone and telegraph	0.9	1.7	+ 0.8
Domestic service	1.5	0.6	− 0.9
Clothing[2]	14.1	8.0	− 6.1
Transportation	9.8	14.2	+ 4.4
User-operated[3]	8.0	13.4	+ 5.4
Purchased local	1.2	0.3	− 0.9
Purchased intercity	0.6	0.5	− 0.1
Airline	0.06	0.40	+ 0.34
Other	0.54	0.09	− 0.45
Recreation[4]	6.2	7.7	+ 1.5
Foreign travel[4]	0.5	1.0	+ 0.5
TV, radio, etc.[5]	0.9	1.5	+ 0.6
Toys, sports equipment, etc.[6]	1.2	1.8	+ 0.6
Admissions to spectator events	1.2	0.6	− 0.6
Personal Services	4.0	6.6	+ 2.6
Personal business	3.2	5.1	+ 1.9
Brokerage	0.15	0.36	+ 0.21
Life insurance	0.88	0.99	+ 0.11
Legal services	0.41	0.77	+ 0.36
Private education	0.80	1.5	+ 0.7
Medical Care	4.5	9.6	+ 5.1
Doctors and dentists	1.8	3.2	+ 1.4
Private hospitals	0.9	4.0	+ 3.1
Health insurance[7]	0.30	0.67	+ 0.37

Sources: Computed by author from data in U.S. Bureau of Economic Analysis *The National Income and Product Accounts of the United States, 1929–1974*, and *Survey of Current Business*, July 1979.

[1]Includes tobacco and alcoholic beverages.

[2]Includes shoes, accessories, and jewelry.

[3]Mostly costs of purchasing, maintaining, and operating automobiles.

[4]Includes expenditures abroad by United States residents.

[5]Radio and television receivers, records, and musical instruments.

[6]Wheel goods, toys, sports equipment, boats, and pleasure aircraft. Includes both durables and nondurables.

[7]For medical care, hospitalization, and income loss. Does not include workmen's compensation. Data pertain to 1948.

At the coarsest level of aggregation, the table shows just about what we expect. Americans are now spending more of their budgets on housing, medical care, private transportation, recreation, and personal services than they were in 1947. At the same time, they are spending less on food, clothing, and public transportation. But if we peer a bit below the surface, some fascinating details emerge.

Food

Spending on virtually every category of food declined in relative importance over this thirty-year period, including even *meals away from home* (which came as a surprise to me). They claimed 6.7¢ out of every dollar in 1947, but only 5.2¢ in 1977. (One can only imagine what the French would think of this!)

The most dramatic decline, again surprisingly, was for *alcoholic beverages*—which accounted for only 2.4 percent of the 1977 budget as against 5.3 percent in 1947. In fact, real consumption of alcoholic beverages per capita increased only 12 percent over the thirty-year period, despite the fact that its price relative to all consumption items fell by 26 percent. Americans are indeed drinking (relatively) less.

Accompanying the decline in relative spending on food came a noticeable *upgrading in diets* (though not necessarily in their nutritive content). As table 6.7 indicates, per capita consumption of beef almost doubled, per capita consumption of chicken almost tripled, and consumption of such luxury and convenience items as ice cream, processed fruits, and processed vegetables registered dramatic increases. Concurrent with these increases came sharp declines in per capita consumption of such obviously inferior goods as pork, lard, potatoes, and cornmeal. Consumption

Table 6.7   Civilian per Capita Consumption of Selected Food Items, 1940 and 1970 (in Pounds per Year)

Year	Beef and Veal	Chicken and Turkey	Processed Fruits[1]	Processed Vegetables[2]	Ice Cream
1940	62	17	34	35	11
1970	117	50	54	74	18

Year	Pork	Lard	Potatoes	Cornmeal and Corn Flour	Fresh Fruit	Fresh Vegetables
1940	74	14	139	22	139	117
1970	66	5	95	7	81	99

Source: U.S. Bureau of the Census, *Historical Statistics of the United States*, vol. 1, Series G881–915.

[1]Canned or frozen fruits and fruit juices; dried fruit.

[2]Canned or frozen.

of fresh fruits and vegetables also declined, though one may legitimately question whether this marked an increase in living standards. (Adelle Davis lives!)

Housing

The costs of owning or renting a home or apartment claimed 15.5 percent of consumer budgets in 1977 as against 9.9 percent in 1947. Almost all of the increase is accounted for by *owner-occupied housing*, as growing income levels and strong incentives set up by the income tax system combined to induce a substantial shift from renting to owning. In 1940 only 44 percent of Americans owned their own home; by 1970, 63 percent did (see table 6.8, part A).

It is worth noting that the rapid escalation of housing prices that we have experienced in recent years was *not* characteristic of the postwar period as a whole. In fact, between 1947 and 1977 housing prices increased only 151 percent while consumer prices in general increased 165 percent. Housing commanded an increasing budget share because real per capita consumption of housing tripled.

Some data compiled by Lebergott (1976) enable us to go somewhat beyond these rather dry statistics (see table 6.8, part A). Between 1940 and 1970, *crowding* diminished significantly. The fraction of housing units with more persons than rooms declined from 20 percent to 8 percent, and the average number of persons per room fell from .74 to .62.

Table 6.8   **Selected Changes in United States Housing, 1940–70**

A. Characteristics of Housing Units

| Year | Average Age (in Years) | % Owner-Occupied | Persons per Room | | Percentage with | |
			Average	Percentage > 1.0	Running Water	Flush Toilets
1940	31.7	44	.74	20.3	70	60
1970	27.7	63	.62	8.0	98	96

B. Characteristics of Household Operation

| Year | Percentage with | | Energy Source for Heating | | Percentage with | |
	Central Heat	Electric Lighting	Wood or Coal	Oil or Gas	Mechanical Refrigerators	Television
1940	42	79	78	22	44	0
1970	78	99	4	82	99	99

Sources: Lebergott 1976; except for average age of (private nonfarm) housing stock and percentage owner-occupied, which came from *Historical Statistics*, Series 217 and 243.

The *quality* of housing also improved. The average age of the housing stock fell by four years, the fraction of housing units with running water increased from 70 percent to 98 percent, and the fraction with flush toilets increased from 60 percent to 96 percent.[15]

Household Operation

Other improvements in the way Americans are housed become apparent only when we look at expenditures on household operation. While the total budget share spent on this category did not change, its composition underwent radical surgery. Table 6.6 shows, for example, that the budget share allocated to *household appliances* fell almost in half between 1947 and 1977. What this conceals is that the very steep decline in the relative prices of these items enabled Americans to have more and more while spending less and less.[16] By 1977, *real* spending per capita on household appliances was more than double what it had been in 1947, and the *stock* of household durables must have increased by much more than this. Lebergott (1976) reports, for example, that the fraction of American families owning mechanical refrigerators increased from 44 percent to 99 percent between 1940 and 1970. The penetration of televisions went from zero in 1940 to virtually 100 percent by 1970.

Sources of power for household operation tell a fascinating tale. Spending on electricity more than doubled despite a decline in its relative price; real spending per capita increased more than fivefold. Concurrently, fuel oil and coal demanded a decreasing share of consumers' budgets despite a sharply increasing relative price. In fact, household usage of fuel oil and coal was unchanged in absolute terms between 1947 and 1977 despite a 53 percent increase in population. There was, in brief, a veritable revolution in the way homes were heated—away from dirty fuels such as coal and wood, which also require considerable effort to use, and toward such cleaner and more convenient fuels as oil, gas, and electricity. Lebergott (1976), for example, reports that the fraction of United States families heating by wood or coal dropped from 78 percent to 4 percent, while the fraction using oil or gas rose from 22 percent to 82 percent, between 1940 and 1970 (see table 6.8, part B).

There were other notable changes as well. The average American used the *telephone* about five and one-half times as much in 1977 as in 1947, but did so while allocating a budget share only twice as large.

One further item which is of trivial importance in consumer budgets nowadays, but is nonetheless interesting for the light it sheds on postwar changes in America, is spending on *domestic service*. In 1947, Americans spent 1.5 percent of their budget on domestic service—a sum almost as large as what they spent on doctors and dentists, and even larger than what they spent on either local public transportation or private education. About one household in fourteen had a domestic employee.

By 1977, the price of domestic service had increased 321 percent (versus 165 percent for consumer prices in general); only about one household in twenty-seven had a domestic worker;[17] and this budget item claimed only 0.6¢ out of every consumer dollar. In real terms, the consumption of domestic services declined *absolutely* by 31 percent (or 55 percent on a per capita basis). In the murder mysteries of the 1970s, the butler was never there to do it.

Clothing

Food, clothing, and shelter are supposed to be the three basic necessities. Like food, clothing gobbled up a smaller and smaller share of the consumer's budget during the postwar period. By 1977, consumers were spending only 8¢ of every dollar on clothing (including shoes, jewelry, and accessories) as compared to 14¢ in 1947. In part, this resulted from a decline in the relative price of clothing (by 28 percent from 1947 to 1977); but even *real* spending on clothing grew noticeably slower than total spending.

Food, clothing, and shelter together, it may be noted, absorbed fully 88 percent of total spending in 1947 but less than 75 percent in 1977. Room was being made for nonnecessities.

Transportation

Spending patterns on transportation goods and services reveal a pattern that is fascinating even though its basic outlines are well known. The almighty *automobile* was already well ensconced on the American scene by 1947—claiming 8 percent of consumer budgets for its purchase, care, and feeding (as compared with only 1.8 percent for all forms of purchased transportation). But the automobilization of America accelerated during the postwar period. By 1977, consumers were spending 13.4¢ out of every dollar on their cars, and a negligible 0.8¢ on purchased transportation.

When we recall that *air travel* was almost nonexistent in 1947, but dominated purchased intercity travel by 1977, the comparison is more dramatic still. Purchased transportation *excluding air travel* took 1.7¢ out of every consumer dollar in 1947, but only 0.4¢ in 1977. It is only a slight exaggeration to say that the postwar period witnessed the death of the train, the bus, and the subway.

Recreation

Spending patterns on recreational goods and services offer some surprises. Even including foreign travel as recreation,[18] the share of recreational spending in consumer budgets increased only 1.5 percentage points during the postwar period. This is much less than Madison Avenue has led us to expect. Furthermore, more than all of this increase was accounted for by only three categories of spending: foreign travel (from 0.5 percent to 1.0 percent); purchases of televisions, radios, and similar goods (from 0.9 percent to 1.5 percent); and purchases of recreational hardgoods such as toys, sports equipment, bicycles, and boats (from 1.2 percent to 1.8 percent). Television sets are particularly remarkable since they claimed an increasing budget share despite a price that fell *absolutely* by 16 percent (that's right!).[19] America's love affair with the television is a notable feature of the postwar period.

Several categories of recreational spending actually made decreasing claims on the consumer's budget, notably *admissions to spectator events* (movies, theater, sports events) which received only 0.6¢ out of every consumer dollar in 1977 as compared to 1.2¢ in 1947. And this occurred despite the fact that prices for such events rose 300 percent (as compared to only 165 percent for overall consumer prices). Real purchases of such admissions actually *declined* 16 percent despite rising population and rising real income. So much for the alleged boom in movies and spectator sports.

Personal Services

Personal services are an odd mixture including such diverse items as private educational spending, life insurance, legal fees, and the costs of stock brokerage. All of these grew rapidly, with spending on stockbrokers displaying the fastest growth (increasing more than eighteenfold) and life insurance costs having the smallest (increasing more than eight-fold).

Medical Care

Everyone knows that Americans are spending more on medical care than they did early in the postwar period (9.6 percent of consumer budgets as compared to 4.5 percent). And everyone knows that consumers are unhappy about the soaring costs of medical care. The tremendous increase in the share of the budget going to medical care is due both to its increasing relative price and to a rapid increase in real consumption of medical services, especially hospital services. While health has improved demonstrably during the last thirty years (more on this in section 6.6), this may have been due more to advances in public health than to increased personal expenditures on medical care.

Summary

During the thirty-year period from 1947 to 1977, real consumption per capita increased by more than 80 percent. As compared to their counterparts in 1947, Americans in 1977 traveled by airplane and watched TV vastly more. They replaced pork, lard, cornmeal, and fresh vegetables in their diets with beef, poultry, and processed fruits and vegetables. They made much greater use of electricity, the telephone, and hospitals, and they spent much more on their own homes—which they heated by gas and oil rather than coal and wood. They bought more toys, sports equipment, and other recreational goods (but not more admission tickets), and devoted a good deal more of their budgets to nurturing their cars.

During the same period, travel by bus, rail, and subway diminished greatly; domestic servants nearly disappeared from the scene; and the basic necessities of life—food, clothing, and shelter—commanded ever decreasing shares of the consumer budget.

One seems forced to the conclusion that the average level of economic well-being both changed in content and improved drastically. Virtually everyone shared in economic growth, but not equally. I turn my attention now to trends in income inequality.

6.4 Trends in Income Inequality

Whereas the level of income was mostly increasing during the postwar period, the central stylized fact about income inequality has been its *constancy*. Table 6.9 displays the basic data that support this fact, and they certainly seem unequivocal. According to the Gini ratio, for example, 1957 was the most equal year and 1961 was the most unequal. Inequality in 1977 was the same as it was in 1947. If we accept these data at face value, there clearly is no postwar trend in income inequality.[20]

Table 6.9   **The Distribution of Income, Families and Unrelated Individuals Pooled, 1947–77**

	Percentage Share						
Year	Lowest Fifth	Second Fifth	Middle Fifth	Fourth Fifth	Highest Fifth	Top 5%	Gini Ratio
1947	3.5	10.6	16.8	23.6	45.5	18.7	.418
1952	3.5	10.9	17.3	24.1	44.3	18.4	.408
1957	3.4	10.9	18.0	24.7	42.9	16.5	.397
1962	3.4	10.4	17.5	24.8	43.9	16.8	.407
1967	3.6	10.6	17.5	24.8	43.4	16.5	.400
1972	3.7	10.0	16.9	24.7	44.8	17.4	.414
1977	3.8	9.7	16.5	24.9	45.2	17.3	.419
Highest	3.9	11.2	18.0	24.9	45.5	18.7	.420
Mean	3.5	10.5	17.3	24.6	44.1	17.2	.408
Lowest	3.1	9.7	16.5	23.6	42.9	16.5	.397

Source: *Current Population Reports*, Series P–60, no. 118, table 13.

But there are a host of very good reasons *not* to accept these data at face value—which is why this section occupies many pages instead of one sentence. First, the changing structure of the United States population by age, sex, and family composition raises questions about the comparability of the data over time. Rough "corrections" for these demographic shifts point to a slight trend toward equality which the raw data mask. Second, attempts to improve the measurement of income by such methods as subtracting taxes or adding transfers in kind seem to produce an income concept whose distribution displays greater equalization over the period than does census income. Third, and most speculatively, it has been suggested that the portion of measured inequality that is simply due to the fact that different people are at different stages in their life cycles has increased over the postwar period so that, if we could measure it, the distribution of *lifetime* incomes would show a greater trend toward equality than the distribution of *annual* incomes.

It turns out, most disagreeably for students of the subject, that the sensitivity of the distribution of income in the United States to subtle changes in the recipient population, the definition of income, or the choice of accounting period is extremely large—much greater in fact than any changes we can find in inequality through time. This, I think, is the most fundamental sense in which we can say that inequality has been relatively constant. But it also explains the urgency of sorting out these seemingly boring issues of definition.

Such issues will occupy the bulk of this section. But before getting buried in the details, I pause briefly to consider a prior question: Does the (relatively constant) postwar income distribution, with its Gini ratio in the .40–.42 range, represent a lot of inequality or a little?

6.4.1   Is the Bottle Half Full or Half Empty?

Clearly, to paraphrase the exceedingly wise words of Rufus Miles, where you stand on this question depends on where you sit in the income distribution. While an "objective" answer is clearly out of the question, let me attempt several ways of providing a frame of reference.

Comparisons over Time

I have already noted that changes in inequality during the postwar period have been too small to provide useful intertemporal comparisons. According to the Gini measure, 1957 had the most equal distribution while 1961 had the least equal. Yet the difference between their Gini ratios is a scant 6 percent (see also fig. 6.1). So if we want to draw useful comparisons through time, we will have to look back further into United States history. Naturally, the quality of the data tails off rather quickly as we do this; but some distributions for earlier years have been constructed. Budd (1967, introduction) has compiled more or less consistent income distributions for several prewar and several postwar years (see table 6.10).[21] The conclusion seems to be that there was substantial equalization during the years of the Great Depression and World War II, but very little change since then. The postwar distribution seems noticeably more equal than the distribution in 1929.

Comparisons over Space

Instead of comparing the postwar income distribution of the United States with the United States income distribution in earlier years, we might compare the United States with other countries at the same time. The hazard here is that different countries use different concepts of income and different definitions of the recipient unit than the United States and, as just mentioned, income distributions can be quite sensitive to these choices. Of the many international comparisons that have been made, two seem worth reporting here. Some years ago Irving Kravis (1960; 1962) made a careful series of binary comparisons by taking the income distributions of ten foreign countries and comparing each one with a *different* United States distribution selected to be conceptually alike. His conclusion was that income inequality in the United States was rather less than in several less developed countries, but somewhere near the middle of a group of modern industrial nations. More recently, a study by Malcolm Sawyer for the OECD (1976) attempted to put the distributional statistics of the various OECD nations on an equal footing so that comparisons could be made. He found the United States and France to have the most income inequality among OECD nations.

The overall conclusion, then, seems to be that income inequality in the United States is higher than in many industrialized nations, but lower than in most less developed countries.

Table 6.10   **Prewar and Postwar Income Distributions**

Year	Lowest Fifth	Second Fifth	Middle Fifth	Fourth Fifth	Highest Fifth	Top 5%	Gini Ratio
	Percentage Share						
1929	3.5	9.0	13.8	19.3	54.4	30.0	.49
1935–36	4.1	9.2	14.1	20.9	51.7	26.5	.47
1941	4.1	9.5	15.3	22.3	48.8	24.0	.44
1947[a]	5.0	11.0	16.0	22.0	46.0	20.9	.40
1962[a]	4.6	10.9	16.3	22.7	45.5	19.6	.40

Source: Budd (1967, table 1, p. xiii).

Note: Families and unrelated individuals, pooled. Based on Office of Business Economics (now Bureau of Economic Analysis) income concept.

[a]These Lorenz curves cross.

Interpreting the 1977 Distribution

Another way to appraise the degree of inequality is to subject the most recent data on income shares to further scrutiny along the following lines (see table 6.11). Data for 1977 tell us that the richest fifth of American families received eight times as much income as the poorest fifth.[22] This 8:1 ratio, which is characteristic of the entire postwar period, strikes me as a very substantial income gap. But some further facts make this inequality seem less severe.

First, it turns out that richer families tend to be larger. The richest fifth of families in 1977 actually included 28 percent more persons than the poorest fifth. Adjusting income to a per capita basis would bring the 8:1 income ratio down to 6.25:1. Second, it turns out that the richest fifth of families in 1977 contained 29 percent of all the wage earners in the country, whereas the poorest fifth contained only 9.5 percent. Thus on a per earner basis, the income ratio was only 2.6:1. And even this ratio can be lowered by considering work effort. The richest fifth of families supplied over 30 percent of the total weeks worked in the economy during 1977, while the poorest fifth supplied only 7.5 percent. Thus, on a per-week-of-work basis, the income ratio between rich and poor was only 2:1. This certainly does not seem like an unreasonable degree of inequality.[23]

Thus we can use the very same data to show that the income gap between the rich and the poor is anything from 8:1 to 2:1—an ambiguity that will make propagandists (from either side) happy. Which ratio is "right"? I certainly do not know. On the one hand, if differences in family size are voluntary (richer parents "buy" more children), and decisions over whether and how much to work are involuntary (due mostly to whether jobs are available), then none of the corrections are warranted and the 8:1 ratio seems most meaningful. On the other hand, if we assume that people voluntarily choose their labor supply but not

Table 6.11   **Characteristics of the Upper and Lower Tails of the Distribution of Family Income, 1977**

Income Group	Percentage Share			
	Income	Persons	Earners	Weeks of Work
Top Fifth	41.6	22.4	28.9	30.4
Bottom Fifth	5.2	17.5	9.5	7.5
Top Tenth	25.6	11.4	15.1	15.7
Bottom Tenth	1.7	8.8	4.0	2.9

Source: *Current Population Reports*, Series P–60, no. 118, table 3, p. 21.

their family size, then all the corrections leading to a 2:1 ratio are appropriate. To state the issue this way is to demonstrate its irresolvability. Clearly, all of these choices have voluntary and involuntary aspects.

6.4.2   Demographic Changes and the Problems They Cause

I turn now to the first of our problems in interpreting the postwar income distribution data and in accepting the conclusion that inequality has not changed: demographic changes.[24] This section makes three main points. First, demographic changes have been substantial.[25] Second, measured income inequality is quite sensitive to the composition of the underlying population of recipient units. Third, many of the demographic changes that occurred were of the sort that raise measured inequality.

Families versus Unrelated Individuals

A logical place to start is with the division of the United States population between families and unrelated individuals. As table 6.12 shows, this division has changed dramatically over the postwar period, and especially over the last decade. In this ten-year period, the population of the United States over the age of sixteen increased 19 percent, but the number of census families increased only 14 percent, and average family size fell from 3.67 to 3.33 persons. By contrast, the number of unrelated individuals grew by an astounding 75 percent in these same ten years. These figures reflect several striking demographic trends, including a growing propensity for both the young and the old to live apart and an increasing incidence of broken marriages.

Table 6.13 shows why these developments are important for interpreting income distribution data. Unrelated individuals have always had much lower and much more unequally distributed incomes than have families, though there was some convergence in both respects during the last decade. Thus the demographic shifts that underlie table 6.12, many of which clearly represent improvements in well-being, lowered

Table 6.12	Composition of Income Units, 1947–77			
	1947	1957	1967	1977
Percentage of Units that are				
Families	82.1	80.8	79.1	71.2
Unrelated individuals	17.9	19.2	20.9	28.8
Percentage of People in				
Families	93.4	93.0	93.3	89.2
Unrelated individuals	6.6	7.0	6.7	10.8

Source: *Current Population Reports*, Series P–60, nos. 59, 114, 118; and Series P–20, nos. 21, 33.

average income and increased income inequality when families and unrelated individuals are pooled in a single distribution.

A first step, therefore, is to look separately at trends in the distributions among families and among unrelated individuals. These are summarized in tables 6.14 and 6.15, but before considering these data one technical point must be made (with due apologies to the casual reader). Data on percentile shares for the years 1958 through 1977 were computed in the obvious way: by ranking consumer units and adding up

Table 6.13   Comparison of Income Distributions among Families and among Unrelated Individuals, 1947–77

	1947	1957	1967	1977
Mean Real Income[1]				
1. Per Family	$9,620	$11,719	$15,974	$18,264
2. Per Unrelated Individual	4,306	4,834	6,403	7,981
3. Ratio (2)/(1)	.45	.41	.40	.44
Gini Ratio				
4. Ratio Among Families	.376	.351	.348	.364
5. Among Unrelated Individuals	.552	.489	.490	.443
6. Ratio (5)/(4)	1.47	1.39	1.41	1.22

Source: *Current Population Reports*, Series P–60, nos. 114, 118.
[1]Mean income in 1977 dollars. Price deflation by Consumer Price Index.

Table 6.14   The Distribution of Income among Families, 1947–77

Year	Lowest Fifth	Second Fifth	Middle Fifth	Fourth Fifth	Highest Fifth	Top 5%	Gini Ratio
1947	5.0	11.9	17.0	23.1	43.0	17.5	.376
1952	4.9	12.3	17.4	23.4	41.9	17.4	.368
1957	5.1	12.7	18.1	23.8	40.4	15.6	.351
1962	5.0	12.1	17.6	24.0	41.3	15.7	.362
1967	5.5	12.4	17.9	23.9	40.4	15.2	.348
1972	5.4	11.9	17.5	23.9	41.4	15.9	.360
1977	5.2	11.6	17.5	24.2	41.5	15.7	.364
Highest	5.6	12.7	18.1	24.2	43.0	17.5	.379
Mean	5.1	12.2	17.6	23.8	41.3	16.0	.361
Lowest	4.5	11.6	17.0	23.1	40.4	15.2	.348

Source: *Current Population Reports*, Series P–60, no. 118, table 13.

Table 6.15   **The Distribution of Income among Unrelated Individuals, 1947–77**

| | Percentage Share | | | | | | |
Year	Lowest Fifth	Second Fifth	Middle Fifth	Fourth Fifth	Highest Fifth	Top 5%	Gini Ratio
1947	2.0	6.2	12.7	22.5	56.6	29.3	.552
1952	2.6	7.7	14.7	25.4	49.7	20.2	.480
1957	2.6	7.3	13.7	25.4	50.9	19.7	.489
1962	2.6	7.5	12.8	24.4	52.7	20.8	.502
1967	3.0	7.5	13.5	24.5	51.5	21.1	.490
1972	3.3	8.2	13.8	23.9	50.9	21.4	.478
1977	4.1	9.0	14.7	24.0	48.2	19.6	.443
Highest	4.2	9.0	14.8	27.0	56.6	29.3	.552
Mean	2.8	7.6	13.7	24.7	51.1	21.0	.489
Lowest	1.4	6.2	12.7	22.5	47.9	18.7	.442

Source: *Current Population Reports*, Series P–60, no. 118, table 13.

their incomes. For the years 1947–57, however, the micro data required to do this were unavailable, so shares were estimated and interpolated from grouped data. The post-1958 data are thus more trustworthy than the pre-1958 data, and we must keep this in mind in looking for trends.[26]

In the case of families, the data show some trend toward equality before 1957 though little since then—which raises the question of whether we are seeing a trend or a statistical illusion. Between 1947 and 1957, there were clear (if modest) upward trends in the shares of the second, middle, and fourth fifths. All of these gains came at the expense of the upper fifth (and especially the top 5 percent), whose shares declined quite markedly. Since 1958, however, there is little trend of any kind. The only development worth noting is the climb of the share of the lowest fifth from the 4.5–5 percent range to around 5.5 percent during the years 1961–66. The host of public assistance policies introduced or expanded around that time is, of course, the leading explanation for this improvement in the lot of poor families.

Using the Gini ratio to summarize these data, all of this can be said more concisely by noting that, once cyclical effects are removed, the Gini ratio exhibits a mild downward trend (about −.002 per year) until 1957 and no trend thereafter.[27]

The story with unrelated individuals seems to have been just the reverse: relative stability until 1957 followed by a marked trend toward equality.[28]

The share of the lowest fifth fluctuated aimlessly through 1957, apparently underwent a shift (not shown in table 6.15) when the nature of the data changed in 1958, and marched steadily upward thereafter. The shares of the second and third fifths did very little until about 1964 and then also started to move up strongly. In total, the combined share of the lower 60 percent of the income distribution increased from 25.4 percent to 28 percent between 1964 and 1975—a substantial improvement. The upper 40 percent, naturally, were the losers. Beginning around 1960 or so, the shares of these two quintiles exhibit a noticeable downward trend.

In sum, the postwar data show:

1. An equalizing trend in the family distribution until 1957 but not after (table 6.14)
2. An equalizing trend in the distribution among unrelated individuals since 1957 but not before (table 6.15)
3. A decrease in the portion of the population in families (table 6.12)
4. A widening of the income gap between families and unrelated individuals between 1947 and 1957 and a narrowing of that gap from 1967 to 1977 (table 6.13)

All of these conflicting forces get amalgamated in the pooled distribution to produce very little overall trend despite some equalization in both component distributions.

The Changing American Family

But we do not solve the problem of demographic change simply by separating families from unrelated individuals. For, as we learned in tables 6.2 and 6.3, both the composition of families and the nature of the unrelated individuals population underwent substantial demographic change during the postwar period. To keep the discussion manageable, I limit myself to families in what follows. But the reader should keep in mind that equally dramatic changes were occurring in the demography of unrelated individuals, with corresponding effects on the income distribution.

Just what were the changes in the structure of the American family, and how did they affect the distribution of income? We can answer these questions with the help of table 6.2 which lists some important demographic changes, and table 6.16, which illustrates the extreme sensitivity of income inequality to the nature of the recipient unit.[29]

Average family size was constant between 1947 and 1967, but fell dramatically during the following ten years due to a sharp decline in the number of children. This means that family income *per capita* grew more rapidly than mean family income. The distribution of families by size shows that most of the statistical "action" came in the two tails. At one extreme the fraction of families with two members drifted up slowly from 1947 to 1967, and then skyrocketed between 1967 and 1977.[30] At the other extreme, the number of families with six or more members also drifted up slowly during the first two postwar decades, but then took a nosedive between 1967 and 1977. Relative to 1947, we now have

Table 6.16   Gini Ratios for Various Types of Families, 1964

A. By Family Size[1]		*D. By Age of Head*[2]		
Two persons	.408	14–24 years	.302	
Three persons	.337	25–34 years	.291	
Four persons	.311	35–44 years	.316	
Five persons	.316	45–54 years	.330	
Six persons	.335	55–64 years	.379	
Seven persons or more	.355	65 years and over	.471	
B. By Family Structure		*E. By Number of Earners*		
Female headed	.434	No earners	.418	
Male headed	.343	One earner	.361	
Married, wife present	.339	Two earners	.297	
Working wife	.290	Three earners or more	.285	
Nonworking wife	.365			
Other marital status	.365	*F. By Head's Work History in 1964*		
		Did not work	.452	
C. By Residence		Worked	.327	
Nonfarm	.347	At full-time jobs	.311	
Farm	.433	At part-time jobs	.444	
		G. By Color		
		White	.349	
		Nonwhite	.399	

Source: U.S. Bureau of the Census, *Trends in the Income of Families and Persons in the United States, 1947–1964*, Technical Paper no. 17 (Washington, D.C.: Government Printing Office), tables 23, 24, 25, 26, 28, 32, and 33.
[1]The Lorenz curves for three-person and six-person families cross between the 60th and 80th percentiles.
[2]The Lorenz curves for ages 14–24 and ages 25–34 cross between the 80th and 95th percentiles. The Lorenz curves for ages 25–34 and ages 35–44 cross between the 40th and 60th percentiles.

more childless couples, fewer families with four children or more, and fewer extended families. But since table 6.16 shows that the greatest degree of inequality is found among the largest and smallest families, it is not clear that these very large demographic shifts had much influence on the trend in inequality.

The next change in family composition worthy of note is the increased incidence of female headship. The fraction of families headed by females, which fluctuated in a range around 10 percent from 1947 to 1967, shot up to 14.4 percent by 1977. Since female-headed families normally have lower incomes than male-headed families, and since table 6.16 shows that they also typically have more unequally distributed incomes, this factor tended to retard the growth of income per family and to increase inequality.

The farm population dwindled remarkably during the postwar period. In 1947, more than one family in six lived on a farm. By 1977, this was down to one family in twenty-six. It is quite likely that this migration from the farm reduced income inequality because farm incomes are much more unequally distributed than nonfarm incomes (see table 6.16) and because farm incomes are typically much lower than nonfarm incomes. However, there is a complication that bears mentioning. Census money income excludes income received in kind, which is probably far more important on farms than elsewhere. Since census data therefore overstate the gap between farm and nonfarm incomes, they probably also overstate the equalization caused by the migration from rural areas.

The age structure of families (as measured by the age of the family head) also changed dramatically. Between 1947 and 1977, the number of young (under 25) and old (65 and over) families grew much faster than the number in the prime earning years, ages 35–64 (table 6.2). Given the facts that families at the extremes of the age distribution always have much lower incomes than those in the middle and that the income distribution among the elderly is quite unequal (table 6.16), this development pushed inequality up.[31]

In summary, the changing age-sex composition of family heads pushed the distribution of income toward greater inequality while the movement off the farm pushed in the opposite direction. In addition, there were a host of other demographic changes, some of which may have had substantial effects on measured income inequality. Indeed, given the extreme sensitivity of income inequality to demography that table 6.16 documents, it is somewhat amazing that the distribution of income among families changed so little during a period when the demographic structure changed so much.

6.4.3 Measured Inequality and the Income Concept

It has already been mentioned that the concept of income used by the Census Bureau is far from ideal. Two obvious questions follow. First, if we could measure income better, would inequality appear less than in the official data? Second, if we could measure income better, would a stronger trend toward equality emerge? This section answers both of these questions in the affirmative.[32]

Specifically, this section deals with five potential improvements in the census income concept: subtracting personal taxes, adding in transfers in kind, adding in other types of income in kind, including capital gains, and correcting for underreporting of income. In addition, the influence of cash transfers on inequality is examined. As in the previous section, we shall see that changes in the definition of income typically cause changes in measured inequality that exceed anything we can find in the time series.

Personal Taxes

We can probably make sense of an income distribution that *excludes* both public transfer payments and taxes or one that *includes* both. But census income is an awkward halfway house which includes transfers but fails to deduct taxes. Thus a first step in improving the census income concept is to subtract personal taxes.[33] In practice, most studies have deducted only *federal* taxes, thus leaving state income taxes in the alleged "posttax" income figures.[34] The federal income tax is decidedly progressive. The payroll tax, while regressive relative to *earnings*, is not quite so regressive relative to *income* because low income groups receive a large proportion of their total income in transfers. Deducting both income and payroll taxes thus *decreases* measured inequality noticeably, as table 6.17 shows.[35]

A similar study by Taussig (1973), using 1967 data and an income concept similar to census income, reported that federal personal taxes reduced the Gini coefficient from .376 to .361. It seems unlikely that including state and local income taxes would change these figures very much, but including sales, excise, and property taxes might.[36] I conclude that the distribution of posttax income in any one year is moderately more equal than the distribution of pretax income. The difference, however, is not dramatic.

Because personal taxes have grown faster than pretax income (table 6.5), it seems obvious that subtracting them from census income each year would increase the trend toward equality. Yet a careful study of the 1950–70 period by Reynolds and Smolensky (1977) belies this supposition. They conclude instead that while taxes equalized the distribution of any one year, taxes had almost no effect on the trend in inequality of aftertax income.[37] Why the discrepancy? Reynolds and Smolensky (1977) show that federal personal taxes became less progressive between 1950 and 1970 for several reasons, the most important of which were (a) the increasing importance of the payroll tax relative to the income tax and (b) the decreasing progressivity of the income tax.

Transfers in Kind

Recent years have witnessed a sharp controversy, both in academic journals and in the popular press, over the extent to which adding transfers in kind to income would change the portrait of inequality in post-

Table 6.17	Effect of Federal Personal Taxes on the Distribution of Family Income, 1972		
Share of:	Before Tax	After Tax	Change
Lowest fifth	4.92	5.26	+0.34
Second fifth	11.59	12.23	+0.64
Middle fifth	17.22	17.69	+0.47
Fourth fifth	23.57	23.87	+0.30
Highest fifth	42.70	40.95	−1.75

Source: Radner 1979.

war America. The controversy is over the *quantitative* dimensions of the effect, not its *qualitative* direction, since no one disputes that (a) transfers in kind have grown much faster than factor incomes[38] and (b) the distribution of transfers in kind is much more favorable to the poor than the distribution of factor incomes. These undisputed facts are enough to conclude that more equality in any given year and a stronger trend toward equality would emerge if the distribution of income were adjusted to include transfers in kind. But how much more?

The reason for the controversy boils down to this. While it is straightforward to estimate the total volume of in-kind programs such as food stamps, public housing, public education, and medical services provided under Medicare and Medicaid, it is not quite so straightforward to distribute these totals among income groups. And it is even more difficult to decide how to price them out. Treating a dollar spent on a transfer in kind as equivalent to a dollar received in cash seems inappropriate unless the transfer in kind provides precisely what the consumer would have used the extra cash to purchase. However, there are two cases in which transfers in kind are just as good as cash.[39] The first is when the government provides goods that the consumer would otherwise have purchased anyway and provides *less* of them than the consumer would have bought for herself. In this case, the transfer in kind does not affect budget allocation decisions and is equivalent to a cash transfer. Food stamps come close to fitting this pattern; it is arguable whether Medicare and Medicaid do. However, it seems clear that public education and public housing are not of this character. The second case is where the good that is distributed can be resold with insubstantial transactions costs (e.g., a transferable ration coupon). It is clear, however, that few, if any, public programs fit this second model.

Apart from these exceptional cases, it is conceptually clear that transfers in kind are worth less to recipients than what they cost to provide.[40] But how much less? This question can only be answered by positing some utility function and assessing the cash equivalent (in utility terms) of each transfer in kind. An excellent recent study by Smolensky et al. (1977) did precisely this, and concluded that the cash equivalent of one dollar in either food stamps or rent supplements was essentially one dollar, but that one dollar spent on either public housing or Medicare/Medicaid was worth substantially less than one dollar to recipients.[41]

Table 6.18 summarizes the results of two conflicting studies of the effects of transfers in kind on the distribution of income in 1972, under the (possibly false) assumption that such transfers should be valued at full cost. The adjustment adds between 1.8 and 2.3 percentage points to the share of the poorest fifth of families, depending on whose assumptions about the volume and distribution of noneducational transfers we

Table 6.18	Effect of Transfers in Kind on the Distribution of Income among Families, 1978	
	Percentage Share	
Income Concept	Lowest Fifth	Highest Fifth
1. Census income	5.40	41.36
2. Census income plus educational transfers	5.97	40.22
3. Census income plus noneducational transfers		
(a) Browning	7.29	40.09
(b) Smeeding	6.75	40.37
4. Census income plus *all* in-kind transfers		
(a) Browning	7.70	39.09
(b) Smeeding	7.21	39.35

Source: Calculated by author from data in Browning (1979) and Smeeding (1979a).

use,[42] and subtracts a like amount from the share of the richest fifth. These are substantial changes. However, the increment to the share of the lowest fifth would be reduced by about one-half percentage point if transfers in kind were valued at 70 percent of cost instead.[43]

We are thus far from agreement over how large the effect of transfers in kind has been on the postwar trend toward equality. After a series of papers by Browning (1976; 1979) and Smeeding (1979a; 1979b), airing this and a number of other issues, it appears (Smeeding 1979b) that Browning's adjustments (including one for transfers in kind) raise the share of the lowest fifth of families in 1972 from 5.4 percent in the raw data all the way to 8.5 percent. Smeeding's corrections, by contrast, raise it only to 6.5 percent. The difference is hardly inconsequential, though only part of it traces to their divergent treatments of transfers in kind.

Cash Transfers

This seems an appropriate time to ask how large an equalizing effect *cash* transfers have had on the distribution of income. Unlike the other concerns of this section, this does not constitute a "correction" of census income, since census income already includes cash transfers; but the issue seems important enough to merit special attention.

By how much do cash transfers reduce income inequality in any given year? A number of studies have tried to answer this question, with relatively good agreement that cash transfers have decreased the Gini ratio by about 12 percent in recent years.[44] Taussig's (1973) study shows that the equalizing impact of cash transfers is much greater than that of taxes. The study by Smolensky et al. (1977) enables us to compare the equalizing effects of cash and in-kind transfers with the following results:

Reduction in the Gini Ratio

From cash transfers	—.046
From in-kind transfers:	
valued at full cost	—.027
valued at cash equivalent	—.016

Clearly cash transfers are much more important as equalizers, even if transfers in kind (including educational transfers) are valued on a dollar for dollar basis. If we adjust for the estimated lower value of certain transfers in kind, the predominance of cash transfers is even clearer.

I conclude that cash transfers are a very major source of income equality—substantially more important than either personal taxes or transfers in kind. The equalization is accomplished mainly by raising the incomes of the lowest fifth. But what of the trend in inequality? As table 6.4 shows, transfers have become an increasingly important source of income since 1957, and especially since 1967. We also know that the lower income strata receive a disproportionately large share of these transfers.[45] Thus it is clear that cash transfers pushed the distribution of income in the direction of greater equality during the postwar period. For example, Danziger and Plotnick (1977) estimated that transfer payments reduced the Gini coefficient by .069 (or 14.4 percent) in 1974 compared to only .048 (or 11 percent) in 1965.

While this is a noticeable effect over so short a period of time, it is surprising that the explosive growth of transfers did not push inequality down even faster. Three reasons suggest themselves. First, transfer payments may create disincentives for earning income that disequalize the distribution of factor income. Second, these transfer payments may have helped finance the splitting up of family units that led to increasing inequality. Third, Reynolds and Smolensky (1978) have suggested that transfers and other government programs follow a typical life-cycle pattern that dulls their initial redistributive thrust. Specifically, as redistributive programs mature and reach a wider clientele, their benefits become less concentrated on the poor. Thus, as the benefits from these programs grow larger in the aggregate, they simultaneously start to be distributed in a manner less favorable to the poor.

Other Income in Kind

Transfers in kind have already been discussed, but some factor payments are also made in kind rather than in cash. Major items here include food and lodging consumed by farmers and farm workers, fringe benefits that are either partially or totally subsidized by employers (e.g., medical insurance, company cars), and the benefits that many self-employed individuals siphon out of their businesses (unbeknownst to the tax collector). On balance, it is quite unclear to me whether including this potpourri of items would increase or decrease measured inequality in any given year, though both Schultz (1975) and Henle (1972) have speculated that they are disequalizing. There are no studies that shed much light on this issue.[46]

Nonetheless, I would still hazard a guess that, were we able to measure it, the addition of (nontransfer) income in kind to the CPS data would lead to a more disequalizing trend. One reason is that food and lodging consumed on farms (which is distributed more favorably for the poor) has declined as a fraction of all income in kind, while fringe benefits (which are distributed in a more prorich pattern) have increased dramatically. Another reason was mentioned earlier: the farm/nonfarm income differential is exaggerated by omission of income in kind.

Capital Gains

It has often been suggested that the CPS understates the degree of income inequality because it excludes capital gains—which accrue almost exclusively to the rich. And the one scrap of evidence we have on this issue supports this idea. When Smeeding (1979a) distributed an aggregate of accrued capital gains constructed by Browning (1976) among families for the year 1972,[47] he found that the share of the highest fifth increased by 1.4 percentage points.

I am dubious about the value of this exercise because many, indeed most, capital gains are not gains of real purchasing power, but simply represent maintenance (or rather partial maintenance) of principle in an inflationary world. Obviously, if the inflation rate is 8 percent, a fifty dollar stock must increase four dollars per year just to maintain its real value. These four-dollar increments, if they occur, are not gains in real terms. A careful study by Eisner (1980) shows that over the 1946–77 period as a whole, the more than three trillion dollars in nominal capital gains that households received failed (by a very small margin) to provide compensation for inflation. "Real" capital gains, in a word, were as often losses as gains.

Because of the extremely prorich pattern by which capital gains are distributed, it is clear that their inclusion would *disequalize* the income distribution in any year for which aggregate real gains are positive (as Smeeding and Browning found). But it is equally clear that including capital gains would *equalize* the distribution of income in any year for which aggregate real gains are negative. Since gains were roughly zero in an "average" postwar year, I conclude that the omission of capital gains in the CPS data is not misleading on average, though it does conceal some sizable variations in inequality from year to year.

What of the trend? Eisner's (1980, table 33) data on real capital gains as a fraction of disposable income show violent fluctuations but absolutely no trend.[48] It is thus highly unlikely that the omission of capital gains distorts our picture of the postwar trend in income inequality.

Underreporting of Income

The CPS is plagued by underreporting of all sorts of income. But the two biggest underreporting problems come at opposite ends of the income distribution: transfer payments (which are received mainly by the poor) and property income (which is received mainly by the rich). As a consequence, a correction for underreporting would raise the incomes of both the poor and the rich relative to the middle class, making it unclear whether measured inequality would rise or fall. What a series of such corrections might do to the postwar trend in inequality is totally obscure.

Summary

Table 6.19 summarizes this section by bringing together estimates, many of them admittedly dubious, of the effects on the distribution of income of all the adjustments discussed here.[49] The overall conclusion seems to be that patching up the census income concept probably would lead to a distribution of income with noticeably more equality in any one year but only a *slightly* stronger trend toward equality over the postwar period as a whole.

While there is a good deal of guesswork involved, it is conceivable that all the adjustments together might reduce the level of the Gini ratio by about .050 in any one year—a change which exceeds by far the difference between the highest and lowest Gini ratios recorded in table 6.14. For the share of the poorest fifth of families, it is clear that transfers in kind are the most important adjustment, though personal taxes and underreporting also matter. For the share of the richest fifth of families, transfers in kind, personal taxes, and (in some years) capital gains, are all quite important.

Where the trend in inequality is concerned, all the adjustments together seem likely to lead to more equalization through time, mainly because of transfers in kind. However, the effects of improving the income definition seem unlikely to be as strong as the effects of the demographic changes discussed in the previous section.

6.4.4   Measured Inequality and the Accounting Period

It is clear that the distribution of income would look more equal if income were measured over an accounting period longer than a year because: (1) some year-to-year fluctuations would be "smoothed out"; and (2) part of the inequality in any one year's income distribution is due to the fact that people are at different stages of their life cycles, and income varies systematically by age.

It is not obvious, however, that these considerations have much bearing on the *trend* in inequality. The fact that there are transitory income fluctuations will distort our picture of the trend only if the variability of income has increased or decreased systematically over time. It is far from evident that this is true. Similarly, the fact that life-cycle influences contribute to measured inequality will alter the trend only if these life-cycle influences have grown more (or less) important over time. Here, however, it has been claimed that this is in fact the case—that the gap between *annual* income inequality and *lifetime* income inequality has increased over the postwar period (Paglin 1975). An examination of this controversy is the major task of this section.

Transitory Income Fluctuations

The natural approach to correcting for transitory fluctuations in income is to follow households through time and average their incomes

Table 6.19   **Effects of Adjustments in the Income Concept on the Distribution of Income**

Adjustment	Effect on Gini Ratio	Effect of Share — Lowest Fifth	Effect of Share — Highest Fifth	Effect on Trend toward Equality[a]
1. Subtract Personal Taxes	−.015[b]	+0.3[c]	−1.7[c]	0
2. Add In-Kind Transfers				
At full value	−.027[d]	+2.0[e]	−2.1[e]	+
At 70% value	−.016[d]	+1.5[e]	−1.6[e]	
3. Add other Income in Kind	?	?	?	−
4. Add Capital Gains	0	0	0	0
5. Adjust for Underreporting	n.a.	+0.3[f]	+0.1[f]	?

Note: n.a. = not available.

[a]+ sign means the correction would *increase* the trend toward *equality*. − sign means the correction would *decrease* the trend toward equality. A zero means approximately no effect.

[b]From Taussig (1973).

[c]From Radner (1979).

[d]From Smolensky et al. (1977).

[e]Computed by author from data in Smeeding (1979a) and Browning (1979). Both educational and noneducational in-kind transfers are included. Since the two sources disagree on the latter, their estimates have been averaged.

[f]Calculated by the author from data in Smeeding (1979a).

over multiyear periods. Up until quite recently, there was a dearth of data with which to do this. Kravis (1962) had studied a panel of households for five years between 1949 and 1954, finding inequality (as measured by the Gini ratio) over five years to be about 10 percent less than inequality in a single year. He had also examined twelve years of Delaware tax returns (1925–36), and found the twelve-year Gini ratio to be 8 percent lower than the average of the one-year Gini ratios.

The availability of several panel studies in the United States in recent years has verified Kravis's findings. Various sets of panel data have been used by Benus and Morgan (1975), Kohen, Parnes, and Shea (1975), Hoffman and Podder (1976), David and Menchik (1979) and others to reach the following general conclusions.

1. Gini ratios for income over three years generally are about 3–5 percent lower than Gini ratios for one year,[50] though reductions as large as 10 percent have been found.[51]

2. If we stretch the accounting period to seven years, the drop in the Gini ratio increases to 9 percent, even if we restrict attention to families with the same head throughout the period (Hoffman and Podder 1976).

3. Because of the specific way it weights reductions in inequality at various points on the Lorenz curve, the Gini ratio seems to decline less as the accounting period is lengthened than do other measures of inequality.[52]

If these sound like small adjustments, it should be remembered that a 10 percent decline in the Gini ratio (e.g., from .360 to .324) is absolutely colossal compared to anything we can find in the time series data (see table 6.14).

Life-Cycle Influences

It is clear that inequality over the lifetime is lower than inequality in any one year, but here the absence of hard data makes it necessary to resort to simulation and estimation techniques.

My simulation study (Blinder 1974) "guesstimated" that inequality in lifetime income was about 30 percent lower than inequality in a single year if the Gini measure was used, but about 40–45 percent lower if the coefficient of variation was used to measure inequality.[53] Lillard (1977) estimated that the Gini ratio for lifetime *earnings* was about 45 percent less than that for annual earnings in a very special group of American men. Gordon (1976) estimated that for a sample of white male heads of households between thirty and fifty-five years of age, the share of the lowest fifth in lifetime income was 8.7 percent, compared to 6.7 percent in annual income. Without actual data, it is hard to know how accurate these estimates are.[54]

Our best guess is thus that the difference between lifetime inequality and annual inequality is very great. But is this important for interpreting the postwar trend in inequality? To answer this, think of a population composed of different age groups. Inequality can increase if: (1) inequality within age groups increases; (2) the distribution of families across age groups shifts toward groups with greater inequality; or (3) income differences by age become more pronounced.[55]

What do the data tell us about each of these factors?

1. Data covering 1947–64 reveal only weak downward trends in age-specific Gini ratios.[56] Danziger, Haveman, and Smolensky (1977) found that if all age-specific Gini ratios had been constant at their 1965 levels, the Gini ratio for 1972 would have been (very slightly) lower than it was. Thus it seems that factor (1) was operative, but very weak.

2. As noted earlier (see page 442 and table 6.2), changes in the age structure of families were substantial and disequalizing. Over 1965–72, Danziger, Haveman, and Smolensky (1977) found that the shifting age distribution added .011 to the Gini coefficient (which increased in total by .016). Blinder and Esaki (1978) created a time series of hypothetical income distributions covering 1947–74 on the counterfactual assumption that the age distribution did not change. They found that the effect of the shifting age distribution on quintile shares, while disequalizing, was very modest.

3. The data do show an increased arching in the age-income profile, as figure 6.3 illustrates.[57] Danziger, Haveman, and Smolensky (1977) attributed a .005 increase in the Gini ratio between 1965 and 1972 to this factor. We lack a study of this factor over a longer period of time.

On balance, it seems clear that the shifting age distribution and the increased curvature of the age-income profile have caused income inequality to increase during the postwar period despite small declines in age-specific inequality. But the magnitude of the effect seems modest.

Yet, in a controversial paper, Paglin (1975) claimed that the shifting age distribution counteracted what would otherwise have been a very strong trend toward greater income equality among families. Whereas the raw data (see table 6.14) show rather little downward trend in income inequality between 1947 and 1972 (a 4 percent decline in the Gini ratio), Gini ratios that Paglin (1975) presented as "corrected" for age factors exhibit a very strong downward trend (dropping 21 percent). It behooves us to examine Paglin's calculations. Is his method a valid way to "remove" the influence of the changing age structure from the data?

Paglin's technique for decomposing the Gini ratio is straightforward. Begin by constructing a hypothetical Lorenz curve on the assumption that all families of the same age (as defined by the family head) have the same income, and use the area between this hypothetical Lorenz curve and the actual Lorenz curve (shaded in fig. 6.4) as a measure of inequality due to factors other than the life cycle. This simple decomposition seems appealing at first, but does not survive closer examination.[58]

Relative Mean Income

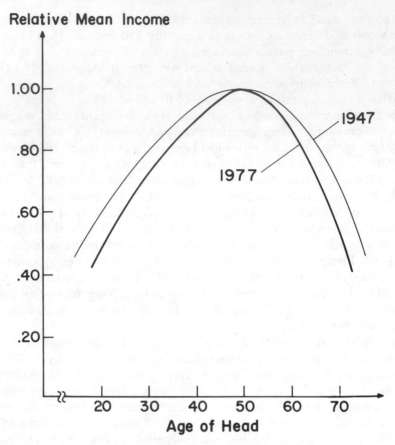

Fig. 6.3   Age-income profiles for families.

Pyatt (1976), and before him Bhattacharya and Mahalanobis (1967), have shown that the Gini ratio can be decomposed into *three* components (not two): (a) a weighted average of the age-specific Gini ratios (or of any other desired grouping), (b) a part dependent on the differences in average incomes across age groups, and (c) a part due to the overlapping of the groups.[59]

Paglin is presumably interested in isolating (a), but by subtracting term (b), he is actually left with parts (a) and (c). Since part (c) has no intuitive interpretation, the Paglin measure of age-corrected inequality can exhibit strange behavior, as Danziger, Haveman, and Smolensky (1977) have shown. In terms of the three age-related factors enumerated in section 6.4.4, Paglin's procedure does not succeed in isolating factor (1), the effects of changing inequality within specific age groups.

I conclude that while Paglin's basic point—that postwar changes in life-cycle influences on income distribution have masked some of the trend toward equality—is correct, he has probably exaggerated its quantitative significance.

Income Equality versus Income Mobility

A related point should be dealt with here. There is considerable churning within the income distribution from year to year. The same families do not, for example, always populate the bottom fifth or the top 5 percent. If our real concern (for welfare purposes) is with income inequality over some lengthy period of time, then it is clear that we can get a good degree of equality in either of two ways:

1. Families could occupy essentially the same relative positions year after year, but the annual distribution (and hence the multiyear distribution) could be quite equal.

2. The annual distribution of income could be quite unequal, but families could move around within the distribution so much that the multiyear distribution of income could be quite equal.

In this sense, income *equality* and income *mobility* are substitutes for one another.[60] In fact, I am certainly not the first to speculate that mo-

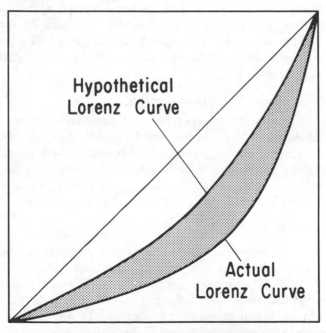

Fig. 6.4   Paglin's decomposition of the Gini ratio.

bility occupies a more exalted place in the American constellation of value judgments than does equality. Americans seem quite willing to tolerate gross disparities in incomes so long as there is a reasonable chance that low-income families in one year can become high-income families in another year. With very little mobility, on the other hand, even a Gini ratio of .300 might be considered intolerable.

The studies cited earlier, and several others as well, seem to suggest a good deal of mobility in the United States income distribution—especially near the bottom of the distribution (Mirer 1975; Benus 1974) and among the young (Kohen, Parnes, and Shea 1975). To cite just one summary statistic, Lane and Morgan (1975) found that the rank correlation for family money income between years one and six of the Panel Study of Income Dynamics was only .47 (or .64 among families with the same head in the two years). While ghetto dwellers rarely trade places with Rockefellers, ours is not a stratified society.

6.5 Special Aspects of Income Inequality

Social scientists and philosophers have long been intrigued by issues relating to equality in the abstract. Laymen and political figures, by contrast, have shown rather less interest in equality than in such related (and more concrete) issues as the plight of the poor, income differentials by race, and income differentials by sex. Each of these special aspects of income inequality has been the focus of a major public policy initiative during the postwar period. For these reasons, each of them merits special attention.

6.5.1   The Special Problem of Poverty

As just noted, the revealed political preferences of the American public show much less concern with inequality than with the plight of the inhabitants of the lower tail of the distribution—the poor. As Lampman (1973) has remarked, this country has never set a target for the Gini ratio. It has, however, declared war on poverty and set specific targets for its reduction. Who is winning the War on Poverty?

Defining Poverty

It turns out, however, not to be so easy to separate the specific problem of poverty from the more general problem of income inequality.[61] The reason is clear enough. Income is a continuous variable, whose distribution can be estimated. Poverty, however, is a dichotomous variable: a family is either poor or it is nonpoor. To decide who is poor, we must place a "poverty line" somewhere in the income distribution, as depicted in figure 6.5, and count how many families (or people) fall below it. Unfortunately, there are many ways to place the line.

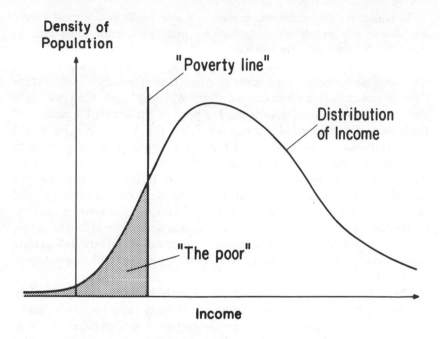

Fig. 6.5   Defining the poverty population.

At one extreme, we could base our poverty line on a *purely absolute standard* of poverty: a family is deemed poor if and only if its income is insufficient to purchase a prescribed bundle of goods and services. Since the bundle is fixed, the poverty line is increased only to adjust for inflation. This concept of poverty, which underlies the official poverty counts of the United States government, has been criticized on many grounds.

1. It seems to contradict public notions of what constitutes poverty. This point is obvious when we consider long periods of time: the rich of centuries ago lacked many of the conveniences that today's poor routinely have. But section 6.3, above, showed how dramatic changes in the standard of living have been even over a period as short as thirty years. It would be surprising indeed if the concept of poverty had not changed accordingly, and evidence from public opinion polls and elsewhere suggests that it has.[62]

2. The bundle of goods and services is inherently arbitrary. Who knows what items every family must have if it is not to be deemed "poor"? Answers to this question are arbitrary at best. Official defini-

tions of poverty in the United States are essentially obtained by defining a food budget and tripling it.[63]

3. It is clear that economic growth will eventually pull almost everyone above any purely absolute poverty line. This definition seems to make the War on Poverty too easy to win.

The unexceptionable idea that what constitutes poverty is culturally, not biologically, determined leads us away from a purely absolute standard of poverty. But where do we stop? We could go all the way to a *purely relative standard* and define the poor as the lowest 20 percent of the income distribution. Under this definition, the War on Poverty would be unwinnable *by definition*; and the Bible would be literally correct: ye have the poor always with you. Personally, I find this to be not an unattractive definition of poverty. However, it does require that we amend the poverty-reduction goal. Counting the poor will no longer do; instead, it is natural to study trends in the share of total income received by the lowest 20 percent. This, of course, has been done at length in this chapter. By this definition, the "special" problem of poverty has already been considered; the conclusion was that poverty has been eroding— but slowly.

There are, of course, intermediate grounds between purely absolute and purely relative standards of poverty. Poverty lines based on "minimum decency" budgets recognize psychological as well as physical needs, and are periodically adjusted to reflect changing norms and mores. Between adjustments, of course, they function just like fixed budgets and so are close cousins to strictly absolute definitions of poverty. They also share the arbitrariness of the fixed budget standard.[64]

A different intermediate choice comes much closer to the purely relative concept of poverty: define the poor as those families with incomes below x percent of the median. Fuchs (1967) suggested such a standard with $x = 50$. While this definition allows the poverty population to shrink or expand *in principle, in practice* it has amounted to defining the poor as the lowest 20 percent (Fuchs 1967, p. 89).

Not Again!

A related set of points is worth making here. If we are to enumerate the poor, we must decide what types of recipient units to count (families? persons?), we must select a definition of income, and we must pick an accounting period. This all sounds familiar. The issues and problems are exactly the same as in our lengthy discussion of income inequality —and so is the sensitivity of the poverty count to the choices we make. Official poverty counts, it should be noted, are based on census income —a concept which, we have seen, apparently hides an upward trend (of uncertain amount) in the share of the bottom fifth. The demographic shifts studied earlier are also worth recalling, since many of them have served to increase the poverty population under official definitions. Finally there is the accounting period. Official poverty counts make no attempt to distinguish those who are permanently poor from those who are temporarily poor (owing, for example, to a large capital loss).[65] Given the amount of mobility that has been found at the lower end of the income distribution, this may be an important problem.

Who Are the Poor?

Having said all this, let us see who the official data classify as poor. According to the latest data (for 1977), 9.3 percent of all families and 22.6 percent of all unrelated individuals fell below the official poverty lines. Persons in families constituted about 80 percent of the poor, and almost half of these were in families headed by a female—a female headship ratio far higher than that for the population as a whole. The poverty rate was only 5.5 percent for male-headed families, but thirty-two percent for female-headed families. Among poor unrelated individuals, almost two-thirds were female.[66] Relative to the population as a whole, the poor were also more frequently black, less educated, and lived in larger families.[67]

Alternative definitions of income or concepts of poverty give rather different poverty counts, however. Table 6.20, for example, shows how the fraction of persons classified as poor changes as we adjust either the income concept or the definition of poverty. The upper left-hand entry is the official poverty count for 1976: just under 12 percent of all persons were considered poor. A relative poverty definition[68] raises the count to 15.4 percent of the population—a 30 percent increase in the number of poor people. Altering the definition of income by deducting direct taxes, adding income in kind, and correcting for underreporting (which, we know, is very serious for transfer income) cuts the poverty count drastically—to only 6.5 percent.

Table 6.20   **The Poverty Count for 1976, by Different Definitions (Percentage of All Persons)**

	Census Income	Census Income Adjusted[1]	Census Income Minus Transfers
Official Poverty Lines	11.8	6.5	21.0
Relative Poverty Standard[2]	15.4	—	24.1

Source: Danziger, Haveman, and Plotnick 1979, table 5, p. 31.
[1]Adjusted for income in kind (both transfers and otherwise), direct taxes, and underreporting by Smeeding (1977).
[2]Defines poor persons as those with income below 44 percent of the median income.

Trends in Poverty Counts

How has the poverty count behaved through time? Figure 6.6 plots four different estimates. The official data, using census income and an absolute definition of poverty, show rapid progress against poverty from 1959 (when the data begin) until 1969. Thereafter, the fraction of *families* who are classified as poor almost levels off (it is 9.7 percent in 1969 and 9.3 percent in 1977), while the fraction of *unrelated individuals* so classified continues to tumble. The other two series use persons as the recipient unit, and are available only since 1965 (and not for every year). There is no discernible trend in relative poverty based on census money income. Absolute poverty based on income adjusted for taxes, in-kind income, and underreporting does show a downward trend, though fluctuations are severe.[69]

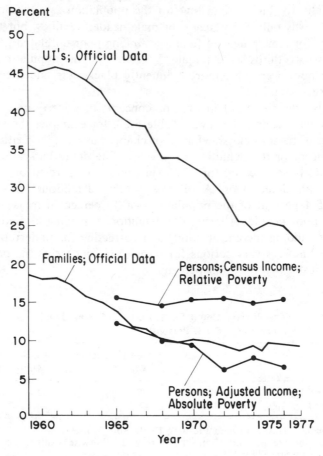

Fig. 6.6   Trends in poverty.

The conclusion, then, seems to run something like this. The official poverty count declined smartly through the 1960s, but has been stagnant since then. This constancy, however, is due to the dominant position of families in the aggregate; the incidence of poverty among unrelated individuals continued to fall. If we fix up some of the pitfalls with census income, there appears to have been considerably more progress in the War on Poverty. But if we adopt a relative poverty concept rather than the official poverty lines, there has been much less.

One final word seems in order. Whether we use official poverty lines or a relative poverty concept, table 6.20 shows that many fewer people are poor after (cash) transfers than before transfers. The trends in pre- and posttransfer poverty are also quite different. By official definitions, the poverty rate for all persons declined 24.4 percent between 1965 and 1976. But, there is almost no trend in the poverty rate based on income minus (cash) transfers (Danziger, Haveman, and Plotnick 1979, table 5, p. 31). Transfers, in a word, have been the chief weapon in the War on Poverty.

6.5.2   Black-White Income Differentials

It is, of course, well known that nonwhite individuals and families typically have lower incomes than whites.[70] For example, the ratio of mean income among nonwhite families and unrelated individuals to that among whites averaged .589 (with standard deviation .057) for the post-war period as a whole.

However, there was a substantial narrowing of the differential during the period. Figure 6.7 charts the behavior of the nonwhite/white income ratio since 1947, for families and unrelated individuals pooled. The upward trend from .52 in 1947 to .68 in 1975 is clear and unmistakable, though there has been some slippage since then. The gains scored by blacks between 1965 and 1968 are particularly impressive.[71]

The economic position of blacks relative to whites is far from uniform across different demographic groups. In 1977, for example, the black/ white mean income ratio was .63 when averaged over all families. But for families with a head aged 18–24, it was .97 while for families headed by a 55–64 year old it was .57. Similarly, the ratio was .76 for male-headed families versus .64 for female-headed families.

Several demographic forces limited the economic gains achieved by blacks, however. First, there was a substantial increase in the fraction of families headed by females—which rose from 28 percent in 1967 to 37 percent by 1976.[72] Second, the labor force participation rate of black men declined somewhat—from 85 percent in 1954 to 71 percent in 1977, with much of the drop accounted for by the elderly (see Richard Freeman, chap. 5 of this volume). This occurred despite an increase in

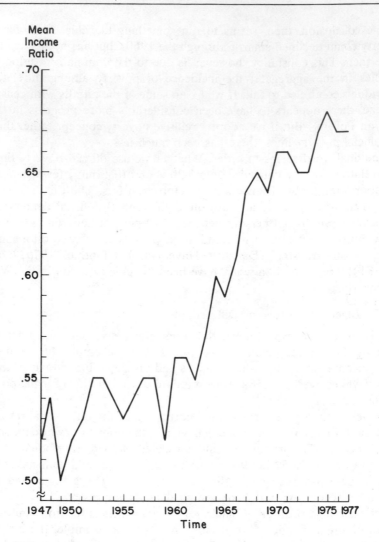

Fig. 6.7   Trend in nonwhite/white mean income ratio, for families and unrelated individuals.

black earning rates relative to those of whites. However, relative earnings gains were greater for women than for men. Indeed, something close to full parity between the races was achieved among females working full time full year. The black/white earnings ratio for such workers rose from .56 in 1955 to .93 in 1977.[73]

Thus the improvement in the black/white income ratio was the net result of a confluence of forces, some of which were equalizing and some of which were disequalizing. On balance, however, there can be no question that the relative economic position of blacks improved substantially during the postwar years. Equally clear is the fact that—except in isolated instances—parity has not yet been achieved.

6.5.3   Male-Female Income Differentials

When we come to consider income differentials between men and women (or between male- and female-headed families) a rather different picture emerges. As figure 6.8 shows, the ratio of female to male

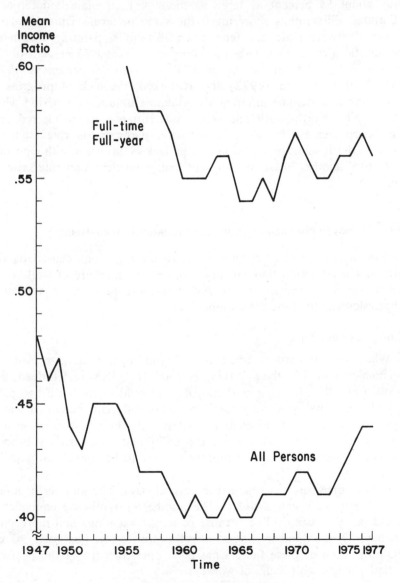

Fig. 6.8   Trends in female/male mean income ratios.

incomes dropped from 48 percent just after World War II to only 40 percent by 1960, hovered in a narrow range between 40 percent and 41 percent between 1960 and 1969, and rose in recent years to 44 percent.

Part of this huge income differential—which is wider than that between blacks and whites—is due to the fact that more women than men work part time or for only part of each year. But figure 6.8 shows that even women who worked full time for a full year typically had incomes only about 55 percent as large as those of their male counterparts. (Earnings differentials show much the same pattern.) Differentials in incomes between male- and female-headed families paint an even more pessimistic picture. Female-headed families averaged 73 percent of the income of male-headed families in 1947, but only 50 percent in 1977. Indeed, as Lampman (1977) has remarked, the lack of progress in narrowing male-female differentials is almost unique in a period when black-white, North-South and other differentials were being reduced. The sharp increase in female labor force participation rates suggests itself as the leading explanation of this lack of progress, although that just raises another question: why did female participation rates rise so much?[74]

6.6   Trends in Nonincome Aspects of Economic Well-Being

This section seeks to remedy some of the omissions caused by the myopic concentration thus far on *income* as the measure of well-being. The discussion is necessarily less systematic, less quantitative, and more impressionistic than the discussion of income.

6.6.1   Leisure Time

When an economist is asked to go beyond income as a measure of economic well-being, the first thing he thinks of is leisure. (Indeed, this is often also the *last* thing he thinks of.) It would seem that if two individuals have the same wage rate[75] but earn different incomes because they voluntarily work different hours, then the best first guess is that they are equally well off. Income inequality that arises from voluntary choices between work and leisure, then, is not to be considered a social "bad."[76]

Leisure time can be expanded in several ways. The number of hours worked per week can shrink.[77] The number of (full-time equivalent) weeks per year can decline because of longer vacations and more paid holidays. Or the number of years of retirement can be increased. As we shall see, each of these factors has been operative during the postwar period. I begin with hours of work.

Hours of Work per Week

It is, of course, well known that the work week has shrunk over the long sweep of history. Indeed, the extent of this shrinkage is often exaggerated. We have probably all heard stories about how a work week of six or seven twelve-hour days was "typical" around the turn of the century. But the data belie these grisly tales. The average manufacturing worker at the turn of the century apparently worked about six ten-hour days per week—an average work week of fifty-nine hours.[78] Hours outside of manufacturing were typically shorter yet, so the average worker in all industries worked only fifty-three hours (Moore and Hedges 1971). From 1900 to 1947 there was a steady downward trend in the average work week among manufacturing workers which reached 40.4 hours by 1947.[79]

It is often claimed that the decline in the typical work week ended around World War II, and that since then American workers have taken their increased leisure in the form of fewer weeks per year. This widely held view derives from looking only at hours per week *in manufacturing,* which by 1977 accounted for just 24 percent of total employment. Here the decline in the work week did indeed halt: it was 40.3 hours long in 1977. But more than three-quarters of the United States labor force works in other industries; and in these industries the decline in the average work week has continued throughout the postwar period, perhaps because of the increased use of part-time workers (see table 6.21). I conclude that American workers decreased their average work week by about 10 percent during the postwar period. Manufacturing workers (a shrinking minority) were a notable exception.

Weeks of Work per Year

Data are scarcer for the number of work weeks (or days) in a year. Lebergott (1976, p. 91) reports that the percent of nonfarm workers taking vacations increased from nearly zero in 1930 to 60 percent in 1950 and 80 percent in 1970. He also cites U.S. Bureau of Labor Statistics data that the typical American worker had seven paid holidays. While we do not know this for a fact, it is not hard to imagine that the

Table 6.21   **Average Weekly Hours in Selected Industries, 1947–77**

Year	All Private Nonagricultural	Manufacturing	Construction	Wholesale and Retail Trade
1947	40.3	40.4	38.2	40.5
1977	36.0	40.3	36.6	32.8

Source: Economic Report of the President (1979), table B–35, p. 224.

spreading incidence of vacations and paid holidays may have reduced the typical work year by two weeks (about 4 percent) or more.

Incidence of Retirement

Another remarkable development of the postwar period has been the increasing prevalence of retirement, especially for men.[80] The labor force participation rate for men 65 years of age and older fell from 47.8 percent in 1947 to only 20.1 percent in 1977; for men aged 55–64, the decline was from 89.6 percent to 74 percent.[81] Reimers (1976) compared men who reached age 65 around 1933 with men who reached age 65 around 1963 and concluded that the younger generation devoted about 2 percent fewer years of its life to work than did the older generation.

It takes more than a little *chutzpah* to combine this guesstimate with my seat-of-the-pants estimate that more vacations decreased the work year by about 4 percent, and with data showing a 10 percent decline in the average work week. But, if we do all this, we are led to conclude that working time over a typical career has decreased about 16 percent during the postwar period. While this is a substantial amount, it probably means that leisure time expanded more slowly than the consumption of market goods and services.[82] Evidence that leisure time is a luxury good is lacking.

Housework

There is, however, one other important aspect of declining work effort that ought not to escape our attention. Lebergott (1976) has estimated that the typical housewife spent about twelve hours on housework per day in 1900, but only five hours in 1966. Stafford and Duncan (1977) cite data from time diaries showing that married women spent about twenty-seven hours per week on work in the home. How much of this decline in the housewife's workday took place since World War II is not known. But if we attribute half of the eight-hour-per-day decline to the postwar period, then the postwar decline in the workday for housewives would be about 50 percent. This may be an overestimate,[83] but it does seem that housewives have improved their lot relative to paid workers in the postwar period.[84] Family leisure thus probably increased faster than leisure time of the principal breadwinner.[85]

The Valuation of Leisure

How much is this increasing leisure worth? There seem to be two basic approaches to the valuation of leisure time, though each has many variants. The first approach tacitly or explicitly posits a utility function that combines both income (or consumption) and leisure time into a composite measure of well-being. The major alternative is to convert leisure time into money by using the market wage. While the utility-function approach is obviously conceptually superior, it faces one (insurmountable?) problem: who knows what the right utility function is?

The Distribution of Leisure and Income

What of the distribution of leisure time? Morgan and Smith (1969), using data from the Panel Study of Income Dynamics, found a slight negative correlation between leisure and income, but a slight positive correlation between leisure and the ratio of income to "needs." Sirageldin (1969) constructed a distribution of economic well-being based on leisure and the ratio of income to "needs" for data from the Productive Americans Survey. He found that well-being so defined was distributed more equally than income. Taussig (1973) valued leisure at the wage, using data from the Survey of Economic Opportunity, and obtained very similar results. "Full income" was slightly more equally distributed than money income. Browning (1976) and Browning and Johnson (forthcoming) made two different adjustments for nonworking time and found very substantial equalizing effects.

The conclusions seem to be, therefore, that (a) leisure is distributed somewhat more equally than income; (b) leisure has a slight negative correlation with income; and (c) more comprehensive measures of economic well-being that include both leisure and income are distributed more equally than income alone.

Involuntary "Leisure"

Having said this, we must not ignore the fact that not all "leisure" time is taken voluntarily. A person who is disabled or involuntarily unemployed does not want to "buy" all the leisure he gets at the going wage rate. For him, the wage clearly *over*estimates the marginal value of leisure time. While there is no satisfactory way at present to decompose unemployment time into "voluntary" and "involuntary" components,[86] it is at least worth pointing out that the incidence of total unemployment is highly uneven. The young, the black, and the female suffer most from unemployment. Involuntary leisure seems concentrated at the lower end of the income distribution. It is hard (for me at least) to imagine that this pattern is entirely the result of free choice.

6.6.2   Wealth

In purchasing the goods and services from which they derive satisfaction, people are not restricted to their current income if they have accumulated wealth on which they can draw. So, if our real concern is with the distribution of economic *well-being*, data on the distribution of wealth are a valuable supplement to data on the distribution of income.[87]

Sources of Data

We know far less about the distribution of wealth in the United States than about the distribution of income. Certainly nothing comparable to the annual CPS exists for wealth. What meager knowledge of the wealth distribution we have comes from three sources.

First, there have been a few surveys of wealth holding, of which the Survey of Financial Characteristics of Consumers (SFCC) for 1962 (Projector and Weiss 1966) is undoubtedly the best. But these surveys have been sporadic, scattered through time, and noncomparable; so they tell us little about trends in wealth inequality. In addition, it is apparently very hard to elicit accurate data on wealth holding from survey respondents: even the assiduously planned and executed SFCC was plagued by underreporting (Projector and Weiss, 1966, pp. 61–62; Lebergott 1976, pp. 217–223). Nonetheless, the SFCC data on the wealth distribution in 1962 is undoubtedly the best "snapshot" information we have.

Second, estimates of the wealth distribution have been made by the estate multiplier method. Briefly, this method involves treating individuals who die in a particular year as a random sample (perhaps after some adjustments) of those who were living in that year. Then estate tax records on the wealth of decedents can be used to infer the distribution of wealth among the living.[88] However, since only estates above a certain amount (which for many years was $60,000) are required to file tax returns, the estate multiplier method can yield information only about the extreme upper tail of the wealth distribution.

Finally, a clever investigator can piece together scraps of information from which he can create an estimate of the distribution of wealth (Lebergott 1976). While this technique may be promising, it involves considerable judgment and perhaps some guesswork in piecing together disparate pieces of information, making time series comparisons very difficult.

The Stylized Facts

The stylized facts of the wealth distribution in the postwar United States are allegedly as follows: (1) Inequality in the wealth distribution far exceeds that in the income distribution. (2) There is no noticeable trend in wealth inequality.

Qualitatively, fact (1) rests on a fairly secure base; but we remain uncertain of its quantitative dimensions owing to the paucity of data. The SFCC found the Gini coefficient for wealth to be .76, as compared to a Gini ratio for income in the same population of .43 (Projector and Weiss 1966, p. 30). Lansing and Sonquist (1969, p. 50) reported Gini ratios for wealth within age cohorts in the 1953 and 1962 Surveys of Consumer Finances ranging from .62 to .69.[89] Feldstein (1976), however, has pointed out that these wealth data exclude an important source of wealth which is both very large in the aggregate and very equally distributed: the discounted present value of future social security benefits. When he added estimates of this "social security wealth" to the fungible wealth of those consumer units in the SFCC with heads between thirty-five and sixty-four years of age, the Gini ratio dropped from .72 to .51. The top 1 percent of wealth holders held 28.4 percent of fungible wealth, but only 18.9 percent of total wealth. This adjustment, as dramatic as it is, does not overturn the conclusion that wealth is more unequally distributed than income.

George Stigler (1973) once asked in another context, "Is this fact in fact a fact?" Our second "fact" may not be. What we know from estate multiplier estimates by Lampman (1962) and Smith and Franklin (1974) is that the share of the very, very wealthy fell somewhat between the 1920s and the 1940s and has been relatively constant since then. Thus the alleged stability of the wealth distribution is based on the experience of the *top 0.5 percent* (or at best the top 1 percent). It hardly needs to be stated that the lower 99.5 percent might have had a different experience. Furthermore, Feldstein (1976) has pointed out that the explosive growth of (very equally distributed) social security wealth doubtless imparted some equalizing trend to the wealth distribution.

Combining Wealth and Income

This look at the wealth distribution was motivated by a need to supplement information on income inequality. For this purpose, however, we need to know the joint distribution of income and wealth across individuals. Only survey data can give us this information. The SFCC data show a strong positive correlation between income and wealth (Projector and Weiss 1966, pp. 6–7), which can hardly be considered surprising.

The most natural way to combine the distributions of wealth (a stock) and income (a flow) is to add the annuity value of net worth to census money income, and then subtract current property income to avoid double-counting. Weisbrod and Hansen (1968) did approximately this in combining the SFCC with the 1962 CPS, but were forced to merge the two data sources in a very crude way. They found that the Gini ratio of .37 for census income became .42 when the annuity value of net worth was added at a 4 percent interest rate and .47 when a 10 percent interest rate was used. Taussig (1973) combined income and net worth information from the same data source, using a 6 percent interest rate, and found that the Gini ratio was almost unchanged unless substantial corrections were made for underreporting of net worth. After those corrections, the Gini ratio rose from .361 to .393. Taking account of the distribution of wealth thus seems to increase the degree of inequality.

6.6.3   Living Apart from Relatives (and Nonrelatives)

Whatever benefits the extended family may have brought to its members, they came at a cost of increasing household congestion and loss of privacy. And, apparently, Americans in the postwar period prized the reduced congestion and increased privacy more than the benefits of the extended family. Data on the rapid growth of the number of unrelated individuals—especially young and old people living alone—were cited earlier in this chapter (see page 437). Table 6.22 offers further data on this subject.

The Census Bureau defines a *subfamily* as either a married couple (with or without children) or a single parent with one or more unmarried children, living in the same household as another family to which they are related. The number of subfamilies so defined thus seems a

Table 6.22   Selected Data on Living Apart and Privacy, 1940–70

A. Data on Subfamilies[1]

Year	Number of Subfamilies (Millions)			Ratio of Subfamilies to Primary Families
	All	Husband-Wife	Other	
1940	2.06	1.55	0.52	.065
1947	3.12	2.33	0.79	.089
1977	1.18	0.51	0.67	.021

B. Data on Married Couples without Own Household

Year	Number (Millions)	Fraction of all Married Couples
1940	1.95	.068
1947	2.93	.087
1977	0.53	.011

C. Data on Secondary Families[2]

Year	Number of Secondary Families (Millions)			Ratio of Secondary Families to Primary Families
	All	Husband-Wife	Other	
1940	0.68	0.40	0.28	.021
1947	0.83	0.60	0.23	.024
1977	0.14	0.03	0.21	.004

Sources: Historical Statistics, p. 41, Series A288–A319; *Current Population Reports*, Series P–20, no. 313, table 5.

[1]Defined by the Census Bureau as "a married couple with or without children, or one parent with one or more unmarried children under 18 years old, living in a household and related to, but not including, the head of the household or his wife."

[2]Defined by the Census Bureau as "two or more persons such as guests, lodgers, or resident employees and their relatives, living in a household and related to each other."

good indicator of the number of extended families, though single grand-parents would not be counted as subfamilies. Part A of table 6.22 shows that the absolute number of subfamilies fell by almost two-thirds between 1947 and 1977.[90] In 1947 almost 9 percent of primary families had another related family living with them. By 1977 this fraction was down to barely over 2 percent. Furthermore, almost three-quarters of these subfamilies in 1947 included both parents, whereas by 1977 less than half of all subfamilies had two parents. Data in Part B of table 6.22 on the number and frequency of married couples living in the household of some other family (not necessarily a related family) tell a similar story.

A phenomenon related to living apart from relatives is the decline in the number of boarders and lodgers in American households—living apart from nonrelatives. According to data put together by Lebergott (1976), the percentage of urban households with a boarder or lodger decreased from 23 percent in 1900 to 14 percent in 1941 and to only 2 percent in 1970. The lodger, in other words, almost disappeared from the scene during the postwar period.

Data germane to this phenomenon appear in Part C of table 6.22. The Census defines a "secondary family" as two or more persons related to one another but not related to the primary family. This category includes guests, lodgers, or resident employees; but since single individuals are not counted as secondary families, most lodgers are excluded in this count. Nonetheless, as many as 2.5 percent of primary families shared their homes with such an unrelated secondary family in 1947. Almost none did by 1970.

6.6.4 Health

It will not be considered heretical to assert that, at equal levels of consumption and leisure, healthier people are better off. And it is quite clear that the health of the American people has improved considerably during the postwar period.

Perhaps the most useful summary statistic representing the state of health is life expectancy. Table 6.23 displays data on life expectancies at birth and at age twenty. Progress in increasing longevity breaks down naturally into three distinct periods. Life expectancies increased dramatically between 1940 and 1955, but improvement in this regard slowed for women and virtually ceased for men during the next fifteen years. However, since 1970 there has been a resurgence in extending life expectancies, especially for adults. In total, life expectancy of a man reaching adulthood increased by 8.5 years over the period 1940–77. For women, the increase was almost 12 years. The reduction in infant mortality was even more dramatic—infant mortality in 1970 was less than half what it was in 1940.[91]

Table 6.23   Changes in Life Expectancy, 1940–77

A. Life Expectancy at Birth (in Years)			B. Life Expectancy at Age 20 (in Years)[b]		
Year	Males	Females	Year	Males	Females
1940	60.8	65.2	1939–41	47.8	51.4
1955	66.7	72.8	1955	50.1	55.8
1970[a]	67.1	74.8	1970[a]	50.2	57.2
1977[a]	69.3	77.1	1977[a]	51.9	59.1
Change 1940–77	+8.5	+11.9	Change 1940–77	+4.1	+7.7

Source: For 1940–45, Historical Statistics, ser. B108–9, B118–19, pp. 55–56; for 1970, U.S. Department of Health, Education and Welfare, Public Health Service, Vital Statistics of the United States, vol. 11, sec. 5, table 5–4 (Washington, D.C.: U.S. Government Printing Office, 1976); for 1977, U.S. Department of Health, Education and Welfare, Monthly Vital Statistics Report, Advance Report: Final Mortality Statistics, 1977. Publication no. (PHS) 79–1120, vol. 28, no. 1, suppl. (Washington, D.C.: U.S. Government Printing Office, 11 May 1979).
Note: Life expectancy is defined as expected years of life remaining.
[a]Excludes deaths of nonresidents of the United States.
[b]Whites only.

Mortality and morbidity from many, but not all, serious diseases has also fallen dramatically in the postwar period, as table 6.24 shows.

6.6.5   Social Indicators

Not all indicators of well-being are pointing upward. As table 6.25 shows, the postwar period has witnessed a stunning increase in the incidence of illegitimate children, a surge in the divorce rate, and little or no

Table 6.24   Selected Data on Illness and Disease, 1940–70

			A. Deaths per 100,000 Population from Selected Diseases			
Year	Tuberculosis	Syphilis	Influenza and Pneumonia	Diabetes	Malignant Neoplasms	Cardiovascular and Renal Diseases
1940	45.9	14.4	70.3	26.6	120.3	485.7
1970	2.6	0.2	30.9	18.9	162.8	496.0

			B. Incidence per 100,000 Population of Selected Diseases			
Year	Tuberculosis	Syphilis	Malaria	Measles	Whooping Cough	Hepatitis
1940	78.0	359.7	59.2	220.7	139.6	2.5[a]
1970	18.3	43.8	1.5	23.2	2.1	32.0

Source: Historical Statistics, Series B149–166; B291–304, pp. 58 and 77.
[a]Data pertain to 1950.

Table 6.25   **Changes in Selected Social Indicators**

Year	Illegitimate Birthrate[1]	Divorce Rate[2]	Suicide Rate[3]	Crime Rate[4]
1940	7.1	8.8	14.4	88.9
1955	19.3	9.3	10.2	79.8/83.5
1970	26.4	14.9	11.6	274.7

[1]Illegitimate live births per 1,000 married females. Data from: *Historical Statistics*, Series B29, p. 52.

[2]Divorces per 1,000 married females 15 years old and over. Data from: *Historical Statistics*, Series B217, p. 64.

[3]Suicides per 100,000 population. Data from: *Historical Statistics*, Series B166, p. 58.

[4]Crimes known to police per 1,000,000 population. Two series are spliced here. The right-hand series pertains to the entire United States, and the number reported for 1955 is actually for 1957. The left-hand series pertains to urban areas only and is constructed by the author from separate data on urban crimes and urban population. (Urban population for 1955 is interpolated between the 1950 and 1960 censuses.) Data from: *Historical Statistics*, Series H952; Series H962, p. 413; Series A57, p. 11.

progress against suicide. Furthermore, crime has been one of our biggest growth industries. There is little cause for cheer in any of this.

6.6.6   Happiness

"Early to bed, early to rise, makes a man healthy, wealthy, and wise." This rhyme, I suppose, is meant to be a formula for happiness. Americans, we have seen, are indeed considerably wealthier and healthier than they were thirty years ago. They are also better educated.[92] Are they happier?

This is not the sort of question an economist feels comfortable with —and with good reason. Nonetheless, a provocative paper by Easterlin (1974) attempted to answer this question by studying opinion poll data on people's self-proclaimed happiness. Easterlin's findings for the United States are easily summarized. At a given point in time, happiness seems clearly to increase with economic status. However, as we look over time, there is little if any upward trend in happiness despite noticeable improvements in the average standard of living.

These findings suggest one of two things. Either "happiness" is a relative concept which depends (only) on each person's situation relative to that of his peers, or that, regardless of how happy people really are in an absolute sense, they tend to answer a survey question like this by rating their happiness relative to that of their contemporaries. There is probably no operational way of distinguishing between these two competing hypotheses, though they are different. For example, if we compare a family with income of $18,264 in 1977 and one with $3,546 in 1947 (the means for the two years), the first hypothesis states that they are equally happy while the second hypothesis states that the 1977 family is happier on an absolute scale, but no more happy on a relative scale—and responds to the questioner by reporting on relative happiness. I personally find the latter interpretation more appealing.

6.7   In Conclusion

> When *I* use a word . . . it means just what I choose it to mean—
> neither more nor less.
>
> Lewis Carroll

We have seen in this essay that, according to the official data, average incomes generally have been *rising* during the postwar period while income inequality has been relatively *constant*. Can we accept these "facts" at face value? What welfare implications, if any, follow from them?

6.7.1   Income Levels and Economic Well-Being

The data show that per capita income and consumption increased roughly 80 percent in real terms between 1947 and 1977. In addition to consuming *more* of most goods and services, Americans changed their patterns of consumption markedly. For the most part, these redirections of spending seem recognizable as improvements in the quality of life. In addition, longevity and health improved, leisure time expanded, and privacy increased. Yet over the same period a number of social indicators such as divorce, illegitimacy, and crime signal a deterioration in the quality of life, and people report themselves no happier than thirty years ago. What are we to make of all this? Must we abandon the use of income as a measure of well-being?

My own impression is that we need not. For one thing, our main use of income as a gauge of well-being is cross-sectional, and it still seems reasonable to view people with higher incomes as "better off" at any moment in time—despite some anomalies. Second, even looking across time, my guess is that rising average income does indeed improve the human lot—though perhaps not by as much as the data suggest. Various nonincome aspects of well-being, such as leisure time and health, may not grow as rapidly as material consumption; growth may produce a variety of well-known disamenities (e.g., pollution and congestion); and we should not entirely ignore the message that "happiness" is perhaps a relativistic concept. While it would be presumptuous to conclude that people are 80 percent "better off" now than they were in 1947, it seems preposterous to conclude that they are no better off.

6.7.2   Income Inequality and Economic Well-Being

Things get quite a bit murkier when we turn our attention to the trend (or lack thereof) in income inequality. During the postwar period, a number of strong, and seemingly autonomous, forces pushed income inequality higher.[93] These include:

1. A shifting age distribution that left the 1977 economy with relatively more old and young (and thus lower paid) members than the 1947 economy.
2. An increasing incidence of female headship of families.[94]
3. Changes in living arrangements that produced more low-income units as extended families broke up, fewer families took in lodgers and boarders, and more young and old people formed their own households.

In brief, when we look at the United States economy from 1947 to 1977, we are not looking at a society unchanging in composition by age, sex, and family structure. And most of the demographic changes that occurred were the sort that produce greater inequality, given our measurement procedures. Two conclusions follow. First, if we could measure the income distribution at fixed demography, a trend toward equality would emerge—a trend that the official data mask. Second, most of the factors that served to increase inequality during the postwar period do not signify deteriorations in economic well-being. Indeed, the opposite seems more likely. Measured income inequality thus seems an unreliable indicator of economic welfare.

Despite these and other disequalizing factors, the overall income distribution—as measured—did not become more unequal. The main reasons seem to have been a variety of government redistributive activities, including:

1. The rapid growth of cash transfers which, we have seen, have been the principal weapon in the War on Poverty.
2. The equally rapid growth of transfers in kind, which are *not* included in the official data (another reason why the official data understate the trend toward equality).
3. Other programs such as affirmative action guidelines, equal opportunity and antidiscrimination laws. These programs have not been dealt with in this chapter because we lack estimates of their effects on income inequality.[95] But I would be remiss not to suggest a possible link between these governmental activities and the observed narrowing of black-white income differentials.

It appears that, on balance, these competing sets of factors—demography versus government—battled to a standoff. Income inequality, as measured in the official data, was unchanged between 1947 and 1977. But I would not want to push the analogy to a tug-of-war too far, because there is reason to suspect that the two sides were not independent. Specifically, government programs designed to equalize posttax posttransfer incomes may well have helped disequalize pretax pretransfer incomes. For example:

It has often been suggested that redistributive tax and transfer schemes have disincentive effects that, e.g., discourage labor supply among beneficiaries (such as the poor or the elderly).[96]

It is conceivable, though here we know much less, that transfer programs such as AFDC and social security may have contributed to some of the changes in family structure and living arrangements that were just labeled as disequalizing factors (e.g., increases in female headship, more elderly people living alone).

It is quite possible that expenditures on public education (an apparently "equalizing" transfer in kind) were among the factors leading to the more pronounced age-income profile—thus contributing to a growing gap between annual and lifetime inequality.

No wonder, then, that in the wonderland of inequality,

> it takes all the running *you* can do, to keep in the same place. If you want to get somewhere else, you must run at least twice as fast as that!
>
> Lewis Carroll

Notes

1. For a detailed treatment of postwar demographic changes, see Easterlin, chapter 4 of this volume.
2. For an extensive discussion of opportunity sets, see Gordon (1977).
3. Conversely, two people with equal incomes may have gotten there from very different opportunity sets.
4. Even the CPS data are not perfectly consistent over time. Minor changes in such factors as definitions and survey techniques have been made. For a more detailed discussion and critique of the census-income concept, see Taussig (1977).
5. On this, see Lebergott (1976, pp. 11–12) or Rivlin (1975).
6. For more detailed technical discussions of this issue, the interested reader is referred to Atkinson (1970), Sen (1973), or Rothschild and Stiglitz (1973).
7. Readers familiar with the Gini ratio may skip the rest of this section, which is a nontechnical explanation for lay readers.
8. By the formula for the area of a triangle, this area is always one-half.
9. But not all, as a well-known paper by Budd (1970) established.
10. A full account of these recessions can be found in the paper by Robert Gordon, chapter 2 of this volume.
11. Defined specifically as personal income plus retained earnings plus contributions for social insurance (both employee's and employer's shares).
12. Defined specifically as disposable income (as in the NIA) plus retained earnings, or alternatively as augmented personal income minus contributions for social insurance minus personal tax and nontax payments.
13. All deflation is done using the implicit deflator for personal consumption expenditures.
14. It hardly needs pointing out that the national income accounts measure *nominal* interest, not *real* interest. The share of interest has risen mainly because there is trend in the inflation rate.

15. Age of the housing stock refers to private nonfarm residential structures containing from one to four units. The increase in the incidence of running water and flush toilets came largely in rural areas.

16. Absolute prices rose only 15 percent over thirty years, which implies that relative prices fell 57 percent.

17. In 1940, there were 2,412,000 private household workers and 34,949,000 households. By 1970, the number of private household workers had fallen slightly to 2,347,000, while the number of households had risen to 63,401,000, according to *Historical Statistics*, Series D–567 and A–288.

18. A procedure the Commerce Department does not follow. I have taken several liberties with their way of organizing the data.

19. This category also includes radios, musical instruments, and records.

20. For detailed discussions of this topic, see Taussig (1977) and Danziger (1977).

21. The income concept underlying this table differs from census income, and so these distributions are not directly comparable to those in table 6.9.

22. Table 6.11 pertains to families, and excludes unrelated individuals.

23. A similar calculation comparing the richest tenth and the poorest tenth brings an apparent 15:1 ratio in the raw data down to only 2.8:1.

24. This issue has been stressed by Kuznets (1974), among others.

25. My discussion of this point is deliberately sketchy. For further details, see Richard Easterlin's chapter 4 of this volume.

26. Blinder and Esaki (1978) report detecting a statistically significant break in the trend for several percentile shares around 1958.

27. A regression was run with the Gini ratio as the dependent variable, and the following independent variables: the unemployment rate; a constant; a dummy variable which is 1 starting in 1958; time; and the interaction of time with the dummy. The coefficient of time was $-.0022$ (with standard error .0004). The sum of the coefficients of time and the interaction term, which is the post-1958 time trend, was $-.0004$ (with standard error .0017).

28. In a regression identical to that reported in note 27, the estimated time trend in the Gini ratio among unrelated individuals was $-.0014$ (standard error $= .0013$) until 1957 and $-.0040$ (standard error .0017) thereafter.

29. Table 6.16 summarizes the whole distribution by the Gini ratio only to keep the volume of data manageable. Inspection of the underlying distributions reveals, fortunately, that there are hardly any instances of crossing Lorenz curves—the circumstance that would render the Gini ratio potentially misleading. The few Lorenz curve crossings that occur are indicated in footnotes to table 6.16. The year 1964 was selected for this table because it comes closest to being a "typical" postwar year.

30. The reader is reminded that, by Census Bureau definitions, there are no one-person families.

31. I will have more to say on the subject of age and the income distribution when I discuss the accounting period, since the problems arise largely from measuring income in a particular year rather than over the lifetime.

32. The section is limited to the family income distribution both to save space and because most of the literature does the same.

33. Let us be clear about what this simple adjustment *does not* do. If we are interested in *income* as an indicator of *well-being*, as we are, then a proper "adjustment" for taxes and transfers really requires resolution of every complex and controversial issue in tax incidence theory. What portion of the value of any transfer payment actually accrues to the recipient? What part of the burden of a

sales tax falls on the consumer of the product? Can the income tax be shifted? It hardly needs saying that questions such as these are well beyond the scope of this chapter and indeed probably also beyond the scope of current economic knowledge. My aim here is much more modest: to get the bookkeeping straight. Specifically, subtraction of individual income tax payments and the employee's share of the payroll tax from census income (the employer's share is already excluded), is *not* meant to imply that the burden of these taxes falls entirely on those who pay them. Nor does the absence of any deduction for indirect taxes imply that they are totally borne by firms.

34. An exception is Smeeding (1979a), who also deducts indirect taxes.

35. This table is drawn from a detailed study of the 1972 distribution using micro data and the old Office of Business Economics (OBE) income concept. The findings correspond closely to those reported earlier by Budd (1967) for 1962. Table 6.17 shows much less redistribution than that implied by the data in Browning (1976).

36. On sales and excise taxes, see Smeeding (1979a). Sales taxes are usually viewed as regressive, but Browning (1978) argues that they should be considered as progressive. Smeeding (1979c) disagrees.

37. Browning (1976) reaches a similar conclusion.

38. According to Browning (1976), transfers in kind (including public education) increased from 7.2 percent of census income in 1952 to 9 percent in 1962 and 14.6 percent in 1972.

39. For further discussion, see Smolensky et al. (1977).

40. Their justification, I presume, is either on some externality argument or on grounds of paternalism.

41. Smolensky et al. (1977) did not try to price out public education by this method, which is difficult because the market for private education is so thin and because public and private education seem to be different products.

42. The volume and distribution of educational transfers are apparently not in dispute.

43. See Smeeding (1979a, p. 941).

44. Lorenz curves for income before and after cash transfers do not cross, so the Gini ratio is probably a satisfactory summary statistic. Studies alluded to include Danziger and Plotnick (1977), Taussig (1973), Smolensky et al. (1977), and Garfinkel and Haveman (1978), and cover years ranging from 1965 to 1974.

45. According to Browning and Johnson (forthcoming, table 1), in 1976 the lowest fifth of families (ranked by total income) received 63 percent of its income in the form of transfers.

46. Smeeding (1979a) attempted an adjustment for employer pension contributions but, as Browning (1979) pointed out, was guilty of double-counting since census income includes income from pensions. In principle, we might want to include *either* pension contributions when made *or* pension income when received, but not both.

47. His distribution assigned 68 percent of the gains to the top fifth and 3 percent to the bottom fifth.

48. Real capital gains as a percentage of disposable income varied from $+38$ percent in 1958 to -54 percent in 1946. A regression of this ratio against time produced a coefficient that was essentially zero.

49. A similar analysis can be found in Danziger (1977).

50. For the "typical" 3–5 percent reduction, see Benus and Morgan's (1975) calculations for a 1968–72 Office of Economic Opportunity panel and for a special

panel designed to study the impact of the 1964 income tax cuts; and Kohen, Parnes, and Shea's (1975) results with the National Longitudinal Survey (NLS) of mature men. Earlier, Vandome (1958) had reported similar results for the United Kingdom.

51. Benus and Morgan (1975) reported a 9 percent reduction in the Gini coefficient in a 1967–70 panel study of purchases of durable goods, and Kohen, Parnes, and Shea (1975) found a 10 percent reduction among the NLS young men.

52. Hoffman and Podder (1976) report declines in several measures of inequality ranging from 13 percent to 21 percent when the accounting period is lengthened from one year to seven years. David and Menchik (1979) find an even stronger effect: the coefficient of variation declines 14 percent when income over three years is used instead of annual income.

53. The coefficient of variation, a common measure of dispersion, is the ratio of the standard deviation to the mean.

54. Soltow's (1965) study of the distributional history of the town of Sarpsborg, Norway from 1928 to 1960 found that the thirty-three-year Gini ratio was 27 percent lower than the average of the one-year Gini ratios. Blomquist (1976) estimated that the Gini ratio for lifetime income among employed males in Sweden was about half as large as the Gini ratio for annual income.

55. This classification follows Danziger, Haveman, and Smolensky (1977).

56. The data are from U.S. Bureau of the Census, Technical Report no. 17, (Washington, D.C.: Government Printing Office), and are not reproduced here.

57. Figure 6.3 shows smooth curves fitted (by eye) to grouped data. Each mean income is expressed as a fraction of the income of families headed by a 45–54 year old.

58. For criticisms of Paglin's method, see Danziger, Haveman, and Smolensky (1977) and Minarik (1977).

59. The third part arises from the fact that the upper part of the low-income groups have higher incomes than the lower parts of the high-income groups. For a lucid explanation of Pyatt's decomposition and a discussion of how it relates to Paglin's technique, see Murray (1978).

60. For further discussion see Shorrocks (1978) or Blinder (1976).

61. For a fuller discussion, see Weinstein and Smolensky (1976).

62. Kilpatrick (1973) used Gallup poll surveys of minimal income needs to argue that the man on the street's concept of the poverty line rises with average income, though less than in strict proportion. Lebergott (1976, pp. 53–60) collected data showing that payments to poor on relief remained about 30 percent of the wage for common labor for more than a century. See also Rainwater (1974, esp. chaps. 3 and 5).

63. Based on the work of Orshansky (1965).

64. Lebergott (1976, pp. 70–76) has objected eloquently to the "scientific" budgets that underlie the minimum decency standard.

65. This is no trivial problem. The CPS each year finds a number of families with *negative* income (and census income *excludes* capital losses). For example, in 1977 the mean income among the 2 percent of families with incomes below $2,000 was −$1,700. One wonders how many families with negative income are "poor" in any meaningful sense.

66. U.S. Bureau of the Census *Current Population Reports*, Series P–60, no. 119.

67. Non-whites constituted 34 percent of all poor persons; among heads of poor families, 63 percent had not finished high school; the average family size was 3.67. See *Current Population Reports*, Series P–60, no. 119.

68. The poor are those below 44 percent of the median income.

69. These fluctuations may be due to inconsistencies in estimation methods over time. See Plotnick and Smeeding (1979, fn. 16).

70. For data on black-white *earnings* differentials, see Richard Freeman, chapter 5 of this volume.

71. The data pertain to "nonwhites," rather than to blacks. However, blacks predominate in this group.

72. Versus 9 percent and 11 percent for white families in the two years. Data are from Danziger and Lampman (1978).

73. The same ratio for men was also .56 in 1955, but improved only to .69 in 1977. See Thurow (1979).

74. Freeman addresses this issue in chapter 5 of this volume.

75. And the same wealth. More on wealth later.

76. The crucial words in these last two sentences, of course, are "voluntarily" and "voluntary." Not all interpersonal differences in hours of work are voluntary. More on this below.

77. Or there can be more leisure time on the job. On this, see Stafford and Duncan (1977).

78. *Historical Statistics.* The work week comes from series D–765, p. 168; the work day is reported as 9.89 hours in Series D–847, p. 172.

79. The older and newer hours series are not entirely comparable, though both display downward trends. The data series cited in my note 78 ends in 1926, when average weekly hours are 50.3. The newer series used for postwar comparisons records a value of 45 for that same year.

80. Gordon and Blinder (forthcoming) explore reasons for this phenomenon.

81. Reimers (1976) shows that these data need not imply that the mean age of retirement *among those who actually retire* has decreased; and she estimates that it has been fairly constant at around 65 years of age. The reason is that there are fewer and fewer people who never retire.

82. Real consumption per capita rose about 80 percent. The percentage *increase* in leisure is the percentage *decrease* in working time multiplied by the initial ratio of work to leisure. If that initial ratio was two, for example, then leisure time rose 32 percent.

83. But it is not clear that it is. Most of the work-saving machinery that has helped the housewife became widespread only after World War II.

84. It should be noted, however, that housewives were more overworked in 1900 than were paid workers. Housewives, it seems, really did work the proverbial six or seven twelve-hour days.

85. Yet one more qualification. Women are spending far more time in the paid work force than they used to. So the reduction in housework often may not represent more leisure time.

86. Taussig (1973) makes an attempt at this. Browning (1976) and Browning and Johnson (forthcoming) treat all nonworking time as voluntary leisure.

87. Were the lifetime used as the interval for measuring income, there would be little need for separate data on wealth. The present value of income would differ from (human plus nonhuman) wealth only to the extent that inheritances differ (in present value) from bequests.

88. For a discussion of the method, and examples of its use, see Lampman (1962) or Smith (1974).

89. Since Gini coefficients within these age cohorts were .70–.71 in the SFCC, the agreement between the two sources is close.

90. The year 1940 is included also to show the increase in living together brought about by the war.

91. Twenty deaths per one thousand live births in 1970 versus forty-seven in 1940.

92. I resist the temptation to equate education with wisdom.

93. The word "autonomous" needs some explanation. I do not mean to imply that these forces were God-given or exogenous in some ultimate sense, but only that they probably were not themselves effects of the changing income distribution.

94. Among the many factors contributing toward this development were higher divorce rates, more illegitimate births, and changing social mores regarding the role of women. For a full discussion, see Ross and Sawhill (1975).

95. They are dealt with by Richard Freeman in chapter 5 of this volume.

96. A possible counterweight to this is that withdrawal of labor supply may push up the relative wages of these groups.

---

2. Irving Kristol

Some Personal Reflections on Economic Well-Being and Income Distribution

It is my understanding, from surveying various studies of trends in income distribution in the United States over the past three decades, that economists have found very little significant change to have taken place. There does seem to have been a slight increase in the proportion of national income received by the very poor, a slight decrease in the proportion received by the very rich. What goes on in between is such a complex muddle that economic analysis can tease few unquestionable inferences from the data. Moreover, the very methodology of studying income distribution has, over these decades, become ever more controversial. Just what is to be included in the concept of "income" becomes less clear every time a new governmental "entitlement" program is launched (whether it involves food, housing, medicine, or whatever). And it has become ever more apparent that in order to take account of normal age differentials in earnings, of changing demographics, and of economic mobility (both up and down), the distribution of "lifetime earnings" would give us a far more valid report than any cross-sectional survey at a moment in time. The trouble is that economists have not come up with any accepted procedure for measuring any such distribution of lifetime earnings, and there are even some grounds for thinking they never will.

Does it matter? What, precisely, is the point of all of these studies and of the interminable controversies they generate?

Irving Kristol is coeditor of *The Public Interest* magazine.

When one raises this issue among economists, one discovers that they tend to feel that, in some way or other, income inequalities *ought* to have a significant relation to other larger issues such as the rate of economic growth, economic stability or instability, social and historical stability or instability, or even that sense of well-being we vaguely call "happiness" or "contentment." And yet it is astonishing how little by way of any such relationships economic and social research have come up with. Increases and decreases in income inequalities, as conventionally measured, appear to be indifferently compatible with social turbulence as with social stability, with economic decline as with economic growth, with political order as with political chaos, with an increase in individual and social pathologies (e.g., suicide, alcoholism, drug addiction, crime) as with a decrease. Inequality, one gets the impression, is an important issue for today's social scientists *despite* the fact that such importance escapes all empirical verification.

To complicate matters even further, any effort to relate income inequality even to strictly economic well-being is plagued by the fact that the concept of economic well-being is itself not so unambiguous as some economists believe. An improvement in economic well-being can be quite rigorously defined as an increase in (actual or potential) purchasing power over the material goods of this world (i.e., the goods that money can buy). But this brute statistical fact is always "processed" through people's minds, and it is the ideas and attitudes in these minds that ultimately determine the meaning we give to any brute statistical fact. Fortunately for the science of economics, those ideas and attitudes are not utterly disparate, incoherent, and inconstant. One can therefore say, with some confidence, that most people, most of the time, and most anywhere, wish to see their purchasing power increase and are pleased when that occurs. Having said that, however, one must also go on to say that particular circumstances can modify or even overwhelm any purely statistical measure of economic well-being. Both poverty and affluence can have ambiguities that escape the strictly economic perspective.

It is an observable fact that not all people who are statistically poor are everywhere equally miserable or have an equal sense of being "badly off." The past and the future always shape our sense of the present. So much, therefore, depends on the hopes one may have for one's children, the faith one may have in the ultimate benignity and "fairness" of Providence, on the assurance and solace one may derive from traditions. Poverty does not always dehumanize, and relative affluence can have its costs in human terms—costs that are actually, if often dimly, felt. Anyone who has seen *Fiddler on the Roof* and contrasted the lives portrayed there with the lives of Jews in Long Island's Great Neck today, will appreciate the immense difficulties involved in disentangling economic well-being from other kinds of well-being.

Similarly, on the street where I lived until recently there was a Chinese family, recent immigrants, who ran a basement laundry. The parents and their five children shared the two tiny rooms at the back of the tiny store, and I shudder to think what this family did to our official poverty statistics. Still, those parents expressed great confidence that their children would "get ahead"—and, in fact, all five ended up as college graduates. Ought not one to incorporate that *prospect* in any estimate of the family's economic well-being? In contrast, on that same street there were several welfare families whose incomes, in cash and kind and services, may well have been larger than that of our Chinese family, but who were in various stages of a dependency-induced corruption, with little family stability and with the children involved in drugs and delinquency. Would an increase in their welfare receipts really have improved their economic well-being? If it had merely accelerated their demoralization, how would that relate to economic well-being?

Or, at the other extreme, take the case of a statistically affluent suburban child who has every advantage, as we say, but who comes to experience those advantages as bars in a "gilded cage," to use Max Weber's prescient phrase. He perceives the improbability of his surpassing his successful father in either economic or professional terms. He finds family and community life empty of meaning, and school a distracting bore. So he "drops out" of the world he was born into and becomes a "bohemian," a pseudobohemian, or a drifter, living—perhaps placidly, perhaps miserably—off handouts and odd jobs. What meaning are we to ascribe to the statistics of his economic well-being, before and after? When affluence can demoralize as vigorously as poverty, can we take the statistics on economic well-being with the solemnity that economists are naturally inclined to do?

And, of course, this matter becomes infinitely more complicated if we try somehow to incorporate the idea of economic equality into the idea of economic well-being, as so many economists think proper. Here, ordinary people seem to have an intuitive respect for existential complexities that economists often seem to lack. The intensity with which economists work out their Gini coefficients, and the subtlety with which they measure income trends in the quintiles or deciles of the population, is matched—so far as I can see—by the utter lack of interest of the average American in their findings. To some extent, perhaps, this is because those findings are never definitive—every piece of research seems to give rise to an exercise in counterresearch, and the arguments soon unravel into microdisputes. But mainly, I think, it is because the average person is far less interested in economic inequality—or is interested in it in quite a different way—than is the average social scientist.

Why? One reason, I would say, is that the social scientist links the issue of inequality to the issue of poverty more rigorously than does the average person. It is certainly true that as a society becomes more afflu-ent, the "poverty line," as popularly perceived, will also move upward. Today, for example, no one would dispute the fact that the absence of private, indoor toilet facilities—an absence our grandparents would have found not at all shocking—is a sure sign of poverty. On the other hand, the average person feels free to distinguish between "needs" and "wants" in ways that the average economist, *qua* economist, is prohib-ited from doing. People who have what are perceived to be minimally adequate food, shelter, and clothing may be seen as poor, but not as *problematically* poor, regardless of how far down they are in the income distribution. And if one looks at poverty in this way, then the percentage of the American people who qualify as poor is small—well under 10 percent. A social scientist might retort that any such "absolute" defini-tion of poverty is arbitrary, as compared with a definition in terms of relative income. But it is precisely this question to which economics can never hope to give an authoritative answer.

This popular perception of poverty is closely linked to a popular perception of opportunity—specifically, the opportunity to move out of poverty. To the degree that poverty is not viewed as a necessarily per-manent condition, it will be of less concern. And the average American is strongly of the opinion that, leaving the physically handicapped (in which one would include the elderly) aside, there really is no reason for anyone in the lowest quintile of the income distribution to interpret his condition as permanent, since opportunities for "bettering one's con-dition" will and do exist. It may be recalled that Adam Smith had ear-lier suggested that the modus operandi of a market economy is such that economic mobility—and the eventual distribution of income as well—would of a certainty be less unequal than in any other kind of society. The reason for this is that the talents requisite for success in such an economy are so mundane, and the role of sheer luck is so great, that economic mobility should be greater, and eventual economic inequali-ties less significant, than in noncapitalist orders. Americans on the whole tend to accept this thesis as a fact of life. Social scientists, in contrast, think it important either to prove or disprove this thesis by research.

I carefully say "social scientists" because sociologists are perhaps even more prominent in this endeavor than economists. It is they who have created a sizable library of ever more technical literature on the question of "social mobility," of which income mobility is the major component. It is an open question whether this literature provides more enlightenment than obfuscation. We do know, without benefit of re-search, that if economic growth tends to create new and better-paying jobs and occupations and professions (as it does), then the statistics will obviously reveal considerable upward social and economic mobility (as they do). But what sociologists appear to be worried most about is whether everyone benefits *equally* from these changes, and they do seem to be especially concerned as to whether those who are already in the top decile manage to hang in there. The statistical procedures of sociologists are such that one begins with a rigorously egalitarian definition of social mobility, one in which the children of upper-class parents are downwardly mobile, while their places are taken by the upwardly mobile—a world turned upside-down indeed!—and then measure the actuality in the light of this "ideal." The fact that there has never been such a society, or that the very idea of such a society is inherently absurd, somehow is lost sight of.

It is sociologists, too, who have popularized the concept of "relative deprivation," which is supposed to explain why people's views of their own economic well-being are inextricably intertwined with the idea of equality. Now, there certainly is such a thing as a sense of relative deprivation, but it turns out to have only a limited connection with the larger idea of equality and to be more intimately related to the idea of justice or fairness ("to each his due"). Thus, there have been innumerable strikes in the United States over pay differentials among workers ("equal pay for equal work!"), yet I do not recall a case of there being a strike over the chief executive officer's very high salary. If sociologists tacitly assume—as practically all seem to do—that a more egalitarian society is (and will be perceived to be) a more just society, that is an assumption which derives from ideology, not from history or contemporary experience.

And much the same is true, I would say, for the way in which—and the intensity with which—economists study income inequalities. One begins blandly with the premise that absolute equality is the ideal state and then one measures degrees of departure from this ideal. Yes, I know, there is nothing "normative" about such a statistical procedure—it is merely a mathematical convenience that zero inequality is taken as the base for all measurements. But is it not odd that it is impossible to point to a study that breathes satisfaction (as distinct from *Schadenfreude*) at discovering an increase in economic inequality? This whole literature is as profoundly suffused with ideology as it is liberally bespattered with statistics.

What, really, is the point of this keen interest among economists and sociologists in the issue of inequality? There is precious little evidence to the effect that it responds to a widespread popular concern and much evidence to the contrary. Indeed, one gets the distinct impression that much of the research is directed toward "raising the consciousness" of the public about the issue—and that the rest of the research is directed toward rebutting such "consciousness raising" efforts. It is hard to believe that even the most casual reader can fail to perceive the essentially ideological nature of this disputation.

My own view—admittedly a bit extreme—is that when you need an economist or a sociologist to bring you intelligence about inequalities of income or social class, that is in itself proof that neither issue is of serious concern to the citizenry. There are simply no "mysteries" to be elucidated about income inequality and social class, since there is no reason to think that common opinion, based on observation and experience and gossip, is likely to be self-deceiving about a matter of such interest to everyone. The very notion that such self-deception is probable derives from the Marxist idea—an ideological conception of the role of ideology—that bourgeois society is constantly at work instilling "false consciousness" into the populace.

At this point a social scientist might object that opinion poll data do reveal that people misconstrue the social and economic reality they inhabit—that, for instance, households with incomes of $100,000 a year blandly report themselves to be "middle class." To this objection, there are two rejoinders.

First, if a $100,000-a-year household thinks itself to be middle class, then it *is* middle class. And the same is true for a $10,000-a-year household. What on earth gives social scientists the authority to dismiss such "subjective" conceptions of class and to impose a presumably more "objective" one? Here again we are dealing with a Marxist derivative that has been unthinkingly adopted by modern social science. Class may (or may not) find phenomenological expression, but at root it is a mode of self-definition. There are aristocrats in England who are as poor as church mice but are definitely "upper class." And there are immigrants to the United States who are also as poor as church mice but are definitely "middle class" from the moment they set foot here. The very thought that there is someone ("up there?") who knows better than we do what class we are in is as breathtaking in its intellectual presumption as it is sterile for all serious purposes of social research.

Second, when poll data reveal vast, apparent misconceptions about *other people*—about how rich or poor they are, or how powerful or weak they are—such data ought not to be taken too seriously. No economic, social, or political system could function for a moment if people actually had wildly unrealistic notions of their economic, social, and political reality. The interesting question here for social research is why people express such opinions and beliefs to pollsters, not why they have them.

My own explanation for the keen interest of social scientists in the nonobvious issue of equality is that this is but one manifestation of how nineteenth-century ideologies—and most especially the socialist ideology —have so decisively shaped modern social science. Thus, it is my understanding that the National Bureau of Economic Research was itself originally founded, back in the 1920s, to take a serious look at the issue of economic inequality—an issue then posed by socialist, quasi-socialist, or "progressive" critics who maintained that, under capitalism, the rich were getting richer while the poor were getting poorer. It was they who defined the issue—and it is they who have been defining it ever since. It is fascinating to note the way in which research does *not* dispose of this issue. One might have thought, as the evidence accumulated to the effect that nothing very novel or exciting has happened to the distribution of income in recent decades—and there is even evidence to suggest that nothing very exciting has happened in the past century—that social scientists would simply lose interest in the question. They have not. Instead the studies become ever more sophisticated, ever more incomprehensible to the noninitiated, ever more "scholastic" in the pejorative sense of that term—and they still don't bring us tidings of significance. The impulse behind such studies can hardly be designated as routinely "scientific."

It can, however, be quite easily recognized as "ideological." The prominence of the issue of equality, I should say, reflects the degree to which egalitarian, quasi-socialist conceptions of justice have permeated our culture, including the thinking of many social scientists who do not regard themselves as in any way socialist but who, as a matter of course, use the ideal of a socialist society—classless and egalitarian—as a proper criterion for the judging of capitalist reality. Of all the social sciences, economics has been the least influenced by this ideological impulse, in part because the discipline of economics is truly more rigorous than the other social sciences; in part because a respect for market processes is indigenous to the methodology of this discipline. But economists are human, and it could not remain unaffected. One has only to recall the ingenuity and persistence with which distinguished professors of economics elaborated quite fanciful justifications for the progressive income tax—for which there is no *economic*, as distinct from moral or political —justification since it involves an interpersonal comparison of utilities which is beyond the scope of economics.

It is understandably irksome to many economists that the science of economics, strictly considered, should not offer answers to many important questions that *appear* to be economic in nature but in fact belong to moral and political theory. Indeed, we have witnessed recently a vigorous dissenting movement by advocates of something called "political economy"—sometimes "normative economics," sometimes simply "radical political economy"—who argue in favor of a candid union of economics with ideology. These are for the most part younger economists who are discontented with the limits of their social-scientific discipline and who wish to import into economics all of those intellectual and moral considerations that used to constitute the body of political philosophy when *that* discipline still flourished. (One such consideration is equality, as an ideal or nonideal for a good society.) One may sympathize with the moral and intellectual passions behind this movement while realizing they are destructive of the integrity of economics as a scientific discipline.

What it comes down to, in the end, is the need for economists to recognize their severe limitations *qua* economists. Economics has many useful and important things to tell us, but it really has nothing to say about the larger features of a good society, or about the status of equality or inequalities in such a society, and it only has something to say about "economic well-being" on a fairly narrow—though not unimportant—definition. Those economic statistics we are being deluged with do tell us something valid about the real world; but they often tell us less of the truth about the real world than economists are—by virtue of their *déformation professionelle*—inclined to think.

3. Wilbur J. Cohen

Economic Well-Being and Income Distribution

I have been asked to present my personal reactions to the issues dealing with income transfer programs as they affected the economic well-being and income distribution during the postwar period. The basis for my comments derives from Alan S. Blinder's broad-gauged and informative essay on this important topic.

I am not quite sure what Martin Feldstein had in mind when he asked me to do this. I assume he thought that one of the significant developments of both the post-1929 depression and the post–World War II economy was the striking growth of transfer payments, public and private, and because of my participation in these developments, I should be prepared to explain and defend my previous actions in this area.

Perhaps it passed through his mind that at this reflective stage of my life as a Senior Citizen I might admit my role in the expansion of our income transfer programs was all a mistake, and I would ask forgiveness for my sins and errors. Or perhaps I might review the postwar developments in these programs and say enough was enough and let's stop, look, and listen before going any further. Or I might express some doubts about the wisdom of some past specific decisions as they affect savings, investment, and productivity.

But then maybe he assumed I would vigorously defend past policy decisions and we could have a rousing controversy about such issues as

Wilbur J. Cohen is the Sid W. Richardson Professor of Public Affairs, L. B. J. School of Public Affairs, University of Texas at Austin.

compulsion, regressive payroll taxes, the adverse impact on work incentives, and the abuse and fraud involved in the programs.

As you will see, I am not going to do any of these things.

There is some advantage in reaching age sixty-five and reflecting about one's past activities. It is easy to conclude that we had complete freedom of choice at each juncture or to conclude that, on the basis of the choices at the time, we chose the only one we could have selected. I really can't—or won't—comment on which of these seems to me now to be the correct one. But I will say that we should be willing to learn from past experience and revise decisions in the light of new developments. But I would quickly add the latter isn't always feasible or simple. Sometimes the good is the enemy of the better. Sometimes it is better not to substitute unknown and untried proposals for known and current evils.

I was seventeen years old in 1930 when I entered the University of Wisconsin. My fellow students were troubled and concerned about the collapse of the economy and the values in which they and their parents believed. Although they did not then utilize the term "quality of life," they embraced the concept. We read Henry Adams, Lincoln Steffens, Thorstein Veblen, and Karl Marx, along with Aristotle, Plato, and Thucydides. We searched for explanations and, of course, permanent solutions to the vexing problems of the times.

Within a short time I gravitated to the Economics Department, where the dominating influences were John R. Commons, Selig Perlman, Edwin E. Witte, and other faculty members who became identified as "institutionalists." After several courses it began to dawn on me that one could improve the quality of life of people by changing, creating, or restructuring some of the institutions, particularly economic ones. John R. Commons had studied and advocated state worker accident compensation programs, health insurance, and unemployment insurance programs. Here were specifics I could comprehend which would improve the quality and standard of living. I believed that the creation of these institutions would improve the health and welfare standard of living and the quality of life.

I was fortunate shortly thereafter to be assigned a minor role in the effort to create the various institutional proposals which eventually became the Social Security Act of 1935 and then later in the additions to it, such as survivors insurance, disability insurance and Medicare, and in 1950–51 to help accelerate the role of the private sector in health, welfare, and pensions as chairman of the Wage Stabilization Board committee in this area.

It is now about forty-five years since I started this work. It has been exciting, controversial, and challenging. Although there are some—even

many—who increasingly doubt the wisdom of specific programs or provisions, I doubt if there are many, or any, who would question the
generalization that the overall health and welfare standard of living has
improved since 1930, 1940, 1950, or 1960, and even since 1970. The
questions of how much of an improvement and for whom may defy
precise measurement. But there certainly is evidence of improvement
in that infant mortality has declined; life expectancy has increased; absolute poverty has declined; individuals have more choice about work,
leisure, and retirement; and more persons have access to education,
medical care, housing, transportation, and recreation.

The questions today are not as simplistic as they were in the thirties.
There are questions as to how and why these improvements occurred
and what would have happened if all of the programs had developed in
the private sector.

There are different ways of looking at the changing standard of living.
Economists look at income, measure it, and compare it over time. We
draw certain conclusions from such measurements. But I think there are
other elements to be considered: the range of choices, continuity of income, future expectations, educational attainment, opportunities for self-
fulfillment, the balance between work and leisure, not to mention clean
air and water, and freedom from chemical and nuclear wastes.

In addition, the predominant lesson to be derived from recent experiences is that we live—and will continue to live—in a very imperfect
world. We have experienced major miscalculations on the part of presi-
dents and other politicians, business, labor, social reformers, and even
economists. We are all living in glass houses. We find we cannot control
the forces around us as simply, quickly, or effectively as we would like.

Alan S. Blinder's essay "The Level and Distribution of Economic
Well-Being" reviews not only a wide range of economic data relating to
the issue of equality and inequality of income in the postwar period,
but in addition he deals with such topics as black-white income differentials, the poor and poverty, leisure time, health, "the privilege of living
apart from relatives," illegitimate birth, divorce, suicide, and crime rates
as social indicators, and even happiness!

This is indeed a wide range of controversial topics. However, I miss
a reference to such other related questions as smoking, abortion, drug
use, and some other questions such as women's use of time in the home
and office, the Equal Rights Amendment, changes in life-styles and other
questions which relate to health, education, welfare, and happiness.

A significant aspect of his paper seems to me the brief inclusion of
some social indicators in an economic review. I had almost given up on
the possibility that economists would attempt to interrelate economic
and social indicators.

One of the key issues in Mr. Blinder's essay is the impact of the income transfer programs on equality and inequality of income. Table C6.1 displays the increases which took place in the twenty-five-year period from 1950 to 1975.

In 1950 all *public* and *private* expenditures for health, education, and welfare were equivalent to 13.4 percent of gross national product. By 1970, this indicator had risen to 21.8 percent, by 1975 to 27 percent, by 1976 to 27.5 percent, but then decreased to 27.1 percent in 1977 and 26.8 percent in 1978.

All income maintenance program expenditures were only 4 percent of GNP in 1950, reached 6 percent in 1960, 7.5 percent in 1970, 10.6 percent in 1975 and peaked at 10.9 percent in 1976 with a decrease to 10.6 percent in 1977 and 10.2 percent in 1978.

Are we at the end of an era of significant expansion of the income maintenance programs? Or will the continued increase in the number and proportion of the aged result in further increases?

Health program expenditures were 4.5 percent of GNP in 1950, then 5.2 percent in 1960, 7.2 percent by 1970, 8.4 percent by 1975 and continued to increase to 8.6 percent in 1976, 9 percent in 1977 and 9.2 percent in 1978. It is likely that this figure will reach 10 percent of GNP during the 1980s.

However, I do not think the overall total of such expenditures as a percentage of GNP will be lower in 1990 than the figure for 1980. The private pension plan area is still expanding. Social security benefits are indexed to increasing wages and prices. The increasing number of aged will increase expenditures for medical services under Medicare and supplementary private arrangements. Proposals for catastrophic health in-

Table C6.1   **Public and Private Expenditures for Social Welfare Purposes, 1950 and 1975, as Percentage of Gross National Product, and Increase, 1975 over 1950**

	1950	1975	Increase, 1975 over 1950
Net Total	13.4	27.0	2.015 times
Income Maintenance	4.0	10.6	2.65 times
Health	4.5	8.4	1.86 times
Education	4.1	6.8	1.66 times
Welfare and Other Services	0.8	1.7	2.13 times

Source: Alfred M. Skolnik and Sophie R. Dales, "Social Welfare Expenditures, 1950–75," *Social Security Bulletin* 39, no. 1 (January 1976): 19, with 1978 revisions from table 2 supplied by the Social Security Administration, Office of Research and Statistics.

Table C6.2 Public and Private Expenditures for Social Welfare Purposes, Selected Fiscal Years, 1950–78

Type of Expenditure	1950	1955	1960	1965	1970	1974	1975	1976	1977	1978[1]
					All Expenditures (in $ Millions)					
Total, Net[2]	35,395	49,957	78,743	117,792	209,330	332,104	392,320	447,154	497,375	548,291
Public	23,508	32,640	52,293	77,175	145,856	239,358	290,332	331,744	361,253	393,897
Private	12,227	17,997	27,829	42,687	67,353	99,592	110,164	124,998	146,769	165,978
Income Maintenance	10,723	17,304	29,827	42,550	72,473	126,373	153,300	177,572	194,093	208,640
Public[3]	9,758	15,409	26,292	36,575	60,813	107,648	131,670	153,166	166,293	177,240
Private	965	1,895	3,535	5,975	11,660	18,725	21,630	24,406	27,800	31,400
Health	12,027	17,330	25,856	38,892	69,201	106,057	122,584	139,316	164,514	186,977
Public	3,065	4,421	6,395	9,535	25,391	41,522	51,236	58,539	67,271	76,199
Private	8,962	12,909	19,461	29,357	43,810	64,535	71,348	80,777	97,243	110,778
Education	10,981	14,206	21,781	34,129	61,746	87,172	99,452	109,487	116,222	124,094
Public	9,366	11,863	18,036	28,149	51,863	73,740	85,266	93,072	98,346	104,594
Private	1,615	2,343	3,745	5,980	9,883	13,432	14,186	16,415	17,876	19,500
Welfare and Other Services	2,004	1,793	2,658	4,291	9,789	19,348	25,160	30,367	33,193	40,164
Public[4]	1,319	947	1,570	2,916	7,789	16,448	22,160	26,967	29,343	35,864
Private	685	850	1,088	1,375	2,000	2,900	3,000	3,400	3,850	4,300
					Public Expenditures as Percentage of Expenditures for Specified Purposes					
Total[5]	65.8	64.5	65.3	64.4	68.4	70.6	72.5	72.6	71.1	70.4
Income Maintenance	91.0	89.0	88.1	86.0	83.9	85.2	85.9	86.3	85.7	85.0
Health	25.5	25.5	24.7	24.5	36.7	39.2	41.8	42.0	40.9	40.8
Education	85.3	83.5	82.8	82.5	84.0	84.6	85.7	85.0	84.6	84.3
Welfare and Other Services	65.8	52.7	59.1	68.0	79.6	85.0	88.1	88.8	88.4	89.3

Table C6.2—*continued*

Type of Expenditure	1950	1955	1960	1965	1970	1974	1975	1976	1977	1978[1]
	All Expenditures as Percentage of Gross National Product									
Total, Net[2]	13.4	13.2	15.8	17.9	21.8	24.4	27.0	27.5	27.1	26.8
Income Maintenance	4.0	4.6	6.0	6.5	7.5	9.3	10.6	10.9	10.6	10.2
Health	4.5	4.6	5.2	5.9	7.2	7.8	8.4	8.6	9.0	9.2
Education	4.1	3.7	4.4	5.2	6.4	6.4	6.8	6.7	6.3	6.1
Welfare and Other Services	.8	.5	.5	.7	1.0	1.4	1.7	1.9	1.8	2.0

[1]Preliminary data.

[2]Total expenditures adjusted to eliminate duplication resulting from use of cash payments received under public and private social welfare programs to purchase medical care and educational services.

[3]Includes cash benefits and administrative costs under social insurance, public assistance, supplemental security income, and veterans' and emergency employment programs. Excludes cost of medical services provided in conjunction with these programs and for other welfare programs.

[4]Includes food stamps, surplus food for the needy and for institutions, child nutrition, institutional care, child welfare, economic opportunity and manpower programs, veterans' welfare services, vocational rehabilitation, and housing.

[5]Before adjustment for elimination of duplication.

surance coverage and for coverage of services for all mothers and children are under Congressional discussion as is welfare reform.

Several years ago I estimated that the total of these expenditures might reach 33 percent of GNP between 1980 and 1990. I am not so sure of this now but I have not withdrawn this speculative projection because I believe the built-in elements related to economic and demographic factors eventually will overweigh the political constraints on growth.

Several possible lines of change, however, must be recognized.

1. Program changes are likely to be considered for reallocating resources in relation to priorities. In health this could take the form of cost constraints in the expansion of health maintenance organizations, for example, and other changes in the health delivery system. In education, it could involve closure of some doctoral programs, closing of some elementary schools, and pressures to constrain salary improvements.

In social security it could involve changes in the retirement age or freezing the minimum benefit for persons with short periods of coverage in the social security system.

I am not sure that all of these changes are necessary, desirable, or feasible, but I do think there will be more questioning of prior decisions and more controversy about priorities, and such issues at the program margins will produce strong emotional responses.

2. There probably will be greater emphasis on redistribution of income measures. The rise in the payroll taxes since 1950 has now resulted in pressures to limit the increase in such taxes and even proposals for a rollback. The recent recommendation of the Advisory Council on Social Security for an earmarked income tax for financing Medicare illustrates this development.

3. Expenditures will continue to expand in the *private* sector. Proposals for catastrophic health insurance will surely involve mandating employer coverage under private health insurance.

As the size and importance of income maintenance and health programs have grown, there has been an increased recognition of the interrelationships between tax, expenditure, economic, and fiscal policy on the one hand and income maintenance policy on the other. But I am not at all sure where we will come out on this matter over the next several years. There is more to the resolution of this issue than economic policy alone: Psychology and politics play important roles. There are, therefore, many different options available to the American people and to the Congress.

While redistribution of income in terms of income classes is of vital concern to economists and some of the American people, redistribution of income over one's own lifetime is probably of greater interest to most working people. The average head of family is concerned about the distribution of his or her income over time for such purposes as purchasing a home; providing for accidents, disability, premature death, or for retirement and medical costs; and, in many cases, meeting the cost of educating his or her children.

Because of the nature of the relationship between the private and public sectors in this country, the resolution of the crucial issues in income maintenance and health has been related more to the philosophy underlying this relationship than to income redistribution. It is therefore essential, in my opinion, for us to comprehend the larger context within which our social welfare programs and expenditures operate rather than judging them solely in relation to the way they affect the Lorenz curve or the Gini ratio.

I believe the size and nature of both national and family obligations and expenditures will determine the choice of options for future policy in health, social security, and welfare reform.

I think that, by and large, in the American situation, there is no substantial political pressure for equality of income, though there is a consensus on equality of opportunity—and that is a very important distinction. There is wide recognition that certain factors in our society impair equality of opportunity—that is, access to jobs, education, health services, or housing. Over the years, those persons who have been advocating improvement in the income maintenance, education, and health programs have not attempted to obtain absolute equality or even to approach equality of income, but rather to provide a greater degree of equality of opportunity, which is what the middle class and the blue-collar workers (as well as others) stress as an important objective.

Summary of Discussion

Peter Peterson expressed unease over the uncertainties surrounding future costs of various United States income transfer programs. Noting that we "operate in a sea of ignorance" about the full, discounted costs of public policies, he suggested that we undertake a policy of "truth-in-spending" as we have "truth-in-lending." Wilbur Cohen shared the concern, adding that until recently the expectation was that continued economic growth would finance the programs.

References

Atkinson, Anthony B. 1970. On the measurement of inequality. *Journal of Economic Theory* 2 (September): 244–63.

Benus, Jacob. 1974. Income instability. In *Five thousand American families*, vol. 1, ed. J. N. Morgan et al. Ann Arbor: Institute for Social Research, University of Michigan.

Benus, Jacob, and Morgan, James N. 1975. Time period, unit of analysis, and income concept in the analysis of income distribution. In *The Personal Distribution of Income and Wealth*, ed. James D. Smith, pp. 209–24. NBER Studies in Income and Wealth, vol. 39. New York: Columbia University Press.

Bhattacharya, N., and Mahalanobis, B. 1967. Regional disparities in household consumption in India. *Journal of the American Statistical Association*, vol. 62 (March).

Blinder, Alan S. 1974. *Toward an economic theory of income distribution*. Cambridge: M.I.T. Press.

———. 1976. Inequality and mobility in the distribution of wealth. *Kyklos* 29, fasc. 4: 607–38.

Blinder, Alan S., and Esaki, Howard Y. 1978. Macroeconomic activity and income distribution in the postwar United States. *Review of Economics and Statistics* 60 (November): pp. 604–9.

Blomquist, N. Soren. 1976. The distribution of lifetime income: A case study of Sweden. Ph.D. diss. Princeton University.

Browning, Edgar K. 1976. The trend toward equality in the distribution of net income. *Southern Economic Journal* 43 (September): 912–23.

———. 1978. The burden of taxation. *Journal of Political Economy* 86, no. 4: 649–71.

———. 1979. On the distribution of net income: Reply. *Southern Economic Journal* 46 (January): 945–59.

Browning, Edgar K., and Johnson, William R. Forthcoming. Taxes, transfers, and income inequality. In *Regulatory change in an atmosphere of crisis: Current implications of the Roosevelt years*, ed. Gary Walton. New York: Academic Press.

Budd, Edward C. 1967. *Inequality and poverty*. New York: Norton.

———. 1970. Postwar changes in the size distribution of income in the U.S. *American Economic Review* 60 (May): 247–60.

Danziger, Sheldon. 1977. Conference overview: Conceptual issues, data issues, and policy implications. *Conference on the trend in income inequality in the U.S.* Madison, Wisc.: Institute for Research on Poverty.

Danziger, Sheldon; Haveman, Robert; and Plotnick, Robert. 1979. Income transfer programs in the United States: An analysis of their structure and impacts. Paper prepared for the Joint Economic Committee of the United States, Special Study on Economic Change (mimeographed). Madison, Wisc. (May).

Danziger, Sheldon; Haveman, Robert; and Smolensky, Eugene. 1977. The measurement and trend of inequality: Comment. *American Economic Review* 67, no. 3 (June): 505–12.

Danziger, Sheldon H., and Lampman, Robert J. 1978. Getting and spending. *Annals of the American Academy of Political and Social Science* 435 (January): 23–39.

Danziger, Sheldon, and Plotnick, Robert. 1977. Demographic change, government transfers, and the distribution of income. *Monthly Labor Review* 100 (April): 7–11.

David, Martin, and Menchik, Paul. 1979. Aspects of the lifetime distribution of income and wealth (mimeographed). Madison, Wisc. (May).

Easterlin, Richard A. 1974. Does economic growth improve the human lot? Some empirical evidence. In *Nations and households in economic growth: Essays in honor of Moses Abramovitz*, ed. P. A. David and M. W. Reder. New York: Academic Press.

Eisner, Robert. 1980. Capital gains and income: Real changes in the value of capital in the United States, 1946–1977. In *The measurement of capital*, ed. Dan Usher. NBER Studies in Income and Wealth, vol. 45. Chicago: University of Chicago Press. Forthcoming.

Feldstein, Martin S. 1976. Social security and the distribution of wealth. *Journal of the American Statistical Association* 71 (December): 800–807.

Fuchs, Victor R. 1967. Redefining poverty and redistributing income. *The Public Interest*, no. 9 (summer).

Garfinkel, Irwin, and Haveman, Robert. 1978. Capacity, choice, and inequality. *Southern Economic Journal* 45, no. 2 (October): 421–31.

Gini, Corrado. 1936. On the measure of concentration with especial reference to income and wealth. Unpublished Cowles Commission paper.

Gordon, Roger H. 1976. Essays on the causes and equitable treatment of differences in earnings and ability. Ph.D. diss., M.I.T.

————. 1977. A search for consistent welfare measures (mimeographed). Princeton University (July).

Gordon, Roger H., and Blinder, Alan S. 1980. Market wages, reservation wages, and retirement decisions. *Journal of Public Economics*, in press.

Henle, Peter, 1972. Exploring the distribution of earned income. *Monthly Labor Review* 95, no. 12 (December): 16–27.

Hoffman, Saul, and Podder, Nripesh. 1976. Income inequality. In *Five thousand American families—patterns of economic progress*, vol. 4, ed. G. J. Duncan and J. N. Morgan, pp. 333–56. Ann Arbor: Institute for Social Research, University of Michigan.

Kilpatrick, Robert W. 1973. The income elasticity of the poverty line. *Review of Economics and Statistics* 55 (August): 327–32.

Kohen, Andrew I.; Parnes, Herbert S.; and Shea, John R. 1975. Income instability among young and middle-aged men. In *The personal distribution of income and wealth*, vol. 39, ed. J. D. Smith, pp. 151–207. New York: Columbia University Press.

Kravis, Irving B. 1960. International differences in the distribution of income. *Review of Economics and Statistics* 42 (November): 408–16.

————. 1962. *The structure of income: Some quantitative essays*. Philadelphia: University of Pennsylvania Press.

Kuznets, Simon. 1974. Demographic aspects of the distribution of income among families: Recent trends in the United States. In *Econometrics and economic theory: Essays in honor of Jan Tinbergen*, ed. Willy Sellekaerts, pp. 223–45. London: Macmillan Press.

Lampman, Robert J. 1962. *The share of top wealth-holders in national wealth 1922–1956*. Princeton: Princeton University Press.

Lampman, Robert J. 1973. Measured inequality of income: What does it mean and what can it tell us? *Annals of the American Academy of Political and Social Science* 409 (September): 81–91.

————. 1977. Changing patterns of income, 1960–1974. In *Toward new human rights: The social policies of the Kennedy and Johnson administrations*, ed. David Warner. Austin: Lyndon B. Johnson School of Public Affairs.

Lane, Jonathan P., and Morgan, James N. 1975. Patterns of change in economic status and family structure. In *Five thousand American families—patterns of economic progress*, vol. 3, ed. G. J. Duncan and J. N. Morgan. Ann Arbor: Institute for Social Research, University of Michigan.

Lansing, John B., and Sonquist, John. 1969. A cohort analysis of changes in the distribution of wealth. In *Six papers on the size distribution of wealth and income*, ed. Lee Soltow. NBER Studies in Income and Wealth, vol. 33. New York: Columbia University Press.

Lebergott, Stanley. 1976. *The American economy: Income, wealth, and want*. Princeton: Princeton University Press.

Lillard, Lee A. 1979. Inequality: Earnings versus human wealth. *American Economic Review* 67 (March): 42–53.

Lorenz, Max O. 1905. Methods for measuring concentration of wealth. *Journal of the American Statistical Association* 9: 209–19.

Minarik, Joseph J. 1977. The measurement and trend of inequality: Comment. *American Economic Review* 67 (June): 513–16.

Mirer, Thad. 1975. Aspects of the variability of family income. In *Five thousand American families—patterns of economic progress*, vol. 4, ed. G. J. Duncan and J. N. Morgan, pp. 201–12. Ann Arbor: Institute for Social Research, University of Michigan.

Moore, Geoffrey H., and Hedges, Janice N. 1971. Trends in labor and leisure. *Monthly Labor Review* 94, no. 2 (February): 3–11.

Morgan, James N., and Smith, James D. 1969. Measures of economic well-offness and their correlates. *American Economic Review* 59 (May): 450–62.

Murray, David. 1978. Sources of income inequality in Australia 1968–69. *Economic Record* 54, no. 146 (August): 159–69.

Orshansky, Mollie. 1965. Counting the poor: Another look at the poverty population. *Social Security Bulletin* 28, no. 1 (January): 3–29.

Paglin, Morton. 1975. The measurement and trend of inequality: A basic revision. *American Economic Review* 65 (September): 598–609.

Pareto, Vilfredo. 1897. *Cours d'economie politique.* Rouge: Lausanne.

Plotnick, Robert, and Smeeding, Timothy. 1979. Poverty and income transfers: Past trends and future prospects. *Public Policy* 17 (summer).

Projector, Dorothy S., and Weiss, Gertrude S. 1966. *Survey of financial characteristics of consumers.* Washington, D.C.: Board of Governors of the Federal Reserve System.

Pyatt, Graham. 1976. On the interpretation and disaggregation of Gini coefficients. *Economic Journal* 86 (June): 243–55.

Radner, Daniel B. 1979. Federal income taxes, social security taxes, and the U.S. distribution of income, 1972. Working Paper no. 7, Office of Research and Statistics, Social Security Administration, Washington, D.C. (April).

Rainwater, Lee. 1974. *What money buys: Inequality and the social meaning of income.* New York: Basic Books.

Reimers, Cordelia. 1976. Is the average age at retirement changing? *Journal of the American Statistical Association* 71, no. 355 (September): 552–58.

Reynolds, Morgan, and Smolensky, Eugene. 1977. *Public expenditures, taxes, and the distribution of income: The U.S., 1950, 1961, 1970.* New York: Academic Press.

———. 1978. The fading effect of government on inequality. *Challenge* 21 (July/August): 32–37.

Rivlin, Alice M. 1975. Income distribution: Can economists help? *American Economic Review* 65 (May): 1–15.

Ross, Heather L., and Sawhill, Isabel V. 1975. *Time of transition.* Washington, D.C.: Urban Institute.

Rothschild, Michael, and Stiglitz, Joseph E. 1973. Some further results on the measurement of inequality. *Journal of Economic Theory,* 6: 188–204.

Sawyer, Malcolm. 1976. Income distribution in OECD countries. *OECD Occasional Studies,* July, pp. 3–36.

Schultz, T. Paul. 1975. Long-term change in personal income distribution: Theoretical approaches, evidence, and explanations. In *The "inequality" controversy*, ed. D. M. Levine and M. J. Bane, pp. 147–69. New York: Basic Books.

Sen, Amartya K. 1973. *On economic inequality.* New York: Norton.

Shorrocks, Anthony. 1978. Income inequality and income mobility. *Journal of Economic Theory* 19 (December): 376–93.

Sirageldin, Ismail. 1969. *Nonmarket components of national income.* Ann Arbor: Survey Research Center, University of Michigan.

Smeeding, Timothy M. 1977. The antipoverty effectiveness of in-kind transfers. *Journal of Human Resources* 12 (summer): 360–78.

———. 1979a. On the distribution of net income: Comment. *Southern Economic Journal* 46 (January): 932–44.

———. 1979b. Still more on the distribution of net income: Further comment (mimeographed). University of Utah.

———. 1979c. Are sales taxes progressive? (mimeographed). University of Utah.

Smith, James D. 1974. The concentration of personal wealth in America, 1969. *The Review of Income and Wealth*, series 20, no. 2, pp. 143–80.

Smith, James D., and Franklin, Stephen D. 1964. The concentration of personal wealth, 1922–1969. *American Economic Review* 64 (May): 162–67.

Smolensky, Eugene, et al. 1977. Adding in-kind transfers to the personal income and outlay account: Implications for the size distribution of income. In *The distribution of economic well-being*, ed. F. Thomas Juster. NBER Studies in Income and Wealth, vol. 41. New York: National Bureau of Economic Research.

Soltow, Lee. 1965. *Toward income equality in Norway.* Madison, Wisc.: University of Wisconsin Press.

Stafford, Frank, and Duncan, Greg. 1977. The use of time and technology by households in the United States (mimeographed). Ann Arbor: University of Michigan (July).

Stigler, George J. 1973. General economic conditions and national elections. *American Economic Review* 63 (May): 160–67.

Taussig, Michael K. 1973. *Alternative measures of the distribution of economic welfare.* Princeton: Industrial Relations Section, Princeton University.

———. 1977. Trends in inequality of well-offness in the United States since World War II. *Conference on the trend in income inequality in the U.S.* Madison, Wisc.: Institute for Research on Poverty.

Thurow, Lester C. 1979. Manpower programs as income redistribution (mimeographed). Cambridge: M.I.T. (July).

United States Bureau of the Census. Various issues. *Current population reports*, series P–20. Washington, D.C.: United States Government Printing Office.

United States Bureau of the Census. Various issues. *Current population reports*, series P–60. Washington, D.C.: United States Government Printing Office.

United States Bureau of the Census. 1975. *Historical statistics of the United States, colonial times to 1970*, part 1 and part 2. Washington, D.C.: United States Government Printing Office.

United States Bureau of the Census. 1967. *Trends in the income of families and persons in the United States: 1947–1964*. Technical Paper no. 17. Washington, D.C.: United States Government Printing Office.

United States Bureau of Economic Analysis. 1976. *The national income and product accounts of the United States, 1929–1974*. Washington, D.C.: United States Government Printing Office.

United States Bureau of Economic Analysis. Various issues. *Survey of Current Business*. Washington, D.C.: United States Government Printing Office.

United States President. 1979. *Economic report of the president, 1979* Washington, D.C.: United States Government Printing Office.

Vandome, Peter. 1958. Aspects of the dynamics of consumer behavior: Income and savings over two years from the 1954 reinterview savings survey. *Bulletin of the Oxford University Institute of Statistics* 20 (February): 65–106.

Weinstein, Michael M., and Smolensky, Eugene. 1976. Poverty (mimeographed) University of Wisconsin (March). Forthcoming in *Dictionary of American economic history*.

Weisbrod, Burton A., and Hansen, W. Lee. 1968. An income–net worth approach to measuring economic welfare. *American Economic Review* 58 (December): 1315–29.

7 The Structure of Industry

1. Richard E. Caves
2. Walter B. Wriston
3. James R. Schlesinger

1. Richard E. Caves

The average citizen sees the economy around him as a confusing welter of transactions, and he may have no conviction about it other than that he himself pays too much for what he buys and receives too little for what he sells. An economist instinctively thinks of the economy as a series of markets in which prices are set by the rivalry of buyers and sellers. Some markets may be hard to define. Some prices may be set by the government or behave in quizzical ways. Nonetheless, the logic of market relationship proves overwhelmingly useful for thinking about the course of economic events and the effects of economic policies.

Our practical concern with the structures of industries stems from the market's value as an analytical tool for thinking about the economy. An "industry" is nothing but the participants on one side of a market. We normally identify an industry as the firms that sell some particular good or service, but the term applies with equal logic to the companies that compete as buyers for some intermediate product, or that engage in both buying and selling (scrap metal, for example). Still, we most often think of an industry as a collection of competing sellers. This chapter presents some data arranged to display key features of the changing structure of industries selling goods and services. The coverage will be economywide, but we omit markets for financial assets and pay little attention to the agricultural sector.

Richard E. Caves is professor of economics at Harvard University.

I am indebted to Scott Bales for research assistance, to P. J. Corcoran, F. M. Scherer, and J. F. Weston for making special tabulations of data available, and to F. M. Scherer and L. W. Weiss for helpful suggestions.

7.1   The Sectoral Composition of the American Economy

The national income of the United States can be regarded as the sum of income originating in each producing sector of the economy—agriculture, mining, construction, manufacturing, and so forth. A useful measure of the importance of these economic sectors, therefore, is how much income is generated by each sector's payments for labor, capital, and natural resources. Table 7.1 shows how major sectors' percentage contributions to national income have changed over time. The figures cover various years since World War II, with 1929 included for an earlier point of reference. We expect to find that primary activities— agriculture, fishing, forestry, mining—have grown proportionally less important over time, and the table confirms that expectation. Agriculture shrank by growing much more efficient, and the other sectors' shrinkage partly reflects the partial exhaustion of our natural resources. Similarly, the table supports the commonplace belief that people spend increasing proportions of their incomes on services as their incomes grow larger. The principal services sectors have increased their share of national income throughout the postwar years, although a decline apparently occurred between 1929 and 1945 in the shares claimed by finance, insurance, and real estate, and in the residual category of services (such as health, education, and legal services). A slight decline has occurred in the share claimed by the wholesale and retail trade sector, perhaps because of the efficiency of chain stores and other large-scale retail outlets. Similarly, innovations have apparently reduced the relative cost of transportation (such as efficient motor vehicles and highways, large and specialized ships). In other service sectors productivity gains come very slowly. Apart from the temporary wartime inflation of the public sector apparent in 1945, the government sector appears to have undergone a large increase in proportional importance—at least until the late 1970s.

The division of sectors shown in table 7.1 is a traditional one, based on kinds of economic activities. For some purposes we may be interested in other bases for classifying the producing sectors of our economy. One basis might be the motives that we suppose chiefly guide the decisions made by their top executives. Do the firms maximize profits, subject to the competitive pressures of Adam Smith's famous "invisible hand" of competition? Are they nonprofit enterprises that pursue some goal other than the greatest possible surplus of revenue over cost (profit)? Are they part of the government sector, making decisions on some politically determined goal? Or are they profit-seeking firms whose decisions are regulated by such officials? Table 7.2 presents a very rough division of our economy's producing sectors according to the type of motivation and the mechanism of social control that chiefly influence

Table 7.1   Percentage Distribution of United States National Income, by Sector of Origin, Selected Years, 1929–78

Sector	1929	1945	1950	1955	1960	1965	1970	1975	1978
Agriculture, forestry, fisheries	10.0	8.4	7.3	4.6	4.2	3.6	3.0	3.4	2.9
Mining	2.4	1.5	2.2	1.8	1.3	1.1	1.0	1.6 }	6.9
Construction	4.4	2.4	4.9	5.0	5.1	5.4	5.5	5.4 }	
Manufacturing	25.2	28.8	31.6	32.6	30.0	30.1	26.8	25.1	26.4
Transportation	7.6	5.8	5.6	4.8	4.3	4.1	3.8	3.6	3.7
Communications	} 3.2	2.3	3.0	3.6	} 2.0	2.0	2.2	2.4	2.3
Electric, gas, sanitary services					2.1	2.0	1.9	2.1	1.9
Wholesale, retail trade	15.6	15.4	17.0	15.8	15.5	15.0	15.2	15.6	15.2
Finance, insurance, real estate	14.7	7.2	9.1	10.3	11.5	11.2	11.4	11.3	11.6
Services	10.1	7.8	9.0	9.4	10.7	11.3	12.8	13.5	13.6
Government, government enterprises	5.9	20.3	9.8	11.5	12.6	13.3	15.8	16.1	14.3
Rest of the world	0.9	0.2	0.5	0.5	0.6	0.8	0.6	0.8	1.0
Total[a]	100.0	100.0	100.0	100.0	100.0	100.0	100.0	100.0	100.0

Sources: U.S. Bureau of the Census, *Historical Statistics of the United States, Colonial Times to 1970* (Washington, D.C.: Government Printing Office, 1975), part 1, p. 239; U.S. Bureau of the Census, *Statistical Abstract of the United States, 1978* (Washington, D.C.: Government Printing Office, 1978), p. 446; *Survey of Current Business* 59 (March 1979): 13.

[a]Percentages may not sum up to 100.0 because of rounding errors.

Table 7.2   **Amount and Percentage Distribution of National Income Originating from Sectors Distinguished by Motivation and Social Control, Selected Years, 1950–75**

Sector		1950	1955	1960	1965	1970	1975
Investor-owned,	Amount[a]	186.6	249.2	306.0	407.8	554.4	847.8
unregulated	Percentage	77.8	75.7	73.6	73.0	69.3	68.7
Investor-owned,	Amount	25.8	35.9	47.3	60.8	88.5	141.7
regulated	Percentage	10.8	10.9	11.4	10.9	11.1	11.5
Nonprofit enterprise[b]	Amount	3.9	6.0	9.5	14.4	29.5	44.7
	Percentage	1.6	1.8	2.3	2.6	3.7	3.6
Government and government	Amount	23.6	38.1	52.7	75.4	127.4	199.9
enterprise	Percentage	9.8	11.6	12.7	13.5	15.9	16.2
Total national income of	Amount	239.9	329.2	415.5	558.4	799.8	1234.1
domestic origin	Percentage[c]	100.0	100.0	100.0	100.0	100.0	100.0

Source: U.S. Bureau of the Census, *Statistical Abstract of the United States, 1973* (Washington, D.C.: Government Printing Office, 1973), p. 325; ibid., *1978*, p. 446. U.S. Bureau of Economic Analysis, *The National Income and Product Accounts of the United States, 1929–74: Statistical Tables* (Washington, D.C.: Government Printing Office, 1977), tables 1.14 and 6.5; *Survey of Current Business* 59 (July 1979): 31, 54.

[a]In billions of current dollars.

[b]Secured by subtracting compensation of employees in private households (table 6.5 of National Income and Product Accounts) from national income originating in households and institutions (table 1.14). It is assumed that none of these nonprofit organizations are in the regulated sector.

[c]Percentages may not add to 100.0 because of rounding errors.

its decisions. The sectors consisting mainly of investor-owned and profit-seeking enterprises are divided into those subject to specific regulation of their prices and other activities and those that are not subject to such detailed economic regulation.[1] The third group of enterprises is described as "nonprofit," meaning that they are not part of the government sector but that they are also not formally organized for the pursuit of profit. Many nonprofit enterprises are devoted to providing health services (hospitals) and education (private colleges), but other diverse services are offered by many voluntary associations. The motives of decision-makers in the nonprofit sector are surely complex and diverse, and so we characterize them by what they are not. The fourth group comprises governments and government enterprises.

Table 7.2 shows that, since World War II, the unregulated investor-owned sector has declined from about three-fourths to two-thirds of our economy (in terms of the national income that it generates). The regulated sector has remained about constant in size while the nonprofit and government sectors have grown appreciably. For the most part these changes did not occur because we reclassified industries among these four sectors. The government sector has taken over certain formerly private activities, but most other changes shown in the table result mainly from the fact that industries classified under the various sectors grew at different rates. Occasionally a major decision of public policy does make it appropriate to reclassify a sector. The airlines are now being deregulated. The petroleum industry was added to table 7.2's regulated sectors for 1975 although no other changes were deemed to affect individual nongovernment sectors during the years 1950–1975.

Our economy's activity could be broken down in many other ways as well. For example, there has been some research on the "information economy," the proportion of economic activity devoted to providing information products and services (as distinguished from the "real" things about which we need to be informed). The provision of information has been said to account for 46 percent of the net income in the economy in 1967—53 percent of all employee income (Porat 1977).

Manufacturing is the largest and most conspicuous of our economy's major sectors, even though its proportional size has declined somewhat in the past two decades. Hence we also provide in table 7.3 a summary of the changing size distribution of the major manufacturing industries between 1954 and 1972 (years when the Census of Manufactures was taken). The changes that have occurred are rather modest. Broadly, the net outputs of nondurable-goods industries have declined a bit in importance (chemicals are an exception) while those of most durable goods have expanded.

7.1.1 Input-Output Relations

So far, we have compared sectors of the economy in terms of the amount of national income that they generate. This approach, however, does not take into account the markets in which these sectors buy and sell. An overview of these market relations is provided by table 7.4, an input-output table describing flows of current goods and services through the United States economy in 1967. An input-output table shows who bought each sector's output and who sold its inputs, as well as its total sales and purchases. Each line of table 7.4 shows the disposition of one sector's 1967 output. Of its total output of $63.1 billion, the agricultural sector sold about half to manufacturers of nondurable goods ($30.2 billion), sold $9.3 billion directly to final demand (private and public consumption and investment), and plowed back $18.5 billion as inputs into other areas of agricultural production.

Similarly, each column of the table shows how a sector distributed its input purchases among other producing sectors, imported goods and services, and "value added" (the primary factors of production). The value of each input purchase for each sector can be divided by that

Table 7.3   Percentage Distribution of Net Output (Value Added) among
                   Major Industries within Manufacturing Sector, 1954 and 1972

Sector	1954	1972
Food and kindred products	11.5%	10.1%
Tobacco manufactures	0.8	0.7
Textile mill products	4.1	3.3
Apparel and related products	4.4	3.8
Lumber and wood products	2.7	2.9
Furniture and fixtures	1.7	1.7
Pulp, paper and products	3.9	3.7
Printing and publishing	5.4	5.7
Chemicals and products	8.1	9.2
Petroleum and coal products	2.2	1.6
Rubber, miscellaneous plastics products	1.6	3.3
Leather and leather products	1.4	0.8
Stone, clay, and glass products	3.3	3.6
Primary metal industries	8.0	6.6
Fabricated metal products	6.5	7.6
Nonelectrical machinery	10.6	10.6
Electrical machinery	6.3	8.6
Transportation equipment	11.9	11.2
Instruments and related products	1.8	3.0
Miscellaneous manufactures	3.8	1.9
Total[a]	100.0	100.0

Sources: U.S. Bureau of the Census, *Census of Manufactures, 1954*, vol. I, *Summary Statistics* (Washington, D.C.: Government Printing Office, 1957), chap. 3, table 1; idem, *Census of Manufactures, 1972*, vol. 1, *Summary and Subject Statistics* (Washington, D.C.: Government Printing Office, 1976), General Summary, table 8.

[a]Percentages may not add to 100.0 because of rounding errors.

sector's total sales in order to secure a set of "input coefficients"—the number of cents spent on any given input per dollar's worth of output sold. For example, manufacturers of nondurable goods spent 11¢ on their sales dollar on outputs of the agricultural sector, 4.7¢ on outputs of the mining sector, and 5.5¢ on transportation and trade. These input coefficients contain information about the technology of production, and we shall use them below to describe how technology has been changing over time.

7.2   The Population of Enterprises

In this section we temporarily turn our attention from the structures of markets to traits of the whole population of business enterprises. We shall be concerned with the various legal forms of enterprises and the relative importance of the largest enterprises.

Table 7.4   The Input-Output Structure of the American Economy, 1967 (Billions of Dollars)

	Agriculture	Mining	Construction	Manufacturing: Durable Goods	Manufacturing: Nondurable Goods	Transportation and Trade	Utilities	Services	Other	Final Demand	Total
Agriculture, etc.	18.5	0	.3	1.1	30.2	.2	0	2.8	.6	9.3	63.1
Mining	.1	1.2	.9	4.4	12.9	a	3.4	.3	.1	1.5	24.9
Construction	.6	.6	a	1.3	1.3	1.8	1.7	8.6	1.8	85.6	103.3
Manufacturing: durable goods	.8	1.6	32.7	111.6	10.9	4.6	.5	9.7	2.0	142.7	317.1
Manufacturing: nondurable goods	7.9	.7	4.8	14.6	79.3	8.7	.6	17.9	6.1	135.6	276.2
Transportation and trade	4.1	.7	10.8	15.8	15.2	11.4	1.0	8.7	6.9	141.5	216.2
Utilities	.5	.5	.4	5.0	4.1	5.0	7.5	9.5	1.3	26.0	59.8
Services	5.0	3.7	6.8	14.6	16.9	26.1	3.3	42.1	2.9	185.9	307.3
Other industries	.1	.3	.8	5.3	2.7	6.7	6.2	8.1	.1	93.7	123.9
Imports	1.0	2.1	.1	9.8	7.4	2.3	.3	.2	3.2	−26.4	0
Value added	24.4	13.5	45.6	133.6	95.4	149.3	35.3	199.5	98.9	—	795.4
Total	63.1	24.9	103.3	317.1	276.2	216.2	59.8	307.3	123.9	795.4	

Source: Unpublished consolidation of the published input-output table for 1967 prepared by the Bureau of Economic Analysis, U.S. Department of Commerce.

aLess than $50 million.

7.2.1   Legal Forms of Enterprise

The chief forms of investor-owned enterprise are the individual proprietorship, the partnership, and the corporation. Legally, the first two are distinguished from the corporation in that the single owner (in the case of the proprietorship) or at least some of the partners (in the case of a partnership) bear unlimited personal responsibility for any debts that the enterprise may incur. The owners of the corporation, by contrast, are limited in their liability for the enterprise's debts to the capital that they have initially subscribed. The limited-liability corporation is the standard large enterprise that we find about us in the economy today. By allowing the individual supplier of equity capital to limit his responsibility for the enterprise, the corporation attains something not possible in the other forms—a division of labor and a specialization between those who manage the company and those who own it. Two other types of enterprises, the cooperative and the government, may be noted briefly here. The cooperative enterprise is owned by persons who are its customers or suppliers. They generally do not enjoy limited liability for the cooperative's debts—they are, in effect, partners, and their equity shares in the cooperative are defined not by the amount of capital they have contributed but by the volume of business they currently do with the cooperative. Finally, a government enterprise may be organized in various ways, but its controlling shareholders in effect are the taxpaying public, who ultimately pay additional taxes if the public firm runs a loss, or who may enjoy a tax reduction if it turns a profit.

The corporation, because many individuals can participate in its ownership without facing excessive risks, is far and away the dominant form of enterprise in the American economy. Table 7.5 shows some features of the corporations in American industry along with their smaller neighbors, the proprietorships and partnerships. The table lists not only the total numbers of these enterprises, but also expresses them as a number per thousand persons in the United States population. It lists the total receipts of each class of enterprises (in current dollars) and the receipts per enterprise in constant dollars (the GNP implicit deflator was used in this calculation). The data on real receipts per enterprise for each type thus give a rough impression of what is happening to the average size of each.

Table 7.5 shows that, over the thirty-five years covered, the numbers of each type of enterprise have grown not only absolutely but also relative to the country's human population. This result is a little surprising, because international studies comparing countries at various levels of economic development show that the number of enterprises per thousand of the population actually tends to decline as the level of development increases (Caves and Uekusa 1976, pp. 101–6). The increase in the

Table 7.5   Trends in Enterprise Structure of the United States Economy, Selected Years, 1940–75

Type and Characteristics of Enterprise	1940	1945	1950	1955	1960	1965	1970	1975
Proprietorships								
Total number (thousands)	2,018	5,689	6,865	8,239	9,090	9,078	9,400	10,882
Number per thousand persons	15.2	40.5	45.1	49.7	50.3	46.7	45.9	51.0
Total receipts (billons of dollars)	31	79	n.a.	139	171	199	238	339
Receipts per proprietorship (thousands of 1958 dollars)	31	23	n.a.	19	18	20	19	17
Partnerships								
Total number (thousands)	271[a]	627	n.a.	n.a.	941	914	936	1,073
Number per thousand persons	2.1[a]	4.5	n.a.	n.a.	5.2	4.7	4.6	5.0
Total receipts (billions of dollars)	13	47	n.a.	n.a.	74	75	93	146
Receipts per partnership (thousands of 1958 dollars)	111	126	n.a.	n.a.	76	74	73	72
Corporations								
Total number (thousands)	473	421	629	807	1,141	1,424	1,665	2,024
Number per thousand persons	3.6	3.0	4.1	4.9	6.3	7.3	8.1	9.5
Total receipts (billions of dollars)	148	255	458	642	849	1,195	1,751	3,199
Receipts per corporation (thousands of 1958 dollars)	635	1,105	908	875	720	757	778	840

Sources: U.S. Bureau of the Census, *Historical Statistics of the United States, Colonial Times to 1970* (Washington, D.C.: Government Printing Office, 1975), part 1, p. 197, and part 2, p. 911; U.S. Bureau of the Census, *Statistical Abstract of the United States, 1978* (Washington, D.C.: Government Printing Office, 1978, pp. 6, 483, 561.

[a]Data pertain to 1939.

number of proprietorships and partnerships has only kept pace with the population of persons during the last two decades, but the corporate population has continued to outgrow the human population. One clue to this pattern appears in the changes in the real size (receipts) of the average enterprise in each class which reflect no growth and, if anything, a decline in the size of each. That decline suggests that the numbers of the smaller enterprises of each type have expanded somewhat faster than the larger ones.

Without further analysis, only some rather general conclusions can be drawn from the patterns shown in table 7.5. The table hardly suggests any withering away of the small-business sector. And it probably reflects changes in legal form of some enterprises (from proprietorship or partnership to corporation) without any change in their function—such as the use of incorporation by high-income professional persons, often undertaken for tax reasons.

7.2.2 Size Distribution of Companies

It is obvious to all that the largest corporations in the American economy are very large indeed, operating economic empires that stretch across many product markets in the United States and abroad. Our society distrusts unregulated concentrations of power (whether in private or public hands), and so there is always a social concern both about the behavior of the largest enterprises and also about their sheer size. Are they growing increasingly dominant, fulfilling Karl Marx's prediction of a "constantly diminishing number of the magnates of capital"? Economists like to distinguish clearly between two ways of treating corporate size. A company's size can be judged by its market share, which is relevant to the working of competitive processes. The concentration of market shares will be described in the next section. Corporate size can also be considered overall, in terms of the share of assets (sales, or some other size measure) accounted for by the largest companies. Overall concentration does not have the same clear significance for economic analysis as does concentration in particular markets, but it undeniably holds interest in the light of our society's concern with bigness and the concentration of influence.

In principle, one can use a variety of strategies for measuring the proportional size of the largest companies. It is logical, first of all, to concentrate on the size distribution of nonfinancial companies and leave financial institutions for separate treatment.[2] The available data are weaker for the whole population of nonfinancial companies than for the manufacturing sector, so we start with manufacturing companies. The Census of Manufactures provides data on the share of total activity in manufacturing accounted for by the largest manufacturing companies. It should be noted that these data do not reflect any nonmanufacturing activities of the largest manufacturing companies (or of their smaller competitors). Nor are their overseas investments included.

There is room for debate over what size variable to employ for measuring the overall concentration of large companies. When we examine the concentration of sellers in particular industries, we are usually concerned with concentration's effect on processes of competition in the marketplace. Sales then become the obvious size measure to use. When we investigate overall concentration, however, there is no such clear motive for the inquiry, and correspondingly no way to know just what measure of companies' size is most revealing. Value added, which we shall mainly use, has the advantage of measuring the income originating with firms of various sizes, and thus it indicates their role as employers of the primary factors of production. The fifty largest manufacturing companies accounted for 25 percent of all value added in manufacturing in 1972. Their share of the value of factory shipments was almost the same, 24 percent. Their share of payroll to employees was smaller, 22 percent, and their share of all manufacturing employees was smaller still, 17 percent. That is, the fifty largest manufacturing companies use proportionally less labor in their production processes than do smaller companies, but their employees earn higher wages (U.S. Bureau of the Census 1975, table 4).[3]

Tables 7.6 and 7.7 show what has happened since 1947 to the concentration of the largest companies. Table 7.6 provides the more reliable data, dealing with the proportion of value added in manufacturing accounted for by the largest companies. The fifty largest companies' share has risen by nearly one-half, and this share has risen somewhat faster than the combined share of the other firms that make up the largest 200. It is surprising, though, that most of the increase took place shortly after World War II. The large wave of conglomerate mergers in the 1960s, which might have been expected to raise the share of the largest companies, was accompanied by a slowing down of the increase in the largest companies' share.

Table 7.6   **Share of Total Value Added by Size of Manufacturing Companies, Selected Years, 1947–72**

Company group	1947	1954	1958	1963	1967	1972
Largest 50	17	23	23	25	25	25
Largest 100	23	30	30	33	33	33
Largest 150	27	34	35	37	38	39
Largest 200	30	37	38	41	42	43

Source: U.S. Bureau of the Census, *Census of Manufactures, 1972, Concentration Ratios in Manufacturing*, Special Report Series MC72(SR)–2 (Washington, D.C.: Government Printing Office, 1975), table 1.

Table 7.7 presents some measures of concentration of the largest companies based on the assets they control rather than their value added; and the table addresses concentration among all nonfinancial companies and not just manufacturing. The concentration of corporate assets in the largest manufacturing companies is likely to be greater than the concentration of value added for several reasons: the largest firms

Table 7.7   **Concentration of Assets of the Largest 200 Manufacturing Companies and the Largest 200 Nonfinancial Companies, Various Years 1956–77, with Alternative Treatments of International Assets**

		Manufacturing Companies		All Nonfinancial Companies, International Assets Included, Companies Ranked by Assets
	Federal Trade Commission	Adjusted Series, International Assets Included on Gross Basis		
Year	Series	Companies Ranked by Assets	Companies Ranked by Sales	
	(1)	(2)	(3)	(4)
1956		52.9	45.4	
1957		54.2	47.1	
1958		55.0	46.4	
1959		54.8	46.4	
1960	56.3	55.4	47.3	40.5
1961		55.7	45.9	
1962		55.2	47.0	
1963		56.0	47.7	
1964		55.4	47.6	
1965	56.7	55.4	47.5	40.1
1966		55.6	47.1	40.5
1967		57.7	48.8	41.2
1968		59.5	50.8	41.5
1969	60.1	59.4	50.7	40.4
1970	60.4	60.0	51.9	40.6
1971	61.0	59.5	52.8	40.8
1972	60.0	58.4	51.5	39.8
1973	56.9[a]	58.8	51.3	39.1
1974	56.7[a]	58.9	53.7	39.5
1975	57.5[a]	59.4	55.1	39.9
1976	58.0[a]	60.0	55.2	
1977	58.4[a]	61.1	56.6	

Sources: Column 1—Federal Trade Commission data from U.S. Bureau of the Census, *Statistical Abstract of the United States, 1978* (Washington, D.C.: Government Printing Office, 1978), p. 576. Columns 2–4—calculated by Professor J. Fred Weston using data from *Fortune*; Federal Trade Commission, *Quarterly Financial Reports*; and U.S. Treasury, *Internal Revenue Service, Statistics of Income, Corporations*.

[a]Not comparable to earlier figures; see text.

are more capital-intensive than are smaller firms; they are more diversified outside of manufacturing; and as multinational companies they hold proportionally more assets abroad. Column 1 of table 7.7 presents data published by the Federal Trade Commission on the concentration of assets in the 200 largest manufacturing companies. This series is distorted because a change after 1972 caused companies to exclude their overseas assets from the data they supply, whereas they had previously included overseas assets in whatever way they saw fit. It is necessary to add about 2.8 percentage points to the 1973–77 figures in column 1 to make them comparable to earlier data (Penn 1976),[4] in which case they show the asset concentration of the 200 largest manufacturing firms to exceed concentration based on value added (compare the last line of table 7.6) but to change little over the last decade.

Prof. J. Fred Weston has estimated in columns 2, 3, and 4 of table 7.7 a series of data that seeks to include the gross foreign assets of United States corporations throughout 1956–77; column 1 excludes foreign assets from 1973 on and includes them erratically before. Column 2 indicates the concentration of assets in the largest manufacturing companies when all companies' international assets are included and companies are ranked by asset size. Column 3 does the same except that it ranks companies by sales; this ranking shows a lower level of concentration but one that continues to increase during the 1970s. Finally, column 4 extends the measurement from manufacturing companies to the 200 largest nonfinancial companies in relation to all nonfinancial companies. The following conclusions seem to follow from tables 7.6 and 7.7: (1) corporate concentration of assets is greater than concentration of sales, which is in turn greater than concentration of value added; (2) concentration is higher with overseas assets included than if they are left out (that is, the larger companies undertake proportionally more investment abroad); (3) although there has clearly been a long-run increase in concentration of the largest companies, the trend may have slowed down in the last decade.

Another social concern about the largest companies is the staying power of the leaders. Is there much turnover among them? Table 7.8 gives some idea of the amount of turnover by analyzing what happened after 1947 to the fifty largest manufacturing companies of 1947, and what happened before 1972 to the fifty largest in 1972. The same companies accounted for half of the top fifty in both years. As for the rest, all but six of the largest fifty in 1947 could be found in the largest 200 for 1972; and all but five of the largest fifty in 1972 were among the largest 200 in 1947. The high survival rate of the 1947 firms may be a little surprising, given the frequency with which firms disappear by merger. On the other hand, acquiring smaller firms is one way to stay on top.

Table 7.8   **Turnover among the Fifty Largest Manufacturing Enterprises, Selected Years 1947–72**

Category	1947	1954	1958	1963	1967	1972
Largest 50 Companies in 1947						
Share of manufacturing value added	17	21	20	21	20	17
Number ranked:						
among the largest 50	50	35	34	30	24	25
among the largest 100	50	47	46	46	41	38
among the largest 200	50	50	50	49	46	44
Largest 50 Companies in 1972						
Share of manufacturing value added	12	19	20	22	23	25
Number ranked:						
among the largest 50	25	33	37	40	42	50
among the largest 100	35	44	43	46	50	50
among the largest 200	45	45	47	49	50	50

Source: U.S. Bureau of the Census, *Census of Manufactures, 1972, Concentration Ratios in Manufacturing*, Special Report Series MC72(SR)–2 (Washington, D.C.: Government Printing Office, 1975), tables 2, 3.

Some conclusions from economists' research on the turnover of large companies help to place table 7.8 in perspective (Collins and Preston 1961; Mermelstein 1969; Stonebraker 1979). When turnover is examined for earlier decades of the twentieth century, it appears that the amount after 1929 was smaller than in earlier years. Economists have wondered what hardening of the economic arteries might be involved. One factor determining corporate turnover is the changing mix of industries in the economy; a firm can rise to the top because it dominates a fast-growing industry, or sink because it is stuck in a slow-growing one, without any change occurring in its position vis-à-vis its immediate competitors. When we control for industry mix, however, the conclusion still holds that the turnover of leading firms slowed after 1929. The slower turnover is also partly explained by the number of major antitrust cases brought in 1911 or shortly afterward, which caused the dismemberment of some of the then leading firms. With this influence also controlled, turnover still appears to have been rather stable since around 1929, but somewhat higher before that time. The explanation for the slower turnover, most economists agree, is that in the 1920s large companies first began to diversify their activities significantly. They improved their chances of staying on top even if one of their industries—or their own activities in some sector—turned sour. If diversification permits a large corporation to ride out economic storms, is that a good or a bad sign for the flexibility and competitiveness of our economy? The question is a subtle one. When resources must be moved from industry A to industry B, they can travel by two different routes. Companies in industry A can shrink or close down, and the resources they employed may find new jobs with different companies in industry B. Or companies in industry A can diversify and make administrative transfers to B of resources in their employ. The results of the two processes need not be the same, and there is no decisive way to determine which is better.

7.3 Structures of Individual Product Markets

The biggest companies in American industry owe their size partly to their tendency to operate in large markets. They also tend to compete in many markets each and to hold high shares of sales in their more important markets, and these properties also help to explain their bigness. We will consider data on market shares in this section and evidence on companies' multimarket activities in the section that follows.

A major public concern over the organization of industry has been with the amounts of monopoly and competition found in the United States economy. It is not easy to match up the structures of actual markets we observe with the theoretical prototypes of monopoly (one seller) and competition (many sellers, none of them large). Most markets contain "some" sellers, perhaps only "a few." Therefore economists usually evaluate the number and size distribution of firms in the market by measuring the share held by the largest few—often the largest four or eight. This "concentration ratio" can be used to measure how concentrated are either the sellers or buyers in a given market.[5]

Our information on seller concentration in the manufacturing sector extends back to the turn of the century. The beginning of the twentieth century was a critical period for the organization of American industry. Transportation and communication had been growing steadily cheaper during the nineteenth century. Markets were becoming more national and integrated, and business firms were discovering new methods of efficient large-scale organization. By 1900 many American manufacturing industries had assumed the shapes that they would retain throughout the century—partly through the wave of mergers mentioned above. One careful attempt was made by Warren Nutter (1951, pp. 35–48, 112–50) to patch together evidence on concentration in manufacturing at the turn of the century.[6] He concluded that 32.9 percent of all national income originating in manufacturing emanated from industries in which the four largest sellers accounted for 50 percent or more of output sometime during 1895–1904. Data provided periodically by the Bureau of the Census allow us readily to calculate a similar figure for present-day conditions. In 1972 it was 29.0 percent; in 1963 it was 33.1 percent.[7] The obvious conclusion is that average seller concentration in manufacturing industries has shown no systematic trend over the twentieth century.

Many economists object to measuring overall concentration in this way—by classifying industries according to whether the largest four sellers hold more or less than 50 percent of shipments. Although industries less concentrated than the 50-percent mark are probably effectively competitive, those ranking above it surely vary a great deal in how closely the rival sellers manage to behave as if they were single monopolists. Therefore concentration is better summarized as a weighted average of the concentration ratios for individual industries. Prof. F. M. Scherer (1980) has provided such a calculation for 1972, the most recent year for which data are available. He found that 6.8 percent of value added in manufacturing came from industries in which the four largest firms account for 80 percent or more of industry shipments, and 21.5 percent of value added originated in industries whose four largest firms account for 60 percent or more of industry output.[8] This figure of 21.5 percent in 1972 can be compared (roughly) to the following figures for earlier years: 15.9 percent in 1947 and 20.7 percent in 1958.[9] The simplest device for summarizing concentration is to average industries' concentration ratios, each weighted by some measure of an industry's importance. Data calculated by Scherer and M. A. Adelman, going back to 1947, are presented in table 7.9. Both the weighted and unweighted average figures suggest that some slight increase in average concentration occurred since World War II, but the rate of change has been slow.

The measures of concentration examined so far reflect the changing mixture of industries in the United States manufacturing sector as well as whatever changes in concentration have occurred in the typical industry. The automobile industry, for example, has grown much larger as a proportion of the manufacturing sector since 1900, and it has become much more concentrated. Measures of average concentration in various

Table 7.9   **Average Seller Concentration, Selected Years, 1947–72, for All Manufacturing Industries, Unweighted and Weighted by Value Added**

	1947	1954	1963	1972
Simple (unweighted) average	39.7	39.5	40.7	41.5
Average weighted by value added[a]	36.3	38.1	37.8	38.5

Source: F. M. Scherer, *Industrial Market Structure and Economic Performance*, 2nd ed. (Chicago: Rand-McNally, 1980), table 3.7.
[a]Each industry's concentration ratio in any given year is weighted by its value added in that year to determine the weighted average.

years tend to register an increase due to both of these changes. For some purposes, however, we would like to abstract from the changing mix of industries in the economy to see what happens over time to concentration in an unchanging group of industries. The Bureau of the Census frustrates that desire by revising its industry definitions from time to time, but we have been able to follow 154 industries that survived unchanged from 1947 to 1972. The mere fact that they survived redefinition suggests that nothing much happened to their structures or technologies over this period. In that sense, they are critical for telling us whether any fundamental forces have been at work changing the level of industries' concentration. In table 7.10 these industries are subdivided according to whether they sell their outputs to producers, consumers, or a mixture of these two groups. Those groups serving consumers are also divided according to whether their products are differentiated or not. (The goods sold by an industry's manufacturers are differentiated if buyers easily distinguish between brands or the goods of different sellers; makers of differentiated goods usually apply brand names to their goods, and advertise and promote these brand names with the public.) These 154 industries on average showed a slight increase in concentration, about like that of the full population covered in table 8. However, concentration in the producer-goods industries fell while concentration in the other industries rose. Among the consumer-goods industries, those showing appreciable amounts of product differentiation grew in concentration much more than did the undifferentiated goods (Mueller and Hamm 1974).[10] Changes in marketing practices (network television?) or in the way consumers buy goods (the rise of supermarkets and dis-

Table 7.10	Changes in Four-Firm Seller Concentration, 1947–72, for Population of 154 Consistently Defined Industries, by Type of Buyer and Degree of Product Differentiation		
	Number of Industries	Change in Concentration 1947–1972	Level of Concentration 1972
All industries	154	+ 1.71	41.5
Producer goods	87	− 1.67	41.3
Consumer goods			
low differentiation	18	+ 3.78	25.3
medium differentiation	22	+ 7.73	42.1
high differentiation	10	+ 8.00	53.9
Mixed industries			
low differentiation	5	+11.80	50.8
medium differentiation	10	+ 2.60	50.5
high differentiation	2	+ 2.50	55.0

Source: F. M. Scherer, *Industrial Market Structure and Economic Performance*, 2nd ed. (Chicago: Rand-McNally, 1980), table 4.8.

count stores?) may have somehow changed the structures of these consumer-goods industries.

Average changes in industries' concentration ratios give us no feeling for how much concentration typically changes for the individual industry. Table 7.11 addresses that question by cross-tabulating the concentration ratios of 196 industries in 1954 and 1972 (1970, for some). Industries that stayed within the same ten-point range appear along the diagonal of the table (italicized figures); industries appearing above the diagonal grew more concentrated, while those below the diagonal became less concentrated. Of the 196, 77 appear on the diagonal and thus saw little change. Concentration fell in 45 industries and rose in 74.[11] The numbers cluster rather closely around the diagonal, implying that for most industries concentration did not change much over two decades. The most common change was for industries with a concentration ratio of less than 30 percent in 1954 to become more concentrated by the 1970s. We have no good explanation of why so many unconcentrated industries underwent proportionally large increases in concentration during this period.

As mentioned above, a description of the structure of industry should in principle give equal time to the buyers' side of the market. Households buying consumer goods are numerous and unconcentrated, but the manufacturer of these goods must first sell them to retail outlets, and those may sometimes be concentrated in local shopping areas. Where buyers are or may be concentrated, that fact takes on importance for predicting how the market will behave. What is more, John Kenneth Galbraith (1952) argued that the concentration of buyers is directly influenced by the concentration of sellers: that the presence of concentrated sellers able to exercise some monopoly bestirs buyers to coalesce and confront them with some countervailing concentration. Galbraith's proposition has not fared well when tested against actual markets. The most concentrated buyers do not seem to have emerged in sectors where sellers are the most concentrated. Even if they had, there is no assurance that the household buyer at the end of the line of transactions benefits from bilateral struggles between concentrated buyers and sellers upstream. In any case, we would like to have evidence on the concentration of buyers facing major manufacturing industries in our economy.

Although such data are not simple to secure, there are two approaches that may be taken to estimate the concentration of industrial buyers facing those industries. The first approach, which is that followed by Guth, Schwartz, and Whitcomb, is to construct data first using the input-output table (see table 7.4) to determine which industries are the big customers for any given selling industry, and then drawing on official data on seller concentration in those industries to determine how concentrated an industry's buyers might be. Their results suggest that buyer

Table 7.11 Distribution of Changes in Four-Firm Seller Concentration Ratios, 196 United States Manufacturing Industries, 1954 to 1970/1972

Concentration Ratio in 1954	Concentration Ratio in 1972									
	0–10	11–20	21–30	31–40	41–50	51–60	61–70	71–80	81–90	91–100
0–10	4	8	1							
11–20	2	20	11	8	1	1				
21–30		5	12	11	2	1				
31–40			7	10	3	1	2			
41–50		1	1	3	13	7	2			
51–60				1	4	5	4	3		
61–70					2	7	5	2	1	
71–80						3	4	3		2
81–90							1	2	4	3
91–100								1	1	1

Source: U.S. Bureau of the Census, *Concentration Ratios in Manufacturing,* Special Report Series MC72(SR)–2 (Washingon, D.C.: Government Printing Office, 1975), table 5.

Note: [a]The period covered is normally 1954 to 1972. However, changes from 1954 to 1970 are shown for industries that were lost through reclassification in the 1972 Census of Manufactures, and for which data for 1954 were available. There are fifteen such industries.

concentration for any given industry is typically quite low; table 7.12 lists the ten manufacturing industries that they found to face the most highly concentrated buyers.[12]

The second approach for estimating buyer concentration is to examine levels of concentration of the retailing sectors that stand between the manufacturer and the final consumer. Of course, information on concentration in retailing and other service sectors is of interest because of the possibility that these sectors might function as concentrated sellers, whatever their behavior as buyers from the manufacturing sector. Table 7.13 lists concentration ratios for a selection of major retailing and service industries. These concentration data pertain only for the United States national market as a whole, and in that form they are appropriate to appraising the concentration of these sectors as buyers in national markets for manufactured goods. They can be quite deceptive, however, as guides to their concentration of sellers. The typical market for most retail stores and service businesses is far from national in scope, and is more likely to be only the size of an individual city or small region. Seller concentration for these sectors in appropriately defined local markets may be substantially higher than is indicated by the figures in table 7.12. On the other hand, some classes of retail businesses compete with other classes, lowering effective concentration.

7.3.1 Company and Plant Concentration

A major concern for public policy is whether existing levels of seller concentration rest on economies of scale. If they do, we could not have

Table 7.12   Selected Manufacturing Industries with High Estimated Buyer Concentration Ratios, 1963

Industry	Buyer Concentration Ratio		
	4-Firm	8-Firm	20-Firm
Tire cord and fabric	60	63	64
Primary aluminum	36	51	55
Padding and upholstery fillings	30	34	38
Synthetic rubber	29	36	39
Primary copper	26	40	48
Secondary nonferrous metals	25	46	74
Aluminum castings	24	26	31
Carbon and graphite products	23	26	34
Miscellaneous fabricated textile products	21	25	30
Collapsible tubes	21	27	29

Source: Louis A. Guth, Robert A. Schwartz, and David K. Whitcomb, "Buyer Concentration Ratios," *Journal of Industrial Economics* 25 (June 1977), tables 1, A.1.

Table 7.13   **Seller Concentration in Selected Service and Distribution Industries, 1972**

Industry	Share of	
	4 Largest	20 Largest
Department stores	38.8%	68.4%
Variety stores	51.1	75.5
Grocery stores	17.5	34.7
Gasoline service stations	3.7	8.0
Women's ready-to-wear stores	11.2	22.8
Furniture stores	4.4	9.0
Drug stores	11.4	28.8
Liquor stores	11.0	19.4
Merchant wholesalers	2.0	5.8
Merchandise agents, brokers	6.9	11.4
Hotels, motels	9.5	18.8
Laundry, cleaning, services	5.4	11.4
Advertising agencies	13.3	38.9
Computing and data processing	18.4	39.4
Automotive rental and leasing	26.4	39.3
Motion picture production, distribution	29.2	55.8
Legal services	0.7	2.7

Sources: U.S. Bureau of the Census, *1972 Census of Retail Trade*, vol. 1, *Summary and Subject Statistics* (Washington, D.C.: Government Printing Office, 1976), chart 1; idem, *1972 Census of Wholesale Trade*, vol. 1, *Summary and Subject Statistics* (Washington, D.C.: Government Printing Office, 1976), chart 4; idem, *1972 Census of Selected Service Industries*, vol. 1, *Summary and Subject Statistics* (Washington, D.C.: Government Printing Office, 1976), chart 1.

smaller firms, and thus more of them in each industry, without incurring higher costs of producing the industry's output. If they do not, more companies and thus more competition could exist without that cost of efficiency. Scale economies do or may exist in many aspects of a company's activities, but the best documented form of scale economies—and probably the most important—is in production activity at the plant level. Therefore we are concerned with the extent to which the leading companies operate more than one plant in their principal industry, and thus may be larger than is warranted by scale economies at the plant level.

Table 7.14 shows, for a number of narrowly defined manufacturing industries, how many plants are operated by the average member of the four largest companies. It shows that the leading companies are single-plant firms only in a small and declining proportion of manufacturing industries. A slight increase typically occurred between 1963 and 1972 in the number of plants per leading company. That change probably stemmed from the general growth of the economy during the decade; it was not the result of mergers in most cases.

Table 7.15 explores the connection between seller concentration and multiplant operations further by relating the number of plants per company (both the four leading companies and all companies in the industry) to levels of seller concentration. Although the number of plants per company seems to increase with concentration for *all* companies in the industry, it shows no such tendency for the four largest companies. If anything, the largest companies in the most concentrated industries tend to operate somewhat fewer plants than the leading companies in less concentrated industries, a fact that suggests some role for scale economies at the plant level in explaining seller concentration.[13]

7.4   The Activities of Large Companies

America's largest nonfinancial companies are conspicuous for the many markets in which they operate. A company can extend its activities beyond its principal or original base market in several directions. It can replicate its base-market activity in another geographic region. It can become active in a market that supplies inputs to or buys outputs from its base activity; the firm then becomes vertically integrated. Or it can enter a market with no direct relation to its base; it becomes diversified and gets called a "conglomerate" if its diversification is quite extensive. Finally, the expanding firm becomes multinational if any of these modes of growth carry it outside the boundaries of the United States (or into the United States from a foreign base of operations).

Table 7.14   Extent of Multiplant Operation for Four Leading Firms in Manufacturing Industries, 1963 and 1972

Average Number of Plants per Company, Four Leading Companies	1963		1972	
	No. of Industries	Percentage of Industries	No. of Industries	Percentage of Industries
1.00 to 1.50 plants	78	18.7	51	11.4
1.75 to 2.50 plants	89	21.3	107	23.9
2.75 to 4.00 plants	87	21.9	98	21.9
4.25 to 7.00 plants	87	21.9	94	21.0
7.25 to 10.00 plants	28	6.7	35	7.8
10.25 to 20.00 plants	35	8.4	46	10.3
More than 20.00 plants	13	3.1	17	3.8
All industries	417	100.0[b]	448	100.0[b]

Sources: U.S. Congress, Senate, Subcommittee on Antitrust and Monopoly, *Concentration Ratios in Manufacturing Industry, 1963*, Part 2, 89th Cong., 1st Sess. (Washington, D.C.: Government Printing Office, 1967), table 27; U.S. Bureau of the Census, *Concentration Ratios in Manufacturing*, Special Report Series MC72 (SR)–2 (Washington, D.C.: Government Printing Office, 1975), table 8.

[a]The gaps in the ranges occur because the leading firms' number of plants must be an integer, so the average number per firm can only take certain fractional values.
[b]Percentages may not add because of rounding errors.

Table 7.15   **Relation between Seller Concentration and Multiplant Operations for 448 Manufacturing Industries, 1972**

Four-Firm Concentration Ratio	Number of Industries	Average Number of Plants per Company	
		All Companies	Four Largest Companies
0–10	22	1.10	5.85
11–20	73	1.11	6.16
21–30	91	1.21	6.02
31–40	72	1.29	6.39
41–50	67	1.28	5.19
51–60	49	1.29	4.17
61–70	29	1.66	8.56
71–80	25	1.52	4.09
81–90	12	1.34	3.87
91–100	8	1.53	5.33

Source: U.S. Bureau of the Census, *1972 Census of Manufactures, Concentration Ratios in Manufacturing*, Special Report Series MC72(SR)–2 (Washington, D.C.: Government Printing Office, 1975), table 8.

The multimarket firm developed late in the history of business organization, and its rise has only recently been traced by business historians. notably Alfred D. Chandler, Jr. (1962 and 1977). Innovations in transportation and communication during the nineteenth century first made possible the coordination of far-flung economic activities by means of the firm's administrative apparatus. The opportunities born of these innovations were seized by large national firms that came to dominate United States national markets by the end of the century. Some of these enterprises discovered early in the twentieth century that they could use their resources (and adapt their administrative structures) to operate successfully in many markets, not just at the site of their initial success. Those discoveries started a process of multimarket expansion by large firms (especially diversification) that has continued to this day. Firms have expanded both by internal growth (organizing and financing new ventures in other industries) and by acquiring independent companies operating in other markets. The multimarket growth of large firms has been a controversial process, especially when carried out through acquisitions and mergers. "Horizontal" mergers between directly competing firms tend to increase the concentration of sellers, and are thus capable of promoting the evils of monopoly. Vertical integration and diversification raise different concerns for public policy. The vertically integrated firm, it is feared by some, can manipulate prices at various stages of production to the disadvantage of its nonintegrated rivals. And the diversified firm which can sustain losses in one of its markets from profits earned elsewhere might use this option to triumph artificially in market warfare with undiversified rivals. The dilemma is that the large firm often seems to make better use of its own—and society's—resources by expanding into multimarket activities, but it may coincidentally attain the power to act in ways that restrain competition. The strength and importance of these counterpoised effects are still much debated among economists, and the issues and evidence are complex. Here we shall provide some background data on the structures of large multimarket companies.

7.4.1   Mergers and Acquisitions

It is convenient to review some evidence on acquisitions and mergers, before turning directly to firms' multimarket activities. The number of mergers among American businesses has shown wide fluctuations over time. This cyclical pattern has been evident from the beginning of the twentieth century. Prof. F. M. Scherer has recently assembled a statistical series that shows the value of corporate assets in manufacturing and mining acquired through merger from 1895 to 1977, with market values adjusted for price changes so as to reveal the real value of the assets acquired. (For the period 1920–48 he was forced to rely on a simple count of the number of mergers.) His results are shown in Figure 7.1. At its peak, the merger movement of the late 1960s involved a larger

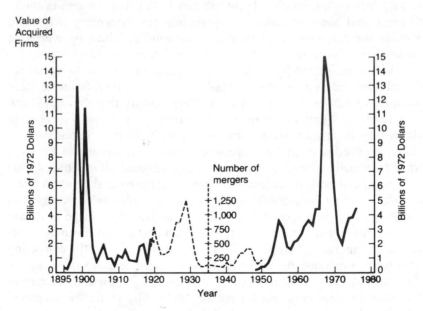

Fig. 7.1.   Volume of manufacturing and mining firm acquisitions, 1895–1977. Based on data from F. M. Scherer, *Industrial Market Structure and Economic Performance*, 2d ed. (Chicago: Rand McNally, 1980), fig. 4.5.

amount of corporate assets than in any previous period. Smaller bursts occurred in the mid-1950s and the latter 1970s. At the beginning of the twentieth century, the amount of corporate assets involved in mergers was almost as great as that of the 1960s despite the fact that the economy was much smaller then. Mergers were also numerous in the late 1920s.

Economists have given some attention to the reasons for these large fluctuations in the volume of corporate assets changing hands (Nelson 1959 and Steiner 1975). For example, fluctuations tend to take place in prosperous periods when large corporations are enjoying large cash flows not needed at the time for reinvestment in their existing activities. Merger waves may be promoted by high prices of common stocks, which encourage the owners of closely held companies to sell out and realize their capital gains.

We mentioned that mergers and acquisitions may serve to combine directly competing firms ("horizontal" mergers), or they may unite firms in different markets. These types of mergers have occurred in varying proportions over time. At the beginning of the twentieth century, for example, most consolidations and acquisitions were horizontal, and they created many of the dominant firms that carry on today as leaders in their industries. Perhaps because of changes in antitrust policy, mergers came more often to involve firms in vertically related markets or in largely unrelated markets. The Federal Trade Commission classifies mergers among large manufacturing and mining companies according to whether they are horizontal, vertical, or conglomerate. And the conglomerate group is further subdivided according to whether an acquisition extends the acquiring firm's activity into a product market somehow related to its previous activities, into a new geographic market for the types of products it already offers, or into some unrelated activity. The distribution of mergers by type is shown in table 7.16. Horizontal mergers declined proportionally after the early 1950s, probably because legislation passed in 1950 (the Celler Kefauver Act) tightened legal restrictions on horizontal mergers. Conglomerate mergers have grown much more prevalent since that time, and product-extension mergers have given way to acquisitions involving more remote diversification.

7.4.2 Diversification

In large part due to conglomerate mergers, most large enterprises have become highly diversified. Diversification is an ambiguous thing to measure across sectors of the economy, because the measure depends on how we define the base activities beyond which a company's output becomes diversified. Suppose that we call a company undiversified if it operates in only one of the 115 manufacturing industries identified in the statistics on enterprises of the Census of Manufactures. Table 7.17

Table 7.16   **Distribution of Assets Acquired in Mergers Involving Large Manufacturing and Mining Companies, by Type of Merger, 1948–77**

Type of Merger	1948–55	1956–63	1964–72	1973–77
Horizontal	36.8%	19.2%	12.4%	15.1%
Vertical	12.8	22.2	7.8	5.8
Conglomerate:				
product extension	44.8	36.0	39.3	24.2
market extension	2.4	6.7	7.3	5.7
other	3.2	15.9	33.2	49.2
Total	100.0	100.0	100.0	100.0

Source: U.S. Congress, Senate, Committee on the Judiciary, Subcommittee on Antitrust and Monopoly, *Economic Concentration*, Hearings pursuant to S. Res. 40, Part 8A (Federal Trade Commission, *Economic Report on Corporate Mergers*) (Washington, D.C.: Government Printing Office, 1969), p. 637; Federal Trade Commission, *Statistical Report on Mergers and Acquisitions* (various issues).

Table 7.17   **Measures of Outbound and Inbound Diversification for Major Sectors of Manufacturing Industry, 1972**

Sector	Outbound Diversification[a]	Inbound Diversification[a]
	(1)	(2)
Rubber products	66.3%	32.6%
Petroleum and coal products	59.9	15.7
Electrical machinery	53.0	43.0
Pulp, paper and products	49.6	45.2
Leather and leather goods	43.5	18.9
Tobacco manufactures	39.9	1.7
Food and kindred products	35.2	28.5
Machinery, except electrical	34.1	41.3
Stone, clay, and glass products	34.0	28.3
Chemicals and products	33.1	31.8
Instruments and related products	31.0	30.5
Fabricated metal products	29.0	41.3
Lumber and wood products	28.2	31.4
Textile mill products	26.2	33.6
Transportation equipment	25.0	15.1
Primary metal industries	24.9	25.8
Miscellaneous manufactures	24.5	27.3
Furniture and fixtures	23.1	24.4
Printing and publishing	21.8	17.7
Apparel and related products	21.0	23.8

Source: U.S. Bureau of the Census, *Enterprise Statistics, 1972*, Part 1, ES72–1 (Washington, D.C.: Government Printing Office, 1977), tables 1, 2.
[a]See text for definitions of the measures. It should be noted that diversification is defined here so as to include vertical integration.

shows (col. 1) what fraction of the shipments of companies classified to each base industry emanate from plants of theirs whose principal outputs are classified to other industries. The table shows weighted averages[14] of these diversification percentages for twenty broad sectors of manufacturing. The sectors are listed in descending order of this variable. We can call the variable "outbound diversification." Column 2 presents a corresponding measure of how much "inbound diversification" has occurred into each sector. That is, it represents the proportion of shipments from the industry in question that come from plants belonging to firms based in other industries that have diversified into this one.

Certain patterns can be detected in table 7.17. The most diversified manufacturing sectors seem to be of two kinds. Some—electrical machinery, pulp and paper, nonelectrical machinery—contain companies that are highly diversified or vertically integrated among industries within the sector. For these sectors the measures of outbound and inbound diversification are both high. Other top-ranking sectors, such as rubber products, petroleum, and tobacco, have diversified heavily into activities in more remote manufacturing sectors—rubber and petroleum into chemicals, tobacco into food products. For these sectors inbound diversification is less than outbound diversification. At the bottom of the list are several sectors dominated by small firms—furniture, printing and publishing, apparel. Throughout the economy, small companies on average are proportionally less diversified than their larger brethren.

Table 7.17 shows the diversification prevailing in 1972, but it gives no feeling for how the pattern has been changing. Table 7.18 illustrates, over the short period 1967 to 1972, how the process of diversification has related to the migration of companies among the economy's major sectors. It tells how many companies classified to an industry in 1967 remained in the same industry[15] in 1972. Roughly two-thirds stayed in place, for all sectors together. Some companies simply went out of business (3 percent). The remainder were strongly affected by the diversification process. Either they were acquired by another company (15 percent) or they themselves changed their activities so much (by acquiring other companies or changing their output mix) as to be reclassified to another industry (14 percent). Table 7.18 suggests that company turnover due to acquisition and reclassification was highest in the mineral and manufacturing industries.

7.4.3   Vertical Integration

Vertical integration is if anything a more ambiguous concept than diversification to measure across the face of American industry. When a firm adds a further stage of fabrication to its activities, we say that it has become more vertically integrated. However, there is no meaningful way to compare the degrees of vertical integration of firms in two different

Table 7.18   Diversification and Turnover among Large Companies, 1967–72

Category of Companies		All Sectors	Mineral Industries	Construction Industries	Manufacturing	Wholesale Trade	Retail Trade	Service Industries
Large companies in 1967	N	5,238	88	298	3,506	177	709	460
	%	100.0	100.0	100.0	100.0	100.0	100.0	100.0
Classified to same industry in 1972	N	3,551	54	200	2,340	99	532	326
	%	67.8	61.4	67.1	66.7	55.9	75.0	70.9
Acquired since 1967 by another company	N	768	17	25	552	27	96	51
	%	14.7	19.3	8.4	15.7	15.2	13.5	11.1
No longer in operation	N	164	1	19	101	4	17	22
	%	3.1	1.1	6.4	2.9	2.3	2.4	4.8
Classified in another industry category in 1972	N	755	16	54	513	47	64	61
	%	14.4	18.2	18.1	14.6	26.6	9.0	13.3

Source: U.S. Bureau of the Census, *Enterprise Statistics, 1972*, Part 1, ES72–1 (Washington, D.C.: Government Printing Office, 1977), p. 324.

industries. Therefore any broadly based measurement of vertical integration must be restricted to its changes over time within particular sectors. Economic theory offers no strong hypotheses about how vertical integration is likely to change in modern industrial economies. On the one hand, the development of the profit-center organization lets the modern corporation coordinate discrete activities more efficiently and so might increase vertical integration. On the other hand, an industry's growth and development may allow production of some necessary inputs to be farmed out more efficiently to independent specialist firms.[16]

If we cannot compare vertical integration among sectors, we can at least measure its changes over time for a given sector. Note that the value of an industry's shipments is equal to the cost of the material inputs it purchases plus the payments that it makes to primary factors of production. If it becomes more integrated (say, by producing some inputs it previously bought on the market), the ratio of payments to primary factors to total sales should rise. Arthur Laffer (1969) calculated this ratio for ten broad sectors of the United States economy in 1929, 1965, and years in between, and derived an index of the changes that have occurred. Overall, his index for 1965 took almost the same value as for 1929, with no systematic fluctuations in between. The manufacturing sector showed some increase in integration (especially in durable goods), but vertical integration declined in contract construction, services, and agriculture. Tucker and Wilder (1977) similarly investigated trends in narrowly defined industries within the manufacturing sector for the years 1954–72. They also found a slight increase of vertical integration in manufacturing, with the average industry's ratio of value added to value of shipments rising roughly from 0.43 to 0.51 (the exact value depending on the weight used to combine individual industries). Their evidence suggests that increases in vertical integration are associated with increases in the size and market share of the industry's leading firms, but it is not clear what causal relation (if any) exists between these changes.

7.4.4 Multinational Companies

An increasingly visible form of multimarket enterprise is the multinational company. Various definitions of the multinational company have been offered; here, we mean simply an enterprise legally resident in one country that controls at least one industrial establishment in some other country. The multinational company is subject to many popular misconceptions. For example, American companies are said to have "gone abroad" only in the years since World War II. However, foreign investment by American enterprise began in the nineteenth century, and the ratio of the book value of American investment abroad to American gross national products was apparently just about the same in 1914 as it was in 1966 (Wilkins 1970, p. 201). Similarly, multinational corporations are thought to be strictly an American specialty. However, other countries (among them Great Britain, the Netherlands and Switzerland) are also the homes of important multinational companies, and in some recent years investment by foreign companies entering the United States was greater than investment by United States companies abroad.[17]

For America's nonfinancial industries as a whole, 15.8 percent of all corporate assets were located abroad in 1972. Table 7.19 shows each sector's percentage of assets located abroad, with the sectors ranked in decreasing order of percentage. Some clear patterns emerge from the rankings. Some heavy foreign investors secure their raw materials overseas (petroleum, mineral industries). In others the leading firms acquire advanced technologies or special skills in differentiating their products.

Table 7.19   **Foreign Assets as a Percentage of Total Assets, United States Industries Ranked by Extent of Foreign Investment, 1972**

Sector	Foreign Assets Percentage of Total Assets
Petroleum and coal products	35.9
Machinery, except electrical	24.9
Food and kindred products	20.8
Rubber products	20.8
Heavy construction	19.2
Instruments and related products	18.4
Chemicals and products	16.8
Transportation equipment	16.5
Mineral industries, total	14.2
Tobacco manufactures	13.3
Stone, clay, and glass products	12.5
Pulp, paper, and products	11.2
Fabricated metal products	10.1
Electrical machinery	9.1
Other construction	8.4
Miscellaneous manufactures	8.3
Primary metal industries	8.0
Furniture and fixtures	6.2
Textile mill products	6.0
Printing and publishing	5.6
Retail trade	5.5
Business services	5.5
Apparel and related products	4.8
Leather and leather goods	3.3
Personal services	2.9
Wholesale trade	2.8
Lumber and wood products	2.4
Total, all industries	15.8

Source: U.S. Bureau of the Census, *Enterprise Statistics, 1972*, Part 1, ES72–1 (Washington, D.C.: Government Printing Office, 1977), pp. 310–15.

Such progressive and differentiated-goods industries include both consumer goods (food, transportation equipment) and producer goods (machinery, instruments). Industries at the low end produce undifferentiated goods (lumber) or serve intrinsically single-country or local markets (printing and publishing, retail trade, personal services).[18]

7.5 Strategic Features of Market Behavior

Industry structures are important because they affect the decisions made by buyers and sellers present in the marketplace. Investment decisions, short-run output and price levels, research, and advertising outlays —not to mention the diversification and foreign-investment decisions just considered—will come out differently for an industry, depending on the market's structure. How structure affects behavior is a complex problem of economic analysis that preoccupies economists working in the field of industrial organization.[19] Here we can only provide data on some of the consequences of these decisions by enterprises.

7.5.1 Advertising Outlays

One controversial category of business outlay is advertising expenditures. Advertising conveys some information that is useful to the consumer and would be more costly to secure in other ways. Even the ad that contains no hard facts may still fulfill an informative function: to show that the maker has enough faith in the product's quality that he will incur the cost of advertising to induce buyers to try it. On the other hand, advertising in some market settings may make competitive processes work less well.[20] And some citizens object to the values that advertising espouses.

Table 7.20 provides information on changes over time in total advertising outlays and the mixture of advertising media used. Each column represents an index (1967 = 100) of current-dollar advertising outlays through the medium in question. In 1977 total outlays on advertising, $38 billion, were 2 percent of gross national product. It does not appear that this percentage has been increasing over time. Table 7.20 shows that total advertising outlays in 1935 were 6.25 percent of their 1970 level. The current-dollar gross national product of the United States in 1935 was only 5.68 percent of its 1970 level. This same impression persists if we examine the ratios of advertising outlays to total sales for selected manufacturing industries that are heavy advertisers. Michael E. Porter matched data on 1935 advertising-sales ratios for thirteen industries to data on these same industries for 1965; the (unweighted) average advertising-to-sales ratio for the thirteen in 1935 was 10.0 percent, but in 1965 it had fallen to 5.0 percent.[21]

Table 7.20   Trends in National Advertising Expenditure, by Medium, 1935–70 (Indexes, 1967 = 100)

Year	Total	Magazines	Network Radio	Spot Radio	Network Television	Spot Television	Newspapers	Business Papers	Outdoor Advertising
1935	7	11	98	5	0	0	16	7	18
1950	31	40	306	43	6	3	57	36	76
1955	52	57	131	43	37	26	79	63	103
1960	70	74	67	71	54	53	89	86	109
1965	91	94	94	88	85	90	93	95	95
1970	112	103	88	118	114	125	108	105	122
1975	162	117	130	179	159	191	160	130	175
Percentage distribution, 1975	100%	8.3%	0.4%	10.3%	12.5%	16.0%	45.7%	5.0%	1.8%

Sources: U.S. Bureau of the Census, *Historical Statistics of the United States, Colonial Times to 1970* (Washington, D.C.: Government Printing Office, 1975), part 2, p. 857; U.S. Bureau of the Census, *Statistical Abstract of the United States, 1978* (Washington, D.C.: Government Printing Office, 1978), p. 855.

How did this decline in the proportional importance of advertising come about? Table 7.20 shows that the mix of advertising media has changed considerably over the period. The big change is, of course, the rise of television at the expense of network radio. For local advertising messages there has apparently been some displacement of newspapers and outdoor advertising by spot radio and television (outdoor advertising has been legally restricted on the interstate highway system since the 1960s). It seems quite possible that television is an efficient medium for disseminating advertising messages, in the sense that the cost of placing a message before a given number of viewers is less than by any other medium. The total number of advertising messages per citizen may have grown substantially, even while the total cost of advertising has fallen in relation to the nation's gross national product.

7.5.2   Research and Development Outlays

In the postwar period American industry has spent heavily on research and development, as developments in basic science were translated into new products and more efficient processes. An industry's "progressiveness" is rightly regarded as one of the most important features of its social performance. The potential for innovation is not evenly spread across the manufacturing sector. Science simply offers more scope for technical innovation in pharmaceuticals, say, than it does in colonial furniture. Accordingly, the proportion of sales revenue spent on research and development varies greatly from industry to industry. Table 7.21 shows the trend over time (1957–76) for a number of manufacturing industries (no benchmark before World War II is available). High rates of research and development (R&D) spending are concentrated in the chemicals, machinery, aircraft, and instruments sectors, where most of the opportunities are found for embodying scientific discovery in useful articles. Even in more traditional sectors, however, appreciable amounts of R&D spending are carried on. Such sectors undertake R&D in quest of products that are new, or provided in new forms, but without depending on any basic scientific advances.

Table 7.21 also shows the trend in rates of R&D expenditure over the past two decades. Some economists have expressed concern over a falling off of R&D spending, clearly apparent in the table. For the manufacturing industry as a whole the spending rate fell by one-third between the mid-1960s and 1976. The decline is unevenly spread among the industries shown in the table, and appears most evident in chemicals, electrical equipment, and aircraft. Some other sectors have held their own or shown increases. This decline in aggregate R&D spending partly reflects cutbacks in the federal government's support of industrial research. During the period 1957–65 federally funded R&D accounted for about 57 percent of total outlays on R&D. Since then the federal pres-

Table 7.21   Research and Development Funds as a Percentage of Net Sales in Manufacturing Companies Performing R&D, by Industry, Selected Years 1957–76

Industry	1957	1963	1965	1967	1969	1971	1973	1974	1975	1976
Food and kindred products	.3	.4	.4	.5	.4	.5	.4	.4	.4	.4
Textiles and apparel	a	.5	.5	.5	.6	.5	.4	.4	.4	.4
Lumber, wood products	a	.5	.4	.3	.4	.7	.7	.8	.7	.7
Paper and allied products	.6	.8	.8	.9	1.0	.8	.7	.8	.9	.9
Chemicals and allied products	3.5	4.3	4.3	5.7	3.9	3.9	3.5	3.5	3.7	3.7
industrial chemicals	5.0	5.1	4.7	4.8	4.0	3.8	3.4	3.2	3.5	3.6
drugs, medicines	3.6	4.7	6.4	8.0	6.0	6.2	6.5	6.3	6.4	6.3
other chemicals	1.3	2.8	2.3	2.3	2.1	1.9	2.0	2.1	2.2	2.1
Petroleum refining, extraction	.7	1.0	1.0	.8	.9	.9	.7	.6	.7	.7
Rubber products	1.7	2.3	1.9	1.9	2.2	2.6	2.6	2.5	2.5	2.4
Stone, clay, glass products	b	1.6	1.6	1.8	1.7	1.8	1.7	1.7	1.2	1.2
Primary metals	.5	.8	.8	.8	.8	.8	.7	.6	.8	.8
ferrous metals, products	a	.7	.7	.8	.7	.7	.5	.5	.6	.6
nonferrous metals, products	a	1.1	.9	1.0	1.0	1.0	.9	1.0	1.2	1.1
Fabricated metal products	1.6	1.6	1.3	1.3	1.3	1.2	1.2	1.2	1.2	1.2
Machinery	3.4	4.2	4.0	4.2	3.8	4.0	4.6	4.6	4.8	4.8
office, computing, accounting machines	a	a	a	a	a	a	11.6	12.6	12.0	11.6
Electrical equipment and communication	7.6	10.1	9.1	8.6	7.9	7.2	6.9	6.6	6.5	6.5

Table **7.21**—*Continued*

Industry	1957	1963	1965	1967	1969	1971	1973	1974	1975	1976
Radio, TV receiving equipment electronic components	c	c	c	1.9	2.2	2.4	1.7	1.7	1.4	1.3
communication equipment	a	13.0	11.4	10.3	9.7	9.2	6.2	6.2	6.9	7.4
other electrical apparatus	a	7.3	7.0	7.3	6.6	6.4	6.3	7.6	7.6	7.4
Motor vehicles, equipment	2.9	3.4	3.1	3.4	3.1	3.1	{ 3.5	3.7	3.5	3.2
Other transportation equipment							1.2	1.3	1.3	1.3
Aircraft and missiles	16.8	26.7	27.0	19.7	20.2	16.2	13.3	14.1	12.7	12.2
Professional and scientific instruments	7.0	5.9	5.9	5.4	6.4	5.7	6.1	6.1	5.9	6.0
Other manufacturing	a	.7	.7	.6	.8	.8	.8	.9	.8	.7
All manufacturing	3.4	4.5	4.3	4.2	4.0	3.5	3.3	3.1	3.1	3.0

Source: National Science Foundation, *Research and Development in Industry, 1976* (Washington, D.C.: National Science Foundation, 1978), table B–35.

[a]Not available separately; included in total.
[b]Included in the other manufacturing industries group.
[c]Included in the other electrical equipment group.

ence in the research laboratory has shrunk steadily, and in 1976 federal funds accounted for only 35 percent of the total. Between 1965 and 1976 company-financed R&D increased by 170 percent (in current dollars), while federal funds rose by only 20 percent, (and thus fell in real terms, given the rising cost of R&D inputs).[22]

Rates of R&D spending differ among large and small companies. One virtue claimed for large corporations is their ability (or inclination) to mount major research and innovative efforts. Most small companies do little or no formal R&D spending. Among medium-size and large companies, however, the rate of R&D spending does not clearly increase with the size of the company. The National Science Foundation issues data on company-financed R&D outlays, as a percentage of sales, by size of company, for those companies that do undertake research. For the years 1972–1976 these figures were as follows:

Fewer than 1,000 employees	1.5 percent
1,000 to 4,999	1.2
5,000 to 9,999	1.5
10,000 to 24,999	1.4
More than 25,000	2.5.

Thus, if the rate of private R&D spending increases with companies' size, it is only for the very largest companies in comparison to all others that perform some R&D. Economists have investigated the relation of R&D activity to size comparing R&D spending rates for companies competing with one another in the same industry. Their studies generally conclude that R&D spending as a percentage of sales does not increase with company size in most industries. Furthermore, their analyses of the productivity of R&D activities, measured by the number of patents issued or the number of major innovations achieved, suggest that the largest companies may be less productive with their R&D outlays than are their medium-size competitors.[23] It should be kept in mind, though, that the proportion of companies doing some research increases with companies' size.

7.5.3 Productivity Growth

A close relation probably exists between research outlays and the growth of productivity in American industry, even though increases in productivity also come from finding better ways to do things or doing them on a larger and more efficient scale, rather than from formal research efforts. Table 7.23 presents three measures of the annual rate of growth of productivity, as well as the growth rate of real output (adjusted for price changes) in each sector. The concept of productivity refers to the amount of ouput secured from a given bundle of inputs; when we say that productivity has grown, we mean that the amount of output has increased more than the amount of all inputs. A popular measure of productivity is labor productivity, which is shown in table 7.22 as the growth of output per unit of labor input. This measure is incomplete because inputs of capital and intermediate goods and services may also have been changing. To compare the growth of output to the growth only of labor inputs is to neglect changes in these other inputs. The column headed Total Factor Productivity partly remedies this problem by making allowance as well for the growth of inputs of capital. The growth of total factor productivity is less than the growth labor productivity if capital inputs have been increasing. Because labor in the highly productive American economy has been getting more expensive relative to capital, entrepreneurs substitute capital for labor, and so we are hardly surprised at the growing role of capital. Nonetheless, table 7.22 shows that output in most sectors has grown faster than inputs of capital (because most figures in the last column are positive). Only if they are negative can the growth of labor productivity. be larger or wholly explained by substitution of capital for labor.

Several interesting patterns emerge in table 7.22. The rates of growth of total output and of total factor productivity are obviously correlated. Causal influence runs both ways between the two variables. Productivity grows because an industry can offer better products or offer its old products more cheaply. People buy more at the lower prices, and output grows faster. Also if demand is growing fast, producers are more likely to take a chance on investments in large-scale plants capable of lower-cost production, and they may be induced to spend more on research. The broad sectors experiencing the greatest gains in productivity are the public utilities and mining industries. The manufacturing sectors with the highest rates of growth of total factor productivity are those with the highest rates of R&D spending (table 7.21). However, productivity growth rates differ among manufacturing industries a good deal less than do rates of R&D spending. In part this fact reflects the sources of productivity growth other than research. Also, the productivity gains from R&D spending often appear not in the industry that does the spending but in the industry that uses the improved equipment or other inputs made possible by the research.

The growth of productivity in the economy feeds back to the structure of industry in a way not shown in table 7.22. Improved production processes not only reduce the labor (and perhaps the capital) required to produce a given output, but they also change the bundle of intermediate goods that the process requires. When a particular intermediate good (plastics, for example) comes to be produced more efficiently, its price usually falls relative to the prices of similar intermediates. Producers substitute it for other inputs, so that its use grows rapidly.

Input-output analysis, described above (see table 7.4), helps us to trace these effects of technological change on the structure of the econ-

Table 7.22   **Annual Percentage Rates of Output Growth and Productivity Growth (Overall, Labor Productivity, Capital Productivity), by Industry, 1948–66**

Sector	Output	Total Factor Productivity	Output per Unit of Labor	Output per Unit of Capital
Manufacturing	4.3	2.5	2.9	0.8
Nondurable goods	3.8	2.6	3.2	0.7
food (excluding beverages)	3.1	3.0	3.4	1.8
beverages	2.7	2.2	2.9	1.0
tobacco	1.9	1.1	2.7	−0.1
textiles	2.8	4.0	4.3	2.7
apparel	3.1	1.9	2.2	−0.9
paper and paper products	5.0	2.5	3.0	1.0
printing	4.1	2.7	2.7	1.8
chemicals	8.2	4.9	6.0	2.8
petroleum refining	4.1	3.0	5.5	1.0
rubber products	7.2	3.9	4.0	3.3
leather products	1.2	1.7	1.7	1.0
Durable goods	4.7	2.4	2.8	0.3
lumber	2.3	3.5	3.9	0.3
furniture	4.3	2.9	2.9	2.7
stone, clay, and glass	3.9	2.4	3.2	−0.2
primary metal products	2.5	1.6	2.1	−0.7
fabricated metals	3.9	1.9	2.2	−0.3
machinery (excluding electric)	4.8	2.6	2.7	1.9
electric machinery	8.0	3.7	4.1	1.5
transportation equipment	6.7	3.2	3.2	1.5
instruments	7.0	2.9	3.7	−0.7
miscellaneous manufactures	4.0	3.5	4.0	0.6
Mining	2.1	4.2	4.6	2.9
Metal	2.0	2.4	2.9	−0.4
Coal	−1.3	5.2	5.8	0.4
Crude oil and natural gas	2.9	3.2	2.3	5.4
Nonmetallic mining and quarrying	4.6	2.6	3.2	−0.2
Contract construction	3.1	1.5	2.0	−3.8
Transportation	2.3	3.4	3.7	0.6
Railroads	0.6	5.2	5.8	0.6
Intercity bus	0.0	n.a.	1.5	n.a.
Intercity trucking	8.5	n.a.	3.1	n.a.
Waterways	0.2	0.5	0.7	−2.1
Air transport	14.6	8.0	8.2	6.1
Pipelines	6.0	n.a.	9.1	n.a.
Communications and public utilities	7.1	4.0	5.8	1.2
Communications	7.0	3.8	5.5	0.7
Electric, gas and sanitary services	7.1	3.9	6.1	1.5

Source: John W. Kendrick, assisted by Maude R. Pech, *Postwar Productivity Trends in the United States, 1948–1969*, National Bureau of Economic Research, General Series, No. 98 (New York: National Bureau of Economic Research, 1973), tables 5.1, 5.5, and 5.6.
n.a.—not available.

omy. Anne P. Carter (1970) analyzed the structure of the American economy in 1961 and showed how input requirements would have differed if the bundle of final goods and services actually purchased in 1961 had been produced with the technology of the American economy as it was in 1958, 1947, or 1939. For the period 1939–1961 her figures indicate that the total requirement of labor inputs needed to produce the 1961 output was falling at a rate of 2.4 percent annually. The capital required to produce the 1961 output was also falling, at a rate of 1.2 percent annually. These changes were accompanied by a very slight increase in the total bundle of intermediate goods needed to produce the 1961 output. Thus, technological progress tended to involve the substitution of intermediate commodities for inputs of *both* capital and labor. Labor was becoming more expensive and capital no cheaper, and so producers economized on these costly primary inputs by using relatively more of the cheaper inputs of intermediate goods ·and services. Another part of the story was that some producing establishments were growing specialized, buying inputs of goods and services from outside suppliers rather than making them in-house.[24]

While inputs of intermediate goods were growing slightly more important overall, rapid changes were taking place in requirements for particular intermediates. From the thirty-eight sectors included in Carter's study, table 7.23 presents the ten intermediate inputs with the most rapidly growing requirements and the ten with the most rapidly shrinking requirements. The annual rate of change in these requirements from 1939–61 is shown. The list indicates the changes in sources of power (electricity for coal) and means of transportation (highways and aircraft for railroads) that were taking place in those years, as well as such materials substitutions as plastics (included in the chemicals sector) for wood and steel. Inputs of communications increased rapidly because of the increasing specialization of individual production units in the economy as well as the cheapening of communication. And the rising inputs of instruments used for measurement and control reflects what we popularly call "automation."[25]

7.5.4   Profits

Profits play a vital role in allocating resources in our economy and in signaling the performance of individual sectors, as well as in determining the distribution of income. The accounting profit that a company reports actually may contain components that differ widely in economic significance. Profit includes the supply price of equity capital—what each sector must pay to bid for its portion of the nation's equity funds. Profit includes windfalls—unexpected gains or losses that occur because economic conditions turned out differently from what people expected. Finally, profit may contain elements of pure surplus or rent—monopoly rents earned by an industry when new competitors are somehow pre-

Table 7.23   Intermediate-Good Sectors of the American Economy
Experiencing the Largest Increases and Decreases in Unit
Input Requirements by Their Users, 1939–61

Sector	Annual Rate of Change of Requirements
Largest Increases	
Aircraft	5.5%
Electric and gas utilities	3.4
Communications	3.1
Scientific and professional instruments, cameras, etc.	3.0
Electrical and service equipment	2.6
Nonelectrical machinery and equipment	2.4
Wholesale and retail trade	2.1
Automobile repair	2.0
Chemicals, synthetic materials, drugs, paint	1.9
Engines and turbines	1.8
Largest Decreases	
Coal mining	−4.5%
Construction	−3.2
Nonferrous metal mining	−2.1
Iron and steel	−1.9
Iron mining	−1.7
Leather and shoes	−1.7
Agriculture, forestry, and fishing	−1.5
Wood and wood products	−1.1
Scrap materials	−0.8
Trains, ships	−0.6

Source: Anne P. Carter, *Structural Change in the American Economy* (Cambridge: Harvard University Press, 1970), p. 39.

vented from entering, or efficiency rents that can accrue to individual firms that happen to be more productive than their competitors. Identifying these components in actual profit figures is a complex and controversial problem of analysis, but most economists agree on two propositions. (1) Profits do perform their function of signaling that resources should be shifted from one sector to another: when demand rises, for example, a sector's profits rise, existing firms expand their output, new firms enter, and the inflated profit rate is competed down. (2) Persistent lumps of monopoly profit arise captured in industries with few sellers who are protected by entry barriers from new entrants. Which of the sources of entry barriers are "unnatural" and call for intervention by public policy is the issue on which there is considerable disagreement.[26] Some economists have tried to measure the real cost of monopoly to the American economy (which is not the same thing as monopoly profit). Most studies report costs that are less than one percent of gross national product, although some have argued for higher numbers (cf. Harberger 1954 and Kamerschen 1966).

Most of the research that economists have done on the profit rates of industries and companies has been designed to test hypotheses about sources of inefficiency or of monopoly in American industry. However contentious may be the debates over these tests, there is no evidence that the results are changing over time. As far as we can tell, the structures of markets and characteristics of firms that produced good (or bad) economic performance three decades ago still do so today. There is a good deal of interest, however, in the levels of companies' profits and their trends over time. This is a complex question because the familiar nominal measures of profits are not the same thing as the economic rate of return on the assets of America's corporations. Table 7.24 shows two measures of nominal profits for all manufacturing corporations—the ratio of profits after income taxes to stockholders' equity and the ratio of profits after income taxes to total sales. A simple average of the annual rates of profit on stockholders' equity for the thirty-two years covered in the table is 11.9 percent. Similarly, profits on sales averaged 5.0 cents on the dollar. Both series fluctuate with the business cycle, but neither shows a clear trend.

These conventional figures do an increasingly poor job of representing a real rate of return on the assets held by United States corporations. Inflation is the main source of distortion, and so nominal profits lately have diverged sharply from a measure of real rates of return. One source of distortion arises because the replacement cost of the wear and tear on its capital equipment must be subtracted from a company's revenues before we can measure its rate of return. Depreciation allowances, which fill this function in the calculation of nominal profits, fail to recognize that inflation may elevate the replacement cost of real corporate assets sharply above their historical cost; in addition, reported depreciation allowances are heavily influenced by tax considerations. A second and similar source of distortion lies in the fact that the real cost of the materials that a company uses from its inventories is the cost of replacing them, whereas nominal profit figures often reflect materials costs at the time the company put the materials into its inventory. (The company makes a capital gain when the price of materials rises. But that is not the same thing as a real return on its capital, and it supplies no incentive for any more capital formation.) Finally, nominal profits fail to reflect the capital losses that companies suffer when the nominal dollars in their balances of cash (and similar assets) depreciate through inflation. The right-hand column of table 7.24 presents a rate of return on the assets of all nonfinancial corporations that is corrected for all three of these distortions. This column cannot be compared directly to the other two,

Table 7.24   Selected Data on Nominal Profit Rates and Real Rates of
                    Return on Corporate Assets, 1947–78 (Percentages)

	Manufacturing Corporations		All Corporations
Year	Profits after Income Taxes Divided by Stockholders' Equity	Profits after Taxes Divided by Total Sales	Income Accruing to Capital Divided by Total Capital (Adjusted for Inflation)
	(1)	(2)	(3)
1947	15.6%	6.7%	4.1%
1948	16.0	7.0	6.9
1949	11.6	5.8	7.5
1950	15.4	7.1	6.4
1951	12.1	4.8	4.7
1952	10.3	4.3	5.3
1953	10.5	4.3	4.8
1954	9.9	4.5	5.3
1955	12.6	5.4	6.7
1956	12.3	5.3	5.4
1957	10.9	4.8	4.8
1958	8.6	4.2	4.3
1959	10.4	4.8	5.7
1960	9.2	4.4	5.4
1961	8.9	4.3	5.3
1962	9.8b	4.5	6.5
1963	10.3	4.7	6.9
1964	11.6	5.2	7.9
1965	13.0	5.6	8.6
1966	13.4	5.6	8.5
1967	11.7	5.0	7.7
1968	12.1	5.1	7.0
1969	11.5	4.8	6.0
1970	9.3	4.0	4.8
1971	9.7	4.1	5.2
1972	10.6	4.3	5.9
1973	12.8	4.7	5.3
1974	14.9a	5.5a	3.3
1975	11.6	4.6	4.3
1976	13.9	5.4	4.8
1977	14.2	5.3	4.9
1978	14.6b	5.3b	4.6

Sources: Columns 1 and 2—*Economic Report of the President, 1979* (Washington, D.C.: Government Printing Office, 1979), table B–83. Column 3—data provided by Patrick J. Corcoran, Federal Reserve Bank of New York, as described in his article "Inflation, Taxes, and Corporate Investment Incentives," *Federal Reserve Bank of New York Quarterly Review*, Autumn 1977, pp. 1–10.

aData from 1974 on are not fully comparable to those for earlier years.
bProvisional figure based on first three quarters.

which pertain only to manufacturing corporations and only to profits on equity capital. Nonetheless, it is safe to conclude that the rising trend in nominal profit rates in recent years is not an accurate reflection of real rates of return, which in the 1970s have lain below their peak in the mid-1960s. Many explanations for this decline in the real rate have been suggested, but no consensus has been reached.

7.6   Summary: Major Trends in Structure and Performance

The structure of industry has not been an area of revolutionary change in the postwar American economy. The mixture of industries and companies that make up our economy does not alter much from year to year. Nonetheless, this survey has uncovered some trends, most of them proceeding at a measured pace, that may have important implications in the long run:

1. Economic activity continues to shift away from the primary and manufacturing sectors and into most service industries and the public sector. Activity within manufacturing has shifted toward the high-technology sectors and those making capital goods and synthetic materials.

2. Economic activity has shifted away from the investor-owned sector subject only to general regulation by the government and into closely regulated, nonprofit, and government-enterprise sectors.

3. In the nonfinancial sector a long-term trend has continued toward the concentration of the assets of nonfinancial corporations in the hands of the largest corporations. This trend stretches back to the 1920s (and probably earlier). It has proceeded rapidly since World War II, especially in the manufacturing sector, but it has not been accelerating lately.

4. The increasing diversification of the largest enterprises is surely a major factor explaining the concentration of assets in the hands of the largest companies, although the merger waves of the 1960s and 1970s have not much affected the proportional importance of the 100 or 200 largest nonfinancial companies.

5. About 16 percent of the assets of United States nonfinancial corporations are now located abroad, and more and more of our larger companies are multinational. Although data are not readily available, it is clear that foreign multinationals have similarly grown more numerous on American soil, and competitive processes in many industries would appear to be growing more international in scope.

6. Whatever one makes of the increased concentration and diversification of the largest enterprises, the population of smaller companies has not been drying up; the population of companies continues to grow faster than the human population.

7. The concentration of sellers in individual markets in manufacturing has shown no trend over the twentieth century as a whole, although

there has been a slight increase since World War II. This average pattern masks a postwar decline in concentration in producer-goods industries and an increase in consumer goods, especially industries selling heavily advertised products.

8. Sales-promotion outlays are a no larger proportion of total industrial sales now than in the 1930s, but the mix of advertising media has shifted toward television and away from other media.

9. Research and development outlays of United States manufacturing, 3 to 4 percent of sales by those companies performing research and development, have dropped proportionally by about one-third since the mid-1960s.

10. The real rate of return to the assets of United States nonfinancial corporations, which averaged 5.8 percent since World War II, was one-third lower in the 1970s than it was during the 1960s.

Notes

1. The regulated sectors are taken to be transportation, public utilities (electricity, gas, communication), banking, and insurance carriers. The intensity with which they are regulated in fact varies a good deal, both between and within these sectors. Insurance, for example, may not on average be regulated more than agriculture. We must recognize that all sectors of the economy are regulated in terms of such factors as their effects on the environment or the health and safety of their employees. All are subject to laws that enforce contracts, define property rights, and prevent violence and fraud. By "unregulated" we mean that their conduct in the marketplace is regulated only by general laws that prevent artificial restrictions on competition (the "antitrust laws").

2. This is the case because the assets of financial corporations are to a significant extent the liabilities (bonds, common shares, liabilities to banks) of the nonfinancial companies; to compare the sizes of financial and nonfinancial companies is thus, in a sense, to double-count.

3. The same conclusions would be reached if we considered the largest 200 rather than the largest 50 companies.

4. Before 1973 the Federal Trade Commission allowed companies to report their international assets in whatever way they wished. Some reported as a corporate asset only their net equity in their foreign subsidiaries, while others consolidated their subsidiaries and thus reported all their subsidiaries' assets. Prof. J. Fred Weston's procedure, which is described in this text, attempts to include all foreign-subsidiary assets on a consolidated or gross basis.

5. For a formal statement of the relation between measures of concentration and economic welfare, see Dansby and Willig (1979).

6. A brilliant qualitative description of the evolution of the modern large company is provided by Chandler (1977).

7. F. M. Scherer (1980, p. 68) calculated these figures from Census of Manufactures data for the years in question.

8. Scherer's data came originally from U.S. Bureau of the Census (1975).

9. Shepherd (1964, table 2). In calculating his average, Shepherd used industry shipments as a weight rather than value added. The 1947 figure is probably atypically low due to the state of the economy immediately after World War II. Compare table 7.7 of this text.

10. This pattern is not apparent among the industries serving a mixture of households and business buyers, but the number of industries involved here is very small.

11. The count of increases and decreases depends on our choice of decile blocks for defining when an industry's concentration is unchanged. A different choice of blocks would change the details of our conclusions but not the general picture.

12. Buyer concentration may typically be low, but its level can nonetheless make a difference for the performance of markets. See Guth, Schwartz, and Whitcomb (1976).

13. The distribution of plants per company for the four largest companies is subject to some inaccuracy because of the form in which the Bureau of the Census publishes the underlying data. The resulting errors should not bias the distribution as a whole up or down, but they may cause a few industries to be misclassified.

14. Each industry's diversification percentage is weighted by the total sales of companies allocated to it.

15. The statistical measure of "base industry" is that underlying table 7.17; the manufacturing sector we mentioned for illustration is divided into 115 industries.

16. Compare Chandler (1962, concluding chapter) and Stigler (1951).

17. Between the beginning of 1971 and the beginning of 1978 the book value of direct investment in the United States grew by 157 percent, that of United States direct investment abroad only 97 percent. At the latter date, however, foreign investment in the United States was still only 23 percent of United States investment abroad (U.S. Bureau of the Census, 1978, pp. 856, 866).

18. These propositions have been tested statistically. See, for example, Pugel (1978, chap. 4).

19. The field is well summarized in Scherer (1980). For a brief account, see Caves (1977).

20. For a recent survey of the economic issues, see Comanor and Wilson (1979).

21. Caves, Porter, and Spence (1980, chap. 6). Porter's sources of data were: Neil Borden, *The Economic Effects of Advertising* (Chicago: Richard D. Irwin, 1942), pp. 62, 442; and United States Internal Revenue Service, *Sourcebook of the Statistics of Income* (Washington, D.C.: IRS 1965).

22. Calculated from National Science Foundation (1978, table B-1). For more information, see chapter 8 of this volume, by Edwin Mansfield.

23. This research is summarized by Kamien and Schwartz (1975, esp. pp. 15–19).

24. Carter (1970, pp. 33–44). The calculated rate of change for the capital inputs is based on the period 1939–1958 rather than 1939–1961.

25. The inputs discussed here and in table 7.23 are only current inputs and do not reflect the capital goods also supplied by some of these sectors. Although changing input requirements have been important for explaining differing rates of output growth among United States industries, we should note that changes in the composition of final demand have apparently been still more important. See Vaccara and Simon (1968, pp. 19–58).

26. A survey of the controversy over profits, monopoly, and efficiency is provided in Goldschmid et al. (1974, chaps. 2, 4).

2. Walter B. Wriston

From the Hall of Mirrors to the Floppy Disk

Public policy in a democracy results from the complex interaction of what people think an economic and political system should be and what they believe it to be at the moment. It is the disparity between what they conceive of as the "ideal" and what they perceive as "real" that fuels the engine of social change. Both concepts, the ideal and the real, have always been influenced by the products of the pamphleteer or his equivalent, which nowadays may range from the studies of a respected think tank to the lines and lyrics of a rock song at a Jane Fonda rally.

The difference between then and now is that the incendiary words of Thomas Paine were read by a few hundred people, but the staged television demonstration at a nuclear plant enters fifty million living rooms on the seven o'clock news with devastating effect.

The impact of this continuous flow of facts, fiction, data, information, and misinformation has had a profound effect on American society in general and on business in particular. We have become the first human society to live in a state of what George Gallup has called "a continuous audit."

In this age of unlimited data proliferation, it is now always possible to look back and find a piece of data somewhere in the memory banks to "prove" that somebody "knew" something years ago and failed to act upon this information responsibly in violation of some law or regulation. As long as the trail is wide and long and prolix, which the computer assures it will be, commentators, lawyers and regulators can dig through a billion pieces of paper, or their electronic equivalents, as they are currently doing in the IBM and American Telephone and Telegraph antitrust suits, until it becomes statistically inevitable that any given proposition can be "proved" after the fact. There is always a piece of data that can be produced and, taken by itself and in hindsight, used to prove that the manager or policy-maker has committed an inexcusable oversight.

This data may range from the presence of a Russian brigade in Cuba that appears and reappears like the Cheshire cat sitting on an international limb, to a loan or investment that goes bad, thereby proving to the critics that it should never have been made in the first place. This continuous audit cannot fail to have a significant and inhibiting effect on the way we conduct our affairs.

Just as we find it increasingly hard to determine *when* we know something, so we also find it harder to determine *what* we know. The line

Walter B. Wriston is chairman of Citicorp.

between "information" and the "real" things about which we need to be informed, in Professor Caves's phrase, has become blurred. Indeed it can be argued that the importance of the legal and regulatory paper trail has made the manual of procedure more important than the act itself. We resemble the French in the line uttered by Professor Higgins in *My Fair Lady*: "the French don't care what you do, actually, so long as you pronounce it properly." We have become so entranced with pronouncing it properly in our electronic data that we sometimes forget what it is we are trying to do. The production of statistics has become an end in itself.

It might add to our perspective a bit if we reminded ourselves of where we got this word "statistics" in the first place. It was given to us by a Scottish gentleman named Sir John Sinclair, who imported it from Germany in 1791 and used it in the title of his book, *A Statistical Account of Scotland*. The German term, he tells us in his preface, did not quite describe his own purposes, because, whereas he himself was interested in "the quantum of happiness enjoyed by the inhabitants and the means of its improvement," in Germany the word was confined to matters concerning the political strength of the state. A case can be made that the original German concept of statistics is now working its way into our country on the back of the technologically driven data explosion.

Underlying the whole process is, of course, the revolution that began with the first electronic computer in 1946—a computer that belonged, by the way, to the Ordnance Corps of the United States Army. Every item in an inventory today leaves a paper trail and an electronic trail —of research, development, design, manufacture, distribution, marketing, and accounting. And we find the laws and regulations concerned more with assuring a clearly marked trail, than with the final results. A single number, which appears to be finite, is itself the end result of many guesses and can be—and often is—communicated worldwide in minutes. We have reached the point where the statistics of the GNP, or the composite index of leading indicators, when released, can cause a major rally or slump on Wall Street.

In this situation, the index is not a statistical report about what is happening in the world: publication of the statistic *is* the happening, even though the probability is that the number will be revised in a few weeks. No business executive prior to the Second World War had to live in such an environment.

Governments have fared no better. There is an old adage that "what you don't know can't hurt you." That would be a precarious rule to follow; nevertheless, there is more than a little truth in the remark of a former British Chancellor of the Exchequer that there was no balance of payments problem in the nineteenth century because there were no balance of payments statistics. In fact, nobody ever attempted to work out the statistic before the 1930s. The old-time policy-makers only dimly realized that it might theoretically exist. They looked instead to the movement of gold reserves, and if this was creating a problem, it was usually something that could at least wait until after lunch.

Today, any government in the world that announces a change in its fiscal or monetary policies can find out in a matter of minutes what the world thinks of the development by watching the cross-rate on their currency, which alters almost instantly in the currency markets in London, Zurich, or Tokyo. The old gold exchange standard of yesterday has in fact been replaced by the electronic information system of today, which can be more or less harsh than the gold standard, but in the end is just as sure and just as certain.

The incessant production of new data and its instantaneous communication throughout the world thus creates a paradox: information, which we have always viewed as the thing that eliminates uncertainty, now increases everybody's feeling of insecurity because of the failure to convert data into knowledge.

There is an insatiable demand, both in public opinion and in the halls of government, to "get things under control." If we subjected our health to the same process, we would take our blood pressure every hour. This drumbeat of data could lead us to the conclusion that we seem to be very sick men and women, when in fact we are only measuring the normal rhythm of life.

The resulting hypochondria is providing a ready market for the peddlers of miracle cures in bottles of all shapes and sizes. What they have in common is almost always a label that reads: "To be taken with large doses of government intervention."

The power of the computer has made possible a flow of data about any perceived "problem" which must then be "solved" by legislation or regulation. We have now reached the level of legal sophistication where it is probable that each of us is now in violation of some law or regulation—we just don't have enough time and money to find out which ones. This state of affairs gives a prosecutor the selective power to accuse anyone of violation of law, usually on page one of the newspapers.

Since a new set of numbers is always being produced somewhere in the world, it is only a matter of time before a law or regulation appears requiring their publication regardless of their utility. Under the banner of protecting the small investor, the SEC now requires reams of data that are so comprehensive that no small investor could possibly get anything out of them. It is clear, upon reflection, that the requirement to produce these data is part of an effort to control the governance of American business, rather than any concern to protect the small investor.

The mere production of all this data affects business decisions no less than government policy: in fact, they feed on each other. Thousands of pages of data are regularly produced with an eye solely to influencing a possible business decision or a government policy and are instantly communicated all over the world in order to measure the reaction. All of this is done without a brick being laid or a dollar changing hands.

This chain of events is pushing business back to an old discredited form of economic policy, which has now been dressed up in new mod fashions which appeal to some modern business managers. It has been packaged most attractively by the president of the United States, who has referred to it in a State of the Union address as a partnership between government, business, and labor.

For such a partnership to exist, we would have to adopt the view that business has become a separate class with separate interests which are independent of the interests of its owners and its employees. We would also have to accept the proposition that the almost three million workers in the Federal government are no longer the servants of the citizens as envisioned by our Constitution, but that they, in effect, also have become a separate estate with interests distinguishable from those of the people whom they are elected or appointed to serve.

Once one swallows that premise, the popular argument that there has been a separation of ownership and management of the American corporation logically follows. This, in turn, may be used to make the argument that the corporation has a life of its own, independent of its owners and their interests, and doubt is thus cast upon the corporation's legitimacy. Data may then be produced to show to the prosecutor's satisfaction that corporate power to influence output, employment, and the income of millions of Americans is growing year by year. The historical justification for private ownership of the means of production, namely that it would produce, via the force of competition in the marketplace, the highest social product, appears to have been undermined. The length of the road we have come can be measured by two incidents. The flap caused in 1953 by the misquotation of Charlie Wilson allegedly saying what was good for General Motors is good for America, has now been enshrined as public policy by the 96th Congress for Chrysler Corporation.

Private ownership has become so subverted that the employees—including the professional managers—have in effect become wards of the state. Indeed the bailout of Chrysler Corporation by the Federal government is a denial of the right of private owners to fail, which follows logically the denial of the right to succeed. If all this is accepted, it becomes clear that so-called excess earnings are now justifiably claimed by government. The chain is complete in which the government has transferred the wealth of savers and equity holders to others in our society. Since markets cannot be fooled over time, this massive income transfer is reflected by the fact that the real rate of return on the Standard and Poors common-stock index has been negative since 1967.

The litany of what we have done to effect this transfer of wealth from the saver to the spender would make Colbert green with envy. Dean Mecking of Rochester put it this way: "It includes what products can be marketed, how they can be advertised, what the terms of sales can be, who can be hired, what kinds of working conditions must be provided, what kind of fringe benefits are allowed, how land can be used, what financial reports must contain, who can be on the board of directors, whether plants can be closed, whether production lines can be altered and whether new production techniques can be introduced."

All this adds up to a kind of modern mercantilism in electronic clothing which is packaged as "partnership." However flattering this "partnership" role might seem to the businessman, and it is very attractive to some, there are at least two things wrong with it. First of all, it contradicts the basic American principle that our society is a collection of individuals, not institutions, and that the basis of our political liberty is individual liberty. Carried to its logical conclusion, this view of society must ultimately replace the idea of the individual as the center of our society with the notion of the *standestaat*. The second thing wrong with the partnership concept is that, to the extent that it succeeds, it will be an economic disaster. It replaces economic competition among various entities with political competition. It creates an environment in which a corporation's well-being depends less and less on its ability to produce a saleable product or service and more and more on its ability to secure a favorable interpretation of some obscure subparagraph in the Federal Register.

Corporations are the economic agents of the people just as surely as governments are their political agents. The failure to preserve this distinction between the proper role of economic agents and political authorities threatens to politicize all economic decision-making. To the extent this occurs, it will, and in fact already has begun to, impair fundamentally the capacity of the business system to provide jobs and raise productivity. Once the economic marketplace is replaced by the political process, what Franklin Roosevelt called the "great arsenal of democracy" will be replaced by a shrinking pie with special-interest political groups fighting over their share. The state will become the receiver in bankruptcy of impotent individual responsibility.

In the short run, some corporate managers are tempted to participate in the political game to curry favor, and many have done so in the belief their enterprises' survival depends on it. But the longer term result of this business/political strategy is to bring all decisions concerning output, employment, and resources allocation to Washington. Once this is achieved, one of the most powerful effects of the resulting flood of regulations and laws and publicity is to create a powerful incentive for us all to avoid risk of any kind. Indeed, risk has already become the regulators' new four-letter word, and is now used as a pejorative, as in risky policy or risky investment even though these phrases are redundant. This process tends to nullify the capital value of organizations designed to make economic decisions on economic grounds. Although there are undoubtedly many reasons for the significant decline in the real market value of American corporations, this phenomenon surely has to rank as one of the most important.

We have revived Colbert's ancient and disastrous "system of restraint and regulation" with an efficiency beyond anything he could have dreamed or imagined. Today it is even more dangerous because we have something Colbert lacked. We have computerized data. The combination of mercantilist ideas with the torrents of information that now inundate American society may be a greater threat to the survival of our system of democratic capitalism than the Great Depression or the Second World War.

Oliver Wendell Holmes once remarked that there are times when "we need education in the obvious more than investigation of the obscure." What needs to be made obvious today is that the solutions concocted by Colbert and Louis XIV will not work any better among the computer banks than they did in the Hall of Mirrors in Versailles.

---

3. James R. Schlesinger

Whither American Industry?

Dramatic changes have taken place both in the position and structure of American industry in the years since World War II. Despite substantial strides in technology and in productivity, there has been a general erosion of the once preeminent position of American industry, which had emerged from World War II with perhaps 60 percent of the world's manufacturing capacity. Some of that relative slippage was both inevitable and desirable with the sought-for revival of other nations, now both competitors and partners, which had suffered a general flattening of industry in the course of the war. By the later 1960s, changed motivations, attitudes, and expectations, combined with the burden of the Vietnam War, the environmental movement, and the course of new

James R. Schlesinger is senior advisor at Lehman Brothers Kuhn Loeb, Inc. and Georgetown Center for Strategic and International Studies.

social and economic programs—embodied, for example, in the Great Society—accelerated the trend towards a more rapid erosion of the position of American industry. By 1980 it had become apparent to all but the most quixotic observers that something more fundamental was wrong with the performance of American industry than could be explained by some mechanism like gap-narrowing or catch-up.

From its elevated position as model for the entire world, American industry had gradually slipped so that some segments (such as steel) were regarded as basket cases, while much of industry, if not yet in the category of basket cases, could only be regarded as having lost entrepreneurial initiative and no longer in the forefront of industrial development. This slippage was, of course, reflected in comparative productivity as well as in a relative drop in income per head. By the later 1970s, the decline of America's industrial fortunes, marked by the virtual cessation of productivity growth and a weakened ability to compete internationally, had become an object of concern to our competitors and industrial allies, who gradually came to fear that neither the American position of international leadership nor the performance of the international economy could be sustained in the absence of more vigorous performance by American industry.

In reviewing dramatic changes, we should also note the truly astonishing alteration in the climate of opinion. In the closing years of the war and the early postwar years, the prevailing expectation was that postwar economic trends would—in the absence of sustaining activity by governments—revert to the conditions of the 1930s. Such expectations were reflected at Bretton Woods and elsewhere. The prevailing wisdom was that a combination of employment policy and exchange rate adjustments would sustain a tolerable level of economic activity and maintain some modest economic growth.

All of this has changed dramatically. Rather than the feeble economic performance that was expected, the postwar period was characterized by an astonishing explosion, marked by an unbelievable expansion of international trade and investment that led to rapid increases in economic activity and standards of living throughout the industrial world. To some extent that explosion depended upon certain noneconomic factors. The paramount position of the United States provided a degree of security for international trade and investment, a corollary of the Pax Americana. The availability of cheap and abundant energy, rapidly exploited by the flow of international investment, permitted rapid industrialization and the significant diminution in backbreaking human labor.

Nonetheless, the change in perspective is still striking. The prevailing view of a declining marginal efficiency of investment has happily proved to be absurdly wrong. Perhaps most significant of all, the concept of a closed economy, even for the United States, has had an increasingly fall-off sound. Policies can no longer be *prudently* pursued on the expectation that international repercussions will be minimal. Moreover, there is substantial reason to doubt whether the very self-equilibrating mechanisms on which we have counted to sustain the international financial system can effectively operate given the explosion of oil prices, the limitations on oil production, and the consequences that have flowed from those developments. Increasingly, achieving balance in international trade, investment, and finance will require mechanisms which we have, as yet, not devised. The defectiveness of self-equilibrating mechanisms in this area of special concern is a far cry from the prevailing faith at Bretton Woods that a satisfactory outcome could be attained through the manipulation of government employment policy and exchange rates.

A large proportion of the economists of the 1940s would scarcely recognize this postwar world. Yet, I suspect that Schumpeter would have done so. With his abiding faith in the *inherent* vigor of the unfettered enterprise system, he would not have been too surprised by the explosive growth we have experienced in the last generation. His concern lay in the long-run smothering effect, stemming from attitudes and institutions which economic prosperity itself tended to foster. The objective performance of the economy provided little protection against the host of critics, who by their ill-conceived actions would sap the motivations and alter the interpretation of reality in a way that would ultimately hobble economic performance.

Neither would Schumpeter have been surprised by the difficulties that we have encountered since the middle 1960s, nor by the flow of superficial and destructive commentary that has marked our political life. Certainly the role of "intellectuals"—reflected, for example in the post-Vietnam, post-Watergate press—would have appeared to him as the chief pitfall lying in the path of necessary economic adjustment and of economic progress. Although we may not yet have reached "capitalism in the oxygen tent"—his abiding fear—the vital signs of the American economic organism are now flickering.

I am, of course, hesitant to introduce into the sanctum of quantitative economics, that is the National Bureau, a view that places principal emphasis upon the sociological setting in which business operates. Yet I see no recourse, for I believe Schumpeter was correct, that the ultimate driving force in this and other industrial societies is the overall culture in which business operates and which it simultaneously reflects and forms.

Of course, I could go back even further to the Adam Smith of *The Theory of Moral Sentiments* (not *The Wealth of Nations*) to underscore a point far better understood by our British brethren: that economic performance in the enterprise economy is not simply the product of a system of self-serving individualistic exchanges among amoral economic men, but rather is something shaped in a larger moral and social context. A free economy, to be acceptable to the participants, must be based upon a set of social habits, motivations, and educated and *socially constrained self-interest*—in short, a set of (normally) accepted social norms and obligations. Otherwise, it will provide justification for Leviathan.

A set of habits perfectly satisfactory in one period, if they become ingrained, may prove to be hollow and pernicious in the next period. Thus to understand the performance of American industry one must examine the overall social context and how it has influenced business motivations. It is this that will determine the evolving position and structure of industry, which Professor Caves has so admirably delineated in his paper. In order to understand this larger culture, one must cast one's net over a broader area than American industry alone. One must examine areas that other speakers will comment on. In particular, one must examine the changing social environment, as it is so heavily influenced by government, as well as the broader international setting that helps determine the range of activities in which American industry can profitably operate.

In the sixties and seventies, American society underwent a set of external shocks and adjustment of internal values that led to the *systematic* weakening of the social order. Over the past two decades, two debilitating trends, somewhat inconsistent, could be observed. These were: a steady rise in the services that the public demands the government perform, and a steady decline in the authority of government.

The business community has rightly questioned the first trend, but it has frequently fostered and exploited the second. Yet, in the long run, the business community will suffer more than most from weakened governmental authority. Like the Irish of old, an attitude of being "agin' the Government," irrespective of function, is surprisingly commonplace among businessmen. Ultimately, however, only government, limited to its proper sphere, can provide the firm social structure in which business can flourish and satisfactory economic performance be attained. No doubt government, driven by public demands and by faulty analysis, has been a principal offender. Yet the business community appropriately should regard the government not as rival but as shield.

Consider the following phenomena:

1. Government, in pursuit of such ends as the equitable distribution of income, the stimulation of purchasing power, and a higher "marginal propensity to consume," has diminished incentives for and reduced the pace of capital formation in the American society substantially below that existing in comparable industrial societies. It has simultaneously imposed upon business such social goals (and economic burdens) as aiding the handicapped, equal employment opportunity, hiring the hardcore unemployed, cleaning up the environment, and eliminating risks to health and safety. In short, business under the purview of government

is to be the vehicle for achieving a just society. It has thereby created a regulatory maze embodying risks that require a higher rate of return to elicit the investment of capital. In short, it has gone a considerable way along the path of killing the goose that lays the golden eggs.

2. Social discipline, properly a major concern of government, has deteriorated. Despite the spread of universal education and the increasing number of high school graduates, it is now necessary for business concerns in some urban areas to teach employees with high school degrees how to count and how to read. Relative to (say) the Japanese, enough American employees are mellow, "laid back," or worse that production and quality control suffer.

3. The post-Watergate, post-Vietnam political framework in the United States has suffered considerable damage. The presidency has been weakened, so that it must devote massive effort and political resources (i.e., side-payments) to attain its necessary goals in foreign policy, not to speak of domestic policy. Social programs have acquired a life of their own beyond the capacity (or perhaps the desire) of the executive branch to control. Discipline within the Congress has broken down. Responding to their own constituencies, the members are less inclined to follow the leadership. Congressional committees, given a weakened executive branch, can reach through to executive branch agencies to achieve objectives, either parochial or emotional, not necessarily in the general interest.

4. Leading businessmen have simultaneously been tantalized, repelled, and enticed by the political process. Enormous energies are devoted by CEO's and others to serial visits to Ways and Means or Finance Committee members, meetings at agencies, and consultations with presidential assistants. From a social standpoint, if not a corporate standpoint, there is unquestionably better use that can be made of that time.

5. The burden seems particularly heavy for those firms—such as steel and automobile producers—under severe pressure either from foreign competition or from regulation. Their time might better be invested in design, production, and marketing. To cite the extreme case, Chrysler's executives' efforts have been diverted from the internal management decisions necessary to salvage the company (if possible) to the political game. At the other end of the spectrum, firms that are especially prosperous, such as oil, are under continued pressure to justify their prosperity. Firms at intermediate points on the spectrum do not suffer such a degree of diversion or harassment. Nonetheless, the upshot is clear: most firms will find it far easier to strike a gusher in Washington than to pursue ordinary production activities.

6. Among traditional bellwethers of American industry, the ability to anticipate the future has not been spectacularly good. The handwriting has been on the wall, at least since 1973, for the mass market for the

heavy, high-acceleration automobile. Yet, without government prodding, the United States industry's general inclination has been to leave the market for fuel-efficient vehicles to its foreign competitors. The consequences are now quite distressing.

In general, there has been limited effort in strategic investment in creating new capabilities and new markets—for example, in creating an effective organization to market abroad. This may reflect that, aside from speeches, government has given precious little support to such activities.

7. Almost alone amongst major industrial nations, the United States government takes a suspicious attitude toward business activities, even those that involve foreign sales. Japan, Incorporated, may be a polar case, but almost all socialist governments have a decent regard for the ability of their firms to produce competitively and sell overseas—for balance of payments reasons. In the relations between the United States government and business, the appropriate balance of cooperation and review has been singularly absent. In the United States the prevailing relationship is one of mutual suspicion, recrimination, and unwarranted harassment. Perhaps these attitudes could somehow be justified when the American economy was preponderant and the balance of payments and strength of the dollar not a source of daily concern. These attitudes can be justified no longer. They have become socially pernicious.

8. In the post-Vietnam world, the United States, under public pressure, has become neglectful of the foreign policy and national security requirements indispensable for the preservation of the existing international economic order. Pax Americana may be finished. Nonetheless, there is a minimum requirement for adequate security and avoidance of basic instabilities if international trade and investment are to flourish. Today, given the obvious risks to energy supplies in the Middle East, the vital interests of the United States and the free world are under threat to a degree that we have not known since World War II.

These are serious and disturbing problems. The economic agenda for the next decade must handle these in a satisfactory way if the enterprise system, indeed free societies, are to survive.

To be concrete, how do these burdens affect the performance and the structure of American industry? Let me cite a few examples from my own governmental experience. In 1973, after the close of the Middle Eastern war, I sought ways to substantially increase tank production. Inventory drawdowns had been sizable, and the lesson of the war was the high prospective rate of attrition in combat. Congress was more lenient with funds, yet I discovered that there was an intractable bottleneck. Much of American foundry capacity, which had been marginal, had been forced to close because of low profitability and the high cost of compliance with the new environmental regulations. For turrets we had to turn to foreign supplies.

No greater change from World War II could be imagined: the great Arsenal of Democracy without foundry capacity! It raises an interesting question. Should the elaboration of social goals, rather haphazardly, be permitted to destroy a segment of industry necessary for the national security? But more generally the episode points to the unanticipated as well as extraordinary burdens recently placed on American industry.

Last spring, after the Iranian oil cutoff, American law hindered the attempt to distribute petroleum supplies evenly. Given the law and the advice of the Antitrust Division, it was impossible for the Department of Energy and the major suppliers jointly to discuss supplies of crude oil and product. Consequently, the immediate problem was intensified by the scarcity of information and by the growth of uncertainty. Given Department of Justice attitudes, the companies quite correctly refused to discuss supply or price. As a result, a handful—I mean a *handful*—of Department of Energy employees were obliged through bilateral conversations with major oil companies to acquire piecemeal an overview of the market, which they could not adequately convey to the participants.

Yet, at that time, we had (for better or worse) a price control system and an impending shortage. The antitrust laws were at best irrelevant in those conditions. Refiners were scampering around looking for crude oil and attempting to provide more product; they could not charge prices higher than the regulations permitted. Nonetheless, the Department of Justice was alert to the possibility of a conspiracy to restrict supply and raise prices. Clearly the effect of the antitrust laws under these circumstances was to frustrate the very purpose for which the legislation was enacted[1] and to worsen the impact of the shortfall. Ingrained habits in novel circumstances have pernicious effects.

Let me cite one further illustration. The crude oil equalization tax (COET) provided a mechanism by which the oil industry could have worked its way out of controls over a number of years, and the economy would have simultaneously benefited from moving to world oil prices. Yet the majors were ambivalent about, and the independents resistant to, any compromise on the COET. They (quite naïvely) expected the whole loaf—and felt it was their just due. The ultimate outcome will be the imposition of a windfall profits tax which, instead of fading out by 1985, will probably be permanent. It will prolong de facto regulation and impose a financial burden during the 1980s alone at least four times as great as that of the COET. Putting aside the serious longer term implications, I can only suggest that industry, no less government, must learn the art of timely compromise.

Internationally the American economy now labors under heavy burdens. Its ability to compete has been significantly weakened. One does not need to spend much time recounting the anecdotes and myths one hears traveling abroad. Generally speaking, foreign manufacturers, who in the past were eager to visit American plants, now feel they have little to learn from such visits, although they still believe they have much to learn from the United States in marketing. Nonetheless, in such areas as process engineering, quality control, cost control, and production the United States in all too many industries no longer has a net advantage.

Ill-conceived protectionist devices have impeded the dynamics of adjustment. To cite one horrendous case, quantitative limits on steel imports have resulted both in the erosion of markets for higher quality steel for American producers and in higher costs for American firms that purchase steel.

For the longer term, the basic goals must be a restored ability to compete and a renewed growth of productivity. Admittedly, movement of exchange rates, in principle, should permit adjustment by the American economy to lower rates of productivity growth. But adjustment of exchange rates is inhibited by the position of the American dollar as the key currency—as a store of value as well as a medium of exchange. We must recognize that a steadily eroding dollar, while solving the problem of higher relative inflation and disparate productivity growth, poses even more serious problems for the maintenance of the international financial structure.

The disabilities under which the United States now labors reflect the alteration of the social framework. The resuscitation of the social framework is the task for the next decade. It is, of course, far easier to describe than to reverse major social trends. Nonetheless, the tasks are clear. We should: (1) rebuild government authority; (2) better confine government activities to those roles which are proper and which government can effectively perform; (3) generally restore social discipline; and (4) achieve a far more effective and harmonious relationship between business and government, especially in the international sphere in which there is no adequate substitute for material support.

If we pursue these goals, the competitive position of American industry will improve, and there will be a better balance amongst the various sectors of American industry. Given the trends of recent years, it will require dedication and imagination to achieve these results. Recent experience has scarcely been encouraging. Nonetheless, the United States continues to be the most resilient society on earth. If it is obliged to adjust, I remain confident that it can adjust.

Note

1. One might add that, under conditions of rigorous international competition, neither the antitrust laws nor the conventional data on *domestic* industrial concentration seem particularly relevant from an economic, as opposed to a sociopolitical, point of view.

Summary of Discussion

Robert Gordon set the theme for much of the discussion by asking whether the trend towards increasing regulation of business is a phenomenon particular to the United States economy. He pointed out that growing regulation in America could not be a major explanation of the decline in United States relative competitiveness if the regulatory process is expanding as well in Europe and Japan. James Schlesinger and Walter Wriston emphasized that a distinctive feature of United States regulation is the regulatory maze which confronts businesses on individual business decisions. As an example, Schlesinger cited the welter of agencies and regulatory bodies now overseeing nuclear energy development. David Packard, Wriston, and Ruben Mettler each noted that their companies' experiences demonstrate a special United States penchant for over-regulation. Packard and Mettler speculated that the traditional concern of European governments for their economies' competitiveness in international trade leads them to a more pragmatic approach to regulation. Jack Sawyer and Irving Kristol pointed out that Europe has a long tradition of government intervention in support of business. Sawyer suggested that the United States regulatory tradition reflected instead the populist hostility to railroads and big business that emerged in the late nineteenth century.

Milton Friedman cautioned against laying the blame for over-regulation on government. Most regulations reflect the wishes of individuals, businesses, or other groups trying to use government to pursue particular private ends. He cited our energy regulations as such a case. In the mid-1950s when foreign oil was cheap, the oil industry sought to block its importation. Then in the 1970s when it became expensive, our regulations actually subsidized its importation.

Arthur Okun worried that in the zest to criticize government regulation, many of the benefits of recent regulations might be overlooked. He pointed out that free markets seem to be quite poor at generating appropriate information for consumers, and cited the truth-in-lending and truth-in-advertising legislation as important examples where regulations have helped to deliver important market information.

Richard Caves took up a second issue raised by Wriston's commentary: whether the increase in information flows following the "information revolution" has harmed economic performance. Caves said that the issues of over-regulation and information are not as closely linked as Wriston argues. While the computer technology may make greater regulation feasible, the example of many poor countries throughout the world demonstrates that extensive regulation does not depend on computer technology. Caves stressed that the new methods of information processing also have a marked positive effect on market efficiency by allowing businesses to take more rapid, accurate decisions.

References

Caves, Richard. 1977. *American industry: Structure, conduct, performance.* 4th ed. Englewood Cliffs: Prentice-Hall.

Caves, Richard E., and Uekusa, Masu. 1976. *Industrial organization in Japan.* Washington, D.C.: Brookings Institution.

Caves, R. E.; Porter, M. E.; and Spence, M. 1980. *Competition in the open economy.* Cambridge: Harvard University Press.

Chandler, Alfred D., Jr. 1962. *Strategy and structure.* Cambridge: M.I.T. Press.

————. 1977. *The visible hand.* Cambridge: Harvard University Press.

Collins, Norman, and Preston, Lee. 1961. The size and structure of the largest industrial firms, 1909–1958. *American Economic Review* 51 (December): 986–1011.

Comanor, William S., and Wilson, Thomas A. 1979. Advertising and competition: A survey. *Journal of Economic Literature* 17 (June): 453–76.

Dansby, R. E., and Willig, R. D. 1979. Industry performance gradient indexes. *American Economic Review* 69 (June): 249–60.

Galbraith, John Kenneth. 1952. *American capitalism: The concept of countervailing power.* Boston: Houghton Mifflin.

Goldschmid, Harvey, et al., eds. 1974. *Industrial concentration: The new learning.* Boston: Little Brown.

Guth, Louis A.; Schwartz, Robert A.; and Whitcomb, David K. 1976. The use of buyer concentration ratios in tests of oligopoly models. *Review of Economics and Statistics* 58 (November): 488–92.

Harberger, Arnold C. 1954. Monopoly and resource allocation. *American Economic Review* 44 (May): 77–87.

Kamerschen, David R. 1966. An estimate of the 'welfare losses' from monopoly in the American economy. *Western Economic Journal* 4 (Summer): 221–37.

Kamien, Morton I., and Schwartz, Nancy L. 1975. Market structure and innovation: A survey. *Journal of Economic Literature* 13 (March): 1–37.

Laffer, Arthur B. 1969. Vertical integration by corporations, 1919–1965. *Review of Economics and Statistics* 51 (February): 91–93.

Mermelstein, David. 1969. Large industrial corporations and asset shares. *American Economic Review* 59 (September): 531–41.

Mueller, Willard F., and Hamm, Larry G. 1974. Trends in industrial market concentration 1947 to 1970. *Review of Economics and Statistics* 56 (November): 511–20.

National Science Foundation. 1978. *Research and development in industry, 1976.* Washington, D.C.: National Science Foundation.

Nelson, Ralph L. 1959. *Merger movements in American industry, 1895–1956.* Princeton: Princeton University Press.

Nutter, G. Warren. 1951. *The extent of enterprise monopoly in the United States: 1899–1939.* Chicago: University of Chicago Press.

Penn, David W. 1976. Aggregate concentration: a statistical note. *Antitrust Bulletin* 21 (Spring): 92–98.

Scherer, F. M. 1980. *Industrial market structure and economic performance.* 2d ed. Chicago: Rand McNally.

Shepherd, William G. 1964. Trends of concentration in American manufacturing industries, 1947–1958. *Review of Economics and Statistics* 46 (May): 200–212.

Steiner, Peter O. 1975. *Mergers: Motives, effects, policies.* Ann Arbor: University of Michigan Press.

Stigler, George J. 1951. The division of labor is limited by the extent of the market. *Journal of Political Economy* 59 (June): 185–93.

Stonebraker, Robert J. 1979. Turnover and mobility among the 100 largest firms: An update. *American Economic Review* 69 (December): 968–73.

Tucker, Irvin B., and Wilder, Ronald P. 1977. Trends in vertical integration in the U.S. manufacturing sector. *Journal of Industrial Economics* 26 (September): 81–94.

U.S. Bureau of the Census. 1975. *Census of manufactures, 1972, concentration ratios in manufacturing.* Special Report Series MC72 (SR)–2. Washington, D.C.: Government Printing Office.

U.S. Bureau of the Census. 1978. *Statistical abstract of the United States, 1978.* Washington, D.C.: Government Printing Office.

Vaccara, Beatrice, and Simon, Nancy. 1968. Factors affecting the postwar industrial composition of real product. In *The industrial composition of income and product*, ed. John W. Kendrick, Studies in Income and Wealth, no. 30, pp. 19–58. New York: National Bureau of Economic Research.

Wilkins, Mira. 1970. *The emergence of multinational enterprise: American business abroad from the colonial era to 1914.* Cambridge: Harvard University Press.

8 Technology and Productivity in the United States

1. Edwin Mansfield
2. Ruben F. Mettler
3. David Packard

1. Edwin Mansfield

8.1 Introduction

Technology consists of society's pool of knowledge concerning the industrial, agricultural, and medical arts. It is made up of knowledge concerning physical and social phenomena, knowledge regarding the application of basic principles to work in the relevant fields or professions, and knowledge of the rules of thumb of practitioners and craftsmen. Although the distinction between science and technology is imprecise, it is important. Science is aimed at understanding, whereas technology is aimed at use. At the outset, it is worth noting that changes in technology often take place as a consequence of inventions that depend on no new scientific principles. Indeed, until the middle of the nineteenth century, there was only a loose connection between science and technology.

The fundamental and widespread effects of technological change are obvious. Technological change has permitted the reduction of working hours, improved working conditions, provided a wide variety of extraordinary new products, increased the flow of old products and added a great many dimensions to the life of our citizens. Its contribution to American economic growth has been very important, as evidenced by Denison's (1962) estimate that about 40 percent of the total increase in national income per person employed during 1929–57 was due to "advance of knowledge."

Edwin Mansfield is professor of economics at the University of Pennsylvania.

My thanks go to Zvi Griliches and Richard Nelson, who commented on a preliminary draft of this paper.

At the same time, technological change also has its darker side. Advances in military technology have enabled modern nation-states to cause human destruction on an unprecedented scale; modern technology has contributed to various kinds of air and water pollution; and advances in industrial technology have sometimes resulted in widespread unemployment in particular occupations and communities. Despite the many benefits that society has reaped from technological change, no one would regard it as an unalloyed blessing. (For example, see National Commission on Technology, Automation, and Economic Progress [1966].)

8.2   Productivity Growth in the United States

Economists and policy makers have long been interested in productivity—the ratio of output to input. The simplest measure of productivity is output per hour of labor, often called labor productivity. Clearly, changes in labor productivity are of fundamental significance, since they are intimately related to, but by no means synonymous with, changes in a country's standard of living. The rate of technological change is one determinant of the rate of growth of labor productivity. Other important determinants of the rate of labor productivity growth are the extent to which capital is substituted for labor, economies of scale, changes in the utilization of productive capacity, and changes in the rate of diffusion of new techniques.

A somewhat more complicated measure of productivity is the total productivity index, which has the advantage that it takes account of both capital and labor inputs. Specifically, this index equals $q \div (zl + vk)$, where q is output (as a percentage of output in some base period), l is labor input (as a percentage of labor input in some base period), k is capital input (as a percentage of capital input in some base period), z is labor's share of the value of output in the base period, and v is capital's share of the value of the output in the base period. Substituting values of q, l, and k over a given period into this formula, one can easily calculate the value of the index for that period.

Labor productivity in the United States has not increased at a constant rate. The rate of growth of output per man-hour was significantly higher after World War I than before and significantly higher after World War II than before. Specifically, based on Kendrick's (1976) figures, the trend rate of growth of real output per man-hour was almost 2.5 percent for the three decades prior to 1948 (after adjustment for the effect of the Great Depression), as compared with over 3 percent from 1948 to 1973. This increase in the rate of growth of labor productivity seems to have been due to a faster increase in real capital per man-hour during 1948–73 than during 1919–48.

During 1966–79, however, there was a notable slowdown in the rate of increase of both output per man-hour and total productivity. Table 8.1 compares the rate of increase of productivity between 1966 and 1973 (both business-cycle peaks) with that during 1948–66. Output per man-hour increased by about 2.3 percent per year during 1966–73, as compared with 3.4 percent per year during 1948–66. Total productivity increased by less than 2 percent per year during 1966–73, as compared with 2.5 percent per year during 1948–66. In most industry divisions (and particularly in electric and gas utilities), there was a fall in the rate of increase of output per man-hour.

Since 1973 the rate of productivity increase in the United States has been even lower than during 1966–73. According to the Council of Economic Advisers (1979), output per man-hour increased by 1.0 percent during 1973–77, as compared with 2.3 percent during 1965–73. And between 1977 and 1978, it increased by only 0.4 percent. According to unpublished data that John Kendrick has made available to me, total productivity in manufacturing fell sharply from 1973 to 1974 and was only slightly higher in 1975 than in 1974. By 1976 it was not much above its 1973 value.

Table 8.1   **Productivity Trends in the United States Private Domestic Economy, 1948–73**

	Average Annual Percentage Rates of Change		
	1948–66	1966–69	1969–73[a]
Total Productivity	2.5	1.1	2.1
Real Product per Man-Hour:			
Private domestic economy	3.4	1.7	2.9
Agriculture	5.6	6.7	5.3
Mining	4.6	1.8	0.2
Contract construction	2.0	0	−0.5
Manufacturing	2.9	2.7	4.5
durable goods	2.8	2.2	—
nondurable goods	3.2	3.4	—
Transportation	3.7	2.2	4.5
Communications	5.5	4.6	4.1
Electric and gas utilities	6.1	4.4	1.0
Trade	2.9	2.1	2.3
wholesale	3.1	3.0	—
retail	2.7	1.0	—
Finance, insurance, and real estate	2.1	−0.4	0.2
Services	1.2	0.4	1.0

Source: Kendrick 1976.
[a]Preliminary.

What factors are responsible for this significant slackening of United States productivity growth? According to Kutscher, Mark, and Norsworthy (1977) of the Bureau of Labor Statistics, one of the major factors has been the increase in the proportion of youths and women in the labor force. Output per man-hour tends to be relatively low among women and among new entrants into the labor force. During the late 1960s, women and new entrants increased as a proportion of the labor force. Based on the Bureau's calculations, this change in labor force composition may have been responsible for 0.2 to 0.3 percentage points of the difference between the average rate of productivity increase in 1947–66 and that in 1966–73. George Perry (1971), in his analysis of the causes of the slowdown, agrees that this factor was important.

A second factor that has been cited in this regard is the rate of growth of the capital-labor ratio. During 1948–73, relatively high rates of private investment resulted in a growth of the capital-labor ratio (net nonresidential capital stock divided by aggregate hours worked in the private nonfarm sector) of almost 3 percent per year. After 1973, relatively low rates of investment resulted in the growth of the capital-labor ratio by only about 1.75 percent per year. According to the Council of Economic Advisers (1979), this reduction in the rate of growth of the capital-labor ratio may have reduced the rate of productivity increase by up to 0.5 percentage points per year. Christensen, Cummings, and Jorgensen (forthcoming), in their study of this topic, also emphasize the decrease in the rate of growth of the capital-labor ratio.

A third factor that has been cited in this regard is increased government regulation. A variety of new types of environmental, health, and safety regulations have been adopted in recent years. Because reduced pollution, enhanced safety, and better health are generally not included in measured output, the use of more of society's resources to meet these regulations is likely to result in a reduction in measured productivity growth. Also, the litigation and uncertainty associated with new regulations may discourage investment and efficiency, and the form of the regulations sometimes may inhibit socially desirable adaptations by firms. According to the Council of Economic Advisers (1979), the direct costs of compliance with environmental health and safety regulations may have reduced the growth of productivity by about 0.4 percentage points per year since 1973.

A fourth factor, cited by John Kendrick (1976) and others, is the reduction in the rate of increase of intangible capital due to the decrease in the proportion of gross national product devoted to research and development (R & D) during the late 1960s and early 1970s. In section 8.3 of this paper, we shall look closely at the changes over time in the level of R & D expenditures in the United States. For now, it is enough to say that United States R & D expenditures decreased, as a percentage of gross national product, from 3.0 percent in 1964 to 2.2 percent in 1978.

A fifth factor, cited by William Nordhaus (1972) and others, is the shift of national output toward services and away from goods. However, there is considerable disagreement over whether this shift in the composition of national output is responsible for much of the productivity slowdown. Michael Grossman and Victor Fuchs (1973), among others, are skeptical of this proposition.

Edward Denison (1978b) has carried out a particularly detailed investigation of the causes of the productivity slowdown. Table 8.2 shows his estimates of the sources of the growth of national income per person employed (NIPPE). According to these estimates, the advance of knowledge was responsible for 1.4 percentage points of the annual growth rate of NIPPE during 1948–69, and 1.6 percentage points of the annual growth rate of NIPPE during 1969–73. The effects of other factors, such as changes in the characteristics of the labor force, changes in

Table 8.2   Sources of Growth of National Income per Person Employed, Nonresidential Business Sector

Item	1948–69	1969–73	1973–76	Change from 1948–69 to 1973–76
Growth Rate of NIPPE	2.6	1.6	−0.5	−3.1
Effect of Irregular Factors	−0.1	−0.5	0.1	0.2
Adjusted Growth Rate	2.7	2.1	−0.6	−3.3
Changes in Labor Characteristics:				
Hours of work	−0.2	−0.3	−0.5	−0.3
Age-sex composition	−0.1	−0.4	−0.3	−0.1
Education	0.5	0.7	0.9	0.4
Changes in Capital and Land per Person Employed:				
Structures and equipment	0.3	0.2	0.2	−0.1
Inventories	0.1	0.1	0.0	−0.1
Land	0.0	−0.1	0.0	0.0
Improved Allocation of Resources[a]	0.4	0.1	0.0	−0.4
Changes in Legal and Human Environment[b]	0.0	−0.2	−0.4	−0.4
Economies of Scale	0.4	0.4	0.2	−0.2
Advances of Knowledge (and Not Elsewhere Classified)	1.4	1.6	−0.7	−2.1

Source: Denison 1978.

Note: Detail may not add to totals due to rounding.

[a]Includes only gains due to the reallocation of labor out of farming and out of self-employment in small nonfarm enterprises.

[b]Includes only effects on output per unit of input of costs incurred to protect the physical environment and the safety and health of workers, and of costs of crime and dishonesty.

capital and land per person employed, and economies of scale, are also estimated in table 8.2.

According to Denison, there was a sharp decline in NIPPE during 1974 and 1975. Such declines were without precedent in the period since World War II. Because of them, the 1973–76 rate of growth of NIPPE was negative (−0.5 percent). When the 1948–69 period is compared with the 1973–76 period, the adjusted rate of growth of NIPPE fell by 3.3 percentage points (from 2.7 percent to −0.6 percent). Denison's findings indicate that 0.4 percentage points of this decline were due to the use of more resources to meet pollution, safety, and health regulations (and to prevent crime). Another 1.2 percentage points of this decline were attributable to six factors: (1) a steeper drop in working hours, (2) an accelerated shift in the age-sex composition of employed labor, (3) a slower growth of fixed capital per worker, (4) a slower growth of inventories per worker, (5) reduced gain from resource reallocation, and (6) reduced gain from economies of scale. Of course, many of these factors have already been cited in earlier paragraphs of this section.

Denison concludes that 2.1 percentage points of the 3.3 point drop in the growth rate of NIPPE remain in the residual called "advances in knowledge and not elsewhere classified." To some extent, this may be due to a slowdown in the rate of technological change and in the rate of innovation. Much more will be said on this score in later sections of this paper. Also, the fact that 1974 and 1975 were the years when big oil price hikes first took effect suggests that their effects may be reflected in the residual. Some observers attribute a substantial proportion of the drop in the rate of productivity increase to the quadrupling of oil prices. Others, like Denison, do not seem to believe that this factor can explain a substantial portion of the decline in the growth rate of NIPPE. The truth is that there is considerable uncertainty regarding the contribution of various factors to the observed productivity slowdown.

8.3 Research and Development

Research and development, as defined by the National Science Foundation, includes activities of three kinds. First, there is basic research, which is "original investigation for the advancement of scientific knowledge . . . which do[es] not have immediate commercial objectives."[1] For example, an economist who constructs an econometric model, without any particular application in mind, is performing basic research. Firms carry out some basic research, but it is a small percentage of their R & D work. Second, there is applied research, which is research that is aimed at a specific practical payoff. For example, a project designed to determine the properties of a new polymer that a chemical firm plans to introduce would be applied research. The dividing line between basic and applied research is unclear at best. The distinction is based on the purpose of the project, applied research being done to promote specific practical and commercial aims, basic research being done to obtain new knowledge for its own sake.

Finally, there is development, which tries to reduce research findings to practice. Major development projects attempt to bring into being entirely new processes and products. Minor development projects attempt to make slight modifications of existing processes and products. Frequently, prototypes must be designed and constructed or pilot plants must be built. The dividing line between research and development often is hazy. Research is oriented toward the pursuit of new knowledge, whereas development is oriented toward the capacity to produce a particular product. The outcome of research is generally more uncertain than the outcome of development. Nonetheless, in development there often is considerable uncertainty regarding cost, time, and the profitability of the result.

To estimate the effects on aggregate output or productivity of the aggregate amount spent on R & D, economists have used econometric techniques to estimate the relationship between output, on the one hand, and labor, capital, and R & D, on the other. Results obtained during the 1960s provide reasonably persuasive evidence that R & D has had a significant effect on the rate of productivity increase in the industries that have been studied. Minasian (1969) and Mansfield (1968a) found that, in chemicals and petroleum, a firm's rate of productivity growth was directly related to its expenditures on R & D. Minasian's results indicated about a 50 percent marginal rate of return from R & D in chemicals. Mansfield's results indicated that the marginal rate of return from R & D was about 40 percent or more in the oil industry, and about 30 percent in chemicals if technical change was capital embodied (but much less if it was disembodied). In agriculture, Griliches (1964) found that, holding other inputs constant, output was related in a statistically significant way to the amount spent on research and extension. Evenson (1968), using time series data, estimated the marginal rate of return from agricultural R & D at about 57 percent.

More recently, Griliches (forthcoming), using data for almost nine hundred manufacturing firms, found that the amount spent by a firm on R & D was directly related to its rate of productivity growth. The private rate of return from R & D was about 17 percent (higher in chemicals and petroleum, lower in aircraft and electrical equipment). Terleckyj's (1974) findings suggest about a 30 percent rate of return from an industry's R & D based only on the effects on its own productivity. Also, his results show a very substantial effect of an industry's R & D on productivity growth in other industries. This, of course, is eminently reasonable since one industry's R & D often results in improved machines and inputs to be used by other industries.

Mansfield (1980) found that there is a direct relationship between the amount of basic research carried out by an industry or firm and its rate of productivity increase when its expenditures on applied R & D are held constant. Whether the relevant distinction is between basic and applied research is by no means clear: basic research may be acting to some extent as a proxy for long-term R & D. Holding constant the amount spent on applied R & D and basic research, an industry's rate of productivity increase during 1948–66 seemed to be directly related to the extent to which its R & D was long term.[2]

The National Science Foundation has published data for many years concerning the amount spent by industry, government, universities, and others on research and development. Table 8.3 shows total R & D expenditures in the United States from 1953 to 1979. Clearly, R & D expenditures grew very rapidly in the 1950s and early 1960s. In 1953 total R & D spending was about $5 billion, or about 1.4 percent of gross national product. By 1964 total R & D spending was about $19 billion, or about 3.0 percent of gross national product. Industry, impressed by the wartime accomplishments of science and technology, increased its R & D spending greatly. So did the federal government, which poured particularly large sums into defense and space R & D.

Table 8.3   **Expenditures on Research and Development, United States, 1953–79 (Billions of Dollars)**

Year	Total R & D Expenditures (Current Dollars)	Total R & D Expenditures (1972 Dollars)	Industry R & D Expenditures (1972 Dollars)	Government R & D Expenditures (1972 Dollars)
1953	5.1	8.7	3.8	4.7
1955	6.2	10.1	4.1	5.8
1957	9.8	15.1	5.3	9.4
1959	12.4	18.3	6.0	11.9
1961	14.3	20.7	6.9	13.4
1963	17.1	23.9	7.6	15.7
1965	20.1	27.0	8.8	17.5
1967	23.2	29.4	10.3	18.2
1969	25.7	29.6	11.5	17.2
1971	26.7	27.9	11.3	15.6
1973	30.4	28.8	12.2	15.5
1975	35.2	27.7	12.1	14.6
1977	42.9	28.2	12.9	14.3
1979[a]	52.4	32.0	15.1	15.8

Source: National Science Foundation 1976; 1977; 1979a.
[a]Preliminary estimate.

The industries that were the leading performers of R & D were aircraft and missiles, electrical equipment, chemicals, motor vehicles, and machinery. These industries accounted for over 80 percent of all R & D performed by industry in 1960, and they continued to do so in 1974. However, it is important to recognize that much of the R & D they performed was (and is) financed by the federal government. During 1964 the government financed about 90 percent of the R & D in the aircraft industry, about 60 percent of the R & D in the electrical equipment industry, about 25 percent of the R & D in the machinery and motor vehicles industries, and about 20 percent of the R & D in the chemical industry. Table 8.4 shows the intersectoral transfer of funds for R & D in 1976.

In the late 1960s, due partly to the tightening of federal fiscal constraints caused by the Vietnam War, federal expenditures on R & D (in 1972 dollars) decreased. From $18.2 billion in 1967, they·fell to $14.5 billion in 1974. Much of this reduction was due to the winding down of the space program and the reduction (in constant dollars) of defense R & D expenditures. During 1975–78, there once again were increases in constant dollars in federal R & D expenditures. The biggest percentage increase occurred in expenditures for energy R & D, which increased (in current dollars) from $1.2 billion in 1975 to $2.9 billion in 1978.

Industry's expenditures on R & D (in 1972 dollars) increased during 1967–78 but at a much slower rate than in 1960–67. In 1960, industry's R & D expenditures (in 1972 dollars) were $6.6 billion; in 1967,

Table 8.4   Intersectoral Transfers of Funds for Research and Development, United States, 1976 (Billions of Dollars)

Sources of Funds	Performers					
	Federal Government	Industry	Universities and Colleges	FFRDCs[a]	Other Nonprofit Institutions	Total
Federal Government	5.6	10.2	2.5	1.1	0.8	20.2
Industry	—	16.3	0.1	—	0.1	16.5
Universities and Colleges	—	—	0.8	—	—	0.8
Other Nonprofit Institutions	—	—	0.3	—	0.3	0.6
Total	5.6	26.5	3.7	1.1	1.2	38.1

Source: National Science Foundation 1976.

[a]Federally funded research and development centers. These are organizations exclusively or substantially financed by the federal government to meet a particular requirement or to provide major facilities for research and training purposes. Those that are administered by industry (such as Oak Ridge National Laboratory or Sandia Laboratory) or nonprofit institutions (such as the Rand Corporation) are included in the respective totals for industry or nonprofit institutions.

they were $10.3 billion; in 1978, they were $14.1 billion. The slower rate of increase since 1967 may have reflected a stabilization or decline of the profitability of R & D. In the chemical and petroleum industries, Mansfield's (1979) results suggest such a change in the profitability of R & D. Also, Beardsley and Mansfield (1978) found, in a study of one of the nation's largest firms, that the private rate of return from its investments in new technology tended to be lower during the late 1960s and early 1970s than during the early 1960s.

The nation's total R & D expenditures (including government, industry, and others), when inflation is taken into account, remained essentially constant from 1966 to 1977. The constant dollar figures are very crude, since the National Science Foundation uses the GNP deflator to deflate R & D expenditures. But it seems to be generally accepted that no appreciable increase in real R & D expenditures took place during this period. As a percentage of gross national product, R & D expenditures fell from about 3.0 percent in 1964 to about 2.2 percent in 1978. This decline occurred almost continuously from 1964 to 1978, each year's percentage generally being lower than the previous year's.

Besides declining as a percentage of gross national product, R & D expenditures seem to have changed in character during the late 1960s and the 1970s. Mansfield (1979), in a survey of over one hundred firms accounting for about one-half of all industrial R & D expenditures in the United States, found that the proportion of company financed R & D expenditures devoted to basic research declined between 1967 and 1977 in practically every industry (Nason, Steger, and Manners 1978 came to essentially the same conclusion). In the sample as a whole, the proportion fell about one-fourth, from 5.6 percent in 1967 to 4.1 percent in 1977.

In four-fifths of the industries, based on a rough measure of the perceived riskiness of projects, there was also a decline between 1967 and 1977 in the proportion of R & D expenditures devoted to relatively risky projects. In metals, chemicals, aircraft, drugs, and rubber this reduction was quite large. In some industries, such as aircraft, chemicals, metals, and rubber there was also a substantial decline in the proportion of R & D expenditures devoted to relatively long-term projects. But in other industries, such as drugs, there was an increase in this proportion.

When asked why they reduced the proportion of their R & D expenditures going for basic research and relatively risky projects, the reason most frequently given by the firms was the increase in government regulations, which they felt had reduced the profitability of such projects. Another reason was that breakthroughs were more difficult to achieve than in the past, because the field has been more thoroughly worked over. Still another reason, emphasized by Nason, Steger, and Manners (1978), is that management has changed its view of how R & D should be managed. In the 1950s and early 1960s, firms frequently did not try to manage R & D in much detail. When some of the results turned out to be disappointing, many firms began to emphasize control, formality in R & D project selection, and short-term effects on profit. The shift in emphasis has tended to reduce the proportion of R & D expenditures going for basic and risky projects. Although there is general agreement that a greater emphasis on detailed management was justified, many observers wonder whether the pendulum may have swung too far.

8.4   Scientific and Engineering Personnel

Engineers and scientists, although they are by no means the sole source of advances in technology, play an important role in bringing about such advances and in fostering their utilization and acceptance. Since World War II, there have been three quite distinct‧periods with regard to the employment of engineers and scientists. The first period, from about 1950 to 1963, was marked by rapid growth of jobs for engineers and scientists. As shown in table 8.5, the employment of engineers and scientists grew by over 6 percent per year, which was far in excess of the rate of growth of total nonfarm employment. In part, this rapid increase was due to increases in defense activities and in the space program. During this period there were many complaints of a shortage of engineers (see Cain, Freeman, and Hansen 1973 and Hansen 1967).

The second period, from about 1963 to 1970, saw the employment of engineers and scientists grow at about the same rate as total nonfarm employment. The employment of scientists grew more rapidly than the employment of engineers, because there was a relatively rapid increase in college enrollments and research programs. The relatively slow rate of increase of engineering employment reflected cutbacks in defense programs and space exploration, among other things.

The third period, from about 1970 to 1974, was marked by a very slow growth of scientific and engineering employment. Whereas total

Table 8.5   **Average Annual Percentage Change in Scientific, Engineering, and Total Nonfarm Employment, 1950–63, 1963–70, and 1970–74**

Type of Employment	1950–63	1963–70	1970–74
Scientists	7.0	4.8	1.4
Engineers	6.5	2.5	0.3
Scientists and Engineers	6.6	3.2	0.7
Nonfarm Wage and Salary Workers	1.7	3.3	2.5

Source: National Science Foundation 1977.

nonfarm employment grew by 2.5 percent per year, the employment of engineers and scientists grew by 0.7 percent per year. (Indeed, between 1970 and 1972, there was a decline of twenty thousand persons in engineering employment.) In considerable part, this was due to a slower growth (or curtailment) of college enrollment, R & D expenditures, and defense activities—particularly in aircraft and related products.

Unemployment rates for scientists and engineers have tended to be very low. During the 1960s, the unemployment rate for these workers was below 1 percent. But in 1971, due partly to the cutbacks in defense spending and some R & D programs, the unemployment rate for scientists and engineers rose to about 3 percent. By 1973, it fell below 1 percent once again. However, in 1975, the unemployment rate for engineers increased to 2.6 percent, due to the recession.

Most engineers and scientists are employed by industry. Over one million were employed in the industrial sector in the mid-1970s, as compared with about three-hundred thousand in universities and colleges, and about two-hundred thousand in the federal government. Table 8.6 shows the allocation of industry's labor force among various work activities. About 37 percent of the scientists and 26 percent of the engineers are involved in R & D or R & D management. However, this does not mean that the others do not play an important role in the process by which technology is developed and applied. The interface between R & D and the rest of the firm is of fundamental importance in determining the rate of innovation, as Freeman (1974), Mansfield et al. (1977a), and others have indicated. Production engineers, sales engineers, and other non-R & D engineers and scientists play a significant part in the innovation process.

An important characteristic of the nation's engineers is their age. Many studies suggest that engineers, particularly those engaged in research and development, tend to experience a reduction in creativity

Table 8.6   **Percentage Distribution of Industry's Scientific and Engineering Labor Force, by Primary Work Activity, 1974**

Primary Work Activity	Scientists	Engineers	Scientists and Engineers
R & D and R & D Management	37	26	29
Management of Non-R & D Activities	15	20	19
Production and Inspection	13	17	16
Design	1	18	14
Computer Applications	19	2	6
Other Activities	15	17	16
Total	100	100	100

Source: National Science Foundation 1977.

after the age of thirty-five or forty, due in part to obsolescence of knowledge. Given the slowdown in the rate of growth of the engineering labor force, one would expect that the proportion of engineers that are young has declined. To see how big this decline has been, Brach and Mansfield (1979) obtained detailed data from six major firms in the aerospace, chemical, and petroleum industries. The results show that the percentage of engineers under thirty-four years decreased from 51 percent in 1960 to 30 percent in 1974, and that the percentage under forty-three years decreased from 78 percent in 1960 to 56 percent in 1974. When the sample was expanded to include eighteen firms in the aerospace, electronics, chemical, and petroleum industries, similar results were obtained. If, as some claim, the rate of innovation in the United States has been slowing down, it is conceivable that this "graying" of industry's engineers may be partly responsible.

Given the slowdown in the demand for engineers, it is not surprising that the percentage of bachelor's (and first professional) degrees awarded in engineering declined continually and significantly between 1960 and 1975. In 1960, engineering degrees were 10 percent of the total; in 1975, they were 4 percent of the total. The percentage of bachelor's (and first professional) degrees in the physical and environmental sciences fell from 4 percent in 1960 to 2 percent in 1975. (In contrast, the percentage in the social sciences increased from 8 percent in 1960 to 14 percent in 1975.) Turning from undergraduates to graduate students, enrollments for advanced degrees in science and engineering decreased from 38 percent of all advanced degree enrollment in 1960 to 25 percent in 1975. And according to the National Science Foundation (1979c), a sizable proportion of the doctoral labor force in science and engineering may have to obtain jobs outside science and engineering in 1982 and 1987.

8.5   Patents and Innovations

The number of patents is sometimes used as a crude index of the rate of invention in a given field during a particular period of time. Used in this way, patent statistics have important disadvantages. For one thing, the average importance of the patents granted at one time and place may differ from those granted at another time and place. For another, the proportion of the total inventions that are patented may vary significantly. Nonetheless, it is worthwhile examing the patent statistics at least briefly.

Table 8.7 shows the changes over time in the number of United States patents granted. The number of patents granted to United States residents rose during the 1960s, reached a peak in 1971, and was about 20 percent lower in 1976 than in 1971. When patents are broken down by

Table 8.7   **United States Patents Granted to United States Residents, by Year of Grant, 1960–76**

Year	Number of Patents (Thousands)	Year	Number of Patents (Thousands)
1960	39.5	1969	50.4
1961	40.2	1970	47.1
1962	45.6	1971	56.0
1963	37.2	1972	51.5
1964	38.4	1973	51.5
1965	50.3	1974	50.6
1966	54.6	1975	56.7
1967	51.3	1976	44.3
1968	45.8		

Source: National Science Foundation 1977.

product field, the results are much the same. For example, the number of patents on electrical equipment, instruments, and communication equipment all reach a peak in 1971. In some product fields, such as machinery and fabricated metals, the peak is reached in the late 1960s. In chemicals, it is reached in 1972. One problem with the data in table 8.7 is that they are influenced by changes over time in how rapidly patent applications are processed.

The number of patents granted is a measure of inventive activity in a previous period, since roughly two years are taken by the Patent Office to process and examine a patent application. To correct for this, table 8.8 shows the number of patents by year of application. There is much less year-to-year fluctuation in the number of patents when application dates rather than grant dates are used. And, as would be expected, the peak patenting rate now occurs in 1969 rather than 1971. When the data are broken down by product field, the results are surprisingly uniform. In machinery, fabricated metals, and electrical equipment, the peak is in 1966; in communication equipment and chemicals, it is in 1969; and in instruments, it is in 1971. In practically all of the fifty-two product fields for which data are available, the patent rate declined during the 1970s. The only exceptions are in drugs, agricultural chemicals, and motorcycles, bicycles, and parts.

From the economist's point of view, innovation is often more relevant than invention. Innovation is generally defined as the first commercial introduction of a new or improved process or product. The rate of innovation depends heavily on the quality of a nation's industrial managers and the way its firms and industries are organized, as well as on the tax laws, regulatory considerations, and a host of other factors influencing the profitability and riskiness of innovative activity. Successful innovation requires a great deal more than the establishment of an R & D laboratory that turns out a lot of good technical output. In many industries, the bulk of the innovations are not based to any significant extent on the firms' R & D. And even in those industries where R & D is important, one of the crucial problems is to effect a proper coupling between R & D, on the one hand, and marketing and production, on the other. Unless this coupling is effective, R & D can be of little use.

To measure the rate of innovation, counts have sometimes been made of the number of major new processes or products introduced in particular periods of time. For example, in the pharmaceutical industry, the number of new chemical entities per year is often used for this purpose. Measures of this sort have important problems. For one thing, it frequently is difficult to find suitable weights for different innovations. (Clearly, all are not of equal importance.) For another thing, such measures overlook the small innovations, which sometimes have a bigger cumulative effect than some of the more spectacular innovations. (For evidence on this score in petroleum and synthetic fibers, see Enos 1958 and Hollander 1965.) Nonetheless, it is worthwhile taking a brief look at results based on data of this sort.

In the pharmaceutical industry, the number of new chemical entities per year (excluding salts or esters of previously marketed drugs) declined from an average of about forty during the 1950s to about twenty during the 1950s to about fifteen during the early 1970s. This decline

Table 8.8   **United States Patents Due to United States Inventors, by Year of Application, 1965–73 (Thousands of Patents)**

	1965	1966	1967	1968	1969	1970	1971	1972	1973
All Patents	42.2	45.0	44.1	45.3	46.3	45.6	45.3	41.9	41.6
Food	0.5	0.5	0.5	0.5	0.5	0.6	0.6	0.4	0.4
Textiles	0.4	0.4	0.5	0.5	0.5	0.5	0.5	0.4	0.3
Chemicals	5.8	6.2	6.1	6.1	6.3	6.2	6.1	5.4	4.9
Drugs	0.6	0.7	0.6	0.6	0.7	0.7	0.7	0.7	0.7
Oil and Gas	0.6	0.7	0.7	0.8	0.8	0.8	0.7	0.6	0.6
Rubber	2.3	2.4	2.4	2.3	2.5	2.3	2.3	2.2	1.8
Stone, Clay, and Glass	1.0	1.0	1.0	1.0	1.1	1.1	1.1	1.0	0.9
Primary Metals	0.5	0.5	0.5	0.5	0.5	0.6	0.5	0.5	0.5
Fabricated Metals Products	5.8	6.4	6.2	6.2	6.2	6.1	6.0	5.6	5.1
Machinery	13.3	14.3	13.8	14.0	14.2	13.9	13.9	12.7	11.7
Electrical Equipment	4.8	5.3	5.1	5.2	5.1	5.1	4.8	4.5	4.3
Communications and Electronics	5.2	5.4	5.1	5.2	5.7	5.5	5.3	5.0	4.7
Transportation Equipment	2.2	2.6	2.5	2.7	2.6	2.6	2.7	2.5	2.5
Aircraft	0.5	0.7	0.7	0.7	0.8	0.7	0.7	0.7	0.7
Instruments	4.5	4.6	4.7	4.8	5.0	5.1	5.2	4.8	4.7

Source: National Science Foundation 1977.
Note: Most of these patents were assigned to United States corporations.

has caused considerable controversy. The drug industry charges that it is due in considerable measure to new government regulations. Others attribute it, at least in part, to the fact that the field is more thoroughly worked over than it was shortly after World War II, and that it has become increasingly difficult and costly to make major advances. As pointed out by Grabowski (1976) and others, available estimates indicate very substantial increases during the 1960s in the costs of developing a new drug.

Counts of innovations have also been used to indicate changes over time in the nature of major innovations introduced by United States firms. The National Science Foundation (1977) reports a study of 277 major innovations marketed by United States manufacturing firms that tried to rate how radical each innovation was. In 1953–59, 36 percent of the innovations were rated as radical breakthroughs (rather than as major technological shifts, improvements, or imitations), as contrasted with 26 percent in 1960–66 and 16 percent in 1967–73. Although the results are of interest, ratings of this sort should be viewed with considerable caution.

8.6   The Diffusion of Innovations

How rapidly productivity increases in response to an innovation depends on the rate of diffusion—the rate at which the use of the innovation spreads. Diffusion, like the earlier stages in the creation and assimilation of new techniques and products, is essentially a learning process. However, instead of being confined to a research laboratory or a few firms, the learning takes place among a considerable number of users and producers. In the United States, how rapidly does the diffusion process go on? According to the available data, it takes about five to ten years, on the average, before one-half of the major firms in an industry begin using an important technique. And in many cases it takes longer. The rate of imitation varies widely (Mansfield 1968b).

To explain the differences among innovations in the rate of imitation, Mansfield (1968a) suggested a simple model that assumes that the probability that a nonuser will use the innovation between time t and time $t+1$ is dependent on the proportion of firms already using the innovation, the profitability of using the innovation, and the investment required to install the innovation. Mansfield tested this model against data for over a dozen innovations in five industries, the results being quite favorable. Hsia (1973) found that this model provides a good fit to data regarding twenty-six innovations in the plastics, textiles, and electronics industries in Hong Kong. Blackman (1971) found this model to be useful in his studies of the United States aircraft industry. Romeo used a variant of this model in his study (in Mansfield et al. 1977a) of numerically controlled machine tools.

To indicate more specifically how rapidly some major innovations have spread in the period since World War II, table 8.9 shows the increase over time in the percentage of (1) steel output produced by the basic oxygen process, (2) ammonia capacity accounted for by large-scale plants (600 tons per day or more), (3) acrylonitrile output produced from propylene, (4) vinyl chloride capacity that uses the oxychlorination process, and (5) value of discrete semiconductors and receiving tubes accounted for by discrete semiconductors. On the average, it took about eight years before half of the output or capacity was accounted for by these innovations.

At least two studies have been made which shed light on whether or not innovations spread more rapidly than they used to. First, when the

Table 8.9   **Rates of Diffusion of Five Major Innovations in the United States**

Year	% Steel Produced by Basic Oxygen Process	% United States Ammonia Capacity: Large-Scale Plants	% Acrylonitrile Produced from Propylene	% Vinyl Chloride Capacity Using Oxy-chlorination	Discrete Semiconductor Output as Percentage of Output of Semiconductors and Receiving Tubes
1953	—	—	—	—	7.4
1954	—	—	—	—	8.0
1955	—	—	—	—	9.5
1956	—	—	—	—	18.8
1957	—	—	—	—	27.4
1958	1.6	—	—	—	—
1959	2.0	—	—	—	51.4
1960	3.4	—	9.1	—	60.9
1961	4.0	—	11.2	—	63.3
1962	5.6	—	15.3	—	64.2
1963	7.8	—	22.0	—	68.2
1964	12.2	—	32.6	—	71.5
1965	17.4	2.5	46.0	32.0	76.1
1966	25.3	6.2	59.5	40.0	79.0
1967	32.6	20.1	86.0	—	81.4
1968	37.1	41.7	88.9	56.0	82.3
1969	42.6	58.3	89.7	70.0	—
1970	48.2	58.8	94.7	—	—
1971	53.1	63.1	100.0	81.0	—
1972	56.0	—	—	83.0	—
1973	55.2	—	—	—	—
1974	56.0	79.2	—	—	—

Source: Mansfield 1977.

profitability of the innovation and the size of the investment required to introduce the innovation are held constant in Mansfield's study, there is an apparent tendency for the rate of diffusion to increase over time. However, this tendency was very weak. The time interval between 20 percent adoption and 80 percent adoption decreased, on the average, by only about four-tenths of 1 percent per year. Further, this observed tendency could easily have been due to chance.

Second, in the case of chemicals, a study (reported in Mansfield et al. 1977a) of the diffusion of twenty-three major processes was carried out by Simon. His results indicate that an innovation's rate of diffusion is affected by the profitability of the innovation to users and by whether or not the firms that imitated the innovator used its process or invented around it. Holding both of these variables constant, there is a tendency for the rate of imitation to be higher for more recent innovations. Moreover, this tendency is statistically significant. Also, holding other factors constant, there seems to be a tendency for new chemical products to be imitated more rapidly than was the case a number of years ago.

Thus, what evidence we have points to an acceleration, rather than a slowdown, in the rate of diffusion. In part, this has probably been due to the growth of more effective mechanisms to transmit and evaluate technical information. For example, the engineering literature is more extensive and detailed, and evaluation techniques are more sophisticated. Turning to international comparisons, the United States seemed to be a leader in accepting some of the innovations in table 8.9. For example, this was the case for semiconductors. But with respect to the basic oxygen process in steel, a number of other countries had a faster rate of acceptance than the United States.

8.7 America's Technological Lead

To understand the changes in America's technological position in the postwar period, it is necessary to compare United States technological capabilities with those in other countries. Based on international comparisons of total productivity and on data indicating which countries have developed and exported new and improved products, there appears to have been a substantial gap between European and American technology. Thus, Denison (1967) concluded that productivity differences between Europe and the United States could not be explained fully by differences in capital per worker, education, or other such variables. And Vernon (1966) and Hufbauer (1970) have demonstrated that, to a large extent, American exports have been in new products which other countries have not yet produced.

This gap does not seem to be new. The available evidence, which is fragmentary, suggests the existence of such a gap in many technological areas prior to 1850. After 1850, total productivity seemed higher in the United States than in Europe, the United States had a strong export position in technically progressive industries, and Europeans tended to imitate American techniques. American inventors were enormously productive during the nineteenth century, and the United States held a technological lead in many major areas of manufacturing.

The technology gap received considerable attention in the 1960s, when many Europeans claimed that superior technology had permitted American firms to get large shares of European markets in such areas as aircraft, space equipment, computers, and other electronic products. In response to the Europeans' concern, the Organization for Economic Cooperation and Development (OECD) carried out a major study (1968) of the nature and causes of the technology gap. The study concluded that a large gap existed in computers and electronic components, but that no general or fundamental gap existed in drugs, bulk plastics, iron and steel, machine tools (other than numerically controlled machine tools), nonferrous metals (other than tantalum and titanium), and scientific instruments (other than electronic test and measuring instruments).

The longstanding technological lead enjoyed by the United States has undoubtedly been due to a variety of factors—such as the favorable social and business climate in the United States, our competitive system, and the values of the American people. According to the OECD studies, the size and homogeneity of the United States market has been an important factor but not a decisive one. Also, the bigness of American firms is considered to be another factor but not a decisive one. Further, the large government expenditures on R & D in the United States have been credited with an important role. In addition, according to the OECD studies, American firms have had a significant lead in managerial techniques, including those involved in managing R & D and in coupling R & D with marketing and production.

More recently, American analysts and policy makers have expressed increasing concern that the United States technological lead is being reduced and in some areas eliminated. At least three types of evidence have been adduced. First, as shown in table 8.10, the percentage increase in American labor productivity has been smaller than in Japan, Germany, France, or the United Kingdom. In Japan, output per man-hour grew by 290 percent during 1960–76, as compared with about 60 percent in the United States. Christenson, Cummings, and Jorgenson (forthcoming) have estimated that the rate of increase of total productivity during 1960–73 was lower in the United States than in Canada, France, Germany, Italy, Japan, Korea, the Netherlands, or the United Kingdom. Although the level of productivity in other countries still tends to be lower than in the United States, results of this kind have been interpreted as evidence of a decline in the American technological lead.

Table 8.10   **Output per Man-Hour in Manufacturing, Selected Countries, 1960–76 (1967 = 100)**

Country	1960	1962	1964	1966	1968	1970	1972	1974	1976
United States	78.8	84.5	95.2	99.7	103.6	104.5	116.0	114.7	122.4
France	68.7	75.2	83.7	94.7	111.4	121.2	135.9	146.1	153.6
Germany	66.4	74.4	84.5	94.0	107.6	116.6	130.3	145.6	162.4
Japan	52.6	61.9	75.9	87.1	112.6	146.5	163.9	187.5	204.6
United Kingdom	76.8	79.3	89.7	95.7	106.9	109.1	121.2	127.9	125.4
Canada	75.5	83.9	90.9	97.2	107.3	115.2	127.4	132.3	137.4

Source: National Science Foundation 1977.

Second, as shown in table 8.11, R & D expenditures as a percentage of gross national product have increased in Japan, Germany, and the Soviet Union, while they have decreased in the United States. But this evidence should be treated with caution. Although the percentage of gross national product devoted to R & D has increased in these countries relative to the United States, the United States percentage is still higher than any country other than the Soviet Union, where the figures are not comparable (and probably inflated relative to ours). Also, as we shall see in the following section of this paper, much of the industrial R & D in some major foreign countries is done by United States-based multinational firms. One-half of the industrial R & D in Canada and one-seventh of the industrial R & D in Germany and the United Kingdom were carried out by United States-based firms in the early 1970s. And more fundamentally, a nation's rate of economic growth depends on how effectively it uses both foreign and domestic technology, and this may not be measured at all well by its ratio of R & D spending to gross national product.

Third, the National Science Foundation (1977) has reported a study which indicates that the United States originated about 80 percent of

Table 8.11   **Expenditures on R & D as a Percentage of Gross National Product, Selected Countries, 1961–75**

Country	1961	1963	1965	1967	1969	1971	1973	1975
United States	2.74	2.87	2.92	2.91	2.75	2.50	2.33	2.32
France	1.38	1.53	1.99	2.16	1.96	1.87	1.73	1.48
Germany	—	1.40	1.72	1.97	2.02	2.36	2.22	2.25
Japan	—	—	1.55	1.55	1.71	1.88	1.92	—
United Kingdom	2.69	—	—	2.69	2.63	—	—	—
Canada	1.01	0.95	1.17	1.33	1.34	1.25	1.11	—
USSR	—	2.37	2.40	2.55	2.62	2.85	3.19	3.18

Source: National Science Foundation 1977.

the major innovations in 1953–58, about 67 percent of the major innovations in 1959–64, and about 57 percent of the major innovations in 1965–73. Without knowing more about the way in which the sample of innovations was drawn, it is hard to tell whether the apparent reduction in the proportion of innovations stemming from the United States is due to the sampling procedures. Also, some attempt might have been made to weight these innovations. Nonetheless, taken at face value, the results suggest a reduction in the United States technological lead.

8.8   International Technology Transfer

In recent years, the international transfer of technology has become of intense interest to analysts and policy makers. A firm can use various channels to transfer its new technology abroad. It can export goods and services that are based on the new technology. Or it can use the new technology in foreign subsidiaries. Or it can license the new technology to other firms, government agencies, or other organizations that utilize it abroad. Or it can engage in joint ventures with other organizations, which have as an objective the utilization of the new technology abroad.

International technology transfer accounts for a substantial proportion of the returns from R & D carried out by United States firms. Based on a study of thirty major firms, Mansfield, Romeo, and Wagner (1979) found that about 30 percent of the returns from these firms' 1974 R & D were expected to come from foreign sales or foreign utilization. During the first five years after the commercialization of the technology, foreign subsidiaries (rather than exports, licensing, or joint ventures) were expected to be the principal channel of transfer in about 70 percent of the cases (table 8.12). This is noteworthy because, according to the tradi-

Table 8.12   **Percentage Distribution of R & D Projects, by Anticipated Channel of International Technology Transfer, First Five Years after Commercialization, Twenty-three Firms, 1974**

Category	Channel of Technology Transfer				
	Foreign Subsidiary	Exports	Licensing	Joint Venture	Total
All R & D Projects:					
Sixteen industrial firms	85	9	5	0	100
Seven major chemical firms	62	21	12	5	100
Projects Aimed at:					
Entirely new product	72	4	24	0	100
Product improvement	69	9	23	0	100
Entirely new process	17	83	0	0	100
Process improvement	45	53	2	1	100

Source: Mansfield, Romeo, and Wagner 1979.

tional view, the first channel of international technology transfer often is exports. Only after the overseas market has been supplied for some time by exports would the new technology be transferred overseas via foreign subsidiaries according to this view.

To some extent, these results seem to reflect an increased tendency for new technology to be transferred directly to overseas subsidiaries, or a tendency for it to be transmitted more quickly to them (in part because more such subsidiaries already exist). Such tendencies have been noted in the drug industry, where many new products developed by United States drug firms have been introduced first by their subsidiaries in Britain and elsewhere. Also, Baranson (1976), based on twenty-five case studies, concludes that American firms of various types are more willing than in the past to send their most recently developed technology overseas. And Davidson and Harrigan (1977) have shown that United States firms introduce their new products in foreign markets much sooner than they used to (table 8.13), and that foreign subsidiaries are used more frequently (and licensing is used less frequently) as a channel of transfer than used to be true.

Mansfield and Romeo (in press) gathered data concerning sixty-five technologies to see whether the proportion of transferred technologies that were less than five years old (at the time of transfer) was greater during 1969–78 than during 1960–68. For technologies transferred to subsidiaries in developed countries, this was the case, and the increase in this proportion (from 27 percent in 1960–68 to 75 percent in 1969–78) was both large and statistically significant. But for technologies transferred to subsidiaries in developing countries or for those transferred through channels other than subsidiaries, there appeared to be no such tendency, at least in this sample. The fact that the technologies licensed to, or jointly exploited with, non-United States firms were no newer in 1969–78 than in 1960–68 is worth noting, since some observers

Table 8.13   **Percentage of New Products Introduced Abroad within One and Five Years of Introduction in the United States, 1945–75**

Period	Number of New Products	Percentage Introduced Abroad	
		Within One Year	Within Five Years
1945–50	161	5.6	22.0
1951–55	115	2.6	29.6
1956–60	134	10.4	36.6
1961–65	133	24.1	55.6
1966–70	115	37.4	60.1
1971–75	75	38.7	64.0

Source: Davidson and Harrigan 1977.

worry that United States firms may have come to share in this way more
and more of their newest technologies with foreigners.

In general, the evidence suggests that the rate of international diffusion of technology has tended to increase. Because of better communication and transportation techniques, as well as other factors, such an
increase is quite understandable. Cooper (1972) has presented some
evidence to this effect. Also, the OECD studies (1968) of the technology gap come to the same conclusion. One of the most recent studies of
this topic was by Schwartz (1979), who investigated the international
diffusion of fifteen plastics innovations, thirteen semiconductor innovations, and nine drug innovations. Holding other factors constant, he
found that the diffusion rate tended to be higher for more recent innovations in each industry, although this tendency was statistically significant only in plastics.

According to the National Science Foundation (1977), data concerning United States receipts and payments of licensing fees and royalties
can be used as an indicator of the amount of know-how transferred by
the United States, as well as the direction of the technology flows.
Tables 8.14 and 8.15 present the latest data published by the National
Science Foundation. According to these figures, the United States received about $3.5 billion from foreign affiliates and about $800 million
from unaffiliated foreign residents in 1975, and paid about $200 million
to foreign affiliates and about $200 million to unaffiliated foreign resi-
dents. Based on tables 8.14 and 8.15, American receipts and payments
of this sort more than tripled during 1966–75, and those to unaffiliated
foreign residents more than doubled during this period.

These figures, while interesting, suffer from many defects. For one
thing, payments of this sort between affiliated firms are influenced by tax
and other considerations. For another, much technology is transferred
internationally without payment because the technology is not patented,
because firms in one country copy (without payment) features of new
products or processes originating in another country, and so on. Nonetheless, tables 8.14 and 8.15 can be used to support at least two important propositions. First, it seems clear that the international transfer of
technology is a large and rapidly growing business. Second, it seems
clear that multinational firms play a very important role in the international transfer of technology.

Studies by Baranson (1976), Caves (1971), Hufbauer (1970), OECD
(1968), Tilton (1971), and others show in much more detail the major
role played by multinational firms in the international transfer of technology. As would be expected, the preponderant flow of technology has
been out of the United States. In recent years, with the trend toward
increased foreign direct investment in the United States, some observers
have worried that such investment might result in foreign firms gaining

Table 8.14 United States Receipts and Payments of Royalties and Fees for Unaffiliated Foreign Residents, 1966–75 (United States Dollars in Millions)

	1966	1967	1968	1969	1970	1971	1972	1973	1974	1975 (preliminary)
Net Receipts										
Total	353	393	437	486	573	618	655	712	751	759
Developed countries	304	342	375	426	505	547	575	633	646	644
Western Europe	186	190	196	222	247	268	270	297	321	343
Canada	30	33	31	28	33	32	38	32	38	37
Japan	70	95	130	155	202	223	240	273	249	227
Other developed countries[a]	18	24	18	21	23	24	27	31	38	37
Developing countries	50	50	59	59	64	62	72	74	94	105
Eastern Europe		1	4	2	4	9	8	5	11	9
Net Payments										
Total	76	104	106	120	114	123	139	176	186	192
Developed countries	72	100	102	116	107	119	134	166	176	184
Western Europe	67	93	94	107	99	110	121	146	156	168
Canada	2	3	4	4	4	5	6	6	7	7
Japan	3	4	4	4	4	4	6	13	12	8
Developing countries	4	3	4	5	7	4	5	9	8	7
Eastern Europe							1	1	2	1

Source: National Science Foundation 1977.

Note: Table represents receipts and payments between United States residents with residents or governments of foreign countries for the use of intangible property such as patents, copyrights, or manufacturing rights. Excludes fees and royalties related to United States foreign direct investments. Excludes film rentals.

[a]Other developed countries included here are Australia, New Zealand, and the Republic of South Africa.

Table 8.15 United States Receipts and Payments of Royalties and Fees for Direct Investment Abroad, 1966-75 (United States Dollars in Millions)

	1966	1967	1968	1969	1970	1971	1972	1973	1974	1975 (preliminary)
Net Receipts[a]										
Total	1,162	1,354	1,431	1,533	1,758	1,927	2,115	2,513	3,071	3,526
Developed countries	854	982	1,027	1,101	1,289	1,429	1,609	1,949	2,389	2,740
Western Europe	496	579	594	651	755	848	971	1,180	1,428	1,722
Canada	246	266	285	287	336	355	377	416	541	566
Japan	43	55	59	66	80	96	114	170	211	231
Other developed countries[b]	69	83	88	97	118	131	147	183	209	221
Developing countries	279	352	377	398	428	452	453	519	631	734
International and unallocated	29	20	27	34	40	46	53	46	51	52
Net Payments[c]										
Total	64	62	80	101	111	118	155	209	212	241
Canada	41	43	47	56	62	64	60	73	83	89
United Kingdom	12	11	21	25	19	11	15	20	16	10
Other European countries	10	8	9	16	23	39	78	113	111	140
Other countries	1	1	3	4	7	4	2	2	2	1

Source: National Science Foundation 1977.

[a]Represents net receipts of payments by U.S. firms from their foreign affiliates for the use of intangible property such as patents, techniques, processes, formulas, designs, trademarks, copyrights, franchises, manufacturing rights, and management ties.

[b]Other developed countries included here are Australia, New Zealand, and the Republic of South Africa.

[c]Payments measure net transactions between U.S. affiliates and their foreign patents. Affiliated payments are not further detailed because in many cases the amounts are too small or would disclose individual company data.

access to important United States technology. According to the National Academy of Engineering (1976), access to American technology is less important than many other factors in prompting such investment.

Another important development in the postwar period has been the growth of overseas R & D by United States-based multinational firms. During the 1960s and early 1970s, the percentage of total company-financed R & D expenditures carried out overseas grew substantially. By the middle 1970s, it had risen to almost 10 percent. (Table 8.16 presents data for fifty-five firms.) According to Mansfield, Teece, and Romeo (1979), much of this R & D is aimed at the special design needs of overseas markets. It tends to be predominantly development rather than research, and aimed at product and process modification rather than at entirely new products or processes.

Firms differ considerably in the extent to which they have integrated their overseas R & D with their domestic R & D. Some firms, such as the IBM Corporation, have integrated their R & D activities on a worldwide basis. Such worldwide integration existed in about half of the firms studied by Mansfield, Teece, and Romeo. Most overseas R & D seems to have some commercial applicability to the firms' United States operations. According to the firms studied by Mansfield, Teece, and Romeo, a dollar's worth of overseas R & D seems to result in benefits to these firms' domestic operations that are equivalent to about fifty cents of R & D carried out in the United States.

Some groups, such as the AFL-CIO, have pressed for measures to regulate the international transfer of technology to prevent our advanced technology from becoming available to competitors in other nations. Thus, in 1971, the AFL-CIO suggested that "the President [be given] clear authority to regulate, supervise, and curb licensing and patent agreements on the basis of Congressionally determined standards."[3] Economists generally seem to have been rather skeptical of such proposals to interfere with the international diffusion of technology. It would be very difficult to stem the diffusion of technology, and even if it could be done, it would invite retaliation. Technology flows both into and out of the United States, and there are mutual benefits from international specialization with respect to technology.

Table 8.16	Percentage of Company-Financed R & D Expenditures Carried out Overseas, 1960–74, Fifty-five Firms				
	1960	1965	1970	1972	1974
Thirty-five-Firm Subsample	2	6	6	8	10
Twenty-Firm Subsample	—	—	4	—	9

Source: Mansfield, Teece, and Romeo 1979.

In addition, if United States firms could not transfer and utilize their technology abroad, they would not carry out as much research and development, with the result that our technological position would be weakened. According to results obtained by Mansfield, Romeo, and Wagner (1979), public policy makers should not assume that decreased opportunities for international technology transfer would have little or no effect on United States R & D expenditures. On the contrary, if United States firms could not transfer their new technology to their foreign subsidiaries, the result might well be a 10 or 15 percent drop in their R & D expenditures.

Some groups have also pressed for government support of R & D in industries where our technological lead seems to be declining. The international competitiveness of particular American industries will depend in the long run on the government's policies with respect to science and technology, but this does not mean that government support for science and technology should be focused on industries experiencing problems in meeting foreign competition. As pointed out in the next section of this paper, whether or not more R & D should be supported or encouraged in a particular industry depends on the extent of the social payoff from additional R & D there, not on whether or not our technological lead there seems to be declining.

8.9 Public Policies toward Civilian Technology

The federal government finances about half of the research and development in the United States. During the 1950s and 1960s, over 80 percent of the government's R & D expenditures went for military and space projects. During the 1970s, this percentage fell to about 63 percent. Federal expenditures on civilian R & D (notably health, energy, environment, transportation, and communication) have increased considerably as a percentage of the total, as shown in table 8.17. This is a noteworthy shift in the composition of federal R & D expenditures.

The rationale for government support of R & D varies from one area of support to another. National security and space exploration, for example, are public goods—goods where it is inefficient (and often impossible) to deny their benefits to a citizen who is unwilling to pay the price. For goods of this sort, since the government must take the primary responsibility for their production, it must also take primary responsibility for the promotion of technological change in relevant areas. Of course, such R & D results in a beneficial spillover to the civilian sector, but the benefits to civilian technology seem decidedly less than if the funds were spent directly on civilian technology.

Market failure of some kind is the rationale for large federally financed R & D expenditures in other areas. In energy, for example, it has been claimed that the social returns from energy R & D exceed the private returns due to the difficulties faced by firms in appropriating the social benefits from their R & D. Further, it has been argued that risk aversion on the part of firms may lead to an underinvestment (from society's point of view) in energy R & D. Also, the availability of energy is often linked to our national security.

As shown in table 8.17, some federally financed R & D is directed toward the general advance of science and technology. Expenditures of this sort seem justified because the private sector will almost certainly invest less than is socially optimal in many of the most fundamental types of research, because the results of such research are unpredictable and frequently of relatively little direct value to the firm supporting the research, although potentially of great value to society as a whole.

Besides its financing of R & D, the federal government influences and supports civilian technology in a variety of other ways. The patent laws, the tax laws, federal regulatory policies, the antitrust laws, and government policies toward education—all have an impact on the rate of technological change. And in the period since World War II, all have been the subject of considerable and widespread debate. At present, much of this debate has surfaced in connection with the Domestic Policy Review on Industrial Innovation, discussed below.

For a variety of reasons, a number of economists, such as Arrow (1962), Griliches (1972), Mansfield (1976), and Nelson, Peck, and Kalachek (1967), have suggested that there may be an underinvestment in civilian R & D in the United States. Because R & D is characterized by substantial external economies, riskiness, and indivisibilities, such a tendency might be expected in a competitive economy. However, on

Table 8.17   **Percentage Distribution of Federal R & D Obligations, by Function, 1969–78**

Function	1969	1972	1974	1976	1978
National Defense	53.5	53.9	51.3	49.1	48.7
Space	23.9	16.4	14.2	13.3	13.1
Health	7.2	9.6	12.0	11.0	11.2
Energy	2.1	2.3	3.5	7.5	11.8
Environment	2.0	3.2	4.0	4.5	3.4
Science and Technology Base	3.3	3.6	4.0	4.0	4.0
Transportation and Communications	2.9	3.7	4.0	3.3	2.9
Natural Resources	1.3	2.1	2.0	2.3	a
Food and Fiber	1.4	1.8	1.7	1.9	1.9
Other	2.5	3.4	3.3	3.1	3.0
Total	100.0	100.0	100.0	100.0	100.0

Source: National Science Foundation 1977; 1978; 1979b.
a Included with environment.

a priori grounds alone, one cannot demonstrate conclusively that this is true in the brand of mixed capitalism found at present in the United States. A number of empirical studies (some of which are cited in section 8.3) have been carried out to estimate the social rate of return from R & D. In general, the results indicate that the marginal social rate of return has been very high, which seems to suggest that some underinvestment may in fact exist. However, existing studies are rough and should be viewed with caution.

To illustrate, Mansfield et al. (1977b) estimated the social and private rates of return from the investments in seventeen industrial innovations, most of them run-of-the-mill advances in the state of the art. The median social rate of return was over 50 percent, while the median private rate of return was 25 percent. In five of these cases, the expected private rate of return was less than 15 percent (before taxes), which indicates that they were quite marginal from the point of view of the firm. Yet their average social rate of return was over 100 percent. This study was replicated by both Nathan Associates and Foster Associates, and the results of their studies are in accord with those given above.

The federal government has made a number of proposals and efforts to stimulate civilian technology. In 1963 the Department of Commerce proposed a Civilian Industrial Technology program to encourage and support additional R & D in industries that it regarded as lagging. It proposed that support be given in important industries, from the point of view of employment, foreign trade, and so forth, which have "limited or dispersed technological resources." Examples cited by the department included textiles, building and construction, machine tools and metal fabrication, lumber, foundries, and castings. The proposal met with little success on Capitol Hill. Industrial groups opposed the bill because they feared that government sponsorship of industrial R & D could upset existing competitive relationships.

In 1972, former President Nixon, in his special message to the Congress on science and technology, established three programs related to federal support of civilian R & D. One was an analytical program at the National Science Foundation to support studies of barriers to innovation and the effects of alternative federal policies on these barriers. This program (the R & D Assessment Program) has provided a substantial addition to fundamental knowledge in this area, and is now part of the Foundation's Division of Policy Research and Analysis. The other two programs, one at the National Science Foundation and one at the National Bureau of Standards, were to be experimental programs to determine effective ways of stimulating innovation. Both of the latter programs no longer exist in their original form, although elements of them remain.

In 1978 and 1979, the federal government carried out a Domestic Policy Review on Industrial Innovation. The Industry Advisory Subcommittee involved in this Review prepared draft reports on (1) federal procurement, (2) direct support of R & D, (3) environmental, health, and safety regulations, (4) industry structure, (5) economic and trade policy, (6) patents, and (7) information policy. These drafts were discussed and criticized by the Academic and Public Interest Subcommittees involved in the review. Further, the Labor Subcommittee presented a report, as did each of a large number of government agencies. The overall result was a large and far-flung effort to come up with policy recommendations.

One theme that ran through the Industry Subcommittee's reports was that many aspects of environmental, health, and safety regulations deter innovation. As pointed out in previous sections, there is a strong feeling that this is the case in a number of industries, although it is recognized that we lack very dependable or precise estimates of the effects of particular regulatory rules on the rate of innovation. However, the recommendations of the Industry Subcommittee with respect to regulatory changes were met with considerable hostility by the Labor and Public Interest Subcommittees.

Another theme found in some of the Industry Subcommittee's reports was that tax credits for R & D expenditures should be considered seriously. Although this mechanism to encourage civilian technology has the advantage that it would entail less direct government control than some of the other possible mechanisms, it would reward firms for doing R & D that they would have done anyway, it would not help firms that have no profits, and it would be likely to encourage the same kind of R & D that is already being done (rather than the more radical and risky work where the shortfall, if it exists, is likely to be greatest). A tax credit for increases in R & D would get around some of these difficulties, but the problem of defining R & D remains. As might be expected, the Treasury Department is particularly concerned about this definitional problem.

In October 1979, President Carter put forth a number of proposals, based on the Domestic Policy Review. He asked Congress to establish a consistent policy with respect to patents arising from government R & D, and advocated exclusive licenses for firms that would commercialize inventions of this sort. He asked the Justice Department to write guidelines indicating the conditions under which firms in the same industry can carry out joint research projects without running afoul of the antitrust laws. Also, to reduce regulatory uncertainties, he asked environmental, health, and safety agencies to formulate a five-year forecast of what rules they think will be adopted.

In addition, President Carter proposed a new unit at the National Technical Information Service to improve the transfer of technology from government laboratories to private industry, and he proposed that the National Science Foundation and several other agencies expand an existing program of grants to firms and universities that carry out collaborative research. He also asked that a program to support innovative small businesses (currently under way at the National Science Foundation) be expanded by $10 million in 1981. And he proposed that government procurement policies put more stress on performance standards rather than specific design specifications.[4]

Although this program may have many beneficial effects, it is hard to believe that it can have a very major impact on the nation's technological position. As its principal architects are the first to admit, it is only a first step. This exercise, like its predecessors in previous administrations, demonstrates that it is not easy to formulate an effective, equitable, and politically acceptable program. Further attempts will almost certainly be made. In formulating future proposals, it seems to be generally agreed that any program should be neither large-scale nor organized on a crash basis, that it should not be focused on helping beleaguered industries, that it should not get the government involved in the latter stages of development work, that a proper coupling should be maintained between technology and the market, and that the advantages of pluralism and decentralized decision-making should be recognized (Mansfield 1976).

Finally, the emergence of technology assessment during the 1960s should be noted. As public awareness of environmental problems grew, more and more emphasis was placed on the costs (such as air and water pollution) associated with technological change in the civilian economy. Policy makers became increasingly interested in technology assessment, which is the process whereby an attempt is made to appraise the technical, political, economic, and social effects of new technologies. In 1972, Congress created the Office of Technology Assessment to help it anticipate, and plan for, the consequences of the uses of new technology. Unfortunately, it is notoriously difficult to forecast the future development and impact of a new technology, and technology assessment has proved very hard to carry out.

Also, the effects of the energy crisis on United States technology policy should be cited. Between 1974 and 1977, federal R & D obligations for energy development and conversion increased at an annual rate of over 50 percent. Between 1977 and 1978, they increased at an annual rate of over 20 percent. Many aspects of the government's R & D policies in the energy area have been controversial. In 1979 one of the biggest issues was whether the government should grant massive subsidies to fund the commercialization of synthetic fuels. As Pindyck (1979), Stobaugh and Yergen (1979), and others have pointed out, there are very considerable problems with some of these proposals. In November 1979, the Senate approved a $19 billion program to develop a synthetic fuels industry.

8.10   Summary and Conclusions

During the thirty-five years that have elapsed since World War II, at least eight very important changes have taken place in American productivity and technology. First, the rate of productivity increase, which was relatively high up until about 1966, fell somewhat during 1966–73 and then took a nosedive in the mid-1970s. Some of this decline can be attributed to changes in the composition of the labor force, reductions in the rate of growth of the capital-labor ratio, and increasingly stringent pollution, safety, and health regulations. But most of the decline during the mid-1970s cannot be explained in this way. To some extent, it may have been due to the disruptions caused by the quadrupling of oil prices and the double-digit inflation of the mid-1970s. To some extent, it may have been due to a slowdown in the rate of innovation. The unfortunate truth is that we do not know how much of the decline is due to each of these factors.

Second, R & D expenditures in the United States increased at a relatively rapid rate until the middle 1960s, after which they remained relatively constant in real terms. After 1967, federal R & D expenditures decreased, due in large part to reductions of space and defense programs, while industry's R & D expenditures increased, but at a much slower rate than before 1967. As a percentage of gross national product, R & D expenditures fell from 3.0 percent in 1964 to 2.2 percent in 1978. Also, there was a substantial decline between 1967 and 1977 in the proportion of company financed R & D expenditures devoted to basic and relatively risky projects. These developments are important because a variety of econometric studies indicate that an industry's or firm's rate of productivity increase is related significantly to the amount it spends on R & D. Also, holding constant the amount spent on R & D, an industry's rate of productivity increase during 1948–66 seemed to be directly related to the extent to which its R & D was long term.

Third, the employment of scientists and engineers grew relatively rapidly from 1950 to 1963, less rapidly from 1963 to 1970, and very slowly from 1970 to 1974. In many major firms, the engineering labor force is much older than in 1960. The percentage of bachelor's (and first professional) degrees awarded in engineering and in the physical and environmental sciences decreased considerably between 1960 and 1975.

Fourth, when patents are classified by date of application, the peak patenting rate for United States residents occurred in 1969, after which it declined. In practically all of the fifty-two product fields for which data are available, the patent rate declined during the 1970s. The only exceptions are in drugs, agricultural chemicals, and motorcycles, bicycles, and parts. Counts of innovations seem to indicate that in some industries, notably pharmaceuticals, the rate of innovation declined during the 1970s. Also, there is some evidence that the percentage of United States innovations that are radical breakthroughs tended to decrease during the 1960s and 1970s.

Fifth, when other factors are held equal, the available evidence indicates that there may have been an increase in the rate of diffusion of innovations. New processes tend to spread more rapidly from firm to firm and to replace old processes more quickly than in the past. Also, there is some evidence that new products are imitated more quickly than in the past. In part, this has probably been due to the growth of more extensive and effective mechanisms to transmit and evaluate technical information.

Sixth, the longstanding technological lead that the United States has maintained in many branches of manufacturing technology seems to be lessening, and in some areas it may no longer exist. Productivity has been increasing less rapidly in the United States than in other major countries since 1960. Rough data seem to indicate a decrease in the proportion of major innovations originating in the United States. Although it is very difficult to make meaningful international comparisons of technology levels, there seems to be widespread concern among policy makers on this score.

Seventh, the rate of international diffusion of technology has tended to increase, due in part to the growth of multinational firms. United States-based firms seemed to transfer newer technology to their overseas subsidiaries more in 1969–78 than in 1960–68. The percentage of R & D carried out overseas has increased considerably, and some major firms organize and integrate their R & D on a worldwide basis. According to a study of thirty major firms, about 30 percent of the returns from these firms' 1974 R & D were expected to come from foreign sales or foreign utilization. And in the bulk of the cases, foreign subsidiaries were expected to be the principal channel of international technology transfer in the first five years after commercialization. Although some groups have pressed for measures to regulate the international transfer of technology, most economists seem to be skeptical of such proposals.

Eighth, the federal government, which supports about half of the R & D in the United States, has reduced the proportion of its R & D going for defense and space, and increased the proportion going for civilian purposes (notably health, energy, environment, transportation, and communication). There is some evidence that there may be an underinvestment in civilian R & D, and that government regulations and policies may have erected unnecessary obstacles to innovation. A series of examinations of United States technology policy has taken place.

Unfortunately, although it is becoming clearer that a variety of problems exists in this area, it is less obvious how much the government can or will do to help solve them. To a considerable extent, this reflects the fact that we know less than is frequently acknowledged concerning the efficacy (and costs) of various policy alternatives that have been proposed.

Finally, it is important to recognize that America's technology policies cannot be separated from its economic policies. Policies which encourage economic growth, saving and investment, and price stability are likely to benefit our technological position. Just as many of our current technological problems can be traced to sources outside engineering and science, so these problems can be ameliorated by policies relating primarily to nontechnological areas. Indeed, the general economic climate in the United States may have more impact on the state of United States technology than many of the specific measures that have been proposed to stimulate technological change.

Notes

1. National Science Foundation, *Methodology of Statistics on Research and Development* (Washington, D.C.: Government Printing Office, 1959), p. 124.

2. When the annual rate of productivity change during 1948–76 is used instead, this relationship no longer exists, but this may be due to the changes over time in the extent to which various industries' R & D have been long term. More work is needed on this point.

3. See A. Biemiller's testimony on 28 July 1971 in *Science, Technology, and the Economy*, Hearings before the U.S. House Subcommittee on Science, Research, and Development (Washington, D.C.: Government Printing Office, 1972), p. 53.

4. Other proposals were made as well. For a more complete account, see *The President's Industrial Innovation Initiatives*, Office of the White House Press Secretary, 31 October 1979.

2. Ruben F. Mettler

Technology: A Powerful Agent for Change

Introduction

An invitation to say a few words about technological changes and their effect on the postwar domestic American economy is certainly a challenge. The subject is rich in opportunity for speculation—and rich in opportunity for error.

Ruben F. Mettler is chairman and chief executive officer of TRW, Inc.

Technological change during the postwar period has been rampant. One need not search far to see powerful and pervasive technological innovations introduced into the economy in recent years, based on fundamental advances in mathematics, physics, chemistry, geology, and biology, and their applications in fields of direct significance to the economy: agriculture and food production; medicine and human health; energy conversion and utilization; transportation; construction and urban development; communications and information processing; instrumentation and control; industrial production; extraction and conversion of raw materials; military development and national security; and earth and space exploration.

Some of the major technological changes have been slow and evolutionary and some have been sudden and dramatic. New scientific and engineering understanding and brilliant inventions only become innovations that significantly influence the economy with the addition of management, capital, marketing, distribution, production, maintenance, and widespread extensions of human skills.

Changes in the American and in the world economy, while heavily influenced by technological change are, of course, more deeply rooted in the world's major political, social, and economic forces, and must be judged and interpreted in the context of:

1. Population growth and the related need for food and shelter and education and jobs, with the resulting pressures on political and social and economic institutions
2. Limitations on the supply and distribution of energy and national resources as well as on related environmental issues
3. Enormous variations in income levels per capita in different parts of the world
4. Dependence on international trade and investment and continuing real economic growth
5. Reconciliation of conflicting cultures and value systems as modern communication and transportation increasingly force them into intimate contact
6. Vulnerability of vital and increasingly complex national and international institutions to disruption by small groups
7. Foreign policy and national security issues related to these major problems in a world possessing nuclear weapons

Rather than discuss technological changes in general terms, I wish to comment on three important changes in our domestic economy which have been heavily influenced by technology during the past thirty years and which are likely to be equally or more important during the next thirty years. In addition, I will comment on a sweeping technological wave of such significance to economic development that it requires special treatment.

I won't comment directly on Edwin Mansfield's excellent background paper on technology and productivity, except to underscore and emphasize his very last paragraph in which he cites the high leverage which sound general policies encouraging economic growth, savings, investment, and price stability have on stimulating technological progress.

International Constraints on Our Domestic Economy

Few changes in the domestic American economy in the postwar period appear to me to be as significant and as inadequately recognized, particularly by national policy makers, as those changes—heavily influenced by technology—which increasingly bind the domestic economy to the rest of the world, and make it a more dependent subelement of a larger and more powerful economic system.

These binding forces exert a discipline on national policy makers by creating significant conflicts between politics and policies which are popular domestically but incompatible with international reality. They force on business executives the recognition that many of their markets are worldwide in scope and that they must compete worldwide to survive in those markets. Some of the puzzles and surprises in postwar domestic economic analysis and modeling may be the result of a preoccupation with internal variables and insufficient recognition of the scope and significance of external international forces on our domestic economy. All of these effects are amplified by our voracious appetite for energy.

Multinational corporations (American and foreign) have been the principal agents for the large increase in international trade in the postwar period and for the dramatic postwar expansion in international investment, credit, and money that now link our domestic economy ever more tightly to the rest of the world.

These linkages and the resulting constraints on our domestic economy have in large part been fashioned by technological changes which are still gaining momentum and may be even more important in the years ahead. Included among the more important technologies working to bind our domestic economy to the rest of the world are those related to agriculture and food production and to finding, producing, transporting, and refining massive quantities of petroleum products. But I'd like to comment today especially on (1) communications and information processing and (2) jet transportation.

In worldwide communications a sudden qualitative change took place in the 1960s when high capacity commercial communication satellites were first launched into orbit. The first such satellite placed in synchronous orbit over the Atlantic provided more communications capacity than all of the transatlantic cables and radio links previously built, at a small fraction of the per-channel cost. In just a few years, satellites equipped with wide-band transmission links came to dominate long distance communication of voice, data, and television to all parts of the globe, at significantly reduced costs.

In parallel with this quick expansion of worldwide communications capacity came the development and volume production of digital computers and related information processing systems, and the rapid development and expansion of the worldwide system of jet transportation.

Communications and computers, backed up by quick and convenient passenger transportation, have been and are essential tools in the international expansion and control of multinational industrial and banking institutions, with their significant effect on the world economy and hence on our domestic economy.

Dramatic Changes in Military Technology

During the postwar period there have been a number of concurrent technological breakthroughs that have dramatically altered the nature and power of military forces. These changes have had a first-order effect not only on the foreign policy of the United States and of its adversaries and allies, but also on the world economy and hence also on our domestic economy. The effects of these changes are now gathering momentum and will be even more significant in the next thirty years.

During the 1950s the almost concurrent development of small nuclear warheads (with unbelievably greater destructive power than even the atomic warheads of the 1940s, which in turn had overshadowed all prior explosives) and large rocket-propelled missiles of intercontinental range, permanently changed the nature and power of strategic military forces. For the first time in history, strategic military forces with the power to completely destroy an industrialized society became an instrument of foreign policy.

During the 1960s and 1970s further development of sensing instruments and control electronics gave these missiles pinpoint accuracy. High accuracy combined with large numbers of missiles and warheads make it possible for an aggressive superpower to aspire to having a first-strike capability able to deliver a knock-out blow, again drastically altering the strategic military equation.

From a position of overwhelming strategic military dominance during the 1950s and early 1960s, the United States followed policies which (it is now widely, though belatedly, recognized) will result in strategic military superiority passing to the Soviet Union during the 1980s, unless vigorous new United States military (nuclear and nonnuclear) development and production programs are initiated and sustained during the next decade. During 1970–78, the Soviet Union spent about $100 billion more (conservatively estimated) on military equipment and facilities and about $40 billion more on military R & D than did the United States. In the crucial category of strategic weapons and R & D, they outspent the United States by more than two to one.

I believe these changes, although difficult to quantify, have already had important effects on our domestic economy in the past several decades and will be even more significant during the next several, particularly when viewed in the context of the increasing vulnerability of our economy to interruption of supplies and our increasing linkage to the world economy and world political forces. If allowed to proceed unchecked, the Soviet Union, under an umbrella of strategic nuclear superiority, could be more aggressive and adventuresome in using conventional military forces and in exerting diplomatic pressure.

Consider first some effects internal to our domestic economy. Even though our military programs have been significantly less aggressive than those of the Soviet Union, they have absorbed federally funded R & D and a significant fraction of industrial technological talent during the 1960s and 1970s, with a resulting penalty to new commercial processes and products and to industrial productivity. As we look to the 1980s, it is now increasingly evident that the United States must step up its military programs or live with Soviet military dominance with all of its unacceptable consequences. In this situation, the negative effects on our domestic economy of large military expenditures will continue and may increase. The Soviet Union, with a smaller and less productive economy than ours and with much larger military programs may also suffer a penalty to domestic productivity and economic strength.

Two of our economic competitors, Germany and Japan, have gained in productivity and relative economic strength in recent decades by holding their military expenditures to a very low level and depending on the United States for strategic military security. Essentially all of their research and development and industrial capacity has been focused on their civilian economy. How significant has this effect been? And what military policies will (or should) they follow during the rest of this century to share in a common defense?

Thinking more broadly, how much of the weakness of the dollar (and the high price of gold) in recent years stems from loss of confidence in the American military capability? What would be the effect on our trading partners, particularly our energy suppliers, if we failed to maintain our position in nuclear and nonnuclear forces? Reasonable political stability is essential to international trade, investment, credit, and economic growth. Hence, should not our foreign policy be more explicitly focused on these matters? Can we get through the next decade without military intervention in the Middle East? How do we cope with almost certain nuclear proliferation to smaller countries, both friendly and unfriendly to the United States?

I have no answer to these questions, but include them because I believe they are too often omitted in considering economic issues and must certainly be included in a discussion of technological development in relation to our domestic economy. There is no reason to believe that technological changes in the military field will stop or slow down. On the contrary, they are more likely to accelerate.

The Next Energy Transition

Few issues have been and will be more important to our domestic economy and to the stability of the world economy than those related to energy supply, utilization, and pricing. During the past thirty years we have gone through an energy transition and during the next thirty years we will go through another.

So much has been written and said (both sense and nonsense) about energy in recent years that one is tempted just to skip it. Yet no serious discussion of technological change and our domestic economy can properly omit energy.

Highly effective technology directly applicable to our major energy issues (both those related to conservation and supply) has been developed during the postwar period. We have the scientific and engineering foundation for significant and much needed improvements in our energy-related technology during the next several decades. Although necessary to a successful energy transition, technology per se is not the real issue. Petroleum-related technology has flourished during the postwar period, but the most startling development is the extent to which our nation has failed to use other available and applicable technology in addressing our major energy needs for conservation and supply and early development of new energy-efficient products. This situation developed in part because economic incentives for its use have been minimal, and disincentives to its use have been actively promoted; and in part because of largely exaggerated fear of unwanted side effects. The failure to permit the price mechanism to function has been particularly noteworthy.

The major energy issue is whether our political, social, and economic institutions (and those of other nations) have the strength and flexibility to adapt to the institutional changes needed, especially those needed to achieve a reasonable definition of the common purpose and the means to work effectively toward achieving it. As the leading industrial nation in the world, one would expect leadership from the United States in this effort.

If man can be defined as "a tool-making animal with foresight" then we have surely failed the test. Even if we make the essential high priority effort to conserve energy and reduce its use per unit of output, energy supply will continue to be central to the growth and efficiency of all industrial economies. For the past ten years, making progress on our energy problems and those of other nations has been regarded as vital to controlling inflation, vital to our national security, essential to economic growth and increased productivity, necessary for protecting our environment, and the only way to achieve a productive and stable foreign policy. If those reasons aren't motivation enough, a few more reasons to pull ourselves together could easily be added.

In the energy field, technological change has been slower than needed, to the detriment of our domestic economy. Future economic growth and improvement in our productivity will depend heavily on stimulating wider and more rapid use of advanced technology in energy.

A Second Industrial Revolution

Developing like a storm during the 1950s, the 1960s, and the 1970s, and now ready to burst forth during the next thirty years is "a second industrial revolution." Its full dimensions are still unclear, but there is no doubt that its scope and power, already highly significant both to our domestic economy and to the world economy, will grow enormously in the years ahead.

The first industrial revolution was heavily based on mechanical engineering in providing tools, machinery, and new sources of power to replace human labor. The second, now developing, is based on a number of concurrent technological changes in the fields of communications and information processing.

Much has been said about the dramatic changes in these fields, but their effects may still be understated. Impressive advances have been taking place simultaneously in a wide range of interrelated technologies, which put together multiply their potential effects on economic development. These interrelated technologies include, listing just a few: transistors, integrated circuits, LSI, microprocessors, VLSI; compact and readily accessible data storage of massive capacity; computers, large and small; digital communication switching and signal processing; advanced programming languages and highly sophisticated programs; satellites as communication stations; audio-visual sensing and displays; word processing and voice coding; optical communication; highly intelligent terminals; and electronic printing. Parallel advances in all of these related aspects of communications and information processing have created an explosion of possible applications.

The 1960s and early 1970s were characterized by a buildup of very large central computing capacity; the late 1970s and 1980s have been and will be characterized by widespread distribution of computing power via communication links to a large number of remote locations, spread through all parts of the economy. Driven by dramatic improvements in performance and very large reductions in costs, there has been an almost explosive demand for more communication and information processing in industrial, financial, government, professional, and educational institutions. (As an example of the dramatic cost reduction, a small computer using a few microprocessors and selling today for about one hundred dollars can outperform a large computer selling for over one million dollars fifteen years ago. Roughly similar cost reductions have occurred in related equipment and systems. By way of perspective, if a corresponding reduction had been made in the price of a Cadillac, you could buy one today for a few dollars.)

In addition to creating new markets and a wealth of new products which have given a boost to economic growth, this new field has made significant contributions to improved productivity. It will be important to our international competitive posture, and a continuing large investment will be needed to maintain our current leadership in these new technologies.

In one sense, synthetic electronic intelligence is being produced and used to extend man's brain—if you like labels, consider "intellectronics." One of the particularly interesting effects of this technology on our economy arises from its potential for both positive and negative effects on how institutions of various types are managed. You heard some comments earlier on some of the negative effects as related to government intervention in our economy. On the positive side, there is a large potential for improving the productivity and profitability of business institutions by effectively using communications and information processing technology. Most studies of productivity underestimate, in my view, the differences in productivity attributable to management skill.

Conclusion

In the context of worldwide political, social, and economic issues, technological change has had a major impact on the domestic American economy during the postwar period and will continue to have a major impact during the next thirty years.

Sound political and economic policies which encourage economic growth, savings, investment, and price stability have high leverage in stimulating technological progress and focusing it on improving productivity and on new markets, products, and related new job opportunities.

Among the most significant changes in the postwar American economy are those which increasingly bind our domestic economy to the rest of the world and make it a more dependent subelement of the larger and more powerful world economic system. This trend has been heavily influenced by technological change. It is given added significance by dramatic changes in military technology and in the relative military strength of the United States and the Soviet Union during the postwar period. It is vital to our national security and our economy that we initiate and sustain vigorous new military (nuclear and nonnuclear) development and production programs during the next decade. The dangers arising from our failure to maintain a proper military posture relative to the Soviet Union have been amplified by our failure to use market incentives to stimulate the use of available technology in addressing our energy needs.

Phenomenal concurrent advances in a wide range of new technologies in the fields of communications and information processing are leading us into "a second industrial revolution" of major importance both to our domestic economy and to the world economy. These changes will reshape some major industries and have significant effects on productivity, on international competitive patterns, and on how both government and business enterprises are managed. Technological change and its effect on our economy should not be expected to slow down. On the contrary, it is more likely to accelerate. Effective use of our scientific and technological resources will be an important, and possibly a crucial, economic issue for the period ahead.

3. David Packard

Productivity and Technical Change

In the two decades that reached from the mid-1940s to the mid-1960s, the United States had a healthy economy, characterized by rapid economic growth and low inflation, and propelled by great technical progress. This technical progress helped general annual increases in productivity in excess of 3 percent and was a major contributor to the overall well-being of the economy.

The economies of Europe and Japan recovered from the destruction of World War II during this period, and by 1965 were growing and achieving annual productivity increases even larger than those in the United States; in the case of Japan alone, productivity was increasing at annual rates of from 6 to 8 percent.

Since about 1970, the rates of improvement in productivity have declined in the major industrial countries of the world, with corresponding declines in the health of their economies from the robust decades following the war. This serious deterioration in the well-being of the free world economy has been of great concern to businessmen, economists, and people in government at many levels. It is difficult to find much to be said that has not already been said about the subject. Yet the problem

David Packard is chairman of the board of the Hewlett-Packard Company.

is so important that it is imperative that the search for answers continue and that action which will improve the situation be identified and undertaken. It seems to be generally agreed among economic scholars, managers, and government executives that improvement in productivity would be helpful in reducing inflation and promoting economic growth.

The productivity of a business enterprise is determined by a number of factors, but the prime influences are management and the application of technological innovation.

Management plays a major role in determining the structure of the organization, influences the quality of supervision, provides training for the workers, and works to motivate employees. There can be significant improvement in productivity from management-directed activity, as shown by the range of productivity that can be measured between well-managed and poorly managed enterprises.

While productivity gains can be made by management leadership that encourages people to work harder and work smarter, technology is the base of most major gains in productivity. The use of better tools, better equipment, and better manufacturing processes is the only way productivity can be improved once management's contribution has been optimized. Even with the handicap of poor management practices, better tools, equipment, and processes will usually improve productivity.

It is not often that one finds a manufacturing facility completely equipped with the latest and most productive tools, machinery, and processes. In the first place, these expensive items are seldom replaced as rapidly as better equipment becomes available. Depreciation policies and inadequate capital generation often limit replacement. Sometimes management strategy does not give the highest priority to productivity improvement, perhaps because the incentives are not right.

Industrial productivity has been higher in Europe and Japan since the war, in part, at least, because new plants employing the most modern equipment were built to replace those destroyed during the war while plants in the United States continued to operate with older, less productive equipment. Also, many of the industries in these countries were playing a catch-up game.

Inflation, coupled with the government's traditional fiscal and tax policies, have made the replacement of older equipment more and more expensive and difficult, although the investment tax credit allowance is a step forward. It is one of the few incentives left to industry to improve productivity through new equipment. A more liberal depreciation policy would also help in the more rapid replacement of older equipment, although to be effective, management would have to place less emphasis on short-term profits.

Nearly every enterprise could improve its productivity by the more extensive use of the newer and more productive equipment that is already available, but the greatest contribution clearly must come from the acceleration of the discovery and the innovative application of new technology. Technology is an important contributor to productivity in areas beyond development of better, more effective equipment and processes. Technology makes its most dramatic contribution to productivity in the creation of entirely new products from which new business enterprises and entirely new industries develop.

The United States has had an outstanding record in being at the forefront of new industry creation throughout the entire twentieth century. Automobiles, aircraft, plastics and chemicals, electronics, communications, and computers are just a few examples of that leadership. Whether the productivity gains that result from new industries based on new technology are properly reflected in the indices we use to measure productivity or not, each of these industries has given us a quantum jump in productivity, however you choose to define it.

The creation of a new industry based on technology requires the innovative application of scientific knowledge to do something that is useful and that needs to be done. The process can involve innovative application of old technology, but the most dramatic examples come from the discovery of new technology. A recent example is the invention of the transistor and related solid-state electronics technology, followed by the development of large-scale integrated circuits.

This new technology has made possible the modern computer industry. Thousands of new products and new business enterprises have been generated in this multi-billion-dollar industry in which again the United States was, and still is, in the lead. Computers have made a considerable contribution to increased productivity throughout industry, although there may be some debate about just how much. The industry itself has achieved productivity gains estimated at 35 percent per year reflected in lower prices and increased performance.

Two ingredients are necessary to make these quantum gains. One is the discovery of new scientific knowledge. The other is the creation of the proper environment, the incentives, and the resources to encourage the innovative application of the new technology to something useful that needs to be done. Both ingredients are necessary to support a productive research and development endeavor.

We often discuss research and development without considering that a very wide range of activities is involved. Research is generally considered to be the search for new knowledge, but more often it involves gaining a better understanding of what is already generally known. Development generally means practical application of scientific knowledge to produce new tools, new processes, and new products. Here, sometimes, research in terms of a search for new knowledge is also needed, and thus no clear line can be drawn between research and development, and indeed they are often linked together.

The worldwide bank of basic scientific knowledge is generally available to scientists and engineers of all nations through widespread publication. Good basic research work is done in the United States, nearly every European country, Japan, and the USSR.

There are some restrictions on the availability of scientific knowledge because of national security considerations, and there is some private control of scientific knowledge, but neither is a serious impediment to the general availability of new scientific knowledge. There is sometimes an advantage to early, and presumably exclusive, access to new knowledge, but is seldom lasts for long.

There has been considerable discussion recently about whether the United States is falling behind in research and development (R & D), but the discussion does not always make a distinction between the discovery of new basic knowledge and the whole host of other activities that goes on under the heading of R & D.

The number of patents issued is often used as an index of the level of R & D, but only a few patents involve new basic knowledge. Most patents involve the use of existing technologies. The number of patents issued may be a general indication of the country's scientific and engineering activity, but this is not a good indication of the level or quality of basic research.

We have by no means used up our basic scientific knowledge. However, common sense tells us we should try to add to scientific knowledge at the same time we utilize what we have. It is never possible to predict a scientific breakthrough to a new field of knowledge. Many times in the past, knowledgeable people have proclaimed that science has already discovered everything that can be discovered, but these forecasters of the future of science have always been proven wrong. New scientific knowledge will bring about the creation of new products and entirely new industries in the future as it has in the past. Furthermore, the payoff will be great, for new scientific knowledge is the cornerstone of technical change. It will continue to contribute to productivity in the future, as it has in the past.

The United States should consider new and more effective ways to increase the level of R & D in domestic industry with particular emphasis on how to encourage a higher level of basic research by industry. We should also look for ways to improve effectiveness of established and continuing federally supported R & D.

One suggestion to encourage an increase in the level of R & D by industry is to allow a federal tax credit for R & D. There is no doubt that the establishment of such a tax credit would encourage management to increase the level of funding and activity. However, unless this credit were established only for increases in R & D above previous levels, we would find that the credit would be used to pay for a great deal of work that would have been done anyway.

Since a substantial part of the cost of R & D is in the instrumentation and equipment required, the investment credit might be increased by an additional percentage, say 10 to 20 percent of cost for machinery and equipment used in R & D. Faster write-off of equipment and facilities used for R & D would also help. There would be some definition problems here, as there would be for tax credits for total or incremental R & D expenditures, but I believe they would be manageable.

Total federal support for R & D is very large, but much of it is for space and defense programs, health, and more recently, energy. These expenditures have had only marginal effect on improving the productivity of the economy.

High-energy physics receives very large federal support, and so far has had very little payout in the areas of productivity, although there has been some. Most solid-state electronics R & D is now funded by private sources, and here the payout in productivity has been tremendous. It will continue to be large in the future. Increased federal funding could be useful in this area, and, in fact, the Department of Defense has plans to put more money into large-scale integrated circuit R & D.

I believe the entire Department of Energy program of support for R & D should be reexamined to make sure all promising areas of basic research are adequately funded. Here the program should be patterned after the brilliant Office of Naval Research (ONR) program established in 1946. This ONR program deserves a great deal of credit for keeping the United States ahead of the world in many areas of technology. Federal support, through the ONR, made it possible for Stanford University to create an outstanding program in electronics in the two decades after the war. Important research work was done in high-frequency vacuum tubes called traveling wave tubes and backward wave oscillators. Later, major contributions to the field of solid-state electronics technology were made at the Stanford laboratories. An outstanding faculty was assembled and fine students were educated. Much of this research and many of the students contributed to the impressive growth of new electronics companies on the San Francisco Peninsula. Stanford could not have made these important contributions in electronics research and education without the funding provided by ONR. The "Silicon Valley" could not have happened without this federal support of Stanford University.

Federal funding of R & D should emphasize basic research, since it has been shown that adequate funding of basic research in all promising areas of technology will have a high payoff over the long run. Development, on the other hand, will be done better by the private business sector.

The imaginative application of scientific knowledge to create new products, new business enterprises, and new industries is called innovation. The economic and social climate of the United States has fostered innovation from the early days of the Republic. Yankee ingenuity it was called in the nineteenth century. The combination of pioneering attitudes, unlimited risk capital, incentives to innovate, and new technical knowledge have always made up the magic formula for the development of new products and the building of new industries, as well as productivity improvement in the old.

Serious questions are being raised as to whether pioneering attitudes are disappearing in the United States: societal attitudes that advocate no growth, claim big is bad, and express increasing dissatisfaction with the material side of life, probably combine to foster the idea that increasing productivity should not have a high priority on the list of human endeavors. The availability of risk capital has been reduced by federal tax policy, and other government policies have reduced incentives and established formidable hurdles in the path of technical innovation.

The changes in federal tax policy in 1970, which increased the capital-gains tax, effectively dried up sources of risk capital for the establishment of new technical enterprises in the United States.

A Small Business Administration study showed that new capital acquired by small firms through public offerings of equity dropped from a level of 548 offerings in 1969, which raised nearly $1.5 billion, to 4 offerings in 1975, which raised $16 million. Fortunately, the capital-gains tax rate was reduced last year, and venture capital is again becoming available for new and small business enterprises, where a great deal of innovation takes place.

During the late 1950s and early 1960s, when a great many new electronics companies were established, the availability of stock options caused many scientists and engineers to leave older established firms and cast their lots with newly formed firms. If the firm became successful, the rewards were great, for when the stock option was exercised, the stock had considerable value. The gain was not taxed until the stock was sold. The recipient could either hold the stock in the hope of further gain or sell it and pay the tax from time to time as funds were needed. This was important because innovative technical people almost always had more freedom to use their expertise and ingenuity in a small firm, especially when they had the great incentive of ownership participation. This may account for the fact that in many industries small and medium-sized firms have often been more innovative.

Congress, in an action to prevent what it thought was a tax loophole, made stock options taxable when exercised, and the recipient usually had to sell the stock to pay the tax. To compound the problem, an SEC regulation prevented the person from selling the stock for a considerable time after it was received if the person involved had a management role. In effect, stock options as incentives for technical people to follow their pioneering spirit were largely eliminated. There is now an effort to restore the stock-option incentive, and to do so would restore an important stimulus for technical people to undertake risky, but potentially profitable ventures in newly established enterprises.

Productivity in older and larger established firms is influenced by technical change in a somewhat different way. Such firms use many engineers and scientists in developing new products, devising new production methods, and designing better production equipment and tooling. The ability of engineers and scientists doing this kind of work to improve productivity has been seriously affected by the unprecedented growth of governmental regulations since 1970. In many cases, technical people have been required to spend much of their time dealing with regulatory problems instead of doing the kind of engineering and scientific work that would otherwise contribute to productivity improvement.

Governmental regulations, in fact, may be the largest and most important factor in the decline of productivity in the United States. Regulations have been a serious problem in every aspect of industrial expansion. The nuclear power industry may represent the worst of this situation.

It should require from four to five years to design, build, and bring on line a new power plant, but regulatory procedures have extended the time required threefold. It now takes from twelve to fifteen years to bring a new plant on line. We may reach the point where it will be impossible to build a nuclear plant or any other major facility in the United States because of excessive regulation.

Regulatory procedures are causing costly delays in even the most noncontroversial projects. I am involved in building an aquarium on the shore of Monterey Bay. Although everyone thinks it is a great idea, it is taking a full year to get approvals from all of the agencies involved. Ten years ago, only a month or so would have been required. It is impossible to keep architects and engineers working productively in this kind of a situation.

Regulations have seriously reduced the productivity of new-product development in every industry. The introduction of new drugs has become much more expensive and time consuming, and even in the development of electronic instruments, which have few health and safety problems, the regulatory agencies involved have increased development time and cost.

The impact of government regulation on small or newly forming enterprises is even more serious. The Occupational Safety and Health Administration code book contains some twenty-eight thousand regulations, and OSHA is only one of many, many regulatory agencies. It is utterly impossible for an individual entrepreneur starting a new business to know, understand, and deal with all of these regulatory matters and still have any time or energy left to deal with the mainstream work of his enterprise. It is not surprising that fewer new technically oriented firms are being started today. What is surprising is that there are any.

We need to find a way to apply more commonsense judgment to matters of regulation so that we can continue to preserve and protect all the important things in our society . . . things like the environment, individual dignity, and the freedom to innovate and produce.

From my experience, I have concluded that there is a significant decline in productivity because of the changes in societal attitudes I have already alluded to and also changes in managerial attitudes and policies. Specifically, if management people were to develop a better appreciation of the influence of technology on productivity, basic research would receive more support in the private sector. If management people were to put more emphasis on long-term performance instead of quarter-to-quarter or even year-to-year results, better decisions that affect productivity would be made.

In conclusion, there are a number of things the federal government can do to improve the productivity of our economy. The government can and should give a higher priority to increasing productivity in every action that is taken which has a significant impact on the economy. This applies to tax policy, regulatory policy, and policies that affect federal support of R & D.

I believe the private sector can and should do a better job as well. I believe productivity would improve if managers were to place more emphasis on long-term performance, as I mentioned earlier.

If both the federal government and the private business sector were to give productivity a higher priority among all of their other concerns, this would also influence the attitude of the general public. It would help bring about a general realization that there can be no improvement in the economic well-being of the average individual without an improvement in the overall productivity of our economy.

I am convinced that, to the extent the importance of productivity improvement to the welfare of the individual is understood and accepted, a better climate for productivity will be established.

Summary of Discussion

A lively debate centered on the appropriate role of the federal government in the area of research and development (R & D). Milton Friedman saw an inconsistent attitude of businessmen in their views about the government's role in R & D. On the one hand, they complain that government regulation stifles R & D while on the other they ask for special government favors for R & D, such as tax credits. Friedman saw no reason why a tax credit on R & D matched by tax increases elsewhere should be any more effective in raising productivity than an end to special tax incentives and a general reduction of tax rates. Friedman disputed the notion that a government role was appropriate for research projects with long lead times. It is the market, and not the government, he declared, which has the longer time horizon.

Arthur Okun held that the free market fails to reward adequately the production of knowledge and therefore generates too low a level of R & D. Government subsidization of R & D (starting with patent laws and grants for basic research) is an economically efficient response. Friedman agreed that the free market is likely to be imperfect in generating R & D but suggested that so too is a system with a large government role. It's a choice of two evils, he declared. Okun responded that it would be remarkable if the "best" system were either all governmental or all private; some mix is inevitable.

Feldstein took issue with Friedman on targeted versus general tax cuts for R & D: a general tax cut might stimulate R & D, but an equal tax cut targeted on R & D should provide a larger stimulus. Friedman answered by observing that the goal is not the stimulation of R & D but of productivity growth. And for the latter goal, he argued, the tax issue is unclear.

Edwin Mansfield shed some more light on the question of tax policy. He noted that a good definition of "research" for tax incentive purposes is very difficult to devise. Moreover, where other countries have attempted to create tax incentives for R & D, the results, according to the little evidence that is available, appear to have been small. He stressed that very little is known about the effects of such programs and that there is a need for much more economic research in this area.

Mettler and Packard cited a number of government-supported programs of basic research that have had significant beneficial effects on technological development. Packard reiterated the favorable experience of the Office of Naval Research.

References

Arrow, Kenneth. 1962. Economic welfare and the allocation of resources for invention. In *The rate and direction of inventive activity*, National Bureau of Economic Research. Princeton: Princeton University Press.

Baranson, Jack. 1976. Technology transfer: Effects on U.S. competitiveness and employment. Report prepared for the U.S. Department of Labor. Washington, D.C.

Beardsley, George, and Mansfield, Edwin. 1978. A note on the accuracy of industrial forecasts of the profitability of new products and processes. *Journal of Business* (January).

Blackman, A. W. 1971. The rate of innovation in the commercial aircraft jet engine market. *Technological Forecasting and Social Change*, nos. 3–4.

Brach, Peter, and Mansfield, Edwin. 1979. Engineering employment by American manufacturing firms. Philadelphia: University of Pennsylvania.

Cain, G., Freeman, R., and Hansen, W. L. 1973. *Labor market analysis of engineers and scientists.* Baltimore: Johns Hopkins University Press.

Caves, Richard. 1971. International corporations: The industrial economics of foreign investment. *Economica* 38 (February): 1–27.

Christensen, L.; Cummings, D.; and Jorgensen, D. Forthcoming. An international comparison of growth of productivity, 1947–73. In *New developments in productivity measurement and analysis.* Chicago: University of Chicago Press.

Cooper, Richard. 1972. Technology and U.S. trade: A historical review. In *Technology and international trade.* Washington, D.C.: National Academy of Engineering.

Council of Economic Advisers. 1979. *Annual Report.* Washington, D.C.: Government Printing Office.

Davidson, W., and Harrigan, R. 1977. Key decisions in international marketing: Introducing new products abroad. *Columbia Journal of World Business* (Winter).

Denison, Edward. 1962. *The sources of economic growth in the United States.* New York: Committee for Economic Development.

———. 1967. *Why growth rates differ.* Washington, D.C.: The Brookings Institution.

———. 1978a. Effects of selected changes in the institutional and human environment upon output per unit of output. *Survey of Current Business* (January).

———. 1978b. The puzzling drop in productivity. *Brookings Bulletin* (fall): Washington, D.C.: The Brookings Institution.

Enos, John. 1958. A measure of the rate of technological progress in the petroleum refining industry. *Journal of Industrial Economics* (June).

Evenson, Robert. 1968. The contribution of agricultural research and extension to agricultural production. Ph.D. diss. University of Chicago.

Freeman, Christopher. 1974. *The economics of industrial innovation.* Baltimore: Penguin.

Freeman, Richard. 1971. *The market for college-trained manpower.* Cambridge: Harvard University Press.

Grabowski, Henry. 1976. *Drug regulation and innovation.* Washington, D.C.: American Enterprise Institute.

Griliches, Zvi. 1964. Research expenditures, education, and the aggregate production function. *American Economic Review* 54 (December): 961–74.

———. 1972. A memorandum on research and growth. In *Research and development and economic growth productivity.* Washington, D.C.: National Science Foundation.

———. Forthcoming. Returns to research and development in the private sector. In *New developments in productivity measurement and analysis.* Chicago: University of Chicago Press.

Grossman, M., and Fuchs, V. 1973. Intersectoral shifts and aggregate productivity change. *Annals of economic and social measurement.* New York: National Bureau of Economic Research.

Hansen, W. L. 1967. The economics of scientific and engineering manpower. *Journal of Human Resources* (spring).

Hollander, S. 1965. *The sources of increased efficiency.* Cambridge: M.I.T. Press.

Hsia, Ronald. 1973. Technological change in the industrial growth of Hong Kong. In *Science and technology in economic growth*, ed. B. Williams. London: Macmillan.

Hufbauer, Gary. 1970. *Synthetic materials and the theory of international trade.* London: Duckworth.

Kendrick, John. 1976. Productivity funds and prospects. In *U.S. economic growth from 1976 to 1986.* Washington, D.C.: Joint Economic Committee of Congress (1 October).

Klein, Burton. 1979. The slowdown in productivity advances: A dynamic explanation. Cambridge: Center for Policy Alternatives, M.I.T. (15 January).

Kutscher, R.; Mark, J.; and Norsworthy, J. 1977. The productivity slowdown and the outlook to 1985. *Monthly Labor Review* (May).

Mansfield, Edwin. 1968a. *Industrial research and technological innovation.* New York: Norton. Published for the Cowles Foundation for Research in Economics at Yale University.

———. 1968b. *The economics of technological change.* New York: Norton.

———. 1976. Federal support of R and D activities in the private sector. In *Priorities and efficiency in federal research and development.* Washington, D.C.: Joint Economic Committee of Congress (29 October).

————. 1977. The diffusion of eight major industrial innovations in the United States. In *The state of science and research*, ed. N. Terleckyj. Boulder: Westview.

————. 1980. Basic research and productivity increase in manufacturing. *American Economic Review.* In press.

Mansfield, Edwin, and Romeo, Anthony. In press. Technology transfer to overseas subsidiaries of U.S.-based firms. *Quarterly Journal of Economics.*

Mansfield, Edwin; Romeo, Anthony; and Wagner, Samuel. 1979. Foreign trade and U.S. research and development. *Review of Economics and Statistics* 61 (February): 49–57.

Mansfield, Edwin; Teece, David; and Romeo, Anthony. 1979. Overseas research and development by U.S.-based firms. *Economica* (May).

Mansfield, Edwin, et al. 1971. *Research and innovation in the modern corporation.* New York: Norton.

————. 1977a. *The production and application of new industrial technology.* New York: Norton.

————. 1977b. Social and private rates of return from industrial innovations. *Quarterly Journal of Economics* 91 (May): 221–40.

Minasian, Jora. 1969. Research and development, production functions, and rates of return. *American Economic Review* 59 (May): 80–85.

Nason, H.; Steger, J.; and Manners, G. 1978. *Support of basic research by industry.* Washington, D.C.: National Science Foundation.

National Academy of Engineering. 1976. *Technology transfer from foreign direct investment in the United States.* Washington, D.C.: National Research Council.

National Commission on Technology, Automation, and Economic progress. 1966. *Report to the President of the United States.* Washington, D.C.: Government Printing Office.

National Science Foundation. 1976. *National patterns of R and D resources, 1953–76.* Washington, D.C.: Government Printing Office.

————. 1977. *Science indicators, 1976.* Washington, D.C.: Government Printing Office.

————. 1978. *An analysis of federal R and D funding by function.* Washington, D.C.: Government Printing Office.

————. 1979a. National R and D spending expected to exceed $57 billion in 1980. *Science Resources Studies Highlights* (8 May).

————. 1979b. Total federal R and D growth slight in 1980 but varies by budget function. *Science Resources Studies Highlights* (25 June).

————. 1979c. *Projections of science and engineering doctorate supply and utilization, 1982 and 1987.* Washington, D.C.: Government Printing Office.

Nelson, Richard; Peck, Merton; and Kalachek, Edward. 1967. *Technol-*

ogy, economic growth, and public policy. Washington, D.C.: The Brookings Institution.

Nordhaus, William. 1972. The recent productivity slowdown. *Brookings Papers on Economic Activity*. Washington, D.C.: The Brookings Institution.

Organization for Economic Cooperation and Development (OECD). 1968. *Gaps in Technology*. Paris: Organization for Economic Cooperation and Development.

Perry, George. 1971. Labor structure, potential output, and productivity. *Brookings Papers on Economic Activity*. Washington, D.C.: The Brookings Institution.

Pindyck, Robert. 1979. Should the federal government subsidize synthetic fuels? Testimony before the Senate Committee on Banking, Housing, and Urban Affairs (25 July).

Schwartz, Mark. 1979. The imitation and diffusion of industrial innovations. Ph.D. diss. University of Pennsylvania.

Stobaugh, R., and Yergen, D. 1979. Testimony before the Senate Subcommittee on Conservation and Solar Applications (27 July).

Terleckyj, Nestor. 1974. *Effects of R & D on the productivity growth of industries: An exploratory study*. Washington, D.C.: National Planning Association.

Tilton, John. 1971. *International diffusion of technology: The case of semiconductors*. Washington, D.C.: The Brookings Institution.

Vernon, Raymond. 1966. International investment and international trade in the product cycle. *Quarterly Journal of Economics* (May).

9 The Role of Government: Taxes, Transfers, and Spending

1. George F. Break
2. George P. Shultz
3. Paul A. Samuelson

1. George F. Break

The role of government during the postwar period has been the subject of much passionate debate and has greatly enlivened the lecture, cocktail, and many other circuits too numerous to mention. The purpose of this paper is not to extend those discussions of what should be done about the government, or to add to the already extensive analyses of why governments grow. Rather it is the more sober one of taking a close look at the revenues and expenditures of United States governments during the past thirty years or so in order to identify the main structural changes that may have occurred during that period. Some of these changes, of course, are already well-known and broadly recognized, others may be less conspicuous, and still others may call forth dispute and discussion.

The focus throughout will be on what may be termed the official fiscal record of governmental spending and taxing. Two sources of data are available for this purpose—the national income and product accounts (NIPA) and the Bureau of the Census, Governmental Finances series (BOC:GF). For the federal government, in addition, there is the annual budget document and the accompanying special analyses. These are the

George F. Break is professor of econmics at the University of California at Berkeley.

I wish to thank David Arsen for assistance in collecting and analyzing the data and Michael J. Boskin and Richard A. Musgrave for their very helpful comments on the first draft of the paper.

statistical series studied, for what they do show, for what they don't show, and for what they could show with suitable adjustments.

9.1   Broad Expenditure Changes

By any of the standard measures, government expenditures have grown significantly during the postwar period. Table 9.1 summarizes the official record for all levels of government together. Bureau of the Census accounts show two broad expenditure measures, one covering general government activities only (table 9.1, section A), and the other adding to general expenditures those of public utilities, government liquor stores, and insurance trust funds (table 9.1, section B). The national income and product accounts show one expenditure series (table

Table 9.1   Alternate Measures of Government Expenditure Growth during the Postwar Period

Expenditure Measures	Terminal Years		Average Annual Growth Rate During Period
A. *BOC:GF General Expenditures*[a]	*1948*	*1976–77*	
1. Nominal dollars (billions)	50.1	514.0	8.4
2. Nominal dollars per capita	342	2,380	7.0
3. Billions of 1972 dollars[b]	89.6	375.7	5.1
4. Constant dollars per capita	900	1,682	2.2
5. Ratio of current dollar expenditures to GNP	.193	.272	1.1
B. *BOC:GF Total Expenditures*[a]	*1948*	*1976–77*	
1. Nominal dollars (billions)	55.1	680.3	9.2
2. Nominal dollars per capita	376	3,150	7.7
3. Billions of 1972 dollars[b]	98.6	497.3	5.8
4. Constant dollars per capita	990	2,229	2.8
5. Ratio of current dollar expenditures to GNP	.213	.360	1.8
C. *NIPA Total Expenditures*[a]	*1947*	*1977*	
1. Nominal dollars (billions)	42.5	621.7	9.3
2. Nominal dollars per capita	295	2,866	7.8
3. Billions of 1972 dollars[b]	80.5	441.9	5.8
4. Constant dollars per capita	559	2,037	4.4
5. Ratio of current dollar expenditures to GNP	.183	.325	1.9

[a]Intergovernmental expenditures are excluded from total expenditures of grantors.
[b]Computed using the NIPA implicit deflator for personal consumption expenditures.

9.1, section C) which differs both in conceptual framework and in measurement procedures from the BOC:GF series.[1]

Absolute dollar expenditures (lines A.1, B.1, and C.1 in table 9.1) show the most striking, and least meaningful, picture of postwar government growth. Clearly, one should make some allowance for the growth of population (lines A.2, B.2, C.2), for increases in the general price level (lines A.3, B.3, C.3), and for both together (lines A.4, B.4, C.4). Neither adjustment, however, is free of ambiguities. Unchanged expenditures on pure public goods yield unchanged public benefits to everyone as population grows, though per capita expenditures thereon decline steadily. Choice of the proper price index to convert different kinds of government expenditures to constant-dollar terms is a complex issue that will be discussed below. For the moment the best single measure of the postwar growth in the total expenditures of all levels of government in this country appears to be their ratio to gross national product (GNP) with both the numerator and denominator measured in nominal (current) dollars (lines A.5, B.5, C.5).[2]

Relative to the size of the economy, then, all three broad expenditure measures have grown significantly during the past thirty years. BOC general expenditures rose from 19 percent of GNP in 1948 to 27 percent in 1976–77, BOC total expenditures rose from 21 to 36 percent of GNP during the same period, and NIPA expenditures increased from 18 to 32.5 percent of GNP between 1947 and 1977.

9.1.1 Economic Composition of Expenditures

The national income accounts distinguish five major economic categories of government expenditure. These show the different ways in which the government goes about its many activities, as distinct from the purposes or functions served thereby, to be discussed later. When the economic structure of all government activities in the country in 1977 or 1978 is compared with the structures in 1948, little change shows up (table 9.2). Purchases of goods and services were 63 percent of the total in all three years, and a modest rise in transfer payments from 29 to 32 percent of the total was matched by an equal fall, from 8 to 4 percent, in net interest payments. Indeed, for those who treat debt interest as one kind of transfer payment there would be virtually no change in the economic structure of government spending (see, for example, Rolph 1948; 1954).

When the federal and state-local sectors are separated, however, three structural changes that merit attention show up. Federal purchases of goods and services shrank from 43 to 33 percent of the budget, while state-local resource using programs grew from 87 to 93 percent, solidifying further their dominant position in that sector. Opposite shifts moved

Table 9.2 Government Expenditures by Major Economic Category (Percentage Distributions), 1948, 1977, and 1978

Category	1948			1977			1978		
	Federal	State and Local	All Levels	Federal	State and Local	All Levels	Federal	State and Local	All Levels
Purchase of Goods and Services	47.8	86.9	63.3	34.2	92.6	63.3	33.2	93.2	63.5
National defense	30.6	—	21.1	22.2	—	15.0	21.5	—	14.4
Nondefense	17.3	86.9	42.2	12.0	92.6	48.3	11.7	93.2	49.1
Transfer Payments	32.8	17.0	28.6	40.9	11.1	32.4	40.3	11.0	31.9
Grants-in-Aid	5.7	—	—	16.0	—	—	16.8	—	—
Net Interest Paid	11.8	0.5	8.3	6.9	-1.8	3.8	7.6	-2.3	4.0
Subsidies less Current Surplus of Government Enterprises	1.8	-4.4	-0.3	1.9	-1.9	-0.5	2.1	-1.8	0.6
Subsidies	—	—	—	1.8	0.0	1.2	2.0	0.1	1.4
Surplus of government enterprises	—	—	—	-0.1	-1.9	-0.7	-0.1	-1.9	-0.7

Source: *Survey of Current Business*, vol. 56 (January 1976), tables 3.2 and 3.4; vol. 59 (July 1979), tables 3.2 and 3.4.

federal transfer payments up from 33 to 40–41 percent of the total and state-local transfer payments down from 17 to 11 percent. The third change, which requires a three-level classification of governments to reveal its full significance, was the rapid increase in federal grants-in-aid, from 6 percent to nearly 17 percent of total federal expenditures.

A different kind of broad economic classification is given in BOC data. There the distinction drawn is between the ordinary activities of government financed by the general fund and the activities of various kinds of public enterprises that have their own revenues and operate more or less independently of the rest of government. These distinctions are hard to make very precisely, but they are clearly an important part of the postwar fiscal record.[3] Table 9.3 highlights one of the most widely recognized and much discussed postwar structural changes in these spending categories—the dramatic rise in insurance trust expenditures, and the corresponding fall in general expenditures.

9.1.2 Government Output

Government purchases of goods and services are particularly important economically because they, unlike the other categories shown in table 9.2, are made to acquire for public use the services of scarce resources. They are in Pigou's apt terminology "exhaustive expenditures."[4] As such, they are part of the economy's total productive activity, and their ratio to GNP shows the government's share of total output during each period.

The postwar record of that share, shown in table 9.4 and figure 9.1, reveals two major structural changes during the period. The first concerns the relation between the federal and state-local shares of total government output. From approximate equality at the beginning of the period, at 5.5 percent of GNP, the two sector shares first diverged

Table 9.3	Percentage Distributions of Total Government Expenditures by Type, 1946, 1948, and 1976–77		
Expenditure	1946	1948	1976–77
General Expenditure	.95	.91	.75
Utility and Liquor Store Expenditure	.02	.04	.03
Insurance Trust Expenditure	.03	.05	.21
Amount in $ Billions	79.7	55.1	680.3

Sources: U.S. Bureau of the Census, *1977 Census of Governments*, vol. 6, *Topical Studies*, no. 4, *Historical Statistics on Governmental Finances and Employment* (Washington, D.C.: Government Printing Office, 1979).

sharply in favor of the national government because of the Korean War. In 1953, however, the federal share began a long-term decline that reached equality with the rising state-local share in the late 1960s and fell further and further behind thereafter. By 1978 federal output was only 7 percent of GNP compared to 13 percent for state and local gov-

Table 9.4   Government Purchases of Goods and Services as a Percentage of GNP, in Current and Constant (1947) Dollars, by Level of Government, 1947–78

Year	Current Dollars (G/GNP)			1947 Dollars (G′/GNP′)		
	Federal	State and Local	All Government	Federal	State and Local	All Government
1947	5.4	5.5	10.9	5.4	5.5	10.9
48	6.4	5.9	12.3	6.1	5.6	11.7
49	7.9	7.0	14.9	7.0	6.3	13.4
50	6.5	6.9	13.4	6.2	6.2	12.4
51	11.6	6.6	18.2	10.0	5.8	15.8
52	15.1	6.7	21.8	12.6	5.7	18.4
53	15.7	6.8	22.5	13.0	5.8	18.9
54	13.1	7.6	20.7	11.0	6.3	17.3
55	11.1	7.6	18.8	9.4	6.4	15.8
56	10.9	8.0	18.9	9.1	6.5	15.6
57	11.3	8.4	19.7	9.3	6.7	16.1
58	12.0	9.2	21.2	9.7	7.4	17.0
59	11.1	9.0	20.1	9.0	7.1	16.2
60	10.6	9.2	19.8	8.7	7.3	16.0
61	11.0	9.7	20.7	9.0	7.5	16.5
62	11.3	9.6	20.9	9.1	7.3	16.5
63	10.9	9.9	20.8	8.7	7.5	16.2
64	10.3	10.2	20.4	8.1	7.6	15.8
65	9.8	10.3	20.1	7.7	7.7	15.4
66	10.5	10.6	20.1	8.1	7.8	15.9
67	11.4	11.2	22.6	8.8	8.0	16.8
68	11.3	11.6	22.9	8.6	8.1	16.8
69	10.4	11.8	22.2	8.0	8.2	16.1
70	9.7	12.5	22.3	7.3	8.5	15.8
71	9.0	12.9	22.0	6.6	8.6	15.2
72	8.7	12.9	21.6	6.2	8.4	14.6
73	7.8	12.9	20.7	5.5	8.3	13.8
74	7.9	13.5	21.4	5.5	8.6	14.1
75	8.0	14.1	22.1	5.6	9.0	14.7
76	7.6	13.5	21.1	5.3	8.6	13.9
77	7.7	13.2	20.9	5.3	8.2	13.5
78	7.3	13.3	20.6	5.0	8.1	13.1

Source: Survey of Current Business, vol. 56 (January 1976); vol. 59 (July 1979).

Fig. 9.1   Data from table 9.4.

ernments in the current-dollar series and 5 compared to 8 percent in the constant-dollar measures.

The second major structural change was the replacement of public sector growth exceeding the rate of growth of the total economy with growth that fell behind it. For the federal government this change occurred in 1953 in both the current- and constant-dollar series, and for the state-local sector it occurred in 1975. For both levels combined the postwar peak ratios to GNP were either in 1953 (constant-dollar measure) or in 1968 (current-dollar measure).

Official measures of government output are subject to a number of well-known limitations (see, for example, Musgrave 1959; Shoup 1947 and 1969). Prominent among these, as far as any assessment of the role of government during the postwar period is concerned, is the omission of government capital formation. Estimates of expanded measures of government product in the United States have recently been made available by Eisner and Nebhut (1979) for the 1946–76 period. Four major imputations are made in their series:

1. Values of the services of government capital are measured as the sum of an interest return and capital consumption allowances at replacement cost
2. Uncompensated factor services, such as those provided by military draftees and jurors, are added
3. Real gains and losses on government capital, or net revaluations, are estimated
4. Work-related expenses, mainly travel expenses of government employees, are estimated and deducted

The resulting ratios to GNP, computed in 1972 dollars, are shown in the first two columns of table 9.5, for government product both gross and net of real capital gains and losses on government capital (current government product). When these two expanded product measures are compared with the official NIPA series for GNP originating in government relative to GNP (both in 1972 dollars), shown in the third column of table 9.5, two main differences stand out. One is the much

Table 9.5   **Alternative Measures of Government Product as a Percentage of GNP, in Constant (1972) Dollars, 1946–76**

| | Eisner and Nebhut Series | | |
Year	Current Product	Gross Product	Official NIPA Series
1946	44.3	37.9	15.9
1947	35.6	39.9	12.4
1948	30.1	33.2	11.9
1949	23.8	24.2	12.7
1950	20.1	20.0	12.1
1951	17.0	18.7	13.7
1952	18.4	17.9	14.3
1953	19.7	20.4	13.7
1954	20.5	20.7	13.7
1955	20.3	25.1	12.9
1956	21.3	22.3	12.9
1957	22.4	23.2	13.1
1958	22.4	22.7	13.3
1959	22.6	22.8	12.7
1960	22.8	23.9	12.9
1961	22.9	24.9	13.0
1962	22.2	22.8	12.8
1963	21.7	22.2	12.6
1964	21.3	22.5	12.4
1965	20.6	21.4	12.1
1966	20.6	21.0	12.3
1967	21.4	21.7	12.6
1968	21.4	21.8	12.5
1969	22.4	23.8	12.5
1970	23.1	24.3	12.6
1971	21.4	22.0	12.3
1972	20.0	22.6	11.7
1973	20.0	24.9	11.2
1974	21.3	24.9	11.7
1975	21.9	22.0	12.0
1976	19.9	19.7	11.5

Sources: Eisner and Nebhut 1979, table 5, p. 42; *Survey of Current Business,* vol. 56 (January 1976); vol. 59 (July 1979).

higher postwar peaks at the very beginning of the period in the expanded series. The other is the similarity in the timing of the peaks during the latter part of the period in all three series, both in the late 1960s and in 1974–75.

9.1.3   Total Expenditures

When the focus is expanded from government purchases to total expenditures, several complications arise. Whereas a G/GNP ratio has a precise meaning—namely, the relative importance of a specific component of total national output—a total expenditure ratio (E/GNP) does not. Transfer expenditures are not necessarily less than GNP, and GNP is only one of a number of measures of the size of the economy that might be used to show the relative growth of government transfer payments. Nevertheless, GNP is the measure commonly used, and that practice will be followed here.

Two more important difficulties in dealing with total government expenditures arise from their heterogeneous character, which complicates the derivation of constant-dollar measures, and their greater sensitivity to economic fluctuations, which may mean that trends are obscured in unadjusted data.

Constant-Dollar Adjustments

Arriving at a good set of constant-dollar adjustments is mainly a problem of measurement for government output expenditures and mainly a problem of choice for all other expenditures. The measurement problems, arising from the intangible nature of many governmental benefits and services, are well known (see, however, Hulten 1979). For example, to adopt a Baumol-type hypothesis of zero productivity growth in the public sector (Baumol 1967), as is often done for simplicity, could be regarded both as too pessimistic or too optimistic. Given a private sector in which labor productivity and money wage rates rise steadily, the lower the rate of productivity growth assumed in the derivation of the constant-dollar government output series, the more rapid the increase in the implicit price deflator for the public sector and the greater the divergence between current- and constant-dollar government output measures. If, as the Baumol hypothesis would suggest, the relative price of government output is rising steadily over time, the government's share of national output will be shown to rise more rapidly by current- than by constant-dollar measures. This, indeed, is the relation shown in table 9.4 above.

The critical question, of course, concerns the quality of the constant-dollar series for government output. Criticizing the Canadian national income accounts for implicitly assuming a zero rate of productivity growth in the government sector, a rate which he regarded as too low,

Stanbury (1973) computed the effects of different degrees of productivity understatement on the relative size of the public sector shown by constant-dollar measures. His results, shown in table 9.6, clearly indicate that constant-dollar government output shares must be interpreted with great care. Since the base year used for the price adjustments was 1961, earlier constant-dollar output shares (G'/GNP') are overstated and later ones understated by any G' measure that uses too low a rate of government output productivity growth. Whereas the Canadian national income accounts, for example, showed a 1926–68 increase in the relative size of the government sector from 13.2 percent to 19.0 percent of GNP, the true increase would have been from 7.3 percent to 21.1 percent if the government sector had in fact experienced a 2 percent average annual rate of productivity growth over that period.

NIPA measures of constant-dollar government purchases in this country are also based on an assumption of zero factor-productivity growth.[5] Use of this standard convention has produced significant differences in the measured rates of price increase in the private and public sectors during the postwar period. These are illustrated in the following tabulation, which compares changes in the implicit price deflators for the government sector as a whole (FSL), the federal sector (F) and the state-local sector (SL) with the deflators for personal consumption expenditures (PCE) and national income (NI).

Table 9.6   **Productivity and the Relative Size of the Public Sector in Canada (in Percentages)**

Alternative Rates of Long-Run Average Annual Productivity in the General Government Sector	Ratio of Government Expenditures on Current Goods and Services and Capital Formation to GNP in 1961 Dollars[a]	
	1926	1968
−1.0	17.5	18.0
−0.5	15.2	18.5
0.0[b]	13.2	19.0
+0.5	11.4	19.5
+1.0	9.8	20.0
+1.5	8.5	20.6
+2.0	7.3	21.1
+2.5	6.3	21.7
+3.0	5.4	22.2

Source: Stanbury 1973.
[a]Note that transfer payments and subsidies have been omitted.
[b]This is the rate implicitly assumed in the Canadian national accounts.

NIPA Implicit Price Deflators (1972 = 100)

Year	FSL	F	SL	PCE	NI
1947	33.8	35.1	32.5	52.8	51.3
1978	157.8	153.3	160.4	150.3	153.4
1978/1947	4.67	4.37	4.94	2.85	2.99

Whether long-term changes in the government's share of total national output are better measured by current-dollar (G/GNP) or by constant-dollar (G'/GNP') ratios remains an open question. For the other kinds of government expenditure, which are mainly transfer and net interest payments (table 9.2), the problem is less one of measurement than one of choice. The real value of these expenditures is determined not by productivity in the public sector but rather by productivity in private markets. They should, in other words, be converted to constant-dollar terms by the use of private, not public, sector price indexes (Dubin 1977). It is what those payments will buy in private markets that determines their real value, and they should be treated accordingly.

This means, for one thing, that there is no simple way to convert total government expenditures into constant-dollar terms. In principle, transfer and interest payments should be deflated by price indexes specific to the different groups receiving them. In practice, such measurement refinements may or may not be worth the costs of making them. To gain some insights into the nature of these tradeoffs three alternative constant-dollar/expenditure-to-GNP ratio series have been constructed and are given in table 9.7, along with the usual current-dollar series. In the first, presented as a standard of reference, all government expenditures, regardless of type, are deflated by the appropriate NIPA implicit price deflators for government output. In the second constant-dollar series, real government purchases of goods and services are taken directly from NIPA sources—i.e., are measured in the same way as in the first series —but all other expenditures are deflated by the NIPA deflator for personal consumption expenditures (PCE). The third series is constructed in the same way as the second except that the Consumer Price Index (CPI) is used in place of the PCE deflator.

Two questions are of particular interest concerning the alternative series shown in table 9.7. What differences, if any, are there in the measured growth rates for the whole postwar period? When do the postwar peaks in the different E/GNP ratios occur? The answer to the first question is shown at the bottom of the table where the 1978 values for each series are given as a ratio to their corresponding 1947 values. Greater rates of growth are shown by the current-dollar series than by any of the others; and among the constant-dollar measures, much the least growth is shown by the conventional series based on the implicit government sector price deflators. Indeed, it shows federal expenditures to have fallen slightly as a percentage of GNP between 1947 and 1978. The growth trends shown by the two expenditure measures deflated in part by alternative consumer price indexes are very similar. Finally, the more rapid growth in state-local, relative to federal, expenditures shows up clearly in all four series.

The years in which the relative size of government, measured by E/GNP ratios, peaked during the postwar period are remarkably con-

Table 9.7   Direct Government Expenditures as a Percentage of GNP: Alternative NIPA Measures, Selected Years 1947–78

Year	Level of Government[a]	Current Dollars	Implicit Deflators for Government Purchases	Implicit Deflator for Personal Consumption Expenditures	Consumer Price Index
1947	F	12.1	19.1	13.9	13.9
	SL	6.2	11.8	9.1	9.1
	FSL	18.3	30.9	23.0	23.0
1948	F	12.7	22.1	14.6	14.5
	SL	6.8	12.2	9.4	9.4
	FSL	19.5	34.2	24.0	23.9
1953	F	20.3	31.8	22.7	22.6
	SL	7.5	11.7	9.5	9.5
	FSL	27.7	43.5	32.2	32.1
1957	F	17.0	25.9	18.7	18.7
	SL	9.0	12.9	10.9	10.9
	FSL	26.0	38.8	29.6	29.6
1967	F	18.6	23.5	19.4	19.5
	SL	11.9	13.3	12.9	12.9
	FSL	30.4	36.8	32.2	32.4
1972	F	17.7	17.7	17.7	17.7
	SL	14.0	14.0	14.0	14.0
	FSL	31.7	31.7	31.7	31.7
1975	F	19.8	20.6	19.8	19.6
	SL	15.1	15.4	14.8	14.8
	FSL	34.9	36.0	34.6	34.4
1978	F	18.0	18.7	18.0	17.6
	SL	14.3	14.8	13.5	13.4
	FSL	32.2	33.5	31.5	31.0
1978/	F	1.49	0.98	1.29	1.27
1947	SL	2.31	1.25	1.48	1.47
Ratios	FSL	1.76	1.08	1.37	1.35

Source: Survey of Current Business, various issues.

Note: Direct government expenditures are those made to provide benefits directly to the private sector. Intergovernmental grant expenditures are accordingly omitted from the series.

[a]F=federal; SL=state-local; FSL=federal, state, and local.

sistent both among the different table 9.7 series and with the output share measures shown in table 9.4. The peak year for the federal government was 1953 in all cases, and for the state-local sector it was 1975. For both governmental levels combined there was more variation, but the same two years show up in all but one of the measures used.

Full Employment Adjustments

Isolating short-term changes in government expenditures and economic activity and eliminating them from all affected measures in order to reveal long-term trends more clearly has long been a major preoccupation of empirical researchers. A good example for the postwar period is provided by Charles Schultze's analysis of federal government spending trends and priorities (1976, pp. 323–69). In his measures, which cover the 1955–77 period, both federal expenditures and GNP are adjusted for recession by computing their hypothetical levels at a constant national rate of unemployment of 5 percent. In addition, any incremental costs of the Vietnam War are subtracted from federal expenditures. These baseline budget expenditures are then divided by nonrecession GNP estimates to provide an improved measure of federal governmental growth. For the period studied Schultze's two adjusted series show a significantly slower rise in the relative size of the federal sector than does the standard unadjusted measure (table 9.8).

Which of these two pictures is the more realistic is debatable. The unadjusted series may be unduly affected by temporary developments; the adjusted series may fail to eliminate these aberrations properly. The Schultze estimates, for example, are based on a constant unemployment rate as the appropriate standard of adjustment,[6] but postwar changes in

		Schultze's Baseline Budget Outlays as a Percentage of Nonrecession GNP	
	Ratio of Federal Budget Outlays		
Fiscal Year	to GNP (%)	Current Dollars	Constant Dollars (1955 = 100)
1955	18.4	18.2	18.2
1960	18.5	18.1	17.0
1965	18.0	18.1	16.4
1970	20.5	19.0	16.1
1975	22.5	19.9	15.9
1977*	22.2	20.1	15.8

Table 9.8   Alternative Federal E/GNP Ratios, 1955–77

Source: Schultze 1976, pp. 327–31.
*Estimated.

the structure of United States labor markets may mean that a weighted rate that varies with changes in the composition of the labor force would be more appropriate (G. Perry 1970). The difficulties the Council of Economic Advisers (CEA) has had recently in distinguishing temporary from long-term changes in the economy's rate of productivity growth indicate clearly the slipperiness of full employment or potential GNP estimates.[7] It is interesting to note that when CEA estimates of full-employment GNP are used to measure growth in the relative size of the federal government, the picture is indeed different (table 9.9). The measures, by Pechman and Hartman (1979), show the full employment federal E/GNP ratio rising from 17.6 percent in 1960 to 21.0 percent in 1979, an increase slightly greater than 19 percent. Actual budget outlays, in contrast, rose from 18.5 to 21.6 percent of actual GNP, a growth of only 17 percent.

GNP Adjustments

A third difficulty with the measures of the size of government under discussion is that there may be some systematic biases in the measurement of GNP over the postwar period. Two sources of these problems, tending to produce opposing biases in measured GNP during the period, have been widely discussed.

The first is especially troublesome because its presence would indicate that the two component terms of the E/GNP ratios are not independent, as unbiased size-of-government estimates require, but rather are negatively correlated. High government expenditures require high tax rates, and higher tax rates may induce many activities and transactions that would ordinarily be recorded in NIPA series to go underground and hence to disappear from measured GNP. How large the underground economy has become is a subject for vigorous current debate,[8] and by its very nature it presents an elusive target for NIPA estimators, not to mention Internal Revenue Service agents. At this point one can only note the distinct possibility that nonrecorded transactions do increase systematically in response to rising tax rates, and that these developments, if significant, impart an inherent upward bias to all E/GNP measures of the size of government.

The other source of postwar bias in the GNP accounts has been created by the steady movement of more and more married women into the labor force (Boskin 1979). This represents a shift from nonmarket production of household services or leisure, neither of which are part of measured GNP, into market production, which is. Over the postwar period, in other words, measured GNP has been rising faster than has total economic activity. This upward bias in the E/GNP denominator offsets, or dominates, the opposite bias created by the growth of the underground economy. The net effect on measures of the relative size

Table 9.9   **Relation of Federal Budget Outlays to the Gross National Product, in Current and Constant Dollars, Fiscal Years 1960–79**

| | Budget Outlays as Percentage of GNP | | | |
| | Current Dollars | | Constant Dollars[c] | |
Fiscal Year[a]	Actual (1)	Full Employ-ment[b] (2)	Actual (3)	Full Employ-ment[b] (4)
1960	18.5	17.6	20.6	19.6
1961	19.2	17.7	21.3	19.6
1962	19.5	18.5	21.6	20.4
1963	19.3	18.4	21.0	20.0
1964	19.2	18.7	20.8	20.2
1965	18.0	17.8	19.3	19.1
1966	18.7	19.0	19.6	20.0
1967	20.4	21.0	21.3	21.9
1968	21.5	22.1	22.3	22.9
1969	20.4	21.1	20.8	21.6
1970	20.5	20.3	20.5	20.3
1971	20.7	19.9	20.5	19.7
1972	20.9	20.1	20.5	19.7
1973	20.0	20.0	19.3	19.3
1974	19.8	19.7	18.8	18.6
1975	22.4	20.5	21.2	19.5
1976	22.6	20.9	21.5	19.9
1977	22.0	20.8	20.5	19.6
1978	22.1	21.3	20.5	19.9
1979[d]	21.6	21.0	19.9	19.5

Sources: *The Budget of the United States Government, Fiscal Year 1980*, pp. 577–78. Full-employment figures are from the Office of Management and Budget.
Note: From Pechman 1979, p. 26.
[a]Ending June 30 for 1960–76 and September 30 for 1977–79.
[b]Full-employment outlays as a percentage of full-employment GNP.
[c]Calculated in fiscal 1972 prices.
[d]Estimated.

of government may be guessed at and speculated about, but quantitative determination seems out of reach, at least for the present.

Conclusion

There is, it seems, no single expenditure series that can be said to predominate as the best measure of changes in the size of the public sector. Each candidate has its own strengths and weaknesses, and no one of them can be relied upon alone. When questions arise as to whether government is becoming more or less important, a procedure similar to the NBER's identification of business cycle phases has much to recommend it. A sustained two- or three-year rise in one particular E/GNP series may be no more indicative of government growth than a two-quarter fall in real GNP is of the occurrence of a national recession. Moreover, expenditures measure only one aspect of the government's total impact on the economy. Tax expenditures, lending and loan guarantee operations, and regulatory activities must also be taken into account. Only when all, or most, of these complex dimensions of the public sector's economic role show a definite expansion can one be sure that government is really growing.

9.2   Trends in Intergovernmental Relations

Prominent among the widely recognized and discussed postwar fiscal changes in this country has been a greatly increased public sector interdependence. The fiscal measure of this trend is the rapid rise in federal and state grants-in-aid. As table 9.10 shows, both types grew much faster than did the economy as a whole; federal grants rose from .05 percent to 3.5 percent of GNP and state grants from 1 percent to 3.5 percent. As a result both state and local governments are now much more dependent on outside funds than they were at the beginning of the postwar period. Figure 9.2 shows the development of this important structural change.

Table 9.10	Federal and State Intergovernmental Grants as a Percentage of GNP, Selected Years, 1946–78	
Year	Federal Grants/GNP	State Grants/GNP
1946	0.5	1.0
1950	0.8	1.5
1955	0.8	1.5
1960	1.3	1.9
1965	1.6	2.2
1970	2.5	3.0
1975	3.6	3.4
1978	3.6	n/a*

Sources: NIPA data for federal grants and for state grants since 1960. *Survey of Current Business*, vol. 56, part 2 (January 1976); May 1978, p. 16; and other issues. State grant data prior to 1960 are from ACIR, *The States and Intergovernmental Aids*, Report A–59 (February 1977), p. 9.

*n/a=not available. In 1976–77 state grants were 3.4 percent of GNP.

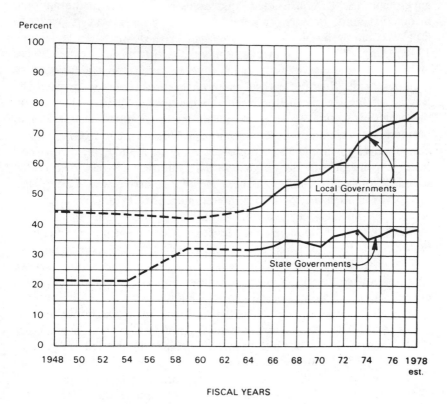

Percent

FISCAL YEARS

Fig. 9.2   The growing state and local dependency on outside aid, selected years 1948–78. (Outside aid as a percentage of general revenue from own sources.) Data from ACIR, *Significant Features of Fiscal Federalism, 1978–79 Edition*, Report M–115 (May 1979), p. 80.

Though no sharp reversal in these trends appears to be imminent, there are signs that here too postwar growth rates may be slowing markedly. Federal grants are projected in the 1981 United States budget to grow less rapidly than the economy, falling to 3.5 percent of GNP in 1979 and to 3.4 percent in 1981.[9] If these projections are realistic, they represent a new phase in intergovernmental relations. With relatively less federal money flowing in, states may slow the growth in their own aid to local governments. It will be some time, however, before the full significance of these developments is revealed.

In a federal fiscal system with significant flows of intergovernmental aid two distinct measures of the relative importance of different levels of government can be constructed. Like transfer payments in the national income accounts, intergovernmental grants may be treated in aggregate fiscal accounting by either the *deduct-add* or the *omission* rule (Rolph 1948). Under the latter they are simply omitted from total expenditures of all grantors. This yields for each level of government a measure of spending made directly for the benefit of the private sector, or what the Bureau of the Census calls direct expenditures. The focus here is on the provision of final services to consumers or intermediate services to business, regardless of whether the financial means came from the operating level of government or from outside sources. Under the *deduct-add* rule, in contrast, intergovernmental expenditures are recorded in the spending totals of grantors but then, in order to arrive at a nonduplicating total for all levels of government, intergovernmental revenues are deducted from the recorded expenditures of grantees. The focus here is on the expenditures made by each level of government that are financed by that same level, or what may be called own-financed expenditures.

The changes that have occurred during the postwar period in both measures of relative fiscal importance are shown in table 9.11. For this purpose BOC measures of general expenditures are used because of their availability for all three levels of government throughout the postwar period. The first change of note, in direct general expenditure (DGE) shares, is the decline in the importance of the federal government as a provider of services to the private sector. Its share fell from 65 percent of total direct general expenditures in 1948 to one of 47 percent in 1976–77. These losses in relative importance were added more or less equally to the state and local DGE shares. As a financing agent, however, the federal government has remained supreme through-

Table 9.11   **Federal, State, and Local Percentage Shares of Direct General Expenditures and Own-Financed General Expenditures, Selected Years, 1948–77**

Years	Direct General Expenditures			Own-Financed General Expenditures		
	Federal	State	Local	Federal	State	Local
1948	65	12	23	66	15	19
1950	62	13	24	67	16	17
1960	65	15	20	71	17	12
1965–66	56	15	28	63	18	19
1970–71	50	19	31	59	22	20
1975–76	46	20	34	59	22	19
1976–77	47	20	33	60	22	18

Sources: U.S. Bureau of Census, *1977 Census of Governments*, vol. 6, *Topical Studies*, no. 4, *Historical Statistics on Governmental Finances and Employment*, tables 3, 5, and 6.

out the postwar period. Its share of own-financed general expenditures (OFGE) did vary from one year to another but never fell much below 60 percent. During the period, state governments steadily increased the relative importance of their financing role from 15 percent of OFGE in 1948 to 22 percent in 1976–77, while local governments stayed close to the 18 to 20 percent range.

Three-level estimates of government receipts and expenditures on a NIPA basis have recently been made available for the 1959–76 period (Levin 1978). Intergovernmental shares for direct and own-financed expenditures, computed from these data, are shown in table 9.12. Some of the same trends show up for both types, but the conceptual and measurement differences between the two sources alter other trends. Federal dominance of direct spending does decline during the period but less rapidly than is shown in BOC data. In 1976 the federal share of direct expenditures was 57 percent on a NIPA basis but only 46–47 percent on a BOC basis. In both series the state share of direct expenditures rises by one-third between 1960 and 1976, but the local share rises by only one-eighth in NIPA data compared to a two-thirds increase in BOC measures. In the own-financed expenditure series the federal government leads the other two sectors by comparably wide margins, but the trends are different. In NIPA measures the federal share is 68 percent in both 1960 and 1976 but declines from the 66 to 71 percent range at the beginning of the period to 60 percent at the end in the BOC measures. The local share stays close to 18–20 percent throughout the period in BOC data (except for 1960), but falls from 17 to 14 percent in NIPA data. In both sets of measures the state share of own-financed expenditures rises during the postwar period.

9.3   Public Sector Functions

Three major changes in the functional structure of government expenditures have occurred during the postwar period: (1) domestic pro-

Table 9.12   **Federal, State, and Local Percentage Shares of NIPA Direct and Own-Financed Expenditures, Selected Years, 1960–76**

	Direct Expenditures			Own-Financed Expenditures		
Year	Federal	State	Local	Federal	State	Local
1960	64	12	24	68	15	17
1965	60	14	26	66	17	17
1970	58	16	26	65	19	16
1975	57	16	27	67	18	15
1976	57	16	27	68	18	14

Source: Levin 1978, pp. 16–17.

grams have gained significantly in relation to defense programs; (2) social security and welfare spending has risen rapidly; and (3) social investment expenditures in health, education, and other areas have also increased in relative importance, but less dramatically.

There are a number of sources that could be used to document these trends. The basic statistical data used here are those given in the NIPA tables on "Government Expenditures by Type and Function" (table 3.14 in recent years). They were chosen because they provide a valuable cross-classification by government ends and means—dividing expenditures into twenty major functional classes and forty-three subclasses, all carried out by the four major economic methods shown earlier in table 9.2.[10] Discussion of these basic data is again supplemented by reference to the fiscal analyses made in the Brookings Institution's *Setting National Priorities* series.

Various measures of the postwar shift from defense to domestic spending, differing in their allocation of particular spending programs to the two broad categories, are readily available. Table 9.13 shows the Pechman-Hartman breakdown, which simply separates national defense budget outlays from all others. In their measures defense spending declines from 49 percent of total federal outlays in fiscal 1960 to 23 percent in 1978 and 1979. Schultze combines federal budget outlays for national defense and foreign affairs in his baseline series and classifies all others as domestic. In this treatment domestic programs rise from 7 to nearly 15 percent of nonrecession GNP between 1955 and 1977, while national security programs fall from 11 percent to 5 percent (table 9.14). A still broader definition of defense spending is used by the Advisory Commission on Intergovernmental Relations (ACIR). It includes national defense, international affairs and finance, space research and technology, and an allocated portion of net federal interest payments. In their tabulations federal domestic own-financed expenditures begin the postwar period in the 6 to 8 percent of GNP range (between 1949 and 1959) and rise to a 15–16 percentage plateau in the late 1970s (table 9.15).

During the past quarter decade, then, government domestic programs have gained significantly with the structural shift away from defense spending. In the nature of the case, that shift could not continue indefinitely, and indeed President Carter's 1981 budget indicates that it may soon be stopped, or even reversed. Within the domestic sector itself, the largest growth in relative importance has occurred in education programs (mainly at the state and local level), and in social security and welfare services (mainly at the federal level). Table 9.16 provides the details. The NIPA tabulations used begin with 1952, but since that year was significantly influenced by the Korean War, 1955 is also given in table 9.16 as an alternative initial year for the identification of postwar

changes in functional shares. Whichever early year is taken, the large
relative decline in national defense expenditures stands out. The other
major fall in relative importance occurred in transportation programs,
but in the state and local sector only. Education expenditures rose from
12 percent of total direct government expenditures in 1955 to 18 percent in 1978, from 36 to 38 percent of state-local direct expenditures,
and from 0.6 to 2.7 percent of total federal expenditures over the same

Table 9.13   Federal Budget Outlays as a Percentage of Total Outlays, by Major Category, Fiscal Years 1960–79

Fiscal Year[a]	Defense	Nondefense				Grants-in-Aid to State and Local Governments[c]
		Total	Payments for Individuals[b]	Net Interest	Other	
1960	49.0	51.0	24.8	7.5	18.7	7.6
1961	47.7	52.3	26.5	6.9	18.9	7.3
1962	45.9	54.1	25.4	6.4	22.3	7.4
1963	45.0	55.0	25.7	6.9	22.4	7.7
1964	43.5	56.5	25.1	6.9	24.5	8.6
1965	40.1	59.9	25.7	7.2	27.0	9.2
1966	40.7	59.3	25.5	7.0	26.8	9.6
1967	43.1	56.9	25.3	6.5	25.1	9.6
1968	44.0	56.0	25.7	6.2	24.1	10. 4
1969	43.0	57.0	28.6	6.9	21.5	11.0
1970	40.0	60.0	30.4	7.3	22.3	12.2
1971	35.9	64.1	35.3	7.0	21.8	13.3
1972	33.0	67.0	36.8	6.7	23.5	14.8
1973	30.2	69.8	38.8	7.0	24.0	16.9
1974	28.8	71.2	41.2	8.0	22.0	16.1
1975	26.2	73.8	43.7	7.1	23.0	15.3
1976	24.4	75.6	45.7	7.3	22.6	16.1
1977	24.2	75.8	45.3	7.4	23.1	17.0
1978	23.3	76.7	43.3	7.9	25.5	17.3
1979[d]	23.2	76.8	43.2	8.7	24.9	16.6

Sources: Office of Management and Budget, "Federal Government Finances" (January 1979), pp. 40–42, 65–67.

Note: From Pechman and Hartman 1979, p. 28.

[a]Ending June 30 for 1960–76 and September 30 for 1977–79.

[b]Payments for retirement, disability, and unemployment (principally social security,
medicare, veterans' pensions and compensation, and unemployment insurance) and
low-income assistance (principally welfare, food stamps, housing, and medicaid).
Includes grants-in-aid to state and local governments that subsequently result in
payments for individuals.

[c]Total grants-in-aid, including grants for payments for individuals.

[d]Estimated.

Table 9.14   **Federal Baseline Budget Outlays for Defense and Domestic Programs, as a Percentage of Nonrecession GNP, Selected Fiscal Years, 1955–77**

| Fiscal Year | Baseline Budget Outlays as Percentage of Nonrecession GNP | | |
	National Defense and Foreign Affairs	Domestic Programs	Total
1955	11.2	7.0	18.2
1960	9.5	8.6	18.1
1965	8.1	10.0	18.1
1970	6.9	12.1	19.0
1975	5.7	14.2	19.9
1977*	5.4	14.7	20.1

Source: Schultze 1976, p. 328.
*Estimated.

period. By far the largest rise, however, was in social security and welfare services. From a 7–11 percent share in 1952–55 for all levels of government combined they vaulted to a 25 percent share in 1978.

A more detailed analysis of federal domestic programs alone is provided by Schultze's baseline budget tabulations, shown in table 9.17. The rapid growth in payments to individuals, both for retirement, disability and unemployment, and for low-income assistance, stands out. It is also interesting to note that while expenditures for Schultze's categories of physical and social investment were both 2.1 percent of nonrecession GNP in 1977, those for physical investment were 1.6 percent of GNP in 1955, while those for social investment were only 0.6 percent.

9.4 Government Revenue Systems

That the governmental revenue structure has changed significantly during the postwar period is not likely to be disputed. Some of the specific dimensions of that change, however, vary with the view one wishes to take of government finance. In the revenue game there are many individual players. While the contribution each has made to the total revenue raised during the postwar period is a matter of record, the significance of each contribution depends on the context in which it is evaluated, and in particular on the performance of its most directly competing contributors.

Three alternative sets of revenue data are presented here for two or three levels of government, depending on the availability of data. The first, given in table 9.18, compares the percentage distributions in 1948 and 1976–77 of BOC:GF total own-source government revenue. For all levels of government combined by far the largest relative increase during the period occurred in insurance trust revenues, from 7 percent of the total in 1948 to 20 percent in 1976–77. General sales taxes were next with a doubling of their percentage share, but it was still only 5.5 percent at the end of the period. The property tax, in contrast, main-

			Federal	
Calendar Year	Sector	Total	Defense	Domestic

Table 9.15   Federal Government Expenditures from Own Funds on Defense and Domestic Programs, Selected Years, 1929–79

Calendar Year	Sector	Total	Defense	Domestic
Amount in Billions of Current Dollars				
1929	10.2	2.6	1.1	1.5
1939	17.4	8.9	1.5	7.4
1949	59.3	41.3	22.0	19.3
1954	97.0	69.8	47.1	22.7
1959	131.0	91.0	53.6	37.4
1964	176.3	118.2	64.0	54.2
1969	285.6	188.4	95.5	92.9
1974	458.2	299.3	105.3	194.0
1975	532.8	356.8	114.5	242.3
1976	570.3	385.2	120.1	265.1
1977	621.8	422.6	129.8	292.8
1978 P	685.0	461.0	141.2	319.8
1979 est.	764.5	507.0	155.0	352.0
As Percentage of GNP				
1929	9.9	2.5	1.1	1.5
1939	19.2	9.8	1.7	8.1
1949	23.0	16.0	8.5	7.5
1954	26.5	19.1	12.9	6.2
1959	26.9	18.7	11.0	7.7
1964	27.7	18.6	10.1	8.5
1969	30.5	20.1	10.2	9.9
1974	32.4	21.2	7.5	13.7
1975	34.9	23.3	7.5	15.8
1976	33.5	22.7	7.1	15.6
1977	32.9	22.4	6.9	15.5
1978 P	32.5	21.9	6.7	15.2
1979 est.	32.6	21.6	6.6	15.0

Source: ACIR, *Significant Features of Fiscal Federalism, 1978–79 Edition*, Report M–115 (May 1979), p. 7.
Note: P = preliminary; est. = estimated.

Table 9.16   Government Expenditures by Major Function, 1952, 1955, and 1978 (Percentage Distributions)

Expenditures	Federal Total Expenditures			Federal Direct Expenditures		
	1952	1955	1978	1952	1955	1978
National Defense	65.8	57.8	23.7	68.2	60.4	28.3
Space Research and Technology	—	—	0.9	—	—	1.0
Central Administration	8.9	9.7	12.0	9.2	10.1	14.3
International Affairs and Finance	3.3	3.3	1.2	3.5	3.5	1.4
Education	0.4	0.6	2.7	0.2	0.6	1.2
Health and Hospitals	0.6	0.4	2.0	0.5	0.3	1.5
Social Security and Special Welfare Services	7.3	12.7	34.1	5.6	11.0	34.5
Civilian Safety	0.0	0.0	0.2	0.0	0.0	0.1
Labor	0.3	0.4	4.8	0.0	0.1	3.0
Veterans Benefits and Services	7.0	7.4	4.3	7.1	7.7	5.2
Regulation of Commerce and Finance	0.0	0.0	0.1	0.0	0.0	0.2
Transportation	1.6	1.8	3.6	0.9	0.8	2.5
Other Commerce and Transportation	0.0	0.0	0.3	0.0	−0.1	0.4
Utilities and Sanitation	—	—	1.2	—	—	0.2
Housing and Community Development	−0.1	−0.4	2.5	−0.1	−0.5	1.2
Nuclear Energy Research and Development	—	—	0.6	—	—	0.6
Postal Services	1.2	0.7	0.5	1.2	0.8	0.6
Agriculture and Agricultural Resources	1.8	4.3	1.6	1.8	4.4	1.7
Natural Resources	1.7	1.2	2.0	1.7	1.1	2.1
General Revenue Sharing	—	—	1.7	—	—	—
Sum	99.8	99.9	100.0	99.8	100.2	100.0
Amount in $ Billions	71.0	68.1	459.7	68.4	65.0	382.4

Sources: U.S. Department of Commerce, Office of Business Economics, *The National Income and Product Accounts of the United States, 1929–65*; Statistical Tables (Washington: Government Printing Office, 1966), table 3.10; and *Survey of Current Business*, vol. 59 (July 1979), table 3.14.

tained a stable share of total revenue while the individual income tax declined slightly. More significant losses in production of revenue were registered by the corporation income tax and excises. If state liquor store profits are combined with them, excise revenues fell from 16 percent of the total in 1948 to less than 7 percent in 1976–77.

When attention is focused on each of the three levels of government, several new dimensions of the total revenue picture appear. The property tax remained the most important source of local government revenue, but its share fell from 60 to 50 percent. The individual income tax

Table 9.16—*continued*

Expenditures	State and Local Direct Expenditures			Federal State and Local Direct Expenditures		
	1952	1955	1978	1952	1955	1978
National Defense	0.5	0.5	0.3	50.0	40.4	15.9
Space and Technology	—	—	0.0	—	—	0.6
Central Administration	9.8	10.1	13.1	9.4	10.1	13.7
International Affairs and Finance	—	—	—	2.5	2.3	0.8
Education	32.7	36.2	38.2	9.0	12.3	17.6
Health and Hospitals	9.0	8.2	9.1	2.8	2.9	4.9
Social Security and Welfare Services	11.2	9.8	13.7	7.1	10.6	25.3
Civilian Safety	7.7	7.5	7.7	2.1	2.6	3.4
Labor	0.8	0.7	2.3	0.2	0.3	2.7
Veterans Benefits	0.6	0.3	0.0	5.4	5.2	2.9
Regulation of Commerce and Finance	1.4	1.3	0.7	0.4	0.5	0.4
Transportation	18.2	18.8	7.5	5.6	6.8	4.7
Other Commerce and Transportation	−0.7	−0.5	−0.2	−0.2	−0.2	0.1
Utilities and Sanitation	3.3	3.3	4.3	0.9	1.0	2.0
Housing and Community Development	1.9	0.2	0.1	0.4	−0.3	0.7
Nuclear Energy Research and Development	—	—	0.1	—	—	0.4
Postal Services	—	—	—	0.9	0.5	0.3
Agriculture	1.2	1.1	0.6	1.6	3.3	1.2
Natural Resources	2.4	2.5	2.5	1.9	1.6	2.3
General Revenue Sharing	—	—	—	—	—	—
Sum	100.0	100.0	100.0	100.0	99.9	99.9
Amount in $ Billions	25.2	32.7	303.6	93.6	97.6	686.0

more than tripled its relative importance at the state level, from 5 to 16 percent, and for local governments it rose from insignificance in 1948 to provide 3 percent of total revenues in 1976–77. Excise tax receipts fell most dramatically at the federal level and significantly at the state level, but rose in relative importance for local governments. Finally, the heterogeneous category "charges and miscellaneous" raised its standing moderately at the state level and significantly among local governments. If user charges make up a large portion of that last category at the local level,[11] the ten percentage point increase in it, accompanied by an equal percentage point decline in the local revenue share of the property tax, provides an intriguing, though no doubt wholly coincidental, adumbration of the two revenue trends most likely to result from California's Proposition 13 and similar local tax limitation measures.

Table 9.17   Federal Expenditures on Domestic Programs, by Category, Selected Fiscal Years, 1955–77

Category	Billions of Dollars						As Percentage of Nonrecession GNP			
	1955	1960	1965	1970	1975	1977	1955	1965	1970	1977
Baseline Domestic Expenditures	26.4	43.8	65.7	115.4	225.8	292.2	7.0	10.1	12.1	14.7
Payments to Individuals	12.1	21.9	31.1	61.3	131.4	167.4	3.2	4.8	6.4	8.4
Retirement, disability, and unemployment	10.4	19.4	27.2	51.8	107.2	136.5	2.8	4.2	5.4	6.9
Low-income assistance	1.7	2.5	3.9	9.5	24.2	30.9	0.5	0.6	1.0	1.5
Physical Investment and Subsidies	6.1	10.7	20.7	23.8	32.5	41.4	1.6	3.2	2.5	2.1
Natural resources and environment	4.7	4.3	6.9	8.8	11.2	16.4	1.2	1.1	0.9	0.8
Transportation	1.0	4.2	5.8	7.0	10.4	15.5	0.3	0.9	0.7	0.8
Commerce, science, research and development, and other	0.4	2.2	8.0	8.0	10.9	9.5	0.1	1.2	0.8	0.5
Social Investment and Services	2.4	3.5	4.9	16.3	32.3	40.9	0.6	0.8	1.7	2.1
Education	1.0	1.0	1.3	6.0	12.2	14.2	0.3	0.2	0.6	0.7
Health	1.0	1.8	2.3	5.0	9.7	12.4	0.3	0.4	0.5	0.6
Manpower training	0.1	0.2	0.5	1.6	2.8	4.7	—	—	0.2	0.2
Social services and other	0.3	0.5	0.8	3.7	7.6	9.6	—	—	0.4	0.5
Revenue Sharing	0.1	0.2	0.2	0.5	7.0	7.4	—	—	—	0.4
Outlays for Net Interest	4.8	6.9	8.6	14.4	23.3	33.0	1.3	1.3	1.5	1.7
Other	1.1	1.8	1.6	1.7	5.7	9.6	0.3	0.2	0.2	0.5
Less: Intragovernmental Transactions, etc.	−0.2	−1.2	−1.4	−2.6	−6.4	−7.5	—	—	—	—
Addendum: Recession-Oriented Expenditures (all classified as "payments to individuals")	0.0	0.0	0.0	−1.7	7.8	14.5	—	—	—	—

Source: Schultze 1976, p. 334.

Table 9.18   **Own-Source Government Revenue, by Type and Level of Government (Percentage Distributions)**

	1948				1976–77			
	All Govern-ments	Fed-eral	State	Local	All Govern-ments	Fed-eral	State	Local
Taxes	76.5	80.1	66.9	68.3	63.8	63.8	64.9	62.7
Property	9.4	—	2.7	60.5	9.5	—	1.4	50.5
Individual income	29.6	40.8	4.9	0.4	28.3	41.0	16.4	3.1
Corporation income	15.3	20.5	5.8	—ᵃ	9.7	14.4	5.9	—ᵃ
Customs duties	0.6	0.8	—	—	0.8	1.4	—	—
General sales & gross receipts	2.8	—	14.7	4.1	5.5	—	19.8	4.5
Excises	14.6	15.3	25.4	—ᵇ	6.4	4.6	13.8	2.4
Motor vehicle & operator's license	0.9	—	5.9	—ᵇ	0.7	—	2.9	0.3
Death & gift	1.3	1.9	—	—ᵇ	1.4	1.9	1.2	—ᵇ
All other	2.1	0.7	7.4	3.1	1.4	0.4	3.5	1.8
Charges & Miscellaneous	12.6	13.5	7.7	13.2	13.3	10.4	12.9	22.8
Utility Revenue	2.3	—	—	16.2	2.2	—	—	11.9
Liquor Store Revenue	1.4	—	8.5	0.9	0.4	—	1.4	0.3
Insurance Trust Revenue	7.2	6.3	17.0	1.4	20.3	25.8	20.8	2.3
Amount in $ Billions	67.0	47.2	10.1	9.7	657.3	382.1	155.8	119.4

Sources: U.S. Bureau of the Census, *1977 Census of Government*, vol. 6, *Topical Studies* no. 4, *Historical Statistics on Governmental Finances and Employment*, tables 1, 3, 5, and 6.
ᵃMinor amount included in individual income tax.
ᵇMinor amount included in "All other" taxes.

Among the revenue sources used by governments taxes clearly attract the most public interest. Postwar changes in the structure of United States tax systems are therefore of special interest. Before these can be elucidated, however, a decision must be made about how to treat the payroll tax for social security. Is it simply a tax, or is it so closely related to benefits-to-be-received that it should be treated as a public price or user charge? The answer, of course, is that it is a rather ambiguous mixture of both of those features (see, for example, Break 1977). Since it cannot readily be classified as the one or the other, the United States tax structure will be shown both ways, with social insurance revenues treated as taxes (total tax revenue in table 9.19) and with those receipts excluded from the tax category (general tax revenue in table 9.19). International tax comparisons must deal with the same troublesome issues (see, for example, D. Perry 1979).

Table 9.19   **Structure of the United States Tax System: Percentage Distributions of Major Sources of Tax Revenue for Selected Years, 1946–78**

Tax	1946	1948	1950	1975	1977	1978
	Total Tax Revenue					
Individual Income	33.5	32.4	27.0	32.3	33.7	34.6
Corporation Income	18.2	21.3	26.4	10.0	11.5	11.9
Sales and Excise	21.2	20.8	20.1	16.6	15.2	14.9
Property	10.0	10.7	11.0	12.2	11.2	10.0
Estate and Gift	1.8	1.9	1.3	1.5	1.6	1.1
Social Insurance	12.2	9.3	10.5	24.9	24.5	25.2
Other	3.1	3.6	3.7	2.4	2.3	2.2
Total	100.0	100.0	100.0	99.9	100.0	99.9
Amounts ($ Billions)	$50.0	$57.4	$67.2	$443.4	$572.4	$650.1
	General Tax Revenue					
Individual Income	38.1	35.7	30.2	43.0	44.6	46.3
Corporation Income	20.7	23.5	29.5	13.3	15.2	15.9
Sales and Excise	24.1	22.9	22.5	22.2	20.1	19.9
Property	11.4	11.8	12.2	16.3	14.8	13.4
Estate and Gift	2.0	2.1	1.4	1.9	2.1	1.5
Other	3.6	3.9	4.2	3.2	3.0	3.0
Total	99.9	99.9	100.0	100.0	99.8	100.0
Amounts ($ Billions)	$43.9	$52.1	$60.2	$332.8	$433.1	$486.0

Source: *Survey of Current Business*, January 1976 and July 1979, tables 3.2 and 3.4.
Notes: All receipts listed in "nontaxes" categories are excluded. Receipts from Federal Reserve banks are excluded from corporation profits tax accruals. Customs duties are included under Sales and Excise taxes and motor vehicle license receipts are included under the Other category.

The main distinction between the two interpretations of tax totals collected by all levels of government during the postwar period lies in the roles played by social insurance contributions and the individual income tax. In the "total tax" structure, social insurance revenue is the big gainer, from 10 percent of total taxes in 1948–50 to 25 percent in 1978, while the individual income tax provided close to a third of total tax revenues at both the beginning and the end of the period. As a source of "general tax" revenue, on the other hand, the individual income tax made a significant gain in its relative position, from 36 percent of the total in 1948 to 46 percent in 1978. In both tabulations the property tax has been falling in relative importance in recent years, and the corporation income tax again shows a significant postwar decline. The sales and excise category combines opposing movements on the part of general sales taxes, which grew considerably, and excises, which lost ground during the period.[12]

While the federal general fund has become almost a single tax system during the postwar period, both state and local governments have significantly diversified their general tax structures. The federal individual income tax provided just over half of all federal government general tax receipts in 1948; in 1978 it provided 66 percent (table 9.20). When the corporate profits tax is added to the picture, the federal government's reliance on income taxation is seen to have increased during the period from 76 percent to 87 percent of total general revenues. Excises provide the only other major source of federal tax receipts, and their share of the total declined from 20 percent in 1948 to 10 percent in 1978.

State governments began the postwar period with heavy reliance on selective sales and general sales taxes (table 9.21). The principal changes during the period were the rapid increase in the importance of individual income taxes (from 7 percent of the total in 1948 to 26 percent in 1978), and the less meteoric rise in the general sales tax (from 22 to 30 percent of the total). Selective sales taxes showed the greatest decline.

In the local government sector individual income and general sales taxes have also increased in relative importance in the last thirty years, but their role is still a minor one compared to the property tax (table 9.22). That venerable levy, which produced 89 percent of total local tax collections in 1948 (as it had in 1902), was still producing 86 percent in 1968, but by 1978 it had declined to an 80 percent share. This may seem a relatively modest rate of decline, but it is, of course, an average for a highly diverse set of individual local government units throughout the country. If city revenue systems are studied by themselves, a very different picture emerges (tables 9.23 and 9.24). Whether one takes only the largest cities or all those with populations above 25,000 in

Table 9.20	General Tax Revenue of the Federal Government, by Major Type, Percentage Distributions for Selected Years, 1948–78 (Amounts in $ Billions)

	Fiscal Year				
Tax	1948	1950	1975	1977	1978*
Individual Income	51.0	44.7	64.4	64.3	65.8
Corporation Income	25.5	29.8	21.4	22.5	21.7
Sales and Excise	20.2	22.3	11.1	9.5	9.9
Property	—	—	—	—	—
Death and Gift	2.3	2.0	2.4	3.0	2.1
Motor Vehicle	—	—	—	—	—
Other	0.9	1.2	0.8	0.7	0.5
Amounts	$37.9	$35.2	$190.2	$243.8	$271.8

Source: ACIR, Significant Features of Fiscal Federalism, 1978–79 Edition, Report M–115 (May 1979), p. 44.
*Estimated.

Table 9.21   State Tax Collections, by Source, Selected Years, 1902–78 (Percentage Distribution)

Year	Total Excluding Employment Taxes	Individual Income Taxes	Corporation Income Taxes	Death and Gift Taxes	General Sales Taxes[a]	Selective Sales and Gross Receipts					Property Taxes	Motor Vehicle and Operators' Licenses	All Other
						Motor Fuel Taxes	Alcoholic Beverage Taxes	Tobacco Taxes	Amusement Taxes	Public Utility Taxes			
1902	100.0	—	—	4.5	—	—	.6	—	—	—	52.6	—	42.9
1913	100.0	—	—	8.6	—	—	—	—	—	—	46.5	1.7	42.5
1922	100.0	4.5	6.1	7.0	—	1.4	—	—	—	—	36.7	16.1	28.3
1927	100.0	4.4	5.7	6.6	—	16.1	—	—	—	—	23.0	18.7	25.5
1932	100.0	3.9	4.2	7.8	.4	27.9	—	1.0	—	—	17.3	17.7	19.7
1934	100.0	4.0	2.5	4.7	8.7	28.5	3.1	1.3	—	—	13.8	15.4	17.9
1936	100.0	5.9	4.3	4.5	13.9	26.2	4.8	1.7	—	—	8.7	13.8	16.3
1938	100.0	6.9	5.3	4.5	14.3	24.8	5.6	1.8	—	—	7.8	11.5	17.5
1940	100.0	6.2	4.7	3.4	15.1	25.3	5.8	2.9	—	—	7.8	11.7	17.0
1942	100.0	6.4	6.9	2.8	16.2	24.1	6.6	3.3	.7	2.6	6.8	11.0	12.6
1944	100.0	7.8	10.9	2.8	17.7	16.8	6.6	3.9	1.3	3.1	6.0	9.7	13.6
1946	100.0	7.9	8.9	2.9	18.2	18.0	8.1	4.0	2.3	2.7	5.0	8.9	13.0
1948	100.0	7.4	8.7	2.7	21.9	18.7	6.3	5.0	1.9	2.3	4.1	8.8	12.3
1950	100.0	9.1	7.4	2.1	21.0	19.5	5.3	5.2	1.5	2.3	3.9	9.5	13.1
1952	100.0	9.3	8.5	2.1	22.6	19.0	4.5	4.5	1.6	2.3	3.7	9.4	12.5
1954	100.0	9.1	7.0	2.2	22.9	20.0	4.2	4.2	1.7	2.4	3.5	9.6	13.0
1956	100.0	10.3	6.7	2.3	22.7	20.1	4.1	3.9	1.6	2.2	3.5	9.7	13.0
1958	100.0	10.3	6.8	2.4	23.5	19.6	3.8	4.1	1.6	2.3	3.6	9.5	12.5
1960	100.0	12.2	6.5	2.3	23.9	18.5	3.6	5.1	1.6	2.0	3.4	8.7	12.1
1961	100.0	12.4	6.6	2.6	23.7	18.0	3.6	5.3	1.6	2.1	3.3	8.6	12.3
1962	100.0	13.3	6.4	2.5	24.9	17.8	3.6	5.2	1.5	2.0	3.1	8.1	11.6

Table 9.21—continued

| Year | Total Excluding Employment Taxes | Individual Income Taxes | Corporation Income Taxes | Death and Gift Taxes | Selective Sales and Gross Receipts | | | | | | Property Taxes | Motor Vehicle and Operators' Licenses | All Other |
					General Sales Taxes[a]	Motor Fuel Taxes	Alcoholic Beverage Taxes	Tobacco Taxes	Amusement Taxes	Public Utility Taxes			
1963	100.0	13.4	6.8	2.7	25.0	17.4	3.6	5.1	1.5	2.0	3.1	8.0	11.3
1964	100.0	14.1	7.0	2.7	25.1	16.7	3.6	4.9	1.6	2.1	3.0	7.9	11.4
1965	100.0	14.0	7.4	2.8	25.7	16.5	3.5	4.9	1.6	1.9	2.9	7.7	11.2
1966	100.0	14.6	6.9	2.8	26.8	15.7	3.4	5.2	1.5	1.9	2.8	7.6	10.8
1967	100.0	15.4	7.0	2.5	27.9	15.2	3.3	5.1	1.4	1.9	2.7	7.2	10.5
1968	100.0	17.1	6.9	2.4	28.7	14.2	3.1	5.2	1.3	1.8	2.5	6.8	9.9
1969	100.0	18.0	7.6	2.4	29.7	13.5	3.0	4.9	1.3	1.8	2.3	6.4	9.3
1970	100.0	19.1	7.8	2.1	29.6	13.1	3.0	4.8	1.2	1.9	2.3	6.2	9.0
1971	100.0	19.7	6.6	2.1	30.0	12.9	3.0	4.9	1.2	2.0	2.2	6.2	9.1
1972	100.0	21.7	7.4	2.2	29.4	12.1	2.8	4.7	1.1	2.0	2.1	5.6	8.9
1973	100.0	22.9	8.0	2.1	29.1	11.8	2.7	4.6	1.0	2.0	1.9	5.3	8.6
1974	100.0	23.0	8.1	1.9	30.5	11.1	2.6	4.4	1.0	1.9	1.8	5.1	8.7
1975	100.0	23.5	8.3	1.8	30.9	10.3	2.4	4.1	1.0	2.2	1.8	4.9	8.8
1976	100.0	24.0	8.1	1.7	30.6	9.7	2.3	4.0	0.9	2.3	2.4	4.9	9.0
1977	100.0	25.2	9.1	1.8	30.6	9.0	2.1	3.5	0.8	2.3	2.2	4.5	8.9
1978 est.	100.0	26.1	9.0	1.8	30.3	9.1	2.1	3.5	0.8	2.4	2.0	4.3	8.6

Source: ACIR, *Significant Features of Fiscal Federalism, 1978–79 Edition*, Report M-115 (May 1979), p. 53.
[a]Includes the collections from the business and occupation taxes levied by Hawaii, Washington, and West Virginia. The amounts in fiscal 1977 were $146 million (est.), $263 million, and $299 million respectively.

Table 9.22 Local Tax Collections, by Major Source, Selected Years 1902–78

Fiscal Year	Total Tax Collections	Property Taxes	Sales and Gross Receipts Taxes		Individual Income Taxes[a]	All Other Taxes
			General	Selective		
Amount (in $ Millions)						
1902	704	624	—	—	—	80
1913	1,308	1,192	—	3	—	113
1922	3,069	2,973	—	20	—	76
1927	4,479	4,360	—	25	—	94
1932	4,274	4,159	—	26	—	89
1936	4,083	3,865	40[b]	50[b]	—	128
1940	4,497	4,170	55[b]	75[b]	18	179
1944	4,703	4,361	60[b]	76[b]	26	180
1948	6,599	5,850	210[b]	190[b]	44	305
1952	9,466	8,282	369	258	85	473
1956	12,992	11,282	546	343	164	657
1960	18,081	15,798	875	464	254	692
1964	23,542	20,519	1,170	635	376	841
1968	31,171	26,835	1,204	728	1,077	1,327
1972	48,930	40,876	2,675	1,562	2,241	1,575
1976	67,557	54,884	4,711	2,445	3,127	2,390
1977	74,794	60,275	5,417	2,815	3,752	2,535
1978[c]	81,500	65,250	6,270	2,730	4,300	2,950
Percentage Distribution						
1902	100.0	88.6	—	—	—	11.4
1913	100.0	91.1	—	0.2	—	8.6
1922	100.0	96.9	—	0.7	—	2.5
1927	100.0	97.3	—	0.6	—	2.1
1932	100.0	97.3	—	0.6	—	2.1
1936	100.0	94.7	1.0	1.2	—	3.1
1940	100.0	92.7	1.2	1.7	0.4	4.0
1944	100.0	92.7	1.3	1.6	0.6	3.8
1948	100.0	88.6	3.2	2.9	0.7	4.6
1952	100.0	87.5	3.9	2.7	0.9	5.0
1956	100.0	86.8	4.2	2.6	1.3	5.1
1960	100.0	87.4	4.8	2.6	1.4	3.8
1964	100.0	87.2	5.0	2.7	1.6	3.6
1968	100.0	86.1	3.9	2.3	3.5	4.3
1972	100.0	83.5	5.5	3.2	4.6	3.2
1976	100.0	81.2	7.0	3.6	4.6	3.5
1977	100.0	80.6	7.2	3.8	5.0	3.4
1978[c]	100.0	80.1	7.7	3.3	5.3	3.6

Source: ACIR, *Significant Features of Fiscal Federalism, 1978–79 Edition*, Report M–115 (May 1979), p. 55.

[a]Includes minor amounts of local corporation income taxes.

[b]The distribution of sales and gross receipts taxes between "General" and "Selective" for the years 1936–48 are estimated.

[c]Partially estimated.

1940 and 50,000 in 1970, the postwar decline in relative importance of the property tax is precipitous. As a source of general revenue, the contribution of the property tax declined from 55 percent in 1947 to 23–26 percent in 1976–77, while within the tax category alone its share fell from 81 to 60 percent for all cities and from 77 to 53 percent for large cities. As noted earlier, city fiscal systems have become more and more dependent on outside aid (20 percent of the total in 1947 and 44 percent in 1976–77), with much more of it coming directly from the federal government.

9.5   Tax Expenditures

No account of postwar changes in government expenditures and revenues would be complete without some discussion of that hybrid category known as federal tax expenditures. Their official definition is "revenue losses attributable to provisions of the federal tax laws which allow a special exclusion, exemption, or deduction from gross income or which provide a special credit, a preferential rate of tax, or a deferral of tax liability."[13] In principle, these are all departures from the "normal"

Table 9.23   **City Revenues, by Major Source, 1947 and 1976–77 (Percentage Distributions)**

	1947[a]	1976–77[b]
General Revenue	100.0	100.0
Taxes, total	69.8	42.8
property	56.4	25.7
general sales and gross receipts	8.0	5.8
selective sales and gross receipts	—[c]	3.8
other	5.4	7.6
Charges and Miscellaneous	10.8	17.5
Intergovernmental Revenue	19.4	39.7
from state governments	18.4	23.4
Amount in $ millions	3,305	60,921

Sources: 1947 data: U.S. Department of Commerce, Bureau of the Census *Compendium of City Government Finances in 1947*, 1949 table 2, p. 6. 1976–77 data: U.S. Department of Commerce, Bureau of the Census. *City Government Finances in 1976–77*, 1979 table 1, p. 5.

[a]1947 data are for 397 cities with 1940 populations greater than 25,000.

[b]1976–77 data are for the 392 cities with 1970 populations greater than 50,000 and a sampling of cities with 1970 population less than 50,000.

[c]Category not listed separately in original source. Amounts included in "other" taxes.

Table 9.24   Large City Revenues, by Major Source, 1947 and 1976–77 (Percentage Distributions)

	1947[a]	1976–77[b]
General Revenue	100.0	100.0
Taxes, total	70.9	42.6
property	54.9	22.6
general sales and gross receipts	10.8	5.7
selective sales and gross receipts	—[c]	4.0
income taxes	—[c]	8.0
other taxes	5.3	2.3
Charges and miscellaneous	8.8	13.9
Intergovernmental revenue	20.3	43.5
from state government	19.3	27.3
Amount in $ millions	2,245	31,520

Sources: 1947 data: U.S. Department of Commerce, Bureau of the Census, Large-City Finances in 1947 (Washington, D.C.: Government Printing Office, 1948), table 1, p. 5. 1976–77 data: U.S. Department of Commerce, Bureau of the Census, City Government Finances in 1976–77 (Washington, D.C.: Government Printing Office, 1979), table 8, p. 97.

[a]1947 data are for 37 cities with 1940 populations greater than 250,000.

[b]1976–77 data are for 46 cities with 1970 populations greater than 300,000.

[c]Category not listed separately in original source. Amounts included in "other" taxes.

structure of individual and corporation income taxes chosen expressly to pursue various public policy objectives. Seen in this light, tax expenditures are "alternatives to budget outlays, credit assistance, or other policy instruments,"[14] and as such should be included in any analysis of federal government expenditure policies or trends. That they merit close attention is indicated by their rapid postwar growth, shown in table 9.25 and figure 9.3.

In dealing with tax expenditures, however, one encounters serious conceptual and measurement difficulties. There is, in the first place, no general consensus as to what the "normal" structure of an income tax is. Of the top ten federal tax expenditures in fiscal 1980, shown in table 9.26, three are debatable candidates for the list. Andrews (1972) has questioned this interpretation of the medical and charitable contribution deductions and Break (in press) has argued that the deductibility of state and local nonbusiness ability-to-pay taxes may be an integral part of a federal structure. Conceptual problems also exist for the most important item on the list—long-term capital gains. Would a shift to the

Table 9.25   Federal Tax Expenditures and Other Measures of Federal Finances 1970–80

	1970	1971	1972	1973	1974	1975	1976	1977	1978	1979[a]	1980[a]
Amounts (in $ Billions)											
Gross national product	959	1,019	1,111	1,238	1,359	1,457	1,622	1,834	2,043	2,289	2,506
Total budget outlays	197	211	232	270	326	366	403	451	493	493	532
Income tax revenue, total	123.2	113.0	126.9	139.4	158.6	163.0	173.0	211.6	241.0	273.9	298.4
Individual income tax	90.4	86.2	94.7	103.2	119.0	122.4	131.6	157.6	181.0	203.6	227.3
Corporation income tax	32.8	26.8	32.2	36.2	38.6	40.6	41.4	54.9	60.0	70.3	71.0
Estimated tax expenditures, total	44.0	51.7	59.8	74.4	82.0	92.9	98.5	111.6	133.9	149.9	169.0
Individual income tax	37.6	41.8	46.5	56.0	62.8	70.6	72.6	83.9	100.7	111.4	126.2
Corporation income tax	6.4	9.9	13.3	18.4	19.2	22.3	25.9	27.7	33.2	38.5	42.8
Indexes (1970 = 100)											
Gross national product	100	106	116	129	142	152	169	191	213	239	261
Total budget outlays	100	108	118	126	137	166	186	205	229	250	270
Income tax revenue, total	100	92	103	113	129	132	140	172	196	222	242
Individual income tax	100	95	105	114	132	135	146	174	200	225	251
Corporation income tax	100	82	98	110	118	124	126	167	182	214	216
Estimated tax expenditures, total	100	118	136	169	186	211	224	254	304	341	384
Individual income tax	100	111	124	149	167	188	193	223	268	296	336
Corporation income tax	100	155	208	288	300	348	405	433	519	602	669

Sources: Data on tax expenditures: for 1970 through 1976, from Joint Committee on Taxation, *Issues in Simplification of the Income Tax Laws* (19 September 1977), table 7; for 1977 through 1980, by summation of detail in table G–1, *Special Analyses, Budget of the United States Government, Fiscal Year 1979* and *Fiscal Year 1980*; other data, from *Budget of the United States Government, Fiscal Year 1980*, tables 16 and 19.

Note: From Manvel 1979, p. 207.

[a] Amounts shown for fiscal year 1979 and 1980 are budget estimates or projections.

"normal" income tax structure simply involve elimination of the present 60 percent exclusion of long-term capital gains, or would it also include full deductibility of capital losses from ordinary income, indexation of capital gains and losses for inflation, and the substitution of a full accrual

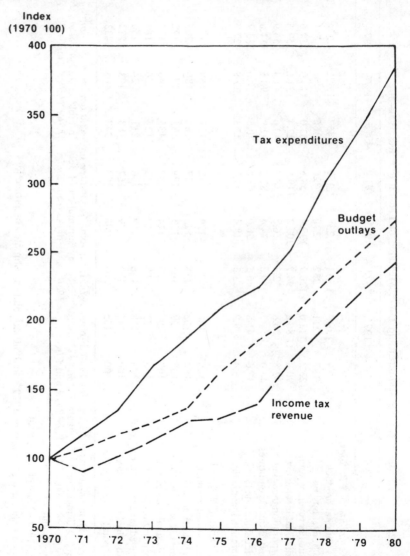

Fig. 9.3   Trends in tax expenditures and other measures of federal finances, 1970–80. Data from table 9.25.

Table 9.26   **The Top Ten Federal Tax Expenditure Categories, Fiscal Year 1980 (Amounts in $ Billions)**

Category[a]	Estimated Revenue Loss: Individuals and Corporations
1. Capital gains	23.3
2. Investment tax credit	19.1
3. State and local nonbusiness taxes	17.7
4. Exclusion of pension contributions and earnings	15.1
5. Medical expense exclusions and deductions	12.7
6. Interest on home mortgages and consumer credit	12.2
7. Charitable contributions	9.0
8. Exclusion of social security and railroad retirement benefits	8.4
9. Interest on state and local debt	7.7
10. Excess of percentage over cost depletion; expensing of exploration and development costs	3.4

Source: *Special Analyses* (1979, pp. 207–11).

[a]Constructed in some cases from separate items in the official tax expenditure list; addition of separate revenue loss estimates subject to the qualifications discussed in the text.

basis for the current realization basis of the tax? The answers given to these questions, which are likely to differ from one expert to another, would make a great deal of difference in the reported size of the capital gains tax expenditure, as indicated by a recent study of corporate capital gains and losses by Feldstein and Slemrod (1978). According to their calculations for 1973 the taxation of real corporate capital gains at ordinary tax rates with full deductibility for real capital losses would have raised only slightly more revenue, assuming no investor reactions to tax change, than did the existing tax law.[15] According to this definition of the "normal" tax structure, then, virtually no capital gains tax expenditure was made in 1973.[16]

Even if all the individual tax expenditure items were, by some ideal standard, correctly defined and measured, further difficulties would be encountered in adding them together to obtain separate totals for particular functional areas or a grand total for the whole set, since the presence of important interactions among them would make the revenue loss from any one of them a function of the tax treatment of various others. The revenue to be gained from eliminating two tax expenditure items, then, may be either larger or smaller than the sum of their individual estimated costs.[17] Official tabulations of tax expenditures, in fact, deliberately omit functional and grand totals. To expect people not to add together the individual items, however, is like expecting no one to climb Mount Everest. They will be added because they are there. What insights may be obtained from such exercises, however, are highly problematical. For the moment it seems best to note the presence and development of federal tax expenditures but not to add them formally to any of the expenditure series discussed earlier.

9.6 Summary

This paper has scrutinized alternative measures of government expenditures and revenues, assessed their usefulness as indicators of postwar fiscal trends, and identified what appear to be the major structural changes that have occurred in this area during the past thirty years. Among these changes are the following:

1. The government sector is larger than it was at the beginning of the period, but in many of its dimensions it has been growing recently less rapidly than the economy as a whole.
2. The federal government's tax-transfer programs have grown rapidly, especially in the domestic program sector.
3. Defense spending has declined significantly, but that trend may be stopped, or reversed, soon.
4. Social insurance expenditures and the payroll taxes that finance them have been major growth components of the public sector.
5. The public sector's share of national output has not grown significantly since 1953, but state and local governments have replaced the federal government as the major partner in these activities.
6. Intergovernmental grants have grown rapidly, and the public sector has consequently become significantly more interdependent.
7. The state-local sector has become more centralized, especially in the financing of its major programs.
8. Federal grants made directly to local governments have become an important part of the intergovernmental picture and have converted traditional hierarchical relations into triangular ones.
9. The federal tax structure has become more homogeneous during the postwar period. Insurance trust programs are mainly financed by payroll taxes and the general fund relies heavily on individual and corporation income taxes.
10. State-local tax systems, in contrast, have become more diversified and more responsive to economic growth and inflation.
11. The property tax remains the dominant contributor to own-source local government revenues, but its position is considerably less secure than it was at the beginning of the period, and there are now wide variations in its relative use among different kinds and sizes of local governments.
12. Federal tax expenditures appear to have grown rapidly, but the significance of these developments cannot readily be discerned.

13. Strong inflationary pressures in recent years have not only complicated the measurement of fiscal trends, but they may also be causing important structural changes that are only beginning to appear on the scene. Extrapolation of past trends is always a dangerous game; it appears to be especially so at this time.

Notes

1. Table 3.18 in the NIPA accounts, published each year in the July issue of the *Survey of Current Business*, shows the relation between NIPA and BOC:GF measures of state and local government receipts and expenditures.

2. Even that measure can be questioned for its choice of the two terminal years used. In principle, one would like two years when the economy was at peacetime levels of full, or comparably high, employment. In practice, one must use single years that fall short of those requirements, averages of several years that may obscure important changes, or single years adjusted to estimate what peacetime full employment values would have been. The terminal years used in table 9.1, while not ideal, seem good enough to show the broad trends sought at this point.

3. See, for example, the discussion of the treatment of federal government sponsored enterprises and of the offsetting of receipts against expenditures for particular programs in the federal budget in the President's Commission on Budget Concepts (1967), pp. 187–95 and 245–76, respectively.

4. This was the term used in the first edition of *A Study in Public Finance*. In the second Pigou changed it to "real" expenditures and in the third to "non-transfer" expenditures. Of the three the most memorable and distinctive is surely the first (Pigou 1947, p. 19).

5. In the 1976 revisions the measurement of real factor inputs in the government sector was changed so as to distinguish, within the limits of data availability, between wage bill increases created by the hiring of better qualified workers or the promotion of employees on the basis of merit, which are interpreted as increases in the quality of government inputs, and wage bill increases resulting from general upward adjustments in the whole pay structure, which are not. Estimates of constant-dollar purchases from business were also improved by the use of new information on prices and the composition of the inputs. *Survey of Current Business*, Part I, January 1976, p. 22.

6. Schultze used a 5 percent rate as a matter of convenience but noted the use of a 4 or a 6 percent rate would have made little difference (1976, pp. 327–28).

7. *Economic Report of the President* 1979, pp. 72–76.

8. *Business Week* 1978, pp. 73–77; 1979, p. 26; the Internal Revenue's first attempt to study tax noncompliance comprehensively, *Estimates of Income Unreported on Individual Income Tax Returns*, was released in September 1979.

9. *Special analyses* (1980, pp. 8, 254).

10. Transfer and interest payments are combined in NIPA table 3.14.

11. Census publications do not provide the needed detail, but NIPA data for the state and local sector show that in 1977, for example, education, health, and hospital charges were 75 percent of the "nontax" category of total receipts.

12. State retail sales taxes were 2.8 percent of total tax revenues in 1948 and 5.8 percent in 1978. The corresponding shares of general tax revenues were 3 per-

cent in 1948 and 7.7 percent in 1978. In addition, local general sales taxes increased from 3 percent of general tax revenues in 1948 to 8 percent in 1978 (table 9.22).

13. *Special analyses* (1979, p. 183).

14. Ibid. The basic conception and its importance for policy analysis was developed by Stanley S. Surrey as assistant treasury secretary in the Johnson administration in 1967 and later (Surrey 1973; see also Feldstein 1975).

15. The amounts were $1,138 million from the 1973 tax law and $1,193 from the revised structure indicated (Feldstein and Slemrod 1978, p. 114).

16. All tax expenditure estimates are impact measures. That is, they take no account of the potential effects on tax revenues of taxpayer reactions to elimination of the particular tax expenditure item under study. In the situation under discussion here, as studies by Feldstein and his associates strongly suggest, any tightening of the capital gains tax rules, while retaining a realization basis, would significantly reduce capital asset sales with correspondingly important effects on federal income tax revenues (Feldstein, Slemrod, and Yitzhaki 1978; Feldstein and Yitzhaki 1978).

17. See for example, *Special analyses* (1979, pp. 189–93).

---

2. George P. Shultz

The Comparative Advantage of Government

No one can question that government's role in the postwar economy has grown tremendously, changed qualitatively, and has affected markedly virtually every aspect of economic activity. We all know that government is legitimate and necessary and that government is here to stay. But, along with other leading institutions in our society, its performance is now widely criticized and reactions to its size, power, and pervasiveness are increasingly sharp.

The postwar surge of its spending, taxing, regulating, and judging has produced some important accomplishments, but also much to worry us. Not least of these worries is the uneasy and widespread feeling that the juggernaut may be out of control—powered by a dynamic of its own, unrelated to our broad concerns almost because of its close relation to our parochial concerns, with results that are as disagreeable for our allies and friends around the world as they are for us. Certain issues stand out that illustrate problems brought about by the role that government has played in changing the postwar American economy. I will discuss five such issues in this commentary.

Issue: Comparative advantage (and disadvantage) in the tasks that government undertakes: the need for limits.

George P. Shultz is vice-chairman of the Bechtel group of companies and professor at the Graduate School of Business, Stanford University.

Even governments need to recognize that a given form of organization or aggregation of people cannot do everything. Competence is important and it demands specialization. But as the reach of government has extended more and more into our economic and private lives, government officials have been led more and more into areas where they have no comparative advantage and may even be out of their element entirely. Government increasingly has come to dominate the production of essential goods and services and their allocation to various uses, substituting a system of bureaucratic command and control for the incentives of private enterprise and the pulls and hauls of the marketplace.

Private enterprises operating in a competitive market have a clear comparative advantage whenever the objective is efficiency in the use of resources, adaptation to variations in local and individual needs, or responsiveness to meet new issues and changed conditions. The superiority of the private market over governmental command and control of large sectors of the economy derives in part from its superiority in the essential tasks of collecting and evaluating information, of giving opportunity for the expression of individual tastes, and of driving producers to seek the lowest cost methods for transforming raw materials into goods that people want and value.

In addition, important managerial distinctions may be drawn between government and private business that bear on their respective areas of comparative advantage. These distinctions start with the deliberately flat organization structure of the federal government, stemming from the very concept of checks and balances. The resulting disposition to delay has been compounded in recent years by the wide distribution of action-stopping power among Congress, the executive branch, the judiciary, and the regulatory agencies. Government action is crablike at best, with an overwhelming emphasis on criticism and on policy formulation as opposed to execution of concrete tasks.

By contrast, the pyramidal structure of organization described in most textbooks does reasonably resemble the reality of business. A "doing" organization must be set up to force the decisiveness that gets action. One of the first lessons I learned in moving from government to business is that in business you must be very careful when you tell people who are working for you to do something, because the probability is high that they will do it. In government, no way! For, among other things, they don't necessarily consider themselves to be really working for you in the first place.

This contrast between "debating" and "criticizing" organizations with their disposition to delay, and "doing" organizations with their spirit of action underlies the comparative disadvantage of government in managing important parts of the economy. And many of our economic problems today result from the large and increasing proportion of economic decisions being made through the political process rather than the market process.

The problem is nowhere better or more tragically illustrated than in the field of energy. Decisions as to price, allocation of supplies, and siting of plants are based heavily on political rather than market considerations. Now the proposed bill, S.1246, if passed, would further extend the government's political intrusion into the allocation of capital within the energy industry. The inevitable result is that a potentially efficient system for producing and consuming energy becomes ensnarled by high-visibility politics, dominated by regional considerations, varying corporate interests and their different abilities to exert political influence, and, importantly, attempts to use the energy system as a means for distributing welfare benefits. By this time, everyone knows the result is a mess.

Perhaps the situation is serious enough and the mess is obvious enough to allow the operation of Katz's law: "When things get bad enough, people will do even obvious and sensible things." If so, government should back off from its areas of comparative disadvantage and spend its time and the taxpayer's money in areas where it has special capabilities and responsibilities. In a field such as energy, these areas include seeing that externalities (e.g., the costs of dealing with pollutants) are reflected in the marketplace and insuring that the markets themselves are competitive.

More generally, government has a clear comparative advantage in the raising and distributing of money. In the postwar period government has in fact become, in considerable measure, an income redistribution system. But to perform this function, government need not, as it has, get into the business of providing health, housing, and a host of other in-kind services, where it operates at a comparative disadvantage. The feeling is widespread today that administration of these efforts is wasteful, unfair, and unwise—a feeling borne out by detailed analysis of the income maintenance system.

But government's special responsibility must primarily be the provision of a framework of law and security for people pursuing their own objectives, and the development of a military capacity able to defend the country's vital interests. We all rely on government to perform well in these areas of comparative advantage and unique responsibility.

Issue: Regulations and, even more, the uncertainties created by the processes of implementing them—a real wild card—inhibit thinking and actions geared to long-term objectives and requiring long-term capital commitments.

Regulations and the regulatory process are receiving increasing attention these days for a number of very good reasons. The problems to which government regulations are addressed are heavily publicized. Sometimes publicity is based on faulty analysis or on dramatization of "horror" stories, both of which invite political overreaction. Nevertheless, many real problems do exist. Government must particularly concern itself with areas where externalities are involved, such as the cases of air and water pollution, although a pricing approach (e.g., an effluent tax) rather than a command and control approach is frequently preferable on grounds of fairness and efficiency. At the same time, one experiment in deregulation, with airlines, is moderately successful and others should be tried, though they may not be. Certainly the time is long past when regulation of the railroads can be justified on the grounds that railroads possess a monopoly in the field of transportation, and there never was any economic justification for the regulation of trucking.

Wide-ranging efforts are being made to estimate the costs of complying with regulation, with contributions coming from the academic, business, and governmental communities. Approximations like "$100 billion per year and growing," conservative in that they take into account only a part of the problem, increasingly force attention to the questions: What are the benefits? And are they really worth it?

Important though it is to question the need for certain regulations and to estimate their costs as well as their benefits, it is even more essential to think through the long-term consequences of the extreme uncertainties inherent in the processes through which regulation is implemented. An individual project can be subject to a myriad of regulations administered by various levels and agencies of government with different jurisdictions and objectives. It often seems impossible to get a definitive decision, especially given the number of intervenors who have standing to interpose legal challenges at almost any stage of a project. It is worth noting that the Alaska Pipeline could only be built after Congress passed a law overriding all previous laws that were blocking its construction. And the proposed Energy Mobilization Board, still another level of bureaucracy, is based on the assumption that a supra-agency is necessary to cut through the maze of red tape if significant energy projects are to get under way.

A well-publicized example of difficulties posed by the regulatory maze involved Sohio's efforts to move oil from the West Coast inland by pipeline. In January 1975 the company began the process of securing necessary permits and government approvals: a total of approximately 700 permits were required from about 140 local, state, federal, or private agencies. On 13 March 1979, fifty months later, the decision was reached to abandon the project. In the interim, Sohio had spent $50 million and managed to secure only 250 of the 700 permits required. When the oil company abandoned the project, it was spending at a rate of $1 million per month in the approval procedures. Governments regulated this project right out of existence.

The volume of permits Sohio had to obtain and of government bodies before whom it had to appear suggest another aspect of the problem. Adam Smith once remarked that specialization increases with the size of the market. Perversely, the vast increase in regulation in recent years has been accompanied by a form of specialization that amounts to a "balkanization" of problems. A whole host of federal, state, and local agencies regulate various aspects of what to a business is one problem.

The legitimate concern is not just a matter of the time involved to go to so many different places for answers. Action can be completely hung up by differences of view among those who represent regulatory interests that are deliberately insulated from each other by statute. A friend of mine once remarked that "whatever is not prohibited nowadays is required." I am forced to amend his statement to "whatever is prohibited may *also* be required."

These regulatory uncertainties continue into the operations phase of any major undertaking, and they are having a devastating impact on major long-term undertakings. The proposition involved here is fairly obvious: *The greater the uncertainty connected with future benefits from an investment, the more these benefits are discounted. The result surely is to skew the investment process into short-term undertakings and to discourage just those kinds of long-term efforts needed to make effective progress on such problems as energy.*

It is sometimes remarked that only the government can handle major undertakings with long-term consequences. That may well describe the world we now live in, but that unappealing situation is created not by the market, not by the inability of private enterprises to organize huge undertakings or by their unwillingness to assume risk. Rather it reflects the facts that government has injected unnecessary uncertainties and risks, including the risks of price and profit controls in the future, and that only government can use compulsion to raise capital for an unprofitable venture or one for which the wild card of regulatory uncertainty looms too large. The impending result: more government activity in areas of its comparative disadvantage. A far better course is to reduce regulatory uncertainty so that private capital can seek out the most promising ventures for the long term.

Issue: High marginal rates of taxation at all income levels bring major distortions in economic activity and increasing resistance at the voting booth and in individual economic behavior.

This problem is all too familiar for middle and high income earners. The distortions of economic activity involved in the avid search for tax shelters and the fact that relatively little revenue is collected at the highest marginal rates testify to their basic futility. The relentless way in which inflation projects middle income earners into ever-higher tax rate brackets has received increasing commentary, so that now the idea of "indexing" the tax system can almost be taken out of quotation marks. Unfortunately, even such a simple and basic change as indexing has not been made. Nevertheless, attention to and recognition of these undesirable consequences suggests that some action may well be in the offing.

Less attention has been paid to the high marginal rates of taxation on the poor and to the fact that they, too, react predictably and negatively. Of course, they can't afford tax lawyers, but they have found effective ways to shelter income. Reliance on government transfer payments instead of employment is one available tax shelter for the poor. Work in the underground economy, where people are paid in kind or cash, not reported for tax or GNP purposes, is another.

Unfortunately, neither the NBER nor anyone else has produced convincing evidence regarding the size and rate of growth of the underground economy. The more enthusiastic estimates range from 10 to 27 percent of the GNP ($200 to $500 billion) with recent growth at rates of from 20 to 40 percent per year. Though I doubt that the high end of these estimates can be taken seriously, this subject deserves much more attention. Intuitively, it is highly plausible that the poor will react to the high direct rates of taxation on earnings (in the form of withdrawal of benefits) and the high indirect taxes on spending by concealing earnings and acquiring goods and services so far as possible in ways that escape much or all indirect tax. Anecdotally, I have seen some astounding examples on a personal level—and not just confined to those in lower income brackets. The other day I noticed a judge insist on payment in cash for performing services at a wedding.

The implications of this government-induced change in the postwar economy are important, if the phenomenon itself is important. A growing underground economy means that, even at the low end of the range mentioned above, the rate of increase in real GNP is being underestimated by one percentage point and levels of unemployment are being significantly overestimated. Such mistakes give an obvious inflationary bias to economic policy.

But I wonder if a different and more powerful point is in the making. The electorate in eleven states has recently voted for greater control of spending or of tax rates at the state and local level, where control can be more direct than at the federal level; and thirty states have endorsed a constitutional amendment calling for a balanced federal budget. At the level of individual economic behavior another manifestation of this political reaction may well be the underground economy. If it is anywhere near as sizable as some estimates suggest, the implied tax revolt is very real indeed. As limits of government's overall size become more real and compelling, decisions about the composition of government activity become as difficult as they are crucial. Increasingly, the answer to "which?" may no longer be "both," even in capitol cities.

Issue: How do we provide for an adequate defense when an already high rate of taxation and expenditure reflects government's major role as the redistributor of income?

The numerical facts involved are well brought out in Professor Break's paper: Total government expenditures have risen from 21 to 36 percent of the GNP during the period 1948 through 1977. These estimates do not take account of off-budget finance or spending required of the private sector by government, both growth areas. Meanwhile, drawing from Professor Break's paper, "domestic programs rise from 7 to nearly 15 percent of nonrecession GNP between 1955 and 1977, while national security programs fall from 11 percent to 5 percent"; "the federal government's tax-transfer programs have grown rapidly, especially in the domestic program sector"; and "social insurance expenditures and the payroll taxes that finance them have been major growth components of the public sector."

As is well known, the chief characteristic of government transfer programs is their "entitlement" nature, with people entitled to a payment based upon such characteristics as income, age, minority status, or place of residence. Sometimes, in fact, they are paid as a result of their ingenuity in beating the system. It is a misnomer to talk of a budget for these programs since the best that can be done is simply to estimate how heavy the drawings will be on the entitlements. With 46 percent of the families in the United States receiving a transfer payment of some kind, it is easy to see that this large and growing sector of the budget has considerable momentum behind it. I speak with some feeling as a former OMB director who, with scars and without success, tried to curtail school lunch spending on behalf of children of middle and upper income parents.

If there is anything to the idea that taxpayers are in a rebellious frame of mind about paying for burgeoning government growth, then the momentum behind the redistributive functions of government can overwhelm our ability to finance an adequate defense. This internally generated threat to our national security deserves sober thought and decisive action. Some way must be found, at a minimum, to make the transfer payment system more internally efficient, as one approach to curbing its growth. In the end, though, the entitlements themselves must be subject to critical scrutiny.

Issue: The escalating rate of inflation is one postwar change in the American economy in which government's role is central and about which it is all too easy to be pessimistic.

Without belaboring the whole gamut of budget, tax, regulatory, and other government actions that raise costs and the chronic monetary accommodation of rising prices, I will simply assert here that inflation, including our current roaring version, is rooted in government policy and behavior. However broad the agreement with this observation, the practical outcome seems to be—almost as though drawn toward it by a magnet—some form of wage and price controls. As these controls move into center stage, unwillingness to conform with them becomes conveniently tagged as the reason for inflation, and those unwilling to conform as the villains. This process of shifting blame from culprit to victim obscures the main point of government responsibility. Economic miseducation is given an added boost when prominent managements feel impelled to make public statements in support of such programs. The activities of OPEC and the political vulnerability of large oil companies offer apparently irresistible opportunities to shift political blame further. Such scapegoating may be good politics, but it is certainly lousy economics.

Inflation has been with us long enough now and has become enough of a preoccupation that many question whether the problem can be dealt with at all. The answer is a clear "yes." Our own prior experience in the fifties and early sixties with relatively stable prices shows that it can be done. And today the experience of other countries has given us evidence that inflation is not an international disease. Even among tightly linked countries like those of the Common Market, rates of inflation vary tremendously (in 1978 the highest rate, in Italy, was over four times the lowest, in West Germany).

We know what to do. Classical economic measures—disciplined fiscal and monetary action and a tax and regulatory environment conducive to capital formation and productivity—have worked for us in the past and work for others at present. The problem is not *what to do* but *how to do it*. The problem is to rearrange the political landscape so that the *necessary* is also the *doable*.

The Bottom Line

Political attitudes may be changing, with the public lowering its expectations about the ability of government to solve problems, insisting that legislators recognize limits to the tolerable level of taxation, give more attention to the importance of investment and productivity, and deal more effectively with high and rising rates of inflation. I hope these changes are for real, in part because such developments would help government do better those things where it has a comparative advantage and where, as citizens, we count on exemplary performance.

One prime objective involves the need in a stable and healthy society to serve the twin objectives of equity and efficiency. Clearly the system of markets and enterprise, driven as it is by competitive pressures, is the way to an efficient society. Beyond efficiency, the market system metes out a great measure of equity and it is a profound respecter of the importance of individual choice. Nevertheless, fairness demands attention to equality of opportunity and to access, at least on some minimum level, to essential goods and services. We have seen many changes sweep through our society, a much more heterogeneous one than most, and yet it has held together. I believe a measure of the credit for this achievement must go to those elements of equity provided through the political process. Transfer payments, with all their faults, are the principal vehicle for the political expression of equity. That equity arguments are all too often used as a guise to support narrow self-interest does not alter the basic appeal to the body politic of the "fair shake." Certainly a key problem for policy is to recognize the legitimacy of concern for the poor and the disadvantaged, but to avoid having the rhetoric of poverty become the servant of well-placed interests.

Unfortunately, when this happens, as it does all too frequently, the systems for equity and efficiency become so entangled as to be almost indistinguishable. By the time our energy industry is transformed into a system for geographic and industrial redistribution of oil, let alone for redistribution of income, it is no wonder that so little progress is made toward solving the energy problem. This form of government effort to redistribute income is subverting the very processes that produce the income in the first place.

Returning to the concept of government's comparative advantage, our system of income maintenance should be simplified drastically, concentrating on cash payments rather than the provision of in-kind benefits. These cash payments should become the principal vehicle through which the political process pursues the goal of equity.

Other changes are as essential if the government role in the decades ahead is to reflect its comparative advantages and disadvantages. These changes call for a reversal of many postwar trends, for reduction and simplification in areas like taxes, spending, and regulation, and for reliance more on the use of market incentives to get the regulatory job done.

Such changes imply a rearrangement of the political landscape since, in the end, government is a mirror of our aspirations, our understanding, and our determination. The hope is, however, that we can follow the idea of comparative advantage: a less comprehensive government role can allow more concentration on areas of prime government responsibility, where first class performance is essential.

3. Paul A. Samuelson

The Public Role in the Modern American Economy

This is not the first time that groups like the NBER have taken a broad look at the cosmic future. Let us hope we are a bit luckier in the present exercise.

One almost hesitates to mention the 1929 *Recent Economic Trends*, commissioned by the confident President Herbert Hoover and blessed by Wesley Clair Mitchell, our founder and patron saint, then at the apex of his scholarly career. That group of economists took a careful look at the United States economy and reported it to be in great shape with a sunny future ahead. That was in 1929!

Then again I recall that, before World War II was over, a National Bureau group consisting of a Harvard statistician and a·Wall Street financier published a volume on the subject I am asked particularly to comment on today: the future state of the government finance. It was a sorry performance. It is easy to see in retrospect how woefully it underestimated the scale of post-1945 fiscal activity. But even at the time, this objective study reeked of wishful thinking and of editorializing in favor of the conservative views of its authors. I remember my old master Alvin Hansen commenting to me that no one alive would ever see a federal budget less than twice this volume's predicted numbers. And, as Hansen later explained to me when I asked him how he thought his prewar doctrine of secular stagnation had actually worked out in the postwar epoch: "Paul, my numbers for federal expenditure, fiscal deficits, and tax revenues—which were considered so outlandish in 1939 and 1944—turned out to be far short of the actual mark. Nature never got the chance to perform the needed experiment for us to know what would have happened if the postwar budget had been always in balance at a low level" (and, I may add in 1980, if the low birthrate had continued after 1939—the only trend anyone had a right to extrapolate in 1939).

So, it is well that I as a commentator am chastened by the demonstrated complexity in forecasting the future and in understanding the present before it has become history. But it is also well that at least some of the scholars who have prepared the surveys that we are all to discuss should have been bold in their speculations and should have nominated theses for us to agree with or try to shoot down. It is part of the eclectic diversity of the National Bureau, preserved in each of its reincarnations, that its authors should differ in substance and style. Thus, Professor Mansfield has cautiously reported some of the available facts about

Paul A. Samuelson is professor of economics at M.I.T.

productivity and research, mentioned a few of the current hypotheses some have put forward to explain them, but has eschewed advancing a grand thesis of his own. Professor Easterlin, from the same university, has perceived the postwar movements in birthrates through the spectacles of his own self-generating every-other-generation cycle, giving his brainchild all the rope it can use. Professor Break, whose paper surveys my topic of government finance, has chosen to present the domestic facts in an analytical mode, so that at least our theories can know what it is they are purporting to explain.

What I want to do today is to examine critically some broad views about government that people outside of economics have been hotly debating. Here is (what, prior to hearing some of the speakers at this conference, I thought to be) a caricature, almost a parody, of what most businessmen believe. In a lower keyed version, but still in essentially the same thesis, I suspect it is a view that the majority of college graduates would essentially subscribe to. The thesis follows:

> The Roosevelt New Deal brought in some needed reforms. But this last half century has witnessed an overshoot of government regulations, taxation, and deficit spending. The vigor of the market economy has thereby been sapped—just as it has been in so many of the mixed economies abroad. United States inflation, stagnation in productivity, class struggle, and popular unrest is the inevitable consequence of the cancerous growth of the public sector engineered by powerseeking bureaucrats and politicians.
>
> Britain provides an archetypical case to prove that the hand of government withers progress and efficiency, and fails to make good on the "equity" it promises. As well, a comparative survey of all the mixed economies will bear out the same perverse correlation between the usurpations of the public sector and shortfalls of economic performance—Switzerland versus Sweden, Japan and West Germany versus Italy and the United States, and so forth.

Notice that I have included nothing in the above statement about the importance of limiting government for the sake of liberty itself. A Hayek, even if you could demonstrate to him a mixed economy where government planning, stabilization, and redistribution really worked well, would reject it in the same way he would reject a well-run jail. Such a view is still a minority view with the electorate, but where it does gain support from fellow travelers is to the degree that the actual "jails"—by which I mean the mixed economies as we know them—are not well run.

Tasting Puddings

What I wish to do here is to display that "respect for the facts" which Arthur Burns once proclaimed must be the National Bureau's watchword.

Is all of the above thesis borne out by the available facts?

Is any of it?

What is the cautious reading of experience on these controversial matters?

These are not easy questions. Since time is scarce, let me reveal at the beginning that I do not think the caricature as stated is unequivocally supported by the historical record. That doesn't mean it's wrong. It might be correct. But a fair-minded jury is under no compulsion to swallow its contentions on the basis of the empirical observations available.

Wishes of Bureaucrats

Here is one part of it that I find farfetched. Bureaucrats would of course like to have their empires grow; and politicians do prefer, other things equal, to be elected rather than defeated. It does not follow from this that I am able to make sense about trends, and to make good predictions, by assuming that it is the desires and psyches of Washington inhabitants that I must look to in explaining actual political happenings.

Social security is a good instance. As George Break observes, it has been one of the fastest growing elements of public expenditure and taxation. Those numerous clerks in Baltimore have been of least importance in the process. I have known most of the head actuaries in that program from the beginning. Their causal role has been, if not negligible, certainly minor. Indeed it was over their objections that so many of the evolving features have become dominant. Why then the growth? It was immanent from the beginning—once the national decision was made to introduce a general insurance scheme. Few of us had the imagination and courage to extrapolate what was immanent. But that is the usual story in these matters. My point is not that this has all been a beneficent thing. Franco Modigliani and Martin Feldstein may turn out to be right that the social security system is the cause of a reduced effective rate of saving and investing in the American economy. My point is that how Main Street and Congress feel about this matter, and not how civil servants do, is what has given us whatever it is we now have.

My old teacher, Josef Schumpeter, tried to set forth a theory of public finance based on the realpolitik of getting elected. I welcome modern revivals of this seminal idea. But all theories of revealed preference must be subject to the check of comparison with empirical data. And the innuendo that it is the power wishes of government officials that explains the police state is not a hypothesis that stands up well to explain the complexity of facts that need explaining.

Post Hoc, but . . .

The middle third of the twentieth century goes into the record book as the era in which the tax share of the public sector soared. The final third, we can confidently predict, is not going to be able to show a similar acceleration. This is so, if only because of the nature of a fraction, which has to be bounded by one. But it is also so because, as the market sector shrinks, one can expect there will be a resistance and backlash rather like that we have begun to see in recent years.

How has real GNP fared in this middle third of the century in which governments grew like a cancer? Would a Hayek have predicted in 1933 that the patient would show the debilitation of cancer? Would a Schumpeter in 1942 have written about "capitalism in an oxygen tent" on its march to socialism? Of course. And that is what I was taught at the University of Chicago was the likely future to look forward to after 1935.

But when we turn to the real world, we see it has been a different story. Of course, the recoveries from the world depression consequent upon deficit financing in North America, Germany, and elsewhere in Europe are easy to understand in terms of short-term fluctuations. But what Schumpeter was writing about in *Capitalism, Socialism and Democracy* was the long pull. If he came back to Vienna, Bonn, and Cambridge today, he would be as surprised as that urbane mind could admit to, by what the Kuznetses and Denisons have measured to be the postwar miracles of growth by the mixed economy.

Am I arguing that, *because* the public sector was burgeoning from 1932 to 1970, that is *why* world GNP outperformed the growth rates previously witnessed under the gales of creative capitalistic destruction? No. What I am precisely warning against in this commentary is such a facile attempt to read into the chaos of facts the theses you want to believe about them (theses which may even have important germs of truth in them).

Thus, Switzerland and Sweden show almost identical paths of Kuznetsian progress. If I gave you their two time series blind, you couldn't tell them apart. More than that. It is a great mistake to think that Switzerland is a Walrasian economy and Sweden a totalitarian state. If you examine the long vector of attributes of these two, you will find them surprisingly alike; and also you will find some surprising reversals of the usual stereotypes.

Debaters and lawyers are always trying to overstate their cases. I recall how, just after the mid-1940s, conservative friends used to point to Belgium and Holland. Belgium, they claimed was a market economy and it was prospering. Holland was allegedly a controlled economy and it was stagnating. If you inquired about the different degrees of bombing of the ports of Antwerp and Rotterdam, they lost patience with your pedantry. But of course in a few years, both economies showed marked departures from laissez-faire; and their relative growth rates showed no simple patterns of dominance.

What is relevant to the present session is to look at the numbers Dr. Break has given for the United States and compare them with similar numbers abroad. Everyone knows that Germany and France, to say nothing of the Low Countries and Scandinavia, have grown more in the postwar than has the United States. Is it then the case, as the above thesis would require, that these fast growing countries show a larger fraction for the market economy than we do? I have just had the occasion to prepare the eleventh edition of my elementary textbook *Economics*. Every four years I get reeducated on the world economy, and an economic historian could do worse—as Bob Gordon has indicated in footnoting his paper for this conference—than to use these successive revisions as a documentary source to chronicle both the change in events and in beliefs about them.

What I found, when preparing a table of comparative shares of GNP that taxes take, was that Switzerland and the United States each tax about the same fraction of national income. That paragon of growth and the free market, West Germany, has a larger total tax fraction than the United States or the United Kingdom do. And Germany, unlike America or Israel, has little call to spend on national defense. The Netherlands and Sweden are two nations whose public sectors have leaped above half their GNPs. Has Providence punished them for this profligacy?

Not yet. Their growth rates have for decades been exceeding our best performances. I happen to think that their future productivity trends will be adversely affected by this heavy load. But that thought of mine is not a National Budget thought: It is not a finding of statistical analysis or even a deducible lemma from a compelling model; but like so many of my best insights it is a Bayesian hunch that could never deserve the Mitchell-Burns imprimatur. If you match your hunches against mine, who is to be the referee to adjudicate between them?

Even Britain cannot serve as the whipping youth for the determined empiricist. For all the talk about the "British sickness," the United Kingdom's government's fraction of GNP expended on goods and services has averaged out to less than those reported for the United States in Dr. Break's tables. And, just to confuse the parable, Britain's productivity trend in the third quarter of the century turns out to have surpassed that of the United States—just as growth rate in the United States production index has outperformed production growth in Switzerland and Germany in the 1970s.

I've made my point: Only ideologues can see simple morals writ large in historical record. The facts tell their own story, but it is not the *simple* story that so many want to hear.

Welfare and Mutual Reinsurance

Thanks to earlier National Bureau authors, we have been reminded that conventional measures of product and productivity do not capture all the elements of welfare that the citizenry are concerned with. William

Nordhaus and James Tobin constructed their rough Measure of Economic Welfare (MEW) to make clear that there are offsets to the reduction in productivity which may result from environmental pollution standards and from occupational safety regulations. My neighbors and I go to the polls and by majority vote make sure that if *we* should happen to be unemployed, or blind, or penuriously old, we shall still receive some minimum of income payments. In agreement with Alan Blinder's paper, even though the ordinary measures of income inequality—e.g., Gini coefficients of Lorenz curves, Pareto-curve parameters—show no strong trends for the last three decades, it is my observation that there has been a perceptible reduction in lifetime inequality. Fewer people do go to bed hungry in present-day America; and life is not so short, nasty, and brutish for the poor as I can remember it being in my youth.

None of this is accomplished in a Pareto Optimal way. From the beginning of time such a state of thermodynamic efficiency has never been remotely approached. If economists were to wait for that day in which income redistributions are done in the Pareto Efficient way, they would wait forever. And society's members would wait with them.

Economists are a minority, no more numerous than chiropractors. Noneconomists go whole hours without thinking about Pareto Optimality. It is noneconomists who constitute our clients. We are their not-so-efficient servants. They are our not-so-clear-thinking masters.

Once democracies decide to second-guess the outcome of the market, the programs take on a momentum of their own. When I was a young student of what was to come to be known as macroeconomics, we all took for granted that F.D.R.'s new expenditures on welfare and unemployment compensation would have to last only so long as the economy remained significantly below its full employment potential. *After* recovery was achieved, those expenditures would recede in the simple anticyclical manner. That was the naïve expectation I shared.

Of course it didn't happen. You might think that this was the result of "politics"—a reflection of the weakness in the voting system that tends to make it easier to expand the economy than to restrain and contract it. Well, you would be wrong in thinking so. There may well be such a political bias in the workings of the mixed economy. But what I came to realize belatedly in the late 1930s—and it came from the writings of Bill Haber of the University of Michigan, writings that did not appear in refereed proper economic journals—that once society decided that people should not fall below certain minimum levels of well-being and income, the total of the welfare load would grow and grow. And so it has, no longer to my surprise, these last forty years.

My Worries

I have reached the age to scold and nag. So I must not fail you. Although for the most part my own value judgments applaud the economic trends that have been the trends of my times, my reason and experience with economic models leave me with a concern. Markets are more effective for many facets of economic activity than people have been able to make fiats and commands be. Any new nation freed from colonial bindings can give itself a socialist constitution and type out a crisp Five-Year Plan. But so often, we know from experience, these good intentions are not worth the paper they are written on.

The mixed economy is *mixed*. That is its strength: to mobilize for human ends the mechanisms of the market and to police those mechanisms to see that they do not wander too far away from the desired common goals.

The market can be a strong horse under us. But every horse has its limits. Those limits may not show up at once. A Sweden or Holland can for a time pile onto the horse ever greater relative loads. No one is wise enough to state exact limits beyond which the mechanism must begin to falter. But that doesn't mean limits are not there.

The problem for the United States, I have come to think, is to move beyond our good intentions. Our challenge is to preserve the useful features of the market—as when we want whatever slack there is in the economy to put effective downward pressure on prices and wage costs. But that should not mean that we have to submit to all the thoughtless consequences of the market's solution. To paraphrase Alfred Marshall of ninety-five years ago, economists need to put their cool heads to the service of their warm hearts. And that's what the American economy itself needs urgently to do in the years ahead.

Summary of Discussion

The discussion turned first to the redistributing role of government. Benjamin Friedman suggested that the tables on income redistribution through government in the Break paper understate its true extent. Government expenditures on goods and services also have a large redistributional component. Procurement policies are often targeted to achieve specific distributional aims. Even military spending has some of this character, as evidenced by the difficulty of removing military bases from some Congressional districts even when the bases are not justified on defense grounds. Friedman asserted that a realistic debate about government would be not about the level of public goods provision but rather about how much redistribution we want. Friedman expressed puzzlement about the failure to debate that issue squarely. Wilbur Cohen suggested in response that redistribution has never captured the imagination of the noneconomist, as it is antithetical to middle class and even populist values. Martin Feldstein emphasized that the net redistribution of income through government is far less than the gross redistribution, given the variety and often conflicting goals of redistributive programs. But since each program has negative incentive effects, the efficiency burden of the programs is related to the extent of gross, and not net, redistribution.

In response to a question, Paul Samuelson reiterated that any inverse correlation between government spending as a proportion of income and the rate of economic growth, is not strong, and that part of any simple correlation is spurious. Since public goods generally have an income elasticity greater than one, wealthier (and presumably slower growing) countries devote a larger share of income to public goods. Milton Friedman declared that these correlations would in any event understate the true burden of government spending on economic welfare, since the income statistics give equal welfare weight to public and private spending. This is because government spending is valued at factor cost and not at market price.

Herbert Giersch challenged Samuelson's comparison of United States and German manufacturing growth. The German manufacturing sector was overgrown in the 1960s because of an undervaluation of the DM exchange rate. It thus could have been expected to decline in the 1970s. While this happened with regard to employment, productivity growth accelerated. A comparison of productivity growth rates between the United States and Germany gave a picture completely different from Samuelson's comparison.

References

Andrews, William D. 1972. Personal deductions in an ideal income tax. *Harvard Law Review* 86: 309–85.

Baumol, William J. 1967. Macroeconomics of unbalanced growth: The anatomy of urban crisis. *American Economic Review* 54: 415–26.

Boskin, Michael J. 1979. Some neglected economic factors behind recent tax and spending limitation movements. *National Tax Journal* 32 (supplement): 37–42.

Break, George F. 1977. Social security as a tax. In *The crisis in social security*, ed. Michael J. Boskin, pp. 107–23. San Francisco: Institute for Contemporary Studies.

————. Forthcoming. Tax principles in a federal system. In *Essays on tax policy*, ed. Henry J. Aaron and Michael J. Boskin. Washington, D.C.: The Brookings Institution.

Business Week. 1978. The fast growth of the underground economy (13 March), pp. 73–77.

————. 1979. A new report expands the "irregular" economy (10 December), p. 26.

Dubin, Elliot. 1977. 'The expanding public sector: Some contrary evidence'—A comment. *National Tax Journal* 30: 95. (The original article of this title by Beck, Morris). 1976. *National Tax Journal* 29 (March): pp. 15–21.

Economic report of the president. 1979. Transmitted to the Congress in January. Washington: Government Printing Office.

Eisner, Robert, and Nebhut, David H. 1979. An extended measure of government product: Preliminary results for the United States, 1946–1976. Paper presented at the Sixteenth General Conference of the International Association for Research in Income and Wealth, Pörtschach, Austria, August.

Feldstein, Martin. 1975. *The theory of tax expenditures.* Discussion Paper no. 435. Harvard Institute of Economic Research, Harvard University.

Feldstein, Martin, and Slemrod, Joel. 1978. Inflation and the excess taxation of capital gains on corporate stock. *National Tax Journal* 31: 107–18.

Feldstein, Martin; Slemrod, Joel; and Yitzhaki, Shlomo. 1978. *The effects of taxation on the selling of corporate stock and the realization of capital gains.* NBER Working Paper no. 250. New York: National Bureau of Economic Research.

Feldstein, Martin, and Yitzhaki, Shlomo. 1978. The effects of the capital gains tax on the selling and switching of common stock. *Journal of Public Economics* 9: 17–36.

Hulten, Charles R. 1979. *A solution to the problem of measuring public sector productivity.* Working Paper no. 1124–06. Washington: The Urban Institute.

Levin, David J. 1978. Receipts and expenditures of state governments and of local governments, 1959–76. *Survey of Current Business* vol. 58 (May), pp. 15–21.

Manvel, Allen D. 1979. Tax expenditures continue to grow. *Tax Notes* 8 (19 February): 207.

Musgrave, Richard A. 1959. *The theory of public finance.* New York: McGraw-Hill, chap. 9.

Pechman, Joseph A., ed. 1979. *Setting national priorities: The 1980 budget.* Washington, D.C.: The Brookings Institution.

Pechman, Joseph A., and Hartman, Robert W. 1979. The 1980 budget and the budget outlook. In *Setting national priorities: The 1980 budget,* ed. Joseph A. Pechman. Washington, D.C.: The Brookings Institution.

Perry, David B. 1979. 1979 international tax comparisons. *Canadian Tax Journal* 27: 212–18, using data from the latest edition of the

Organization for Economic Co-operation and Development's *Revenue statistics of OECD member countries.*

Perry, George L. 1970. Changing labor markets and inflation. *Brookings papers on economic activity* 3: 1970, pp. 411–41.

Pigou, A. C. 1947. *A study in public finance.* 3d ed. rev. New York: Macmillan.

President's Commission on Budget Concepts. 1967. *Staff papers and other materials reviewed by the president's commission* (October). Washington, D.C.: Government Printing Office.

Rolph, Earl R. 1948. The concept of transfers in national income estimates. *Quarterly Journal of Economics* 62: 327–60.

———. 1954. *The theory of fiscal economics.* Berkeley and Los Angeles: University of California Press, chap. 4.

Schultze, Charles L. 1976. Federal spending: Past, present, and future. In *Setting national priorities: The next ten years*, ed. Henry Owen and Charles L. Schultze. Washington, D.C.: The Brookings Institution.

Shoup, Carl S. 1947. *Principles of national income analysis.* New York: Houghton-Mifflin, chap. 7.

———. 1969. *Public finance.* Chicago: Aldine, chap. 20.

Special analyses. 1979. *Budget of the United States government. Fiscal year 1980.* Washington, D.C.: Government Printing Office, pp. 183–93, 207–11, 225.

———. 1980. *Budget of the United States government: Fiscal year 1981.* Washington, D.C.: Government Printing Office.

Stanbury, William T. 1973. *Productivity and the measurement of the relative size of the public sector.* Working Paper no. 189. Faculty of Commerce and Business Administration, University of British Columbia.

Surrey, Stanley S. 1973. *Pathways to tax reform.* Cambridge: Harvard University Press.

U.S. Department of Commerce, Bureau of Economic Analysis. *Survey of Current Business.* Various issues.

Concluding Comments

Arthur F. Burns

The National Bureau of Economic Research literally owes its origin to a concern on the part of two remarkable individuals with the problem of income distribution. In early 1917 a discussion took place between Dr. N. I. Stone, who at that time was reputed to be a radical, and Malcolm Rorty, then an executive of the American Telephone and Telegraph Company. The subject of their discussion was the distribution of income in the United States—a matter on which they differed. They agreed, however, that reliable information on that vital subject was meager and that it would serve the public interest to establish an organization that would undertake objective studies of the size and distribution of the national income. The war intervened and this project was delayed until 1920, when the NBER was launched. Its first two publications reported on a pathbreaking statistical study of the national income and its distribution. Since then the NBER's research undertakings have expanded in numerous directions, but the original interest in the size and distribution of the national income remains a major concern—as this conference has again demonstrated.

In the course of this conference, the major trends of the postwar economy in our country have been effectively delineated and discussed.

Some of the trends during this period were clearly favorable. First, entrepreneurship has flourished. The number of independent enterprises in our country grew from about seven million in 1945 to fourteen million in 1975 and perhaps sixteen or seventeen million at present. Second, our economy has generated an extraordinary number of new jobs. Third, in comparison with preceding decades, the unemployment rate has remained quite low. Fourth, the trend of overall production has been both

Arthur F. Burns is Distinguished Scholar in Residence at the American Enterprise Institute.

upward and fairly rapid. Fifth, poverty as we knew it before the 1940s has been practically eliminated in our country. Sixth, homeownership has expanded materially, and so too have the capital goods that fill American homes. Seventh, racial discrimination has been reduced, and we have achieved a much closer approach to equality of economic opportunity than we had before World War II. In short, the postwar period has been marked by many remarkable economic advances.

There were, however, some trends during all or the latter part of the postwar period that many of us, perhaps all of us, would regard as unfortunate. First of all, we have experienced a loosening of family ties, and this has already had enormous implications for our economic society. Second, the American people have come to rely increasingly on government for the solution of economic and social problems. This has led during the past thirty-odd years to a rapid increase in government expenditures, to huge and persistent federal deficits, and to intricate government regulations over our business and personal lives. Third, we have experienced since the mid-sixties a depression in true corporate profits, and this has naturally been accompanied by a depressed stock market. Venture capital investment during much of this period nearly dried up. More important still, we have had a decline of stock ownership, especially among young people, and this has inevitably raised doubts about the future of capitalism in our country. Fourth, the trend of productivity improvement has definitely flattened out since the mid-sixties, and this is a worrisome development. Fifth, we have experienced persistent inflation since the end of World War II and at a pace that has dangerously accelerated over the past fifteen years. Sixth, we have lost our independence in the field of energy. Partly but by no means solely for that reason, we have experienced a decline in our balance of trade and in the dollar's standing in foreign exchange markets. Seventh, our nation's prestige and influence around the world have diminished—and this too is a fact of profound economic significance.

This list of unfavorable or dubious trends can be lengthened, but I want to close these brief remarks by noting a highly constructive development in our country. We as a people now know what our problems are, and we have begun to do something about them. Inflation is now accepted as our nation's number one economic problem. The zeal for government regulation is diminishing. The importance of encouraging saving and business capital investment is no longer questioned. Expenditures on research and development are again rising in real terms. We are no longer neglecting defense spending as we did for a number of years. A conservative financial trend is developing in our country, and I think it is gathering momentum. The next two or three years are likely to be difficult for our economy, but I am confident that we will end the decade of the 1980s on a happier note than we are beginning.

Contributors

Alan S. Blinder
Department of Economics
Princeton University
Princeton, New Jersey 08544

William H. Branson
Woodrow Wilson School
Princeton University
Princeton, New Jersey 08544

George F. Break
Department of Economics
University of California at Berkeley
Berkeley, California 94720

Arthur F. Burns
American Enterprise Institute
1150 Seventeenth Street
Washington, D.C. 20036

Richard E. Caves
Department of Economics
Harvard University
Littauer Center 210
Cambridge, Massachusetts 02138

Alden W. Clausen
President
Bank of America, N.T. and S.A.
P.O. Box 37000
San Francisco, California 94137

Wilbur J. Cohen
Lyndon Baines Johnson School
   of Public Affairs
University of Texas at Austin
Austin, Texas 78712

John T. Dunlop
Harvard Business School
Boston, Massachusetts 02163

Richard A. Easterlin
Department of Economics
University of Pennsylvania
Philadelphia, Pennsylvania 19104

Martin Feldstein
National Bureau of Economic
   Research
1050 Massachusetts Avenue
Cambridge, Massachusetts 02138

Richard B. Freeman
National Bureau of Economic
   Research
1050 Massachusetts Avenue
Cambridge, Massachusetts 02138

Benjamin M. Friedman
Department of Economics
Harvard University
Littauer Center 127
Cambridge, Massachusetts 02138

Milton Friedman
Hoover Institution
Stanford University
Stanford, California 94305

Victor R. Fuchs
National Bureau of Economic
    Research
204 Junipero Serra Boulevard
Stanford, California 94305

Herbert Giersch
Universitat Kiel
Dusternbrooker Weg
Kiel 120/122
West Germany

Robert J. Gordon
Department of Economics
Northwestern University
Evanston, Illinois 60201

Irving Kristol
The Public Interest
10 East 53d Street
New York, New York 10022

Simon Kuznets
67 Francis Avenue
Cambridge, Massachusetts 02138

Edwin Mansfield
Department of Economics
University of Pennsylvania
Philadelphia, Pennsylvania 19104

Ruben F. Mettler
Chairman
TRW, Inc.
One Space Park
Redondo Beach, California 90278

Arthur M. Okun (deceased)
The Brookings Institution
1175 Massachusetts Avenue
Washington, D.C. 20036

David Packard
Chairman of the Board
Hewlett-Packard Company
1501 Page Mill Road
Palo Alto, California 94304

Peter G. Peterson
Lehman Brothers, Kuhn, Loeb
One William Street
New York, New York 10004

Paul A. Samuelson
Department of Economics
Massachusetts Institute of
    Technology
Cambridge, Massachusetts 02139

James R. Schlesinger
Georgetown University
Center for Strategic and Inter-
    national Studies
International Club Building
1800 K Street
Washington, D.C. 20006

Richard F. Schubert
Vice-Chairman
Bethlehem Steel Company
Bethlehem, Pennsylvania 18106

George P. Shultz
President
Bechtel Corporation
50 Beale Street
San Francisco, California 94105

Herbert Stein
2500 Virginia Avenue, N.W.
Washington, D.C. 20037

Walter B. Wriston
Chairman
Citicorp
399 Park Avenue
New York, New York 10043

Since this volume is a record of conference proceedings, it has been exempted from the rules governing critical review of manuscripts by the Board of Directors of the National Bureau (resolution adopted 6 July 1948, as revised 21 November 1949 and 20 April 1968).

Author Index

Subject Index

Abortion laws, 277
Accident rates and mortality, 300, 331
Advertising expenditures, 531–33, 544
Advisory Committee Act, 401
Advisory Committee on Intergovernmental Relations (ACIR), 636
Affirmative action programs, 376–79, 473
Age: distributions (*see* Age distributions); earnings gap, 286–92, 317, 339, 451, 459; and fertility, 295–96; and mortality, 297–98, 300–301, 320; structure of families, 424, 442; and unemployment, 144, 386–87
Age Discrimination in Employment Act, 381
Age distributions: engineers and scientists, 574–75; female labor force, 281, 288, 314, 357; labor force, 338, 349–50, 356–59, 361–62, 408; male population, 319; unrelated individuals, 425
Agglomeration economies, 308, 310
Agriculture: free trade, 258; input-output relations, 505, 507; national income share, 502, 503; population in, decline of, 365, 441–42; prices, and inflation, 142–43, 152, 166; productivity, 565, 569; trade balances, 207, 208–9, 212, 256 n, 266; vertical integration, 529
Aid to Families with Dependent Children (AFDC), 380–81, 474
Aircraft industry: employment, 366;

patents, 577; R&D expenditures, 533, 535, 569, 571, 572; technology gap, 581
Airlines: consumer use, 427, 431; regulation, 505, 659
Alaska pipeline, 659
Alcoholic beverages: consumer expenditures, 427, 428
Alcoholism, 292
American Federation of Labor–Congress of Industrial Organizations (AFL–CIO), 369, 372, 400, 588
Antibias laws, 376–79, 473
Antibiotics and mortality, 297, 299
Antitrust laws, 525, 557, 592
Appliances, household: consumer expenditures, 427, 430; trade balances, 225, 229, 230
Austria, 355
Auto Agreement of 1965, 197, 199, 219–20
Automation, 539
Automobile: consumer expenditures, 427, 431; and population dispersion, 309
Automobile industry: sales boom in 1950s, 117; seller concentration, 516; trade balances, 207, 209–11, 216–20; 232, 256 n; unions, 398; U.S. competitiveness, 555–56

Baby boom, 31, 350, 357, 383. *See also* Population growth
Bank of America, 87–93 passim

11, 162–63, 165, 168; in 1947–57,
111, 115–16, 120–21, 122; in 1957–
67, 126–28, 129–30, 132; in 1967–73,
136, 137, 139, 140, 145; in 1973–79,
146, 149–50, 152; share of OECD
total, 185–86; transfer payment share,
489–92; and unreported income, 630,
661

Hansen, Alvin, 665
Happiness and economic well-being,
471–72
Hayek, Friedrich, 666, 668
Health and economic well-being, 469–
71
Health and safety laws, 379, 566, 568,
592
Health programs, 489–92. *See also*
Transfer payments and programs
Heckscher-Ohlin model of comparative
advantage, 232–33, 261
Hicksian IS-LM model, 111, 114
Hiring: antibias regulations, 376–79;
computerization, 379; federal man-
power programs, 380; and unionism,
371
Holmes, Oliver Wendell, 551
Homicide rate, 292–93, 300, 318, 331
Hong Kong, 192, 193
Hoover, Herbert, 122
Household: consumption patterns, 426–
32; indebtedness, 16, 20, 26–30, 37–
42; technology, 361. *See also* Individ-
uals
Housework, decline in amount of, 464
Human capital, 212, 232–35, 259; and
education, investment in, 362–63,
383; and lifetime income, 419

Ideology, 483–86
Illegitimacy rates, 293, 329–30, 470–
71
Immigration, 276, 294–95, 301–5, 311
Immigration Act of 1965, 302
Income, personal: and debt ratio, 29;
and economic mobility, 453–54; and
fringe benefits, 384–85, 386, 403,
447; growth, 308, 309, 311, 422–24,
472; lifetime, 419, 434, 449–53; measuring, 418–19, 442–48; sources, 424–
25; underreporting, 448, 630; uses,
425–26

Income inequality, 416, 433–62, 670;
and age, 286–92, 317, 339, 383, 451,
459; black-white, 381, 459–61; and
capital gains, 447–49; and demographics, 437–42 (*see also* Families);
and education, 362–63, 382–83; and
income in kind, 447, 449; of industrial nations, 435; and leisure, 465;
male-female, 461–62; measuring,
419–21, 433–37; motive in studying,
479–86; and taxes, 442–43, and
transfers, 443–47, 486–93; and
wealth distribution, 466–67
Income tax, 63, 443, 485; corporate,
108, 109; individual, 108, 381, 423,
443, 639–40, 644, 645; surcharge,
134, 136–38, 145–46
Indexation: contracts, 84, 86; tax, 84,
661; wages, 147
India, 302
Individuals: growth in numbers, 437,
468; income trends (*see* Income inequality); poverty level, 457, 458.
See also Families; Household
Industrial loans, 46
Industrial Revolution, 308, 311, 602–3,
604
Industrial supplies: trade balances, 207,
208–9, 211, 212, 232
Industry, 501–58; classification, 506–
10; concentration ratios, 515–22; defined, 501; growth trends, 502–4,
543; input-output relations, 505–7;
sectoral shifts and productivity, 353–
54; U.S. leadership, 551–58, 606
Inflation: and capital replacement, 605;
and equities investment, 40, 41; and
indebtedness rise, 24–25, 63; postwar acceleration, 13–14, 81–85, 109–
10, 135, 140, 142–43, 151–52, 165–
68, 174, 662–63; and price movement inertia, 118–19, 128, 129, 148,
167; and profits, 541; wage, 140–42,
147, 153, 351, 385, 391–92, 394; and
wage and price controls, 140–43; and
unemployment, 68, 108–11, 120–21,
129–30, 134–35, 144, 152, 170–74,
351, 391–92
Information processing industries, 505,
546–51, 598–99, 602–3
Innovation: and creativity, 574–75; diffusion rates, 578–80, 595; and inven-